Sexuality,
State, and
Civil Society
in Germany,
1700–1815

"Hope would remain within." Detail from frontispiece to *Journal des Luxus und der Moden* 24.1 (1806). Courtesy of the Department of Special Collections, Stanford University Libraries.

Sexuality, State, and Civil Society in Germany, 1700–1815

ISABEL V. HULL

Cornell University Press ITHACA AND LONDON

This book has been supported by a grant from the National
Endowment for the Humanities, an independent federal agency.

First published 1996 by Cornell University Press.
First printing, Cornell Paperbacks, 1997.

Printed in the United States of America

Library of Congress Cataloging-in-Publication Data
Hull, Isabel V.
    Sexuality, state, and civil society in Germany, 1700–1815 / Isabel V. Hull
        p.   cm.
    Includes bibliographical references and index.
    ISBN 0-8014-3126-3 (alk. paper)
    ISBN 0-8014-8253-4 (pbk.: alk. paper)
        1. Sex customs—Germany—History. 2. Sexual ethics—Germany—History.
    3. Civil society—Germany—History. I. Title.
HQ18.G3H84   1995
306.7´0943—dc20   95-31511

Cloth printing   10 9 8 7 6 5 4 3 2

Paperback printing   10 9 8 7 6 5 4 3 2 1

For Inge

Contents

❖ Contents ❖

❧ Contents ❧

Acknowledgments

I have accumulated many debts in the course of this long project and it is a great pleasure to be able to thank those who helped me.

For their financial support over the years, I thank the Alexander von Humboldt Stiftung, the American Association of University Women, the American Council of Learned Societies, Cornell University, and the John Simon Guggenheim Foundation. My thanks also to Karin Hausen, who served as my sponsor for the Humboldt Stiftung.

I thank the staffs of the many libraries and archives I have used, but especially the people at the Generallandesarchiv in Karlsruhe and the Niedersächsische Staats- und Universitätsbibliothek Göttingen for their patience and friendliness. I am also greatly indebted to Klaus Schmidt and the coworkers at the Zeitschriftenindex project in Göttingen for sharing with me their vast knowledge of eighteenth-century published works and generously permitting me to use their computer and raw data before the project results were yet available to the public.

Joan W. Scott rescued me from isolation and arranged for me to use the facilities and profit from the intellectual exchange at the Institute for Advanced Studies in Princeton, even though I was not a fellow. Rudolf Vierhaus and his successor, Hartmut Lehmann, were equally generous in permitting me, without official affiliation, to use the library of the Max-Planck-Institut für Geschichte in Göttingen and to take part in its seminars. I thank all three very much.

I have learned a great deal from the many colleagues and friends with whom I have discussed parts of this project over the years. I thank them all and want especially to mention in this connection Carola Lipp.

Several people were unfortunate enough to have to read an earlier, even longer version of this book. My friend Mary Beth Norton counseled me wisely on cutting; Jonathan Knudsen patiently and kindly analyzed the sections on civil society. I owe most to the three people whose detailed, careful, and generous criticism guided me through the rewrite: Laura Engelstein, David W. Sabean, and Mack Walker. It was wonderful to engage with their ideas. These readers saved me from many errors. I am deeply grateful to all of them for helping me make this a better book than I ever could have without them.

I. V. H.

Abbreviations

ADB	*Allgemeine Deutsche Bibliothek*
Alm.f.Ä.	*Almanach für Ärzte und NichtÄrzte*
Bald.Mag.	*Baldingers Neues Magazin für Ärzte*
Bay HStA	Bayerisches Hauptstaatsarchiv München
Beitr.z.B.	*Beiträge zur Beruhigung und Aufklärung*
Berl.Mon.	*Berliner Monatsschrift*
Braun.J.	*Braunschweigisches Journal*
Chron.	*Chronologen*
Fränk.Samm.	*Fränkische Sammlungen*
Dt.Mon.	*Deutsche Monatsschrift*
Dt.Mag.	*Deutsches Magazin*
Dt.Mus.	*Deutsches Museum*
GLA	Generallandesarchiv Karlsruhe
Hann.Mag.	*Hannoversches Magazin*
Hann.G.A.	*Hannoverische Gelehrter Anzeiger*
Hyp.Br.	*Hyperborëische Briefe*
JaJ	*Journal aller Journale*
JdL	*Journal des Luxus und der Moden*
Mag.z.Er.	*Magazin zur Erfahrungsseelenkunde*
NADB	*Neue Allgemeine Deutsche Bibliothek*
N.Hann.Mag.	*Neues Hannoverisches Magazin*
N.Mannig.	*Neueste Mannigfaltigkeiten*
NTM	*Neuer Teutscher Merkur*
Schl.Prov.Bl.	*Schlesische Provinzial-Blätter*
Schlesw.J.	*Schleswigisches Journal*
TM	*Teutscher Merkur*

*Sexuality,
State, and
Civil Society
in Germany,
1700–1815*

Introduction

The great transformation from absolutism to the earliest form of the modern state redrafted the "sexual system." By sexual system I mean the patterned ways in which sexual behavior is shaped and given meaning through institutions. It is not surprising that the new configurations of state and social institutions in German-speaking central Europe in the late eighteenth and early nineteenth centuries should have profoundly affected the sexual system; however, because sexual behavior is at the heart of social reproduction and is symbolically central to social classification and the interpretation of order, the sexual system also shaped state and society as both of these changed. The reciprocal (but uneven) relation of these three terms is my subject. I take their reciprocity seriously; thus I interpret the sexual system both as a function of state and society and as an important force helping to (re)organize and develop them.

In order to bring the relation of state, society, and sexual system into the sharpest focus, I have concentrated on the "public" interest in sexual behavior, that is, the judgment of how relevant sexual behavior is to the "public good" (*Gemeinwohl*). The clearest indicator of this judgment is sexual regulation: what agents regulate which behavior in what social groups for which real or ostensible reasons? The transformation from the absolutist to the modern sexual system is an aspect of the transformation of the "public" itself, for when the absolutist state reformed itself by relinquishing its monopoly over public life, encouraging and indeed presiding over the creation of a civil society independent of it, the state also purposely relinquished its previous, theoretically unlimited responsibility to police sexual behavior and granted to the active citizens of civil society, again theoretically, the right to define large sections of the sexual system themselves. In other words, an important line demarcating state from civil society, and thus defining each, ran along the boundary of regulating accepted versus nonaccepted sexual expression.

Besides regulation, a second major indicator of the "public" interest in sexual behavior is the use of sexual categories to organize, classify, and interpret social facts, whether via argumentation (on the basis of putative sexual characteristics) or via (often unreflected) metaphor. Mary Douglas has pointed out how bodily symbols, including sexual ones, become especially salient in times of crisis or sociopolitical reorganization.[1] In fact those engaged in the immense enterprise of

[1] *Purity and Danger: An Analysis of the Concepts of Pollution and Taboo* (London, 1989), 120–22. Also, Pat Caplan, "Introduction," in *The Cultural Construction of Sexuality*, ed. Caplan (London, 1987), 14–15.

putting society and state on a new footing found sexual argumentation very useful in redrawing social lines (for example, by elevating the bourgeoisie above the nobility on the grounds of superior sexual morality, by redefining the poor as the victims of their own sexual incontinence, or by disqualifying women from expanding political participation on sexual-biological grounds), and sexual metaphor helped provide the model, based on putative male sexual drive, defining the new citizen of civil society. The usefulness of sexual argument and metaphors in supplying guidelines for the construction of civil society partly explains the peculiar importance contemporaries ascribed to sexual behavior as diagnostic of social productivity and stability, and of state resilience—an importance that subsequently distinguished the modern sexual system from its absolutist predecessor.

The book's two poles are therefore state and (nascent) civil society. Its sources are also twofold. I have used state documents—on criminal and civil law, poverty, sumptuary legislation, paternity and child-support suits, granting citizenship, and relations of church and state—which reveal the lengthy discussions among officials at all levels of government on various (often hidden) aspects of sexual behavior and state interest. These documents chart the course of the territorial state bureaucracies from seventeenth-century absolutism, which was unlimited in theory but inefficient in practice, to the tinkerings of early Enlightened reform in the mid eighteenth century and the fundamental legal transformations envisioned by state officials of late Enlightened reform absolutism and finally realized during the Napoleonic period. Since the German states were hardly uniform, I have found it necessary to examine several states with different religious, demographic, economic, and administrative characteristics. The archival documentation supporting this study covers Baden-Baden, Baden-Durlach, Bavaria, Hamburg, and (nineteenth-century) Prussia from about 1600 to 1848. The huge size of this undertaking has forced this book to end at 1815, by which time the distinction between the modern state and modern civil society had already been drawn and the main lines of the modern sexual system largely laid down. As it happens, the material from Hamburg and what was available to me from Prussia (during the days of the Democratic Republic) concerns the years after 1815. My materials for the years before 1815 are from Bavaria, Baden-Baden, and Baden-Durlach. Fortunately, a handful of careful studies of (among other things) sexual matters in other localities, as well as the published laws and commentaries of other states, are now available to supplement these sources. My object, in any case, was not to write a series of exhaustive local histories, but to present a general picture of the offical sexual system in central Europe. I can only hope that the south German bias in my sources has not significantly distorted my findings.

Documenting the development of civil society is less a matter of archival record than of written public opinion. As I discuss in detail in Chapters 4 and 5, "civil society" (*bürgerliche Gesellschaft*) here denotes both the goal of Enlightenment reforms and the actual and ever widening new form of social life characteristic of the literate strata, especially males, both bourgeois and noble, in towns and administrative centers. I follow most historians in accepting as the first manifestations of this latter, really existing civil society the numerous reading groups, patriotic societies, and other voluntary organizations of the late eighteenth century and the flood of journals in which local patriots traded expertise and opinions with their fellows in other regions and thereby fashioned national careers and national consensus.

Restoring the sexual dimension to state and society alters much received wisdom about absolutism and civil society. I have found that in practice absolutism was much more permeable and sensitive to accepted sexual custom than the "social disciplinary" model suggests. Furthermore, where absolutism did impose new sexual norms, these were more inclined toward gender equality than those of the liberal, civil society that succeeded it.

Absolutism's actual interest in sexual regulation was, furthermore, extremely limited compared to that of the church, from which it took over much sexual legislation. Despite its Reformation-inspired pretension that it was the caretaker of its subjects' morals, the German ancien régime restricted its active intervention generally to out-of-wedlock births. Its regulatory focus was thus narrowly heterosexual and procreative, its framework marital. That it was perceived to have failed at even this limited moral enterprise was a chief reason that officials concluded absolutism had failed generally and thus that Enlightened legal reform was necessary. Late Enlightened absolutist reformers consequently moved to reduce the penalties for, if not ultimately to decriminalize, extramarital consensual sexual offenses. Dedication to natural law principles and administrative uniformity also encouraged the relatively equal treatment of women and men before the law. The legacy of Enlightened-absolutist reform law proved to be a stronger guarantor of freedom of sexual expression (particularly regarding gender equality) than the consensus forming in the new civil society. Thus German legal reformers, such as Anselm Feuerbach, produced law codes more completely dedicated to moral agnosticism and therefore freer of sexual and gendered values than those drafted by liberals whose referent was civil society and the ideals thought to undergird it.

Civil society, too, looks different examined through the lens of sex. In company with some other recent historians, I argue that civil society in Germany was quite well developed by the end of the eighteenth century. The preponderance of state officials among the German educated public did not necessarily mean subservience to the state, but rather greater familiarity with actual social, including sexual, issues; greater circulation of ideas (bureaucrats typically served first one state and then another); greater penetration of Enlightened reform ideas into precisely those circuits of power in a position to act on them; and paradoxically, more governmental readiness to rely on "public opinion" (since the officials identified themselves with the public) and to grant it widened, protected status as independent civil society.

In Germany, growing reliance on public opinion, especially regarding moral (including sexual) matters, constituted the major argument for instituting civil society and limiting state power (Kant). The moral politics of absolutism had rested

3

upon two foundations: the restrictive principles appropriate to a subsistence economy (such as in sumptuary laws, which had strong analogues in sexual legislation), and the presumed moral unity linking religion, government and subject.[2] In order to restructure state, economy, and society along more modern lines, both absolutist reformers and the "practitioners of civil society," as I call them, found it necessary to replace the ethic of abstention with an ethic of production and consumption. The moral unity that had formed the ideological basis of sex-crime law was shattered when the right of religion to set moral standards and the right of government to enforce them was called into question. Paradoxically, reformers understood this process as itself moral, for the resulting split between law and morality, as Kant and Feuerbach argued, created the sphere of freedom necessary for true moral choice and therefore individual moral development.[3] Thus the new, reformed state was supposed to (and did) relinquish much of its traditional responsibility for upholding the moral order to the new civil society. Decriminalization of many former delicts did not end moral politics, however. Not only did civil society exercise its own informal moral regime, but once the Napoleonic legal reforms had legally defined and guaranteed civil society, many voices speaking on its behalf demanded that the state reenter the moral sphere to uphold its values. Throughout these fluctuations the church and the police acted as expanding or contracting buffer zones, where the untidy line of moral responsibility could be cleaned up. The gradual shift from absolutism to civil society also transformed the standard of the moral good from a conflation of Christian principles with the public good (*Gemeinwohl*),[4] to a secularized concept of the public good that toward the end of the century was supplemented by reference to the good of the private individual.[5] This nascent ideological split between public and private became in the nineteenth century the chief organizing principle behind moral and political decision making.

It is important to underscore the extent to which late-eighteenth-century reformers understood politics morally, for later observers have been prone to misinterpret contemporary moral argumentation and categorization as proof that German civil society was privatist and apolitical. It was neither; rather, its practitioners understood politics as encompassing fundamental social relations and duties which it interpreted in a moral framework; this conviction granted sexual behavior important political status and meaning.

German circumstances also caused the practitioners of civil society to focus with

[2] Dietmar Willoweit, "Struktur und Funktion intermediärer Gewalten im Ancien Régime," in *Gesellschaftliche Strukturen als Verfassungsproblem,* supplemental issue of *Der Staat* 2 (1978): 24–25.

[3] Johannes Kunisch, *Absolutismus. Europäische Geschichte vom westfälischen Frieden bis zur Krise des Ancien Régime* (Göttingen, 1986), 41, 173–74. This split is also the subject of Reinhard Koselleck, *Kritik und Krise. Eine Studie zur Pathogenese der bürgerlichen Welt* (Frankfurt, 1973).

[4] Marc Raeff traces the shifting justification for state ordinances from reference to God's order to the public good in his *Well-Ordered Police State: Social and Institutional Change through Law in the Germanies and Russia, 1600–1800* (New Haven, Conn., 1983).

[5] See Michael Stolleis, *Pecunia Nervus Rerum. Zur Staatsfinanzierung der frühen Neuzeit* (Frankfurt, 1983), 127–28, for a good discussion of the changing meaning of *Gemeinwohl* and its usefulness to the state.

peculiar intensity on certain sexual themes, such as masturbation (a pedagogical nightmare) and infanticide. These popular debates in fact functioned as thought experiments that organized reflection on difficult issues encountered in the transition from state tutelage to civil freedom. For example, the debate on masturbation threshed out the problem of the new male citizen (the pleasures and dangers of untrammeled individualism loosed from their social mooring, the temptations of the all-male civil society, the need for wise education, the putative sexual-biological foundations of male superiority). The debate on infanticide, to take another example, rehearsed the new standards of motherhood needed to found civil society as a thing apart from absolutism, the vulnerability of women to male power under the new order, and the role of law in the regulation of moral behavior.

Whereas certain themes figured more prominently in the German discourse than elsewhere, two were common to western Europe generally: the male sexual model of citizenship and the public/private split. Where collective estate, or (*Stand*), had once organized society, the individual citizen now founded civil society. Stripped of social status and regional inflection, the citizen had to be based on universal principles adhering to the only distinguishing feature he had left: his body. Not surprisingly, an older model of male sexual essence was now reformed to provide knowledge of this new being. The degree to which the model citizen was based not on (bourgeois) class but on gender can be seen if one analyzes the successive steps by which the older male sexual model was refashioned, or if one carefully examines in practice the defining characteristic of relations between civil society and the state, namely the split between public and private. The Napoleonic reforms in Baden show clearly that the protection from state intervention which constituted this boundary was designed to accrue only to the citizen, who was always understood as married, heterosexual and male. Furthermore, he enjoyed these freedoms by virtue of his private familial, not his public status, whereas women were denied the same protection by virtue of their public, not private familial status. Above all, the split between the "public" and the "private" was a powerful symbol system used to bring order to emerging posttraditional relations. It helped generate differentiated norms appropriate to a society newly consecrated to complexity and specialization. It provided a flexible framework within which rights, privileges, duties, and responsibilities could be newly constituted, distributed, and later transformed. And there was no stronger constituent of this dichotomy than the sexual system.

The sexual musings of the practitioners of civil society were not idle. The principles they derived from their conclusions about the differing sexual natures of men and women, or adults and children; about heterosexual attraction as the original socially binding force; about the sexual drive and sexual desire as the analogues of economic productivity and consumption; about sexual expression as the culmination of the fully developed individual personality—all these principles helped shape the laws and through them basic social and even political relations in the emerging new society of the early nineteenth century. The great turning point was the moment when civil society was legally guaranteed (by criminal law reform and sometimes by constitutions) in the Napoleonic period, and state officials accepted it as the legitimate source for positive law in both the civil and criminal realms. The moral opinions of civil society henceforth replaced the abstract guidelines of the state bureaucracy, and the early liberalism characteristic of late-eighteenth-century reformers matured into the liberalism of the early-nineteenth-century variety, with its recognizable moral program of gender and sexual exclusions. Nineteenth-century liberalism reintroduced moral content into positive law and thus canceled the moral project of late Enlightened reform absolutism, which had aimed to promote morality by reducing moral-legal coercion.

If we discover significant new aspects of both the state and civil society, through the lens of sex, then I argue that the sexual system itself cannot be understood at all except in relation to them. Neither the sexual system nor specific sexual behavior has intrinsic meaning, and scholars who analyze either one in a vacuum do so at their peril. There are of course many other aspects of the history of sexuality that merit and have received valuable scholarly attention. The sexual system, as I have defined it here, is only one facet; what follows is not a history of the body or actual sexual behavior, or emotional life. It is instead the history of the changing public interest in sexual behavior at the moment of fundamental transformation toward the modern.

I intend here to demonstrate the interconnection of the sexual system, the state, and civil society in different degrees depending on specific circumstances. I hope to retain the complexity of this shifting interaction and to highlight the paradoxes created as different systems or aspects of the same system clashed and as seeming continuities (such as putative male sexual desire, "morality," and stereotypical female nature, for example) were subtly changed by their differing location in the state–society–sexual system nexus.

A word about words. Although the term "sexuality" appears in the title of the book, it will rarely appear in the text. I agree with Foucault's view that "sexuality" is a construction of precisely the sociopolitical changes that I examine.[6] It would be anachronistic and methodologically misleading to use it for the period before 1815. It is also too much to expect the reader to understand the term in Foucault's sense, rather than in its customary usage as a legitimate, neutral expression for individual sexual potential or sexual subjects generally. Therefore, I avoid using it and substitute the inelegant, but more accurate, phrases "sexual behavior" or "sexual matters." For the same reason I use the adjective "sexual" rather than the more modern-sounding "sex." Although this choice leads to some infelicities, I hope it will discourage readers from interpreting early modern categories according to modern standards.

"Gender," in the context of scholarship about sexual matters, usually means the

---

[6] Michel Foucault, *History of Sexuality*, vol. 1, *An Introduction*, trans. Robert Hurley (New York, 1978), 154. See also Ellen Ross and Rayna Rapp, "Sex and Society: A Research Note from Social History and Anthropology," in *Powers of Desire: The Politics of Sexuality*, ed. Ann Snitow, Christine Stansell, and Sharon Thompson (New York, 1983), 51–73.

culturally determined differences between men and women.[7] It has replaced "sex," which many felt suggested that these differences were biologically determined. (This distinction cannot be made in German.) In a book on sexual matters, the word "sex" must be reserved for genital activity (which is closer to the early modern usage), whereas "gender" will refer to the perception of men and women as different classes of people, regardless of whether the persons about whom I am writing saw the origin of that difference in nature, culture, or a combination of the two. Where relevant, their opinions will be made clear. On the rare occasions when "sex" is supposed to mean the difference between men and women (as in "the fair sex"), it will always be preceded by a clarifying adjective.

Finally, since gender plays such a central role in the changes under examination here, "his" and "her" will be used literally. Where "his" has appeared in this introduction, for example, it has referred exclusively to males. When "people's" is meant, "his/her" or some equally cumbersome, but clear, phrase will be used.

[7] See Joan W. Scott, "Introduction" and "Gender: A Useful Category of Historical Analysis," in *Gender and the Politics of History* (New York, 1988), 1–11, 28–50.

I

The Church,
Traditional Society,
and the Regulation of Sex

Although this book focuses on the efforts at sexual regulation undertaken by the German states and developing civil society, these were not the only sources of systematic engagement in that project. The church and the social nexus in which people lived—their family, neighbors, and fellow workers—exerted for a long time a stronger and more effective sexual discipline than the rudimentary state or than civil society (which did not even exist until the late eighteenth century). The church set the basic framework within which the absolutist territorial state later exercised regulation. From the secular standpoint, the church's two most powerful contributions were the great significance it ascribed to sexual (mis)behavior and the paramount position it accorded to marriage as the only locus of accepted sexual expression. Following these principles (among others) the church carefully developed the hierarchy of sexual offenses that absolutist penal codes later adopted from canon law. Finally, the church's ecclesiastical courts also functioned as model and helpmate for secular institutions at the central and local (*Gemeinde*) levels.

But the church's importance was not merely negatively regulatory; it also positively shaped later developments. By assigning great significance to sexual desire, it also made room for the positive valuation of (marital) sexual expression as a sign of God's love for his creatures and, in any case, as a human necessity (as influential churchmen of the twelfth century and Reformation argued). By recognizing all souls as equal before God, it laid foundations for gender equality. Furthermore, the Reformation anticipated, even defined, the moral dilemma that ultimately encouraged absolutism to devolve moral authority upon civil society. On the one hand, religious reformers demanded a "reform of life," which among other things featured higher standards of sexual comportment, and they set up experimental institutions (marriage courts, morals courts, "discipline-masters") to effect this reform. On the other hand, they recognized that genuine moral improvement could not be coerced. Although some of these ecclesiastical courts charged the secular authorities with the task of sexual regulation, the moral boundary these religious reformers drew favoring internal, voluntary moral improvement over external coercive moral control provided the ideological escape route legal reformers took to relieve the state of its burdensome involvement in the regulation of morals.

In the sixteenth and seventeenth centuries secular authorities depended heavily on church officials, parents (especially fathers), and village leaders to define and implement the state's regulatory agenda; one could say that the absolutist sexual system as a whole was a partnership. But the partners had agendas of their own, and these did not necessarily coincide with the state's interests. Just as the church had worked out its sexual doctrine with surprising indifference to its potential effects on the *ständisch* society the state was sworn to uphold, so parents and *Gemeinde* elites had focused on making sexual behavior coincide with inheritance structures and local subsistence needs with surprising indifference to some of the symbolic uses of sexual conformity with which state officials wished to demonstrate their authority and order in the abstract. The state's partners were therefore also its competitors. These patterns of partnership and competition determined the contours and practical limits of state regulation.

The Christian Church and Sexual Regulation

In the beginning was the Church. At least virtually all histories of sexuality hold Christianity responsible for laying down the principal sexual norms that have guided behavior in the West to the present time. Over hundreds of years the church hammered out the central tenets of sexual ethics: distrust of sexual pleasure, exaltation of celibacy and virginity, restriction of permissible sexual relations to monogamous, procreative, heterosexual marriage. It also created the primary disciplinary methods to uphold these standards: confession, penance, the ecclesiastical courts, and canon law. More important, Christianity invested sexual behavior with extraordinary importance. It was not merely that salvation or damnation might hang from a single sexual act, but that these ultimate conditions might be most vividly expressed in a sexual vocabulary. That is, the body and its sexual possibilities bore enormous symbolic weight; they became saturated with meanings belonging to systems of faith, of order and hierarchy in a Christian community, of signs revealing eternity. The negative evaluation of sex does not distinguish Christianity from other cultures as much as does the excessive significance it attached and attaches to sexual matters. This symbolic overload was Christianity's chief contribution to forming the Western sexual system.

Christian Sexual Doctrine

Peter Brown has theorized that millenarianism grounded Christianity's charged, renunciatory attitude toward the body and sex.[1] Early believers expected Christ's imminent return. His advent would end history, in which humankind had been

---

[1] *The Body and Society: Men, Women, and Sexual Renunciation in Early Christianity* (New York, 1988).

imprisoned since the Fall. To prepare for that coming, the faithful might anticipate the end of earthly bondage by themselves interrupting the biological cycle that perpetuated it, that is, by refraining from sexual relations. This was as close as they might come to escaping earthly chains, for renouncing sex not only thwarted procreation, the start of the unavoidable journey toward death, but it also withdrew one from the community, whose main bonds were affinal, and freed one to pursue divine contemplation. It signified freedom of the will from the dictates of impulse, instinct, and pleasure. And it prepared one for the coming of God by cleansing one of the ritual impurity ancient society associated with sexual acts.[2] Renouncing sex was therefore not self-denial, but self-liberation. —> freedom from desire

Christian sexual asceticism was promoted by various groups, among them desert mystics, radical sectarians, and regular monastics, but sexual renunciation never triumphed over sexual expression inside the Christian community, which after all centered on and was literally reproduced by married couples. There were always two competing sexual expectations inside Christianity, one for the laity and another, stricter one for clerics. The need to minister to the laity's real lives guaranteed that there would always be moderate voices tempering the tendency toward ascetic extremism.

According to the foremost authority on ecclesiastical sexual law, James Brundage, Christian sexual doctrine first began to solidify in the fifth and sixth centuries A.D., as Christianity assumed the institutional form appropriate to a state religion. Thence to the twelfth century, when doctrine underwent a substantial transformation, Christian sexual dogma was chiseled into shape by moralists and legists, whose preoccupations never quite coincided. Their different emphases, changes over time, and the spectrum of opinion characteristic of any large organization, make generalization hazardous; nonetheless, for our purposes it is possible to sum up Christian sexual doctrine down to the twelfth century under three headings. ✓

The first was the continuing rejection of sex for mere pleasure. Fears of ritual ①
impurity and devilish enticement branded sex for pleasure a mortal sin. From this reject
principle a whole series of further elaborations flowed. Occasions for legitimate sex for
marital intercourse were sharply circumscribed to avoid both religious ritual occa- pleasure
sions and the ritual defilement associated with the female reproductive cycle. Jean-
Louis Flandrin has calculated that an observant couple of average fertility could
have engaged in legitimate sex only about once a week under these circumstances.[3]
Any activity or supplement thought to increase sexual pleasure, or to aim for it
exclusively, was also barred. Interdicted therefore were unusual positions; oral and
anal sex; visual stimuli including total nudity and sex by daylight; sex in unusual or
ritually holy places; food, drink, or potions thought to be aphrodisiacs; implements;
sex with partners where procreation was impossible or clearly not the goal: same-

[2] Thomas N. Tentler, *Sin and Confession on the Eve of the Reformation* (Princeton, N.J., 1977), 165–66.
[3] *Un temps pour embrasser. Aux origines de la morale sexuelle occidentale (VIe-XIe siècle)* (Paris, 1983), 41–71; cited in James A. Brundage, *Law, Sex, and Christian Society in Medieval Europe* (Chicago, 1987), 154–64. My account follows Brundage.

sex liasions, prostitution, bestiality and so on. The list was limited only by human inventiveness. Different moralists compiled different lists and different hierarchies of the forbidden. The expansive possibilities of this rubric made it an important one for innovations in sexual doctrine.

If sex for pleasure was not possible, the only acceptable "excuses" for sexual activity were procreation and human weakness, both of which were to be contained exclusively within the second heading, marriage, whose exclusive claim to legitimacy (under church sexual doctrine) rendered everything else illegitimate. Chief among the sexual delicts were thus fornication, that is sex (usually heterosexual) between two unmarried persons, and adultery. But marriage itself was also hedged around with prohibitions. In addition to the acts the church condemned even if they were performed by husband and wife, there were incest prohibitions to the seventh degree (after 1215 to the fourth degree), strict monogamy enforced by prohibition of divorce,[4] and discouragement of remarriage after the death of a spouse, all of which testify to the only grudging approval granted even to marriage as a sexual outlet. Until around the tenth century, however, the church in practice did not control marriage. After that time, the church extended its temporal grasp and began the long battle with secular authorities over this most central of social institutions. Although peripheral to this study, the sexual arguments adduced by both sides in their struggle illuminate and helped form the reigning sexual ideology of the moment.

Whereas the first two summary headings of church sexual ideology concerned outright prohibition of sex for pleasure and grudging tolerance of sex within marriage, the third is the only category in which the church outright required sexual intercourse: the marital debt.[5] The marital debt was actually a way to permit sex for pleasure, but it was defined negatively as surrender to (the partner's) compulsive temptation. If the marital debt were not rendered, then the partner would be driven to fornication or worse. The church seems to have assumed that despite all its efforts, sexual temptation was too strong for most believers to resist. Thus, even marital sex remained somewhat sinful in the eyes of most clerical writers. The remarkable aspect of marital debt was its gender equality. It is one of the few instances in the history of European norms and laws where men and women were held to have exactly equal obligations and rights. That this should be true precisely in sexual relations is clearly significant, but unraveling why requires further study.

Around the twelfth century the Christian sexual doctrine sketched above shifted in a slightly more sex-positive direction.[6] The new consensus deemed sex in mar-

---

[4] Annulment and separation were difficult, but possible; neither, however, permitted legitimate sexual relations thereafter.

[5] See Brundage, *Law*, 93.

[6] Scholars are uncertain why this occurred or how the upward valuation of intercourse in marriage affected the church's view of other sexual acts. Cf. Brundage, *Law*, 323, 333, 359, 364; Tentler, *Confession*, 167–68, 224, 178–79, 184; John Boswell, *Christianity, Social Tolerance, and Homosexuality:*

riage not merely the best of evils, but under circumstances a positive good promoting love and affection between spouses and thus strengthening their bond. The marital debt was now interpreted so expansively that it drove out prohibitions against sex during ritual moments in the church calendar or ritually "impure" times in the female biological cycle.[7] And for the first time, moralists rescued sex for pleasure by demoting it from a mortal to a venial sin, if it were performed in marriage.[8]

[handwritten margin note: shift to positive]

Church sexual doctrine, as it recrystallized in the twelfth and thirteenth centuries and was set down in Gratian's definitive canon law code (1140), remained fairly constant down to the Reformation. Its hierarchy of sexual sins defined the normative sexual landscape of Europe. Gratian's law code ranked "unnatural acts" (which, in the widest definition, included same-sex contacts, bestiality, masturbation, and oral and anal sex) as the most heinous, followed by incest, adultery, and fornication.[9] This was the conventional order. Moralists usually went into greater detail and listed more acts condemned under the rubric *luxuria* (extravagance or lust), than did legists.[10] Tentler sums up the sixteen grades of sin listed in the *General and Brief Confession*, which is notable not for the order of "vileness," which is standard, but for its exemplary pedantry. The author enumerates, beginning with the most wicked (the first five qualifying as "sins against nature"):

1. bestiality
2. "sodomy" (same-sex relations)[11]
3. improper organ (such as anal or oral sex)
4. improper manner (forbidden position)
5. masturbation
6. incest (to the fourth degree after 1215)
7. rape, or sexual abduction of a nun
8. rape, or sexual abduction of a married woman
9. rape, or sexual abduction of a virgin
10. consensual sex with a religious person
11. double adultery (both partners married)
12. simple adultery (one partner married)
13. defloration, or seduction of a virgin
14. fornication

Gay People in Western Europe from the Beginning of the Christian Era to the Fourteenth Century (Chicago, 1980), 216–17, 240–41, 243–66, 270–72. Also Michael Goodich, "Sodomy in Ecclesiastical Law and Theory," *Journal of Homosexuality* 1 (Summer 1976): 432.

[7] Tentler, *Confession*, 213.

[8] Ibid., 175, 175 n. 19.

[9] Brundage, *Law*, 245–51.

[10] For example, the very influential "Canones poenitentiales" (Astesani), reprinted in Hermann Joseph Schmitz, *Die Bussbücher und die Bussdisciplin der Kirche* (Mainz, 1883), 800. For Aquinas's opinion that homosexuality was not *luxuria*, see Goodich, "Sodomy in Ecclesiastical Law," 430.

[11] The later, secular legal texts we will examine usually use "sodomy" more broadly to include bestiality, same-sex relations among humans, and anal intercourse.

15. unchaste touch
16. unchaste kiss[12]

This is a handy summary of the calculus of the impermissible as it had crystallized before the Reformation.

Enforcement

Doctrine is not practice. Enforcement, while being the practice of an institution, does not usually result in uniform, normed behavior on the part of the population being regulated. Nonetheless, enforcement reveals a great deal about the importance of a subject to an institution, and it is not without effect. The two main tools by which the church tried to enforce its sexual doctrine were confession and the ecclesiastical courts.

Despite the importance that some historians of sexuality accord to confession, its efficacy in changing popular sexual behavior is largely unknown. By the Reformation, individual confession was usually practiced only once yearly (at Easter).[13] The long interval between confessions and the press to accommodate all parishioners at the same holiday, the uneven and often poor education of the local priests, and the peasant resistance to interference in their (married) sexual lives that social historians have discovered, all suggest that confession's effects must at best have been small and gradual over centuries.[14]

I find confession significant for two reasons. It was the primary setting in which the church developed its sexual doctrine, and its punishments created the same problems (and solutions) that absolutist officials later encountered when they attempted sexual regulation.

In the confessional sexual behavior came under sustained scrutiny as it did in no other church institution. Because by its nature confession dealt with negatives, the reflection about sex that it inspired was also wholly negative; that is, it concentrated on misdeeds. To aid confessors in their delicate interrogations and chastisements, guidebooks, called penitentials, were developed in the fifth and sixth to eleventh centuries. According to Brundage, "sexual offenses constituted the largest single category of behavior that the penitentials treated."[15] Indeed, the penitentials elaborated for the first time the hierarchy of sexual sins. The penitential writers became the church's first experts on sexual misdeeds, for their opinions were subsequently adopted by canon lawyers, who had not dissected the subject of sexual transgression in such detail themselves.[16] Although these manuals influenced canon law, the emphasis expressed in them differed from that of canon law. The penitentials

[12]Tentler, *Confession*, 141–42.
[13]My understanding of the history of confession comes largely from Tentler's excellent study.
[14]Flandrin, *Temps pour embrasser*, 153–58.
[15]Brundage, *Law*, 153.
[16]Ibid., 169, 172.

tended to be more specific in delineating sexual misdeeds,[17] harsher in their judgment of appropriate penance, and much more concerned with nonmarital and nonprocreative acts, especially male homosexuality and masturbation.[18] Their preoccupation with these "secret" sins is probably due to their authors' own position as monks and confessors to priests,[19] whose unsuccessful struggles with celibacy would have ended in these acts. The peculiarities of especially the monastic and clerical confessional thus encouraged church sexual doctrine to develop more in response to internal considerations (of the clerical writers) than to the actual circumstances of layfolk. Penitential literature, and thus to some extent canon law, elaborated an abstract system of sexual prohibitions irrelevant to lay life and often unsuited to practical enforcement.

The penances set by the penitentials, while not absolutely uniform, were draconian: on average the manuals dictated for mortal sins ("unnatural" sex, or sex with clergy, for example) at least seven years of fasting (that is, a diet of bread and water periodically supplemented by other fare), fifteen years of excommunication, and lifelong prohibition of sexual activity.[20] Lesser sexual sins received lesser penances, but all were stringent.[21] As the absolutist states would later do, the church creatively adjusted these unrealistic penalties. Although the heavy penances were repeatedly cited by moralists and legists alike, in fact they were systematically replaced by lesser, arbitrary punishments; by split penances—whereby an easy, mandatory penance that often could be performed immediately was combined with a voluntary, tougher penance; and, finally, by indulgences.[22] This practice of mitigation made it possible to salvage dogma and achieve perhaps an educational effect without in fact demanding more from people than they were capable of rendering or willing to undergo.

The ecclesiastical courts were the second, more formal way by which the church tried to enforce its sexual doctrine. Canon law and the procedures and rules of evidence of ecclesiastical courts were far more advanced than the comparable legal structures of secular authorities, and thus canon law had a major influence on secular legal developments.

Canon law condemned masturbation, incorrect position, sodomy, bestiality, and the like, but its clearest, most elaborated articles, as well as the majority of sexually related cases appearing before church courts, concerned adultery and fornication, with clerical concubinage, incest, and rape/abduction coming next. That is, canon

---

[17] For example, Gratian did not bother to stipulate the penalties for "unnatural" sex, though he condemned it. Ibid., 250–51.

[18] This difference is clear throughout Brundage's account.

[19] Friedrich Wilhelm Hermann Wasserschleben, *Die Bussordnungen der abendländischen Kirche nebst einer rechtsgeschichtlichen Einleitung* (Halle, 1851), 6–10, where he speculates about the importance of the monastic provenience of the genre.

[20] Flandrin, *Temps pour embrasser*, 129.

[21] Brundage, *Law*, 164–65, cites penitentials calling for one to two years' fasting for simple fornication.

[22] Tentler, *Confession*, 328–38.

law was most concerned to regulate heterosexual cases in which the social relation of the partners was the problem. A very similar pattern of priorities existed for secular authorities, and for the same reason. Unlawful sexual activity that also disrupted social relations was doubly bad. Since the church was in charge of disciplining its own clergy, and since in the eleventh and twelfth centuries the church had extended its temporal jurisdiction to cover marriage, the secular authorities were relieved of the obligation to prosecute concubinage and most cases of incest. But adultery, fornication, and rape had potentially serious family and property consequences that went to the heart of the state's mandate to prevent violence among its subjects and to uphold the security of existing social institutions. Since the religious and the secular orders sustained each other, a number of delicts threatening both were "mixed," or of "mixed jurisdiction" (*mixti fori*). That is, they were shared and could be investigated and tried, and the culprits could be punished by either ecclesiastical or secular courts or, indeed, by both. Sacrilege, usury, witchcraft, and perjury fell into this category. But sexual sins were the classical example of mixed delicts.[23]

In *Die geistliche Gerichtsbarkeit* Georg May examines church/state cooperation in Erfurt just before the Reformation. Whereas the lower ecclesiastical court (*Sendgericht*) handled minor sins of the flesh, the higher ecclesiastical court (*Generalgericht*) focused on "stuprum [impregnation of an unmarried woman of good moral reputation], fornication, concubinage, incest, adultery, bigamy."[24] At the same time, however, worldly authorities were also punishing cases of adultery and bigamy. May indicates that although jurisdictional conflict occasionally erupted between church and state, in general the system operated effectively, without firm principles or undivided legal authority ever being worked out.[25]

The ecclesiastical penalty system was very like that of absolutist secular practice. Although canon law threatened drastic punishments, the actual sentences were generally far lighter and achieved through finely graded categories of penalties that were carefully mixed to match the sin. Small monetary fines were often imposed. This pattern apparently also held for sexual crimes, though more studies would be welcome to establish past practice exactly.[26]

At some point the aim of reconciliation spawned another church procedure, the *Kirchenbuße* (church atonement). This practice may have originated in the public atonement ceremony performed by penitents on the Thursday before Easter (*Gründonnerstag*).[27] The church recommended yearly confession at Easter, and upon completion of confession, penitents were readmitted as communicants in a mass ceremony of atonement. This rite seems to have it become especially, though

[23] Georg May, *Die geistliche Gerichtsbarkeit des Erzbischofs von Mainz im Thüringen des späten Mittelalters. Das Generalgericht zu Erfurt* (Leipzig, 1956), 209. Brundage, *Law*, 319.
[24] May, *Geistliche Gerichtsbarkeit*, 209–10.
[25] Ibid., 327.
[26] Ibid., 212–24.
[27] The surmise of Dietrich Kluge, "Die 'Kirchenbuße' als staatliches Zuchtmittel im 15.–18. Jahrhundert," *Jahrbuch für westfälische Kirchengeschichte* 70 (1977): 57.

never exclusively, associated with sins of the flesh. The guilty fornicant or adulterer, after having shown contrition and perhaps having accomplished some other act of atonement, would stand in church before the congregation, in penitential garb (sackcloth or a white smock) with a burning, often black candle in one hand, sometimes a flagellant's whip in the other, a straw wreath perhaps on her head, if the miscreant were a woman, and possibly a sign around the neck. This ceremony was not intended to induce shame in the penitent, but to express the shame and contrition he or she already felt and which was the prerequisite to proper confession and forgiveness.[28] The *Kirchenbuße* was merely the opportunity to demonstrate atonement. Beginning in the fifteenth century, however, secular authorities particularly in cities began handing down the *Kirchenbuße* themselves. The secular framework changed the meaning. The purpose now was to induce shame via public humiliation, thus producing a cheap, but effective alternative to more drastic bodily punishments.[29] Used this way, the *Kirchenbuße* punished, but did not reconcile. The transformation of the *Kirchenbuße*, which will occupy us again, illustrates how the differing interests of church and state could give entirely different meaning to the same institution.

[margin note: 2 diff uses of Kirchen-buße]

The pre-Reformation Christian legacy to secular authorities consisted in having compiled and defined the list of sexual misdeeds and their fitting punishments. But the church had done so according to doctrinal, not practical criteria. Its second legacy therefore was to solve the resulting enforcement problem by silently narrowing regulatory focus to acts with social consequences and mitigating the actual penalties.

[margin note: legacy of pre-Ref church]

The Reformation

The Reformation transformed these legacies. Its urgent emphasis on moral reform had two important aspects: it linked Christian moral behavior with civic strength, and it focused on the real lives of the laity. Consequently, the reformers revalued marriage as the moral crucible tempering human (sexual) nature into godliness and civic responsibility. The upward valuation of marriage and marital sex shortened the list of sexual misdeeds to those more suitable to external regulation, and the reformers' moral fervor impelled them to press for real enforcement. Out of this atmosphere and on Reformation institutions the absolutist states built the foundations of secular regulation.

[margin note: (+) view of marriage marital sex]

What began as a reform of church doctrine and institutions swiftly became a demand for reform of life. Scholars debate whether doctrinal reform (*reformatio doctrinae*), which is associated with Martin Luther, was really so different from reform of life (*reformatio vitae*), associated with John Calvin and Huldrych Zwingli,

---

[28] See Tentler, *Confession*, 250–63, on contrition as the sine quo non for confession.
[29] Kluge, "Kirchenbuße," 56–63.

that the latter should be called a "second reformation."[30] It seems clear that Calvinist and Zwinglian dominated areas did try more assiduously than their Lutheran counterparts to saturate secular life with reformed Christian principles; they were consequently more interventionist regarding sexual behavior, as well. But scholars agree that the Reformation everywhere sent powerful shock waves into the secular landscape. The Reformation was not a purely religious phenomenon, however; it was carried and put into practice by guilds and merchants, city councils, territorial princes, and fathers anxious to have their authority over wife and children bolstered by reformed doctrine. The intertwining of late medieval church and state, which we have observed in the example of tangled legal jurisdiction over sexual offenses, continued in the Reformation. In fact, it became more intense as reformers explicitly recognized the independence of secular authorities (Luther's "two empires" doctrine), while simultaneously insisting that reformed religious principles ground actual life and governance in the community. Not only Protestant, but also Catholic secular authorities in cities and territories readily accepted this challenge, which may have burdened them with greater governmental duties, but which also vastly increased their power over subjects, while justifying that power in the strongest possible terms as a duty to God. In short, there is no meaningful way to sever the religious from the secular in the Reformation. Nonetheless, certain institutions, regulatory preoccupations, and chastisements can be identified as more clearly serving either religious or secular ends.

In the reformers's eyes, none of the church's failings loomed larger than its perceived inability to enforce orderly sexual lives on either laity or clergy. In the time-honored Christian tradition of reading from sexual behavior to the condition of the soul, reformers interpreted sexual chaos as indicating the thoroughgoing moral decay of the old church. The main symptoms lay in marriage, clerical concubinage, and widespread flouting of sexual decorum, especially publicly tolerated prostitution. These three "symptoms" were widespread, visible social practices, not arcane or hidden sins, like those penalized by the penitentials or the more abstract sections of canon law. Reforming them meant provoking practical, social change. The Reformation set about to overhaul all three problems, but the very heart of the new moral regime was the reform of marriage.

As Lyndal Roper put it: "When, in 1532, Luther meditated on the central goals of the reformation of the church which he had set in motion, he numbered the changes in the institution of marriage as amongst the most important."[31] Reform of marriage was the keystone of the Protestant social edifice. Reformers declared the

---

[30] See the discussion and bibliographical footnotes in Heinz Schilling, ed., *Die reformierte Konfessionalisierung in Deutschland—Das Problem der "Zweiten Reformation." Wissenschaftliches Symposion des Vereins für Reformationsgeschichte 1985* (Gütersloh, 1986).

[31] "Luther: Sex, Marriage and Motherhood," *History Today*, December 1983, 33.

basic unit of Christian society to be not the individual but the married couple.[32] Marriage, far from being a necessary evil, or at most a limited good for loving individuals, was redefined as the most appropriate conduit for one's relation to God[33] and, finally, the original link in the chain of analogies justifying the sociopolitical hierarchy. Marriage was God-given; it was the natural condition for all humans, lay and clerical. Luther called it "a godly and blessed estate" and "not only . . . the equal of all other estates, but rather . . . before and above them, whether they be emperors, princes, bishops, or whoever."[34] Calvin wrote that "the institution of marriage may be taken as an inviolable law."[35] The Strasbourg reformer Martin Bucer deduced a universal right to marriage, contravention of which was an offense against God;[36] the preachers in Ulm (1531) went farther and suggested "the principle of a duty to marry, unless impotence or a special calling should hinder this."[37]

It is as if reformers were intent on making marriage a commandment to compensate for having removed it as a sacrament. By recognizing marriage as a worldly thing they increased its significance as the institution where the divine and the human meet. In marriage, God's order for individuals and society becomes fully congruent. That is, marriage both fulfills God's plan for human destiny and justifies the social order on religious principles. For the relation of man and wife, spiritually equal, carries with it nonetheless religious and social domination. The husband is the religious leader of the household and the authority over wife, children, and servants. The wife shares power and responsibility over children and servants, but is otherwise subject to her husband.[38] This correct family order is the explicit analogue to the obedience all subjects owe their superiors. On the subject of obedience, Calvin wrote that honoring one's father and mother "means that God wants the order He has ordained to be upheld, [it means] that we must observe the degrees of preeminence as He has given them to us."[39] Luther, characteristically blunter, described how marriage lay the personal foundations for the entire social order: "No, my dear fellow," he wrote, "once you are bound to a wife, you are no

---

[32] André Biéler, *L'Homme et la femme dans la morale Calviniste. La doctrine réformée zur l'amour, le mariage, le célibat, le divorce, l'adultère et la prostitution, considérée dans sons cadre historique* (Geneva, 1962), 146–48.

[33] Thus, Calvin, cited in Biéler, *Morale Calviniste,* 38–39; and Martin Luther, "The Estate of Marriage (1522)," trans. Walther I. Brandt, in *Luther's Works,* ed. Helmut T. Lehmann, vol. 45, *The Christian in Society,* ed. Walther I. Brandt (Philadelphia, 1962), 42, 46.

[34] "Der große Katechismus (1529)," in *Dr. Martin Luthers sämmtliche Werke,* vol. 21, *Dr. Martin Luthers katechetische deutsche Schriften* (Erlangen, 1932), 70.

[35] *Comm. Nouveau Testament,* Matt. 19:4; cited in Biéler, *Morale Calviniste,* 64.

[36] *De regno Christi libri duo,* ed. François Wendel, vol. 15 of *Martini Buceri opera latina* (Paris, 1955), 2.45, 226–31, cited in Brundage, *Law,* 554.

[37] Walther Köhler, *Zürcher Ehegericht und Genfer Konsistorium,* vol. 2, *Das Ehe- und Sittengericht in den süddeutschen Reichsstädten, dem Herzogtum Württemberg und in Genf* (Leipzig, 1942), 48–49. Cf. this statement with Theodor von Hippel's view in chapter 6, p. 242.

[38] For Luther on relations of domination and authority in the household, see Roper, "Luther," 38.

[39] *Institution* (1560), 2. 8. 35, cited in Biéler, *Morale Calviniste,* 95.

longer a free master: God demands that you stay by wife and child, nourishing and disciplining them, and that you obey your authorities and help and advise your neighbors."[40] Divorce and bolstered parental consent, two other far-reaching aspects of Protestant marriage reform, were both designed to strengthen that institution.[41]

Marriage, however, was not merely a social institution, it was also a sexual union. The Reformation consequently marks another upward revaluation of sexual behavior. As in the twelfth century, the process of revaluation was channeled exclusively into marriage and consequently changed that institution, while also altering the hierarchy of sexual delicts outside it.

Reformers were unanimous about two points. First, they accepted sexual desire as a universal human appetite that could only very rarely be successfully stifled.[42] Encouraging celibacy was fruitless and promoted hypocrisy, or worse: "Whenever men try to resist this, it remains irresistible nonetheless and goes its way through fornication, adultery, and secret sins, for this is a matter of nature and not of choice," wrote Luther.[43] Further, neither virginity nor celibacy were holy attributes. That central assumption of the desert mystics, which lived on in Roman Catholicism in the guise of priestly celibacy after the Council of Trent, was wholly rejected by Protestants.[44] Second, not only was sex in marriage not a sin, the capacity for sexual joy was "a sign of [God's] goodness and infinite sweetness" (Calvin).[45] It was a positive good in itself, because it was a gift of God. It was thus no longer necessary to justify sexual pleasure by positing procreation as its goal; both Calvin and Luther explicitly rejected that utilitarian rationalization.[46]

Protestant sexual doctrine built upon several pillars: the acceptance and even affirmation of sex within marriage; the ideal of marriage as the exclusive, natural arrangement for all Christians; and the expectation that doctrine would voluntarily be lived—that is, for each individual, family, Church community, and civic society itself, external coercion would be replaced by pious self-regulation.

[40] "Von Ehesachen (1530)," in *Dr. Martin Luther's sämmtliche Werke*, vol. 23, *Dr. Martin Luthers katechetische deutsche Schriften* (Erlangen, 1938), 147.

[41] Martin Luther, "That Parents Should Neither Compel nor Hinder the Marriage of Their Children and That Children Should not Become Engaged Without Their Parents' Consent (1524)," trans. Walther I. Brandt, in *Luther's Works*, 45:379–93. Protestants universally recognized adultery as a ground for divorce because of the grave importance they assigned sexual conduct; see Roderick Phillips, *Untying the Knot: A Short History of Divorce* (Cambridge, 1991), 12–19.

[42] Luther accepted the inevitability of sexual desire without attributing to it any aspect of the sublime. See Roper, "Luther," 34–35.

[43] "Estate of Marriage," 18, also 45.

[44] Ibid., 46–47, and the list of his tracts against celibacy in "An Exhortation to the Knights of the Teutonic Order That They Lay Aside False Chastity and Assume the True Chastity of Wedlock (1523)," in *Luther's Works*, 45:141 n. 3; Jean Calvin, *Institutes of the Christian Religion*, 2 vols., trans. Henry Beveridge (Grand Rapids, Mich., 1957), bk. 4, chap. 12, secs. 23–28 (I have used Beveridge's translation throughout); Roper, "Luther," 35; Biéler, *Morale Calviniste*, 61.

[45] Calvin, *Comm. Moïse*, Deut. 24:5, cited in Biéler, *Morale Calviniste*, 61.

[46] Roper, "Luther," 35; Biéler, *Morale Calviniste*, 37–38. Still, Luther often used the phrase "God's ordinance to produce seed and to multiply" to mean sexual desire or energy. Cf. "Estate of Marriage," 19, 45.

❧ The Church, Traditional Society, and the Regulation of Sex ❧

The rejection of celibacy, the centrality of marriage to Christian life and community, and the upward valuation of marital sex made the Protestant vision even more resolutely heterosexual and family-centered than had previously been the case. As Calvin reasoned, God "has also sanctified [the institution of marriage]. *Hence,* it is evident, that any mode of cohabitation different from marriage is cursed in his sight."[47] Celibacy was especially noxious because it contravened the natural order and encouraged perversion.[48] As Luther put it, without marriage, "it is simply impossible for you to remain righteous."[49] The Protestant reformers were so firmly fixed on marital or heterosexual sex, however, that they had relatively little to say about sodomy, bestiality, and masturbation, apart from their broadsides against the putatively celibate clergy. They did not approve of these acts, but nonrelational, nonheterosexual activity was too marginal to the central project of reforming marriage to count for very much. The married Protestant clergy itself was presumably less concerned with overcoming these temptations, and less likely to project them onto their congregations. The clergy now shared with their parishioners the problems characteristic of marital sex and turned their corrective attention instead on "adultery, loose living, and fornication," that is, on extramarital heterosexual activities that directly threatened marriage.[50]

The abolition of confession must also have wrought changes in Protestant sexual doctrine. Calvinists and Zwinglians abolished individual confession altogether; Lutherans kept a vestige of it, but even then, as Roper writes, "it was not obligatory and it was not to probe the sexual life of husband and wife."[51] Whereas confessional inquiry had previously focused on uncovering each individual, sinful act, it now concentrated on general sinfulness. Given this shift in emphasis, "some of the obsessions of [the confessional] literature . . . inevitably disappeared, such as sinful thoughts, nocturnal emission, or the motivation and position of the marital act."[52]

There was thus a threefold shift in preoccupation or interest: from general sexual prohibition to positive specific sexual expectation; from "secret," nonrelational acts to (heterosexual, that is socially relevant) relational ones; from errors of desire and intention to actual public or socially relevant acts.[53] The last two shifts made the Reformation understanding of sexual behavior more appropriate to successful regulation by focusing on fewer, but more visible acts.

Despite these fundamental changes, there were nonetheless continuities in the hierarchy of sexual sins in Protestant doctrine. The only approved locus of sexual expression was still marriage. And within marriage, not every act was acceptable.

---

[47] *Institutes,* bk. 2, chap. 8, sec. 41, emphasis mine.

[48] Ibid., bk. 4, chap. 13, sec. 21; Luther, "Estate of Marriage," 18.

[49] "Estate of Marriage," 19.

[50] Lyndal Roper, *The Holy Household: Women and Morals in Reformation Augsburg* (Oxford, 1989), 67–68.

[51] "Luther," 36.

[52] Tentler, *Confession,* 357.

[53] Roper has a nice discussion of some aspects of this shift, and especially of the influence of secular government in it. See *Holy Household,* 64–68.

Calvin wrote that couples should "live chastely in their marriage, with appropriate modesty; and that the husband should have intercourse with his wife in all chastity and moderation, and that their bed must not be profaned with immodest lasciviousness."[54] Luther was somewhat more old-fashioned than Calvin, and his list of prohibited sexual acts generally followed the traditional, penitential ladder: first sacrilege, and then in descending order, incest, adultery, abduction, deflowering, promiscuity, and fornication. He too believed that marital love could be overly ardent, and he even mentioned "unnatural" vice, nocturnal emissions, and sinful words.[55] The basic catalog of prohibitions was thus by no means overcome. It lived on, if in paler, partly rearranged form.

Although the reorientation of sexual expectation (and therefore of prohibition) along the marital/heterosexual axis eclipsed the earlier regulatory focus on certain acts, it also brought others to the fore. Luther and Bucer both called for the death penalty for adultery,[56] a sign of the increased importance it merited by virtue of the revised spiritual and social place of marriage. Sexual fidelity was so critical to marriage that adultery became one of the few unchallenged grounds for divorce.[57] Prostitution, like adultery, also threatened the newly exalted estate of marriage. Previously condemned in theory but tolerated in fact, it became a major target for reformers, who succeeded in getting the secular authorities to outlaw prostitution wherever the Reformation extended.[58]

The Catholic Church reacted to its Protestant critics by holding fast to most objects of criticism and thus sharpening the differences between it and the breakaway Protestants. The Catholic doctrinal response to the Reformation was recorded at the Council of Trent (1545–63).[59] Trent rejected divorce and retained marriage as a sacrament, clerical celibacy, the principle of the couple's mutual consent as sufficient for valid marriage (as opposed to requiring parental consent and sexual consummation), and the rather lower valuation of sexual intercourse, which was taken neither to enhance the couple's love for one another and thus further to cement marriage, nor to be a sign of God's love for His human creatures. The Reformation had not gone by completely unnoticed, however. Betrothals had to be witnessed (to cut back on clandestine marriage). The upward revaluation of marriage also caused the Catholic Church to condemn lay concubinage. And Brundage

---

[54] *Comm. Nouveau Testament*, Hebrews 8:4, cited in Biéler, *Morale Calviniste*, 63. Luther agreed: "A Sermon on the Estate of Marriage (1519)," trans. James Atkinson, in *Luther's Works*, ed. Helmut T. Lehmann, vol. 44, ed. James Atkinson (Philadelphia, 1966), 10. Moderation was central to the positive sexual estimation of the practitioners of later civil society.

[55] *D. Martin Luther's Werke. Kritische Gesammtausgabe*, ed. J.K.F. Knaake et al. (Weimar, 1883; rpt., Graz, 1966) 1:482–99, cited in Tentler, *Confession*, 358–59 n. 17.

[56] Brundage, *Law*, 557, 558 n. 35; Ulrich Zwingli, "Ordinance and Notice. How Matters Concerning Marriage shall be Conducted in the City of Zurich" (1525), in *Selected Works*, trans. Samuel Macauley Jackson (Philadelphia, 1901; rpt. 1972), 122. Adultery was not, in fact, punished so harshly, and Luther, "Estate of Marriage," 32–33, clearly thought that draconian punishment was impossible in practice.

[57] Zwingli, "Ordinance," 121–22; Luther, "Estate of Marriage," 30–32.

[58] Roper, *Holy Household*, 89–131.

[59] Brundage, *Law*, 565–67.

finds a slight tendency to be more positive toward sex in marriage. Otherwise, Rome held its ground.

Brundage sums up the post-Tridentine Roman Catholic attitude toward sex as more negative than that of Protestants, to the extent that it continued to associate sex with impurity and the generally sinful condition of humanity.[60] This assessment is accurate, but incomplete. For the Protestants' higher regard for the psychologically and socially binding capacity of marital sex had three developmental possibilities that might encourage greater sexual regulation than did the skeptical, Catholic attitude. First, Protestants used natural law extensively to justify marriage and heterosexual, marital intercourse. This justification went beyond the minimal position, with which Catholics agreed, that marriage was the only acceptable place for sex. The Protestant view claimed a natural, narrowly focussed sexual desire. The Catholic viewpoint tended to imagine sexual desire as protean and apt to flow anywhere. Centuries of learned reflection had worked out a hierarchy of sexual misdeeds and even labeled some of them "unnatural," but this hierarchy had to do with doctrine and God's will, not with the human capacity for sin. That is, Catholic sexual negativism tended to see sexual acts as having a single source in original sin, and to see human beings as (potentially) capable of committing any of these acts. Against this view, Protestants invented a sexually narrower human being, one whose sexual desire was already naturally programmed toward marital heterosexuality, deviations from which were the products either of bad environment or inborn deficiency. The Protestant view created a solid axis of differentiation among sinful acts, encouraged intervention to restore the rightful, natural condition, and suggested a coherence between the sexual act and the person committing it.

Second, in the moment that Protestantism accorded marital sex a positive role in creating and guaranteeing the fundamental social unit, it provided new justification for placing sexual behavior altogether into a social context. The relative indifference of the pre-Reformation church to the social consequences of its sexual doctrine had been heavily criticized by reformers. They had been especially severe about the inconsistency of clerical celibacy as a doctrine and clerical concubinage as a practice and the encouragement the mutual consent doctrine gave to troublesome clandestine marriages. Their own efforts to reconcile doctrine with social effects encouraged a reverse logic: if good sexual behavior contributed positively to society, then bad sexual behavior must hurt it. Therefore, some social problems might best be attacked by changing sexual behavior. In short, the Protestant's positive valuation of sex held the paradoxical potential for greater sexual interventionism in the name of society than did Catholic negativism, which was more strongly doctrinal than social.

Third, the stress on *reformatio vitae* predisposed Protestants to interventionism in order to bring about a community based on functioning Christian principles, including sexual ones. None of the reformers believed they would fully succeed, but

---

[60] Ibid., 574–75.

all of them believed it was a Christian's duty to try. This element was missing from Roman Catholic pastoral and disciplinary practice. Peter Lang has worked through the records of Roman Catholic church visitations in the sixteenth and seventeenth centuries. He discovered that Roman Catholic visitors, like their Protestant counterparts, concentrated during the sixteenth century on controlling clerical behavior and ensuring that sacraments were properly administered and sermons were doctrinally sound. Once these issues had been brought under control, the focus shifted after 1600 to education in the catechism and, slightly, to the behavior of the parishioners. Lang concludes, "The Church overseers worried very little about the morality of the parish. Insofar as they dealt with it at all, they concentrated on sexual failings and after that occasionally on superstitions like magic or fortune-telling."[61] Thus, although the Roman Catholic Church was certainly not indifferent to sexual misdeeds, its focus remained essentially doctrinal.

Despite the Roman Catholic Church's doctrinal steadfastness, Catholic rulers were as impressed as their Protestant colleagues by the new atmosphere of moral zeal and by the postulated social and political relevance of sexual acts, as judged on the marital scale. Catholic and Protestant absolutist states were therefore very similar in their moral legislation and secular efforts at sexual regulation.[62] As all absolutist territorial states built on the foundations Protestantism laid for sexual regulation, so did the eighteenth-century practitioners of civil society build on the Protestant revaluation of sexual nature.[63]

Altogether, the Reformation stimulated secular authorities to pay closer attention to the classical sexual offenses (that is, those defined as socially relevant), to overhaul legislation dealing with sexual delicts, and to punish miscreants more harshly. The Reformation also created new institutions to create or maintain good morals. These new regulatory institutions developed from two sources in Protestant doctrine. One was the duty of individuals and individual communities of believers (congregations) to police themselves. Truly moral behavior occurred not via external constraint, but through the exercise of free will, helped along by the internalization of moral precepts and, in cases of errors, by persuasion. Morality in this sense was the purview of the church.[64]

---

[61] "Reform im Wandel. Die katholischen Visitationsinterrogatorien des 16. und 17. Jahrhunderts," in *Kirche und Visitation. Beiträge zur Erforschung des frühneuzeitlichen Visitationswesens in Europa*, ed. Walter Zeeden and Peter Lang (Stuttgart, 1984), 141.

[62] I discuss this more fully in Chapter 2. On the interpenetration of post-Tridentine Catholicism and absolutism in Bavaria, see Philip M. Soergel, *Wondrous in His Saints: Counter-Reform Propaganda in Bavaria* (Berkeley, Calif., 1993), esp. 75–98.

[63] See Chapter 6, pp. 236–45.

[64] Biéler, *Morale Calviniste*, 54–56. For the institutions of church and parishioner self-regulation regarding sexual behavior, see Paul Münch, *Zucht und Ordnung. Reformierte Kirchenverfassungen im 16. und 17. Jahrhundert (Nassau-Dillenburg, Kurpfalz, Hessen-Kassel)* (Stuttgart, 1978); Heinz Schilling, "Reformierte Kirchenzucht als Sozialdisziplinierung. Die Tätigkeit des Emder Presbyteriums in den Jahren 1557–1562," in *Niederlande und Nordwestdeutschland. Studien zur Regional- und Stadtgeschichte Nordwestkontinentaleuropas im Mittelalter und in der Neuzeit*, ed. Wilfried Ehbrecht and Heinz Schilling

❦ The Church, Traditional Society, and the Regulation of Sex ❦

The reformers, however, believed the state was equally, though differently, critical to a functioning, Christian life. As Calvin wrote of civil government:

> Its object is not merely . . . to enable men to breathe, eat, drink, and be warmed . . . but it is, that no idolatry, no blasphemy against the name of God, no calumnies against his truth, nor other offences to religion, break out and be disseminated among the people; that the public quiet be not disturbed, that every man's property be kept secure, that men may carry on innocent commerce with each other, that honesty and modesty be cultivated; in short, that a public form of religion may exist among Christians, and humanity among men.[65]

The secular authorities had the duty to ensure the practice of a Christian life, that is, the "public form of religion," which includes "honesty and modesty." This external order was inferior to the internal order emanating from the society of the faithful, but it was necessary to maintain it as a bulwark against the chaos that would result from gross violations of God's commandments. Laws and police should rule over this terrain.

The Reformation created the first great codification of the rules of public order. Reflecting the conviction that civic and moral well-being were interchangeable, these rules were variously called "discipline ordinance" (*Zuchtordnung*, in Saxony, Augsburg, Constance, Memmingen, and elsewhere), "church ordinance" (*Kirchenordnung*, in Ulm), or "reformation ordinance" (*Reformationsordnung*, in Basel) and combined regular police regulations with moral dicta and marriage laws.[66] The discipline ordinances bequeathed to the absolutist state its basic sexual laws. The ordinances also established the two quintessential moral regulatory institutions of the Reformation: the marriage courts and the discipline masters.

(Cologne, 1983), 261–327; Heinz Schilling, *Konfessionskonflikt und Staatsbildung. Eine Fallstudie über das Verhältnis von religiösem und sozialem Wandel in der Frühneuzeit am Beispiel der Grafschaft Lippe* (Gütersloh, 1981); Paul Münch, "Kirchenzucht und Nachbarschaft. Zur sozialen Problematik des calvinistischen Seniorats um 1600," in *Kirche und Visitation. Beiträge zur Erforschung des frühneuzeitlichen Visitationswesens in Europa*, ed. Ernst Walter Zeeden and Peter Thaddäus Lang (Stuttgart, 1984), 216–48; Heinz Schilling and Helmut Sydow, "Calvinistische Presbyterien in Städten der Frühneuzeit—eine kirchliche Alternativform zur bürgerlichen Repräsentation? (Mit einer quantifizierenden Untersuchung zur Holländischen Stadt Leiden)," in *Städtische Führungsgruppen und Gemeinde in der werdenden Neuzeit*, ed. Wilfried Ehbrecht (Cologne, 1980), 385–444; Paul Münch, "Volkskultur und Calvinismus. Zu Theorie und Praxis der 'reformatio vitae' während der 'Zweiten Reformation,'" in *Die reformierte Konfessionalisierung in Deutschland—Das Problem der "Zweiten Reformation." Wissenschaftliches Symposion des Vereins für Reformationsgeschichte 1985*, ed. Heinz Schilling (Gütersloh, 1986); Heinz Schilling, "'Geschichte der Sünde' oder 'Geschichte des Verbrechens'? Überlegungen zur Gesellschaftsgeschichte der frühneuzeitlichen Kirchenzucht," *Annali dell' Istituto storico italo-germanico in Trente* 12 (1986): 169–92; Ernst Walter Zeeden et al., eds., *Repertorium der Kirchenvisitationsakten aus dem 16. und 17. Jahrhundert in Archiven der Bundesrepublik Deutschland*, 2 vols. to date (Stuttgart, 1982–); and Helga Schnabel-Schüle, "Kirchenleitung und Kirchenvisitation in Territorien des deutschen Südwestens," in Zeeden et al., *Repertorium der Kirchenvisitationsakten*, 2. 2. 13–104.

[65] *Institutes*, bk. 4, chap. 22, sec. 3.

[66] Morals offenses typically included such delicts as swearing, drunkenness, curfew violations, gambling, heresy (Anabaptism), usury, sorcery, violations of the clothing ordinance, fornication, adultery, illegitimacy, and certain folk customs associated with sexual license or unapproved pairing.

Marriage courts replaced ecclesiastical courts in Protestant regions. Marking the gradual shift from ecclesiastical to secular control of marriage, membership on the marriage court was normally divided between secular representatives (from the large and small city councils or the county commissars) and (outnumbered) clergy.[67] In Augsburg, there were no clergy on the *Ehegericht* at all.[68] Most marriage courts functioned like regular civil courts, handing down legally binding decisions on the validity of marriages, marriages without parental consent, divorces, claims for redress for loss of virginity (under promise of marriage), and claims for child support.[69] Appeals might go either to the city council or a higher secular court; however, since marriage defined the boundaries of sexual morality, it perforce defined sexual misconduct as well. Therefore, marriage courts often handled sexual delicts as well, including many we no longer regard as marriage-related. Ravensburg's marriage court, for example, was given sole jurisdiction over marriages without parental consent (*Winkelehen*), but also over fornication, unwed pregnancy, rape [!], and *stuprum*. The marriage court shared with the city council jurisdiction over delicts leading to divorce or arising in matters of divorce, whereas the city council alone was to handle *Kuppelei* (providing a place for illicit heterosexual trysts), repeated promiscuity, adultery, and desertion.[70] The Zurich marriage court swiftly developed an alternate persona as morals court (*Sittengericht*). In less than a year after its founding (1525) it had begun punishing prostitutes, *Kuppler,* and adulterers; it warned women not to permit men to visit them in the absence of their husbands.[71] Soon it began holding morals hearings with separate records from its usual marriage court proceedings.[72]

Zurich was a bit unusual, however. Most south German cities and not a few northern ones experimented with another institution, the discipline masters (*Zuchtherren*), who were to oversee morality, including but not limited to sexual propriety. The institution of the discipline master was inspired by two sources. The

[67] Walther Köhler, *Zürcher Ehegericht und Genfer Konsistorium,* vol. 1, *Das Zürcher Ehegericht und seine Auswirkung in der deutschen Schweiz zur Zeit Zwinglis* (Leipzig, 1932), 35 (Zurich); Köhler, *Zürcher Ehegericht und Genfer Konsistorium,* vol. 2, *Das Ehe- und Sittengericht in den süddeutschen Reichsstädten, dem Herzogtum Württemberg und in Genf* (Leipzig, 1942), 658 (Lindau, Stuttgart); Schilling, "Geschichte der Sünde," 187 (Emden); Paul Warmbrunn, *Zwei Konfessionen in einer Stadt. Das Zusammenleben von Katholiken und Protestanten in den paritätischen Reichsstädten Augsburg, Biberach, Ravensburg und Dinkelsbühl von 1548 bis 1648* (Wiesbaden, 1983), 272 (Dinkelsbühl); Thomas Max Safley, *Let No Man Put Asunder. The Control of Marriage in the German Southwest: A Comparative Study, 1550–1600* (Kirksville, Mo., 1984), 123–24 (Basel).

[68] Roper, *Holy Household,* 168 n. 3.

[69] Ibid., 63; Köhler, *Zürcher Ehegericht,* 2:43–44, 81–85 (on Ulm). Münster was apparently an exception; there, the marriage court was empowered to mediate marital conflict but not to decide on divorce. Martin Brecht, "Die Ulmer Kirchenordnung von 1531, Die Basler Reformationsordnung von 1629 und die Münsteraner Zuchtordnung von 1533," in *Niederlande und Nordwestdeutschland. Studien zur Regional- und Stadtgeschichte Nordwestkontinentaleuropas im Mittelalter und in der Neuzeit,* ed. Wilfried Ehbrecht and Heinz Schilling (Cologne, 1983), 161.

[70] Warmbrunn, *Zwei Konfessionen,* 275. This division of labor was only theoretical since political events overtook its actual operation.

[71] Köhler, *Zürcher Ehegericht,* 1:148.

[72] Ibid., 2:144.

first, the secular *Einunger* (or *Ainunger*),[73] common in south Germany, was a town's lowest level investigative unit in charge of policing minor delicts. In Ulm, at least, its two stewards were permitted to enter suspects' houses at night and to employ assistants and "spies." According to Walther Köhler, "Breaking open doors blocked to them was their right."[74] The second inspiration was the new presbyterial form of visitations to miscreants by worthy church elders; here, admonishment and recon-ciliation were preferable to punishment, and "secrecy" (or privacy) preferable to publicity, because the object was to achieve voluntary, not forced compliance with moral norms.

When the religious representatives of eight Protestant cities met in Memmingen in 1531 to draft a model discipline ordinance, they outlined the division of labor they envisioned. "The Christian [secular] authorities shall punish 'all sins, which should be punished by excommunication, thus blasphemy, usury, adultery and other such, because they are contrary to God and his community, and also harmful and contrary to the common good and civic unit [*gemainen nutz und bürgerlichem wesen*]." In addition to this fully secular responsibility of Christian government, the reformers in Memmingen wanted the authorities to appoint *Zuchtherren*, who would make sure "that each and every scandal [*Ergernussen*], sin and act, which is against God, against the common good or against a third party [*wider den nechsten*]" was countered. Clearly, the goals of regular criminal justice and the new *Zuchtherren* were the same, but their methods were different. The latter were to confront the miscreant "at first either personally or through intermediaries 'silently and secretly, with true, fatherly warning.'" Men and women, residents and foreigners, would be treated equally. If the warning did not suffice, then the *Zuchtherren* were to turn the matter over to the city council, "as long as the matter is still secret." The council should also handle the matter secretly, and only if they failed or the misdeed became known, should regular punishment follow, "such that god and people may see that one abhors scandal and sin."[75] The *Zuchtherren* were thus to function as a secular court of first instance.

The Memmingen resolution then outlined a third disciplinary track: a religious one aimed at reconciliation. The conferees at Memmingen proposed a committee of equal representatives from the city council, the preachers, and the people, who with moral suasion and by withholding communion would try to move persons who had been punished by the *Zuchtherren* or the council, to repent and rejoin the Christian community.[76]

The example of Ulm shows how this religious impetus gave rise to a secular institution.[77] In Ulm preachers inspired by Zwingli drafted several proposed disciplinary codes (*Zuchtordnungen*) that all respected the rule of secular authority

[73] In Ravensburg the titles were interchangeable. Ibid., 2:337.
[74] Ibid., 2:4.
[75] Memminger Beschluß of 1531, cited in ibid., 2:26–27, 27–28.
[76] Ibid., 2:34–36.
[77] This discussion follows Köhler, ibid., 2:3–88.

over actual crimes and marriage law, but called for a lower, finer-meshed disciplinary system underneath, on the model of the Memmingen resolution. These *Bannherren* (the title came from *Bann,* excommunication) were church members empowered to pursue public morals cases involving violations of the Ten Commandments.[78] If their efforts at suasion were unsuccessful, the miscreant would be handed over for actual punishment to the city council, or to the guilds. Although the city council ultimately accepted the Memmingen resolution, it secularized the *Bannherren* by retaining all power to punish in its own hands, including the right to excommunicate.[79] To underline the secular nature of its authority, the council gave the *Bannherren* the title *Zuchtherren,* which has no religious overtones. It removed the guilds, too, from the disciplinary process. In the end, a dual disciplinary system emerged. So-called *Warnherren* (warning masters) with jurisdiction over "secret sins" and armed only with persuasion represented the church. They were the faint echo of what the *Bannherren* were supposed to have been. Meanwhile, the *Zuchtherren* continued to function as low-level, secular police, handing out fines and light punishments.

As in Ulm, the discipline masters normally developed into secular police; they often employed "informants" (*Kundschafter*), or "denouncers";[80] they levied fines and imposed short imprisonment terms. Their intrusive methods soon met with popular resistance.[81]

There is one further aspect of Reformation sexual regulation to consider—the gender differential. Roper found the Augsburg discipline masters particularly zealous in questioning women about their sexual misdeeds. She concluded that "an abiding legacy of the Reformation was the obsession with women's sexual experience," which strengthened "the belief that women's lusts were to be feared as unbridled and demonic."[82] This matter deserves further study, since the Augsburg moral police also prosecuted men for consorting with prostitutes and charged them more frequently than women with fornication and adultery. And distrust of women's sexual desires was fed from plenty of sources in earlier Christian writings, popular myth, and learned tracts. The Reformation's exact contribution needs to be ascertained and its interest in prosecuting men kept in mind. It seems reasonable, however, that the reformed stress on heterosexual delicts and their social effects should have encouraged lopsidedness in sexual prosecution. In his study of Calvinist moral (presbyterial) proceedings in north Germany from 1550 to 1650 Heinz Schilling found sharp gender differences. Whereas men violated sexual and marital/family norms more frequently than did women, their generally greater lawlessness meant that specifically sexual offenses accounted for proportionately

---

[78] For *Bannherren* in Basel, see Safley, *Let No Man Put Asunder,* 126–27.

[79] See Brecht, "Die Ulmer Kirchenordnung von 1531," for more on the relation of church to secular authorities in Reformation morals legislation.

[80] On informants, see Roper, *Holy Household,* 64 n. 22; on denouncers, see Köhler, *Zürcher Ehegericht,* 1:155, 155 n. 6.

[81] Köhler, *Zürcher Ehegericht,* 2:115, 188, 659.

[82] Roper, *Holy Household,* 131.

fewer brushes with church elders than was true for women. That is, though women were better behaved sexually and maritally than men, they were proportionately more likely to be chastised for sexual failings,[83] which would only have strengthened the already well developed cultural appraisal of women's honor and duty (and therefore also their dishonor and misdeeds) as peculiarly sexual.[84] That widespread association should also have been upheld by the reformers' acute interest in civic order, which most social groups interpreted as meaning fundamentally different duties according to gender. Whether the Reformation's greater social transparency and moral zeal in fact translated into an "obsession with women's sexual experience" requires more investigation.

The Reformation left behind a changed regulatory landscape.[85] Ironically, the religious impetus to infuse zealous Christian moral standards into society bestowed more power on secular authorities to uphold that heightened moral condition. These enlarged responsibilities, codified and institutionalized, were neither easily forgotten nor, as mandates from God, easily shed. The twinning of the secular and the religious did not stop at the level of mutual institutional involvement, but changed the very way sexual behavior was evaluated. Christian marriage anchored both individual *and* civic life. Marital sexual intercourse grounded both institutions and was doubly valued as a result, whereas illicit, relational intercourse became doubly threatening. This situation recast official sexual expectations. And these expectations, of a direct link between certain kinds of sexual behavior and communal well-being could now be translated into practice more completely than ever before. It is impossible to discern whether religious or civic motivation was paramount in driving this mutually sustaining process during the Reformation. By its end, however, the institutional and legal weight lay clearly with the secular authorities (Protestant and Catholic), who, building on the religious-ideological foundation, would pursue sexual regulation more and more in response to secular forces, in society and inside government itself.

The Regulatory Networks of the Secular Community

There was, at this time, a thicket of traditional social institutions which guided actual sexual behavior more closely and with greater effect, because they suffused people's lives more completely than the best efforts of either church or state. Family, community (*Gemeinde*), peer group, and guild formed the contexts within which people acted sexually; they interpreted the material constraints on reproduction, pronounced the principles of popular morality, and set the goals toward which desire would (unconsciously) tend. The state's formal efforts to order its subjects'

---

[83] Schilling, "Reformierte Kirchenzucht," 304–5.

[84] See Chapter 2, pp. 82–89, 91–92, for women's sexual honor and how state laws took that into account.

[85] For comparative purposes, see the excellent study by Martin Ingram, *Church Courts, Sex and Marriage in England, 1570–1640* (Cambridge, 1987).

sexual activities always occurred in relation—antagonistic, supportive, (mis)interpretive, placative—to these traditional networks. They represent the limits to the absolutist state's attempt at moral hegemony.

What we know about these networks is the result of the scholarly focus on their most apparent aspects, those most directly concerned with social and biological reproduction. Clearly, no society survives if it fails to reproduce its population; all societies therefore "regulate" reproduction in some fashion.[86] For the historian, births are like buoys marking the channel of the courtships and marriages that precede them. Heterosexual acts culminating in births, and the social practices associated with these acts, leave traces for demographers to analyze in the aggregate. The "demographic systems" that emerge from these scholarly efforts are not, however, as demographers too often assume, coterminous with sexual activity *tout court;* they describe neither the pattern of all sexual practices nor the complete system(s) of informal sexual regulation. Nonetheless, biological reproduction opens an important window into a society's system of sexual ordering.

Social reproduction is an equally important avenue toward deciphering how informal networks order sexual behavior. Social reproduction occurs not as an elaborate choreography of harmonious interaction, but is rather the uncertain and uneven result of the clashing efforts of social groups "to create and perpetuate their unity, and thus their existence as groups, which is almost always, and in all societies, the condition of the perpetuation of their position in the social space." As Pierre Bourdieu puts it: "In short, groups—family groups or other sorts—are things you have to keep going at the cost of a permanent effort of maintenance."[87] Sexual conduct is critical to the social reproduction of groups: it helps define them, since acceptable, customary sexual behavior (morals) typically distinguishes among classes, *Stände*, regions, religious sects, and so on; it makes and perpetuates connections within groups (for example, through marriage); it establishes the chief conduit for transferring wealth from generation to generation (via inheritance to offspring); and it defines the locus within which the knowledge peculiar to the group, its cultural capital, is inculcated into the young (in the family). The vantage point of social reproduction is therefore well suited to reveal especially the social meanings attached to sexual behavior.

It should be clear from the above why these two scholarly concentrations (on biological and social reproduction) analyze the sexual system primarily through the lens of marriage. Marriage was in fact the key social/sexual institution of the early modern period. It organized the basic units of economic production and ownership: the farmstead, the workshop, the estate. None of these could be operated by the labor of a single person. Guilds often recognized this fact by making marriage a formal requirement of mastership. In the countryside, where at least three-quarters

---

[86] E. A. Wrigley, "Fertility Strategy for the Individual and the Group," in *Historical Studies of Changing Fertility,* ed. Charles Tilly (Princeton, 1978), 148.

[87] "From Rules to Strategems," in *In Other Words: Essays Towards a Reflexive Sociology* (Stanford, 1990), 75.

of the population lived and worked, inheriting a farm meant having a spouse to share the labor and oversight of servants. And, vice versa, only those with prospects of inheriting land (or, in towns, of being admitted into a guild) were permitted to marry. Peasant and artisan widows and widowers remarried as quickly as possible. Government was based on marriage, since it taxed according to households, and only the (married, male) owners of property participated in village (*Gemeinde*) government, in city councils, in territorial Estates. There was, in short, no route to economic independence and social status other than through marriage. Heidi Rosenbaum explains, "Remaining intentionally unmarried opened . . . neither social nor economic prospects. Thus, marriage was self-evident and the status of husband or wife a general goal."[88] Alas, it was a condition not everyone could attain, since marriage and guaranteed subsistence were synonymous. The conundrum was this: to lead an independent and materially secure life, one needed to be married, but to be permitted to marry, one needed to demonstrate that one could materially support one's family (either through certain or actual inheritance, by having saved up one's servant wages, or by promise of admission to a guild).

Synchronizing marriage with a material base was perhaps the chief regulative chore of the traditional networks. The simultaneity of marriage and property became even more complex through the addition of sexual monopoly. Marriage (or courtship leading to marriage) was the only framework for legitimate, socially approved sexual expression. This meant that marriage was a colossally overdetermined institution carrying an unsurpassed density of social meanings. Wealth, social standing, adulthood, independence, livelihood, communal responsibility, (for males) political representation, and sexual expression were all joined symbolically in this one estate, which meant that any one of these social meanings might stand for any other. The embeddedness of sex in this constellation, particularly its connection with property and marriage, constitutes its chief characteristic in the early modern period and also the main difficulty modern writers have had in interpreting it in its historical context. We will return to this problem at the end of the chapter. First, we must examine how the traditional networks juggled these complexities.

The Family

The family's interventions in the sexual activities of children are generally presented as limited to (dis)approving potential spouses and, if custom demanded, ensuring the sexual reputation and thus marriageability of female offspring. Even if one agrees that the motive for such family intervention was to preserve the family line and its material well-being, the enormous differences among families in *Stand*, wealth, inheritance customs, number of children and other peculiar circumstances strongly affected the marital strategies they pursued and the interventions into

[88] Heidi Rosenbaum, *Formen der Familie. Untersuchungen zum Zusammenhang von Familienverhältnissen, Sozialstruktur und sozialem Wandel in der deutschen Gesellschaft des 19. Jahrhunderts* (Frankfurt, 1982), 70 (peasants), 145–46 (artisans), 215–16 (proto-industrial workers).

sexual behavior these demanded.[89] The fixation on protecting (usually landed) property was not an end in itself, but the guarantor of livelihood (*Nahrung*) for the next and future generations. Achieving material security for the children might require one sibling to inherit and thus also to marry (within the same social group) and another to remain celibate. This delicate calculation rarely depended solely on the particular inheritance system, but included a myriad of other cultural considerations.[90]

Family sexual intervention thus occurred primarily in relation to marriage: first, when deciding whether offspring would be allowed to marry at all, and second, when deciding on the suitability of the spouse. Fathers were not the only interested party or sole, determining voice.[91] Even in areas characterized by partible inheritance and small plots, such as Württemberg, all the siblings (and even the in-laws) pressed their continuing interest in the marriages of their fellow inheritors.[92] For all strata, direct material considerations of inheritance were supplemented by questions of stratum- and gender-specific honor. A poorly chosen spouse (a "foreigner," a person of lesser status, a drunkard, a profligate) or an illegitimate birth might diminish the family's community standing and endanger its ties of mutual support with its neighbors. Therefore, the entire family had high stakes in the behavior of its members.

The very denseness of the web of mutual dependence, the limited horizon of

[89] Bourdieu's early view overstressed systems of nondivisible inheritance. See Pierre Bourdieu, "Célibat et condition paysanne," *Études rurales* 4–6 (1962): 33–34, cited in Martine Segalen, *Historical Anthropology of the Family*, trans. J. C. Whitehouse and Sarah Matthews (Cambridge, 1986), 123. Later he observed that marital strategies are themselves only part of larger social strategies pursued by (family) groups. See Pierre Bourdieu, "Les stratégies matrimoniales dans le système de reproduction," *Annales, Économies, Sociales, Culturelles* 27.4–5 (1972): 1125. Cf. the sexual/marriage control strategies of wealthy peasants in the impartible-inheritance area of east Westphalia (Josef Mooser, *Ländliche Klassengesellschaft 1770–1848. Bauern und Unterschichten, Landwirtschaft und Gewerbe im östlichen Westfalen* [Göttingen, 1984], 190–97); of land-owning peasants in the partible inheritance (*Realverteilung*) village of Neckarhausen (David W. Sabean, *Property, Production, and Family in Neckarhausen, 1700–1870* [Cambridge, 1990], 329–34); and of poor proto-industrial workers in the German southwest (Peter Kriedtke, Hans Medick, and Jürgen Schlumbohm, *Industrialization before Industrialization: Rural Industry in the Genesis of Capitalism*, trans. Beate Schempp [Cambridge, 1981], 53–63).

[90] Sabean, *Neckarhausen*, 185–86; Lutz K. Berkner and Franklin F. Mendels, "Inheritance Systems, Family Structure, and Demographic Patterns in Western Europe, 1700–1900," *Historical Studies of Changing Fertility*, ed. Charles Tilly (Princeton, 1978), 209–24.

[91] Heinz Reif, "Väterliche Gewalt und 'kindliche Narrheit.' Familienkonflikte im katholischen Adel Westfalens vor der Französischen Revolution," in *Die Familie in der Geschichte*, ed. Reif (Göttingen, 1982), here 90–91.

[92] David W. Sabean, "'Junge Immen im leeren Korb': Beziehungen zwischen Schwägern in einem schwäbischen Dorf," in *Emotionen und materielle Interessen. Sozialanthropologische und historische Beiträge zur Familienforschung*, ed. Hans Medick and David Sabean (Göttingen, 1984), 231–50; Sabean, *Neckarhausen*, 329–34; Albert Ilien and Utz Jeggle, *Leben auf dem Dorfe. Zur Sozialgeschichte des Dorfes und Sozialpsychologie seiner Bewohner* (Opladen, 1978), 78–79, 87–88; Josef Mooser, "Soziale Mobilität und familiale Plazierung bei Bauern und Unterschichten. Aspekte der Sozialstruktur der ländlichen Gesellschaft im 19. Jahrhundert am Beispiel des Kirchspiels Quernheim im östlichen Westfalen," in *Familien zwischen Tradition und Moderne. Studien zur Geschichte der Familie in Deutschland und Frankreich vom 16. bis zum 20. Jahrhundert*, ed. Neithard Bulst, Joseph Goy, and Jochen Hoock (Göttingen, 1981), 191.

(economic, personal, and collective) life possibilities, and thus the congruity of shared interest probably meant that relatively few children aspired to marry spouses utterly unacceptable to their parents, siblings, and in-laws. Recalcitrance, when it did occur, might be overcome by threats of disinheritance or, more subtly, by promises of speedy inheritance, larger dowry, smooth family relations, and thus a greater chance of material and status success with a more suitable partner.

Courtship was the main forum in which the family exercised sexual guidance. In the countryside, courtship rituals took place with the knowledge and approval of the families of those involved.[93] Acceptable courtships often began at community-sponsored events, such as dances, or the *Spinnstuben*, where young, unmarried villagers combined work and conviviality during winter evenings.[94] In most, or surely a great many, localities in central Europe, if the courtship proceeded, it would include sexual activity. What distinguished family-approved courtship from clandestine liaisons was not the type of sexual activity, but its location. In courtship with the goal of family-approved marriage, sexual activity often took place in the woman's bed, rather than outdoors (the other typical locus of pre- or extramarital sex).[95] Such courtship sex might occur either before or after a formal engagement, or it might be taken as a sign of such.[96] Pregnancy then resulted in a hurried wedding.

The timing of sexual relations between the engaged was the main area of continuous disagreement between the families on the one side and the church and state on the other. The church, followed by the post-Reformation state, insisted that sex occur only after the religious wedding ceremony. The family, its eyes on the social-material aspects of marriage and its powers of surveillance and sanction strong, was relatively indifferent to legal and religious nicety. The high prenuptial pregnancy rate clearly shows the predominance of the authority of the family over that of the state or church in questions of legitimate sexual expression in the absolutist period.[97]

The post-Reformation states strengthened familial authority by making parental approval a precondition for marriage before one reached a certain age, often twenty-

---

[93] For excellent descriptions of two types of ritual courtship, see Rainer Beck, "Illegitimität und voreheliche Sexualität auf dem Land. Unterfinning, 1671–1770," in *Kultur der einfachen Leute. Bayerisches Volksleben vom 16. zum 19. Jahrhundert*, ed. Richard van Dülmen (Munich, 1983), 112–50, esp. 140–42, and Christian Simon, *Untertanenverhalten und obrigkeitliche Moralpolitik. Studien zum Verhältnis zwischen Stadt und Land im ausgehenden 18. Jahrhundert am Beispiel Basels* (Basel, 1981), 234–36.

[94] Hans Medick, "Spinnstuben auf dem Dorf. Jugendliche Sexualkultur und Feierabendbrauch in der ländlichen Gesellschaft der frühen Neuzeit," in *Sozialgeschichte der Freizeit. Untersuchungen zum Wandel der Alltagskultur in Deutschland*, ed. Gerhard Huck (Wuppertal, 1980), 19–49.

[95] Sabean, *Neckarhausen*, 329–31; Peter Becker, *Leben und Lieben in einem kalten Land. Sexualität im Spannungsfeld von Ökonomie und Demographie. Das Beispiel St. Lambrecht 1600–1850* (Frankfurt, 1990), 293; Simon, *Moralpolitik*, 228.

[96] Cf. Simon, *Moralpolitik*, 234–35; Beck, "Illegitimität," 140–42; and Thomas Robisheaux, *Rural Society and the Search for Order in Early Modern Germany* (Cambridge, 1989), 114.

[97] See the tables for Germany in Michael W. Flinn, *The European Demographic System, 1500–1820* (Baltimore, 1981), 122–23.

four or twenty-five for men and twenty for women.[98] In the interests of social stability secular authorities thus tried to counteract Roman Catholic religious tradition, which stressed the free choice of the future spouses.[99] Altogether, family interests, coinciding as they did with material considerations, custom, the pressure of other traditional networks (such as the village), and statute, were doubtless weightier than Christian dogma. Nonetheless, the cleft between them opened a certain free space in which children could negotiate their marital destiny.[100]

Once courtship had run its course, the sexual stewardship of the family seems to have stopped. Parents, siblings, and in-laws might intervene in marital disputes, but not, it appears, to uphold sexual standards; instead, the goal was to preserve the relationship itself. What influence, if any, the family typically had over sexual experimentation outside courtship (such as masturbation, same-sex encounters, casual sex, or in rural areas, bestiality), or over matters such as birth control or sexual "knowledge" generally, is not known. The picture we have at present portrays the family's interest in sexual guidance as primarily relational (that is, connected to object choice and the social relations that entailed), rather than strictly sexual.

The Hausvater / Hausmutter

The family, in the sense used in the preceding section, was in charge of guiding its own offspring. But the parents, as house- and landholders, also bore responsibility for the servants who worked and lived with them on the farm. In the official language of handbooks and statute, this position was that of *Hausvater* or *Hausmutter*.[101] It was an important position because of the huge numbers of young men and women who were in service at some time in their lives. It is likely that a majority of early modern Europeans between the ages of fifteen and twenty-nine were servants; it is known that servants made up at least 10 percent of the population at any one time.[102] Service provided necessary rural labor, taught skills, and permitted servants to earn their own keep while saving money for marriage and independence. And it kept the lid on the Pandora's box of youthful energy typical of the unmar-

---

[98] Safley, *Let No Man Put Asunder*, 32; Robisheaux, *Rural Society*, 106–12.

[99] Brundage, *Law*, 437–39, 443, 498–500, 552–53, 564; Jean-Louis Flandrin, *Families in Former Times: Kinship, Household and Sexuality*, trans. Richard Southern (Cambridge, 1979), 130–33.

[100] Roper, *Holy Household*, 159.

[101] These words were seldom used by heads of households to describe themselves, which is indirect testimony to the discrepancy between statute and reality. Sabean, *Neckarhausen*, 111–15. On handbooks, see Otto Brunner, *Handwörterbuch der Sozialwissenschaften* (1956), s.v. "Hausväterliteratur"; Gotthardt Frühsorge, "Die Begründung der 'väterlichen Gesellschaft' in der europäischen oeconomia christiana. Zur Rolle des Vaters in der 'Hausväterliteratur' des 16. bis 18. Jahrhunderts in Deutschland," in *Das Vaterbild im Abendland I: Rom, Frühes Christentum, Mittelalter, Neuzeit, Gegenwart*, ed. Hubertus Tellenbach (Stuttgart, 1978), 110–23; and Gotthardt Frühsorge, "Die Einheit aller Geschäfte. Tradition und Veränderung des 'Hausmutter'-Bildes in der deutschen Ökonomieliteratur des 18. Jahrhunderts," *Wolfenbütteler Studien zur Aufklärung* 3 (1976): 137–57.

[102] Michael Mitterauer, "Gesindedienst und Jugendphase im europäischen Vergleich," *Geschichte und Gesellschaft* 11.2 (1985): 185, 187.

ried, for servanthood was the estate of single youths and young adults. Servants were the primary targets of state sexual regulation; edicts exhorted *Hausväter* and *Hausmütter* to control their charges closely, to keep them celibate, God-fearing, and hard-working. This task was easier when servants lived and worked closely with the householders. As wealthier farmers (and Bürger in towns) began to develop a more rigid sense of social status in the eighteenth century, they increasingly distanced themselves from their servants and presumably lessened their regulatory effectiveness.[103] Nonetheless, *Hausväter* in Prussia retained the legal right to punish their servants physically, for example by whipping, until 1918. The state preserved this right explicitly for "moral" (*sittlich*) reasons.[104]

Evidence of the efficacy of *Hausvater/-mutter* control of the sexual behavior of their servants is mixed, however. On the one hand, it is true that illegitimacy among female servants did rise at about the time that householders were reducing their personal contact with their servants (after 1750). But the rise in illegitimacy is far too complex a phenomenon to be interpreted so unidimensionally. It is also true, however, that whenever a labor shortage allowed servants to make demands on their employers, they pushed for sleeping arrangements favorable to sexual contact, directly contradicting the repeated admonishments of state ordinances to keep servants' quarters separated by gender.[105] Such demands suggest that householders sometimes did try to curtail their servants' sexual activities and, further, that in general servants identified sexual expression with adulthood and independence[106] and resented interference, especially when the labor market must have made the prospects for future marriage seem brighter. As Dr. Peter Otto Kürn observed in a late-eighteenth-century prize essay on the cause of moral ruination among servants: "They all want to marry early and be their own master."[107]

On the other hand, *Hausväter/-mütter* were undependable agents of state-inspired moral regulation. The ability to absorb the future labor power of servants' illegitimate children may have softened the householders' condemnation of pre- or nonmarital sex.[108] Lack of space meant servants were often thrown together, where younger ones could learn from the relative sexual expertise of older ones.

[103] Rolf Engelsing, "Zur Stellung der Dienstboten in der bürgerlichen Familie im 18. und 19. Jahrhundert," in *Seminar: Familie und Gesellschaftsstruktur. Materialien zu den sozioökonomischen Bedingungen von Familienformen*, ed. Heidi Rosenbaum (Frankfurt, 1978), 419, 421–22.

[104] Reinhart Koselleck, *Preußen zwischen Reform und Revolution* (Stuttgart, 1967), 648–49, 652.

[105] Becker, *Leben und Lieben*, 309. The Bavarian decree of 14 May 1653 (forbidding shared sleeping quarters) noted that servants pressured masters not to follow such edicts. Bayerisches Haupt-Staatsarchiv, General Register Fasz. 321, Nr.7, hereafter Bay HStA, GR 321/7.

[106] Cf. Mooser, *Ländliche Klassengesellschaft*, 306.

[107] "Preisschrift über das Sittenverderben des Gesindes," in *Verhandlungen und Schriften der Hamburgischen Gesellschaft zur Beförderung der Künste und nützlichen Gewerbe* (Hamburg, 1793), 2:124.

[108] See Becker, *Leben und Lieben*, 247, for the eighteenth century; David Sabean, "Unehelichkeit: Ein Aspekt sozialer Reproduktion kleinbäuerlicher Produzenten. Zu einer Analyse dörflicher Quellen um 1800," in *Klassen und Kultur. Sozialanthropologische Perspektiven in der Geschichtsschreibung*, ed. Robert Berdahl (Frankfurt, 1982), 54–76; and Regina Schulte, "Kindsmörderinnen auf dem Lande," in *Emotionen und materielle Interessen. Sozialanthropologische und historische Beiträge zur Familienforschung*, ed. Hans Medick and David Sabean (Göttingen, 1984), 113–42, esp. 123–25, for the nineteenth century.

Eighteenth-century writers and later historians also speculated about the possible sexual abuse of female servants by *Hausväter*.[109] This subject still needs to be systematically researched, but illegitimacy data for central Europe do not support this suspicion.[110] The unreliability of *Hausväter* probably expressed itself in more prosaic ways.

The Village, "Gemeinde," or Community

The home, indeed the world, for most early modern central Europeans was the village, which might consist of as few as twelve or thirteen households, or as many as fifty or more.[111] Regardless of its size, it enjoyed a distinct but changing place in the complex hierarchy of power, authority, duty, and obligation characteristic of the absolutist period. In its legal guise, it was the *Gemeinde*, or community, the smallest administrative unit of the state, but simultaneously also the forum for direct representation of and by the male landowners, in the *Gemeindeversammlung*.[112] In its religious aspect, the *Pfarrgemeinde* was the local parish, whose interest in guiding the community members' sexual behavior we have already examined. Materially, the *Gemeinde* disposed over "communal land, building- and firewood, the rights to run the local pub [*Schankrechte*], trading privileges, buying rights to farms without

[109] At the turn of the nineteenth century, Pastor Schwager bemoaned how poor children "rented themselves to farmers, where they come together with more loose servants" and "impure conversations" result. J. M. Schwager, "Über den Ravensberger Bauer," *Westfälisches Magazin* 2, no. 5, 1786: 57–58. Cissie Fairchilds, "Female Sexual Attitudes and the Rise of Illegitimacy: A Case Study," in *Marriage and Fertility. Studies in Interdisciplinary History*, ed. Robert I. Rotberg and Theodore K. Rabb (Princeton, 1980), 163–204, esp. 172–76. Despite his criticisms of Fairchilds, Flandrin seems disposed to accept widespread sexual coercion of maids by their masters. See also in Rotberg and Rabb, Jean-Louis Flandrin, "Comment and Controversy. A Case of Naiveté in the Use of Statistics," 205–11, esp. 209. See also Jacques Depauw, "Illicit Sexual Activity and Society in Eighteenth-Century Nantes," in *Family and Society*, ed. Robert Forster and Orest Ranum (Baltimore, 1976), 159. Helmut Möller, *Die klein-bürgerliche Familie im 18. Jahrhundert* (Berlin, 1969), 297–98; Rosenbaum, *Formen der Familie*, 87, 161, 512 n. 154; Becker, *Leben und Lieben*, 40–41. Hannelore Westphal believes (by extrapolation from accounts of Junker behavior) that rural *Hausvater*/maid exploitation was ubiquitous into the twentieth century. See Westphal, *Die Liebe auf dem Dorf. Vom Wandel der Sexualmoral und der Prostitution auf dem Lande* (Braunschweig, 1988), 32–37.

[110] See the excellent discussion in Otto Ulbricht, *Kindsmord und Aufklärung in Deutschland* (Munich, 1990), 76–84; and seventy-two cases of illegitimacy from 1837 to 1862 evaluated by Mooser, "Soziale Mobilität," 198–99 n. 21.

[111] John Theibault, "Community and *Herrschaft* in the Seventeenth-Century German Village," *Journal of Modern History* 64 (March 1992): 1–21, esp. 11–13; Sabean, *Neckarhausen*, 7; Robisheaux, *Rural Society*, 23.

[112] The definition of the *Gemeinde* and its legal and administrative functions and its relation to "village," "community," and "neighborhood" are more complex than I have presented them here. See the excellent studies by Karl Siegfried Bader, *Dorfgenossenschaft und Dorfgemeinde* (Cologne, 1962); Heide Wunder, *Die bäuerliche Gemeinde in Deutschland* (Göttingen, 1986); Karl-Sigismund Kramer, *Die Nachbarschaft als bäuerliche Gemeinschaft. Ein Beitrag zur rechtlichen Volkskunde mit besonderer Berücksichtigung Bayerns* (Munich, 1954); and Karl Bosl, "Eine Geschichte der deutschen Landgemeinde," *Zeitschrift für Agrargeschichte und Agrarsoziologie* 9.2 (1961): 129–42, esp. 137–41, for definitions and distinctions. For contemporaries' various understandings of *Gemeinde*, see Theibault, "Community," 6–7.

inheritors,"[113] water rights, poor relief,[114] and so forth. It supervised the paying of taxes and other duties. In short, it was the warp into which one's existence was woven. And that is the final meaning of *Gemeinde* or community: the "culturally defined way of life"[115] taken for granted by those who lived it. In this cultural sense, community custom, the "binding energy of community consciousness,"[116] emerged from the repeated social solutions to perennial problems facing the village. Upholding and modifying custom was an endless task of self-regulation, which depended on what C.J. Calhoun calls the "dense, multiplex bonds" joining villagers together: "These are bonds of many strands, so that actors linked in one context or through one institution are also linked in and through others. This makes it more difficult for one actor to cross another in any specific context than it would be if there were only that single dimension to their relationship."[117] For example, the man whom you suspect of adultery is not merely your neighbor, but a second cousin, who joined you in a lawsuit over right of way, but who has owed you money for some time and whose young son worked as a servant on your farm for six months. These facts are known to you, to him, and to everyone else, and they determine how you will respond to your suspicions. Though modern observers may be prone to overestimate how much villagers knew about one another, still, the density of village relations must have made possible a strong system of mutual control, especially regarding repetitive behavior or acts with social consequences.[118]

This cycle of mutual determination was weighted to the advantage of the married, male property-owner,[119] whom the state regarded (as *Hausvater*) as the rock upon which order was built. As independent owner he participated in the *Gemeindeversammlung*, which set and interpreted rules and resolved disputes.[120] The *Hausväter* naturally interpreted the *Gemeinde* interest as preserving the material and social status quo. That meant preventing three chief dangers: drains on the community poor chest, the addition of "poor householders" into the ranks of property owners and family heads, and social divisiveness. Sexual behavior played an important part in all three considerations. Illegitimate children were a major internal threat to the poor chest.[121] So, in the end, were poor householders, whose lack of capital, laziness, profligacy, or bad judgment might ruin a farm, diminishing

---

[113] Kramer, *Nachbarschaft*, 21.

[114] Poor-relief administration differed from region to region, though the right to welfare from the community poor chest, when it existed, was critical to one's survival in hard times. See Bader, *Dorfgenossenschaft*, 381, 444–48; and Wolfram Fischer, *Armut in der Geschichte. Erscheinungsformen und Lösungsversuche der "Sozialen Frage" in Europa seit dem Mittelalter* (Göttingen, 1982), 10–56.

[115] C. J. Calhoun, "Community: Toward a Variable Conceptualization for Comparative Research," *Social History* 5.1 (1980): 120.

[116] Kramer, *Nachbarschaft*, 37.

[117] "Community," 115.

[118] I am grateful to David Sabean for his cautionary remarks on villagers' mutual knowledge. See also Ilien and Jeggle, *Leben auf dem Dorfe*, 55, on villagers not acting on their knowledge.

[119] Robisheaux, *Rural Society*, 106–7.

[120] Theibault, "Community," 12.

[121] See, for example, Becker, *Leben und Lieben*, 139–40, 248–75.

the tax base while adding more demands on charity.[122] Preventing the economically marginal from marrying was consequently a major interest of other *Hausväter*, who, together with state officials and other villagers, often applied the sexually loaded terms "loose" or "incontinent" *leichtfertig, liederlich* to describe incompetent house-holders.[123] In the eighteenth and nineteenth centuries, the poorest villagers became increasingly identified as sexually marginal as well.[124] Whole families acquired the reputation of being sexually dishonorable; their daughters became "village whores" (*Dorfhuren*), open for sexual exploitation but unmarriageable.[125] Finally, disputes surrounding courtship, promises of marriage, and adultery were common causes of social conflict, the damage from which the *Gemeinde* was intent on minimizing, if the causes themselves could not be eliminated.

It would be wrong to think, however, that the *Hausväter*, or "neighbors," as they were known,[126] in fact set the *Gemeinde* agenda or determined custom and rule. The early modern *Gemeinde* was like a small boat on a perilous sea. Everyone needed it to stay afloat, and everyone contributed, differently, to ensuring that it would. The two biggest incentives to cooperate in the elaborate exercise of mutual determination were therefore economic necessity and the fact that the *Gemeinde* had a conceptual monopoly of the possible. Indeed, endogamy rates of 80 percent and above show that people tended to accept their village as their "community of fate" (*Schicksalsgemeinschaft*).[127]

The *Gemeinde* was interested in a wider range of sexual behavior than the family was. It, too, closely monitored courtship, but was also concerned to uphold domestic harmony after marriage (for instance, by chastising adultery) and to promote "proper" sexual demeanor generally, as part of the well-ordered system of estates. Community order might define "proper" in ways different from church or state, however. To maintain a sexually acceptable status quo locally, the *Gemeinde* developed formal and informal mechanisms to encourage good behavior and chastise bad. These sometimes involved all the members of the *Gemeinde;* more often they involved only small groups acting in its name. Since these regulatory activities served only the interests of the community, not surprisingly they only sometimes harmonized with the interests of the state or church; they might just as well contradict them. As the church and state began to encroach on the *Gemeinde*, the community learned to use official institutions for its own ends.

---

[122] Sabean, *Neckarhausen*, 101–16.

[123] See the discussion in Chapter 2, pp. 93–94 and Chapter 3, pp. 116–19; and cf. Sabean, *Neckarhausen*, 144–45.

[124] Simon, *Moralpolitik*, 232; Michael Fintan Phayer, *Sexual Liberation and Religion in Nineteenth Century Europe* (London, 1977), 48.

[125] Ilien and Jeggle, *Leben auf dem Dorfe*, 81–82.

[126] Kramer, *Nachbarschaft*, 15; Theibault, "Community," 12.

[127] Ilien and Jeggle, *Leben im Dorfe*, 79 (91.6 percent for the village Hausen in Swabia, 1651–1700); Segalen, *Historical Anthropology*, 120. See also Hermann Hörger, *Kirche, Dorfreligion und bäuerliche Gesellschaft*, 2 parts, in *Studien zur altbayerischen Kirchengeschichte*, vols. 5 and 7 (Munich, 1978, 1983), vol. 5:108.

❧ The Church, Traditional Society, and the Regulation of Sex ❧

The most effective of the *Gemeinde*'s own institutions were those that channeled sexual expression into the safe harbors of domesticity. The spinning bees (*Spinnstuben*), courtship rites (*Kiltgang, zu Licht gehen, Lichtkarz*, and so on), and seasonal dances and village celebrations provided occasions for marriageable youth to find socially and emotionally appropriate partners from within the village.[128] Admission to these events and adherence to the local rules of moral comportment were carefully monitored, either by the "neighbor" in whose house the spinning bee was held or by the participants themselves, both male and female.[129] Breaches of custom dishonored those present. Honor was the coin of the realm of early modern villagers, whose sense of morality, of fitting custom, was as well developed and jealously guarded as that of any nobleman or king.[130] Consequently, dishonorable behavior could earn the miscreant a savage beating from the women as well as the men.[131]

Honor

Less violent forms of ritual chastisement, such as charivaris (*Haberfeldtreiben*) and the like, used shame to force conformity,[132] especially regarding sexual misbehavior. Adulterers, clergymen with concubines, or unwed expectant mothers might awake to the cacophony of banging pots and pans and the shouting of scandalous verses. These nocturnal irregulars were usually a definable subset of the entire village: adolescent males, or women only,[133] or "youth." Their actions are not always easy to interpret from the sexual point of view, however. Charivaris lent themselves to misuse, by individuals or groups bent on private revenge, who cloaked themselves in community righteousness. Further, most of our information about *Haberfeldtreiben* comes from the nineteenth century, when the social meaning and purpose of such events had changed from its early modern form. But most of all, one must be mindful that the language of shame was (and is) highly sexualized, and thus the vocabulary of chastisement was often sexual, even when the trespass it punished was not. A common example is the bossy wife, whose effigy presented her as sexually aggressive (the initiator of sex, or having intercourse on top of the man), and her henpecked husband (the obverse), which describes not their actual sexual

shame

[128] Although Edward Shorter's interpretations are wide of the mark, his description of courtship rituals is good. See Edward Shorter, *The Making of the Modern Family* (New York, 1975), 121–38.

[129] Medick, "Spinnstuben," 38.

[130] Samuel Huggel, *Die Einschlagsbewegung in der Basler Landschaft. Gründe und Folgen der wichtigsten agrarischen Neuerung im Ancien Régime* (Liestal, 1979), 484–87, for an excellent discussion of the resilience of rural honor codes under absolutism.

[131] Medick, "Spinnstuben," 38–40; Martin Scharfe, "'Soziale Kontrolle' im Dorf des vorindustriellen Zeitalters. Beitrag zur rechtlichen Volkskunde im ehemaligen Zeller Stab," *Württembergisches Jahrbuch für Volkskunde* (1961/1964), 81; Braun, *Industrialisation and Everyday Life*, trans. Sarah Hanbury Tenison (Cambridge, 1990), 90–91.

[132] Elmar A.M. Schieder, *Das Haberfeldtreiben: Ursprung, Wesen, Deutung* (Munich, 1983); Wilhelm Kaltenstadler, *Das Haberfeldtreiben. Brauch/Kult/Geheimbund, Volksjustiz im 19. Jahrhundert* (Munich, 1971); Helga Ettenhuber, "Charivari in Bayern. Das Miesbacher Haberfeldtreiben von 1893," in *Kultur der einfachen Leute*, ed. Richard van Dülmen (Munich, 1983), 180–207; Georg Queri, *Bauernerotik und Bauernfehme in Oberbayern* (1911; Munich, 1975); Shorter, *Modern Family*, 218–27; Scharfe, "Soziale Kontrolle," 79.

[133] Robisheaux, *Rural Society*, 113–14.

habits but their social relations, expressed in sexual metaphor. One must be sure not to confuse the two.[134]

Aside from formal institutions, like courtship rites or charivaris, the *Gemeinde* had numerous informal ways to guide its members' sexual behavior. The most effective of these must have been the readiness to render real economic or physical help in emergencies. Straying villagers could not afford to drift too far from the common moral mooring, lest their isolation put them in peril when catastrophe struck.[135] "Respectable" villagers could equally ill afford to monitor their neighbors too closely, however, lest they wake to find their fences ripped apart and woodpiles scattered.[136] Spying and "self-righteousness" were not village virtues.[137] There was always a delicate balance to be trod between upholding customary morality and minding your own business. Thus transgressions on either side of the moral line were punishable physically. They were also subject to verbal control, especially gossip. This, too, was a serious matter, because it affected one's general reputation and honor, on which social standing and material security depended. Verbal attacks, especially by women, seem to have been judged to be as harmful as beatings.[138] Although talk leaves few traces for the historian, it was surely the most common and supple method for guiding the behavior of the *Gemeinde*.

The discussion so far has not really differentiated among the many faces of the *Gemeinde*: the collection of *Hausväter*, the interlocking network of kin, the womenfolk versus the menfolk, youth, peer groups, and, in the course of the eighteenthcentury, the wealthier owners versus the less wealthy. All of these groups could and did speak for the *Gemeinde* at various times. In this respect the *Gemeinde* was a convenient fiction behind which clashing interests struggled. It is no wonder that state bureaucrats and social observers, whose viewpoints will preoccupy us for the remainder of this book, had trouble interpreting what they saw there.

The ambiguity hidden within the *Gemeinde* is nowhere more clearly illustrated than by the peer groups, which played a leading role in sexual regulation via courtship rituals, charivaris, and violent sanctions, as we have seen. On the one hand, these formal institutions were firmly anchored in village life and helped perpetuate its social structures and culture. On the other hand, the members of this peer group (of eligible unmarrieds) pursued their own interests: a chance to marry in a limited, endogamous system.[139] Under certain circumstances, such as growing class stratification within the village, this hunger for marriage would directly clash

[134] See Martine Segalen's discussion of European charivaris and their relation to sexual behavior and metaphor in Segalen, *Love and Power in the Peasant Family: Rural France in the Nineteenth Century* (Chicago, 1983), 42–49.

[135] Kramer, *Nachbarschaft*, 54–55.

[136] Fear of revenge kept more people from serving on *Sittengerichte* or on local disciplinary commissions as *Rüger*. See also Braun, *Industrialisation*, 83.

[137] On fines for spying on neighbors, see Kramer, *Nachbarschaft*, 38.

[138] For the relation between physical violence and verbal violence, see Sabean, *Neckarhausen*, 133–46, 334–40.

[139] Medick, "Spinnstuben," 42.

with the marital strategies of the village elite.[140] The elite might then, in its struggle against the peer group, undermine the customary structures of sexual socialization. Similarly, the state, although interested in village stability and orderly sexual life, was prone to interpret peer group activity as harmful rather than helpful. Bureaucrats distrusted fatherless and masterless self-regulation (which was formally contrary to the principles of monarchy and bureaucratic tutelage) and feared the periodic outbursts of violence when peer groups resorted to force to uphold custom. Violence, after all, was the prerogative of the state. Therefore, village elites could enlist state help to weaken the very institutions that ordered early modern sexual life.

Guilds

Whereas most early modern Germans lived in the countryside, towns housed the remaining ten to twenty-five percent.[141] Of these, a majority lived in small towns of at most several thousand inhabitants, though many were no bigger than large villages.[142] Such "home towns," in Mack Walker's phrase, were run in early modern times politically and economically by guildsmen, who accounted for most of their "citizens" (*Bürger*), the town equivalent of *Hausväter:* property-owning males, usually married, with rights of political representation and obligations to uphold the social order.[143] Guild domination of small and middle-sized towns was so complete that urban culture there was largely guild culture, that is, it was structured by guild habits and assumptions.[144] Under absolutism, territorial states whittled away at the independence of towns, but rarely succeeded in fully usurping their prerogatives, any more than the steady decline of the guilds themselves ended in their oblivion, even to this day.[145]

Just as the guilds did not pass away, neither did their sexual attitudes, which lived on, transformed of course, in a threefold legacy. First, the guilds had a major impact on sexual legislation. They were instrumental in drafting the urban statutes of the fourteenth and fifteenth centuries and in shaping the moral ordinances of the

[handwritten marginal note: ① Guild impact on sexual legislation]

---

[140] See Sabean, *Neckarhausen*, 23, 89, 245–46, 420, 424, on class endogamy in the *Gemeinde*.

[141] Opinions differ on the percentage. Hans-Ulrich Wehler, *Deutsche Gesellschaftsgeschichte*, vol. 1, *Vom Feudalismus des Alten Reiches bis zur Defensiven Modernisierung der Reformära, 1700–1815* (Munich, 1987), 70, writes 10 percent. Figured differently, he arrives at 25 percent living in towns in 1800 (180), the same figure Mack Walker uses in *German Home Towns: Community, State, and General Estate, 1648–1871* (Ithaca, N.Y., 1971), 32.

[142] Wehler, *Gesellschaftsgeschichte*, 1:180, writes that 90 percent of German towns contained one thousand or fewer people. Cf. Walker, *German Home Towns*, 26–33; and Thomas Munck, *Seventeenth Century Europe: State, Conflict and Social Order in Europe, 1598–1700* (London, 1990), 169–70.

[143] Munck, *Seventeenth Century Europe*, 171; Rudolf Wissell, *Des alten Handwerks Recht und Gewohnheit*, 2 ed., ed. Ernst Schraepler, 7 vols. (Berlin, 1971–), 1:88–96.

[144] Walker, *German Home Towns*, 34–107.

[145] On the guilds generally, see Wissell, *Alten Handwerks;* Michael Stürmer, ed., *Herbst des alten Handwerks. Meister, Gesellen und Obrigkeit im 18. Jahrhundert* (Munich, 1986), esp. 335–42; and Wolfram Fischer, *Handwerksrecht und Handwerkswirtschaft um 1800* (Berlin, 1955).

Reformation.[146] These served as models for later territorial and imperial ordinances and thus helped set the foundations for sex-crime law. Second, the guilds' narrow, family-centered, gender-divided understanding of social order suffused the reception, success, and ideological form of the Reformation, which in turn reorganized the meaning of sexual behavior in early modern Germany.[147] Finally, the social-sexual habits that grew out of and were embedded in guild family life were steadily reproduced, becoming characteristic of this *Stand,* and then of the class that succeeded it: the lower middle class, or petit bourgeoisie.[148] This class, of course, played a central role, actually and mythically, in the formation of bourgeois sexual morality. The guild was thus a key institution in the system of sexual regulation.

The bonds sustaining the guilds were just as dense and mutually reinforcing as those in the village: the overlap of family and economic unit of production was complete—no single person could run a workshop; the guild exercised (in the town) a monopoly over training and livelihood; guild families were endogamous (not within, but among guilds);[149] master status meant simultaneously marriage, social prestige, and political power; and towns were usually small enough to offer the same transparency as villages.[150] But unlike villages, guilds were also sustained by formal organizations with written statutes. Writing froze the guilds' moral strictures, making them easier to apply and thus more durable,[151] but also harder to adapt to changing times.

The main principle driving guild morality was exclusion. Convinced that the economy was saturated, the guilds strove to regulate producers and production so perfectly that the status quo would be exactly replicated. This minute attention to social reproduction encouraged the guilds' virtually defining twin obsessions: ritual and honor.[152] Ritual sustained the sense of belonging to the corporate body and helped socialize younger members and renew their bonds; honor was the essence of the corporation, what distinguished it, bestowed upon it social and economic power, and made it worth striving and sacrificing for. Because only the corporation be-

[146] For example, Adrian Staehelin, "Sittenzucht und Sittengerichtsbarkeit in Basel," *Zeitschrift der Savigny-Stiftung für Rechtsgeschichte,* Germanische Abteilung 85 (1968): 78–103, esp. 82; and Ernst Ziegler, *Sitte und Moral in früheren Zeiten. Zur Rechtsgeschichte der Reichsstadt und Republik St. Gallen* (Sigmaringen, 1991), 18–20.

[147] Roper, *Holy Household.* Ziegler, *Sitte und Moral,* 31–33; Peter Ziegler, *Zürcher Sittenmandate* (Zurich, 1978), 20; Alfons Felber, "Unzucht und Kindsmord in der Rechtsprechung der freien Reichsstadt Nördlingen vom 15. bis 19.Jahrhundert" (J.S.D. diss., Universität Bonn, 1961), 12–14, 42–43.

[148] Möller, *Die kleinbürgerliche Familie.*

[149] Only five to seven percent of the apprentices in Augsburg in the eighteenth century did *not* come from artisanal families. Roland Bettger, *Das Handwerk in Augsburg beim Übergang der Stadt an das Königreich Bayern. Städtisches Gewerbe unter dem Einfluß politischer Veränderungen* (Augsburg, 1979), 94.

[150] Wissell, *Des alten Handwerks,* 1:145.

[151] Jack Goody, *The Logic of Writing and the Organization of Society* (Cambridge, 1986), 175; Wissell, *Des alten Handwerks,* 1:246.

[152] Friedrich Zunkel, "Ehre, Reputation," in *Geschichtliche Grundbegriffe. Historisches Lexikon zur politisch-sozialen Sprache in Deutschland,* ed. Otto Brunner, Werner Conze, and Reinhart Koselleck (Stuttgart, 1975), 2:1–63, esp. 5–6, 44–48; and Wissell, *Des alten Handwerks,* 1:145–65.

stowed (and rescinded) honor, the concept of honor acted as a powerful lever producing conformity.[153]

The content of guild sexual morality was formed overwhelmingly by the exclusionary dictates of honor, expressed in extremely high standards of sexual purity. Legitimacy was the guilds' obsession. Only those of unquestionably legitimate birth could become masters; this requirement was often verified even before admission as an apprentice. As with all ritual systems of purity, this one tended to spread the exclusionary taboo beyond the mere guildmember himself and beyond the original demand for legitimacy. The master's wife not only had to prove legitimate birth, she also was required to be a virgin upon marriage. A birth occurring less than nine months after the wedding routinely led to ouster from the guild. In fact, premature birth and later legitimation were merely illegitimacy in another form, as far as the guilds were concerned. Church and state tried for several hundred years to force the guilds to interpret legitimacy less strictly, but they remained adamant.[154]

The same absolute standards applied to adultery by either party. Once again the ferocity of the guilds far outstripped what church or state either demanded or wanted. Both church and state deplored adultery, but they wanted the master to remain economically solvent and the couple to reconcile for the sake of social and familial stability. Guild honor demanded the opposite; the adulterous master had to lose his livelihood, his family had to fall into poverty, the adulterous wife could not be forgiven, but rather had to be divorced and cut off from all social contact with her former world. Further, even the legitimate children of an adulterous master were excluded from future membership in the guild.[155] The body of the master, his family, his workshop, and guild property were to be held clean of sexual contamination. Guild rules normally forbade members to have contact with women of questionable reputation, to invite them to guild premises, to sit next to them, to offer them a drink from the common cup, or even to be seen with them on the street.[156]

It should be clear from the foregoing that these were not primarily sexual rules at all; that is, they were not designed with sexual ends in mind, but with particular social (and economic) ones. Written statutes, recited at every formal admission to membership, and jealous, mutual policing by fellow guilds kept the strictures alive and vibrant, as active symbols of social purity, group solidarity, rootedness in the community, and submission to exacting standards.[157] The guilds illustrate the stunning particularity of sexual organization. On the surface one might have thought that such devotion to morality would have pleased church and state. But the guilds' ritual sexual purity was not calculated with the same ends in view, and

[153] Walker, *German Home Towns*, 105–6.
[154] Wissell, *Des alten Handwerks*, 1:233–36, 242–43, 251–54.
[155] Ibid., 1:272.
[156] Ibid., 2:140, 144.
[157] Ibid., 1:269, also 246, 252.

thus it constituted a different and antagonistic sexual subsystem: too unforgiving for the church and too costly for the state.

The Traditional Networks and Sexual "Control"

When demographers look at the aggregate pattern produced by the interactions of all these levels of sexual ordering they can synthesize a "European demographic system" for the early modern period.[158] This was characterized by comparatively late marriage (at the age of twenty for women and twenty-four or above for men), high celibacy (20 percent of the adult population), low illegitimacy (hovering around 2 percent of births before 1750), and slow, but flexible population growth sensitively tailored to the limits of sustenance (*Nahrung*). As useful as this information is, it provides only a pale background for an understanding of the sexual behavior and interpretive systems of any given group. All scholars acknowledge that within the "European demographic system" there was enormous regional variation, even in the variables coarse enough to be measured,[159] which suggests that in the subtler realms of cultural expression the picture was mottled indeed.

Nonetheless, our brief survey of the literature has highlighted several features common to the early modern organization of sexual life as people lived it, rather than as ideology might have it. First, sex was completely embedded in the socioeconomic circumstances of their lives; it was not a thing-in-itself, nor did it have value or meaning except in its various contexts. Second, because of its centrality in organizing socioeconomic life, marriage also exercised a kind of conceptual monopoly over sexual expression; that is, not only was marriage frequently held to be synonymous with sexual expression altogether (because it was the only framework for legitimate sexual activity), but "illicit" sex also tended to be judged by its relation to marriage (the threat it posed, for example). Third, because the system was so strongly social, people's attention tended to focus on the relational aspects of sexual behavior, on *who* was being linked, rather than on *what* they were doing. This meant that acts with few social-relational consequences (not ending in the production of a child, not ending in a long-term relationship, not with a person at all) tended to disappear from view as insignificant. Fourth, privacy was not a value in this system, in several senses. Although efforts were made to shield sexual acts from others' eyes (under cover of darkness, beneath covers or behind bed curtains), cramped quarters meant that secrecy was rarely possible. More important, no one expected "privacy" in the modern sense, where solitude is simultaneously a sign that the sexual act is nobody's business, that it is not social. Early modern Europeans assumed just the reverse; transparency was therefore not just the product of limited spatial resources (few separate bedrooms), it was positively desirable. In Simmel's words, everyone lived with the "knowledge of determining others and of

---

[158] Flinn, *European Demographic System.*
[159] Ibid., 26; Segalen, *Love and Power,* 15; Phayer, *Sexual Liberation,* 42–48.

being determined by them,"[160] and sex was not radically different from other aspects of life in this respect.

The above is not an exhaustive list of common principles, and it ignores entirely the subtle language and syntax of sexual meanings peculiar to different cultural groups.[161] But it does isolate large structures the state, and, later, civil society would encounter when they tried to reform what they took to be sexual custom.

Since much of the rest of this book concerns the question of state and social "control" or "regulation," it is important, finally, to discuss some of the assumptions in the secondary literature about the nature of the "control" or "regulation" that the traditional, non-state networks exercised over sexual behavior.

When contemporaries in the bureaucracy and especially in the church looked at popular sexual customs in village and town, they saw the failure of regulation everywhere and imagined rampant licentiousness.[162] Historians have tended to see the opposite. They have been struck precisely by the power that material and social considerations exercised over sexual behavior, and many have concluded that these dictates must have crushed sexual desire, tender emotion, and erotic expression. Edward Shorter has expressed this view most clearly: "There was an abiding suspiciousness of sexuality," which had resulted in "collective sexual repression," in lives that were "resolutely unerotic," because "traditional society succeeded quite effectively in suppressing (sublimating, if you prefer) the sex drives of the unmarried." "Emotionless courtship" developed into "marital lovelessness," characterized by bleak, fantasy-less, reproduction-oriented sex.[163] Despite their criticisms of Shorter's other hypotheses,[164] many scholars are inclined to agree with this view. Extrapolating from evidence such as limited choice of spouse, age differences of spouses, the expectation of early death, formulaic courtship, rapid remarriage, highly defined gender roles, the testimony of outside (usually bourgeois) observers, and the physical difficulty of life before industrialization, they judge that the emotional range of early modern people was either underdeveloped or that emotional inclination rarely coincided with the life-partner they drew, that consequently "there was hardly room for emotionally fulfilled intimate relations,"[165] and that therefore, as Heidi Rosenbaum sums up for the nineteenth-century peasantry, marital sexual relations were "seldom coupled with tenderness. They were directed

---

[160] "How Is Society Possible?" in *Georg Simmel on Individuality and Social Forms*, ed. D. Levine (Chicago, 1972), 7, cited in Calhoun, "Community," 114. Also, Huggel on the "narrowness" (*Engnis*) of circumstances; Ilien and Jeggle, *Leben auf dem Dorfe*, 55. Cf. Shorter's tendentious interpretation in *Modern Family*, 39–44.

[161] Such as the meanings given to certain gestures, expressions, or objects; assumptions about men versus women, about age-appropriate sexual expression, about the health or wisdom of sex in certain places or times of year, and so on.

[162] The phrase was always that sexual irregularities were "out of control" (*über Hand nehmen*).

[163] *Modern Family*, 20, 51, 99, 99, 138, 60, and for the quality of marital sex, 245–48.

[164] Cf. Rosenbaum, *Formen der Familie*, 225–27.

[165] Gerhard Wurzbacher and Hilde Kipp, "Das Verhältnis von Familie und öffentlichem Raum unter besonderer Berücksichtigung der Bundesrepublik Deutschland," in *Die Familie als Sozialisationsfaktor. Der Mensch als soziales und personales Wesen*, ed. Gerhard Wurzbacher (Stuttgart, 1968), 3:32.

toward quick and immediate genital satisfaction. The satisfaction of psychological needs was secondary."[166] The same conclusion holds for artisans, or any other group for whom material considerations outweighed emotional and romantic ones.[167] Therefore, only "the dissolution of indentured [dingliche] bonds and patriarchal controls" could produce "not only a personalization and individualization of partner choice and courtship, but also a 'transformation of the world of erotic feeling.'"[168]

There are several assumptions behind these extrapolations, held in different degrees by different scholars. The simplest is that sexual energy is a biological drive, if not equally present then certainly present to some degree in all individuals; if it is not permitted to run its course, then it must perforce have been "repressed," dammed up, with deleterious consequences.[169] The commonly held emotional model is the reverse: emotions are assumed to require development, practice, and expression, otherwise they wither and die. The trickiest assumption links the two, whereby sexual activity is seen primarily as a means to express emotional intimacy;[170] not used to this end, it is interpreted as deficient or undeveloped. Further down this chain of speculation, emotional intimacy then appears as perpetually at odds with society,[171] as the province of individuals, as "self-realization— accomplished through sexual gratification."[172] Finally, the chain ends at the daring correlation of sexual acts with degrees of intimacy: sexual intercourse, conducted at leisure, while naked, lying down, in private, playful, at unusual seasons or times, with foreplay and fantasy—these methods and settings are taken as especially characteristic of emotional attachment and erotic "free choice."[173]

---

[166] Formen der Familie, 87.

[167] Ibid., 145, 152–53, 157. Rosenbaum discusses the secondary literature on emotions and sexual relations critically and sensitively for each social stratum. For other examples: on coldness among noble family members, see Reif, "Väterliche Gewalt," 103. For an argument close to Shorter's, but with better German data, see Phayer, Sexual Liberation, esp. 14–15, and Michael F. Phayer, "Lower-Class Morality: The Case of Bavaria," Journal of Social History 8.1 (1974): 79–95. For artisans, see Möller, Kleinbürgerliche Familie, 285–97. For the repressive hypothesis on peasants, see Günther Pallaver, Das Ende der schamlosen Zeit. Die Verdrängung der Sexualität in der frühen Neuzeit am Beispiel Tirols (Vienna, 1987); Ilien and Jeggle, Leben auf dem Dorfe, 59–60, 80, interpret "repression" and lack of emotion as effects of subsistence.

[168] Hans Medick, "Haushalts-und Familienstruktur als Momente des Produktions- und Reproduktionsprozesses," in Familie und Gesellschaftsstruktur. Materialien zu den sozioökonomischen Bedingungen von Familienformen, ed. Heidi Rosenbaum (Frankfurt, 1978), 298. Medick expands on the famous argument of Rudolf Braun, in Industrialisation, 41–47; see his criticism of Braun, 302 n. 12. Cf. the insightful critique in Rosenbaum, Formen der Familie, 219–22.

[169] Becker writes, for example, of the "need for sexuality" which in the seventeenth and eighteenth centuries was "confronted with a marriage system that excluded significant parts of the population," creating a situation of "misproportions," Leben und Lieben, 233. Cf. Mitterauer, "Gesindedienst und Jugendphase," 203, and Braun, Industrialisation, 44 and 83: "It is not surprising that people broke out and went astray when they had the freedom to indulge the most elementary and human desires."

[170] Shorter, Modern Family, 161, 166.

[171] Braun, Industrialisation, 46–47.

[172] Shorter, Modern Family, 167, also 20.

[173] Ibid., 157–61, 165–67, 245; Fairchilds, "Female Sexual Attitudes," 163–204, 191–93; Huggel, Einschlagsbewegung, 494–95; Rosenbaum, Formen der Familie, 86–87.

❧ The Church, Traditional Society, and the Regulation of Sex ❧

Michel Foucault has clearly analyzed how closely these assumptions dovetail with our own sexual ideology.[174] If we try to strip away the sticky residue of our own social imaginings, a task we alas can never entirely accomplish, then we glimpse how truly different the early modern world was from our own. The axis from repression to free choice is wholly inadequate to comprehend that world.[175] Then, as now, sexual desire and its possible modes of expression were fashioned within the contours of one's particular life condition. These conditions were material, mental, physical, social, and accidental, and they differed by *Stand*, wealth, gender, age, and so on. It is possible to view these conditions as constraints, since they are particular and thus limited; an artisan is *not* a nobleman, a peasant is not a priest. But these are trivial observations and useless to historical analysis, since all people must exist as particulars. Desire is not a "force" that must be constrained, but something that actually comes into being within a set of circumstances. It is an act of will, but is never free. It is how a person walks through the landscape in which she finds herself, it is the course he sails with the winds and currents that surround him. With every step that landscape changes, with every correction of the rudder that sea, those winds, are subtly influenced, but never cease to press upon the traveler.

This inextricable mix of necessity and activity means, first, that sexual desire is one way a person negotiates his or her social place. In the sterile language of social science, desire is a way to express and attain personal interest, to maximize one's standing, power, and security in the community. In the early modern period, this was achieved most surely within a system of (heterosexual) marital hegemony. One desired a "good match"; indeed, one desired marriage itself. Pastor Schwager used the word "lust after" (*so lüstern nach*) to describe how much the unmarried young village women in his Westfalian parish wanted to be married themselves.[176] They experienced desire, not constraint. The same principle applies to sexual object choice more narrowly. A limited selection of possible marriage partners is not a sign of lovelessness. As Bourdieu puts it: "But the surest guarantor of homogamy and, thereby, of social reproduction, is the spontaneous affinity (experienced as a feeling of friendly warmth) which binds together the agents endowed with dispositions or tastes that are similar, and thus produced from similar social conditions and conditionings. . . . [L]ove can be described as a form of *amor fati*: to love is always to some extent to love in someone else another way of fulfilling one's own social destiny."[177] This is more than merely the eroticization of necessity, since desire is the mark that individual will makes on necessity, as it operates within necessity to its own advantage.

Thus, as Reinhard Sieder sums up for peasants, "It would be a mistake to separate the 'sexuality' of peasants from its 'socioeconomic'[*hauswirtschaftlichen*]

---

[174] *History of Sexuality*, vol. 1.

[175] As it is, moreover, inadequate to describe our own, despite its usefulness as a fiction.

[176] "Über den Ravensberger Bauer," 63–64.

[177] "From Rules to Strategems," 71; see also the sensitive discussion in Rosenbaum, *Formen der Familie*, 77, 225–27.

determinacy and to want to interpret it 'for its own sake.'"[178] This is true for other groups, and for emotions as well as for sexual habits: "There is no pure, unmediated attraction between individuals."[179] And just as there is no single determinant of either sexual behavior or emotional economy, neither is there a set relation between emotion and sexual expression. Sex is a vocabulary that can express many things. For the historian this complexity of origin, goal, and expression counsels interpretive caution. For the individual, it means that the sheer number of variables that go into producing desire overwhelm any effort at purely rational "calculation." What historians view after the fact as design, the pattern of spousal endogamy, or overwhelming heterosexuality, for instance, is experienced by the individual as, and therefore for subjective purposes is, spontaneous, authentic, and unreflected.[180]

Second, because desire is created out of so many different strands of necessity, not all of which tend in the same direction, it can develop at odds with the prevailing social or erotic system. Further, idiosyncratic discovery or accidental (sexual) innovation can also ruffle the smooth feathers of a desire in conformity with social destiny. But whatever the forces sustaining conformity, the early modern popular sexual systems had room for idiosyncracy and palliatives for sexual dissatisfaction. The vast cornucopia of popular medicine lay at hand to help one inflame or cool desire, as one wished, or to cure other sexual ills.[181] More important were the places of structural refuge within the system, the large tracts of social irrelevancy where certain manifestations of sexual desire seem to have been relatively underinterpreted, such as masturbation, positions, bestiality, possibly rural same-sex relations that remained undiscovered, genital touching, and so on. This is a difficult subject to research and one should be wary of confusing silence with tolerance. Nonetheless, the early modern sexual map had sufficient white space to accommodate errant wandering, some of which would not even have been classified by contemporaries as sexual. Finally, lack of sexual fulfillment was not made worse, as it is today, by an ideology proclaiming it a basic human right and a sign of personhood. Sex was the privilege of those in certain social positions; it was not a right. The absence of sexual expression was therefore not generally a social humiliation. Consequently, sexual dissatisfaction was not compounded by the same string of meanings and personal associations as nowadays. It was literally not "important" in the same way.

Third, early modern sexual desire formed in the absence of a number of obsessions that troubled the nineteenth and twentieth centuries. One searches in vain for the myth that females lacked passion or that sex was harmful or for the morbid fixation on venereal disease (though there was plenty objectively present), for embarrassment about bodily functions, nakedness, or lack of privacy. This is *not* to

---

[178] *Sozialgeschichte der Familie* (Frankfurt, 1987), 59–60.

[179] Sabean, "Junge Immen," 232. See also Sieder, *Sozialgeschichte der Familie*, 113, on artisans and emotion; and Becker, *Leben und Lieben*, 191, 195, 199–201, 203, on emotions in the early modern rural marriage.

[180] Bourdieu, "Stratégies matrimoniales," 1124.

[181] Angus McLaren, *A History of Contraception from Antiquity to the Present Day* (Cambridge, 1990), 111.

say that the desires of earlier generations were "healthier" or "freer," merely that they developed in circumstances almost unimaginable to us, in a completely different complex of meanings and taboos.

Finally, when desire had formed out of its myriad sources, it expressed itself sexually in a language and syntax foreign not only to us, but often also to contemporaries from other social groups. The vocabulary was rich, replete with natural allusion, and often concrete. Herbs, branches, pocket knives, coins, and handsqueezing were all signs in the language of affection.[182] Many a bureaucrat lost his way in this thicket of meanings and, for example, confused a token of engagement with payment for prostitution.[183] If a contemporary could go so thoroughly wrong in such a relatively clear matter, imagine the possibilities for interpretive error hidden in differences as fundamental as defining what is sexual in the first place. This is the dilemma confronting the modern observer, whose own definition of sex is narrowly genital and globally emotional. As one acute observer of rural life notes, "Love as it was recognised in past times in rural society was something different from the eroticised and exhibitionist form of it that we have today."[184] It may be that, in the long years before one could marry or for those who could never marry at all, genital sexual expression occurred rarely.[185] But as Rainer Beck points out, even if abstinence were widespread,[186] the number of erotic outlets short of procreative intercourse multiplied. Intricate rural courtship practices were "for the young men and women of that era attractive and varied enough that they could devote themselves to them for many years without leaving the path of [sexual] honor."[187] Only our own habits label theirs "unerotic" or sexually underdeveloped.

Therefore, inquiring about the quantity or quality of early modern sexual lives is misguided. We must accept them as complete expressions of their own universe(s). Absolutist traditional sexual ordering was not more or less disciplined or repressed, more or less erotic, more or less open to choice, more or less satisfying, than our own; it was merely different.

The State and the Traditional Networks

The absolutist state was not absolute. Its bureaucracy, although ambitious, was thin and uneven. It depended not only for its efficiency but, more important, for its information on the traditional networks. As we have seen, these were maddeningly

[182] For examples, see Shorter, *Modern Family*, 133; Segalen, *Anthropology of the Family*, 129–30; and Segalen, *Love and Power*, 18–19.

[183] See Chapter 10, p. 404–5.

[184] Segalen, *Anthropology of the Family*, 129.

[185] This is what Becker, *Leben und Lieben*, 295, found in St. Lambert, but his sources are too thin to make a general conclusion.

[186] Flandrin believes that, on the contrary, non-procreative forms of sexual expression were common among rural people as replacement for forbidden heterosexual intercourse. Jean-Louis Flandrin, "Répression et changement dans la vie sexuelle des jeunes," in *Le sexe et l'Occident. Évolution des attitudes et des comportements* (Paris, 1981), 279–302. In "Lower-Class Morality," 88, Phayer agrees with Beck, but interprets the significance of abstention differently.

[187] Beck, "Illegitimität," 140, also 120.

complex, cross-cutting, and often mutually contradictory, and most fatal of all from the state's viewpoint, they followed their own dynamics and interests. They also frequently spoke another language; their symbols and gestures might be completely opaque to a representative of the central bureaucracy, whose class, native dialect, home region, and training blinded him to their arguments and necessities. Two exemplary areas of disagreement and misunderstanding were prenuptial coupling and illegitimacy. State bureaucrats took a dim view of peer group courtship regulation, especially when it erupted into violence, and since the Reformation they disapproved of sexual activity between the engaged. The latter was untroubling to village and family, so long as these were strong enough to make sure a marriage ultimately occurred. Illegitimacy was a problem of a different kind. Insofar as some rural areas could absorb illegitimate children as needed laborers, the early absolutist state, worried as it was about moral and abstract economic matters, might be more distressed by illegitimacy than the community. Still, the same economic motives—this time to provide employment for illegitimate offspring in the towns, plus an Enlightened change of heart in the eighteenth century, moved the state to be more lenient than the guilds. These two examples simply illustrate that the various systems of sexual regulation were quite distinct. If the state's object was to bring them into harmony (which is only partly true), then it had a wearying task before it.

Nevertheless, the state was not merely bent on having its own way. Despite its reputation among scholars as having imposed "civilization" by force on its subjects, destroying in the process popular culture, the absolutist state was genuinely intent on safeguarding the villages and families (less so the guilds), on which it felt its own prosperity and security depended, not to mention its duty before God. Besides, its bureaucrats shared many of the same religious, economic, social, and therefore sexual assumptions of the fathers of village and town. Finally, even when these two factors did not result in policies acceptable to the traditional structures, the state's superior enforcement mechanisms could still prove useful for other, local purposes. In short, the relationship between the state and traditional networks was not always antagonistic; it was just always complicated. Only complete immersion in local sources enables one to distinguish when the state sought to override local custom, when locals turned state initiatives to their own advantage, when, indeed, local elites actually caused the state to intervene, and when locals thwarted the state from pursuing disagreeable policies.

Befitting its own hierarchical structure and the widespread analogy between monarch and father, which it of course assiduously polished, the territorial state preferred to strengthen *Hausväter.* It considered them its emissaries in the little realm of the family, upholders of property, order, and godliness. Accordingly, it bestowed upon them (and parents generally) increased formal power to veto their children's spouses.[188] In ordinance after ordinance it held *Hausväter* and *-mütter* responsible for the sexual conduct of their children and servants, as though they

---

[188] Robisheaux, *Rural Society,* 110, 112.

were the first-line police force of the state. It encouraged their power against that of peer groups and neighbors[189] and thus contributed to the decline of those intermediate local authorities.[190] But state adulation of the family father had its limits. As Sabean discovered, "Local officials had to be concerned with satisfying allied groups represented by a particular marriage and had to provide for the smooth running of households, so that no threats to the security of property could get out of hand. Therefore, complaints about cruelty or about the inappropriate use of force got full hearing. Patriarchal values, however central for the eighteenth century, were negotiable."[191]

If the absolutist state depended on *Hausväter* for local sexual order, it depended equally on the other traditional structures, perhaps more than it knew. The prosecution of sexual crimes was at the mercy of the local populace: they provided the original information for indictment, the testimony at the trial, and the audience for public punishments. If the parties to a dispute arising from sexual behavior could solve the problem among themselves, then the authorities might never hear of it.[192] Or they would hear carefully tailored rumors, which, like *Haberfeldtreiben*, cloaked those involved in anonymity.[193] Rumor was a rein that villagers pulled to make the authorities turn to their liking. It was particularly useful when the village itself was divided. The local authorities had to tread carefully, however, because rumor, *Haberfeldtreiben*, and other informal methods of sanction did not always reflect community opinion; they were open to misuse by the vengeful and the personally interested.[194]

The possibilities for mutual misuse and manipulation on the part of the state and the traditional networks should not blind us to the fact that many of the sexual attitudes they were variously enforcing were common to both. This agreement is particularly clear in cases of, for example, father-daughter incest, which was universally and unhesitatingly condemned.[195] It is clear in the shared interest of property owners and state officials in regulating spouse choice for economic reasons, in the shared interest of the *Gemeinde* and the state in discouraging illegitimacy for fiscal reasons, and in the (at least) symbolic interest of the community of the married in punishing adultery. It is clear, too, in the general, unreflected assumption of heterosexuality, and in the expectation that sexual activity was inextricably bound up with social relations and stability.

We are used to thinking of the state as an ungainly apparatus extending its tentacles down into the society beneath it. We are less prepared to imagine society as possessing far more tentacles than the state, but that is surely so. From now on in

---

[189] As in the fight against customary courtship practices and marriages without parental approval.
[190] See Flandrin, *Families in Former Times*, 216, for neighborhood weakening in favor of family ties.
[191] Sabean, *Neckarhausen*, 134.
[192] Becker, *Leben und Lieben*, 260–65, 280–81, 284.
[193] Ibid., 266; Beck, "Illegitimität," 130; David Sabean, *Power in the Blood: Popular Culture and Discourse in Early Modern Germany* (Cambridge, 1983), 148–49, 164, 166, 173, 195.
[194] Scharfe, "Soziale Kontrolle," 82–83; Beck, "Illegitimität," 130.
[195] Beck, "Illegitimität," 130, 131; Simon, *Moralpolitik*, 274.

this book, the writhing below will be obscured by the focus on state officials and then on the self-appointed spokesmen of the new (civil) society. But the reader should never forget that that turbulence was always present, and that state efforts to regulate sexual activity rested on the most insecure and convoluted of foundations. Or, to exchange the octopus for an animal with which more early modern people were familiar, in the words of a Swiss pastor (1816) charged with sexual regulation, "Who is going to supervise a sieve full of fleas?"[196]

[196] Cited in Braun, *Industrialisation*, 42.

2

The Absolutist States and the Regulation of Sex

The Reformation and the wars of religion ended with an immense increase in the power of the German territorial states. They arrogated to themselves duties formerly undertaken by the church. State bureaucracies, blazing a trail toward ever greater extraction of wealth and more uniform administration, hacked at the myriad intermediate authorities (such as the Gemeinde, guilds, families) which formed the thicket of traditional networks of sexual regulation. Where the central state did not supplant these authorities, it tended to instrumentalize them for its own purposes.[1] The weakening of intermediate institutions transformed the relation between the central state and its subjects; the latter became increasingly exposed to the state's direct attention and thus more completely objects of administration. This new target of official tutelage and police (*Polizey*) welfare acquired a new and fitting name, "subject" (*Untertan*), which replaced the medieval "common man" and was replaced by the "citizen" of civil society, thus demarcating the peculiar epoch known as absolutism.[2]

However thorough these changes were in actual practice, there can be no doubt about the sweeping responsibilities the states assumed regarding the conduct of their subjects' lives. As Willoweit puts it, the absolutist state "was a . . . form peculiar to itself because, after the demise of the imperial idea and before the triumph of Enlightenment, it tried, out of *ständisch*-corporatist and political conviction, to realize for the last time the unity of individual and public morality."[3] The secular states, including those headed by Roman Catholic princes, had undertaken this enormous task under the impact of the Reformation; "The political path [upon which they embarked] seems the correlate of the Christian virtues and the consequence of Christian obedience."[4] But in addition to its religious convictions and legitimation, the absolutist state had a distinctly secular political, economic, and social aspect that assumed a certain relation of state and society and aspired to

---

[1] Heide Wunder, *"Er ist die Sonn', sie ist der Mond." Frauen in der Frühen Neuzeit* (Munich, 1992), 251.
[2] Peter Blickle, "Untertanen in der Frühneuzeit. Zur Rekonstruktion der politischen Kultur und der sozialen Wirklichkeit Deutschlands im 17. Jahrhundert," *Vierteljahrschrift für Sozial- und Wirtschaftsgeschichte* 70 (1983): 483–522.
[3] "Struktur und Funktion intermediärer Gewalten," 26.
[4] Ibid., 24.

greater productive power. As Johannes Kunisch sums it up, "The assumption was still determinant, that individual and public morality formed just as much a unity as state and society. Thus it was the disciplining grasp of the absolutist authoritarian state [*Obrigkeitsstaat*] which led the old society of estates via the monopolization of all social and economic opportunity in the prince's hand, to modern competitive society."[5]

"Social disciplining" (*Sozialdisziplinierung*) is the phrase made famous by Gerhard Oestreich to describe the state's mostly coercive efforts to transform its subjects' behavior.[6] Although Oestreich nowhere mentioned sexual behavior as an equal object of the state's disciplining scrutiny, his model clearly includes it:

> The person was disciplined in his desires [*Wollen*] and his expression. . . . The social process precipitated out in the city, territorial, and imperial police ordinances. The very concept, police, is itself an expression of this: the later police science, as the science of the domestic life of the state in the seventeenth and eighteenth centuries wanted discipline and order to rule the ever increasing public life. These territorial and police ordinances are a way to understand the impetus to discipline. At first seemingly only following the goal of protecting or reestablishing the old, Christian discipline and respectability [*Ehrbarkeit*], they soon reached deeply into private life [*Privatleben*] and brought rules and pedagogical guidelines to every conceivable area. The idea of common welfare [*gemeinen Wohlfahrt*] and good police were closely connected to the idea of discipline.[7]

Oestreich's concept of "social disciplining" has been quite influential, suggesting as it did an alternative to institutional history and a way to understand absolutism's relation to the social, economic, and political forms that succeeded it.[8]

"Social disciplining" has important implications for the interpretation of absolutist sexual regulation. It suggests that the territorial states tried to impose an alien system of norms onto preexisting value structures operating in society. As R. Po-Chia Hsia explains it, "The moral regime of the state had its clear limits because it was in direct competition with another moral system: the village as an autonomous unit of ethical-economic behavior, defined by neighborly mutual help, and anchored in the family and community."[9] Whether one judges the states' attempts as successes or failures, the assumption is that the state marched to a different drummer.

A second implication of "social disciplining" is that state regulation targeted behavior for its own sake, not because of its negative social consequences. Thus, the

---

[5] *Absolutismus*, 41.

[6] Gerhard Oestreich, "Strukturprobleme des europäischen Absolutismus," in *Geist und Gestalt des frühmodernen Staates* (Berlin, 1969), 179–97; Winfried Schulze, "Gerhard Oestreichs Begriff 'Sozialdisziplinierung in der frühen Neuzeit,'" *Zeitschrift für historische Forschung* 14.3 (1987): 265–302.

[7] "Strukturprobleme," 193.

[8] "Social disciplining" focuses on the more coercive aspects of the "civilizing process" as Norbert Elias explored them in *The Civilizing Process*, 2 vols., trans. Edmund Jephcott (New York, 1978–82). Although Oestreich concentrated on its military uses, historians of the economic transformation from subsistence to capitalism have found it equally useful; see Leonhard Bauer and Herbert Matis, *Geburt der Neuzeit. Vom Feudalsystem zur Marktgesellschaft* (Munich, 1988), 315–44.

[9] *Social Discipline in the Reformation: Central Europe, 1550–1750* (London, 1989), 137.

state seemed less interested in preventing illegitimacy than in correcting immorality. This suggests that the state was as interested in punishing all sexually immoral/illegal conduct as the church had presumably been before it.

Third, consonant with the idea of forced imposition of unpopular norms, the state's actions appear mostly coercive. The draconian punishments associated with absolutism—the death penalty for sodomy or repeated fornication, for example— seem characteristic of a violent and undifferentiated system of external coercion.[10]

Fourth, the punitive hand of the absolutist state seems to have rested especially heavily on women and the unpropertied. Again, Hsia: "One social consequence [of absolutist regulation of sexual behavior] was greater repression of female sexuality and a widening gap between bourgeois families and the lower classes. The suppression of premarital sex and illegitimacy represented a logical extension of the establishment of patriarchy in early modern Germany."[11] Much of the work on absolutist sexual regulation has focused on gender and social inequities.[12]

Finally, the "social disciplining" model assumes the dichotomy between "public" and "private." The state's activities are then taken to have smashed through this wholesome distinction and injured private life. Kunisch observes "in all of these early modern state-building procedures, a process of all-inclusive disciplining of the entirety of public and private life."[13]

The "social disciplinary" model has undergone much criticism and modification since Oestreich introduced it in 1969. Above all, the cleft separating central from local bureaucrats has emerged as an important consideration, on the one hand, and on the other, so has the reliance of even local bureaucrats on village information and assistance in order to proceed with their regulatory efforts: "Official mandates . . . could only work with the co-operation of the local elites and the acquiescence of the populace."[14] These insights produce a picture of a weaker and more fragmented absolutist state. But they have not displaced "social disciplining" from its position as the main, if often unacknowledged, framework within which scholars attempt to analyze sexual regulation.

The world of absolutist sexual regulation I have discovered differs considerably from that portrayed by Oestreich. The German absolutist territorial states appear in a much closer symbiosis with their "subjects" than the social-disciplinary model suggests. The sexual norms officials tried to enforce were largely shared by the

---

[10] This is, of course, the model Foucault made famous; see Michel Foucault, *Discipline and Punish: The Birth of the Prison*, trans. Alan Sheridan (New York, 1977), beginning his account with the gruesome execution of the regicide Damiens in France in 1757.

[11] *Social Discipline*, 149.

[12] See Roper, *Holy Household;* the essays in Heide Wunder and Christina Vanja, eds., *Wandel der Geschlechterbeziehungen zu Beginn der Neuzeit* (Frankfurt, 1991), and in Karin Hausen and Heide Wunder, eds., *Frauengeschichte-Geschlechtergeschichte* (Frankfurt, 1992), esp. 131–83; and Ulrike Gleixner, "Dörfliche und obrigkeitliche Ordnungen. Die Konstruktion von Geschlecht in 'Unzuchtsverfahren' im 18. Jahrhundert in Preußen (Altmark 1700–1750)" (Ph.D. diss., Freie Universität Berlin, 1992).

[13] *Absolutismus*, 39. Similarly, Oestreich, "Strukturprobleme," 181, 187, 188, 192, 193.

[14] Hsia, *Social Discipline*, 138.

population, at least partly because officials focused narrowly on those acts most likely to harm the local economy and social stability. Although government regulation was certainly by definition coercive, it was also nuanced, sensitive to local circumstances, and flexible. It was precisely this sensitivity to social expectation that produced the different treatment of men and women in sex-crime law. The social-*ständisch* calculation of proper behavior according to a complex grid formed by axes of gender, marital status, *Stand*, and so on, had left a strong, customary legacy in the laws officials then enforced. When officials innovated, they tended to contradict this system of customary, *ständisch* (and therefore also gender) differentiation in the somewhat abstract interest of administrative efficiency, namely, of interchangeability and potentially, of equality. Furthermore, innovation occurred not merely from the top down, but also from local officials, meaning that absolutism was less centrally *dirigiste* than it has often appeared. Finally, absolutism did not penetrate into the "private sphere," because that did not yet exist; indeed, the private sphere was at least partly produced by the failure of the absolutist regulatory system.

In the following discussion of absolutist sexual regulation I focus largely on the territorial states. Although cities, with their concise records, have attracted previous scholarly attention, the territorial states ruled the vast majority of the population, carried through the chief Enlightened reforms of the next century, and were administratively and legally the basis for the modern split between state and society. Not wishing to anticipate those developments, I have tried to distinguish among the three levels of government, central, provincial, and local, where possible. The central officials are of particular importance because in the course of drafting ordinances and coordinating enforcement, they developed a sense of responsibility for public welfare in the abstract. Their point of view ultimately merited the title "state," and occasionally I have used the term to refer to their higher, all-encompassing viewpoint. Occasionally, I use the term "state" to refer to the collective activities of all three levels of government. In later sections of this book, when Germans had begun discussing 'civil society' and its relation to "state" [*Staat*], I use "state" in the more theoretical sense common to political theory.

Legislation as the Barometer of State Regulatory Interest

Although officials upheld (or subverted) aspects of the sexual system in all sorts of ways (through marriage ordinances, inheritance rules, taxation, controlling access to citizen's rights [*Bürgerrecht*]), the penal laws and the bureaucrats' discussions concerning their execution and reform give the most explicit account of what the central state tried to achieve in sexual matters. It was in criminal ordinances that the central government set forth its assumptions about sexual behavior and its effects on the "common good" (*Gemeinwohl*). That is why legislation forms the main source for analyzing the government's viewpoint on these matters. To understand how the regulatory system worked, we must turn to a brief overview of the early modern legal landscape.

The Levels of Statute

The early modern legal situation was so complicated that many state officials apparently never quite grasped it. Most of them, especially those working at the central level, busied themselves with the ordinances and mandates they helped to draft and whose execution they were supposed to oversee. But below, and often contradicting the ordinances, was an entire thicket of mostly unrecorded common law, differing from district to district and even village to village. There are strong indications that customary law remained at the very least sporadically active in determining the treatment of offenders against the sexual order even as late as the early nineteenth century.[15] Customary law is barely visible at the central level, and then usually as deviations from statute in practice, rather than as a system in itself.

What gradually replaced the checkerboard of customary law, whether by codification of the practice of one locality and its extension to all others, or by reform, were the territorial legal codes—or their urban equivalents. The latter were passed by the city councils, usually at an earlier date than the former, which were simply promulgated by the prince after a bureaucratic procedure of collection, discussion, and possibly emendation. Scholarly discussions of early modern sexual regulation have until recently tended to rely on city codes and judicial practice, which has possibly overemphasized how quickly and completely nonurban, territorial codes came into being and how stringently they were enforced.[16] At any rate, territorial codification occurred sporadically, with the results usually left unamended for years. But the codes were in fact constantly tinkered with through a cascade of ordinances and administrative pronouncements issuing forth from the prince and his uppermost bureaucrats. The ordinances were the stream of consciousness of central-state thinking on sexual matters, the seismograph of state interest in sexual regulation. These documents bear various names: *Verordnung, Reskript, Edikt, Mandat, Dekret,* and so forth. Technically, each was produced by a

[15] On customary versus Roman law, see Gerald Strauss, *Law, Resistance, and the State: The Opposition to Roman Law in Reformation Germany* (Princeton, N.J., 1986), esp. 96–135. On the existence of customary or common law in localities: see for Baden, Karl S. Bader, "Verbrechen, Strafe und Strafvollzug in der Landgrafschaft Heiligenberg," *Monatsschrift für Kriminologie und Strafrechtsreform* 50 (March 1967): 198; for the Altmark Brandenburg (Prussia), Gleixner, "Dörfliche und obrigkeitliche Ordnungen," 42; for Bavaria, Stefan Breit, *"Leichtfertigkeit" und ländliche Gesellschaft. Voreheliche Sexualität in der frühen Neuzeit* (Munich, 1991), 132 n. 113, insofar as he correctly remarks that the fornication fine was not specified in the moral mandates of 1635 or 1727, nor in the Bavarian criminal code of 1751, but rather given as the "customary fine." A reconstruction of the parameters of customary handling of sexual delicts would be extremely useful.

[16] Richard van Dülmen has synthesized much of this earlier work, not especially for sexual delicts, though these are included, but for executions and punishment generally. Most of his statistics are accordingly urban. See Richard van Dülmen, *Theater des Schreckens. Gerichtspraxis und Strafrituale in der frühen Neuzeit* (Munich, 1988).

slightly different bureaucratic procedure and targeted a different audience. In the seventeenth and eighteenth centuries, however, "the distinctions were quite arbitrary," as Marc Raeff remarks, and do not always reliably indicate what authority issued the order, or what procedure preceded the decision or characterized its enforcement. Since contemporaries did not distinguish administrative orders from laws or criminal delicts from police violations, all of these documents were equally legal and will be discussed interchangeably here.[17]

At the most abstract level, in several senses of the word, were the sixteenth-century Constitutio Criminalis Carolina (the criminal code for the Holy Roman Empire) and the Imperial Police Ordinances (RPO) from the same century. These explicitly did *not* supersede territorial, urban, or other local law. The Carolina and the RPO might supplement local statute by providing guidelines where the local code was either unclear or inadequate. Some territories, including Hamburg and Baden, had adopted the Carolina as their own, in lieu of a protracted and difficult legal reform of their own institutions.[18] But the Carolina is much less important as a practical code, since even where it was nominally in effect, it was honored more in the breach than in the observance, than it is important as an indicator of the direction of sixteenth-century governmental reform.

The Courts

Most consensual sexual delicts were handled by the lower courts (*Niedergerichte*). These lower, or local, courts were permitted to inflict "civil punishments" (*bürgerliche Strafen*) which ranged from fines, to work punishments, jail (as opposed to prison), corporal punishment by the rod, and public humiliation.[19] Only higher courts might hand down "painful punishments" (*peinliche Strafen*), which included mutilation, imprisonment (*Zuchthaus*), and death in all its permutations: by sword, fire, drowning, and so on. These penalties were reserved for serious offenses like murder, manslaughter, and rape and for repeat offenses, which might include sexual crimes like second- or third-time adultery or fornication.

Although the range of punishments was generally quite similar for lower courts throughout Germany, court personnel differed wildly. In some areas, like Württem-

[17]Raeff, *Well-Ordered Police State*, 9. For the exact differences among these documents in governmental provenience and grammatical style and form, see Heinrich Otto Meisner, *Archivalienkunde vom 16. Jahrhundert bis 1918* (Göttingen, 1969), 137–69, and H.-J. Becker, "Mandat," in *Handwörterbuch zur deutschen Rechtsgeschichte*, 4 vols. to date, ed. Adalbert Erler and Ekkehard Kaufmann (Berlin, 1971–90), vol., 3, col. 231.

[18]John H. Langbein, *Prosecuting Crime in the Renaissance: England, Germany, France* (Cambridge, Mass., 1974), 166, 198; Eberhard Schmidt, *Einführung in die Geschichte der deutschen Strafrechtspflege*, 3 ed. (Göttingen, 1965), 141–44; and Robert von Hippel, *Deutsches Strafrecht* (Berlin, 1925), 1:222–25.

[19]For the most recent account of punishments and their meaning to early moderns, see Dülmen, *Theater des Schreckens*, 62–80, 108–20. The older classic is by Hans von Hentig, *Die Strafe*, 2 vols. (Berlin, 1954–55); published in English under the title *Punishment: Its Origins, Purpose and Psychology* (London, 1937). Also, Rudolf Quanter, *Die Schand- und Ehrenstrafen in der deutschen Rechtspflege* (1901; Aalen, 1970). I discuss the various punishments for sexual delicts in greater detail in the section on ordinances in this chapter.

berg, the (land-owning peasant) citizens of a village elected the judge and jurors. In other places, the privilege of patrimonial jurisdiction meant that the landowner, on whose land the villagers lived, had the right and duty to dispense justice, which was usually twinned with police and administrative power as well. The landowner could be a noble, the Roman Catholic Church (the Protestant churches having lost the privilege of patrimonial jurisdiction to the princes), or even a corporation with historically recognized rights. Under patrimonial jurisdiction, the possessor himself might wield judicial power, but he was more likely to have divested, or sold, this right to a proxy. Whether either the possessor or his proxy had judicial training depended on local circumstances and the assiduousness with which the central government could demand such training. Finally, there were court districts, often on the prince's own domain lands, in which the judge was appointed by the prince. In most regions of Germany, there was no territory-wide uniformity in the composition of early modern courts—they had grown like topsy and had had their status confirmed by legal-contractual agreement. How a case of adultery or fornication was handled depended entirely on where it was committed.[20]

There were other court-like institutions operating on the village level. Often called *Rüge-* or *Frevelgerichte,* these misdemeanor courts were run by a minor official and perhaps a local worthy, as in Baden, or, as in Württemberg, they might contain the same elected village notables who made up the regular court. These courts typically met once a year to settle community disputes. Although very occasionally they decided cases of sexual misbehavior, generally they focused on economic and other police (*Polizey*) matters. And in most areas, they seem gradually to have fallen into disuse.[21] Their impact on the early modern sexual system was small and dwindling, and therefore we can conveniently ignore them for our purposes.

Above the local courts were the *Malefizgerichte,* which judged capital offenses.

[20] For good, recent descriptions of the workings of lower courts, see, for Bavaria, Breit, *Leichtfertigkeit,* 24–25, 42, 128, 254–63, and Wolfang Behringer, "Mörder, Diebe, Ehebrecher. Verbrechen und Strafen in Kurbayern vom 16. bis 18. Jahrhundert," in *Verbrechen, Strafen und soziale Kontrolle. Studien zur historischen Kulturforschung,* ed. Richard van Dülmen (Frankfurt 1990), 85–132, esp. 87–89. For Baden, see Peter Wettmann-Jungblut, "'Stelen inn rechter hungersnodtt.' Diebstahl, Eigentumsschutz und strafrechtliche Kontrolle im vorindustriellen Baden 1600–1850," also in Dülmen, 133–77, esp. 140–41. For the Altmark Brandenburg, see Gleixner, "Dörfliche und obrigkeitliche Ordnungen," 35–43, and for Württemberg, Sabean, *Power in the Blood,* 14–17, 174–98. Useful older studies for Bavaria and Baden are Max von Seydel, *Bayerisches Staatsrecht,* 2d ed., with Josef von Grassmann and Robert Piloty (Tübingen, 1913), 1:7–11; Eduard Rosenthal, *Geschichte des Gerichtswesens und der Verwaltungsorgnisation Bayerns,* vol. 2 (Würzburg, 1906); and Rudolf Carlebach, *Badische Rechtsgeschichte* (Heidelberg, 1906–9), 2:80–89.

[21] For Württemberg, see Sabean, *Power in the Blood,* 15; for the history of Rügegerichte in Baden, see Landvogtei Dilsberg Amtsgericht memorandum of 7 December 1803, Generallandesarchiv Karlsruhe, Abteilung Kreisregierungen (313), Faszikel 2793 (hereafter GLA 313/2793); Directorium of the Dreysam-Kreis to Ministry of the Interior, Freiburg, 11 July 1823, GLA Abt. Innenministerium (236)/3155 and GLA 236/3156–57; and Isabel V. Hull, "Private Acts/Public Control in Emergent Bourgeois Society: The Revival of Religious Morals Courts [*Sittengerichte*] in Napoleonic Baden" (paper presented at the Berkshire Conference on the History of Women, Vassar College, Poughkeepsie, N.Y., June 1993), 2–6.

Cases of violent sexual crimes, sodomy, and repeated consensual offenses came before these higher courts. Befitting the more serious crimes on their docket, *Malefizgerichte* might more often resort to torture to achieve confession.[22] Wolfgang Behringer has found, however, that the Bavarian authorities at least seldom used torture in sexual cases, and when they did, they generally confined themselves to displaying to the accused the instruments of torture, rather than actually applying them. Sodomy was an exception to this gentler rule; sodomites, like the accused witches with whom they had much in common, were not spared torture.[23]

Neither the use of torture in legal investigation nor the execution of a capital sentence could occur without the highest authorities' approval. And so the court council (*Hofrat*) was the apex of the judicial pyramid. Requests to apply torture, completed cases awaiting execution of a capital sentence, and appeals were sent in written form to the court council, that is, to the highest central administrative officials who convened as a court. Under certain circumstances their decisions were checked by the prince's closest advisers, the privy council (*Geheimer Rat*), which normally shared some members with the Hofrat. Behringer discovered that the Bavarian court council decided cases of rape, sodomy, adultery, incest, concubinage, and even such relatively minor matters as fornication, "suspicious carriage," and "*Kuppelei*." Presumably many of the minor delicts were cases of repeaters, or cases where other issues had combined to bring the matter to the Hofrat's attention.[24] In Baden-Durlach and Baden-Baden the Hofrat (called the *Regierung* in the latter) was simply the criminal court for the land. All criminal cases were supposed to be forwarded to it for decision. Therefore, it routinely decided fornication cases, which constituted a "standard rubric" of its activities as a court.[25] Both Baden and Bavaria show how seriously the central state treated sexual delicts and how fluid were the legal boundaries delineating court jurisdictions and defining the seriousness of offenses.

In some areas of Germany there was one final appeal—to the legal faculties at universities, who might be called upon to render an opinion in serious cases awaiting execution of sentence. Württemberg typically turned to its home university, Tübingen, for such judgments; Schleswig-Holstein was one of many states that reached beyond its borders, while Bavaria never adopted this system at all and kept

---

[22] Dülmen, *Theater des Schreckens*, 23–37, is excellent in revising the stereotypical view of the early modern use of torture. Torture was a means of last resort to obtain confessions, which, in the absence of extensive police surveillance and investigation, seemed to be the only guarantee of the truth. Torture was sparingly and carefully used, always under supervision and according to elaborate legal safeguards (which, of course, did not lessen the pain for the victims).

[23] Behringer, "Mörder," 110.

[24] Behringer suggests, however, that the Hofrat before 1660 was hearing even minor sexual offenses. Ibid., 96, 106. Forster found similar practices by the court council in the bishopric of Speyer. See Marc Forster, *The Counter-Reformation in the Villages: Religion and Reform in the Bishopric of Speyer, 1560–1720* (Ithaca, N.Y., 1992), 98, 98 n. 14.

[25] Eberhard Gothein, "Beiträge zur Verwaltungsgeschichte der Markgrafschaft Baden unter Karl Friedrich," *Zeitschrift für die Geschichte des Oberrheins*, n.s., 26 (1911): 385; Wolfgang Windelband, *Die Verwaltung der Markgrafschaft Baden zur Zeit Karl Friedrichs* (Leipzig, 1917), 240–41, 285.

the court council as the court of last resort. At the beginning of the Thirty Years' War, the law faculty at Helmstedt (Brunswick) delivered 850 separate judgments in a single year, though the average number for early modern university faculties appears to have been between 150 and 200. That sexual cases were sometimes included in these judgments is clear from the published accounts of these *Konsilien*, though they make up a small percentage of the total caseload.[26]

Before turning to the territorial ordinances, we might begin by briefly examining the imperial legislation, which had been completed in the sixteenth century, about one hundred years before our inquiry really begins.

The Constitutio Criminalis Carolina and the Imperial Police Ordinances

In 1532, under Holy Roman Emperor Charles V, German legal scholars finished drafting and the Reichstag adopted a model law code for the empire known thereafter as the Constitutio Criminalis Carolina (the "Carolina"). Although it did not replace existing territorial or city criminal laws, it was meant to be a guide for reform, or when local law was undeveloped or unclear, and it was regarded in this spirit by German governments. Its greatest innovations, indeed the bulk of the Carolina altogether, lay in procedural questions. Of the remaining sixty-two paragraphs detailing actual crimes, only eight concerned sexual delicts.[27] Legal historians have been uninterested in interpreting these eight articles or in explaining what relation they bear to the Carolina as a whole. They have generally assumed that there was a sudden need for them, that is, that the moral behavior of the populace had recently degenerated, or, alternatively, that the articles were simply leftovers from earlier ecclesiastical or secular law.[28] It seems more likely that the legal experts' views on sexual behavior, rather than the behavior itself, had changed; and the canonical or secular legal provisions were included, not absent-mindedly, but after considerable discussion.

---

[26] On the practice of appealing to legal faculties, see Karl Kroeschell, *Deutsche Rechtsgeschichte* (Opladen, 1986–89), 3:56–58, and August Hegler, *Die praktische Tätigkeit der Juristenfakultäten des 17. und 18. Jahrhunderts* (Freiburg, 1899). For a list of published *Konsilien*, see Heinrich Gehrke, "Deutsches Reich," in *Handbuch der Quellen und Literatur der neueren europäischen Privatrechtsgeschichte*, ed. Helmut Coing (Munich, 1976), vol. 2, part 2, 1384–92. For examples of sex crimes handled by university faculties, see Johann Hieronymus Hermann, *Sammlung allerhand auserlesener Responsorum* (Jena, 1733–34), part 2, 4–15 (bigamy); part 2, 181–215 (impregnation); and part 2, 285–86 (adultery). Also see Christian Wildvogel, *Responsa et Consilia* (Jena, 1717), on adultery, 1:102–3, 185–87, 195–97, 230–232, on premature coitus (that is, intercourse before the couple had married), 2:602. The vast majority of published cases deal with property and other matters, not with sexual delicts. I thank David Sabean for bringing these works to my attention.

[27] There are many editions of the Carolina. I have found the most helpful and accurate to be by Heinrich M. Zoepfl, *Die peinliche Gerichtsordnung Kaiser Karls V. nebst der Bamberger und der Brandenburger Halsgerichtsordnung* (Heidelberg, 1842).

[28] See, for example, Josef Segall, *Geschichte und Strafrecht der Reichspolizeiordnungen von 1530, 1548 und 1577* (Kirchhain, 1914), 35–37, on the origins of the legal codes of the early sixteenth century, and Langbein, *Prosecuting Crime in the Renaissance*, 168.

The principal author of the Carolina was the legal scholar and later Luther sympathizer Johann Freiherr von Schwarzenberg und Hohenlandsberg, who had drafted a criminal code for Bamberg in 1507 (the "Bambergensis"). The Bambergensis was adopted with slight changes by Brandenburg in 1516 and served as the model for the committee working on the Carolina. The committee produced two drafts (1521 and 1529) before agreeing on the finished form in 1532.[29] About twenty percent of the Bambergensian articles were dropped and a very few added for the Carolina. As John Langbein remarks, revisions were "minor," which makes it all the more noteworthy that revisions were common among the articles on sex, so much so that in two instances changes failed to be recorded elsewhere in the document, making it internally inconsistent.[30]

Without pushing the material farther than it will go in the absence of further research, there are still some discernible trends in the Carolina's articles on sex. First, there appeared to be little discussion or disagreement about rape and "unnatural" sexual practices (bestiality, male *and* female same-sex relations).[31] These are the only articles that stayed the same. A man who committed rape, of either a married or unmarried woman of good character, was punished by death by the sword, on the analogy of a robber, because he had stolen the victim's honor. The complainant would be neither the husband nor father, but the victim herself. Persons guilty of bestiality or same-sex relations were to suffer death by fire.

The remaining delicts specified in the Carolina were incest;[32] abduction of wives, maidens, or nuns; adultery; bigamy; permitting one's own wife or children to be used sexually for one's own gain; and *Kuppelei*. The Carolina extended to these delicts its general practice of retaining the death penalty only where Roman law had called for it, but at the same time undercutting Roman harshness by widening the judge's (or legal expert's) discretionary power to impose some lesser punishment. This reforming practice had two main motives, neither specifically connected to sex. First, making possible lighter punishments increased the probability of reliable, uniform prosecution.[33] Second, widening the discretionary power of judicial experts was part of the Carolina's pedagogical intent to produce a class of bu-

---

[29] Zoepfl, *Die peinliche Gerichtsordnung,* reprints all four stages plus the end product.

[30] *Prosecuting Crime in the Renaissance,* 163–64 nn. 95 and 96. Langbein does not interpret the revisions of the sex regulations or their significance.

[31] "Sodomy" was the more usual legal appellation for "unnatural sexual practices" and in the early modern period included three acts that modern opinion distinguishes: bestiality, male and female same-sex relations, and heterosexual intercourse without possibility of impregnation, especially anal intercourse.

[32] In recent times, incest has taken on a more specific meaning than it had for the period covered by this book. Now it refers usually to parent/child, usually father/daughter relations, or more rarely to sex between siblings. The earlier understanding of incest incorporated these instances, too, but more often referred to sexual contact between in-laws or more distant relations, relations forbidden by canon law. See Brundage, *Law,* on canon law prohibitions, and Jack Goody, "A Comparative Approach to Incest and Adultery," *British Journal of Sociology* 7 (1956): 286–305, for an anthropological perspective.

[33] Segall, *Reichspolizeiordnungen,* 83–84, 91, and Bruce Lenman and Geoffrey Parker, "Introduction," in *Crime and the Law: The Social History of Crime in Western Europe since 1500,* ed. V.A.C. Gatrell, Bruce Lenman, and Geoffrey Parker (Salem, N.H., 1980), 45.

reaucrats learned in the law, whose knowledge would offset the unpredictability and prejudice of lay jurors and thus extend the rule of law as decreed by the state.[34]

Another principle the Carolina applied to criminal law was simplification, that is, it eliminated in many cases the elaboration of circumstance and detail characteristic of earlier drafts. In the course of simplifying the sex laws, it followed two further principles of interest to us. The Carolina (and the Bambergensis) tended to permit women to bring the complaint where they were the victims (in, for example, rape and the husband's adultery). Perhaps by oversight, the article on abduction for sexual purposes retained the older practice, whereby the responsible male relative, husband or father, initiated the legal proceedings. More remarkable still was the Carolina's clear reluctance to include those aspects of Roman law that treated men and women differently for the same sexual delicts. Roman law, while ignoring male adultery altogether, punished the unfaithful wife severely. This bias was evident in the Bambergensis, but entirely expunged in the Carolina. Where the Bambergensis already handled both genders equally (bigamy), the Carolina kept its provisions. Josef Segall is probably correct in attributing the gender evenhandedness to the influence of canon law (or religious sentiment generally); thus he interprets the Carolina as a victory of canon law over Roman law in matters sexual.[35]

Gender equality was hardly complete in the Carolina, of course. It occurred apparently where contemporaries could conceive of both sexes giving offense: in homosexual relations, bestiality, faithlessness (adultery), fraud (bigamy), and *Kuppelei*. There is, further, a hint that children of both genders were considered vulnerable to their father's willingness to sell their sexual services.[36] But there were also sexual crimes exclusively associated with one gender: for males, abduction for sexual purposes, rape, incest (the statute is written with a male offender in view), and sale of sexual access to one's wife or children. The Carolina included no sexual acts deemed peculiarly female. Prostitution, which might have been a candidate for such an honor, went unmentioned. Nevertheless, there were two articles pertaining only to women that concerned the results of heterosexual activity: the Carolina lists abandoning or killing children as purely female crimes. Another possible result of heterosexual activity, abortion, equaled homicide, but the language of the law imagined the perpetrator as either male or female.

Reasoning from mere statute is hazardous, so the conclusions we draw about the Carolina must be modest and tentative. First, sexual delicts form an important category in the imperial law (13 percent). With the exception of rape and forcible abduction (abduction usually occurred with the abductee's consent), most sexual offenses in the Carolina concerned consensual acts, where the injured party was not one of the principals, but a spouse or relative, or more likely, religious or moral opinion. In assuming responsibility for policing some consensual acts, the state was

---

[34] This is Langbein's argument throughout *Prosecuting Crime in the Renaissance.*

[35] *Reichspolizeiordnungen*, 160.

[36] Compare Carolina, article 122, with the Bambergensis, article 147, and drafts 1 and 2, in Zoepfl, *Die peinliche Gerichtsordnung*, 49, 164, 237.

encroaching on territory that formerly had belonged to, or had been shared with, the church. Nonetheless, the panoply of possible sexual crimes the Carolina punished was narrow and incomplete, even by contemporary standards. For example, fornication was absent, though canon and local secular laws forbade it. It is less surprising that prostitution went unmentioned, since it was only beginning to lose the tolerated status it had enjoyed in medieval times, as reformatory religious conviction pressed to outlaw it.[37]

Although it is unclear how influential canon versus earlier secular law was in determining delicts and punishments, one of the chief criteria guiding imperial lawmakers was obvious: most delicts concerned some breach of marital or family relations. Thus, the second conclusion is that marriage was the primary organizing principle for sex-crime legislation.

Third, the laws were remarkably evenhanded toward males and females in their conception of delicts and the punishments they pronounced; indeed, from the number of sexual crimes conceived of as exclusively male, it seems that lawmakers assumed men were more sexually dangerous to society than women. Unfortunately, it is impossible to tell anything further about this assumption or its possible corollaries from the terse language of statute.

Fourth, the unusual degree of revision in the paragraphs dealing with sexual activity suggests that these matters were controversial. Most likely, the lawmakers were doubly ensnared in the great Reformational transformation: both the higher standards to which moral (and thus also sexual) behavior was to be held in this life, on the one hand, and thus the greater responsibility of the secular authorities for upholding these standards, on the other, made it imperative for the law to strike out in new directions. Finally, the direction of the revisions was toward (slightly) lighter penalties, often by providing the judge or legal expert with the power to punish arbitrarily. This trend, too, was a harbinger of the future.

The Carolina was not the only imperial law in the sixteenth century. Complementing it were the Imperial Police Ordinances (RPO) of 1530, 1548, and 1577.[38] They regulated daily life more minutely than the Carolina, though they occasionally overlapped with it. Their purview encompassed trade and commerce, foreigners, vagabonds, clothing regulations appropriate to each *Stand,* and other, less weighty matters.[39] Such a broad charge reflected the original meaning of "police" as that state institution responsible for establishing and maintaining the material conditions necessary for the "common good" (*Gemeinwohl*). This included public health, economic regulation, transportation, social welfare, and everyday conduct, including mundane sexual behavior.

[37] Beate Schuster, "Frauenhandel und Frauenhäuser im 15. und 16. Jahrhundert," *Vierteljahrschrift für Sozial- und Wirtschaftsgeschichte* 78 (1991): 172–89; Lyndal Roper, "Discipline and Respectability: Prostitution and the Reformation in Augsburg," *History Workshop Journal* 19 (Spring 1985): 3–28; Wunder, *Er ist die Sonn',* 58–67; and the study for France, Leah Lydia Otis, *Prostitution in Medieval Society: The History of an Urban Institution in Lanquedoc* (Chicago, 1985).

[38] These are the subjects of Segall's study, *Reichspolizeiordnungen.*

[39] Hippel, *Deutsches Strafrecht,* 1:213–20.

Three sexual delicts fell under the Imperial Police Ordinances of the sixteenth century: concubinage, public adultery (*öffentliche Ehebruch*), and *Kuppelei*. The first was punished arbitrarily by the police "according to circumstance" (*nach Gebühr*);[40] the others called for a "serious penalty" of either corporal punishment and/or some property confiscation.[41] The Imperial Police Ordinances, which, like the Carolina, did not supersede local or customary *Polizey*, are more important as indicators than as actualities. They delineated an avenue of state authority over sexual conduct outside the courts with their increasingly cumbersome procedures, but of course, also with their growing safeguards for defendants' rights. Police power could be much more direct and arbitrary, though the penalties it could levy were usually more limited than those of the law courts and could be made milder still if the police chose.[42] As we shall see, the possibilities of circumventing the law courts by using police procedures instead were not fully developed (or necessary) until the nineteenth century. In the early modern jurisdictional jumble, the police, the local administrator (*Amtmann*, or *Ortsvorgesetzter*), and even the lower court judge might be the same person. As Wettmann-Jungblut describes for Baden:

> On the local level the village administrator had police power, but he at the same time continued to pursue his profession and was responsible for all organizational concerns. In most smaller localities only the civil watch and the day and night watchman exercized police duties. Actual salaried policemen only existed in bigger localities and cities. In 1787 Baden's largest city, Mannheim, employed eleven "police subalterns," four of whom were scribes [*Viertelschreiber*], three inspectors, and four poor-relief administrators. They were all so poorly paid, "that in order to survive, they had to search for another job on the side, meaning they could not devote themselves exclusively and fully to their difficult office."[43]

Polizey in practice often only amounted to an expression for the ordering duties of the local administrator. *Polizey* was more powerful as an ideal of orderly community life, than it was as an actual tool creating such an order.

The Imperial Police Ordinances contain a second significant trend for our purposes, in their criminalization of "public adultery." "Public adultery" is not mentioned in the Carolina, which clearly assumes that the complaint for adultery will be brought by the injured party. The injured party in "public adultery," however, was not the spouse, but outraged public opinion, and the *Polizey* was to proceed on its own initiative. How did this new crime come to be invented? Segall argues convincingly that it was not so much the inexorable drive of the state to expand as it was the result of the German legislators' desire to punish men equally with women for adultery.[44] The first Imperial Police Ordinance (1530) preceded the Carolina by two years. It therefore addressed itself to the unreformed legal situation in which, following Roman law, adultery by the wife met with life-long punishment, but the

[margin note: harm against public opinion]

---

[40] Segall, *Reichspolizeiordnungen*, 158.
[41] Ibid., 162.
[42] Hippel, *Deutsches Strafrecht*, 1:219.
[43] Wettmann-Jungblut, "Stelen," 169. Internal quotation from GLA 213/2403.
[44] Segall, *Reichspolizeiordnungen*, 158–62. This discussion follows Segall.

husband's adultery was considered the equivalent of mere fornication, or concubinage, both of which carried much lighter penalties. To redress this inequity, the Imperial Police Ordinance of 1530 created a new category, adultery carried out in a public way, that is, where the adulterer lived together with a new mate before the community's eyes. This offense would be "seriously punished."

Even when the Carolina established parity between men and women in adultery penalties, the two later revisions of the Imperial Police Ordinances kept "public adultery" on the books. Doing so permitted the *Polizey* to pursue adultery independently, even against the desire of the spouse. It is further noteworthy that the Imperial Police Ordinances extended the heavier penalty to both parties, rather than the lighter. The equality they extended was therefore the equality of discipline, not the extension of rights. As Ursula Flossmann has remarked about the sixteenth-century Austrian territorial police ordinances, "The police commandment of equal treament of the sexes was essentially oriented to the duty of all subjects [*Untertanen*] vis-à-vis the territorial prince's right to command. An equal right of all subjects in the sense of a reforming new distribution of rights to men and women was far removed from any police goals. The 'new' law did not give more rights to women, but simply more duties to men."[45]

The Ordinances

The real mark of official interest in sexual regulation was not imperial law or imperial police ordinances, but the stream of orders the territorial states themselves loosed on their subjects. It is idle to attempt to distinguish political from religious motives here. Centralization of authority, bureaucratic expansion, elimination or cooption of intermediary institutions, attempted penetration into community life, these were all partly impelled, partly legitimized by the prince's newly assumed duty to enforce Christian living upon his subjects. Nowhere did religion leave a stronger mark than in law, and nowhere in law more strongly than in sexual legislation. As Robert von Hippel puts it, "The Bible, especially the Mosaic law, was regarded as divine positive law and thus as the determining source of justice. This is especially clear in [laws against] blasphemy, manslaughter and morals offenses [*Sittlichkeitsdelikten*]."[46] The conflation of God's will and the ruler's made disobedience doubly criminal. The legal historian Eberhard Schmidt, paraphrasing the most famous exemplar of this viewpoint, the draconian Saxon codifier Benedikt Carpzow, explains, "State and authority rest on God's commandment and will. . . . Crime therefore has not only the judicial meaning of a trespass against state norms, it is always also a sin against God."[47] The Reformation's higher standards for

[45] "Geschlechtsspezifische Diskriminierung und Gleichbehandlungsgebot als Strukturelemente frühneuzeitlicher Rechtsordnungen," in *Festschrift für Louis Carlen zum 60. Geburtstag*, ed. Louis C. Morsak and Markus Escher (Zürich, 1989), 624–25.

[46] *Deutsches Strafrecht*, 1:232.

[47] *Strafrechtspflege*, 163.

66

behavior on earth led to the wholesale importation of church prohibitions into secular law. Catholic states did not lag behind Protestant ones in criminalizing sin.

The widespread early modern view of religious obedience as a kind of exchange was echoed in the territorial states' understanding of obedience to law. As its subjects expected to trade the regular fulfillment of ritual duties (communion, pilgrimages, and so on) for escape from harm, the central state expected orderly behavior to achieve the same goal. Except, of course, that it always put the matter negatively: disobedience called forth God's wrath. This theory appeared with monotonous regularity in the supporting documents and preambles to seventeenth-century and early eighteenth-century ordinances on sexual crimes. Bavaria's immense 1635 codification of its morals laws explained:

> Because, if these grave sins are not prevented or punished with all possible energy and seriousness, almighty God will be greatly offended and angered and will be moved to send and inflict all manner of serious, immediate war, unrest and other country-wide punishments, therefore we are dutybound by patriarchal conscientiousness [*Landts Fürstlicher Vätterlicher Sorgfalt*] to remedy and prevent by all means such rapidly increasingly vices of indecency and blasphemy.[48]

By the eighteenth century, decrees tended to stress "patriarchal conscientiousness," rather than religious obligation. A Badenese decree of 1754 typically explained that the prince and his administration were forced to uphold sexual standards "because our governmental responsibilities specially [*vornehmlich*] have as their purview the well-being of our dear subjects, the observation and maintenance of good laws and regulations and also the elimination of harmful vices and abuses."[49] Sex-crime law therefore underwent the same transition from more religious to more secular-materialist inspiration and legitimation as other criminal and especially welfare laws.[50] But from the beginning of morals legislation, the assumption that morality somehow produced material happiness or, more often, that immorality produced disaster was a basic principle that permeated theories of government and its proper relation to society far into the Enlightenment and beyond.

Another long-lasting effect of the conflation of the sacred and secular was harder to see. Having once adopted (more stringent) religious sexual standards as law, the authority of the state became synonymous with upholding these standards. Moral lapses had suddenly become offenses against the government and its officials. Even when the original religious motivation had paled,[51] immoral behavior was considered no less a threat to order and authority, as long as the government identified itself through law with specific moral standards. This situation made it possible for

---

[48] Bavarian decree of 20 September 1635 against fornication, adultery, swearing, and so on. Bayerisches Hauptstaatsarchiv, München, General Registratur Faszikel 321 Nummer 7 (hereafter, Bay HStA, GR 321/7).

[49] Baden-Durlach decree of 13 March 1754 against fornication and adultery, GLA 74/3919.

[50] Raeff, *Well-Ordered Police State*.

[51] In fact, religious preambles to sexual ordinances continued past the mid-eighteenth century. The most recent one I found was in an appendix to a government recommendation (Baden-Baden) of 24 January 1760, GLA 74/3923.

unruly and dissatisfied subjects in fact to express their disdain for authority in sexual ways,[52] but worse, it predisposed officials to misinterpret sexual slips as evidence of deeper, political dissatisfaction and as a wider failure of government and social order than was warranted. In short, by melding sacred and secular, government abruptly widened the potential social-political meaning of sexual behavior and made it more significant. Particularly, sexual *mis*behavior had become identified as an indicator of general (dis)order. Unlike the central state, which had previously devoted little thought to the matter, the church had elaborated its thinking on sexual matters over centuries. By incorporating some of this elaboration into law, that is, by specifying the content of consensual sexual crime, the prince and his officials had widened the field of potential disorder. In its effort to create order, therefore, the state had necessarily also done the reverse.[53]

The Sexual Delicts

We must begin with the specific content of criminalized sexual acts. Offenses involving force or violence, such as rape or forcible abduction, had for a long time fallen under the classic purview of the state's duty to preserve peace (or in Max Weber's negative formulation, the state's monopoly on violence). The overwhelming majority of sexual delicts in seventeenth-century laws, however, concerned consensual acts. These are in any event the most fruitful to study closely, because, especially in the absence of an injured third party (for example, a wronged spouse in adultery), official intervention was justified not by the usual grounds of physical protection or redress of injury, but by more abstract reference to some definition of the common good or to customary morality, that is, to the very assumptions about the proper relation of state to society in sexual matters that we wish to uncover.

Reformation laws regulating sexual activity typically described a spectrum of offenses beginning with forcible sex (rape and forced abduction) and then moving to prohibitions against "sodomy" or "unnatural practices," generally meaning same-sex relations (usually both between men and between women) and bestiality;[54] to the range of forbidden heterosexual acts: between unmarried persons

---

[52] In *Leichtfertigkeit*, 182–90, Breit explains some cases of Bavarian illegitimacy as overt rejection of governmental authority.

[53] Mary Douglas explains this principle in the introduction to *Purity and Danger*, 1–6.

[54] Wiguleus Xaver Alois, Freiherr von Kreittmayr, *Codex Juris Bavarici Criminalis de anno 1751, 1753 [nebst] Anmerckungen* (Munich, 1751–54), 33, which defines "Sodomiterey" as "Fleischliche Vermischung mit dem Viehe, todten Cörpern, oder Leuthen einerley Geschlechts, als Mann mit Mann, Weib mit Weib." Kreittmayr's inclusion of necrophilia represents an elaboration typical of the modern tendency to become more and more specific in enumerating (forbidden) sexual acts, and thus extending the range of possible delicts. Anselm Feuerbach (1826) specifically noted the Carolina's restricted definition, which did *not* include nonprocreational heterosexual acts, necrophilia, or masturbation. Feuerbach believed (incorrectly) the Carolina did not intend to criminalize female-female sexual relations (see article 116); perhaps he was unaware that German states did occasionally execute women for this crime. Paul Johann Anselm Feuerbach, *Lehrbuch des gemeinen in Deutschland gültigen peinlichen Rechts*, 9th ed. (Giessen, 1826), par. 468, pp. 392–93; Brigitte Eriksson, "A Lesbian Execution in

(fornication, called, variously, *Unzucht, Leichtfertigkeit,* or *Liederlichkeit*); between unmarried persons who set up house together (concubinage—*Konkubinat*);[55] between those engaged but not yet officially wed (*früher Beischlaf*); adultery; sexual relations with nuns or priests, or across authority lines (in prison, schools, with godchildren); or with persons deemed unable to consent by virtue of youth, illness, or indisposition (for example, drunkenness); incest (defined according to canon law); prostitution (this was not in every place illegal and referred exclusively to women having sexual relations with men indiscriminately and for money); *Kuppelei;* and bigamy. Of this list, *früher Beischlaf* was a new invention, part of the state's effort (following in the footsteps of the church) to define and control more precisely access to marriage. Secular law also criminalized four specifically female crimes associated with sexual behavior: child abandonment, abortion, infanticide, and hiding one's (out-of-wedlock) pregnancy, which officials interpreted as the possible prelude to infanticide. All of the above delicts appeared in land-wide criminal codes, which usually dated from the end of the sixteenth or beginning of the seventeenth century and were not revised again until the mid-eighteenth century or even later.

In fact, however, revisions occurred constantly in the form of ordinances that tinkered with penalties, chastised indolent officials, admonished pastors and heads of households, modified court jurisdictions, warned of dire consequences, and sighed with exasperation. Given the sheer number of these ordinances, it is noteworthy that certain delicts, such as those involving force, or, among consensual acts, homosexuality (sodomy) and bestiality, virtually never appeared in these official documents. The absence of sodomy and bestiality suggests that these delicts were uncontroversial in several respects. There appears to have been widespread social and governmental agreement on how they should be handled. Unlike in cases of hidden pregnancy and infanticide, there is little evidence that popular opinion, judges, or state officials felt the punishment (death) did not fit the crime.[56] Or if that certainty were gradually changing, the resulting tensions between written law

Germany, 1721: The Trial Records," in *Historical Perspectives on Homosexuality,* ed. Salvatore J. Licata and Robert P. Petersen (New York, 1980–81, 27–40; Louis Crompton, "The Myth of Lesbian Impunity: Capital Laws from 1270–1791," also in Licata and Petersen, 11–25; Michael Goodich, *The Unmentionable Vice: Homosexuality in the Later Medieval Period* (Oxford, 1979); Bernd-Ulrich Hergemöller, "Homosexuellenverfolgung im Mittelalter. Erscheinungsformen und Kausalfaktoren des gesellschaftlichen Kampfes gegen die 'Sodomiter,'" in *Randgruppen der spätmittelalterlichen Gesellschaft,* ed. Hergemöller (Warendorf, 1990), esp. his bibliography.

[55] Proscriptions against concubinage (*Konkubinat*) may originally have been directed against Catholic priests, who frequently lived in such arrangements, until in the wake of the Council of Trent, the church undertook massive, ultimately successful efforts to stem the practice. But the delict concubinage was increasingly used to prosecute lay family arrangements without official sanction. On the common and accepted practice of priestly concubinage into the sixteenth century, see Forster, *Counter-Reformation,* 107.

[56] Alarmed at the sudden rise of infanticide cases resulting from sharpened government attention to that delict, the Bavarian *Hofrat* rescinded its 1685 mandate on the subject, just three years after issuing it. Behringer, "Mörder," 107–8. Dülmen, *Theater des Schreckens,* 158, reports numerous incidents of popular disturbance at the executions of infanticides in the eighteenth century.

and customary practice were being satisfactorily reconciled by the courts. Further, consensual homosexual acts or bestiality would usually have left no traces, such as pregnancy, to attract official attention. Apparently, whatever threat these acts posed was adequately addressed by the promise of draconian punishment and its occasional execution, and thus they were left in silence until a projected redrafting of the entire criminal code put them on the agenda again.

Other consensual acts, such as incest, bigamy, or prostitution, occasionally showed up among the ordinances, but the vast preponderance of them concerned adultery, fornication, premature coitus (*früher Beischlaf*), and increasingly after the early eighteenth century, hidden pregnancy of unmarried women. These four heterosexual delicts were the ones that interested the central state when it busied itself with sexual behavior, which it began to do in earnest after 1600 in a burst of activity that usually continued for ten or twenty years after the Peace of Westphalia, then subsided until the 1720s or 1730s, when it briefly picked up once more.[57] In Baden-Durlach, the state began with an adultery ordinance of 28 May 1613, which was repeated in 1624 and then after much deliberation sharpened and expanded to include fornication, premature coitus, and hidden pregnancy in a mammoth morals mandate of 13 March 1654.[58] The Bavarian territorial code of 1553 mentioned fornication for the first time, but by 1616 the central government was admonishing its officials to punish offenders "seriously"[59] in a new territorial and police code that ushered in a series of repeated and then sharpened ordinances and other measures.[60] This sort of activity was typical of territorial states in the same period.

How "seriously," in fact, did states pursue sexual offenses? This question cannot be answered in absolute terms. Nonetheless, a number of indicators show that princes and officials judged the sexual order an important aspect of the general order and therefore concluded that upholding the sexual order was worth investing significant official time and resources. Otherwise, it is difficult to explain the repeated decrees and rescripts or the number of official discussions among central bureaucrats devoted to reissuing, amending, improving, and ensuring their execution. Most social historians who have examined these documents interpret them as indications these efforts may have failed, but certainly not that no effort had ever been made. On the contrary, historians of popular sexual behavior have generally

---

[57] The volume of both ordinances and intragovernmental correspondence on sexual behavior charts these fluctuations, though the archives' completeness is too doubtful to permit quantification. The Bavarian material is quite extensive even for the seventeenth century, but Baden's records seem spotty until around 1720.

[58] Ordinances of 28 May 1613, 18 December 1624, and 13 March 1654 in GLA 74/3919. Meanwhile, adultery, fornication, prostitution, suspicious carriage, premature coitus, *Kuppelei*, bigamy, incest, and "unnatural" sex practices, together with forcible sex crimes, were specified in the territorial code of 1622; see *Landrecht und Ordnung der Fürstenthumben der Marggraveschafften Baden und Hochberg* (Durlach, 1622), part 7, titles 29–45. The *Landrecht* is commonly known as the *Malefizordnung*.

[59] Breit, *Leichtfertigkeit*, 79.

[60] Bavarian officials seem to have considered their string of decrees to have begun on 1 October 1626 (against fornication). See the Appendix to the government report (*Relation*) of 17 July 1645, in Bay HStA, GR 321/7.

concluded that state governments were indeed energetic, by early modern standards, in trying to thwart sexual misbehavior.[61]

Occasionally one catches a glimpse of extraordinary dedication to this elusive goal. In 1629 the Bavarian elector Maximilian (1597–1651), convinced of the importance of controlling premarital heterosexual intercourse, established a two-man commission with one representative of the court council (*Hofrat*) and one from the council of state (*Staatsrat*), charged "with energetic inquiry and examination of such delinquent males and females" (presumably in Munich). They were to see that the delinquents and their accomplices were duly punished and to report their observations to the elector himself.[62] When after two or three reports, they flagged in these duties, the elector sent a sharp reminder to the *Hofrat*, which he badgered periodically thereafter to keep him better informed.[63] The commissioners in turn appointed "spies" (*Spione*), and the elector decreed that the commission was also to pursue cursers and consorts of priests. Although the commissioners could report that those who were charged with these various delicts were being punished properly, they had to admit the spies were a failure: "The said spies excuse themselves," they reported, "no such clerical concubines or secret trysting spots have come to their attention."[64] We have already met sexual "spies" in the preceding chapter. They were a Reformation institution, common especially to southern German cities, here making their appearance in Catholic Bavaria at the instigation of the prince. The religious motivation animating the elector is clear from his inclusion of priestly concubinage and blasphemers among their targets. Whatever the motivation, obviously he felt that fornication and concubinage were sufficiently disorderly for him to assign two top members of his central government to this task and to keep them at it for eight years. Nor was this the last episode of its kind in Bavaria. There were further admonishments in 1653 and 1654 to local authorities to send the prescribed quarterly reports on sexual delicts to the central administration.[65] In the early 1680s the central authorities must have renewed this request, for local reports claiming to list all persons punished in the past year for adultery and fornication found their way to Munich.[66] The following century was also punctu-

---

[61] Alas, few social historians have been equally interested in both offical action and popular behavior. Gleixner, "Dörfliche und obrigkeitliche Ordnungen," who is exceptionally attentive to local officials, notes for the Altmark Brandenburg "the construction of an, for early modern circumstances, an astonishingly comprehensive apparatus for the control and surveillance of nonmarital reproduction," 64, also 240. Most sexual-historical studies concentrate on popular behavior only, and all assume pervasive, but not necessarily successful, official intervention; recent studies include Breit, *Leichtfertigkeit;* Becker, *Leben und Lieben;* and Pallaver, *Verdrängung der Sexualität,* which resurrects the old repressive hypothesis and blames the church more than the state; older studies include Shorter, *Modern Family,* 49–53, and Phayer, "Lower-Class Morality."

[62] Decree of 3 February 1629; citation from decree of 8 March 1630, Bay HStA, GR 321/7.

[63] Decrees of 10 October 1631 and 14 March 1632, Bay HStA, GR 321/7.

[64] Commissioners' report to the Elector, 10 February 1637, Bay HStA, GR 321/7.

[65] Regent Kurfürstin Maria Anna to Court Council, 15 December 1654, Bay HStA, GR 321/7.

[66] Eighteen reports from various *Land-*, *Pflege-*, and *Hofmarchgerichte* for 1682 and/or 1683, Bay HStA, GR 321/7.

ated by occasional questionnaires and demands for statistics directed to all local administrators, showing the continuing, periodic upsurge in central government interest in regulating sexual behavior.[67]

Another indicator of the authorities' earnestness is the relative weight of sexual delicts among all crimes prosecuted. This is a very inexact measure. Statistics were rarely kept during the absolutist period and early modern crime has not been thoroughly studied. Record-keeping was improving, but still uneven. The data give no hint of the percentage of prosecutions to crimes committed. We are left only with the (often faulty) record of official activity, not with its efficacy. This short-coming confines us to two very modest conclusions. First, throughout the period there was a wide discrepancy among localities (villages, towns) in how energetically they went after sexual offenders. Peter Wettmann-Jungblut, comparing the rural duchy of Klettgau between 1605 and 1612 with the ecclesiastical town of St. Peter and the imperial city Ulm for approximately the same period, found the percentage of sexual offenses per crimes prosecuted to vary from 5 percent in Klettgau to 11.8 percent in St. Peter and 17.5 percent in Ulm.[68] Or, another example, where the comparison is more even: in Nuremberg between 1561 and 1700, fornication and adultery accounted for 5.9 percent of that city's executions; in Frankfurt for the same period, the percentage was over twice as high: 12.7 percent.[69] One can harbor all sorts of reservations about statistics such as these, but they do at least testify to very different microcultures of sexual prosecution. A myriad of local conditions must have determined the enigmatic figures historical research generates; in no particular order: population pressure, religious fervor, rival factions, number of foreigners (who were always more vigorously prosecuted), need for labor, disposition of the local judge or *Amtmann,* type of local economy, local courting customs, need to raise money from fines, and so on. These sorts of causes of a local, sexual system operated into the nineteenth century and probably beyond.[70]

Second, if the data cannot be taken to tell us about the relation of prosecution to "criminal" behavior (that is, whether most delicts committed were actually punished), they do accurately convey the relative focus of state correctional activity. If we return to Wettmann-Jungblut's figures, in Klettgau, where sexual delicts were only 5 percent of total prosecutions, *Sittlichkeit* ranked also low, sixth out of seven, among the rubrics of prosecuted crime. That is, Klettgau's administrators considered slander, offenses against public order, injury, property offenses other than theft, and theft all more pressing than sexual offenses. Presumably, such an outcome would be typical of other localities where few sexual offenses were pursued. But, in Wettmann-Jungblut's other figures, even though the percentages (11.8 percent and 17.5 percent) are not very high, *Sittlichkeit* emerges as a major focus of juridical-administrative attention. In Ulm, *Sittlichkeit* ranked second after theft. In

[67] This is true for both Bavaria and Baden, see Chapter 3, pp. 107–11.
[68] "Stelen," 139, 143.
[69] Dülmen, *Theater des Schreckens,* tables 1 and 2, pp. 187–88.
[70] See Chapter 9, 367–68.

Saint Peter, the ecclesiastical overlords were primarily absorbed in witchcraft cases during 1601–31; the next three categories of offense, theft, violence, and sexual offenses, were almost evenly split (13.7 percent for the first two, 11.8 percent for *Sittlichkeit*).[71] Wettmann-Jungblut also tallied the figures for eighteenth-century Salem, adding together lower and higher (*Malefiz*) jurisdictions: for the entire century, sexual offenses were tied with all property offenses reckoned together for first place; for 1751–58, *Sittlichkeit* was second after injury; for the 1780s, slander, public disorder, and *Sittlichkeit* were first, second, and third, but only differed by a single percentage point.[72] In early modern Frankfurt and Nuremberg the same pattern emerges for noncapital crimes. In Frankfurt, theft and fraud were first and second; adultery, fornication, and "whoring" (*Hurerey*)[73] took places three, four and five on a list of eleven. If one combines the sexual offenses into a single category, *Sittlichkeit, it ranks second overall.*[74] Of seventeen crimes meriting corporal punishment in Nuremberg from 1578 to 1615, theft ranked first, followed by *Hurerey*, fraud, *Unzucht*, whoring-thievery (*Diebshure*), *Kuppelei*, and bigamy in that order.[75] The pattern from these data shows sexual offenses regularly appearing as the second or third most prosecuted crimes.[76]

Wolfgang Behringer has found even more striking evidence of this tendency at the central state level. He examined the court council records (*Hofratsprotokolle*) for seventeenth- and eighteenth-century Bavaria. The court council, functioning as the land's highest court, had amassed jurisdiction over an astonishing array of sexual offenses, not just rape and sodomy (the classical capital sexual offenses), but bigamy, adultery, incest, and even fornication, concubinage, "loose living" (*liederliches Leben*), "suspicious carriage," and *Kuppelei*. It is inconceivable that the court council actually monopolized prosecution of especially the last four acts; one suspects that it must have seen cases of repeat offenders.[77] Nevertheless, when Behringer tallied the cases the court council handled from 1600 to 1650, sexual delicts topped the list. The court council had spent 30 percent of its judicial energy on these cases. At the beginning of the eighteenth century, that percentage had dropped, but *Sittlichkeit* was still third in importance behind crimes against property and crimes of violence, and more important than crimes against religion and even against the

[71] Wettmann-Jungblut, "Stelen," 143, 139.

[72] Ibid., 144.

[73] It is unclear how Frankfurt distinguished *Unzucht* from *Hurerey*, since these terms were often used interchangeably to refer simply to nonmarital heterosexual intercourse.

[74] Dülmen, *Theater des Schreckens,* 67.

[75] Ibid., 208–9 n. 8.

[76] Statistics of executions, a staple of writings on early modern crime prosecution, tend to obscure the importance of *Sittlichkeit* delicts in prosecutions in general, because a much higher percentage of sexual offenses were punished by combinations of fines, corporal punishments, shaming, and imprisonment, than was true for theft, murder, manslaughter, fraud, and witchcraft. See Dülmen, *Theater des Schreckens,* 67; see also Behringer, "Mörder," 95, 110.

[77] In "Mörder," 96, 99, however, Behringer gives the impression that the court council saw even first offenses.

state.[78] The reason for this, of course, was that *Sittlichkeit* was already a crime against both religion and the state, and as such, state officials took it very seriously indeed.

The *Sittlichkeit* ordinances expose the content of the state's interest in sexual regulation in six ways that merit our particular attention: the centrality of marriage in defining sex crime; the nature of the inequity in the treatment of men and women; the relationship between state-sponsored sexual norms and assumptions and those customarily supported by its subjects; the relation between sexual crimes and other offenses with which they were frequently associated in the mandates; the absence of the distinction between public and private; and the dynamic of reform within the legal system.

The Organizing Principle = Marriage

Marriage was the organizing principle of sexual crime. This was true even for forcible crimes, which were recognized as occurring only outside marriage (rape, for example.) But it was even plainer in the case of nonmarital, consensual acts, all of which the monopoly of marriage over legitimate sexual activity made criminal. Because the Reformation had proclaimed marriage "the first order of God and the central order of society,"[79] secular law protected marriage as a *Rechtsgut,* that is, as an institution especially worthy of state protection. Since marriage in Christian thought literally defined all sexual acts against two axes in relation to itself: namely by providing the only locus for legitimate acts and the only legitimate end for them (procreation) as well, protecting marriage as an institution required protecting the particular definitions of permissible and impermissible sexual behavior that went along with it. Secular law therefore adopted Christianity's injunction of heterosexual exclusivity (outlawing same-sex relations, bestiality, and nonprocreative acts) and its rejection of all non or extramarital relations. Among heterosexual, consensual acts, marriage as *Rechtsgut* determined the hierarchy of offenses most injurious to it: adultery, fornication, and premature coitus (*früher Beischlaf*). Adultery shook the institution most gravely and thus was most severely punished. Next came fornication, which was worse than premature coitus, because the latter at least ended up safely within marital confines, even if the timing was askew. Thus Bavaria's grand morals ordinance of 20 September 1635 called for five years banishment for the first offense of double adultery (that is, where both parties were married) and death for repeaters, whereas mere fornicators received a fine and humiliation.[80] A decree of 2 September 1651 made it clear that if the fornicators married, they would receive a lesser penalty still.[81] Similarly, during discussions to change Baden's sex-crime penalties, officials carefully tried to keep the relations

[78] Ibid., 99, 110.
[79] Wunder, *Er ist die Sonn',* 88.
[80] Bay HStA, GR 321/7.
[81] Ibid.

among these crimes the same. One bureaucrat's schema called for a four-week prison term, public humiliation, and then banishment for first-time adultery, whereas a fornicator received half that prison term plus public humiliation only.[82] Premature coitus (usually just fined) was always penalized less than fornication. In the eighteenth century the penalty for premature coitus finally settled at one-half of that for fornication.[83] Although the proportion among these three delicts may not have stayed exactly the same as the penalties changed during the seventeenth and eighteenth centuries, there was a clear understanding of their proper relation, which meant that they were understood as a system and therefore pressure to sharpen or lighten any single penalty inevitably affected the others as well. This systemic quality had far-reaching consequences later in the eighteenth century.

Whereas the secular regulatory agenda had been set by Christian principles, within the boundaries of those principles, however, secular interests in maintaining the social and economic order set enforcement priorities. So, for example, after the law had duly forbidden homosexual acts and sex with animals, officials rarely mentioned those subjects again and wasted no resources on enforcement. It is true that individuals occasionally fell afoul of these provisions; isolated executions for sodomy occurred, especially in the German city-states throughout the seventeenth and eighteenth centuries—in Frankfurt in the 134 years from 1562 to 1696, one sodomite and one sodomite/thief were executed; Nuremberg also burned to death two sodomites during the seventeenth century (1600–92).[84] But in no sense did either cities or territories direct their energy against these delicts as happened in the late nineteenth or twentieth centuries. One should draw from this fact no conclusions about the prevalence of homosexual activity or bestiality, about which we know very little. Rather, one should recognize official preoccupation with heterosexual acts, most particularly with those potentially leading to procreation. Whereas for the Christian churches, marriage was important because it provided an outlet to prevent sexual sin, mutual aid and comfort for the spouses, and the framework for begetting and rearing children;[85] for government, marriage was foremost a social institution. Its putative encouragement of individual morality was, of course, welcome, but the central state's devotion to marriage flagged only slightly once the moral foundation began to weaken (in the late eighteenth century). The states protected marriage for reasons of social order, social reproduction, and fiscal utilitarianism, hence their nearly exclusive focus on procreative sexual acts; the repeated

[82] [Illegible] to Margrave Friedrich V (Baden-Durlach), Emmentingen, 28 March 1654, GLA 74/3919.

[83] Excerpt from Baden's privy council (Geheimer Rat) protocol, 3 August 1803, no. 4162, GLA 234/602.

[84] Dülmen, *Theater des Schreckens*, 190–93. More research might turn up more cases, especially if it should turn out that sodomy prosecution records were kept separately and in a secret place, as they were in early modern Dutch cities: see Theo van der Meer, "The Persecutions of Sodomites in Eighteenth-Century Amsterdam: Changing Perceptions of Sodomy," *Journal of Homosexuality* 16 (1988): 264.

[85] See the discussion of Counter-Reformation Catholic and Puritan attitudes in Edmund Leites, *The Puritan Conscience and Modern Sexuality* (New Haven, Conn., 1986), 77–94.

ordinances on adultery, fornication, and premature coitus; and the silence on everything else.

In practice, this legislation had an even narrower target: pregnancy. This will become clearer when we come to discuss the reality of official regulation, but this assumption is already plain in the language of the ordinances and their supporting documents. They typically complain about "one dishonorable childbirth after the other . . . and . . . many single women seen running around pregnant,"[86] or "the spreading vice of adultery [and] illegitimate pregnancy."[87] Few sexual delicts that did not end in pregnancy were prosecuted in the early modern period. Some historians interpret this as evidence not of limited official interest, but of limited grasp. Lacking adequate investigative ability, this argument runs, the absolutist states settled for punishing only the sexual crimes that could be relied upon to reveal themselves. It is certainly true that pregnancy made the officials' jobs easier for them; it is also true that when other sexual crimes were brought to official attention (through denunciation or being caught *in flagrante delicto*), the judicial process duly ground to its end. But, of course, it had to, once the central state had identified its authority with suppressing all sexual miscreancy. Illegitimate pregnancy carried with it social consequences that made it in fact more practically threatening to the early modern social order than other forms of sexual misbehavior, and which therefore dictated the special interest of officials.

One aspect of this special interest in illegitimacy was economic. Since lords and localities (*Gemeinden*) limited access to marriage to those deemed prosperous enough to support children, marriage safeguarded local treasuries from what was often their largest expense: poor relief. Illegitimate pregnancies forced the local official, the *Gemeinde,* and often the pregnant woman, to scramble to dun the father or his relatives and thus disburden the community. The entire subsistence balance between population and sustenance (*Nahrung*) was jeopardized by out-of-wedlock pregnancies. The population recovery from the Thirty Years' War must have encouraged the focus on procreative delicts and, with it, the tendency for officials to identify sexual misbehavior generally with uncontrolled pregnancy.[88]

As important as economic considerations were, they probably took a back seat to concern for social order and social reproduction. Fornication and premature coitus both challenged the system whereby parents, the *Gemeinde*, the church, and the local official all helped one another control access to the central social institution:

[86] Bavarian decree of 3 February 1629, Bay HStA, GR 321/7.

[87] Head of the Vice Commission Georg Brandlecht to Elector Maximilian, 1 February 1641, Bay HStA, GR 321/7.

[88] For further examples of the equation of sexual misbehavior with illegitimate pregnancy, see the Rastatt government to Margrave Ludwig Georg (Baden-Baden), 7 March 1758, GLA 74/3932; the project to redraft the sex-crime laws (Baden-Baden), 24 January 1760, GLA 74/3932; the Innenministerium memorandum of 11 February 1791 defining *früher Beischlaf* and fornication in terms of illegitimate pregnancy, GLA 236/8479; the Bavarian decree of 11 June 1727, in *Sammlung der Churpfalz-Baierischen allgemeinen und besondern Landes-Verordnungen von Sr. churfürstl. Durchlaucht Maximilian Joseph IV in Justiz-, Finanz-, Landschafts-, Mauth-, Polizey-, Religions-, Militärs-, und vermischten Sachen,* ed. Georg Karl Mayr, (Munich, 1784–1802) 3:116; and the decree of 11 August 1756, also in Mayr, 1:204.

marriage. Marriage was after all a primary *Stand* in the *Ständestaat*. In English, too, we are accustomed to speak of the "matrimonial estate" without reflecting upon what that once meant in a society of ascriptive estates (*Stände*). Like noble, bourgeois, peasant, and clergy, the category married/unmarried/widowed formed an axis along which every inhabitant found his or her proper place, an axis neatly dividing the prescribed from the proscribed. These particulars ranged from the petty details of dress catalogued in the clothing ordinances (*Kleiderordnungen*), to the entire reach of social custom and occupation, to how one was treated under law, whose punishments were tailored to the offender's status. We have already noted the early modern conflation of entrance into marriage with acquisition of citizenship (*Bürgerrecht*), settlement rights (*Ansässigmachung*), economic independence, and changed juridical status.[89] In short, the nexus of political, social and authority relations was charted as much by the marital *Stand* as by the other *Stände*. When young people arrogated the right of sexual expression without having been sanctioned to do so (fornication) or without fulfilling the proper formal requirements (premature coitus), they challenged basic, interlocking systems of social stability. No wonder, then, that sexual acts deemed to diminish the rights of marriage and the married would be prosecuted as harmful to social and political authority relations.

Punishments According to Gender and Stand

Early modern criminal law, like early modern religion, was based on a model of exchange. Where earlier, extended families had made sure that injuries done to their members were paid in full by the wrongdoer, tit for tat, government now inserted itself into this reciprocal relation. It reestablished harmony by demanding of the criminal recompense (punishment) which exactly expunged the injury. This was the basis for the "mirroring punishments" typical of absolutism, where a thief might lose the hand that had stolen, a blasphemer, the tongue, or where a score of different methods of execution were carefully fitted to different crimes and criminals.[90] The calculus of injury was made according to two axes: the seriousness of the crime, and the qualities of the criminal. The second was as important as the first because part of the tear in the social fabric resulted from the duties and expectations the criminal had violated. And those duties, in turn, varied in specific ways, by *Stand*, gender, marital status, age, occupation, and on down the list of social conditions constituting early modern society. The notion of equality, meaning interchangeability, was alien to this system. Justice—the reestablishment of harmony—was achieved precisely by factoring in social difference; equality would have been unjust and ineffective.

During the absolutist period, however, state officials began to abandon the *ständisch* model of justice via social differentiation and to move toward the model of equal treatment. Their hesitant and uneven efforts conflicted with *ständisch*-

[89] See Chapter 1, pp. 30–31.
[90] Dülmen, *Theater des Schreckens*, 11, 74.

inspired, customary laws that still reflected socially differentiated conceptions of sexual duties, nature, honor, and danger. From the bureaucratic perspective, consensual sexual acts must have illuminated especially clearly the tension between the two different principles of justice, since in cases of adultery and fornication men and women were by definition equally guilty but in practice differently punished. To disentangle the old from the new in this process of change, we must first examine the hierarchy of penalties prescribed by seventeenth-century laws and ordinances. These were not necessarily synonymous with the penalties actually exacted, for judicial discretion plus the absolutist habit of pronouncing a draconian penalty and then demonstrating official power precisely by commuting it produced discrepancies between judgment and execution. Nonetheless, the punishments set out in statute do describe in their negative way the system of sexual order the central state attempted to reestablish or establish.

At the apex of punishment stood the death penalty, which by the seventeenth century, was in sexual crime reserved for rape, homosexuality, bestiality, incest between the closest relatives, and repeat offenders in adultery, and perhaps fornication.[91] The next heaviest punishment was banishment, which could be forever or for several years (usually five to seven) and might apply to a locality, district, or to the entire territory. The next three punishments, imprisonment (with or without restriction to bread and water, with or without an added work requirement, which the eighteenth century increasingly favored), corporal punishment (beating), and public humiliation are difficult to order according to severity. Prison conditions throughout the seventeenth and eighteenth centuries were so horrendous that they were indistinguishable from corporal punishment, and both could be equally lethal for any but the truly robust. The same applied to forced labor on public works projects (*opera publica*), which usually meant building fortifications.[92] Prison (*Zuchthaus*) differed from jail (*Amtshaus* or *Thurm*); the former dishonored the inmate and the stay was usually longer and the conditions worse than the latter, where the brief discipline for first- or second-time fornication was usually meted out.

Public humiliation might spare the body, but it damaged the reputation, on which everything depended in small, traditional communities. Public humiliation could be either secular or religious. The secular variety consisted of public display, sometimes tied to a large pillory (*Pranger*) before the village hall (*Amtshaus*), attached to the "vice stone" (*Lasterstein*), or wearing a wooden (*Geige*) or iron (*Halseisen*) device around the neck, or wearing on the head a ring with bells on it [*Springer*]. The *Geige* typically adorned women, the *Springer*, men, and judges

---

[91] Bavarian law was more draconian than Badenese; it called for death for second-time adulterers, whereas Baden did so for third-time offenders only. Cf. Bavarian mandate of 20 September 1635, Bay HStA, GR 321/7, with the Baden-Durlach *Malefizordnung* of 1622, title 29. Dülmen's statistics for executions performed by Frankfurt and Nuremberg combine adultery and fornication and do not specify whether the executed were repeaters. *Theater des Schreckens*, 187–89.

[92] See Wolfram Peitzsch, *Kriminalpolitik in Bayern unter der Geltung des Codex Juris Criminalis Bavarici von 1751* (Munich, 1968), 78–81, 96–137, and Hentig, *Punishment*, 172–78, 202–14.

sometimes ordered delinquents to wear these devices at home, rather than in front of the court. I described the religious variant, the *Kirchenbuße*, in Chapter 1. In the seventeenth century Protestant secular states adopted this practice as an additional penalty for adultery, fornication, and premature coitus.[93]

The public humiliation punishments (*Ehrenstrafen*) have not been easy to interpret. Most historians have thought they were especially associated with (consensual) sexual offenses and more often applied to women than to men. These hypotheses are probably generally true and perhaps truer for the eighteenth century than before. But one should use caution in interpreting what this means. For one thing, although the *Kirchenbuß* and the other humiliation rituals were typically used against sexual criminals, they were not exclusively so. Blasphemers also atoned before the church,[94] whereas thieves, frauds, and others were displayed at the *Pranger*. Furthermore, humiliation penalties commonly substituted for harsher punishments (like death or corporal punishment); what may appear as discriminatory treatment (of women), may in fact have been intended as relative leniency. In any event, many men suffered humiliation penalties; Dülmen writes that the *Halseisen*, for example, was equally apportioned to both sexes.[95]

It has proved very difficult to determine how, and how well, humiliation penalties actually worked. As "dishonoring punishments" (*Ehrenstrafen*), they depended on the community's response to be effective, since in the final instance it was the community that bestowed and removed honor. Sometimes community reaction was so vehement that public humiliation became corporal punishment, as irate passersby hurled objects at those on display. But if, for example, community sexual standards were really as at odds with those of the state as some social historians claim, how effective could dishonoring punishments have been? Some scholars still believe, though no evidence supports this conclusion, that fear of public humiliation was so great that it drove women to infanticide,[96] but the tendency has been rather to downplay this older view that assumed dishonor, once achieved, was complete and eternal. The system of early modern honor and dishonor was surely as complex as the myriad distinctions at work in the society. Dülmen believes that none of the humiliation rites meted out for sexual offenses automatically meant exclusion from the community, that is, permanent and utter dishonor, though all were *ehrenrührig*, that is, they sullied one's honor. He ranks the punishments in descending order of severity: *Pranger* or *Halseisen*, the "vice stone," the straw wreath, and, finally, the *Geige*.[97] (He does not interpret the fact that the three least permanently destructive forms of humiliation were more likely to be visited upon women.) Dülmen believes that only in combination with other punishments, such

[margin note: Dülmer]

[93] Winther to Margrave Friedrich, Röttlen, 19 January 1654, GLA 74/3919. Peitzsch, *Kriminalpolitik*, 90–91; Hentig, *Punishment*, 226–31. See the discussion in Chapter 1, pp. 16–17.
[94] Bavarian mandate of 20 September 1635, Bay HStA, GR 321/7.
[95] Dülmen, *Theater des Schreckens*, 74.
[96] Cf. Breit, *Leichtfertigkeit*, 290, and Dülmen, *Theater des Schreckens*, 77. Women accused of infanticide never mentioned honor as a motive for their crime. Ulbricht, *Kindsmord*, 170.
[97] *Theater des Schreckens*, 65, 71–75, 79.

as beating, would the humiliation rites lead to exclusion. Rainer Beck agrees: "Fear of the 'simple' fornication punishment surely was limited. Presumably the scandal and derision caused by wearing the *(Hals)eisen* or *Geige* were only temporary, or depended upon whether the village had its own reasons to take advantage of the humiliation. Nonetheless, people were not indifferent to these punishments."[98] Behringer goes even further, comparing the *Kirchenbuße* to "parking tickets."[99] This judgment is probably exaggerated in the other direction, for there is too much information indicating how glad people were to escape humiliation punishments. The point should not be that these rites were not dishonoring at all, but that they were only temporarily so, and afterward the punished returned to village life, a picture consistent with our knowledge that many illegitimate mothers later wed and that couples guilty of premature coitus seem not to have suffered long-term consequences.

As historians did after them, contemporary officials also debated long and hard whether imprisonment, public labor, corporal punishment, or public humiliation was more feared and thus a more successful deterrent. They tended to believe that public humiliation was far more effective than fines.[100] Some, like one member of Bavaria's court council (*Hofrat*) even regarded the *Kirchenbuße* as more powerful than hard labor on public works: "The common man holds working on fortifications or other common labor penalty for easier than being displayed before the church, indeed for no punishment at all as with all punishments which do not defame. Single men caught in simple adultery flee such a punishment [i.e., the *Kirchenbuße*] by leaving the country."[101] Eighteenth-century enlightened officials became virtually obsessed with the colossal damage they thought public humiliation wrought—they imagined that fear of dishonor drove pregnant servant girls to murder (infanticide), a notion that became the quintessential example for the strength of popular honor and the perniciousness of public humiliation. Several factors joined to create this view, which became so influential to public policy and later historiography. Officials correctly perceived that shaming penalties were unpopular; they did harm one's reputation for a while, and they doubtless provided ammunition for one's enemies.[102] They were a handicap best avoided, but only a handicap. Officials, however, exaggerated this correct perception of village reality by projecting onto it their own conception of honor, which, being internal, was not subject to forgetfulness, and therefore incorporated the permanent self-direction and self-discipline befitting developing civil society, not village society. They were

---

[98] "Illegitimität," 128.

[99] "Mörder," 121.

[100] Winther to Margrave Friedrich, Röttlen, 19 January 1654, GLA 74/3919.

[101] Decree of Kurfürstin Maria Anna, 30 March 1654, summarizing a previous report of the court council, Bay HStA, GR 321/7. See also court council president and councillors to Kurfürstin Maria Anna, 30 December 1653, Bay HStaA, GR 321/7.

[102] In colonial America, at least, past sexual misdeeds were flung in people's faces years later when neighbors fought over other things. Mary Beth Norton, "Gender and Defamation in Seventeenth-Century Maryland," *William and Mary Quarterly*, 3d ser., 44 (January 1987): 3–39.

especially likely to expect such a thing in the sexual realm from women, hence their fixation on infanticide, a woman's crime.[103] Thus, as in so many other things, public humiliation penalties developed inside a complicated (mis)understanding between officialdom and subjects. Finally, it is possible that certain localities had developed sexual microcultures in which consensual heterosexual misbehavior brought more long-lasting dishonor with it than was true elsewhere.

Clearly the "easiest" punishment, that is, the one most preferred by offenders, was the fine. In the seventeenth century fines for sexual delicts were usually one part of compound punishments whose others parts might consist of imprisonment and forced labor, public humiliation, and/or banishment. Judicial discretion decided whether all or some of these possibilities best fit the particular circumstance. The pressure to levy fines in place of other penalties came both from below and above. Even poorer people preferred to pay fines rather than undergo any alternative punishment.[104] Fines were set in statute to be "palpable" (*empfindlich*), in official jargon; the threshold varied considerably, however. In the Altmark Brandenburg, the simple fornication penalty seems to have been an entire year's income for a maidservant; in Heiligenberg (property of the Fürstenberg princely family, later part of Baden) it may have amounted to the yearly wages of a cook; whereas in Bavaria, a servant would have paid around one to two month's income—the highest fine a lower court gave out.[105] But those were the fines on the books. In practice, judges often reduced the fine to fit the miscreant's circumstances, permitted payment in installments over a long period, or both.[106] Judges were loath to give up fines altogether, because they had three virtues for government. They provided income, both for the state and often for the judge. In Bavaria the fornication fine brought in more money for the lower court than any other source.[107] Fines were also simple to enforce, and they lacked the potentially deleterious side effects that officials feared from other penalties (that is, people were not driven to rash acts to avoid them).

The penalties for sexual crimes changed slowly in the centuries after the Carolina and this change described, with some fluctuations, the same progress from draco-

---

[103] See Chapter 3 on infanticide, and Chapter 5 on civil society.

[104] Winther to Margrave Friedrich, Röttlen, 19 January 1654, GLA 74/3919; Baden-Durlach decree of 13 March 1754, GLA 74/3919; Bavarian court council president to Kurfürstin Maria Anna, 30 December 1653, Bay HStA, GR 321/7; Gleixner, "Dörfliche und obrigkeitliche Ordnungen," 53.

[105] Concerning Altmark, see Gleixner, "Dörfliche und obrigkeitliche Ordnungen," 52 n. 164. For Heiligenberg, Bader, "Verbrechen," 201, lists the fine in 1647 at ten taler, which he calls "high." According to Herbert Rittmann, *Auf Heller und Pfennig* (Munich, 1976), 43, ten taler is about what a cook would have earned in a year. Concerning Bavaria, see Breit, *Leichtfertigkeit*, 133–34.

[106] Bader, "Verbrechen," 204 n. 61, 207. Flossmann, "Geschlechtsspezifische Diskriminierung," 623 n. 27. Breit found that the judges in the three districts he surveyed did not reduce fines, which may have been less necessary in Bavaria, where they were relatively lower than elsewhere. Bavarian judges, like those in Baden, Brandenburg, and elsewhere, simply excused the very poor from paying them. Breit, *Leichtfertigkeit*, 133.

[107] Breit, *Leichtfertigkeit*, 12. Fornication fines in the Altmark went to the judge and helped make the job desirable. Gleixner, "Dörfliche und obrigkeitliche Ordnungen," 37, 51. Cf. Bader, "Verbrechen," 207, and Beck, "Illegitimität," 131.

nian to restrained that one discovers in criminal law altogether. But the path that punishment for sexual crimes took from the death penalty to fines and even decriminalization diverged now and again from general legal developments, for sex laws featured unusual punishments (like public humiliation), which raised unusual issues, and they raised more centrally than other criminal laws the question of the relative guilt and punishment proper to gender and to *Stand.*

It is a widespread scholarly opinion that women were treated more harshly than men by early modern sex-crime law.[108] It is certainly true that women were more likely to be prosecuted for sexual offenses than for other delicts (thievery, violence, and so on), and in eras when government focused on sexual crimes, as under absolutism, the percentage of women drawn into the criminal court system rose.[109] When the practical definition of sexual crime is both heterosexual and procreative, as it was under absolutism, that, too, will ensure that women will be well represented among the "criminals"; in early modern Bavaria, they made up slightly more than half of those brought up on charges of *Unsittlichkeit.*[110] It is also true that women were indeed treated differently from men, as befitted a *ständisch* legal system—that is, different was not unfair in a *ständisch* world. In order to sort through the complexities of gendered legal treatment, we must examine its three facets. Statute allows one to see the *ständisch*-customary origins of gender differentiation, to appreciate how gender formed and was in turn formed by other social-hierarchical grids (especially marital *Stand*), and to glimpse the sexual assumptions contemporaries associated with gender. Actual judicial practice illuminates, first, the official strivings to achieve fairness in a system of differentiation and, second, the tendency of local officials to replace gender differentiation with equal treatment. Legal reform, finally, incorporated the egalitarian principles.

The Bavarian statutes are typical of the early modern gendered pattern in the main consensual delicts, fornication and adultery. The mammoth morals mandate of 1635 set the first fornication penalty for men at "the usual fine" plus eight to fourteen days in the *Springer* or *(Hals)eisen*, whereas women received "the usual fine" and four to five days in the *Geige*, "which they will be permitted to wear at home so they may work." The man therefore received the higher punishment. Not so for adultery: "Because the adultery of women is not less, but rather much more harmful" than that of men, it merited heavier punishment.[111] This meant two things. First, a married women received the same punishment (five years banishment, unless she were noble) for breaking her wedding vows with any man, married or single. A married man, however, received a lighter sentence if his partner was an unmarried woman—they were said to have committed simple rather than com-

---

[108] *Er ist die Sonn',* 249, for Wunder's summary of this train of thought.

[109] Behringer found that women made up 30 percent of those prosecuted in Bavaria in the first half of the seventeenth century, but only 20 percent in 1800. "Mörder," 101–2.

[110] Ibid.

[111] Both fornication and adultery penalties from the mandate of 20 September 1635, Bay HStA, GR 321/7.

[margin handwritten note: marital status of greater concern than gender]

pound adultery. Single men involved with married women also received the harsher compound adultery punishment. It was therefore the woman's marital *status* that determined the penalty, not her gender. In fact, the woman's marital status was such a strong force that it caused the lawmakers to forget altogether the punishment of single women with married men, and it almost obliterated legal consideration of nonmarital *Stand.* Married men committing adultery with unmarried women were punished according to four social gradations: impoverished common peasants or citizens of a town; men of these same *Stände,* but who had some disposable money; citizens of repute or who held municipal office ("die Geschlechter aber/Rathsver-wandte/oder andere ansehnliche Bürger"); and noblemen. Married women guilty of the same offense, however, were lumped into only two categories: noble or urban-patrician, and non-noble.

Several principles can be discerned in this welter of detail. First, the law judged men more culpable for fornication than women. The questions judges routinely put to those charged with *Unzucht,* their judgments in such cases, and how they decided to award civil payments to women in suits arising from *Unzucht* all make it clear that officials assumed men were responsible for taking the sexual initiative, whereas women, unless the man could prove the contrary, were taken to be the "passive" partner.[112] The sexual aggressiveness of men was a foundational assumption; Gleixner has discovered in a careful reading of fornication trials in the Altmark, that judges never asked men why they had illicit sex, but always asked women. For men, the desire for sexual expression was simply taken for granted.[113]

Second, the law judged women's adultery as worse than men's, though this was in fact barely apparent in the punishments female adulterers received. The complexity of the paragraph on adultery and the slip of simply forgetting to punish the single woman who slept with a married man,[114] both indicate that the principle here was the marital *Stand,* not so much the woman. She became important because she literally embodied that *Stand* in a way men obviously did not, and so protecting it, thus also her, from depradation, meant that both single and married men should be punished equally for its/her violation. That this identification of marital *Stand* with the body of the man was not made is clear from the penalties a married man received for adultery, which depended on the marital state of his partner. Finally, clearly the marital *Stand* so defined a woman that it eliminated most other, social gradations in *ständisch* society: with the exception of nobles and the city patriciate, all married women received the same punishment. The fate of the exempt adultresses alerts us to the shorthand for this second principle, namely, female honor. The mandate tells us that noblewomen and those from the oldest families in

---

[112] Both Breit and Gleixner have found this pattern uniformly for Bavaria and Brandenburg respectively, and it is borne out in the government discussions behind the scenes, and later, in the eighteenth-century discussions of infanticide and seduction. Breit, *Leichtfertigkeit,* 128–29, 143; Gleixner, "Dörfliche und obrigkeitliche Ordnungen," 74–77, 84, 87.

[113] "Dörfliche und obrigkeitliche Ordnungen," 77, 78–81.

[114] The mandate of 20 September 1635 is the largest single document of its kind that I have discovered in the archives. It clearly strove for exhaustive completeness.

cities "are to have their honor removed, they are not permitted to attend weddings or other honorable occasions, they are to be entirely robbed [*ganzlichen beraubt*] of their [*Stand*-specific] clothing and jewelry, which they previously were permitted to wear, and also of their dowry and the wedding gift [*Heyrath Guts/Widerleg/Morgengab:* the latter was originally a sign of the bride's honorable, virgin status which she traded for the different honor of marriage]." Adultery destroyed a woman's honor; the statute's silence concerning men is eloquent testimony that adultery did not do the same for them.

The sexual nature of a woman's honor is also clear from the distinction the Bavarian mandate made, a distinction common to almost all early modern legislation, between honorable and dishonorable single women who became impregnated.

> It is equally Our earnest will and opinion that Our officials and police ordinance should distinguish a single, honorable woman, who was brought to fall via *Kupplerey*, alcohol [*Schankungen*], promises, intoxicating drink or false promise of marriage; and this should be taken into consideration and the punishment dictated accordingly and under circumstances made more or less. In particular however We want and order that Our officials should see to it that those common women who prostitute themselves with anyone, and do these persons' will, except in the above circumstances, should not only receive the usual banishment and public humiliation punishments, but be beaten with the rod.

"Prostitute" here means promiscuity, not commercial sex, as the phrase doing any man's "will" makes plain. The continuity in a woman's sexual honor contained in statute was her fidelity. So long as she gave her body to a single man, even if she were unmarried, she was not necessarily dishonored in the eyes of the law. For it assumed that she was by nature sexually passive and that it was likely the active "will" of the man had taken advantage of her. Once she was married, the content of her sexual honor, fidelity, remained the same, but became even more socially important and, for her, determining.

That law was much more specific about women's sexual honor than about men's does not mean that men had none. As Lyndal Roper has written, men's sexual honor in the early modern period consisted of sexual capacity, or virility.[115] That is why judges never asked men to explain why they had engaged in premarital or extramarital sexual relations, and it is one reason why they never asked illegitimate fathers if they had slept with more than one woman;[116] and it is why male adultery did not, of itself, dishonor men. Extreme promiscuity and refusal to accept social responsibility for illegitimate children one had fathered probably damaged a man's sexual reputation in the village.[117] But men's sexual honor was not the object of law. It may have been a silent subject of law, however, insofar as a wife's adultery cast aspersions on her husband's capacity, and thus on the foundation of his sexual

---

[115] "'Wille' und 'Ehre': Sexualität, Sprache und Macht in Augsburger Kriminalprozessen," in *Wandel der geschlechterbeziehungen zu Beginn der Neuzeit*, ed. Heide Wunder and Christina Vanja (Frankfurt, 1991), 193.

[116] Gleixner, "Dörfliche und obrigkeitliche Ordnungen," 104 n. 114.

[117] Ibid., 101–2, 235; Sabean, *Neckarhausen*, 144.

honor. Most adultery laws, if they explained at all why "the adultery of women is not less, but rather much more harmful" than men's, averred that the "foreign" children slipped into the household were the major problem. But the legislators' horror at female adultery may well have had another basis, their identification with the cuckolded husband's loss of sexual honor.[118]

Early modern statute therefore contained the outlines of a sexual system in which women's sexual honor (and therefore her sexual duty) was specified and made the overt object of law, whereas men's was not, and in which a different and rather contrary sexual nature was postulated for women and men respectively. It is worth pointing out that these assumptions were only faintly present in the seventeenth century; in fact, the differences in statutory punishment for men and women committing the same crime were not great. But they existed.

Where did they come from? Were they the product of central state initiative? No, their origins lay in customary law. The telltale phrase in the 1635 mandate describing the fornication fine as the "customary fine" is indicative. Breit has managed to reconstruct what it was from court usage: three *Pfund Pfennige* for the man, two for the woman. He dubs such inequality (in this case in the woman's favor) a leftover of "medieval influence."[119] Ursula Flossmann makes that medieval provenience more precise: it lay in the "patriarchal social order" and customary laws proceeding from that foundation "occasionally froze in the form of written legal monuments, but [in any case] as practical, lived law, they possessed general validity."[120] Gender inequality was thus characteristic of laws emanating from the Estates, not from the central state, and where the central state extended its grasp, women received more nearly equal treatment than they did elsewhere. This is why criminal law was more evenhanded than civil law, for there the state had established its monopoly and made women legal persons, something they continued not to be in civil law. Flossmann explains, "Relicts of unequal, gendered treatment existed where the territorial prince's power of command did not move in a zone 'free of [already existing] law,' but instead could only assume the task of honing 'good old law.'"[121] It must be repeated that the central state did not set out to create gender equality because it thought men and women were equals, and certainly not because it wished to grant women more freedom, but rather because of the administrative dynamic of interchangeability and the moral vision of equally important duties that women and men owed to social harmony, which it was in turn the state's duty to supervise. Their equal subjection to the state, therefore, gave women and men the measure of equality they enjoyed in the negative realm of criminal law.

We have already observed this tendency of central state codifications to move in a

gender =ity to maintain social harmony

---

[118] Susanna Burghartz, "Rechte Jungfrauen oder unverschämte Töchter? Zur weiblichen Ehre im 16. Jahrhundert," in Hausen and Wunder, *Frauengeschichte-Geschlechtergeschichte*, 180.

[119] *Leichtfertigkeit*, 79, 132–33.

[120] "Geschlechtsspezifische Diskriminierung," 619.

[121] Ibid., 623–24. On the early modern state's monopoly over criminal law, but not civil law, see Strauss, *Law*, 124; on women's relatively worse position in civil law, see Wunder, *Er ist die Sonn'*, 247.

less gendered direction in the Carolina and Imperial Police Ordinances. Not surprisingly, those states more influenced by the Carolina moved more decisively along these lines than those, like Bavaria, which hewed closer to their own, customary law. Both Catholic Baden-Baden and Protestant Baden-Durlach were heavily indebted to imperial law,[122] and even when their seventeenth-century ordinances modified or widened it, they did not retreat to greater gender inequality.[123] Thus, in Baden-Durlach's *Malefizordnung* of 1622, the penalties for adultery and premature coitus were the same for women and men and no gender distinctions appeared in the paragraphs on concubinage, *Kuppelei*, suspicion of fornication, aiding seduction ("*anlas unnd understehung der Unzucht*"), bigamy, incest, or "unnatural" practices. Gender divisons showed up in only three places—twice in the fornication statute and then in the conception of certain delicts as peculiar to one sex.[124] As in Bavaria and for the same gendered assumptions we have already examined, men were punished slightly more heavily than women were in fornication cases. We also find the same distinction between women of good character ("sonst unverschreyter Personen") and the promiscuous. Once again, however, the difference in punishment was very slight (four days arrest) and should not be overinterpreted.

The extension of public humiliation to women but not to men in fornication cases in the late seventeenth and early eighteenth centuries has suggested that women were subjected to "more intensified" prosecution for consensual sexual crimes.[125] This widespread phenomenon was not limited to Baden. In the Altmark and in Schwäbisch-Hall judges increasingly sentenced more, and finally only, women to the *Pranger*. In 1722 a revised Bavarian ordinance made possible a "sharpened" humiliation penalty for fornication, which, as it turns out, was rarely used, but then usually against women.[126] And, again in Bavaria, Breit has observed that lower courts (whether under territorial or noble jurisdiction) often exceeded the maximum penalties statute pronounced for women in fornication cases, but they never did so against men.[127]

On the one hand, there is no question that the customary closer association of women's sexual honor and duty with continence will have encouraged judges and drafters of laws to regard public humiliation as an especially fitting punishment to express women's loss of (sexual) honor. On the other hand, that need not have been their principle motive—which is what we find to be the case in Baden. In Baden-Durlach women of "otherwise good character" convicted of fornication could be

---

[122] Carlebach, *Badische Rechtsgeschichte*, 2:89–94, 181–83, and Hippel, *Strafrecht*, 1:223.

[123] Wilhelm Brauer, "Ueber die Fortbildung der Badischen Strafgesetzgebung seit dem Jahr 1789" (1842), in GLA 234/7580.

[124] Baden-Durlach's statutes conceived only of women as prostitutes or victims of sexual coercion, and only of men as rapists, abductors, and coercers of women under their power or protection. Where force was involved, Baden-Durlach assumed a male culprit; in consensual acts, except prostitution, it kept a fairly open mind. Cf. Baden-Durlach *Malefizordnung* (1622), titles 31, 32, 41–45.

[125] Gleixner, "Dörfliche und obrigkeitliche Ordnungen," 64.

[126] On Altmark, see ibid., 53–54; for Schwäbisch Hall, see Renate Dürr's dissertation on servant maids, cited by Gleixner; also see Breit, *Leichtfertigkeit*, 135–36.

[127] *Leichtfertigkeit*, 255–56, 261.

sentenced to public humiliation as a possible substitute for a jail sentence of four days, half the time served by their male partners.[128] It does not seem that Baden-Durlach intended to punish women more than men, but to provide a suitable alternative to a prison sentence. The statute does not explain if imprisonment was unsuitable because of lack of a women's jail (specifically called for by the statute), physical disability caused by pregnancy, by official assumption of female physical weakness, the inadvisability of pulling female delinquents from their family responsibilities, or for some other reasons.

Because early modern law favored compound penalties generally, it easily developed a system of substitutions among them. In this Baden-Durlach case, the substitution was public humiliation for prison,[129] but in many other places, public humiliation was convertible to fines and vice versa. Women's child-support suits, wage figures for servants, and other indicators suggest that single women were often poorer than single men of the same *Stand*, and penalty convertibility may well have had the unintended consequence of forcing them to "choose" public humiliation, thus perpetuating the connection between women's sexual misdeeds and dishonor. One should avoid overinterpreting this as the actual goal of official policy. It was, instead, the product of the confluence of two factors: the central state's unexamined and unreflexive acceptance of the customary judgment about women's sexual honor by providing for it in public humiliation penalties (applicable, however, to both men and women), and the operation of larger patterns of gender difference in economy, society, and so on. The central state's larger intention of holding both men and women equally to their somewhat different duties to the moral and social order was therefore constantly at risk of perpetuating an inequality inappropriate to that end.

The tension between statutes incorporating customary punishment principles and the goal of equal accountability led to paradoxical results. For instance, Bavarian judges' propensity to exceed the maximum punishment for female fornicators but never doing so for men seems at first blush a clear example of discrimination. It was the very opposite. Befitting the customary assumption that men were more sexually aggressive, Bavaria's fornication statute punished them harder than it did women. Early modern judges were in fact attempting to hold men and women to the same standards—this is made especially clear in the lower courts run by nobles, who allowed themselves the greatest latitude in departing from statute, and where in the early eighteenth century they stretched matters so far that they gave women the same punishments as men, but never more.[130]

The early modern system of sexual regulation was thus a complex hybrid in which partly institutionalized, *ständisch*-ascriptive assumptions of gender differ-

---

[128] Public humiliation occurred two other places in Baden-Durlach's morals laws: against women in prostitution and against women and men for second-time adultery. It was therefore not exclusively a female penalty.

[129] In Bavaria, the thrice-repeated *Kirchenbuße* substituted for five years' territorial banishment in adultery cases. Decree of 30 March 1654, Bay HStA, GR 321/7.

[130] Breit, *Leichtfertigkeit*, 256, 261, 262.

ence jostled with official tendencies toward more nearly equal accountability. The former by no means always worked against women's interests either. Statute and judicial practice both agreed with customary conceptions making it dishonorable for single men to father illegitimate children without taking responsibility for both mother and child, either by marrying her, or by paying her damages (sufficient to dower her so that she could honorably marry another) and child support (*Alimentation*). Early modern courts consistently hunted down illegitimate fathers, discounted their excuses of having been seduced, rejected their defamatory claims that the illegitimate mother was promiscuous, and dunned the men for payment.[131] This process willy-nilly involved the courts in lengthy interrogations of both parties, in the course of which, as Ulrike Gleixner has sensitively shown, the prevailing gendered assumptions about male versus female sexual nature, duty, and therefore honor became not only reinforced through repetition, but also elaborated upon and changed. Although the state was the stronger partner in this dialogue, it did not "control" the process of elaboration, which developed in ways unforeseen by all interlocutors.

The tension between *ständisch* and administrative-egalitarian moments in state law was especially evident in sexual legislation. We have already seen how marital estate acted to reduce the differences in treatment by *Stand* in Bavarian legislation. Once again, Baden-Durlach, more influenced by the Carolina, was also more explicit about punishing sexual offenders equally, regardless of *Stand:* most of its provisions applied to "all of our subjects and inhabitants, young and old, man and woman, whatever *Stand* they may be."[132] But what did uniform subjection to moral legislation mean in a nonuniform society? Distinctions in *Stand* consisted mostly of trade-offs in prescribed punishments whereby public humiliation substituted either for hard labor or fines (for the unhealthy and poor), and higher fines and loss of honorable office and social function took the place of public humiliation, hard labor, or imprisonment for moneyed citizens or nobles. The constant here is loss of honor: public humiliation for the poor and ordinary; loss of honorable office, the right to wear distinctive clothes and/or attend honorable social events (such as weddings) for the socially distinguished. Such distinctions make clear that state officials saw sexual transgressions as sullying the honor of people of all *Stände*, men as well as women. The problem was that the external signs of honor and the public that bestowed, recognized, and could withhold honor, differed for each *Stand* and for women and men. The law therefore struggled to concoct equally weighty punishments in a system of unequal and incommensurable weights. This struggle pro-

---

[131] In Chapter 10 I detail the difficult dismantling of the father's responsibility in Napoleonic Baden. For an excellent account of the court's handling of illegitimate fathers, see Gleixner, "Dörfliche und obrigkeitliche Ordnungen," 83–121, esp. 100, 106. Gleixner (71) finds that in the 1740s, Prussia began to let more single fathers escape into the army. I believe this was a peculiarly Prussian practice and not characteristic of other areas.

[132] Baden-Durlach *Malefizordnung* (1622), title 30: "Vom leichtfertigen unehelichen Beysitz." No *Stand*-distinctions in sexual delicts appear in the *Malefizordnung*.

duced, for example, clothing proscriptions that applied only to women, not in order to punish them more or more publicly, but because a woman's sexual-social honor was conventionally expressed in her dress (in gold or silk trimmings, or a wreath at weddings), whereas a man's sexual honor usually was not. This difference may be due to the closer customary identification of a woman's honor with her body (bodily integrity). In any event, a man's dishonor had to be displayed in a different arena (like forbidding his attendance at public guesthouses or pubs).[133] Similarly, public humiliation before an entire community was appropriate to the common *Stände*, whose honor derived from that public. Such ceremonies were literally unseemly for the bourgeois patriciate or nobility because a narrower public (namely their own *Stand*) had social jurisdiction over their reputations. Confounding those two publics would have upset the social order more profoundly than whatever sexual disorderliness the dishonored might have committed. And ultimately state officials tried to use social custom via honor precisely to reinforce the social order, not to undermine it. It was not until the Enlightenment with its ideas of a universal human psychology and a wider, abstract public that the seventeenth-century state's particularist efforts at equal punishment were found unequal and therefore unjust.

Stand distinctions were written into the law of sex crime in more structural ways, too. Because seventeenth-century marriage was a closed estate, that is, one had to pass certain wealth, settlement, and occupation standards to be admitted to it, fornication statutes tended to be aimed at those too poor, too young, or too occupationally marginal to fulfill these criteria. Sometimes the preambles make this plain by singling out, for instance in Bavaria, "single servants and other common people in the countryside" as the chief offenders.[134] Despite specific provisions, for example targeting noble offenders,[135] the sociological and demographic contexts made fornication primarily an offense of the youthful and the poor.[136] Premature coitus, a new crime of the Reformation, penalized through the eighteenth century especially rural commoners whose courting practices clashed with the Reformation's narrower definition of when marriage began and thus when sexual congress was permissible.[137] Adultery, however, was more liable to encompass broader social strata—perhaps one more reason that one finds careful delineation of punishments according to *Stand* in statutes pertaining to adultery but rarely in those pertaining to fornication.

---

[133] Baden-Durlach *Malefizordnung* (1622), title 29; Beverly Ann Tlusty, "Gender and Alcohol Use in Early Modern Germany" (unpublished).

[134] Mandate of 20 September 1635. See also decree of 12 June 1665, both in Bay HStA, GR 321/7.

[135] For example, *Relation* of 25 August 1651 and decree of 2 September 1651, Bay HStA, GR 321/7.

[136] Breit has discovered, however, that historians have underestimated the number of fornicants from better-off peasant families, who in Bavaria at least were better represented among servants, the chief group at risk for running afoul of fornication statutes, than historians have believed. Breit's work also shows how many different motives might lie behind sexual transgression, beyond the simple picture suggested by aggregate statistics. *Leichtfertigkeit*, 178–82, 224.

[137] Robisheaux, *Rural Society*, 105–16, shows how family fathers used this legislation to control their offsprings' marital choices.

Statute versus Custom

With the exception of more strictly defining when marriage begins, a redefinition that rural youths contested for well over a century, and with the possible further exception of outlawing prostitution, which in medieval times had been tolerated although hardly encouraged, the central state did not impose alien or elite sexual views onto the populace. There appears to have been a very broad basis of often unarticulated and unreflected agreement between officials and subjects on a whole range of sexual matters, especially rape; sodomy; bigamy; incest between close family members; female promiscuity; the assumption of a basic heterosexual drive; the assumption that sexual activity was not a human right, but a *ständisch* privilege (that is, dependent upon status, age, gender, condition); the assumption that a general sexual nature was and ought to be expressed somewhat differently by men and women, hence the expectation of male sexual aggression with its danger to society and the need to protect women from it; and the assumption that marriage was the best, most orderly place for sex to occur.[138] Such broad agreement was doubtless the product of previous centuries of negotiation between church and parishioners and between governors and subjects; but by the early modern period, there was a recognizable landscape of common opinion that existed independent of official prodding. That this landscape of common opinion might be honored in the breach as well as in the observance does not gainsay its existence or normative character. Sexual miscreants commonly proclaimed their acceptance of sexual norms, when they excused their behavior by exclaiming, "The devil must have ridden me"—meaning a more powerful force had overwhelmed their own sense of moral right.

In addition to this wider agreement, which officials and subjects alike simply took as given, there was a narrower one between officials and the local possessors of wealth (peasant, Bürger, and noble alike)—the honorable housefathers, the *Ehrbarkeit*—designed to uphold the specific, sexual aspects of social reproduction. This is what largely determined the pattern of legislation on premature coitus, adultery, and fornication. Here the central state identified its interests in order and productivity with those of local elites, chiefly through upholding their control over entry into marriage.[139] But the state's commitment to system (which meant, for instance, that it could champion the wife's interest against the husband's)[140] and to confirming its authority via the reliable prosecution of statute left plenty of room

---

[138] Concerning consensus on sodomy, see Wettmann-Jungblut, "Stelen," 174; on infanticide and *Sittlichkeit*, as demonstrated by villagers turning in their fellows to the courts, see Dülmen, *Theater des Schreckens*, 15; on out-of-wedlock pregnancy, also demonstrated by denunciation, see Gleixner, "Dörfliche und obrigkeitliche Ordnungen," 233–34; on self-denunciation for sexual offenses, see Beck, "Illegitimität," 130; on villagers' slightly stigmatizing illegitimate children, see Breit, *Leichtfertigkeit*, 243.

[139] The state pulled in the same direction as parents: Breit, *Leichtfertigkeit*, 166, 234, 236, found an example of parents who punished a sexually profligate son by reducing his inheritance.

[140] Sabean, *Neckarhausen*, 134.

for disappointment and potential disagreement with the male representatives of the social groups it supported.[141] And within the village, factions, peer groups, clusters of relatives, and situational differences broke up the uniformity one might have expected the alliance of officials and local elites to have produced.

Because of government's too slender local infrastructure and because it counted on wide moral consensus and on cooperation from householders, the absolutist state consciously relied on structures it did not control to execute or interpret its ordinances. The adoption of dishonoring punishments for sexual delicts is an excellent example, since they only worked if the appropriate public played along. Of course, the public could do so for its own, village or group-internal reasons; nevertheless, there are no indications that the appropriate publics for humiliation rituals refused to do their part in bestowing at least transitory dishonor on the delinquents whom officials delivered up to them. Unlike public executions, which got so out of hand the central state was forced to abandon them,[142] public humiliations troubled officials for the opposite reason, they seemed all too successful.[143] Although bureaucrats complained, as illegitimacy continued, that no punishments seemed successfully to deter, they never claimed that shaming penalties failed to shame. The symbiosis between the punishing state and the punishing public is hard to disentangle. On the one hand, by trying to coopt the sexual honor system of the *ständisch*-appropriate public, the states acknowledged that one already existed and that it upheld the same general norms and assumptions the states wished to foster, otherwise cooption would have been unthinkable. In other words, the states' public humiliation penalties provided the occasion for marking[144] or underscoring, but not creating, a dishonorable condition that the misdeed had already caused in the transgression of popularly accepted norms. On the other hand, the ritual authority the state amassed also affected the nonstate honor system on which it was based. Lower officials and judges received many cases only because informal village mechanisms had failed to adjudicate these themselves. Courts therefore operated as arbitration chambers in cases where the honor system was unclear, or where, for instance, a man's and woman's respective claims to honor clashed. The court's judgment in such cases presumably decided the point—a woman could "get her honor back" by having her claims to *Alimentation* upheld by a court. But even here the symbiosis still operated, for the court's decision was based upon whether she had behaved "honorably" by *ständisch*-specific standards, that is, whether the history and the manner of her offense indicated that the liaison was tolerated as a

---

[141] Ordinances ceaselessly admonished householders to exercise stricter surveillance of their servants and, in exasperation, threatened lax masters and mistresses with punishments for failing to do so.

[142] Dülmen, *Theater des Schreckens*, 121, 153–60.

[143] See Chapter 3 on the infanticide debate. Church officials were unhappy that the *Kirchenbuße* occasioned disruptive behavior during the service.

[144] Gleixner, "Dörfliche und obrigkeitliche Ordnungen," uses the word *markiert*, 54, to describe this process. Elsewhere (66–67, 76), she seems to suggest, however, that the court's judgment actually bestowed honor or dishonor.

prelude to marriage.[145] By forcing the performance of dishonor in a ritual, the authorities made the honor system more palpable, probably stronger, and possibly more tendentious, insofar as some sexual transgressions and transgressors received disproportionate ritual attention. But regardless how powerful ritual performance is, it cannot operate at all unless the meanings it incorporates and vivifies make sense to the audience (and to the performer). Thus, the state's considerable power to wield ritual was ultimately bestowed upon it by its subjects, once in their acceptance of the system of meanings the ritual expressed and again in their recognition of the state as a proper overseer and producer of the ritual.[146]

Even the judgment itself served a ritual function. It distilled the information the village had fed it and brought the process of rumor and discussion to a definitive end. Once the judge pronounced upon paternity, for example, the matter was closed for the village.[147] The judgment was an official keystone crowning the pillars built largely of villagers' own fashioning—the reputations they set, the rumors they passed along, the stories they agreed to tell before the court. The keystone is necessary to the arch, it helps hold the parts together and gives them form, but it cannot stand without the stones that support it.

Sittlichkeit: The Moral Context of Sexual Crime

Sexual crime was part of the larger field of *Sittlichkeitsdelikte*, or moral crimes. Morality was not synonymous with sexual conduct. In the seventeenth and early eighteenth centuries *Sittlichkeit* (coming from *Sitte*, custom) had a wide, inclusive meaning encompassing Christian tenets of behavior and religious observance as well as a broad range of social customs. Sexual conduct was merely a subcategory of *Sittlichkeit* in both religious and secular senses; it was not yet taken to be the epitome of morality.

We have already seen how the Bavarian elector and his officials included in the same mandates and administrative orders both consensual sexual delicts (adultery and fornication) and swearing and cursing.[148] This association was commonplace. It illustrates once again the Christian origins of many sexual prohibitions, but more important, it underscores how sexual (mis)behavior was embedded in a larger, nonsexual context. As we have seen in the preceding chapter, the Christian conception of *Sittlichkeit* anchored sexual (mis)behavior in a constellation of impious acts ranging from cursing, to violating the Sabbath, to un-Christian deportment especially on holy days. Drinking (in pubs), gambling, and dancing were particularly

---

[145] Ibid., 54, 66–67, 76, 85, 115. On women going to court to recoup their honor, see Burghartz, "Rechte Jungfrauen," 175.

[146] The latter capacity came from the state's role as lawgiver and bringer of order. On the wide acceptance of this idea in early modern times, see Strauss, *Law*, 126–27.

[147] Gleixner, "Dörfliche und obrigkeitliche Ordnungen," 115.

[148] Mandate of 20 September 1635, report of the Vice Commission, 10 February 1637; report of the Vice Commission, 1 February 1641; court council to Elector, 16 October 1643; court council memorandum, 3 November 1694 and 4 August 1699, all in Bay HStA, GR 321/7.

singled out as common forms of Sabbath and holy day desecration, and as likely to lead to cursing and sexual vice. The particular acts in this constellation of immorality were not considered equal, but they were considered closely related; where one was found, the others were thought to be not far behind. The Christian constellation of *Sittlichkeit* produced the most popular symbolic system of vice, in which these particular acts recalled one another or even stood in for one another metaphorically. In the seventeenth century the moral constellation of Christian *Sittlichkeit* was fairly stable and evenly balanced among all its elements. In no case did the sexual components assume pride of place.

The other axis of *Sittlichkeit* was the more secular one of prodigality. Two categories of official epithets elaborated this theme. The first identified especially pre- or nonmarital sex with luxury, that is with spending or display inappropriate to one's *Stand*. It is thus typical that the 1626 Bavarian decree against fornication, which officials remembered as the first in the series, bore the title: "Preventing luxuriousness especially among persons of the unmarried estate."[149] Similar examples abound.[150] Even more prevalent were the labels "liederlich" and "leichtfertig" to describe fornicants. These elastic terms cover a range of meanings from sexual looseness and disorder to negligence, fecklessness, laziness, and unproductivity.[151] *Liederlich* was the operative adjective in four legal epithets describing (and linking) prostitutes, beggars, troublesome rural servants, and profligate householders in ordinances from the sixteenth century to the nineteenth.[152]

The tenacious mutual association of heterosexual, especially premarital, sexual disconduct, luxury, laziness, wasteful habits (drinking and gambling), and poverty (beggary) suggest that the laws forbidding heterosexual consensual acts outside marriage can be seen as the biological-procreative equivalent of the sumptuary legislation that had begun in the fourteenth century, but reached its height in the sixteenth to early eighteenth centuries. Sumptuary legislation aimed to control all

---

[149] Decree of 1 October 1626, Bay HStA, GR 321/7. See also decree of 21 October 1626, GR 1187/55.

[150] Baden-Durlach *Malefizordnung* (1622), title 36; Winther to Margrave Friedrich, Röttlen, 19 January 1654, GLA 74/3919; mandate of 20 September 1635, Bay HStA, GR 321/7.

[151] Josua Maaler, *Die Teütsch spraach. Dictionarium Germanicolatinum novum* (orig. 1561; rpt., Hildesheim, 1971), 267–73; Jacob Grimm and Wilhelm Grimm, *Deutsches Wörterbuch* (Leipzig, 1877). The cameralist Veit Ludwig von Seckendorff used *liederlich* to describe lazy artisans in *Christen-Stat . . .* (Leipzig, 1685), chap. 13, sec. 7–8, pp. 443–48; cited in Kurt Zielenziger, *Die alten deutschen Kameralisten. Ein Beitrag zur Geschichte der Nationalökonomie und zum Problem des Merkantilismus* (Jena, 1914), 370. For Badenese officials' changing use of *liederlich*, see Albert Straub, *Das badische Oberland im 18. Jahrhundert. Die Transformation einer bäuerlichen Gesellschaft vor der Industrialisierung* (Husum, 1977), 156–59; for Bavarian official usage of *leichtfertig*, see Breit, *Leichtfertigkeit*, 5. On popular usage of *liederlich* and *leichtfertig*, see Sabean, *Neckarhausen*, 144–45; Gleixner, "Dörfliche und obrigkeitliche Ordnungen," 98–99 (who finds the term usually applied to women); and Schulte, "Kindsmörderinnen," 141.

[152] Cf. Fischer, *Armut in der Geschichte*, 35; Baden-Durlach rescript of 25 March 1682, GLA 74/6354; Bavaria decree of 3 August 1772, in Mayr, *Sammlung der . . . allgemeinen und besonderen Landes-Verordnungen*, 1:54; decree of 21 January 1763 against "liederliche Hauswirth . . . ," in *Sammlung der neuest und merkwürdigsten churbaierischen Generalien und Landesverordnungen*, ed. Georg Karl Mayr (Munich, 1771), 448.

consumption, recreational activities, or conspicuous display that went beyond the fulfillment of subsistence needs for the broad population, or of *Stand* requirements for the bourgeois patriciate and nobility. Thus, clothing, imported foods, brewed drink, guests at weddings, funerals, or other festivities, the number and length of dances, the size of dance bands and the like were all subject to strict regulation according to *Stand*.[153] As with laws controlling sexual behavior, religious and secular interests were largely congruent, or better, shared a worldview shaped within the narrow confines of a subsistence culture. The Christian life of modesty, the economic life of regular work to cover one's own needs, the social life appropriately circumscribed to fit each ascriptive *Stand*, all more or less coincided in the effort to uphold the delicate balance of existence in an uncertain world.

Ordinances regulating consumption, consensual sexual acts, and irreligious behavior, in short, *Sittlichkeit*-ordinances, were the product of a subsistence mentality that identified all three forms of misbehavior as mere aspects of the same threat. A Palatine ordinance of 1680 voiced the fear of a "domino effect" inherent in this older view of *Sittlichkeit*: it enjoined everyone (singling out soldiers especially) to avoid "whore-houses and similar assignation spots wherever they are along with other troublesome and suspicious societies and also shameful and inhuman drunkenness from which much disharmony, murder, and manslaughter and also cursing and all manner of sins and scandals usually arise, and these and other disorders are to be eliminated and absolutely not tolerated."[154]

Toward the end of the seventeenth century most scholars of sumptuary laws observe a waning of religious motivation behind the regulations and, instead, an increased central state focus on those aspects of consumption that affect the economic and social order.[155] These secular purposes still aimed to conserve accumulated wealth inside the territorial borders, to uphold the external signs of *ständisch* distinction, and to prevent wealthy nobles or bourgeois from indulging in lavish display that might rival that of the Court.[156] In the eighteenth century this conservatism was transformed as states encouraged economic production and increased consumption, thus undermining the subsistence foundations of the older conception of *Sittlichkeit*. The peculiar seventeenth-century *Sittlichkeits*-constellation remained typical of religious, especially Roman Catholic opinion, whereas secular, state-oriented impetuses caused this idea-cluster to change radically.

---

[153] On sumptuary laws, see Werner Sombart, *Luxus und Kapitalismus*, vol. 1 of his *Studien zur Entwicklungsgeschichte des modernen Kapitalismus* (Munich, 1913); Karin Plodeck, "Zur sozialgeschichtlichen Bedeutung der absolutistischen Polizei- und Landesordnungen," *Zeitschrift für bayerische Landesgeschichte* 39.1 (1976): 79–125; Kent R. Greenfield, *Sumptuary Law in Nürnberg: A Study in Paternal Government* (Baltimore, 1918); Silvia Bovenschen, ed., *Die Listen der Mode* (Frankfurt, 1986); Liselotte C. Eisenbart, *Kleiderordnungen der deutschen Städte zwischen 1350 und 1700. Ein Beitrag zur Kulturgeschichte des deutschen Bürgertums* (Göttingen, 1962); J. M. Vincent, "European Blue Laws," *Annual Report of the American Historical Association* (1897): 355–73.

[154] Decree of 16 November 1680, GLA 77/5075.

[155] Plodeck, "Polizei- und Landesordnungen," 96, and Veronika Baur, *Kleiderordnungen in Bayern vom 14. bis zum 19. Jahrhundert* (Munich, 1975), 124.

[156] This is Plodeck's major argument in "Polizei- und Landesordnungen."

❀ Absolutist States and the Regulation of Sex ❀

In the course of the eighteenth and into the nineteenth century, *Sittlichkeit*
became more and more identified with matters exclusively sexual. This transformation also characterized the word "leichtfertig." As the Grimms noted: (for "Sittlichkeit") "Often the word is limited to sexual respectability or morality"; and (for
"leichtfertig") "In recent usage leichtfertig is often understood as loose in sexual
relations, for which there are also older examples."[157] The Grimms' examples of
this shift in usage toward the narrowly sexual are literary sources from the late
eighteenth century (Wieland, Schiller, Goethe). Had the Grimms included more
legal sources, they would have seen that the "older examples" of the more sexual
usage are typical of legal discourse and that this usage was then, in the late eighteenth century, taken over by the literary shapers of civil society, who developed the
sexual accent even further and, by the nineteenth century, had surpassed official
usage, which still continued to retain some of the diffuseness characteristic of
earlier times. In the following pages we will see this pattern again, whereby the state
shaped and accentuated a way of interpreting or using sexual behavior, passed this
along to nascent civil society, which in its turn developed this interpretation or
usage independently of the state. This incomplete dialectic describes the formation
of our modern conception of "sexuality."

Public and Private

It should be clear now that the early modern absolutist state theoretically at least
shrank from nothing in its pretense to supervise and control the intimate, personal
behavior of its subjects. Nothing they might do,[158] consensually or victimlessly,
nothing they consumed or produced, nothing they said or did, was exempt from
"public," that is, "official," scrutiny. This sweeping claim to power was partly
derived from the prince's duties as a Christian lord and partly from the *Polizey*-
patriarchal duties of the lord to protect his subjects from the harm they might—
through ignorance or weakness—bring upon themselves. Some historians have
been tempted to interpret the central state's grandiose regulatory claims as incur-
sions on the "private" sphere. Reinhold Dorwart claims, for example, that sumptuary legislation failed because "people in all eras of history resent and evade efforts to
regulate personal . . . habits . . . [and this leads to] public evasion of this type of
intrusion into private life."[159] Such a judgment is anachronistic. There is no
evidence for such a conception of "private life" in the late seventeenth or early
eighteenth centuries. No official blushed at the penetration of state power into the
subjects' sleeping quarters. No bureaucrat justified regulation with arguments
designed to defend against the charge of intrusion into a "private" sphere. No

[157] *Deutsches Wörterbuch*, 1272 (*Sittlichkeit*), 643 (*leichtfertig*).
[158] Ordinances forbade boys and girls sharing a bed, or males and females bathing together. See the
Baden ordinances of 20 August 1731, 20 June 1743, 11 July 1745, GLA 74/6361, and the ordinance of
15 April 1752 in GLA 74/4522, as well as the Bavarian ordinance of 20 September 1635 (sleeping
quarters of servants), Bay HStA, GR 321/7, repeated periodically.
[159] Reinhold August Dorwart, *The Prussian Welfare State Before 1740* (Cambridge, 1971), 26.

petitions poured into the central administration begging to preserve privacy. It is certainly true that people evaded regulation and struggled against officials' efforts. But they did so not in the name of individual liberty, but in the name of collective custom and rights, which they perceived to be abridged or threatened by the state's mania for reform. There was an early modern understanding of "private" in the sense of private law, meaning agreements taking place outside the state's purview. This "private" world was not a world of individuals, however, but of collectivities: *Stände*, guilds, families, and the like. Actions in this world, even matters such as "private" display (*privater Aufwand*),[160] took place in "public" in two senses. First, the proximity of others was difficult to escape, even in the "privacy" of the home, in which separate rooms were only beginning to appear. Second, the *ständisch* grid defined with fair completeness the range of possible, expected behavior. There was, of course, some eccentricity; no human-made grid is ever complete. But lacking the normative idea of an individual apart from society, behavior of concrete individuals was conceived less in relation to themselves, than in relation to the particular, *ständisch* collectivity to which each belonged. Just as the concrete individual was dissolved into (*aufgehoben*) the *Stand*, the *Stände* were dissolved into the state, at least in theory. For the state was the organized expression of, and responsible for upholding and protecting, their higher collectivity. This is why the "public" in the sense of "state" flowed effortlessly across *ständisch* borders. No "private" in the sense of individual solitude and apartness or in the sense of a protected place in which that might occur (the house) existed. The emergence of such a peculiar concept transformed this mental, moral, and legal world utterly. Reinterpreting sexual behavior and its relation to society was a major part of this transformation, but we shall be unable to recognize this process if we (mis)interpret the early modern word "private" in its nineteenth- and twentieth-century sense.[161]

Trends in Punishment

Compared with the frequent call for the death penalty characteristic of the Carolina, even the written statutes of the seventeenth and early eighteenth centuries were lenient. Still, the central state's heightened interest in sexual behavior produced a wave of slightly increased penalties for sexual misconduct from the late seventeenth to the early eighteenth century, especially for the three delicts that dominated official attention: adultery, fornication, and premature coitus. Occasionally an exasperated sovereign would even call for restoring the Carolina[162] or

[160] Plodeck, "Polizei- und Landesverordnungen," 96.

[161] See Chapter 4, pp. 157–72 and Chapter 5, 215–16, for an extended discussion of the early modern and eighteenth-century understandings of state and civil society.

[162] Francisca Sybilla Augusta, markgravin of Baden, decree of 12 August 1713, GLA 74/3923. This decree was never published and therefore never acted upon.

applying torture to extract confessions from the "obviously guilty,"[163] but in fact sharpened penalties took the form of increases in the types of punishment already called for, that is lengthened terms of imprisonment or higher fines. The incessant fiddling with the penalties in the seventeenth century shows three trends we have already observed. First, in midcentury, the central states called explicitly for punishing the wealthy and the nobility as well as the common peasants and Bürger who had been targeted before. Graduated fines and the prohibition on wearing the external signs or enjoying the social fruits of elevated *Stand* were designed to tailor punishment to the socially privileged.[164] Second, as the central state began to identify its own power and welfare more closely with economic production, it sought to replace banishment or idleness in prison with work penalties. This was the beginning of a trend that flourished in one form or another for two hundred years. It had the unintended consequence, third, of striking men and women differently, since judges deemed women less able to withstand the rigors of forced labor and imposed sentences of public humiliation in its place.

A more important feature of seventeenth-century punishment for sexual offenses was the pattern of discrepancy between written statute and actual judicial practice. To explore this, we now turn from the qualified chaos of written legislation to the luxuriant chaos of the courts.

The Actual Practice of State Regulation in the Seventeenth Century

Although the absolutist state claimed the right and duty to regulate sexual misdeeds, its theoretical reach exceeded its practical grasp. Local administrators and the patchwork of uneven jurisdictions were not solely to blame for the disjuncture between theory and practice. The central bureaucracy occasionally neglected to publish its ordinances; Baden-Durlach's major legal codification of 1622 was not widely circulated until 1654, by which time some of its provisions had been superseded by intervening mandates. Even then, only three hundred copies of it existed, hardly enough to keep all localities supplied for the 181 years that elapsed until the next codification.[165] The central bureaucrats themselves could not always keep

---

[163] As in Bavaria in 1660: see court council president to elector, 22 May 1660, draft of decree of 7 June 1660, and decree of 11 August 1660, in Bay HStA, GR 321/7. The final decree settled for establishing a punishment for "suspicion" of adultery or fornication.

[164] See Winther to Margrave Friedrich, Röttlen, 19 January 1654 and 28 March 1654, GLA 74/3919, and Bavarian decree of 1 June 1651 and *Relation* of 25 August 1651, Bay HStA, GR 321/7.

[165] Engelbert Strobel, *Neuaufbau der Verwaltung und Wirtschaft der Markgrafschaft Baden-Durlach nach dem Dreissigjährigen Krieg bis zum Regierungsantritt Karl Wilhelms (1648–1709)* (Berlin, 1935), 18. See also Raeff's discussion, *Well-Ordered Police State*, 51–52. For an example of an unpublished ordinance on sexual crime, see document 4, undated, but circa 1715, signed by Evers, GLA 74/3925, which confirmed that the decree of 12 August 1713 had never been put into effect for this reason. The decree of 3 May 1714, concerning fines and wedding dress restrictions for pregnant brides suffered a similar fate. See the memorandum of 30 April 1754, GLA 74/3924.

track of what they had done, as internal inconsistences in the lengthy series of mandates, the repetition of outdated decrees regardless of recent revision,[166] and the common references in bureaucratic correspondence to the same ordinance under different dates all attest.

In the early eighteenth century, central governments, oblivious to their own complicity in the problem, typically began surveying local authorities, to check if practice accorded with statute in the prosecution of sexual crimes. Such surveys took the form of questions about procedure, punishments, or jurisdiction directed to the local and middle-level instances, the more energetic of whom actually researched their records back into the seventeenth century before answering. The results of surveys undertaken in Bavaria in 1722 and 1730–33, a much narrower inquiry in Baden in 1740, and a Badenese compilation, made about the same time, of incest cases from 1682 to 1725 reveal not only discrepancies between mandates and judicial practice, but local particularity, shoddy (or, indeed, no) record-keeping, and jurisdictional confusion.[167]

Under the circumstances, one must ask what relation the mandates bore to real practice? The answers to the inquiries mentioned above and the results of scholarly studies of localities indicate that mandates set the outside limit to punishment and, since they usually mentioned more than one penalty, provided the alternatives among which local judges chose in arriving at sentences. The degree to which judges adhered to these mandates varied from place to place and time to time.[168] Unless judges were trying to equalize penalties for men and women, they rarely erred by exceeding mandated punishments, however.[169] Departure from statute was almost entirely in the direction of leniency.

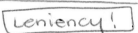

---

[166] For example, the Bavarian government on 2 September 1651 repeated the mandate of 20 September 1635 as though they were unaware they had sharpened penalties in 1643 and 1645. See *Relation* of 17 July 1645, Bay HStA, GR 321/7.

[167] Responses by local authorities to the government survey of 17 April 1722 are in Bay HStA, GR 321/7; responses to the survey of 16 July 1730 and afterward sporadically into 1733, in Bay HStA, GR 322/8; treasury (*Rentcammer*) and court council (*Hofrat*) memoranda of 4 August 1740 and 18 June 1740, in GLA 74/3920; and "Kurze aus den Acten gezogene Nachricht von einigen in den Hzgl. Baden Durl. Landen vorgefallenen Blutschändereyen und deren Bestrafung," undated, in GLA 74/3931. These documents form the basis for many of the conclusions that follow. The scope and number of responses from Bavaria make that documentation much more solid than what I have been able to find in Baden for the seventeenth century. In the eighteenth century, the Badenese material burgeons, however, and this unevenness between the two lands disappears.

See also the court council protocol of 3 November 1694 complaining of unevenness in the local punishment of swearers, an associated group of *Sittlichkeit*-miscreants, in Bay HStA, GR 321/7.

[168] For example in Bavaria, cf. Beck, "Illegitimität," 128, 235 n. 28, who found in the three localities he studied that judges were pretty true to law; whereas Breit, *Leichtfertigkeit*, 257, 264, 284, found discrepancies.

[169] I have found only one case in Baden among those reported to the central authorities, in which the locals exceeded the penalty set by the mandate, and this merely involved raising a fine for fornication from 16 gulden to 19 gulden 2 kreutzer. "Gegen Memoriale" of the treasury (*Rentcammer*) to the privy council (*Geheim-Rats-Collegium*), 18 June 1740, GLA 74/3920.

De Facto Judicial Reform of Sexual Statute

Case by case, and increasing over time, judges *de facto* reformed the laws pertaining to sexual behavior. In Bavaria, in cases of first-time simple adultery, the 1635 mandate as revised in 1643, 1645, and 1654 called for four weeks' imprisonment, a *Kirchenbuße* repeated three times and, depending on the wealth of the adulterer, a fine. If the responses to the 1722 and 1730 inquiries are representative, then a clear tendency toward mildness developed and seems to have followed two stages. In the first, around the turn of the seventeenth/eighteenth centuries, imprisonment withered away, leaving public humiliation and fines.[170] Then, during the first half of the eighteenth century, fines more and more replaced public humiliation.[171] In cases where the couple married, public humiliation was silently dropped; after 1780, when a revision finally substituted a discretionary atonement (*Buße*) for public humiliation in these cases, in fact, the *Buße* was never instituted.[172]

In Baden the tendency toward fines in lieu of any other punishment was doubtless hastened because judges had interpreted the law to give adulterers and fornicators the right to chose fines as substitution, if they could pay them.[173] Bureaucratic correspondence from early eighteenth-century Baden suggests that fines had in this way become very widespread and no longer distinguished fornication from adultery in some locales.[174] Twelve incest cases that the Baden-Durlach bureaucracy culled from the records for 1682 to 1725 show the same pattern, even where fines were not involved.[175] No one received the full measure of the law, which called for public humiliation, beating, eternal banishment, and confiscation of property. In the cases of six individuals an original judgment of banishment was either quickly recalled or mitigated; for two others confiscation decrees were softened. In the remaining cases routinely one or two sorts of punishment made do for the mandated set of four. Unlike the case of fines for adultery or fornication, which seemed to have spread by popular demand and local judicial accommodation, leniency in these incest cases frequently came from the central government, which reviewed sentences deviating from statute and often made them milder still.[176]

---

[170] Landshut provincial government (*Rentamt*) to court council (*Hofrat*), 12 February 1723, Bay HStA, GR 321/7; Mindelheim local government to court council, 14 August 1730, Bay HStA, GR 322/8.

[171] Aybling to court council, 11 August 1730; Mindelheimb to court council, 14 August 1730; Landshut to court council, 9 January 1732; Weissenstein to court council, 10 March 1732, Bay HStA, GR 322/8.

[172] Breit, *Leichtfertigkeit*, 257, 264.

[173] See the preamble to the decree of 13 March 1754 lamenting this procedure, in GLA 74/3919.

[174] Privy council (*Geheimer Rat*) to margrave, 28 November 1739; treasury (*Rentcammer*) to privy council (*Geheim-Rats-Collegium*), 18 June 1740; privy council to treasury, 4 August 1740; "Memoriale ad Concilium Aulicum," 4 August 1740, all in GLA 74/3920.

[175] It is not clear why this summary was collated. Eight cases involved in-laws (the commonest form of prosecuted incest in early modern Europe), none concerned parent-child incest among blood relatives, though two involved fathers with stepdaughters.

[176] GLA 74/3920, and *Malefizordnung* of 1622 (and 1654), title 39.

Gleixner's study of the early-eighteenth-century Altmark (Brandenburg) charts a similar movement. After 1745, although prison sentences for *Unzucht* were handed down more frequently, they were not served for the complete time. After 1750 the humiliation penalty for women dropped out of use, replaced by a stint in the mildest form of jail (the *Vogtei* instead of the *Turm*). After 1755 jail sentences became more and more irregular, and soon fines also disappeared.[177]

The remarkable thing about this development is that, as Breit remarks for Bavaria, "in the rule local courts were a step ahead of state legislation in adopting lighter penalties."[178] Of course, threatening draconian punishment and then graciously granting reprieves was a hallmark of early modern justice; but this feature would produce simple discrepancy, not the progressively milder practice one observes. Although this matter deserves more study, it appears that the cause lay in precisely the nexus of custom and law we have already examined. Local courts conceived of their function as "settling conflicts."[179] Doing so required a sensitive feel for the social pulse of a village. Courts placed great store in a defendant's public reputation and status in the community. They paid particular attention to the number of people who interceded on a defendant's behalf, and, in the absence of effective investigative police, courts were beholden to local public opinion for information concerning and even knowledge of the crime in the first place. This receptivity to the actual circumstances of life as these were interpreted for officials by village discourse seems to have led courts, unevenly but steadily, in the direction of lighter and lighter penalties for consensual sexual delicts.[180] The chasm that ultimately gaped between law and judicial practice was, as we shall see, one of the major impetuses for legal reform in the eighteenth century, and one of the main reasons that there was a space for Enlightenment theory, which acted as a retrospective legitimation for developments that had already occurred where law and life simply did not match.

Pregnancy

A second major hallmark of actual state practice in regulating sexual behavior in the late seventeenth century was its focus: pregnancy. Here the verbal preoccupations of the mandates fell closer to reality. There was a double economic reason behind this congruence. The authorities at all levels were anxious to avoid the public costs of maintaining illegitimate children. They sought to achieve this end either by discouraging illegitimacy altogether through (especially exemplary) punishment of nonmarital heterosexual activity, or by offsetting welfare costs through fines collected from those whom they caught, or child-support payments by the

[177] Gleixner, "Dörfliche und obrigkeitliche Ordnungen," 54.
[178] *Leichtfertigkeit*, 284, also 129 on procedural matters.
[179] Behringer, "Mörder," 123.
[180] Wettmann-Jungblut, "Stelen," 141, 172–74; Behringer, "Mörder," 123–24; Beck, "Illegitimät," 129; Becker, *Leben und Lieben*, 303.

father. In all three cases, the pregnant, single woman was the "problem" that needed a solution.

The state's fiscal straits also meant its police forces were tiny. The only sure method of detecting the commission of an illegal sexual act was the pregnancy of an unmarried woman. Proving sexual misbehavior in the absence of pregnancy was most difficult, as the Bavarian authorities in 1660 discovered with adultery, which they likened in its secrecy to poisoning. They complained that adulterers, against whom the evidence "was so strong that nothing remained except the confession, are nonetheless frequently getting off and avoiding trial by premeditated denial."[181] The court council president, obviously under pressure from the elector, thought torture might be the answer in selected cases, since threat of torture had had no effect,[182] but in the end the court council rejected that alternative as unbefitting a crime no longer deemed a capital offense.[183]

This Bavarian contretemps makes clear why the most common and legally surest means of discovery remained pregnancy, an involuntary and *public* form of self-incrimination. The reader will recall how the Imperial Police Ordinances had introduced public annoyance as a ground for state intervention in a new offense, "public adultery." As a(n inescapably) public act, extramarital pregnancy challenged the state's self-imposed, but universally recognized, responsibility to uphold public order and seemliness.

For all of these reasons illegitimate pregnancy was the main actual target of regulatory efforts. There are indications that this may have been increasingly the case as one moved from the seventeenth into the eighteenth centuries, but only detailed social histories on the local level would be able to confirm this impression.[184] In any event, the centrality of pregnancy to prosecution had a number of effects. It meant that a very large proportion of official investigations must have begun by focusing on single women. Significantly, however, early modern investigations did not stop there, but continued until they reached the male partner, too. Because men were more likely to find employment and acceptance elsewhere than were pregnant women, they had more opportunity to escape the hand of the law by fleeing. In states with large armies, they could disappear into the prince's service,

---

[181] Court council president (*Hofratspräsident*) to elector, 22 May 1660, Bay HStA, GR 321/7.

[182] Bay HStA, GR 321/7

[183] Draft of decree of 7 June 1660. Ultimately, mere suspicion of adultery and fornication were punished according to the decree of 11 August 1660, Bay HStA, GR 321/7.

[184] In the Bavarian responses to the 1722 inquiry on adultery, pregnancy is only mentioned in cases after 1689, though, probably because the inquiry centered on jurisdictional problems rather than on punishment, pregnancy is not mentioned frequently even then. See the responses of Neustatt, Wambding, Wasserburg, Weissstein, Pfaffenhofen, Schongau, Kölz, and Landshut, 1722–23, Bay HStA, GR 321/7. The same pattern occurs in the incest cases collected in Baden, "Kurze Nachricht," GLA 74/3931. Data collected by central governments improve in quality for the eighteenth century and repeatedly show what a large number of cases of sexual crime, especially fornication, involved pregnancy. For example, in a protocol of fornication cases from 1796 in Wolfratshausen, involving sixty-three persons, pregnancy figured in 91.5 percent of the cases. "Leichtfertigkeits-Protokoll," Wolfratshausen, 24 July 1796, Bay HStA, GR 322/8.

where they were safe from prosecution.[185] There were therefore always likely to be slightly more single mothers than single fathers prosecuted. This outcome was not what either officials or villages desired, however, and both made strenuous and generally successful efforts to avoid it. In the 3095 cases of fornication Breit studied in Bavaria, only one in forty putative fathers ran away. They were more likely to stay and dispute the charges, but in fact, few even did that: between 75 and 90 percent of them agreed to pay *Alimentation* without quarrel.[186] Unless military impediments intervened, both village networks and state courts successfully pressed to find the male culprit. And once officials found him, they rarely exonerated him.[187] In the inquiry results we have cited above and in scattered other references throughout the bureaucratic correspondence it is unusual to find women mentioned by themselves. The fact that the woman's pregnancy alerted officials to the commission of a heterosexual offense did not cause them to hold her alone responsible. Here, again state practice reflected local, customary opinion.

The pregnancy diagnosis for sexual misbehavior may even have had the unintended consequence of bringing to light many more cases of married male than married female adultery. The pregnancy of the servant girl or neighbor's daughter exposed the married man, whereas her own married status cloaked in respectability the adulterous pregnancy of the married woman. It is certainly the case that simple adultery, that is, intercourse involving one married and one unmarried person, was overwhelmingly a male crime in prosecution, regardless of the fact that mandates, which typically called for greater punishments for female offenders, seem to have taken wives' adultery more seriously. Bureaucratic correspondence almost always has a male offender in mind, when it discusses the effects of adultery penalties.[188] When the Landshut authorities enumerated thirty-nine simple adultery cases for the late seventeenth and early eighteenth centuries, they identified twenty-seven married men but only six married women as the culprits. For Pfaffenhofen, the ratio was five to one.[189] Of course, this discrepancy might reflect instead a social acceptability of, or a greater tendency or simply opportunity for, married men to commit adultery. In the absence of evidence for these three propositions, however, one should avoid rushing to embrace them, particularly since they describe sociocultural assumptions more characteristic of the nineteenth and twentieth centuries than of the seventeenth and eighteenth. It is furthermore a valuable intellectual

---

[185] Gleixner found this pattern accelerating in Prussia after 1740. See "Dörfliche und obrigkeitlichen Ordnungen," 109–13. See also Peter K. Taylor, "Military System and Rural Social Change in Eighteenth-Century Hesse-Cassel," *Journal of Social History* 25.3 (1992): 479–504, esp. 495.

[186] *Leichtfertigkeit*, 126, 149. On 144, Breit remarks that "accused fathers rarely were prepared immediately to pay child support costs," but this refers to that (small) group of fathers whom mothers had had to drag into court to recover damages. This group ranged from 9 percent to 27 percent of single fathers in Breit's study. Ibid., 149.

[187] Ibid., 130; Gleixner, "Dörfliche und obrigkeitliche Ordnungen," 100, 106.

[188] For example, court council president (*Hofratspräsident*) and councillors to Kurfürstin, 30 December 1653, Bay HStA. GR 321/7.

[189] Landshut to court council (*Hofrat*), 12 February 1723; and Pfaffenhouen [Pfaffenhofen] Regierung to Court Council, 10 May 1722, Bay HStA, GR 321/7.

exercise to remind ourselves of the double-edged quality of most sexual regulation: in this case, focusing on nonmarital pregnancy not only exposed female fornication more readily than male, but, male adultery more readily than female.

A final, paradoxical effect of recognizing sexual crime largely through the medium of illicit pregnancy has surfaced before in our discussion of the mandates, but it was equally true in practice: pregnant women were deemed less able to withstand physical punishment or imprisonment than their male partners, and consequently either were punished less, not at all, or received public humiliation penalties as substitutes. Sometimes equal punishment would be ordered postponed until after the birth of the child; it would be instructive to learn how often such penalties were actually carried out.[190] In any event, the pregnant sexual delinquent developed into the central state's legal nightmare in the following century; she organized its thoughts about sex-crime law and legal reform generally.

Order for Order's Sake

For all their worries about pregnancy, state bureaucrats did not argue for or against sexual regulation on the grounds that a bigger, smaller, or better population would result. Given the devastating impact of the Thirty Years' War on central European populations, one might understand why overpopulation would not have been a worry. But even lands deemed by their own governments to be underpopulated, such as Baden and Bavaria, pursued sexual regulation that could only have worked, if at all, to retard population growth. For seventeenth-century Baden and Bavaria I have found only two ordinances, both by Margrave Friedrich of Baden, designed to use sexual regulation to encourage population growth.[191] One, in 1678, decried the "large number of single and unmarried but nonetheless marriageable citizen's sons" (that is, who fulfilled subsistence—*Nahrung*—requirements) who "because of the hardships and fear of war have not wanted to commit themselves to marriage and householding." To encourage them, the margrave offered two year's exemption from taxes if they married after publication of the mandate. In 1687 he extended this largesse to men who married widows.[192]

This legislation is significant for two reasons. First, there is so little of it. Most governments tried to address their perceived underpopulation problem via immigration, not by relaxing sexual regulations. Second, these Badenese decrees were aimed only to encourage earlier marriage among those elements who, under normal circumstances, would have married anyway—it did not extend the privilege to other groups, who were still left the alternatives of abstinence or penalized fornication. That is, these decrees left the sexual regulation system with its subsistence assumptions entirely intact. Maintaining order, including moral order, was far more important for seventeenth-century governments than population considerations.

[190] An example is case 3 in "Kurze Nachricht," GLA 74/3931.
[191] Strobel, *Neuaufbau der Verwaltung*, 81–83, also located only these two.
[192] Decree of 10 June 1678 in GLA 74/3457; decree of 20 May 1687, GLA 74/3460.

Indeed, the territorial government regarded the latter through local lenses; fears about the local poor chest determined the central bureaucrats' conception of larger state interest. That meant that no demographic standpoint really existed, since demographics is an aggregate, an abstraction relating to the entire territory. Seventeenth-century state sexual regulation was thus anchored in local, concrete subsistence concerns; it was conceived defensively, statically, and for its own sake.

Self-Conscious Failure

The most important characteristic of regulatory practice in the seventeenth century was its failure. And more important than its objective failure was the subjective conviction on the part of central governments that their efforts were in vain. This gradual realization punctured an illusion common to early modern territorial governments, an illusion that was really a kind of theory of government. It held that just as the king's touch might cure scrofula, the king's word might bring order to the land. The mere royal expression of a pious wish in the form of a legal commandment read from every pulpit in the land would suffice to bring society in line with Christian principles and thus also discharge the prince's duty as a ruler by divine right. The mandates' magical quality may also help explain the discrepancy between their often draconian language and the loopholes built into them via judicial discretion, either in the form of "arbitrary," that is judge-determined penalties, or the judge's express right to act more leniently than the written law.[193] It was as if the sentence alone, and not its execution, fulfilled the ritual function of the mandate. Thus, in the incest cases from Baden, the sentence usually was first spoken in its extremity and then afterward made milder.[194]

Through the entire seventeenth and long into the eighteenth century, the magical mandates revealed their impotence to the lawgivers. As early as 1624 Margrave Friedrich V of Baden expressed his exasperation:

Although Our honored and revered ancestors, the margraves of Baden and Hochberg placed punishments on all sorts of misdeeds and crimes, in addition to those penalties prescribed in divine commandments and imperial law, through various published mandates and orders, statutes and ordinances, particularly against fornication [*Hurerey*] and adultery, and these punishments have been earnestly executed against the criminals, without regard to person, such that everyone should have been entirely deterred from any loose life [*leichtfertigen leben*], not to speak of fornication and adultery [*Unzucht, Hurerey auch Ehebruch*].

However, We have alas variously discovered, with extreme displeasure and consternation, since We took office, that in these more than difficult and sad times, along with many other highly punishable sins, disgraces and vices, in particular damnable fornication and

[193] Judicial discretion is expressly provided for, for example, in title 39 (incest) of the Baden-Durlach *Malefizordnung* of 1622, and articles 117 (incest), 118 (abduction for sexual purposes), 119 (rape), 123 (*Kuppelei*), and 123 (abortion) in the Carolina. On the systematic use of clemency in early modern law, see Dülmen, *Theater des Schreckens*, 39, 44–47.

[194] "Kurze Nachricht," GLA 74/3931.

adultery have so increased and proliferated [*so weit eingerissen unnd oberhand genommen*], that they are scarcely held to be sins anymore and that the penalties for them are in general regarded with disdain and, indeed, barely held to be penalties at all.[195]

After 130 years of efforts, the preambles to the mandates still complained: "Because We have often noticed, with great displeasure, the strongly increasing frequency [*die allzustark einreisende Frequenz*] of the vices of fornication and adultery, We have decided to put a serious stop to this."[196] The phrases "proliferating" (*überhandnehmen*), "energetically increasing" (*ganz in Schwung gehen*), and "becoming common" (*gemein werden*) were formulas appearing in virtually every ordinance on sexual behavior of the period:

> Because We have had to observe for some time in Our lands, to what degree the grave vices of fornication and impregnations among the single people, and not less the highly punishable vice of adultery among married persons have become common [*gemein werden*], and then finally how the vexing [*ärgerliche*] vice of incest has been energetically increasing [*sehr im Schwung gehet*] among the common people, and because the penalty for such crimes in the territorial laws, police ordinance, and various mandates and decrees is not sufficient to deter people, indeed the penalty is scarcely given heed.[197]

These ubiquitous, despairing preambles are important, for they indicate that the ceaseless repetition of the mandates resulted more from their perceived failure than from early modern distribution and publication practices, "the transition from an oral to a written culture," or other reasons that scholars have adduced to explain the repetition of laws in the seventeenth and eighteenth centuries.[198]

Recurrent complaints in the mandates about the lethargy of local bureaucrats is another sign that failure was uppermost in the lawgivers' minds.[199] Despite such complaints, we should not imagine that only the central bureaucrats worried about the failure of sexual regulation. The bureaucratic correspondence shows that many central decrees resulted from local entreaties or inquiries, to which the higher levels of government merely responded by loosing another repetitive ordinance.[200] The perception of failure was thus certainly stronger at the central level of government, but by no means restricted to it.

At what did the authorities think they had failed? They had failed, first, literally to order sexual behavior, as the phrase "disorderly mixing" [*unordentliche Ver-*

---

[195] Mandate of 18 December 1624, GLA 74/3921.

[196] Mandate of 13 March 1754, GLA 74/3919.

[197] Ordinance of 11 June 1727, Bay HStA, GR 322/8.

[198] See Raeff's pithy discussion, *Well-Ordered Police State*, 51–54, and his citation on 52. Dorwart reads the evidence flatly as a uniform sign of administrative failure. *Prussian Welfare State*, 26, 27, 71, 73–75, 111, 295. See also Baur, *Kleiderordnungen*, 79–80, for methods the state used to publicize its laws.

[199] For complaints that local governments were not enforcing the regulations on sexual behavior, see the decree of 3 February 1629, and 14 March 1632, the mandate of 20 September 1635, and the decree of 1 June 1651 and 2 September 1651, in Bay HStA, GR 321/7.

[200] See, for instance, prosecutor and councillors (*Anwalt* und *Räthe*) of Munich to elector, 16 October 1643, relaying the request of the authorities at Amberg; court council memorandum of 4 August 1699, concerning a report from Schongau; Landshut authorities to the Kurfürstin, 4 March 1654, all in Bay HStA, GR 321/7.

mischungen] makes clear.[201] But they had failed to impose another kind of order, too, and that was the absolute, systematic, and reliable functioning of the bureaucratic hierarchy from top to bottom. Both sorts of disorder challenged the pretensions of the early modern state to divine origins and, from that, to total responsibility. In the course of the eighteenth century, the central state handled these two challenges separately, indeed almost oppositely. That is, it scaled back its responsibilities while making its machinery more efficient. The perception of failure, which sexual regulation exemplified especially well, encouraged eighteenth-century bureaucrats to engage in fundamental self-criticism, which finally led to a reconception of the proper relation of government to the governed.

[201] The authorities at Emmentingen to margrave, 28 March 1654, GLA 74/3919. The phrase referred to nonmarital sexual activity ("so ausserhalb der Ehe getrieben").

3

Rethinking Regulation,
1740–1800

In the course of the eighteenth century, the German territorial states slowly modified the absolutist pattern of sexual regulation. They did so hesitantly, often spurred on by local officials. And they did so almost solely in reference to women—the unwed pregnant mother. By century's end, sex-crime laws were significantly milder, but most officials still shrank from ending regulation altogether, though the logic of their piecemeal reforms led them inexorably in this direction. Nonetheless, by the 1790s officials had silently abandoned many of the central tenets of absolutist regulation and found themselves following the reform initiatives of the extra-governmental voices of civil society.

The Patterns of State Control in the Early Eighteenth Century

The first half of the eighteenth century saw the last efforts of the absolutist states to be truly absolute in their control over the (hetero)sexual behavior of their subjects. In addition to repeating the seventeenth-century ordinances, governments often modified them by substituting labor for monetary fines for poor people. That substitution characterized all eighteenth-century penal codes and had nothing to do with sexual crimes per se. However, some central governments also slightly sharpened their sex-crime laws, as Bavaria did in its last mammoth ordinance on the subject (11 June 1727) by adding public humiliation for the poor or "fresh," and harsher punishments for noble miscreants.[1] The authorities proclaimed that they were "determined . . . in future to punish with more earnestness and hardness than has been the case to date."[2] As that sentiment indicates, the thinking behind the

---

[1] Despite a few changes, the ordinance of 11 June 1727 basically repeated the punishments of 1635 as amended in 1654. Mayr, *Sammlung der . . . allgemeinen und besondern Landes-Verordnungen,* 3:116–22. Original in Bay HStA, GR 322/8. The famous Prussian edict of 8 February 1765 claimed to stiffen penalties, but did not. See the *Novum Corpus Constitutionum Prussico-Brandenburgensium praecipue Marchicarum, oder Neue Sammlung Königl. Preuß. und Churfürstl. Brandenburgischer, sonderlich in der Chur- und Marck-Brandenburg, Wie auch andern Provintzien, publicirten und ergangenen Ordnungen, Edicten, Mandaten, Rescriptien etc., et. Vom Anfang des Jahrs 1751 und folgenden Zeiten* (hereafter *NCC* by volume and column number) (Berlin, 1753–1806), vol. 3, col. 583.

[2] On penalties for noble adulterers see the ordinance of 11 June 1727, in Mayr, *Sammlung der . . . allgemeinen und besondern Landes-Verordnungen,* 3:118; for public humiliation see p. 123 n. 61, below.

ordinances remained the same: "Therefore [we announce these laws] so that our intended goal, staving off the wrath of God and establishing a good, honorable police, may be better achieved and may serve to warn and cause fear in all [our subjects]."

Territories known for their openness to Enlightenment innovation clung as tightly as others did to the absolutist presumption of control. Protestant Baden-Durlach, under the leadership of its famous Enlightened margrave Karl Friedrich (1746–1811),[3] abandoned the religious justification for controlling sexual behavior and stressed instead Enlightened government's concern for the "good of our dear subjects, the maintenance of good laws and order, as well as the elimination of harmful vices and abuses."[4] But he, too, was frustrated that government efforts were so unsuccessful. Thinking the cause might lie in the fines culprits preferred and regularly substituted for prison sentences, the margrave recommended in 1754 public work penalties instead. They combined the Enlightened absolutist state's fondness for squeezing gain from its subjects, and for inculcating industriousness generally, with its lingering faith in deterrence by "example." The principle of equal punishment for male and female offenders was not to be compromised, though the margrave understood that pregnancy or other physical disabilities peculiar to women might interfere with equal treatment.[5]

If the margrave had wanted to eradicate monetary fines, he failed, just as he failed in written statute at least, to halt the banishment of women convicted of fornication for the third time. He had hoped to find a workable substitute for banishment, which, as a female petitioner pointed out, drove Protestant women to seek shelter in neighboring Catholic lands at the cost of their forced religious conversion. The privy councillors, however, blocked legal reform because "these punishments have a judicious relation to one another" and changing one would require fiddling with the entire system of punishments.[6] They were also not unhappy to have the land "cleansed of such disreputable people." This moral judgment coincided with their unspoken financial interest in incurring no more expenses for bastard children, the same interest that disinclined them to give up monetary fines. In short, until after midcentury, princely attention to sex-crime legislation was limited to (unsuccessful) tinkering that never challenged the basic assumptions set down in the seventeenth century.

The central assumption, of course, was the undisputed interest of the prince or government in regulating sexual behavior. The constant reiteration of mandates and

---

[3] For the extent of Karl Friedrich's reputation, see Wolfgang Leiser, "Fürstenruhm und staatliche Integration: Geschichtsschreibung und Gesetzgebung unter Karl Friedrich von Baden," *Zeitschrift für die Geschichte des Oberrheins* 133 (1985): 211–20.

[4] Karl Friedrich, rescript of 13 March 1754, GLA 74/3919.

[5] "From now on also those women who, despite having committed this vice [fornication], have not become pregnant, or have aborted [their fetus], or have borne a dead child, and for whom all considerable grounds for meting out a less severe corporal punishment than for men do not exist, are to be condemned to exactly as many days in jail [*Thurn*] or at work as is usual for males." Ibid.

[6] Extract from the privy council (*Geheimer Rat*) meeting of 1 March 1755, GLA 74/3920.

the tinkering with penalties characteristic of the early eighteenth century show that this interest was undiminished in the early Enlightenment. Central governments continued to devote considerable attention to sexual regulation, though some princes were more active in this pursuit than others. One such was Margrave Ludwig Georg of Baden-Baden (1727–61). The first years of his reign (1707–27) were spent under the regency of his mother, Margravin Augusta Sybilla, a woman famous for both her baroque piety and her energy. Whether her religious convictions encouraged her son's later devotion to the cause of sexual propriety is unclear. It is noteworthy, however, that as late as 1760 officials still included the formulaic phrases about the "justified wrath of God" in Baden-Baden's sex-crime laws.[7] It is even more unusual in this period to find the monarch explain (in a 1743 rescript on fornication) that "We therefore recognize that We are bound and obligated by conscience to regulate such sinful and highly disturbing vices, especially since We have an inborn most sensitive and enormous repulsion for such things."[8]

Whatever his personal motives, Ludwig's zeal matched his aggravation. Ordinance followed upon ordinance,[9] while a detailed correspondence developed with the military authorities in the residence and garrison city Rastatt in the early 1750s. This flurry of activity was noteworthy for its new targets. The main focus of Ludwig's attention was not the rural population, as in most seventeenth-century edicts, but soldiers and their consorts. In order to escape pension costs and demands for higher pay and to increase mobility, Baden-Baden, like other German territories, had forbidden most ordinary soldiers from marrying. Consequently, their heterosexual activity, much of it apparently in the form of long-lasting monogamous relationships,[10] was illegal. The government labeled it "whoring," regardless of the character of the relationship or whether money exchanged hands. The military authorities of Baden-Baden meted out brutal beatings, and when those failed, they experimented with exile to unpopular garrisons. Their measures were sometimes cleared in advance with the privy council and margrave, who might change them slightly to accord with their own penal experiments, for example by adding or substituting public humiliation.[11] While the military concentrated on the

[handwritten margin note: will involv. in cex. regulation]

---

[7] Government "Projekt," 24 January 1760, GLA 74/3923.

[8] Rescript of 16 October 1743, GLA 74/3925.

[9] These ordinances were issued on 5 June 1737, 26 January 1741, 10 January 1742, 16 October and 12 November 1743, 11 February and 12 May 1745, 16 March and 5 April 1746, 1 July 1748, and 16 December 1749. Not all of these ordinances still exist in the archives, though they are mentioned in the ordinances of 1 July 1748 and 25 January 1754, GLA 74/3923. These and other sex-crime ordinances can be found in GLA 74/3923, 3925, 3929, and 3932.

[10] Oberamt Karlsruhe to Margrave Karl Friedrich, Karlsruhe, 7 March 1798, GLA 74/3926, which refers to the marriage-like living patterns of many soldiers in the Badenese army (which by 1798 included both Baden-Baden and Baden-Durlach).

[11] See Major Dreger to margrave, Rastatt, 24 January 1749; margrave to Major Dreger, 27 January 1749; von Dürheimb's memorandum, probably 1752; ordinance of 13 October 1752; margrave to Oberstleutnant Dreger, 7 December 1752; and ordinance of 30 July 1754; all in GLA 74/3923. Most of the earlier ordinances were also clearly aimed at soldiers.

men under its jurisdiction, the civil authorities and the margrave penned general ordinances targeting especially the pregnant female consorts of the soldiers.[12] Gender discrepancy thus entered statute and became more pronounced as exasperation created harder penalties for the women, and later, when the army silently gave up punishing soldier offenders altogether, yet the laws specifically mentioning women remained.[13]

A second pattern emerging from Ludwig of Baden-Baden's efforts to control his subjects' sexual behavior concerns his bureaucrats' refusal to reform the sexual laws in the ways he wanted. Their first refusal reflected the standard fiscal motives we have seen at the heart of absolutist sex-crime law. In 1746, Ludwig learned that the bishop of Speyer had replaced all fines for fornication with (equal) public humiliation ceremonies for male and female offenders. He wanted to introduce this experiment into the territories Speyer and Baden-Baden shared.[14] The councillors objected, since the money supporting foundlings came "solely and completely from these money fines." They even suggested raising the fines, but Ludwig overruled them and adopted the Speyer experiment.[15]

A few years later, in 1754, Ludwig's frustration at being unable to stem what he saw as the growing wave of fornication and "whoring" erupted in his demand for heightened penalties, especially against women. His central officials agreed to double the fornication fine (from fifteen to thirty gulden), but otherwise they merely repeating the old laws, which included men and thus they held the line against greater gender bias.[16] It is safe to say that Ludwig's bureaucrats produced a much less draconian piece of legislation than he wanted. In good Enlightened style, they hoped that wider publication of the old laws would bring better results.

Therefore, in 1754 the central officials of Baden-Baden clearly wanted to break the absolutist cycle of repetitions, threatened sharpenings of the law, and frustrated experiments with first one combination of penalties and then another. Their disenchantment with absolutist regulation was typical, for at about the same time other German territories also began to abandon the old prescriptions of absolutist control over sexual behavior.

The prospect of loosening controls occasioned much anxiety among princes, officials, and the self-appointed overseers of the social order among the growing educated bourgeoisie. Not surprisingly, reform was a gradual and ambivalent pro-

---

[12] See, for example, the ordinances of 5 June 1737, GLA 74/1925, and 10 January 1742, GLA 74/3923.

[13] Rescripts of 10 January 1742 and 1 July 1748, GLA 74/3923, and Oberamt Karlsruhe to margrave, 7 March 1798, GLA 74/3926. Cf. similar rescripts for Baden-Durlach: Karl Wilhelm, rescripts of 18 December 1732 and 17 December 1742, GLA 74/3926.

[14] The county of Eberstein (*Oberamt* Gernsbach) was jointly owned by Speyer and Baden-Baden until 1803. See Albert Krieger, *Topographisches Wörterbuch des Großherzogtums Baden* (Karlsruhe, 1898), 194.

[15] Margrave Ludwig to Regierung, 16 March 1746, Rastatt; Regierung to Margrave Ludwig 22 March 1746, Rastatt; Margrave Ludwig to Regierung, 26 March 1746, Rastatt, all in GLA 74/3925.

[16] Margrave Ludwig to Regierung, 9 January 1754, Rastatt, GLA 74/3929; Regierung to Margrave Ludwig, 25 January 1754, GLA 74/3923.

cess; it was accompanied by a long discussion preparing the way, arguing the pros and cons, predicting the future, assessing the past. As is often the case with fundamental shifts of this nature, the debate was less than completely straightforward. In most territories this discussion centered around a single offense, which then served as a metaphor for the sexual system and its legal ramifications as a whole, a metaphor permitting contemporaries to speculate about the social, biological, and psychological causes of sexual behavior and about the interaction among, and thus the proper relation of, state law, social custom, and the individual. The offense that served these purposes in the eighteenth century was infanticide.

The Infanticide Debate

The great German jurist Gustav Radbruch called infanticide the "key delict to all efforts at criminal law reform in the eighteenth century."[17] It was key not only because reformers used it widely to argue for abolishing the death penalty, but because infanticide was the crime that officials, legal reformers, and social critics used to discuss the pros and cons of sexual law reform generally. And sexual law reform, thought necessary to eliminate the causes of infanticide, was a major impetus for general reform of all criminal laws during the Enlightenment.

The infanticide debate was a peculiarly German phenomenon. Although infanticide was a subject of concern in all European countries during the eighteenth century, in no other place did it capture the attention of dramatists, novelists. and essayists as it did in Germany.[18] Indeed, in July 1780 over four hundred essayists responded to a prize invitation from the *Rheinische Beiträge zur Gelehrsamkeit* to answer the question, "What are the best and most practical means to prevent infanticide?" Even in a century that could barely contain its zeal to answer prize questions, this outpouring of interest was extraordinary.[19]

[17] Gustav Radbruch and Heinrich Gwinner, *Geschichte des Verbrechens* (Stuttgart, 1951), 242, cited in Wilhelm Wächtershäuser, *Das Verbrechen des Kindesmordes im Zeitalter der Aufklärung. Eine rechtsgeschichtliche Untersuchung der dogmatischen, prozessualen und rechtssoziologischen Aspekte* (Berlin, 1973), 28 n. 2.

[18] Ulbricht, *Kindsmord*. Belles lettres discovered the theme in the mid 1770s and developed it into a major motif of the *Sturm and Drang*. See J. M. Rameckers, *Der Kindermord in der Literatur der Sturm- und Drangperiode* (Rotterdam, 1927). Goethe seems to have been the first to have adopted the theme, in his *Faust* (written 1772–75); H. L. Wagner, J.M.R. Lenz, and Maler Müller wrote or published on infanticide in 1776; A. M. Sprickmann, in 1777; Schiller, in 1781; Lenz, again, in 1782; O. H. Freiherr von Gemmingen, in 1782; F. M. Klinger, in 1791. See the list in Rameckers, *Kindermord*, 4; also see Herbert A. Frenzel and Elisabeth Frenzel, *Daten deutscher Dichtung. Chronologischer Abriß der deutschen Literaturgeschichte*, 5th ed. (Munich, 1969), 1:200–229, and Horst Albert Glaser, "Drama des Sturm und Drang," in *Deutsche Literatur. Eine Sozialgeschichte*, ed. Glaser (Hamburg, 1980), 4:317–19, and the chronology, on 4:363–77.

[19] See the long list of non-belletristic writings on infanticide (with dates of publication) in Philipp Bopp, "Kindermord. Verheimlichung der Schwangerschaft und Geburt. Abtreibung der Leibesfrucht. Kinderaussetzung," in *Staats-Lexikon, oder Encyklopädie der Staatswissenschaft*, ed. Karl Rotteck and Carl Theodor Welcker (Altona, 1834–43), 9:253–55. This list begins with a work from 1778. See Ulbricht's careful discussion of the debate in *Kindsmord*, 217–328.

Why did infanticide strike such a social nerve at this time? Most contemporary commentators (and many later historians) claimed that the incidence of infanticide rose to worrisome heights throughout the century, prompting this public response. In his social history of infanticide in eighteenth-century Schleswig-Holstein, Otto Ulbricht shows that such a precipitate rise has never been demonstrated and is unlikely; furthermore, he demonstrates that the actual infanticide rate seems to have remained relatively low.[20] It is also questionable whether concern for the infants' lives was as paramount as the verbiage suggests. Little was done to lower the appallingly high rate of infant mortality generally, and most people continued to believe that illegitimate children were less "useful" to state, society, and economy than legitimate ones. The pedagogue Heinrich Pestalozzi even claimed that the state was secretly happy to be rid of such troublesome infants.[21] One need not go this far to wonder why infanticide should have seemed more important than the great swell of infant deaths due to other causes. The preoccupation was not with death but with a form of life. There was in the last third of the century a recognized rise in illegitimate births, which both contemporaries and the law identified as the necessary and proximate cause of infanticide. Illegitimacy, the product of disorderly sexual behavior, was from the beginning the core of the infanticide debate,[22] which went on to discuss the full range of sexual topics from the nature of the sexual drive to relations between men and women, to marriage, to the biological exigencies of pregnancy, to the relation between sexual behavior and the social order, to the limits of the state's duty to regulate sexual behavior. The utility of such a debate in a period of social reorganization is clear, and I return to it in Chapters 6 and 7.

The uses to which the infanticide debate were put might be quite different from the reasons it began in the first place, but our interest here is in any event utilitarian: how professed concern over that delict pressured officials to lighten (or abolish) fornication penalties. The outpouring of ink on infanticide in the late 1770s and 1780s has created the impression that public debate caused the legal changes. Wilhelm Wächtershäuser's influential study of infanticide and the law in eighteenth-century Germany states that legal reform must "be ascribed mainly to the influence of the extralegal literature."[23] Besides the rejection of the death penalty, spurred by the Italian lawyer Cesare Beccaria[24] but championed as well by

---

[20] Ulbricht, *Kindsmord,* 176–88.

[21] *Über Gesetzgebung und Kindermord. Wahrheiten und Träume, Nachforschungen und Bilder,* in *Heinrich Pestalozzi; Werke . . . Gedenkausgabe zu seinem zweihundertsten Geburtstage,* ed. Paul Baumgartner (Erlenbach, 1944–49), 4:382–83.

[22] "The only theoretical question that was always handled [by the contestants in the 1780 prize contest] was whether one had to fear negative consequences in the realm of morality [*Sittlichkeit*], that is, whether the suggested means [to end infanticide] would lead to more 'whoring' [*Hurerei*]." Ulbricht, *Kindsmord,* 231.

[23] *Das Verbrechen,* 144.

[24] Cesare Beccaria, *On Crimes and Punishment,* was published in 1764 but not translated into German until 1778, when it was published under the title *Des Herrn Marquis von Beccaria unsterbliches Werk von Verbrechen und Strafen. Auf das Neue selbst aus dem Italiänischen übersetzt mit durchgängigen Anmerkungen des Ordinarius zu Leipzig Herrn Hofrath Hommels* (Breslau, 1778). For the relation between the death

Enlightened writers generally, a new emphasis on the criminal and his or her psychological motivations or intent underlay the call for legal reform. Nonlawyers, mostly bourgeois writers and social observers, were responsible for the new interest in psychology, which, Wächtershäuser claims, was the heart of the matter.

The burden of this mountain of extralegal prose was that women committed infanticide to escape the shame of giving birth out of wedlock. The writers imagined that young women gave in to the importunings of their suitors out of love, were then cynically abandoned, and, facing the penalties of public humiliation called for by law, knowing that this shame would ruin their chances to marry and lead honorable lives, suffering the psychological and physical infirmities of pregnancy and childbirth, in desperation were driven to commit murder. The writers sympathized with the women and censured the perfidious fathers, hypocritical society (upholder of the sexual double standard), and injudicious law. The law, they felt, was especially to blame, because it enshrined male sexual dominance and, far from deterring crime, actually caused it. They recommended removing humiliating penalties for fornication (proof of which was the birth of a bastard child), as well as a series of other reform measures. In the end, they succeeded in making infanticide a "privileged" delict.[25] In the process of doing so they also undermined the bedrock on which rested the laws punishing fornication and, by extension, other consensual heterosexual acts.[26]

Because Wächtershäuser and other scholars have examined the infanticide debate either as an isolated curiosity or against the backdrop of belles lettres, they have missed its significance for the reform of sexual legislation and they have misidentified Enlightened, bourgeois public opinion as the lever moving the state to reform. Long before extragovernmental voices discovered the issue, state officials, often beginning at its lowest judicial levels, struggled against the legal fetters forged by both infanticide and fornication legislation. A brief look at the legal developments will clarify why infanticide was so mixed up with fornication.

Originally, infanticide was a species of kin murder that could only be committed by a woman. By 1532, in the criminal code of Charles V for the Holy Roman Empire, the crime had acquired some leeway for acquittal in cases where the woman claimed the child had been born dead. The indices of suspicion were carefully laid out and room left for alibi and the testimony of (presumably medical) experts.[27] Such punctiliousness not only cleared a path to acquittal, it also revealed another trend: toward confining the delict to unmarried mothers. Only they would have the

---

penalty debate and infanticide, see Manfred Schwarz, *Wechselnde Beurteilung von Straftaten in Kultur und Recht*, vol. 1, *Die Kindestötung* (Berlin, 1935), 76–83, and Ulbricht, *Kindsmord*, 307–13.

[25] Wächtershäuser, *Das Verbrechen*, 146.

[26] Perhaps because of their focus, Wächtershäuser (decidedly) and Schwarz (hesitantly) both write that little actual change occured in sexual legislation as a direct result of the infanticide debate. Wächtershäuser, *Das Verbrechen*, 125–37; Schwarz, *Kindestötung*, 94–104.

[27] Paragraph 131 of *Die Peinliche Gerichtsordnung Kaiser Karls V. von 1532*, ed. Gustav Radbruch (Stuttgart, 1975). Wächtershäuser, *Das Verbrechen*, 23, also noted these changes, though he does not interpret them as indicating a long trend toward "privileging" infanticide.

social reasons to hide the pregnancy and birth, which the law viewed as the incriminating circumstances that virtually defined the crime. During the next two hundred years this trend continued until, if statutes did not declare outright that infanticide was a crime limited to unwed mothers, the courts operated according to this assumption in practice.[28] Infanticide was thus, for the law, a by-product of fornication. As a Bavarian decree of 1629 complained: "Many single women have been seen running around pregnant, who then disappear and lose themselves, so that one cannot know what has happened to the fruit of their body, whether it has not been killed and hidden."[29]

Whereas the fornication ordinances tried (and failed) to halt the necessary first cause of infanticide (illegitimate conception),[30] the seventeenth- and eighteenth-century laws focused on the pregnant, single woman who might be tempted to murder. Befitting the absolutist faith in threatened coercion, the laws sternly declared that single, pregnant women who hid their pregnancies and childbirth, and whose newborns were then discovered dead, would automatically, regardless of circumstance, be presumed to have committed infanticide and condemned to death.[31] Since the only witness to infanticide was generally the mother, the law burdened her with the responsibility of reporting her pregnancy (and thus her fornication) to the authorities. The letter of the laws was harsh and ringed the

---

[28] Among those statutes explicitly defining infanticide as a delict committed by unwed mothers are Hamburg, 1724, in J. Klefeker, *Sammlung der Hamburgische Gesetze und Verfassungen in Bürger- und kirchlichen, auch Cammer-Handlungs- und übrigen Policey-Angelegenheiten und Geschäften somit historischen Einleitungen* (Hamburg, 1765–73), part 5 (1768), 504; Bavaria, 7 April 1728, 29 December 1738, 14 December 1793, in Bay HStA, GR 1187/58; Palatinate, 28 June 1703, 18 February 1726, 5 November 1734, 19 December 1736, and so on, in GLA 77/6491; Prussia, 8 August 1720 and 22 November 1723, in Christian Otto Mylius, ed., *Corpus constitutionem Marchicarum, oder Königl. Preußis. und Churfürst. Brandenburgische. . . . Ordnungen, Edicta, Mandata, Rescripta, etc. Von Zeiten Friedrichs I . . . biss ietzo unter der Regierung Friedrich Wilhelms . . . an annum 1736* (hereafter *CCM*), 6 vols. in 8 (Berlin, 1737–51), II Theil, III. Abteilung, Spalten 121–24, 131–34. Kreittmayr's Code of 1751 does not specify single mothers but already mentions the putative motive that only they could have: "Weibs-Personen, welche ihre Leibs-Frucht aus Furcht der Schand und Straff mit Fleiß in der Geburt ersticken . . . ," and so on, Kreittmayr, *Codex Juris Bavarici Criminalis*, "Capitul" 3, par. 19, p. 21. See Schwarz, *Kindestötung*, 4–22, for this restrictive definition of the delict. Married mothers who murdered their infants fell under the statute pertaining to the murder of relatives.

[29] Bavarian decree of 3 February 1629, Bay HStA, GR 321/7.

[30] The actual social, economic, and other causes of infanticide in eighteenth-century Germany are sensitively analyzed in Ulbricht, *Kindsmord*, 92–174.

[31] Schwarz, *Kindestötung*, 18–19, lists the first such ordinance as a Württemberg edict of 1 March 1658. The first such Bavarian law I have uncovered dates from 21 May 1684, repeated again (with 3,000 copies) in 7 April 1728, in 21 February 1739, inscribed in Kreittmayr's 1751 codification (Cap. 3, para. 21), and repeated once more on 14 December 1793. See for Bavaria Bay HStA, GR 1187/58, and Mayr, *Sammlung der . . . allgemeinen und besondern Landes-Verordnungen*, 3:112–15 and 5:30; for the Palatinate, 3 August 1702, 18 February 1726 (renewed in 1734 and 1739), see GLA 77/6491; for Baden-Baden, 16 October 1749, see GLA 74/3929, and for 11 February 1754 and 28 July 1758, see GLA 74/3923. See also Ulbricht, *Kindsmord*, 240–44 and 338–54, for a summary of infanticide legislation; Bartz, "Ueber die Strafbarkeit der verheimlichten Schwangerschaft und Geburt," in *Archiv des Criminalrechts* (Halle) 6.2 (1805): 63–84, and Carl Joseph Anton Mittermaier, "Beyträge zur Lehre vom Verbrechen des Kindermords und der Verheimlichung der Schwangerschaft," in *Neues Archiv des Criminalrechts* (Halle) 7.1 (1824): 1–45; 7.2 (1825): 304–27; 7.3 (1825): 493–522.

woman with penalties: public humiliation for admitted fornication, death if she tried to escape the pregnancy that proved her guilt. This harshness was also a straitjacket for the authorities who had to apply the law, and long before the public criticism of these laws became commonplace in the 1770s and 1780s, judicial officials at the local and central levels had begun to try to wriggle out of their difficult position. They interpreted the demands of evidence overly strictly, they misinterpreted harsh statutes in a milder light, they adduced honorable excuses for not reporting out-of-wedlock pregnancies, they acquitted women on technicalities, they petitioned the ruler for clemency.[32] Case-by-case they tried to make principled statute more congruent with women's actual behavior and circumstances. Practical judicial leniency gained momentum as the century advanced, especially once the public debate began.[33]

Judges and magistrates began to press for the removal of the state-sponsored shame they thought drove women to commit infanticide,[34] that is to reform the fornication laws or abolish them entirely. In the long term, by the mid-nineteenth century, fornication was decriminalized in virtually all German states.[35] This

---

[32] The 1684 Bavarian ordinance caused skirmishes between the local authorities, mediated and supported by the central government, and the Kurfürst almost from its inception and for ninety years thereafter. See the decrees of 12 December 1687, 7 April 1728, 29 December 1738, and 23 June 1774 in Mayr, *Sammlung der . . . allgemeinen und besondern Landes-Verordnungen*, 3:114–15. Schwarz, *Kindestötung*, 35–36, interprets these documents as evidence of the law's harshness, thus missing the bureaucracy's resistance to the law, which is what necessitated the other decrees. See also Wächtershäuser, *Das Verbrechen*, 68–69, on Bavaria. In 1757 the court council of Baden-Baden explained to Margrave Ludwig Georg how a woman might mistake her pregnancy or hide it for honorable reasons: Regierung to margrave, 23 February 1757, GLA 74/3929. They used reasons that Thomasius had already honed in 1681 (first published in 1720) as a consultant in an infanticide case. Christian Thomasius, *Ernsthaffte/aber doch Muntere und Vernünfftige Gedanken u. Errinnerungen über allerhand außerlesene Juristische Händel* (Halle, 1720), part 1, 59–60.

[33] Ulbricht's detailed study of Schleswig-Holstein has found this pattern there, where local courts consistently petitioned for lesser penalties for convicted child murderers. Ulbricht dates this trend from 1770, but several of the cases he cites date to the 1760s. *Kindsmord*, 338–39, 359–65. For other examples of courts avoiding the death penalty see Wächtershäuser, *Das Verbrechen*, 73–79, 98.

[34] Whether shame was truly the motive behind infanticide in the eighteenth century is unclear. Even if it was, it is probable that the publicists, officials, and unwed pregnant women each had different conceptions of shame and honor. In actual court cases shame was rarely adduced as a motive by the accused, nor did it appear in the official judgments. See the discussion in Ulbricht, *Kindsmord*, 161–73. For court judgments, see Wächtershäuser, *Das Verbrechen*, 100–101.

[35] Fornication was entirely decriminalized in Prussia (1765 for pregnant women, 1794 generally); Schleswig-Holstein (1772, revoked in 1772, and reintroduced in 1857); Hannover (1772 in a draft reform code, for first- and second-time fornication in 1824, altogether by 1840); Saxe-Weimar (1786 for women, men received a small fine); Anhalt-Bernburg (1799); Baden (1813 for pregnant women, 1820 for all); Bavaria (by ordinance 1808, in criminal code 1813); and Hesse (1821). Penalties for fornication were mitigated, bringing them more in line with actual judicial practice in Baden-Durlach (1761); Baden (1773, 1781); Altenburg (12 May 1741, slightly); Austria (1769, women to be punished secretly and mildly); Bavaria (1780); Saxe-Weimar (1781); Schleswig-Holstein (1798). Württemberg was one of the last major territories to abolish fornication penalties. It had gradually replaced prison with money fines and reduced these, on 31 January 1795, 31 July 1806, and 22 July 1836, but it did not abolish them from the criminal code altogther until 1 March 1839. See Schwarz, *Kindestötung*, 96, 102–4; Ulbricht, *Kindsmord*, 319–20; Wächtershäuser, *Das Verbrechen*, 125–37; Friedrich Thudichum, *Ueber unzulässige Beschränkungen des Rechts der Verehelichung* (Tübingen, 1866), 141–42; Wilhelm Ebel, ed., *Friedrich*

[handwritten marginalia: "b&k" of "private" sphere"]

change tended to spread by analogy to decriminalize other consensual sexual acts as well. These developments freed a sphere of sexual behavior from the grasp of state regulation and placed it under the responsibility of the individual and/or society at large. This achievement was a difficult one, however, since states relinquished their pretense to regulation only reluctantly. Thus, for a longer or shorter time depending on the state, statute might remain absolutist, while judicial practice and social and bureaucratic pressure mounted to temper the laws or abolish them entirely. The exact nature of bureaucratic ambivalence, the arguments officials used successfully for reform, the arguments opponents used to retard reform, and the assumptions behind the officials' actions reward a closer look at these first steps toward regulating sexual behavior in a "modern" way. There were three ways a state might respond to the pressure for reform: radically, by eliminating fornication penalties altogether; stubbornly, by permitting no reform at all; or hesitantly, by moving incrementally toward but not attaining radical reform. It should come as no surprise that the first steps were hesitant, and it is to these that we now turn.

Pre-Debate Reform Attempts in Baden

By the 1730s, a generation or more before the public debate on infanticide in the 1780s, the argument that shaming penalties for fornication caused infanticide and should therefore be abolished was already being heard in some areas. Wächtershäuser cites the case of the elector of Saxony who in 1732 wanted to reintroduce the *Kirchenbuße* for fornication. The Protestant Church Konsistorium in Wittenberg advised against this, citing as its first objection the danger of infanticide.[36] In 1739 Elector Karl Philipp of the Palatinate, at the behest of his court council, inaugurated a course that many other governments emulated later. He decreed "when in future a wench [*Dirne*] either from human weakness or seduction allows herself to become infatuated and pregnant (which, however, she should guard against), but reports her pregnancy to the local authorities in time, one should handle her more mildly, keeping in mind the possibility of restoring her honor either through later marriage or in some other way."[37]

This edict shows a number of interesting tendencies. Although it retained the word "Dirne," which contemporaries used indiscriminately to mean "prostitute," as well as (sexually) loose woman, it removed the opprobrium formerly attached to her by defining her motive as "human weakness" (not *female* weakness, as the early nineteenth century was inclined to do) and redefining her as the victim of male seduction. It acknowledged that she did "allow herself to become infatuated and

Esajas Pufendorfs Entwurf eines hannoverschen Landrechts (vom Jahre 1772) (Hildesheim, 1970); *Sammlung der Gesetze, Verordnungen und Ausschreibungen für das Königreich Hannover vom Jahre 1824* (Hannover, 1824); and *Das Strafgesetzbuch für das Königreich Württemberg vom 1. März 1839*, ed. Otto Schwab (Stuttgart, 1849).

36 Wächtershäuser, *Das Verbrechen*, 130.

37 Hofrat to Churfürst, Mannheim, 21 November 1739, and decree of 12 December 1739, both in GLA 77/6491.

pregnant" but abandoned the undifferentiated censure that used to attach to the act
of fornication for an emphasis rather on the person who committed the act. The
concept "human weakness" seems balanced between the religious idea of original
sin, which was capacious enough to imagine that even children might experience
sexual temptation[38] and the idea of an almost irresistible sexual drive, which contemporaries would debate toward the end of the century. The Palatine edict of 1739
also shows an increased practical interest in encouraging the (re)integration of the
woman into society, that is, into marriage, which was a much cheaper and more
satisfactory outcome than blocking this avenue via a shaming penalty and con-
demning her and her illegitimate child to the local welfare rolls and/or to further
illegal activity, such as begging or prostitution. In short, the government wanted to
encourage a productive social, not an ethical or legal, solution to the problem. Many
early absolutist laws had granted reduced fornication penalties to couples who
agreed to marry,[39] so it cannot be said that the states ever had entirely ignored the
cheaper, social outcome, but they came to stress this more regularly in the course of
the eighteenth century.[40] Similarly, the 1739 edict and the row of edicts on infanticide preceding and following it all tried to share the burden of prevention (via
spying and reporting on possibly pregnant women) with the parents, employers of
servants, and any other knowledgeable persons, on penalty of punishment if they
refused to do so.[41] This tacit acknowledgement that officials actually could not
oversee unwed pregnancies by themselves helped lead to the conclusion that *only*
society could effectively police morals.

The arguments in the 1739 Palatine edict formed the standard repertory that
bureaucrats elsewhere repeated and elaborated in their territories, though most of
them hesitated to take them to their ultimate conclusion, that is, the abandonment
of legal penalties for fornication. The court council's "Projekt" for reforming the
sex-crime laws of Baden-Baden in 1760 is a splendid example of both the powerful
attraction and the anxiety that Enlightened ideas exercised on central state officials.
We have seen how Ludwig's personal interest in the sexual propriety of his subjects
had spurred his government to energetic measures that by the 1750s, had put the
judiciary in the unrealistic position of demanding a thirty gulden fine for fornication (which was twice the customary penalty in effect at the beginning of the

[38] See, for example, a rescript from the bishop of Speyer, 5 May 1743, GLA 74/4521, in which he
admonishes parents not to engage in sexual acts in the presence of their children, but instead "to lead
your children in their tender years on the path of the commandments of God and to prevent your own
sensuality and bad example from pulling them into illegal and vicious habits."

[39] For example, Bavarian ordinance of 2 September 1651 and the Baden-Baden ordinance of 24
January 1760, GLA 74/3923. The (lower) fine for *früher Beischlaf* expressed the state's interest in
channeling illegitimacy into marriage.

[40] Ulbricht, *Kindsmord*, 379–85, has found that local courts of Schleswig-Holstein were only too
happy to encourage the petitions of imprisoned child-murderers who sought early release on the
grounds that some man had offered to marry them.

[41] See GLA 77/6491 for the Palatine edicts of 18 February 1726, 8 February 1732, 5 November 1734,
20 November 1735, 23 August 1741, 10 October 1747, 14 April 1750, 13 July 1753, 9 July 1760, and 9
April 1767.

century) and, worse, a sharp, corporal punishment for women who kept their pregnancies hidden.[42] The councillors, who were also the judicial instance of last appeal, used specific cases to argue "repeatedly," as Margrave Ludwig complained, "that the criminal penalties are too hard and in one or another cases require explication."[43] The councillors were especially interested in lowering the fornication fine for couples who married and in exempting women who became pregnant after a promise of marriage or who actually did then marry, from the draconian penalties facing women who hid their pregnancies.[44] Ludwig rightfully pointed out that such a loophole would "if not entirely, certainly in the majority of cases nullify the edict."[45] With the margrave's objections well in mind, the councillors produced the "Projekt" of 24 January 1760 to reform all the sex-crime legislation.[46] Their cover letter to Ludwig stressed that they had reached their conclusions only after "repeated deliberation."

> From the very first, we must obediently remark that, as disgraceful as simple fornication is, and as much as it angers the Almighty, still it is a principle of most civilized peoples that it can only be lessened by limiting the opportunities for it, but in no wise can it be annihilated by the sharpness of the legal penalties attached to it. . . . . It is certainly true that, unfortunately!, all too much disorder comes from out-of-wedlock intercourse, among which abortion and the killing of the womb's fruit [infanticide] are the most regrettable. Both could most quickly be disposed of if it could be brought about that the unfortunate woman, after she had not shied away from secret sin, would report her pregnancy to the authorities.
>
> However! Your Excellency, reporting oneself to the secular authorities, and subjecting oneself to punishment and public chastisement seems to surpass general human weakness [*die gemeine menschliche Schwachheit*] too much to be demanded by a general law. . . . We know of no territory in Germany where such a strict law is actually applied [*in vigore*].

As the most recent legal authority they approvingly cited the Bavarian codifier Kreittmayr, who

> found it too difficult to oblige a woman [*Weibsbild*], [at the cost of] her great dishonor and prostitution [*Schand und prostitution*], to report a pregnancy before its time, which often without her own guilt can end through sickness or otherwise. In addition [to Kreittmayr's observation], the confusions of such a woman [*Weibspersohn*], who has just begun to notice her pregnancy, and who envisions the loss of her public honor [*äuserlichen Ehre*], the public chastisement, the often hard behavior of her parents, and other negative results of her premature sensuality [*übereilten Sinnlichkeit*], are usually too mighty to overcome the natural public sense of shame [*natürliche äußerliche Schamhaftigkeit*] and fear and permit her to decide to report herself to the court for having committed vice. Experience

[42] Regierung to Margrave Ludwig, 25 January 1754, and edict of 8 March 1757, referred to in Regierung to Margrave Ludwig, 7 March 1758, GLA 74/3923.

[43] Margrave Ludwig to Regierung, 14 November 1759, GLA 74/3923.

[44] Regierung to Margrave Ludwig, 7 March 1758, and Margrave Ludwig to Regierung, 14 November 1759, GLA 74/3923.

[45] Margrave Ludwig to Regierung, 14 November 1759, GLA 74/3923.

[46] Regierung to Margrave Ludwig, 24 January 1760 (covering letter) and "Projekt" of same date, GLA 74/3923.

and the cases that have already arisen all confirm . . . that the greatest number of those women who will become impregnated in the future will either have to be whipped [*fustigiret*—and thus shamed], or the penal sanction will remain unexecuted and without effect, in both cases however, one must fear much disorder and evil results.

Here the central bureaucrats of Baden-Baden made a purely formal obeisance to religious scruple before embracing the Enlightened maxim that only prevention, not punishment, could stop crimes of the flesh. Religion echoes briefly in the word "sin" (*sündigen*), but the rest of the arguments are secular, psychological, and practical. As in the Palatinate, they assumed a "general human" (not specifically female) "weakness," of which any useful law must take account. They imagined the psychological terror the young woman must feel as she contemplates her future. The origins of that terror were legal/social (public loss of her honor) and familial/ interpersonal (the disapproval of her parents and the loss of their physical support). The officials did not yet think of pregnancy as an illness with negative psychological effects of its own. The impulses moving the woman to deny her pregnancy were honorable ("natural sense of shame") or at least understandably human ("fear"). It may be that part of this psychological portrait came from the testimony of female appellants ("experience and the cases that have already arisen"), who themselves may have tailored their declarations to suit the expectations of judges.[47] It is clear, however, that this new interest in the psychological state of the defendant demanded that the bureaucrats try to put themselves into her place and, given the gender, age, and, usually, the *Stand* differences in separating them, this process was marked less by accuracy than projection, as we shall see. In this case it is noteworthy that the only authority the councillors cited for their psychological musing was their fellow legal official, Kreittmayr.

In addition to the psychological arguments, these officials produced practical reasons to abandon the absolutist terror penalties. If these were actually followed, the women were shamed for life, they thought, with the implication that they were thus lost to society. More likely, they felt, the penalties would not be applied, and law as a principle would be undermined. Neither alternative was desirable. It was much better to restrict severe punishments to the few women who seemed especially likely to commit abortion or infanticide and to entice the rest to report their pregnancies by reducing the fine for fornication, "insofar as partly the hope of getting a reduced fine may often work better than a high one." The purpose of law was thus not to frighten through empty threats, but to be systematically workable in the real world. Anything less undermined state authority.

Given these arguments, it is at first glance surprising that the councillors did not recommend outright abolition of fornication penalties, or at the very least, public humiliation for women. Clearly one great hindrance to such a logical step was the opposition they (correctly) anticipated from the margrave. But it is also unlikely

---

[47] Ulbricht, *Kindsmord*, 162, notes how quickly female defendants learned to recite the litany of motives that would have the greatest positive effect on the judicial authorities.

gradually & control

that they would have felt comfortable leaping from the pretense of total control to none at all. Instead, they created a loophole designed to let most female (and male) delinquents pay the older, lower fine (fifteen gulden) and escape public humiliation altogether. They did this by keeping the outline of the law as the margrave wanted it and adding to it a provision that if a promise of marriage had occurred, or if one or both parties married (not necessarily to each other), then they would pay half the usual penalty, the man would be sentenced to two-months at public works and the woman would be spared public humiliation. A woman reporting to the authorities her illegitimate pregnancy before the seventh month would be treated similarly.[48] This created by fiat two categories of delinquents: "loose" sinners acting from base motives, and "honest" folk striving (if ineptly) after marriage. Those who still felt it was the state's duty to enforce Christian morality could be mollified that the old laws were still on the books, but the vast majority of delinquents (as the margrave had pointed out the previous year) would be handled in a modern manner.[49] Finally, it should not go unremarked that all this reforming was done primarily with (pregnant) women in mind; thinking about male delinquents and their penalties was more or less after the fact and by analogy.

If the reforming bureaucrats imagined that this clever scheme of inscribed ambivalence would ensure passage of the legislation, they were met with a less clever, but nonetheless effective parry by the margrave. He approved the new law(s), "but at the moment [I] have held back from publishing them and making them official," though he circulated them to the various local government officials.[50] Not surprisingly, this hesitation caused "in one or another cases much trouble," as the

---

[48] The exact penalties were for first-time fornication, a thirty gulden fine for each, or if too poor (as most of the population was), two months at public works for the man (*Schantz-Arbeit*) and public humiliation outside the church for the woman. Male second offenders received both penalties doubled; female second offenders, double the fine plus public humiliation, or if poor, only public humiliation but in a sharpened form (pulling the garbage cart through town and wearing a shaming sign, rather than merely standing outside the church in a straw hat holding a burning candle). Third offenders would receive unspecified corporal punishment or banishment. After a promise of marriage, the fine was reduced to fifteen gulden for each. Men were also sentenced to one month's public work; women, to a work penalty or confinement (*Einthurmung*).

[49] The margrave was surely right that most women would claim a promise of marriage had preceded (and legitimized) their sexual relations. Ulbricht, *Kindsmord*, 86–87, found that 82 percent of the accused child murderers in Schleswig-Holstein in the eighteenth century claimed just that. He is inclined to believe them, since their social profile is the same as that of illegitimate mothers in general, whose sexual experience seems usually to have begun in this fashion. Other, scattered statistics show the same pattern: Cissie Fairchilds, "Female Sexual Attitudes," 177, found the number to be 80 percent (until 1750); Carola Lipp, "Dörfliche Formen generativer und sozialer Reproduktion," in Wolfgang Kaschuba and Carola Lipp, *Dörfliches Überleben. Zur Geschichte materieller und sozialer Reproduktion ländlicher Gesellschaft im 19. und frühen 20. Jahrhundert*, (Tübingen, 1982), 409, found it to be 75 percent (mid-nineteenth-century Württemberg); Herma Klar, "Verbrechen aus verlorener Ehre? Kindmörderinnen. Eine Untersuchung aufgrund von material aus der ländlichen Unterschicht Nordwürttembergs im 19. Jahrhundert" (master's thesis, Universität Tübingen, 1984), argues a much lower figure of 9 percent, based on a small sample of 11. See the discussion in Ulbricht, *Kindsmord*, 76–77, 84–92.

[50] Ludwig von Baden Generale, 12 February 1760, GLA 74/3923.

councillors noted the following year, when they again urged the margrave to publish the laws.[51] Alas, he could bring himself to do nothing more than to direct the local officials to follow the new laws, especially on his royal domains, but he still refused general publication. In the same directive he could not refrain from ordering the officials in Rastatt to remove the "loose [*liederlichen*], unemployed riff-raff," who, presumably, were the main culprits in fornication cases there. That is, Ludwig could not order a softening of the law with one hand without cracking down with the other. This was the confused state of written legislation in Baden-Baden when it was taken over by Baden-Durlach in 1771.[52]

When the new authorities, especially the new treasury officials eager to collect fines, tried to sort out the situation in Baden-Baden, they discovered that actual practice varied from place to place. In at least several areas (named in the surviving documents are the counties [*Oberämter*] of Gernsbach and Ebenstein and the city of Ettlingen) local officials had established the loophole as the general rule, that is, all delinquents received half the fornication penalty, and then by analogy they went on to allow those who married later to pay only half of that (that is, one-quarter of what the statute called for).[53] This is a clear indication of the pressure in the localities to adopt lower penalties. This trend appeared so well established to the privy council of the new state of Baden, that it let the (illegal) practice continue.[54]

In 1779, the year before the *Rheinische Beiträge* published its essay prize announcement, the Badenese government began to consider systematically infanticide and the delicts related to it. The impetus, again, came from below in the form of a case involving "the unfortunate [Magdalena] Niederhaltin," whose life the city governor of Durlach (*Amtsmann*) Johann Friedrich Posselt wished to save.[55] His efforts unleashed several years of questionnaires and governmental discussions. Although this activity centered around the advisability of abolishing the death penalty for infanticide and the official questionnaires sent to each *Amt* and *Specialat* (church district) focused exclusively on that issue, fornication punishments inevitably were drawn into the discussion. Many official respondents expressed their opinions on whether fornication should continue to be punished, and Court Councillor J. N. Brauer, who later became the chief architect of Baden's laws during the

---

[51] Regierung to Margrave Ludwig, 10 April 1761, GLA 74/3923.

[52] Baden-Durlach's own fornication laws had undergone an ambivalent relaxation in 1761 when the margrave canceled the provision that second time female offenders would be shamed by dragging the "whore's cart" (*Hurenkarren*) through town. This did not abolish shaming penalties altogether, however, since poor women unable to pay the fine for their first offense, might still be condemned to a tour with the whore's cart. See Paul Lenel, *Badens Rechtsverwaltung und Rechtsverfassung unter Markgraf Karl Friedrich, 1738–1803* (Karlsruhe, 1913), 180–81, 181 n. 331.

[53] See, in GLA 74/3932, Heydecker memorandum, Karlsruhe, 3 August 1773; treasury (*Rentkammer*) memorandum, Karlsruhe, 1 September 1775; and court council (*Hofrat*) protocol of 23 November 1775.

[54] Court council protocol of 30 November 1775, GLA 74/3932.

[55] Memorandum of Hofrath Posselt, Durlach, 2 August 1779, and his covering letter of 2 November 1779, in GLA 74/3902. See Lenel, *Badens Rechtsverwaltung*, 187–95, for a discussion of the legal effects of Posselt's efforts on the death penalty and legal reform.

Napoleonic reform period, remembered the discussions and the mass of material that poured in as having been about reform of the fornication statutes as much as about infanticide.[56] No wonder, since a hesitant moderation of the former was all that emerged from all the exertion. Whereas opinions about the death penalty differed wildly and seemed to cancel one another out,[57] most reporters who mentioned the subject favored relaxing or abolishing fornication penalties, especially for women, and most especially for women who reported their pregnancies or delivered live children. Church authorities were particularly eloquent in championing this view.[58] Consequently, in October 1781 the lower penalties in Baden-Baden were confirmed and the Baden-Durlach regulations reformed in the same direction in December.[59] The precedent set for the pregnant female fornicant quickly became the model for men and for similar (hetero)sexual offenses. Four years later the male fornicant who reported his lover's pregnancy received the same dispensation, and the following year (1786) the benefit spread by legal analogy to male and female adulterers.[60]

---

[56] Brauer memorandum, 17 May 1799, GLA 74/3920.

[57] Lenel, *Badens Rechtsverwaltung*, 194.

[58] The following reports favored some reform of fornication statutes: in GLA 74/3902, Posselt's covering letter of 2 November 1779; extract of the royal church council (*Kirchenrat*) protocols, 3 December 1779; Report from OAmt Rastatt, 13 November 1779; essay "Honor and Shame," by Schwarzenau [?], a member of the church consistory, 1779; OAmt Karlsruhe, 14 December 1781; report of Carl W.L.F. Drais von Sauerbronn (member of the church consistory and court councillor and appellate judge [*Geh. Reg. Oberhofrichter*]), Karlsruhe, 20 November 1779; Privy Councillor and Court Chaplain (*Oberhofprediger*) Johann Leonhard Walz, Karlsruhe, 17 November 1779; Privy Councillors Friedrich Wilhelm Preuschen and Christoph Wohnlich, Karlsruhe, 29 September 1785; OAmt Ettlingen, 29 November 1781; Amt Bühl, 21 November 1781; in GLA 74/3903, Amt Birkenfeld, 6 December 1781; Amt Winterburg, 14 December 1781; Spezialat Pforzheim, 20 December 1781—for ending Kirchenbuße only; Spezialat Rötteln, Lörrach, 14 December 1781. Although many respondents favored penalizing male fornicants harder, none favored raising *Unzucht* penalties generally. Johann Georg Schlosser (OAmt Hochberg), 7 January 1782, felt fornication fines were irrelevant to infanticide; the OAmt Pforzheim, 11 February 1782, felt they were useless, since they "always allow hope of deliverance, liberation, or the chance that they will be mitigated." Since the questionnaire did not specifically ask about fornication statutes, many respondents were silent on the subject, so it is impossible to know if their views differed from those who did speak up. Given the unanimity above, however, it is unlikely that many would have favored sharper penalties, the usual response of government in earlier times.

[59] In Baden-Baden the fornication fine was fifteen gulden for both man and woman; the woman who reported her out-of-wedlock pregnancy before the seventh month paid a reduced fine of ten gulden, *Früher Beischlaf* was penalized by seven gulden, thirty kreutzer. Added to the laws was a section on persons suspected of leading irregular sexual lives (*verdächtige Zuwandel*), who were fined five gulden. Hofrat protocol of 10 October 1781, GLA 74/3932, printed in *Wesentlicher Inhalt des beträchtlichsten Theils der neueren Hochfürstlich-Markgräflich-Badischen Gesezgebung, oder alphabetischer Auszug aus den in den Carlsruher und Rastatter Wochenblättern befindlichen, auch mehrern andern dazu gehörigen, noch nicht gedruckten Hochfürstlich-Markgräflich-Badischen Verordnungen.* (Carlsruhe, 1782), 593. The 15 December 1781 ordinance for Baden-Durlach, also in *Wesentlicher Inhalt*, 593–94, lowered the fornication fine by one-quarter for women reporting their pregnancies. The fifteen gulden fine for fornication in Baden-Baden was proclaimed for both parts of the grand duchy in Brauer's Eighth Organizational Edict of 1803, para. 62.

[60] Ordinance of 10 August 1785; rescript of 23 October 1786; the latter as extract of the protocol of 23 October 1786, all in GLA 74/3920.

The Pattern of Ambivalence Repeats Itself: Bavaria (1781)

In almost the same year Bavaria went through a very similar spasm of ambivalence. It ended in two contradictory edicts, which effectively left policy to local interpretation. Even the government debate shows that fornication had ceased to be considered a serious offense, yet so long as it remained criminalized, it created embarrassment for law enforcement and official authority.

Bavaria's all-inclusive sex-crime ordinance of 1727 had set the legal framework for most of the eighteenth century by essentially repeating seventeenth-century rescripts on the various crimes.[61] Freiherr von Kreittmayr's 1751 code hewed closely to previous edicts, which accorded less and less well with real administrative practices. One year after the general reorganization of government in Bavaria in 1779,[62] the problem of handling fornication arose in two different forums.[63] The first concerned a conference of his highest bureaucrats called by the elector to try to curb vagrancy.[64] The second was a complaint from the treasury that some districts (they mentioned the Upper Palatinate as particular offenders) were circumventing the fornication laws by commuting humiliation, work, and larger monetary fines to small monetary fines. Since defendants could choose the district where they would be punished, treasury officials feared that a kind of trade in fornicants had developed, whereby the districts promising the greatest relief from corporal punishment via the substitution of fines lured delinquents to themselves and made a profit from the money they collected.[65] The elector asked his central government to make a recommendation on both issues.

The conference on vagrancy recommended that all public humiliation penalties for fornication be abolished. The central government (Oberlandesregierung) reported, "The assembled deputies found this to be good, useful, and necessary. Neither the court council nor the treasury had the least qualms to append to the

---

[61] Wealthy men received the "customary monetary fine" ("gewöhnlichen Geldstraf") (which Stefan Breit, Leichtfertigkeit, 133, has discovered to have been 3 pfd pfennige for men, and 2 pfd pfennige for women) and eight to fourteen days in the Springer or Eisen at home. Men too poor to pay the fine (or who were considered "fresh") received public humiliation in the Springer and a work penalty. Wealthy women received a fine and four to five days in a similar contraption (the Geigen) at home. Poor women (or "fresh" ones) received public humiliation (street-cleaning while in the Geigen or something similar). New in 1727 were the work penalty and public humiliation for the poor and impudent. Male second offenders received a double fine and were banished from the locality (Gericht- or Hofmarch). Female second offenders received the doubled fine and the doubled (public) humiliation. Male third-time offenders were banished from the county (Rentsamt); women, from the locality. Mandate of 11 June 1727, in Mayr, Sammlung der . . . allgemeinen und besondern Landes-Verordnungen, 3:116–17.

[62] In 1779 the Oberlandesregierung had replaced the Hofrat as the central administrative organ of Bavarian government.

[63] Bavaria is one of the few territories where infanticide played only a secondary role in the eighteenth-century discussion of reform of sexual legislation.

[64] Begging and idleness were the main rubrics, but infanticide was a major theme, as well.

[65] Treasury to elector, 30 October 1780. The government of the Rentamt Schwaben thoroughly agreed. "They are handling the punishment of fornicants as if it were a business, and through mitigating or even abandoning all corporal punishment one assures oneself of getting the largest run of clients [den größten Zuspruch]." Bay HStA, GR 322/8.

[conference] report; what is more, the former [court council] reported that it had long wished for such a decree."[66] On 10 January 1780 the central government sent its recommendation to the elector—who did not respond.

While they waited to hear from him, the treasury mobilized itself on the second issue in a way that countered the recommended leniency. They proposed to stop the practice of permitting defendants in sex-crime cases from choosing where they would fulfill their sentences and to force "the actual execution of the statutory corporal punishments." The Oberlandesregierung objected:

> To date fornicants have been able to have themselves punished in a distant place where they are little known, if at all. Otherwise, they would almost inevitably have to submit themselves for punishment to their usual authority; the shame would be greater; the infanticides, abortions, and secret births would be multiplied; the path to future subsistence and maintenance of people who had committed carnal delicts would be made even more difficult, and thus begging and indolence would be increased and other vices and evils caused.[67]

The elector was unable to choose between these alternatives. He finally brought himself to agree with his central officials that first-time fornication, "committed more from weakness than looseness [*Leichtfertigkeit*]" should, for poor and rich alike, "be handled compassionately, thus with no *public* punishment, but instead an arbitrary atonement [*Buße*] at home."[68] By not abolishing all penalties, the government retained its position as moral arbiter, but loosened the laws to make room for the new interpretation of delinquency based on human weakness, rather than unmitigated sin. Rather than hammer out an agreement between the officials and the elector, however, the exact punishment was left to the local judge. The treasury lost its bid to end the custom of choosing the place of punishment, but the elector balked at a purely lenient reform. He insisted the central government draft two ordinances faithfully reflecting the opposing alternatives.[69] One ordinance removed all shaming penalties for first-time fornication,[70] and the other enjoined all localities to punish all fornicants "in no other way than the monetary and physical [*Leibstrafen*] punishments set forth in the laws of the land or in specific ordinances, without any leniency or mitigation."[71] Significantly, the more restrictive edict, which had been approved after the milder reform, was published a month earlier.

As in Baden-Baden, this demonstrated ambivalence created confusion in practice and encouraged local authorities to continue in their own way. As one provincial authority complained, "The self-interest and greed of many authorities cause them to follow either one ordinance or the other, depending on which is more useful in

[66] Oberlandesregierung to elector, 21 March 1780, Bay HStA, GR 322/8.
[67] Ibid.
[68] Elector to Oberlandesregierung, 19 June 1780, Bay HStA, GR 322/8. Emphasis in the original.
[69] Oberlandesregierung to Elector, 25 August 1780, Bay HStA, GR 322/8.
[70] Ordinance of 25 October 1780, in Mayr, *Sammlung der . . . allgemeinen und besondern Landes-Verordnungen*, 1:197.
[71] Ordinance of 25 September 1780, in Mayr, *Sammlung der . . . allgemeinen und besondern Landes-Verordnungen*, 1:195, original in Bay HStA, GR 322/8.

covering their illicit motives; and many an honest, conscientious local official is misled and does not know how to behave; the subject, however, has no idea any more what degree of punishment your excellency's legislation places on fornication."[72] The treasury remained unmollified because the lowest levels of jurisdiction continued to monopolize fornication cases and thus siphoned off both the fines and the court fees from the higher courts. This particularly offended the treasury officials' cameralist sensibilities, since the higher courts passed along their money to the central treasury, but the lower courts did not.[73]

Both more and less reform-minded officials found the legal muddle untenable. Whereas less progressive officials, forced to acquiesce to the new arguments for leniency, responded by stringent moral line-drawing, their more Enlightened colleagues fretted about the deleterious consequences for state authority generally and for shaping citizen-subjects. From the cameralist-absolutist side, the treasury was forced to concede that "public shaming penalties do not do much for the honor and reputation of a country, and can have a very unfortunate and negative effect on people, otherwise honest children [*sonst honeten Kinderen*] who have been seduced for the first time." The category of the naively seduced was thus firmly entrenched in the bureaucratic mind, which forced the treasury to stress the older category of fornicant-sinner and argue that leniency toward innocent seducees "should not universally be extended to those whose reputations show they are already loose and dissolute [*leichtfertig und ausschweifende*]."[74] Like Margrave Ludwig of Baden-Baden, they wanted to preserve a (sizable) category of sexually disreputable delinquents, whose existence might define the "honest children."

Meanwhile, the district government of Schwaben used Enlightened language to lament the fornicants' ability to choose the venue of punishment.[75] They called it an "unreasonable freedom" that undermined the purpose of laws:

> According to the accepted principles of legislation, the purpose of criminal laws is not only to hinder the subjects' misdeeds [*Vergehen*] and vices [*Laster*], which are dangerous to civil society [*bürgerl. Gesellschaft*], but also and primarily to destroy the sources of these misdeeds, the bad, unfortunate tendencies and passions, and finally to make the effects of already committed crimes [*Verbrechen*] as undestructive as possible to the doer as well as to the state.

This argument built on absolutist, police-state foundations, by which the state was responsible for creating conditions that furthered the common good, but went beyond these in an Enlightened way. The criminal laws now received a preemptive, educative function to target the psychological/physical sources of crime. Furthermore, the sufferer was now not only civil society and the state, but also the perpetrator him- or herself.

---

[72] Rentamt Schwaben to elector, 5 February 1783, Bay HStA, GR 322/8.
[73] "And because we have made many conscientious objections on account of Your Majesty's cameral interests . . . ," treasury to elector, 30 October 1780, Bay HStA, GR 322/8.
[74] Ibid.
[75] Rentamt Schwaben to elector, 5 February 1783, Bay HStA, GR 322/8.

The Schwaben officials obviously thought the psychological aspects were important, for they explained them in some detail. The possibility of choosing the judicial forum had created a kind of game (*Possen spielen*) that delinquents could play against the authorities, and which could "become a secret spur and stimulation for coarse and perverse temperaments [bey rohen und verkehrten Gemütheren einen geheimen Abtrib, und Reiz]." Especially the lax practices in the Munich courts encouraged delinquent men and women to go there to be (lightly) "punished," to return to the countryside and continue in their old ways, so that "for them the memory of their punishment serves more as a dangerous pleasure [*gefährl. Vergnügen*], than a useful warning." Not only was the government inadvertently creating perversity among its inhabitants, its own officials were psychological victims of this situation. The major goal of all this legislation was to make sure that "not only the children receive the requisite care and be brought safely into the world, but also be raised into useful, hard-working citizens, and the mother be restored to her usual work as quickly as possible and kept there. But what authority would gladly bother with persons who had previously offended it and handled it in an impudent manner?" The Schwaben authorities were clearly themselves offended by the freedom fornicants exercised against them and by the decline of decorum and contrition proper to a subject. They did not want sexual delinquents to "play games" with them or get pleasure by evading government regulations and then be assured of automatic sustenance. In short, they wanted people who combined the pleasant qualities of obedient, acquiescent subjects with active, economically productive citizens (the word "Bürger" occurs in the memorandum only in conjunction with productive labor). It is also clear from the last few sentences that, though the phraseology uses "persons" throughout, the most troublesome object of this memo was the woman and her illegitimate children.

None of these musings would have been possible or necessary if fornication had been universally condemned as a serious offense. But a growing consensus among high and low agreed that it was not. Otherwise, it would have been impossible for the courts of lowest jurisdiction (*Niedergerichtbarkeit*) in Bavaria to have usurped these cases from higher courts, as they had been doing since the late seventeenth century. All bureaucrats agreed that fornication was a far less serious offense than infanticide and, as we have seen in Bavaria, than begging and vagrancy. Even the officials in Schwaben (Bavaria), who maintained a hard line on fornication, had to admit that "fornication offenses are not so serious [*beträchtlich*] that a citizen should be robbed of his freedom or arrested [*festgemacht*] on that account."[76] The problem was to find a balance, which meant deciding what was a proper, reasonable, and workable role for the government to play. Although officials agreed that fornication was a relatively minor offense, there was no consensus, either among government officials (and rulers), or writers and opinion-makers, about how it should be handled, if at all.

---

[76] Ibid.

Other Alternatives: Decriminalization Versus Unreformed Regulation

The pressure for reform of the sex-crime laws coming from lower judicial admin-
istrations and, increasingly, from "public opinion" could result in tangled, ambivalent reform, clear-cut reform, or no reform at all. In a land where the ruler was of
one mind and unafraid to assert himself against his bureaucrats, it was possible to
chart a clearer course than in territories like Baden or Bavaria. The best-known
example of this in eighteenth-century Germany was Prussia, where Frederick the
Great issued his famous decree of 1765 abolishing "all shaming penalties for women
[*Hurenstrafen*], regardless of type . . . [and proclaiming further that] the women are
not to receive any punishment for this slip [*Fehltritt*], nor any recrimination, nor
any shame."[77] This was indeed the logical consequence of the Enlightened arguments concerning infanticide, and Frederick had moved steadily, if not swiftly,
in this direction since his accession to the throne in 1740. In 1746 he had abolished the *Kirchenbußen*, because "they embitter rather than improve, and occasion
scandals and even more evil consequences."[78] Despite his convictions that the
woman was the victim of seduction and killed to escape shame, Frederick moved
no further for nineteen years, until just after the devastating Seven Year's War had
ended (1763). The timing of the edict suggests that a desire to restore Prussia's
population might have emboldened him to take the next step. While the decree was
radical in that it was not limited to pregnant women, but applied to women generally, and eradicated all penalties, not just shaming ones, it did not decriminalize
fornication altogether. That happened first in 1794 in the *Allgemeines Landrecht*, a
codification and reform project Frederick ordered but did not live to see completed.
The *Allgemeines Landrecht* confined itself to enjoining (at exhaustive length) parents, masters, teachers, and others to prevent the seduction of youths into early
sexual activity, but it penalized neither women nor men for doing so.[79] Unlike
seventeenth-century lawgivers, the codifers of the *Allgemeines Landrecht* assumed a
world in which all subjects were married, and thus fornication became strictly an
offense of not-yet-married youths. In the 1760s, however, the infanticide model did
not propel Frederick further than decriminalizing fornication for the female delinquent, whom he assumed to be pregnant. Like many of Frederick's activities, the
edict of 1765 became widely known and cited in the public domain[80] and by many

[77] Decree on infanticide of 8 February 1765, *NCC*, 3:583–92.

[78] Circular of 20 June 1746, *NCC*, 3:1245ff., cited in Schwarz, *Kindestötung*, 71. Sentiment to abolish
Kirchenbußen was strongly growing in the mid eighteenth century, not the least in church circles, who
felt that *Kirchenbußen* encouraged infanticide and ruined the decorum of church services. On the
abolition of *Kirchenbußen*, see Ulbricht, *Kindsmord*, 274, 278–83, and Michael Muster, *Das Ende der
Kirchenbuße. Dargestellt an der Verordnung über die Aufhebung der Kirchenbuße in den Braunschweig-
Wolfenbüttelschen Landen vom 6. März 1775* (Hannover, 1983).

[79] *Allgemeines Landrecht für die Preussischen Staaten* (Berlin, 1804), vol. 4, part 2, sec. 12 ("carnal
delicts"), par. 992–98, pp. 628–29.

[80] See Schwarz, *Kindestötung*, 71–83, for a discussion of Prussia's role in the infanticide debate.

bureaucrats in internal correspondence. It provided contemporaries with a stark model whose risks and advantages they could contemplate for their own territories. Friedrich E. Pufendorf's projected law code for Hannover (1772) abolished all fornication penalties for both women and men, unless a servant seduced the daughter of his master (!), or unless intercourse followed a marriage promise.[81] Many contemporaries also seem to have interpreted the Palatine edict of 1739, which was continuously repeated throughout the century, as a virtual abolition of all punishment for pregnant fornicants.[82] But more governments evaded this logic than followed it.

The third and largest group of states seems to have dared neither hesitant nor radical reform. Throughout the eighteenth century they clung instead to their old sex-crime laws. The nonreformers include most Protestant states of northwest Germany, Württemberg, Basel, and so on.[83] One should avoid concluding prematurely, however, that no change in the written laws means that no attempt was made to change those laws or their execution. As we have seen, judicial practice often diverged from written mandate, indeed, almost always did so in countries where no recent codification had occurred and hoary laws, often derived from the Carolina, were still on the books. Furthermore, without examining the court council minutes and other archival sources, it is impossible to tell if reform efforts were not actually begun but then squelched before they left a published mark.[84] To my knowledge there is only one local study sufficiently detailed and nuanced to give an accurate picture of an area where no reform of sex-crime laws took place— Christian Simon's study on the moral politics of eighteenth-century Basel, *Untertanen Verhalten und Obrigkeitliche Moralpolitik*.

Despite the infanticide debate, whose echoes reached Basel, no legal reform occurred there. As Simon explains,

> Whether because the taboos surrounding all norms relating to marriage were too strong, or because men of this [Enlightened, reform] inclination lacked decisive influence on lawmaking in moral [*sittlich*] matters, fundamental changes in the law were not attempted. The trend toward ever more regulation of [sexual] behavior continued throughout the [eighteenth] century. All influential circles were convinced that the existing laws created a dam which alone protected society from a deluge created by the sins and vices of the subjects and which made ruling possible."[85]

---

[81] Ebel, *Friedrich Esaias Pufendorfs Entwurf,* title 123, par. 1–4. F. E. Pufendorf was the grand nephew of the famous natural law theorist, Samuel Pufendorf.

[82] Perhaps it actually functioned in that way. See Johann Georg Krünitz, *Oekonomisch-technologische Encyklopädie, oder Allgemeines System der Staats-, Stadt-, Haus- und Landwirthschaft, in alphabetischer Ordnung,* 242 vols. (Berlin, 1773–1858), 26th part, (Berlin, 1794), 704–6 ("Hure"). The officials in Straubing used the Palatine edict to argue for abolition of all punishments for first-time fornication, 26 September 1794, Bay HStA, GR 322/8.

[83] Most historians assume that no reform was characteristic of the majority of German states. Wächtershäuser, *Das Verbrechen,* 129–30; Schwarz, *Kindestötung,* 209–12; Ulbricht, *Kindsmord,* 320–21.

[84] Lenel, *Badens Rechtsverwaltung,* 180–81, names Baden (erroneously) as a case where reform did not take place.

[85] *Moralpolitik,* 149.

Simon's first two reasons are most likely products of the third, the conviction that "society," that is, the ruling bourgeois patriciate, was threatened by sexual (and other) behavior by the rural lower orders. Simon's research makes clear that the urban/rural axis described the flow of power, including *Moralpolitik*, exercised by the city of Basel on the countryside. Because the patriciate was loathe to pay for an extensive state surveillance apparatus, *Moralpolitik* rested practically on the local church authorities, and thus more largely on a consensus between secular and churchly authorities. "The close dovetailing between these two areas . . . meant that the governing system [*Herrschaftssystem*] could not function without a very wide-ranging consensus about the norms which had to be maintained among the ruled."[86] Simon interprets his material to mean that the secular authorities had more or less abandoned the initiative in matters pertaining to sexual crimes to the church, and since the church never contemplated milder reforms,[87] none occurred. He presents a picture of a retrograde and hidebound community that fought to maintain an old order.

But it is possible to understand these events differently. Basel may well have been "progressive" in the sense that it had already developed a self-conscious, well-to-do, closely knit bourgeois society. Bourgeois norms, among which sexual norms played a predominant role, were well established and agreed upon. The strongly Christian emphasis might be considered old-fashioned, but it is characteristic of the Protestant tendency to see sexual behavior as a much more telling sign of morality and a more central marital cement than the Catholic Church was inclined to do until the 1830s or 1840s. In those decades of intentional religious revival the differences between Protestants and Catholics on sexual matters was largely erased, and Christian morality could play a much stronger role in moral political argument than was possible in the heyday of the often anticlerical Enlightenment. In short, some of the fundamental features underlying the repressive *Moralpolitik* of late-eighteenth-century Basel are structurally similar to developments that only a generation or two later shaped the social policies of other areas in central Europe. Thus Basel may be an early example of the repressive possibilities exercised not primarily by the state bureaucracy, but by bourgeois society itself. Well-developed and functioning bourgeois society may have been more interested in controlling the sexual behavior especially of the lower social orders than were the late absolutist states.[88]

If Basel's laws remained the same, its actual judicial practice, however, diverged in a milder direction. Simon found that local judges routinely took poverty into account when meting out fines for adultery, and consensual heterosexual crimes had

---

[86] Ibid., 150–51.

[87] Simon does not make clear whether the church opposed reforms so adamantly because of religious tenet, class makeup, authoritarian habit, or for other reasons.

[88] According to Rainer Koch, *Grundlagen bürgerlicher Herrschaft. Verfassungs- und sozialgeschichtliche Studien zur bürgerlichen Gesellschaft in Frankfurt am Main (1612–1866)* (Wiesbaden, 1983), Frankfurt am Main's mixture of strong bourgeois society and tight moral control is similar to Basel's. Not all such functioning, stable bourgeois societies would be necessarily interested in sexual control. Cities, such as Hamburg, heavily involved in overseas trade, with transient populations of noncitizens, might simply take perceived sexual license for granted, so long as it was confined to certain areas of the city.

generally become "cavalier delicts" by century's end.[89] These typical developments illustrate once again the inexorable trend toward mildness. They show, too, that law reform was not strictly necessary if judges could be relied upon to mediate between written law and social custom. The more convergence between the leading groups in a society and its administrative/judical apparatus, the more likely satisfactory mediation was to occur and the less necessary it was to lose moral face by altering the law.

We need more detailed studies of other areas before we can safely distinguish between those states which held on to regulation out of excess of absolutism and those whose regulatory zeal stemmed instead from a relatively early development of bourgeois society, perhaps typical of Protestant cities and territories. In any event, lack of reform should not be mistaken for lack of movement.

The Last Reform Efforts before Napoleon: The Cases of Baden and Bavaria

Governments struggling to reform sex-crime law made their last attempts in this direction in the 1790s before the French Revolutionary Wars changed matters for them. Both Baden (1798/99) and Bavaria (1794/1799) seriously contemplated further, milder reforms, partly in order to clear up the chaos stemming from their earlier actions, partly because the precedents they had set for first-time fornicants seemed to demand extension to other sexual delicts, and in Baden, partly to establish uniform laws for Baden-Durlach and Baden-Baden.

The Badenese reforms of 1781 had established an umbrella of relative leniency for first- and second-time fornicants and unwed pregnant women whose condition was made known to the authorities. In the following years the model of the self-reporting pregnant woman was extended to cover her male partner and adulterers. But this left third- and fourth-time repeaters subject to the older punishments, including public humiliation. There is some indication that in fact more people may have been committing repeated fornication in the last third of the eighteenth century than had done so before.[90] Local governments were certainly under this impression, given instances of pregnant women with several, living illegitimate children. Since men bore no visible signs of illicit intercourse, they presented less of a bureaucratic problem. Badenese law condemned such women to prison (*Zuchthaus*). As the number of such cases rose, prison became too expensive since the locality had to pay not only transportation costs to prison, but maintainance for the miscreant's other illegitimate children as well, since they could hardly be sent to

---

[89] Simon, *Moralpolitik*, 244–47.

[90] Ulbricht, *Kindsmord*, 67, found that in Schleswig-Holstein most cases of a second- or third-offense of illegitimacy date from the last quarter of the eighteenth century or later. Lipp, "Reproduktion," 394–95, found this pattern continuing into the nineteenth century. See also Peter Laslett, *Family Life and Illicit Love in Earlier Generations: Essays in Historical Sociology* (Cambridge, 1977), 147–49. More work needs to be done with the general illegitimacy statistics before we can make social sense of them.

prison with her. Fiscally, the law was counterproductive. Morally, the matter foundered in complexity. The sexual moral order seemed to demand a harsher penalty with each repetition of the offense, but harsher penalties were either too expensive to the offended community or, like public humiliation, apparently encouraged infanticide.

In 1798 the *Oberamt* Hochberg presented this dilemma squarely to the Badenese Hofrat,[91] which had apparently been contemplating the state of sexual legislation on its own. Spurred by the fiscal arguments of the locality and its alternative suggestions (which they rejected), the directory of the Hofrat Collegium in April 1799

> submitted the results of its own contemplation, which proceeded [on the assumption] of a more lenient punishment and were discussed both in a written vote as well as in repeated oral conferences. [They concluded] that in the case of this carnal delict [fornication] punishment cannot easily enough deter [people] from the crime, and that crime and punishment in this case must not necessarily easily stand in exact proportion [to one another], however some penalty should be retained as a public notice of moral sensibility.[92]

After much debate they proposed uniform legislation for the entire duchy:

1. "So that the fiscal interest does not suffer too much," they simplified fornication punishment by eliminating everything but a uniform monetary fine of twelve fl. [gulden] for the first offense and four fl. [gulden] for each further repetition for both men and women. Men unable to pay would complete a public work tour; women a confinement [*Einthurmung*, not *Zuchthaus*] in which they would spin. Both would last eight days for the first offense with two days added for each repetition.

2. All public humiliation [*Lasterstein*] would stop.

3. Both man and woman would receive half the penalty if someone informed the authorities of her pregnancy.

4. "In order to heighten the impact of the punishment and to make clearer the difference between respectability and immorality [*Erbarkeit (sic) und Sittenlosigkeit*]" the third-time female repeater and the adulteress would be forbidden from all public dances until the former married or unless the latter were forgiven [*condonirt*] by her husband.

5. The harsher penalty for women in paragraph (4) would not take place if successive illegitimate children were the product of a continuous relationship with the same man.

6. All punishment of fornication cases, whether in money or work penalties, was the responsiblity of the local administrative level and should not be referred by them to higher authorities in order to mitigate a punishment.

---

[91] Extract from the Hofrat's protocol of 19 February 1798, no. 10918, bound in the Hofrat protocol of 19 April 1799, GLA 61/3322.

[92] Extract from the Hofrat protocol of 19 April 1799, GLA 61/3322.

7. The state should consider reducing punishment in incest cases.
8. The state should also consider whether the pregnant woman [*Dirne*] should be permitted "private satisfaction," that is, recourse to civil suit against her impregnator.[93]

These suggestions, as befits their date, are delicately poised between strict Enlightenment and post-Enlightenment liberalism. On the one hand, they drastically and refreshingly simplified the chaotic legislation on fornication, following a combination of fiscal and moral-political interests. They eliminated the old public humiliation punishments. The reasoning behind the fornication statutes became a model for other sexual delicts, adultery and incest, as well. And they indicated their weariness with the efforts of local governments to press for leniency in these cases, as well as their tacit conviction that such matters were no longer weighty enough to require the attention of the central government, by attempting to restrict them entirely to the local level. On the other hand, they could not accept the principle that the central administration had no responsibility whatever to demonstrate to its subjects its own "moral sensibility." It was committed to upholding "respectability," yet it wished to do so as much as possible in a social context, not a state one. Hence, not condemnation *to* prison, but banishment *from* social functions, became the sentence. The responsibility for upholding respectability was thus shared with, or even sloughed off onto, society at large. The institution of marriage washed the disreputable clean and returned them to the social fold. Furthermore, sexual respectability was conceived as more important to the reputation of females than males, since only the former were subject to this new restriction. Although such a dichotomous view of sexual reputation has an old tradition in Europe, it was being revivified and used for different purposes by the late eighteenth century. In any case, this notion was foreign to Baden's laws, where the new views were being proposed for the first time. Finally, it was also new to suggest civil law as the proper arena for disputes arising from sexual intercourse ("private satisfaction"). As consensual heterosexual behavior slipped from the criminal law, it came to rest in civil law, where it was subject to different rules and operated in a different way.

At the privy council meeting of 23 May 1799 the plans of the Hofrat directory met a broadside penned by Privy Councillor Johann Nicolaus Brauer,[94] the moderately conservative official who had emerged as the main legal adviser to Margrave Karl Friedrich (1738–1811) and who went on to codify (but not reform) Baden's laws in 1803.[95] Brauer's major legal reservation was that reforming just the sex-crime laws would create "disproportion" between them and the rest of the criminal laws "which bring[s] so many unpredictable consequences and, for the government,

---

[93] I have condensed some of the points in the original document, which contained twelve items.
[94] Extract from the privy council protocol of 23 May 1799, GLA 74/3920. Brauer's report of 17 May 1799 is in GLA 74/3920.
[95] J.N.F. Brauer (1754–1813), privy councillor, director of the consistory, and director of Baden's separate court of highest appeal, the *Hofgericht* (1790). Lenel, *Badens Rechtsverwaltung*, 203–6.

negative popular impressions in [its] wake."[96] He also doubted that sufficient consensus existed to chart a clear reform, so he wanted all the *Oberämter* and church districts (*Specialate*) canvassed for their opinions. Given the apparent unanimity of the Hofrat and the unanimity shown by the *Ämter*, *Oberämter*, and *Specialate*, when they opined about sexual legislation in 1781, Brauer may have overestimated opposition to milder reform.[97] Since he opposed reform himself, he may have done so on purpose. In any event, the Hofrat, daunted by his arguments and by the prospect of canvassing once again all the localities, postponed their reform plans. The eighteenth century ended with the laws of 1781 in place.

The Bavarians made their last, futile pre-Napoleonic reform attempt in 1794. The central government (*Oberlandesregierung*)[98] intended a definitive, overarching reform according to archetypically enlightened standards; other central officials in the court council (*Hofrat*) thwarted the project, fearing the social, political, and symbolic effects of further leniency.

The Oberlandesregierung had prepared to tinker piecemeal with the existing laws on fornication and had questioned its district governments about the actual practice under their authority, but in consultation with the reform-minded Elector Karl Theodor, they had ultimately agreed to issue no further patchwork decrees "until this entire part of the criminal laws [that is, carnal delicts] has undergone the necessary improvement."[99] These improvements the government listed as:

1. Punishments proportional to the degree of the crime.
2. An appropriate punishment instead of banning, against which so many well-founded reservations exist.
3. The necessary care, so that not too much is left to the discretion of the judge.
4. [Removing] the evil consequences of the defendant choosing his/her place of judgment.
5. [Addressing] the circumstance, that these penalties often are seen as a not inconsiderable income for the districts.
6. [Remedying] the inappropriateness and harmfulness of both monetary and public shaming penalties.
7. Laws generally binding, and not limited merely to one class [*Klasse*] of people.
8. Adequate prevention of rising immorality [*überhandnehmende Unsittlichkeit*] in the cities and countryside.
9. [Mitigating] the current large monetary fine for adultery.
10. Clarifying the demarcation line between higher and lower jurisdictions and describing the powers of each.

Some of these points were designed to solve the problems the government had

[96] Brauer memorandum of 17 May 1799, GLA 74/3920.

[97] In any event Brauer confused the lack of agreement over the death penalty with the relative agreement of those who ventured an opinion on the subject of sex-crime legislation in 1781.

[98] The Oberlandesregierung was the new, highest institution of central administration, created in 1799.

[99] Karl Theodor, rescript of 7 July 1794, Bay HStA, GR 322/8.

ducked (or created) in 1780. In general, however, no more succinct list of Enlightened legal principles could be imagined. Proportional punishment; fixed laws (limited judicial discretion); fixed, systematic and clear jurisdiction; equality of subjects/citizens before the law; and a clear distinction between taxes and punishments are all hallmarks of Enlightened government. It is thus significant that "adequate prevention of rising immorality in the cities and countryside" is included in the list, for this shows the compatibility of Enlightened principles with the older absolutist duty of the state to police morals (the expression "überhandnehmende" is a classic topos of absolutist decrees), only now the accent has shifted more firmly to prevention. This telltale "überhandnehmende" also betrays the reluctance of the government to relinquish its old right to regulate.

To achieve these ends, the district governments were asked to report their opinions and suggestions for reform.[100] The central government then gave these lengthy documents to the court council, which, since the administrative changes of 1779, was the court of last appeal and the fount of legal opinion in the government. After two years of fruitless waiting, the central government prodded the court council to act. The latter found two excuses, one for its dilatoriness ("a few pressing matters which arrived in the meantime, as well as the intervening war and the absence of the expert adviser [Referent]"), and another for avoiding reform "[O]ne was nonetheless after many sessions and deliberations on this matter unable to decide [whether to lower or raise penalties], as long as one is not sure what effect the certainly well-meant ordinance of 1780 had").[101] They wanted therefore to canvass four or five courts in each district (Rentamt) and compare the number of sex crimes committed in the ten years before and after the 1780 edict. (This was a tactically similar move to Brauer's arguments in Baden two years later.)

The harder the Oberlandesregierung pushed for reform, the more obstinate the Hofrat became. In 1798 the Hofrat neatly summed up its opposition. The matter of sex law reform was

in no way mature enough [reif genug] or prepared enough, on the contrary, one must discuss and reflect carefully upon the circumstance [Umstand], whether the recent actually practiced exaggerated leniency of a number of judges, prejudiced by modern sensibilities, is adequate any more, has brought forth good effects, or rather has harmed, and indeed caused perverse and very bad effects, and that through this leniency, in these times which are already in all respects undisciplined, the common bond of dutiful respect and appeal [Casition(sic)] toward authority and laws has been ripped apart and the door to unpunished transgression opened wide, and in the end an open dissolution of morals has been caused; and whether therefore, in light of these circumstances, which must be

---

[100] The rescript of 7 July 1794 was originally sent to the Rentämter Burghausen, Straubing, and Landshut, whose lengthy reports are in the archives. In November Adam Freiherr von Aretin urged the elector to question the government of the Upper Palatinate and the judicial senate in Neuburg, too. The elector agreed to send a questionnaire to the Upper Palatinate, but its response, if it sent one, has been lost. Aretin to Elector, 7 November 1794, and the elector's reply of 18 November 1794, both in Bay HStA, GR 322/8.

[101] Hofrat to Oberlandesregierung, 24 January 1797, Bay HStA, GR 322/8.

discussed in the meantime, a mitigation or an increase in the laws is now more necessary and advisable.[102]

For the court council sexual (mis)behavior had become an issue of high political importance. Their enemy was now no longer just the ideologues in the Oberlandesregierung, but the actual practice of judges ruined by "modern sensibilities." The court council, though it did not say so explicitly, obviously wanted to return to the pre-1780 status quo, that is, the court council had overshot mere conservatism and landed among the reactionaries. The French Revolution and its effects in Germany were powerful spurs to their ideological retreat, as the reference to the "undisciplined times" shows. More significant, they correlated uncontrolled sexual behavior with loss of state authority, which of course in the most literal sense was true. By giving up its pretense of control and allowing certain types of formerly punished behavior to go unpunished, the state actually diminished its power relative to the subject and increased the subject's sphere of choice and action. Moreover, sexual license (like revolution) was difficult, if not impossible to stop, and misguided leniency led inexorably to "open moral dissolution."

In its reply to the court council's stubbornness, the Oberlandesregierung made clear that it agreed with the court council about the importance of sexual behavior and the legislation devoted to it: "this matter which is so important to the entire state."[103] Like the court council, they had devoted much time to this subject, for "among the criminal laws, of which so many (as with civil laws) need improvement and entire transformation, we found those which dealt with offences of the flesh to be worthy of [our] main attention." Indeed, reform of sex-crime laws was meant to be the wedge leading law reform in general.[104] For this reason the Oberlandesregierung wanted action as soon as possible, and they begged the elector to ignore the court council and get on with reform. In rejecting the court council's desire to canvass the courts, the Oberlandesregierung was not simply being impatient, it was also acting from a different set of principles and assumptions. As the Oberlandesregierung explained:

> The times are past [it wrote] when one could simply decree a law and imagine that one had thereby accomplished everything. Law has an equally holy goal, to improve and as far as possible to deter crime [An unknown official noted in the margin: "this last object belongs more to the police than to justice."], to penetrate into the nature of crime, to restore the matter to its true aspect [*Gesichtspunkt*], to search for the cause of the problem, and then to counter that with appropriate means via education and appropriate enlightenment, etc. [marginal note: "enlightenment in the usual sense doesn't help in carnal delicts"], and to mix these means with fair criminal laws fitting the offender. The attention of the lawmaker must concern itself [with these goals]; no inventories are

---

[102] Hofrat to Oberlandesregierung, 3 February 1798, Bay HStA, GR 322/8. "Casition" is probably an idiosyncratic spelling of *Cassation*, meaning appeal (for judicial grace, or leniency). I thank Mack Walker for this suggestion.

[103] Oberlandesregierung to elector, 26 June 1799, Bay HStA, GR 322/8.

[104] Peitzsch, *Kriminalpolitik*, 95.

necessary, which, except for [telling] the number of offenses, give not the slightest information, and in the case of carnal delicts, can show even less the level of moral perfection and morality, since the results [*Resultate*—by which they mean of the cases that actually come before the courts] of these offenses depend too much on chance.[105]

This passage represents the highest development of the late Enlightened reform absolutist state at the moment when it was about to be surpassed. These bureaucrats saw no cause to solicit statistics or opinions from the lower bureaucracy, or anybody else, because their own right reason was sufficient to penetrate the "true aspect" and cause of crime. They were not uncomfortable with enunciating laws from the center, according to a priori principles of reason; that is, the Enlightened government itself could and should be the source of progressive reform.

The court council's position was more ambiguous. It was partly disingenuous, designed simply to grind reform to a halt. But it also contained a conservative principle with interesting, and perhaps unintended, developmental potential for the nineteenth century. The Oberlandesregierung summed this principle up as follows: "One can never collect too many of the various concepts [of the local courts] when one is fashioning new laws, because only the number and variety of these permits the lawmaker to make useful laws, through intelligent choice according to general principles, from among the suggestions that differ according to national, local, and temporal conditions."[106] This, of course, built upon Montesquieu[107] and was thus a product of Enlightenment thinking, but it was a theory that could be used to limit the ability of a central authority simply to decree law as it saw fit. The court council hoped that local courts would disavow the lenient principles of the Oberlandesregierung, which is surprising, given their perception that local judges also had fallen prey to insidious modern tendencies. Perhaps they simply grasped at a straw in the wind. But the position of judge as the closest official to real social conditions, and thus as the mediator between general principle and social reality (in both directions), a kind of Landrat of the law, was a central point of contention in legal debates in the nineteenth century. The more classically Enlightened lawyers wanted less judicial discretion than those more critical of the Enlightenment. If we go one step further, we see that the mediating position of the judge might soon be usurped by that of the elected legislator or the civilian expert, whose opinions became crucial to legitimating the lawgiving process in the next century. Laws that reflected "society" (in its different forms: via judicial opinion, "public opinion" from mostly bourgeois writers, men elected under restricted suffrage, "experts" on social issues, and so on) could follow quite different principles at different times. In the nineteenth century sex-crime law was considerably affected when the voices of society, or "public opinion," became more "conservative" (that is less lenient or tolerant) about sexual matters than the central bureaucrats.

[105] Oberlandesregierung to elector, 26 June 1799, Bay HStA, GR 322/8.
[106] Ibid.
[107] Montesquieu, *The Spirit of the Laws*, trans. Anne M. Cohler, Basia Carolyn Miller, and Harold Samuel Stone (Cambridge, 1989).

The Views of the Upper and Middle Bureaucracies on State Control of Sexual Behavior at the End of the Eighteenth Century

If the reform efforts in Baden and Bavaria in the 1790s were frustrated, the documentation they produced makes clear how many changes had occurred in the previous fifteen to twenty years in the attitudes of the central bureaucrats toward sexual crimes and state regulation. We should now turn to those documents to assess the nature of those changes and the limits to them. Although not all the documents have been recovered, the four surviving reports, three from the main district governments (*Rentämter*) in Bavaria and Brauer's memorandum,[108] are all of unusual length and detail.[109] Brauer filled sixteen folio pages with his small script; the Bavarian reports range from forty-one to sixty pages long. All the reports ponder at length and often philosophically the nature of sexual crime and the public interest in regulating sexual behavior. They were composed in a rare moment of reflective stock-taking on the principles underlying state action.

Better still, the spectrum of political possibilities is well represented. The Bavarian reports are all to some extent group products and therefore are probably representative of broad currents of opinion among middle- to upper-level bureaucrats. The directorate (*Vorstand*) of the district government at Burghausen, for example, went to great lengths to "locate the relevant criminal court documents stored in the record office, so that four counsellors [*Räte*] from the directorate could read the older criminal records and prepare a report on the various delicts, so that thereafter a thorough report on this subject by the entire government [*in pleno regiminis*] could be made and the final report, reflecting the necessary thorough reflection, might be sent to the Oberlandesregierung." The final version appears to have been drafted by a single person, but it contains the deliberations of the entire body. Brauer's memorandum is written entirely in his own voice. It was designed to refute point by point arguments for further relaxation and general reform of the sex-crime laws adduced by the Hofrat directory, written by its director, Privy Councilor Ernst Sigmund Herzog. Herzog's report, alas, is missing, though its argumentation can be pieced together from Brauer's refutation.

Neither the Bavarian reports nor Brauer's memorandum is entirely consistent. This inconsistency may reflect differences of opinion among the bureaucrats them-

---

[108] Brauer's memorandum of 17 May 1799 (GLA 74/3920) was a reply to a memorandum by Ernst Sigmund Herzog (1747–1820), director of the *Hofratscollegium*. Herzog's memorandum must have been a lengthy justification of the April 1799 recommendations of the government. Unfortunately, neither in the protocols of the Hofrat (GLA 61/3322–23) nor the Geheimer Rat (privy council) (GLA 61/1806–1807) for April–June 1799, nor in the records of changes in the *Unzucht* legislation (GLA 74/3919–3920), where Brauer's reply is located, could a copy of Herzog's own report be found. I thank Herr Rupp and other staff members of the Generallandesarchiv Karlsruhe for their help in searching (in vain) for this document.

[109] Straubing report of 26 September 1794; Burghausen report of "the last days of October 1794"; Landshut report of 29 December 1794; all in Bay HStA, GR 322/8. Brauer's report, no. 89 1/2, "Ueber den Regierungsvorschlag zu einer ganz neuen Legislatur über die Unzuchtsstrafen," 17 May 1799, GLA 74/3920.

selves; it doubtless results from the state of ideological flux that existed at the end of the eighteenth century. Lines were not as clearly drawn as they would be just a short while later. Nonetheless, the reports fall fairly distinctly along a spectrum ranging from traditional (Burghausen), through transitional (Landshut), to liberal/ Enlightened (Straubing), to enlightened conservative (Brauer).[110] I follow Karl Mannheim's distinction whereby "traditional" refers to a political position that accepts the status quo and the religious and authoritarian ideas behind it in an uncritical and undefensive way.[111] Conservatism, on the contrary, is a modern product of the Enlightenment and early liberalism and self-consciously criticizes some of the principles of late Enlightenment/early liberalism, while inevitably using many of those same principles, notably systematic argument, appeals to reason, and so forth. Nonetheless, "conservative" is too one-dimensional a term to describe Brauer accurately. He was a careful, moderate reformer whose commitment to Enlightened principles caused him later to champion fairly enthusiastically the introduction of the Code Napoléon into Baden. But Brauer was skeptical of the abstract, utopian strand of Enlightenment and was thus a bitter critic of the unfair treatment of women he (rightly) saw emerging from the blueprints of Enlightened-liberal enthusiasts. Because the gender issue was central to sex-crime law, Brauer's 1794 memorandum highlights his skeptical side and foregrounds objections to certain Enlightenment tendencies coming, however, from an Enlightened perspective—hence the term "Enlightened conservative."

What I have called the liberal/Enlightened position (Straubing) also needs explanation. This position was one variant of late Enlightened reform absolutism. It was a form of eudaemonistic liberalism housed within the state and thus it often carried within it significant contradictions, especially concerning the extent of state power versus individual freedom. Nevertheless, those who held this position, such as the authors of the Straubing report, were officials whose ultimate goals for government and society and whose knowledge about how to attain those goals came by the 1790s from the public discourse of early liberal civil society.[112] The political valence of their opinions is complex in two respects. First, as the Straubing report illustrates, many such officials were unaware how marching to civil society's drumbeat undermined the legitimacy of state tutelage; in the 1790s they found no discrepancy between the self-consciously modern principles they embraced and their duties as governors. Second, these modern principles were not universally emancipatory; precisely at the intersection of sex and gender, the opinions of liberal civil society laid strong foundations both for the unequal treatment of men and women as well as for the reintroduction of state regulation on behalf of civil-social

---

[110] Both Peitzsch, using criteria from legal philosophy, and Breit arrived at the same ranking for the Bavarian reports, though their terminology is different. They designate the most old-fashioned reporter (Burghausen) as "conservative." (Peitzsch also tends to lump Burghausen and Landshut together.) Peitzsch, *Kriminalpolitik*, 88–89; Breit, *Leichtfertigkeit*, 284.

[111] Karl Mannheim, *Konservatismus. Ein Beitrag zur Soziologie des Wissens*, ed. David Kettler, Volker Meja, and Nico Stehr (Frankfurt, 1984), 92–98.

[112] I discuss civil society in greater detail in Chapter 5.

values. It is therefore not always easy to distinguish a late enlightened reform absolutist of the Straubing stripe from a post-Napoleonic reform liberal when it comes to moral politics, for both derived their moral value system from civil society and both thought the duty of the state was to uphold these moral values. There was another sort of late Enlightened reform absolutist, who did not traverse this road to civil-social moral politics, but instead either remained skeptical of the content of civil-social morality (for example, Brauer and Theodor von Hippel) and thus was not tempted to elevate it to legal principle, or else regarded law precisely as the epitome of the nonmoral and thus as the bulwark against moral politics (Anselm Feuerbach).[113] Either way, this second sort of late enlightened reform absolutist erected a barrier between the opinions of civil society and the content of law.

The political spectrum represented in these reports on sex-crime law reform was largely caused by the degree to which the particular officials had accepted civil-social opinion on sexual matters; and thus, rather than speak of variants within late Enlightened reform absolutism, it seems simpler to distinguish these official viewpoints by direct reference to civil society, hence along the somewhat simplified spectrum ranging from traditional to liberal/Enlightened to Enlightened conservative.

These internal government reports from the 1790s permit us to assess how far the late absolutist German bureaucracies had moved in reassessing the public interest in sexual behavior just before the transformations caused by the French Revolution. There were two main aspects to this reassessment: how far were officials willing to relinquish state regulation for civil self-regulation? and how far did civil society already set the content of sexual expectations that law would somehow reflect?

State- versus Self-Regulation of Sexual Behavior

Absolutist habits died hard. Despite the logic of reform and despite their differences, the official reporters all agreed that the state had an important role to play in regulating (hetero)sexual behavior. They also knew that many fellow officials and legal scholars disagreed.[114] Two reporters felt it necessary to discredit their

[113] On Hippel, see Chapter 8; on Feuerbach, Chapter 9.

[114] Among the authors favoring decriminalization of fornication were Johann David Michaelis (a professor at Göttingen), *Mosaisches Recht* (Biehl, 1777), part 6, p. 46.; Karl Ferdinand Hommel, trans. and ed., *Cesare Beccaria, Vom Verbrechen und Strafen* (Breslau, 1778), notes, par. 27, p. 126; Ludwig von Heß (Swedish governmental councillor), *Eine Antwort auf die Preisfrage: Welches sind die beßten ausführbaren Mittel dem Kindermorde Einhalt zu thun?* (Hamburg, 1780), 20–35; Nicolaus Waßda, *Lauter Wunsch für diejenigen Personen weiblichen Geschlechts, welche zu Falle kommen* (Frankfurt, 1781); Johann Jakob Cella (Amtmann), *Von Strafen unehelicher Schwängerungen, besonders von den diessfalls gebräuchlichen Zwangskopulationen* (Erlangen, 1783), and *Über Verbrechen und Strafe in Unzuchtsfällen* (Saarbrücken, 1787); Hans Ernst von Globig and Johann Georg Huster (Globig was in the Saxon privy council; Huster was the Saxon electoral privy finance-secretary in Dresden), *Abhandlungen von der Criminal-Gesetzgebung* (Zürich, 1783), 241–42; Julius von Soden, *Geist der peinlichen Gesetzgebung Teutschlands* (Frankfurt, 1792), vol. 2, paras. 371 and 375; Krünitz, "Hure," 699, 817–18, 823; Waldemar Friedrich Graf von Schmettau, "Ueber den Kindermord," in *Kleine Schriften* (Altona, 1795), 54–55.

opponents: "I know, of course, that most 'Naturalists'[115] and other writers who flatter the carnal lusts want to remove for different fake reasons [*Scheingründen*] all penalties from the satisfaction of the sexual drive." [116] The Burghausen government lamely protested that such a notion contravened "the principles of the Roman Catholic religion and the old Bavarian ordinances." The liberal Straubinger were more explicit about the modern legal argument for decriminalization: "[The argument] that these crimes, insofar as they are committed without violence or harm to the acquired rights or property of a third person, should not be punished at all, has in recent times not been without defenders." But apparently they could not logically contradict it any better than the traditionalists. They contented themselves with declaring "we consider it completely unnecessary to prove here the criminal nature [*das Strafbare*] of these offences, or to enlarge upon their generally recognized harm."

Their defensiveness is made even clearer by the new justifications they adduced for state regulation. They now argued in the voice of civil society that the biological welfare and private happiness of the individual miscreant required state intervention. The Landshuter decried the "evil effects for the private [*Privat*] and general welfare" that fornication produced, and the Burghausen reporters adduced the latest medical/pedagogical literature on masturbation and venereal disease to support criminalization. "Through such overdone excesses, if they are not prevented by law, young people [*junge Leute*, but the writers clearly have only young men in mind] would often so exhaust their energies that even before they enter marriage they become incapable of begetting children, or they would have contracted venereal disease and infected others."

Although the upper officials still struggled to keep a niche for legal regulation, the internal governmental and public debates on infanticide had succeeded in convincing administrators of all stripes that "in this world, no improvement in morality is achieved by harshness, but on the contrary, by moderation in the laws."[117] None of the reports favored increasing legal punishments, though the traditionalists in Burghausen and the conservative Brauer held the line against extending leniency any further. Official reluctance to enter the brave new world of deregulation had a number of different sources. Ever since secular authorities had

[115] "Naturalists" were those who argued for decriminalization of some or all consensual sexual acts on the grounds that sexual drive was natural and could not be arbitrarily forbidden by state or church law. On the title page of his book *Über Verbrechen und Strafe in Unzuchtsfällen* (1787), Cella cited Beccaria's succinct statement of the "naturalist" position: "Carnal crimes arise from the misuse of an eternal need that is common to all of nature; a need which antedates society and for which it laid the basis; other [nonsexual] delicts lead to the destruction of societies and spring from the passion of a moment rather than from natural needs."

[116] Burghausen report, October 1794, Bay HStA, GR 322/8.

[117] Ibid. This remark comes in the context of adultery. The Burghausener officials coupled "moderation in the laws" with "the most possible containment of the natural freedom of imperfect people [*fehlerhaften Menschen*] via prison sentences [*Zuchthausstrafen*] of several years or even for life." Clearly "moderation" for the quasi-absolutists from Burghausen was considerably less moderate than for reform or even conservative bureaucrats.

accepted the Reformation's challenge to read social from sexual disorder and identified government authority with obedience to sexual laws, disobedience had been a serious affront to authority in general. Officials still felt that way, as the Landshut report on repeated fornication makes plain. "The third offense clearly assumes a great deal of impudence [*Unverschämtheit*], depraved habits, and stubbornness [*Hartnäckigkeit*] vis-à-vis the authorities' [concern for] subsistence." It was hard for officials to condone their own loss of authority. Officials clung, too, to the old association of sexual misbehavior with luxury, waste, and idleness. They used that association to epitomize the chaos that deregulation might cause. But there were non-symbolic problems confronting judicial reformers, problems that made them hesitate before adopting radical reforms. Would leniency encourage the rise of immoral behavior? Should men and women, indeed all *Stände* and classes, be treated equally? Should judicial discretion be encouraged or clipped? These were difficult questions all reformers, even radical ones, debated at length. Until the French Revolution cleared the legal landscape, leniency was as far as most officials were prepared to go.

Despite the opportunity these reports gave officials to reflect on the principles behind sexual regulation, the writers had remarkably little to say about relations between the state and the individual. Their attitudes were instead embedded implicitly in what they wrote. Whether they argued from public security or individual welfare, none of the reporters thought it theoretically improper for the state to intervene in "private" life. None wrote that even proper, marital sexual behavior should be a privileged haven from state interference. In short, there is no sign of the "private sphere" in its nineteenth-century usage. The most traditional reporters in Burghausen had no hesitation in asserting that (for sexual crimes) "the main purpose [of laws] is general security . . . the secondary aim . . . [is] the improvement of the criminal." Since they assumed that sexual misdeeds harmed the state as well as the individual, "therefore, [even though] he would like to make the use of his natural senses a flattering right, the [individual] person must simply put up with the limitation of his external actions, if by this limitation the public is usefully served [*dem Publico ein Nutzen zugienge*]." In the context of their argument the public utility in this case was keeping (male) citizens capable of entering marriage, having children, and avoiding venereal disease.[118] The reports more influenced by modern arguments, such as the report from Landshut, reversed the order: "The concept and nature of laws have always as their purpose the improvement of the criminal, security for the person offended, and examples for the rest." Like the Burghausener, Brauer also put security in first place, but general education came next.

The word "private" occurs only twice in these reports and still carries its old dual meaning of "individual" or "nonstate." The Landshut officials referred to the

---

[118] The Burghausen report is the only one to mention venereal disease, a favorite obsession of the nineteenth century.

"private" as opposed to the "general welfare." Brauer used "private life" to mean generally that portion of life not regulated by the state, though he gave it an interesting twist. In his argument against shaming penalties, Brauer remarked that for the lower orders shame accrued far less to prison sentences (which were considered most dishonorable by members of the bourgeoisie) "than to the taint of [a dishonorable] private life [*Privatleben*], which is precisely not dependent on the state and which cannot be undermined without absolutely encouraging immoral behavior." "Private life" was in Brauer's usage not the sphere of the individual monad, but the realm where community standards reigned independent of state action. Private life and the honor or shame attached to it were thus highly "public."

Although upper-level officials had not yet realized, much less embraced, the principle behind the separation of state and society, they had already accepted one of the chief tenets that would shortly establish that principle in practice. For all reports agreed that law was an inadequate or even fruitless way to "solve" immorality. It was a short step from here to the conclusion that the state ought to abandon moral supervision to civil society. "One can put a stop to vice through punishment, but habits or custom, which is what really counts, cannot be improved in this way," opined the Straubinger. All reporters, in one way or another, shared the general Enlightened view that education was the only secure way to change people's moral behavior. The Landshut officials agreed that the moral behavior of individuals was more a product of inner conviction, than external force: "The single art [*Kunst*] capable of destroying vice . . . lies in this: when other principles, opinions and tendencies in the state become dominant." Once they had identified individual conviction as the key to morality, upper-level officials naturally focused on education as the fundamental guarantor of *Sittlichkeit*. Education the officials interpreted variously to mean the mere copying of the (hopefully good) example of parents (Straubing and Landshut), teachers (Straubing), and clergy (Landshut); the establishment of popular education (Burghausen); or the use of law itself as a guide to proper behavior. Brauer was eloquent on the last point. Laws do not deter, he said. At most one can "work against recklessness [*Leichtsinn*] regarding punishable acts from earliest youth on, by a manifestation of the retributive earnestness of the authorities in proportion to the danger the offence presents to human welfare." That is, "the penalty expresses the degree of disapproval by its proportions, both in relation to other criminal acts and to general morality, and in this way . . . [the law] correctly shapes the civil, moral being of the citizen [*der (sic) bürgerlich sittliche Sein des Staatsbürgers richtig gebildet wird*]." Brauer's formulation was a most important one, for the law as teacher of civil/bourgeois morality became the most popular conservative argument of the nineteenth century for retaining overt state regulation of "private" acts.

These opinions mark a shift from using law negatively as simple coercion, to using it positively to encourage morally desirable public opinion and useful non-state institutions. The most astonishing proof of this shift was the officials' universal call for marriage for the poor. This was a departure from traditional practice, since most states had long-standing laws forbidding marriage to those unable to demonstrate steady work and some savings.[119] These subsistence-based ordinances the central bureaucrats now condemned. "As long as a state lacks the energy or courage to overcome everything in today's constitution that hinders marriage . . . then every other method of stopping the stream of rising immorality [*über Hand nehmenden Leichtfertigkeit*] will be in vain," wrote Brauer. Even traditionalist Burghausen was prepared optimistically to overlook the old, subsistence worries blocking marriage of the poor. Their prescriptions were straight from the pages of the cameralists: "Those means which seem to us the best for encouraging marriage are none other than those which increase food, because when the food supply in a state increases, more people can feed themselves and attain their honorable livelihood, and thus guarantee [feeding] their legitimate children, and thus one achieves the promotion of marriage."[120] To achieve this happy state they proposed reducing feudal dues, introducing land reform, building factories, and breaking up monopolies in cities and market towns. The liberals in Straubing were less specific, but spoke to the same concerns when they claimed that "anyone who can work is not poor; it all depends on giving people love for work and the opportunity to work. The first can often be achieved by small inducements; opportunity for work can soon be found by anyone who seeks it; one needs merely to help a bit and fill in a few holes [*einige Lücken ausfüllen*]."

This optimistic belief in inevitable economic expansion permitted upper-level officials to forget the poor chest and encourage marriage as a universal institution, which in turn established a new relationship between the individual and the state. Formerly, subsistence fears and legal coercion had created sexual criminals estranged from the moral order; now prosperity and wise laws harnessed sexual energy to bind the individual more strongly to the moral order. To this end the Landshuter recommended "all means must be used to encourage marriage, so that marriages increase, whereby [earlier fornicators] tie a knot [*knipfen ein Band*] which their former excesses had hindered, a knot that fastens them closer to the state and which is intended to improve the education of their children." In other words, by allowing more generously the opportunity for legitimate sexual activity, government successfully maneuvered people into an institution (marriage) from which it and society benefited. At the same time that people married each other, they also "married" the state, as the expression "tie the knot" indicates. (The word "state" [*Staat*] in these reports followed contemporary usage and meant the organized social order, not simply government; officials aimed to encourage moral, productive members of society, not the automata of twentieth-century imagining.)[121] Charac-

---

[119] Klaus-Jürgen Matz, *Pauperismus und Bevölkerung. Die gesetzlichen Ehebeschränkungen in den süddeutschen Staaten während des 19. Jahrhunderts* (Stuttgart, 1980), 29–33.

[120] Most respondents to the infanticide prize question also favored marriage as a panacea to prevent illegitimate births. Ulbricht, *Kindsmord*, 272–73, remarks that this unanimity probably occurred when several tendencies flowed together: cameralism, Enlightenment, early liberalism (which saw marriage as a natural right), and south German protest against marriage restriction for the poor.

[121] For more on the use of *Staat*, see Chapter 4, pp. 157–59.

teristically, the liberals in Straubing underlined the sexual aspect of this new relationship between subject and state. "One should think less about repressing the sexual drive than about ordering it for the good of the state. As long as excessive luxury cannot be unlimited, as long as marriage for the poor is forbidden by law, it will be useless to set limits to fornication [*Unzucht und Leichtfertigkeit*]."

Two interesting assumptions underlie these thoughts. First, unlike the officials of the seventeenth century, who apparently believed that sexual expression could successfully be repressed, these officials felt it virtually inevitable that people would engage in sexual activity. Sexual desire was too strong to resist. Second, a reasonable government would therefore see to it that that natural desire was channeled into an institution government now controlled (civil marriage), in which subsidiary problems (child-rearing, infanticide, promiscuity) could be avoided, and the interests of the married persons became identical with those of the state and society (gratitude at being permitted guaranteed sexual expression, self-identification with the moral order and its principles, such as monogamy, industriousness, and so on). Except for Brauer's memorandum, where the remarks on marriage occur in a passage urging tougher legal prosecution of male sexual offenders, the other three reports all considered marriage in the context of productive work and good citizenship. This was, of course, a very old connection, but whereas before productive work was supposed to be guaranteed before marriage and acceptance as a citizen of a village, now marriage came to be seen as almost a panacea guaranteeing the will to work and ordering society from the inside, so to speak, through the volition and self-interest of the individual. It was not far to the next stage where marriage (which the evolving ideology still held identical with legitimate sexual expression) came to be seen as a right of all citizens.[122]

If officials moved cautiously toward relaxing state regulation of sexual behavior, still, by the 1790s they had moved far along this road and far away from central absolutist assumptions. Whereas previously officials had responded to the failure of sexual regulation by raising or tinkering with penalties, now officials doubted law could achieve much in this realm at all. Whereas religion had once been a prime motive and justification for sexual laws, secular goals and increasingly public opinion set, or canceled, the regulatory agenda. Even a moderately conservative moralist like Brauer did not appeal to religion as a fount of authority for sex-crime legislation. He argued that "as long as nothing better can happen, one [that is, the government] at least should not, by making the laws more lenient still, brand oneself on the forehead publicly, before the more religious part of the public, as participating in the irresponsible view of this excessive growth of sensuality." Religious scruple or princely Christian duty had withered to respect for religious public opinion, an altogether different principle.

Whereas subsistence had set the frame for absolutist regulation, the enthusiasm

---

[122] On marriage as a right, indeed duty, of the citizen of civil society, see Chapter 6, pp. 240–42, and Chapter 7, pp. 285–93.

of upper-level officials for the marriage of the poor shows that overpopulation had ceased to be a fear. In the early nineteenth century the dislocations of war, incomplete economic reform, and a rise in population revived this fear, but not before some of the principles of relaxed state control had been inscribed into law. Three factors had helped unseat the tyranny of subsistence in the minds of late-eighteenth-century upper-level officials. One was faith in economic growth, the result of liberal economic reforms that were the counterpart to and guarantee of civil society. Another was the incessant teaching of cameralists that population equaled state power. The third was a change in the horizon of central and middle-level administrators. The day-to-day concerns that still dominated the outlook of local officials had largely vanished for their higher colleagues. Where local officials still counted the coins in the poor chest, higher officials had lifted their sights to the territorial level, where particular economic hitches evened out in a statistics of general prosperity.[123] Upper officials, partly under cameralist influence, had developed a sense of an aggregate, or even abstract, state, and of themselves as its dedicated administrators, if necessary, even against the ruler's wishes (*vide* Baden-Baden). As central officials conceived themselves as an independent bureaucracy dedicated to principles potentially at variance with those dear to local administrators or to the prince, they laid the foundations for the radical reforms of the Napoleonic period.[124] But they achieved their self-consciousness as independent servants of the abstract state (of law) necessarily in tandem with the growth of civil society.

The difference between absolutist assumptions and those of the 1790s was due both to 150 years of administrative evolution and to the permeation of bureaucracy with extragovernmental ideas coming from civil society. It is striking how strongly "public opinion" shaped upper-bureaucratic thinking. The reports show that the sex and gender ideology being worked out in late Enlightenment journals provided even stodgy and tradition-minded officials with the (contradictory) model of sexual nature, with its assumptions about biology, gender, and the putative public impact of sexual behavior, that guided their recommendations on sexual regulation.

Learning from Civil Society: The Views of the Upper and Middle Officials on Sex and Gender

The more influenced he was by liberal Enlightened public discourse (either as a supporter or as an informed critic), the more likely the official was to speculate about the nature of the sexual drive, its occurrence in males and females, its health or biological risks, and its social or antisocial potential. Of the four reports we are comparing, traditional Burghausen had the least to say on this subject. Officials

---

[123] Nineteenth-century local administrators battled their middle and central-level colleagues for fifty years over whether the poor had a right to wed.

[124] The classic study of the bureaucracy's developing independence is Hans Rosenberg, *Bureaucracy, Aristocracy, Autocracy: The Prussian Experience, 1660–1815* (Cambridge, Mass., 1958).

there were acquainted with the gist of the medical and pedagogical literature on masturbation and firmly believed that too much sexual activity (for males) at too young an age, made (males) unable to have children and thus unsuited for marriage. Otherwise, the Burghausener satisfied themselves with remarking that marriage was the proper place for sexual activity, and that was that.

This was remarkable reticence, or uninterest, compared to the other three reports. Landshut, but especially Straubing, succumbed to all manner of speculation taken as fact. Both were clearly well versed in the burgeoning essayistic and belletristic writings that were beginning to congeal into a coherent sexual ideology.

Let us begin with the common denominators of official agreement on matters sexual. All four reports agreed that sexual passion was a natural urge that the authorities should discourage until the individual had reached the biological and social maturity necessary for marriage. The exact encouragement depended upon the reporter's degree of Enlightenment: not surprisingly the absolutists at Burghausen worried about old bugaboos like dancing and pubs and recommended such old remedies as clothing regulations for servants and "secret overseers" to spy on sexual offenders; their more modern colleagues at Landshut for example, targeted fashionable "impudent clothing" and "premature novel reading, which upsets the head and heart and only serves sentimentality, not mature thinking and action [*die Herz und Kopf verstimmen, die nur zum empfindeln, nicht zum reiffen denken und handeln dienen*]," whereas others feared the bad example of parents, teachers, and priests.

If all these officials agreed that sexual desire was natural, they did not necessarily believe it was equally distributed between men and women. Consonant with pre-Enlightened assumptions about sexual nature, the old-fashioned spirits of Burghausen seem implicitly to have felt that sexual drive was a human quality shared in equal measure by both men and women.[125] The more liberal reporters from Landshut and Straubing were inclined to associate sexual expression with women, whereas the conservative Brauer identified men as the main source of sexual miscreancy. Thus, the more Enlightened or post-Enlightened views were more likely to assume gender differences in sexual nature. They were not yet likely, however, to assume differences among classes. Unlike many nineteenth-century writers, who imagined that the lower orders were closer to animal nature and thus possessed a stronger sexual drive than their social betters, the Landshuter explicitly remarked that "people of the lowest popular classes [*der nidrigsten Volksklaße*] . . . are driven by the same passions as others ["distinguished persons"] and are entitled to the same laws." The other reports implicitly shared this opinion and were doubtless strengthened in that conviction by the prevailing doctrine of equality under the law.

The most important difference of opinion among officials concerned the relation

---

[125] The gender inequality in the laws recommended by Burghausen did not reflect assumptions about differences in sexual biology between men and women, but rather their attachment to older, customary law (which treated gender differentially, as a *Stand*), their perception of men's and women's different moral responsibilities, and their judgment that men and women were differently able to withstand harsh corporal punishment.

of sex to gender. Befitting the political-ideological typology I have suggested, the more liberal officials at Straubing were especially generous with their speculation on this subject, illustrating nicely how unreflected absolutist regulatory preoccupations could become reformed as liberal sexual ideology.

The Straubinger greatly admired the new model Prussian law code (*Allgemeines Landrecht*), which had just gone into effect. They too favored its decriminalization of first-time fornication for females. But instead of resting content with the old argument of thus discouraging infanticide, they preferred sexual-psychological reasons to justify forgiveness:

> There are many causes which together recommend especially in the case of women an indulgent leniency. First, this offence occurs mostly in youth, when the character has no solidity, when temperament and principle, sensuality and reason, premeditation and example struggle with one another and alternately gain the upper hand. Second, the crime occurs in a condition of the strongest passion, when all reflection and power of deliberation is lamed.

These grounds, which might just as easily have applied to men, were thus peculiarly reserved for women, who had been the traditional targets of absolutist sexual reform. Abandoning the reason of infanticide for sexual argumentation thus tended to associate women with irresistible sexual passion. Several pages later, when the reporters needed to justify extending leniency to male fornicators too, they had to return to other, contradictory assertions about sexual nature:

> The claim that the woman is the weaker party can scarcely be applied to moral character [*sittlichen Charackter*]; agreed, the female sex, at least the greater part of it, is used to acting with less forethought; but it is a great question whether in the spontaneous moment when the sex drive destroys all other sensations, the man is more capable of deliberation than the woman. The latter has the advantage that nature has equipped woman with a higher degree of modesty in order to moderate the wild fire of the man. The man appears to be more culpable only in first-time fornication, because here for the most part an inexperienced maiden is surprised by the audacity of her lover, or is seduced by dazzling promises. There are low men who, after having satisfied their sensual lusts, leave the pregnant woman to her fate and try to avoid the costs of compensation by denial. The worry that the fear of punishment could mislead [men] to more such base behavior is the basis for our opinion that the man, too, should be handled with the same leniency for first-time fornication.

The views in this passage were the standard ones widely discussed in the public press. The contradictions were equally standard: the woman was both more prone to sexual indulgence ("acts with less forethought") and less ("higher degree of modesty"); similarly, the man's sexual desire was both more urgent ("wild fire") than hers, but more controllable (he acts with more forethought). Whereas he was associated with sexual potency *and* with rationality, she was at worst irrational and at best not moral, for her modesty was a gift of nature, not the product of her rational will. Reform absolutist solicitude for the unwed pregnant woman encouraged this dichotomous picture of female weakness and male power, but it did not require the speculation about sexual nature.

In another section of their report, the Straubing officials again entered new theoretical territory. Like countless absolutist judges before them, they imagined the illegitimate mother as "surprised" by her lover's importunings or "blinded" by promises, that is, moved to intercourse by interpersonal or social reasons, while they reduced the fathers' motives to the lapidary formula: "satisfaction of their sensual lusts." Male sexual desire was simple and needed no further explanation. But under the direct influence of the pedagogical/masturbation debate, male sexual desire suddenly became problematic. "When the wild fire of sensual desire breaks out before its time, and leads to secret sins [masturbation], the results for the unhappy subjects as well as for the state are dreadful and horrible," the reporters opined, worrying about (male) teachers seducing (male) pupils to the solitary vice.[126] Following the preoccupations of the pedagogues, the officials also believed the danger was not homosexual attraction, but biological depletion. The masturbation model had the curious effect of prolonging the legal life of the male seducer and of making males the possible victims of seduction. After almost a century of reform absolutist legal writing centered on women and sexual law, in which she was the weak victim and he, the sexually and rationally powerful seducer, decriminalizing fornication had freed him from punishment as a seducer of women. But the even stronger need of civil society to conceive of males as both sexually potent and rationally calculating, caused the male seducer to reappear as the ruiner of boys. Males were now entering the sexual-legal discussion in formally similar ways to women as victims of seduction and injudicious laws (insofar as the Straubinger feared male fornicants would be "misled to more such base behavior" by fear of punishment).

The picture of sexual drive the Straubinger report presents functioned in legal discourse in several ways. It established a biological difference between men and women and identified the latter more strongly with sexual susceptibility than the former, though it hesitated to enshrine such a difference in the law. It identified sexual susceptibility as antithetical to reason. By focusing on the seduced young woman and the seduced male child/adolescent/pupil, it cast the (formerly) sexually active miscreants as victims of both their (natural) biological potential and of unscrupulous, experienced men. By playing on their alleged weakness, it provided an avenue for their escape from punishment, but at the same time it underscored their potential need for official supervision or tutelage. These developmental possibilities are only hints in the Straubing report, but they show that pieces of the later

---

[126] This is clear from the fact that discussions of education in the eighteenth century almost always refer to boys, who were more usually pupils than were girls. See Mary Jo Maynes, *Schooling for the People: Comparative Local Studies of Schooling History in France and Germany, 1750–1850* (New York, 1985), 104, 114, 130. Furthermore, the antimasturbation literature, which was the source of information on this subject for the Straubing and Burghausen officials, focused on male pupils. I discuss this further in Chapter 7.

sexual-legal matrix were already present in the minds of upper officials whom the Napoleonic breakthrough would shortly put in the position of redrafting laws.

Yet, there was also criticism of these developmental possibilities within the bureaucracy. The moderate conservative Brauer, for example, was aware of the latest arguments surrounding sexual behavior and for the most part did not accept them. Brauer's bureaucratic interlocutor Herzog[127] had arrayed a string of mostly late-enlightened maxims to guide sex-crime law reform.[128] He had pleaded for (geographically) uniform laws that could actually be applied in practice, not just educative or terror-inspiring edicts. He had argued that laws were unlikely ever to eradicate fornication. He had favored eased marriage for the poor. Most of all, he had wanted to match the law more closely with public opinion (as he saw it) and to use the latter where the former was powerless to act.[129] It was this move away from the state and toward society that opened the door to what Brauer felt were immoral, misguided, and misogynist principles. For one thing, the high importance Herzog ascribed to public opinion led him to champion public humiliation as a better deterrent than other punishments, thus flying in the face of all the arguments in the past fifty years. More than this, Herzog had wanted to follow what he took to be conventional wisdom and punish the woman sexual miscreant more than the man. This principle had never existed in Badenese law, so Herzog was not returning to an older tradition; his call for inscribing the sexual double standard into law instead reflected the new "knowledge" about sexual nature emerging from the public discussions in civil society.

Brauer was quite unwilling to follow the logic of modern public opinion in replacing equality before the law with the double standard. The double standard, he wrote, "which claims that fornication by men should be less strongly judged than fornication by women . . . undermines the basis of all morality, contradicts the example of all truly wise legislation, and would decree injustice of a most unusual sort [die aparteste Ungerechtigkeit statuirt]." Brauer went further and analyzed the problem in sociological terms.

> According to conventional ideas, more dishonor accrues to women than to men for the misuse of the sexual drive [Misbrauch des Geschlechtstriebes]—that is true; but this conventional opinion comes about because the male sex sets the tone of society [als das Tongebende], and, thanks to egoism, the reigning failure of mankind, would prefer to forgive its own misdeeds in this point, than those of women. But this opinion itself is a product of degenerate sensuality [der entarteten Sinnlichkeit] and, far from being nourished by the lawmaker, should on the contrary be strongly counteracted.

[127] His arguments can be reconstructed from Brauer's reply, which (apparently) takes them up seriatim and begins with a paraphrase of what Brauer goes on to demolish. Brauer, "Ueber den Regierungsvorschlag."

[128] The writer was not entirely consistent. He retained public humiliation, for example. He also argued that laws worked by causing fear in would-be offenders, but he used this absolutist premise not to call for harsher laws, but to claim that even the harsh laws had not worked and should be abandoned. It may be that he kept this non-Enlightened argument in order to argue an Enlightened cause.

[129] See pp. 131–32 for the actual recommendations of the Hofrat Collegium.

It may at first seem surprising to read such an analysis from the pen of a moderate conservative, accustomed as we are to imagining that the progress of liberalism is a universally emancipatory process that frees women as well as men.[130] But there were good, structural reasons for Brauer's striking gender egalitarianism. First, Brauer's was a moral argument whose form (and content) remained close to their religious antecedents. Brauer was not inclined to see men as superior to women simply because of the catalog of virtues the emerging gender-polarity ideology[131] ascribed to men. Reason, physical strength, activity, inventiveness, education, and so forth were not necessarily better in the eyes of a moderate conservative than the qualities ascribed to women. Particularity and difference could be virtues in their own right.[132] The differences between the two sexes (and Brauer believed there were many) did not produce moral differences, either in God's eyes, or the law's. Second, Brauer was highly skeptical of those doctors and popular writers who were so active in producing the new version of gender inequality. Whereas literati, he wrote, "look at the world as if it were bathed in moonlight [*mit Mondscheinsgefühl*]," doctors arrived at their scurrilous view of women because they saw only the "basest" women, those "who fall into their hands because of their office," or who were prostitutes. Both of these extremes were as far removed from reality, in Brauer's view, as were the imaginings of legal reformers who concocted their schemes via "mere a priori reflection." Brauer despised all these forms of knowledge based, he thought, upon incomplete, or indeed, no experience. Brauer's own picture of women came from years of experience as an administrator, and, it would seem, from his own happy marriage, if we may judge from his acid remark that the distorted view of the medical men might impress his opponent "as an unmarried man lacking also the experience of having served in family court [*Ehegericht*]."

For skeptics like Brauer, then, "public opinion" was not a reliable source of legal principle because it was particular and masculine, not truly universal, and adhered to the laws of (masculine) self-interest, not Enlightened principles of judicial equality. Its medical experts extrapolated from incomplete knowledge, its utopian legal reformers from abstractions; neither source was as good as experience reflected through intelligence.

But Enlightened skeptics had a hard time arguing successfully against the sexual model that had congealed as public opinion. The difficulties become clear in Brauer's attempt to answer two further reasons that the would-be reformer Herzog adduced for using public humiliation to punish women more harshly than men for sexual misdeeds. First, "nature had surrendered the female sex to a higher degree of

---

[130] Ludwig von Heß, a liberal reformer in the employ of the Swedish government, made an analysis of male sexual hypocrisy and the law very close to Brauer's, demonstrating the critical principles of Enlightenment, if Enlighteners wished to employ them. Whether Brauer was familiar with Heß's book is uncertain. Heß, *Eine Antwort*, 69–71.

[131] The classic article on this subject remains Karin Hausen, "Family and Role-Division: The Polarisation of Sexual Stereotypes in the Nineteenth Century—an Aspect of the Dissociation of Work and Family Life," in *The German Family*, ed. R. J. Evans and W. R. Lee (London, 1981), 51–83.

[132] Mannheim, *Konservatismus*, 111–12.

physical and moral degradation by giving it a wider field of sensual pleasure [*durch Einräumung eines breiteren Feldes des Wollustgenusses*], and thus a dam must be erected against this through [legal] stronger antidotes." Second, only women engaged in prostitution. Brauer tried to dispatch this second argument by claiming that men were less often prostitutes not because of greater morality, but "partly because of the greater vehemence of their own drives, partly because of easier opportunity to engage in other economic pursuits, and partly because of the impotence of their own staying power [*jener Ohnmacht ihrer eigenen Ausdauer*]."

Brauer's reply to the first assertion gave him the rare opportunity to explain his own views on the sexual nature of men and women. As we have seen, he rejected the empirical basis for the allegation that women had more capacity for sexual pleasure than did men. Medical men, he felt, worked from a skewed sample of the worst women, and Herzog was unmarried and thus had no personal experience of women. Brauer's life as a married man and experienced official had led him to the exactly opposite conclusion:

> Among one hundred men who engage in sexual depravity, there will be hardly one, who will be driven by some other reason than the sexual drive itself. However, among ten women who fall, there will be barely two, for whom that will have been the immediate reason. For the rest it will have been sensuality *in general* [*Sinnlichkeit im Allgemeinen*], either they need money for necessities related to clothing or food [*zu Bedürfnissen für Staat und Gaumen*], or a provision in order to make ends meet more easily in the future, or they hope to fulfill other intentions in this manner (through misuse of the sexual drive). Therefore, if there were not men who wanted to satisfy their sexual drive at this price, eight-tenths of the fornication cases would not occur. Only this much is true about the above assertion: when woman are once seduced [*verleitet*] by other passions to the frequent misuse of that drive, they can go much farther toward immoderation, because they can be active or passive at will, and thus do not feel exhaustion so quickly. Once they are used to such immoderate stimulation [*Unmaase des Reizes*], they are less hindered than men are by natural impotence [*Ohnmacht der Natur*], which gave an apparent reason for the false conclusion of many writers. That conclusion is then applied entirely out of its context when one asserts a moral ruin commensurate with the physical depravity that [thus] would occur primarily among women. One would indeed have reason to assert that the inverse proportion [would be true], namely that moral ruin would be greater in men the more they were restrained by [mere] natural impotence.[133]

Brauer's rebuttals are interesting for what they concede to the new arguments about sexual nature as well as for what they withhold. Despite his desire to contradict their conclusions and reasoning processes, Brauer finds himself subscribing to the rudiments of the ideology of sexual/gender difference. He went farthest in this direction when he speculated about "the greater vehemence of [men's] own [sexual] drives." A similar concession is present in his silence about the sexual pleasure women might derive from nonmarital sexual acts. Brauer's analysis of the varying motives of men and women therefore identified overt sexual motivation

[133] Emphasis in the original.

more with men. For the most part, however, Brauer acknowledged sexual differences between men and women only in the indisputable fact that women could engage in "normal" heterosexual intercourse "passively," that is without being themselves excited, which was impossible for men, and which meant that women could tolerate more such activity than men could.

Brauer's concessions to the new ideology were thus carefully limited. From whatever biological differences he admitted, he deduced neither moral difference nor legal conclusion. Unlike more liberal officials, he was disinclined to argue according to women's natural modesty, or their sex drive, emotions, or moral development. He may have thought that fornication and other sexual misdeeds occurred when people got carried away by their biological needs or emotional vulnerability, but he did not make that the center of his explanatory picture. Indeed, although Brauer discussed biological difference, he viewed illicit sexual relations in a primarily social context. The ideology surrounding such relations, the "double standard," came from men's preeminent social position, he felt. The economic ability to satisfy their desires gave men the opportunity to initiate nonmarital acts, whereas women's subsistence needs (*Bedürfnisse*) disposed them to cooperate.

Brauer was the only one of the officials of 1794 to interpret sexual behavior in such a markedly social way. Even the Straubinger, the only others to come even close to such an interpretation, tended to privatize the (social) motives, that is, men promised women something in order to get their way, but their promises appear as individual ploys sundered from their social context (which would presumably have been marriage). The extent to which Brauer saw illicit sex as a social product was the exact extent to which it was not the result of an irresistible, biological urge. Brauer thus fought a rearguard action on three fronts: he resisted purely biological arguments, he countered logical abstraction with concrete experience, and he rejected the assertion that men and women were fundamentally different in ways that law should reflect. His resistance was strengthened by his disdain for modern medical and lay writers, his suspicion of schematic philosophizing, his adherence to Badenese legal tradition, which was egalitarian, and his religious scruples, which dictated moral equality between men and women.

A thorough victory of the new ideas inside government was hindered by a number of factors, including the ones motivating Brauer. Neither the modernists in Straubing nor their fairly progressive colleagues in Landshut advocated overturning the tenet of equal treatment for men and women under the law, which had meanwhile become thoroughly entrenched as a bureaucratic principle. Equal treatment in the abstract was of course also a tenet of liberal civil society, in contradiction to the legal burden of its sexual ideas. That contradiction made it harder for reform-minded officials easily to champion the legal double standard. In fact, the most unequal of the four reports was from Burghausen, where the traditionalists clung to the mild gender inequalities inscribed into customary law and not yet reformed. All other reporters were egalitarians. Effective administration by itself seemed to demand systematic and equal application of law; this bureaucratic imperative kept the law from completely reflecting the new sex/gender system even in the nineteenth century.

The reports of the 1790s show how important extragovernmental ideas had become as guides to official action in the matter of sexual regulation. Whereas at the beginning and middle of the eighteenth century, officials had initiated reforms from their own, administrative perspective, by century's end they were to a large degree responding to views coming from civil society. The initiative had changed hands. To understand how this change had come about we must now turn to the state's new interlocutor: civil society.

4

✿

The Cameralist Theory of Civil Society

The cameralists were the first theorists of German civil society.[1] Mostly upper-level bureaucrats, they wrote handbooks of good government for princes and fellow state administrators. Their tracts, which number some fourteen thousand,[2] embody a genre unique to Germany. Certain peculiarities of German government, economy and society explain why this was so. First, in the seventeenth and eighteenth centuries Germans could look to developments in England and Holland and judge the advantages and disadvantages of commercial capitalism. Cameralism[3] therefore reflected on a foreign present in order to fashion a domestic future bursting with the advantages of a thriving economy but without its disruptive social consequences. Second, no Jean Bodin or Niccolo Macchiavelli flourished here because no German prince could consider, or even imagine, shaking himself loose from the myriad legal obligations, to the Holy Roman Empire, to neighboring territories, to the Estates, to city charters, corporations, and noble families, that collectively clipped the wings of his heraldic eagles. Yet public authority in Germany, especially in the cities, was historically responsible for virtually the entire gamut of human activity: health, safety, the trade and consumption of food and drink, clothing, decorum, and so on. This was the realm of the early modern "police" (*Polizey*); as the territorial princes expanded their power in the Thirty Years' War, they acquired this extensive police responsibility for the practical running of everyday life.[4] German princes' power was thus both limited in fact and absolute in theory. This muddle was made worse by the growing exploitative power of princely taxation, which mightily strained relations between the princes and the taxed. Cameralism was an attempt to solve this muddle, to integrate and balance these conflicting vectors of power and responsibility.

---

[1] The best modern introduction to the cameralists is by Erhard Dittrich, *Die deutschen und österreichischen Kameralisten* (Darmstadt, 1974). Also see Angela Raupach, "Zum Verhältnis von Politik und Ökonomie im Kameralismus—Ein Beitrag zur sozialen Theoriebildung in Deutschland in ihrer Genese als Polizei" (Ph.D. diss., Universität Hamburg, 1982); Albion Woodbury Small, *The Cameralists, the Pioneers of German Social Polity* (Chicago, 1909); Zielenziger, *Kameralisten;* and Louise Sommer, *Die österreichischen Kameralisten in dogmengeschichtlicher Darstellung* (Vienna, 1920).

[2] Raupach, "Zum Verhältnis," 11.

[3] The name was retrospective, applied to these writers by the early eighteenth century.

[4] On the concept and practice of early modern "police," see Raeff, *Well-Ordered Police State* and Hans Maier, *Die ältere deutsche Staats- und Verwaltungslehre*, 2d ed. (Munich, 1986).

On the one hand, cameralists served their masters by advancing schemes of economic growth and efficient administration to augment the prince's wealth and power.[5] On the other hand, they anchored the prince to the existing network of legal obligation, but more than that, to an ideal of the common good (*Gemeinwohl*) that public authority was to serve and guarantee. This is not the place to recount the scholarly debate over whether the concept of "Gemeinwohl" was meant to be a genuine curb on princely power or merely a justification for its unlimited extension. For our purposes the important point is that cameralism produced the first home-grown theory of the proper relation between state and society, and that it did so from within a framework of collectivity and mutual obligation. That framework was, further, both practical and utopian. Practical, because the cameralists aimed to provide down-to-earth advice for real administrators on how to run real governments. Political theory has largely disdained their efforts, because they had little to say, and then nothing original, on such matters as the social contract or constitutionalism.[6] They had little need for origin myths or abstract legal theory; they could and did take for granted public authority (government) and social order because, despite the ravages of the Thirty Years' War, neither had been existentially shaken by civil war (as in England or Holland) or by vain, crushing centralism (as in France). The problem was not to ground state or society, but to bring them into harmony by encouraging their "common good." Despite their lack of theoretical sophistication, the cameralists introduced the concept of "citizen" (*Staatsbürger*) to Germany and laid the foundations for an independent judiciary and thus for the *Rechtsstaat;*[7] and in the course of reflecting on how government ("police") should relate to society, some later cameralists postulated for the first time a private sphere shielded from public intervention and proceeded to ponder the new sort of "public," the civil society, that might arise from these new relations.

Alongside its practicality, then, cameralism also engaged in a doubly utopian speculation. First, it dwelt in the future; it was forward-looking and interested in change, even as it sought to uphold many elements of the status quo. Second, it was literally utopian, or "eudaemonistic," in the contemporary phrase. It aimed at the continuous improvement of government, society, and individual, until each had helped the other to achieve perfection. As Christian Wolff explained, "Since nature requires us to strive toward the best as far as we are able, therefore we must also have a conception of the best or most perfect, so we can judge toward what we must strive."[8] That is, the future contained moral content to guide the actions of state, society, and the individual in the imperfect meantime.

---

[5] Some writers, stressing this aspect, misrepresent the cameralists as simple apologists for the untrammeled growth of state power.

[6] Raupach, "Zum Verhältnis," 75–76, 250.

[7] Georg-Christoph von Unruh, "Polizei, Polizeiwissenschaft und Kameralistik," in *Deutsche Verwaltungsgeschichte. Vom Spätmittelalter bis zum Ende des Reiches*, ed. Kurt G. A. Jeserich, Hans Pohl, and Georg-Christoph von Unruh (Stuttgart, 1983), 1:415–16.

[8] *Vernünfftige Gedancken von dem Gesellschafftlichen Leben der Menschen und insonderheit dem gemeinen Wesen. Zur Beförderung der Glückseeligkeit des menschlichen Geschlechtes, den Liebhabern der Wahrheit mitgetheilet*, 4th ed. (Frankfurt, 1736), par. 226, p. 170.

❖ The Cameralist Theory of Civil Society ❖

In their effort to define and harmonize relations between government and civil society, the cameralists all, at greater or lesser length, pondered how the sexual drive and sexual relations fitted into the grand scheme. These thoughts are the first explicit reflections on how sexual life relates to the public interest in the transition to "modern times." The answer to the question of which member of the triad of state, society, and individual was responsible for making sex "orderly" was largely determined by another triad on which cameralist thinking rested: the collective nature of *Gemeinwohl*, obligation as the foundation for rights, and morality as the guide to action.

Scholars have disagreed about whom to consider a bona fide cameralist.[9] To the indisputable authors of treatises on practical government and police science (*Polizeywissenschaft*), I add the famous "Enlighteners" Christian Thomasius (1655–1728) and Christian Wolff (1679–1754), both of whom wrote influential treatises on morality and society.[10] Because of his enormous influence on Thomasius and others, I also include the only early modern German thinker normally ranked among "real" political theorists, Samuel Pufendorf (1632–94).

Listing cameralists, however, does not define cameralism. Not only did contemporary cameralists disagree on numerous points, cameralism as a whole developed from its seventeenth-century, early absolutist beginnings, through its elevation as a recognized "science" taught formally at universities (beginning in 1727), to its decline in the late eighteenth and disappearance in the early nineteenth century. Since my purpose is not to relate the internal history of cameralism but to examine how the cameralists judged sexual behavior in its public context, my use of their writings will be strictly instrumental. Readers interested in the more usual themes associated with cameralism: mercantilism, capitalism, princely authority, administrative differentiation, and so on, should turn to the secondary literature already cited and to the works of the cameralists themselves.

I begin with the cameralists' views on civil society (*bürgerliche Gesellschaft*), for it was within this context that they evaluated the importance of sexual behavior.

The Cameralists on the Nature of Civil Society

"The state is a society," wrote Austria's most famous cameralist, Joseph von Sonnenfels (1733–1817), in 1777.[11] This conviction he shared with all his colleagues, early and late. This view was not the unthinking imitation of ancient political theorists. It was an attempt to solve in a single stroke precisely the problem that absolutism posed, namely, that government threatened to become widely separated from the governed and needed to be brought (back) into alignment.[12] Indeed, the

---

[9] Compare Zielenziger, *Kameralisten,* 85–110, 114–34, 202–3, 207, 216, 222, 265, 301, 395, with Raupach, "Zum Verhältnis," 17–41.

[10] According to Karl Gottlob Rößig, *Versuch einer pragmatischen Geschichte der Oekonomie- Policey- und Cameralwissenschaften seit dem sechzehnten Jahrhunderte bis zu unsern Zeiten. Deutschland* (Leipzig, 1781), part 1, 35 n. Thomasius was the first to teach cameral science at a university.

[11] In his "Über das Verhältnis der Stände," in *Politische Abhandlungen* (Vienna, 1777), 108.

[12] Raupach, "Zum Verhältnis," 77.

very word "state" was in ill-repute. That is why the author of "the most popular handbook on German politics,"[13] Veit Ludwig von Seckendorff (1626–92) had to apologize for using the word at all: "Although *Stand* and state [*Stat*] should have the identical meaning, the former is more of a personal quality. . . . However, I by no means use the word state as it is often understood nowadays, by which practically all disloyalty, disgrace and profligacy in many perverse places is excused by reference to state, reason of state or state interest [*Statssachen*]."[14]

To set matters right, the cameralists aimed to demonstrate to their princely masters "how the prosperity of the country or the welfare of its subjects is inseparably bound up with the interest of their head, and this is the true and single principle of all of cameralist science."[15] Others admonished regents even more unmistakably. Johann Joachim Becher (1625–82) summed up his advice and definition in a single sentence: "In short, everything which weakens human society [*Gesellschaft*] is to be eliminated and punished: if I wanted to define a state [*Stadt*] correctly, I would call it a *populous, prosperous community* [*nahrhaffte Gemein*]."[16]

The postulated unity of state and civil society meant that the common good (*Gemeinwohl*) was literally common to both; gouging taxes and unsound policies were doubly ruinous "because the duties and rights of a regent of such a state consist in this: ever to maintain and encourage the secure and comfortable life of both his subjects and himself, as the head of them, in the interests of the best for the entire state or for this body, [which is] in head and limbs in every way inseparable."[17]

This inseparability did not mean that the cameralists had forgotten about administration or "Regierung," what we now call the "state." On the contrary, the "entire internal administration" they termed "police."[18] The police oversaw, as Theodor Ludwig Lau (1670–1740) put it, "the internal and external constitution of a state," of which "the internal consists in 1. a satisfied society [*vergnügten Gesellschaft*], which 2. leads a satisfied life. The society becomes strong through a growth in inhabitants and a happy populace."[19] Befitting central Europe's subsistence condition, cameralist theory concentrated strongly on promoting general material prosperity, but it did so in a way designed to overcome the deadlock of the subsistence

---

[13] According to Leopold von Ranke, *Neun Bücher preußischer Geschichte* (1847), 1:45 n. 1; cited in Zielenziger, *Kameralisten*, 335.

[14] *Teutscher Fürsten Stat/ Oder: Gründliche und kurtze Beschreibung/welcher Gestalt Fürstenthümer/ Graff- und Herrschafften im H. Römischen Reich Teutscher Nation, welche Landes, Fürstliche unnd hohe obrigkeitliche Regalia haben/von Rechts- und löblicher Gewonheit wegen beschaffen zu seyn/Regieret/ mit Ordnungen und Satzungen/Geheimen und Iustitz Cantzeleyen/Consistoriis und andern hohen und niedern Gerichts-Instantien, Aemptern und Diensten/verfasset und versehen/ auch wie deroselben Cammer- und Hoffsachen bestellt zu werden pflegen.* (Hanau, 1657) iii.

[15] Johann Georg Leib (1708), *Von Verbesserung*, cited in Zielenziger, *Kameralisten*, 374.

[16] *Politische Discurs* (1673), cited in Zielenziger, *Kameralisten*, 210.

[17] Georg Heinrich Zincke (1692–1768 or 1769), *Anfangsgründe der Cameralwissenschaft, worinne dessen Grundriß weiter ausgeführet und verbessert wird* (Leipzig, 1755), 1:12–13.

[18] Zielenziger (about Theodor Ludwig Lau, but it is equally true for all cameralists until Justi, and for most cameralists after him), *Kameralisten*, 401.

[19] *Entwurff einer Wohl-eingerichteten Policey* (1717), cited in Zielenziger, *Kameralisten*, 401.

worldview. The cameralists dared imagine that population growth would result not in poverty but in increased production and trade, which in turn would nourish more people, with more needs, encouraging further production, and so on, in a continuous spiral of expansion and enrichment. The cameralist enthusiasm for population growth[20] set them apart from their nervous contemporaries in administration and removed one ancient reason to oversee (hetero)sexual behavior closely, though, as we shall see, few of the cameralists grasped this opportunity to promote relaxed oversight.[21]

More important, and more potentially subversive to the subsistence worldview, was their identification of consumption as the motor driving prosperity and the tie binding civil society together.[22] "In a word," wrote Becher in 1673, "consumption maintains these three *Stände* [peasants, merchants, and artisans], consumption is their soul . . . indeed, it is because of consumption that the merchant-*Stand* is so necessary to the community [*Gemeind*], and the peasant-*Stand* so large, since while the latter increases populousness, the former nourishes it."[23]

Encouraging consumption (and population growth) loosed a dynamic that ended in the rejection of subsistence thinking and its values.[24] Wolff drew the logical conclusion: "If one did not demand anything other than what was necessary for survival, then the greatest number of businesses [*Handthierungen*] would collapse, and many people would have no work with which to earn the bare necessities."[25] Therefore, the whole matter of luxury had to be rethought. Although the cameralists always favored moderation, they redefined luxury, once thought a sin, as a good deed. They did so hesitantly; many clung to the old moral equation of luxury-idleness-profligacy-sexual misbehavior, or they promoted domestically produced luxury items but not imports, or they cherished some sumptuary laws, but not others.[26] But in the end the law that equated increased consumption with the common good (*Gemeinwohl*) drove them relentlessly to the conclusion that "[luxury] is a blessing [*Wohlthat*] for society."[27]

From sin to blessing: this volte-face was one consequence of the logic of con-

---

[20] For bibliography on the cameralists' population policy, see Dittrich, *Die deutschen und österreichischen Kameralisten*, 43–44, 52, 61, 67, 74, 92, 96–97, 99, 107, 111–12.

[21] See, for instance, Joseph von Sonnenfels, "Über das Wort Bevölkerung," in his *Politische Abhandlungen*, 231–70, esp. 247–48.

[22] Cf. Sonnenfels, "Der Stände," 99–100.

[23] *Politische Discurs* (1673), cited in Zielenziger, *Kameralisten*, 223.

[24] Raupach, "Zum Verhältnis," 74.

[25] *Vernünfftige Gedancken*, 367.

[26] Johann Joachim Becher, *Psychosophia oder Seelen-Weißheit / Wie nemlich ein jeder Mensch auß Betrachtung seiner Seelen selbst allein alle Wissenschafft und Weißheit gründlich und beständig erlangen könne*, 2d ed. (Hamburg, 1705), 96–97; Christian Thomasius, *Von der Artzeney Wider die unvernünftige Liebe, und der zuvor nöthigen Erkäntniß Sein Selbst. Oder: Ausübung der Sitten-Lehre, Nebst einem Beschluß, Vorinnen der Autor den vielfältigen Nutzen seiner Sitten-Lehre zeiget und von seinem Begrif der Christlichen Sitten-Lehre ein aufrichtiges Bekäntniß thut*, 8th ed. (Halle, 1726), part 8, par. 45, pp. 210–11; Zielenziger, *Kameralisten*, 312 (on Wilhelm von Schröder); Wolff, *Vernünfftige Gedancken*, sec. 384–87, pp. 366–74.

[27] Sonnenfels, "Bevölkerung," 248–49.

sumption. Expansion, that is, inevitable, continuous change, was a second. This death knell to the status quo and central characteristic of coming capitalism was doubtless ill understood by the cameralists, though they assiduously prepared its path with their advice.[28]

A third and even more corrosive corollary to consumptionism was the centrality of desire. For, cut loose from necessity, consumption rested wholly on the fulfillment of individual desire. Cameralists, like many natural-law theorists, interpreted desire as a longing for pleasure and comfort, that is, as a longing for material happiness. That assumption returned them to the problem of luxury, contemplation of which produced the baldest cameralist statement of the materialist goals of the "state." Johann Heinrich Gottlob von Justi (1720–71) in his classic textbook on police science, *Grundsätze der Policey-Wissenschaft* (1759), summed up where the innocent principles of cameralism led in state theory: "All luxury [*Ueppigkeit*] basically aims to make life comfortable and pleasant. This concept already shows that luxury is not something that a government [*Regierung*] can eliminate by itself. The end goal of all states [*Staaten*] is the happiness of the subjects, and to this belongs without doubt, [the possibility of making] one's life comfortable and pleasant."[29]

This transition from the negative principles of subsistence and protection from harm and suffering to the positive principles of happiness and pleasure is also clear in the reasons cameralists gave for the founding of the state/society. Although early cameralists all included well-being (*Wohlfahrt, Nahrung*) as fundamental to the origins of the state,[30] the basic impetus was "to build protection around themselves against the evils that threaten man from man," as Pufendorf, following Hobbes, wrote in 1673.[31] "Civil society [*bürgerliche Gesellschaft*] would not have arisen, if one had not begun to fear loveless people [*lieblosen Leuten*] and sought protection from their hatred," wrote Christian Thomasius in 1692.[32] Ten years later the

[28] See Hans Medick, *Naturzustand und Naturgeschichte der bürgerlichen Gesellschaft. Die Ursprünge der bürgerlichen Sozialtheorie als Geschichtsphilosophie und Sozialwissenschaft bei Samuel Pufendorf, John Locke und Adam Smith* (Göttingen, 1973), 34–5, 61, on the relation of natural-law theories to early capitalism and Raupach, "Kameralisten," 275–76, on their innocence in relation to capitalism.

[29] *Grundsätze der Policey-Wissenschaft in einem vernünftigen, auf den Endzweck der Policey gegründeten, Zusammenhange und zum Gebrauch academischer Vorlesungen abgefasset*, 2d ed. (Göttingen, 1759), par. 308, p. 229; also see par. 195, and Justi, *Die Grundfeste zu der Macht und Glückseligkeiten der Staaten; oder ausführliche Vorstellung der gesamten Policey-Wissenschaft* (Königsberg, 1760), vol. 1, sec. 257 note, sec. 793.

[30] Seckendorff, *Fürsten-Stat*, preface, not paginated, uses the term "Wolfart"; Becher, *Politische Discurs* (1673), cited in Zielenziger, *Kameralisten*, 210 uses "nahrhaffte Gemein"; Philipp Wilhelm von Hörnigk, *Österreich über alles, wenn es nur will* (1684) ed. Gustav Otruba (Vienna, 1964), 185, uses "bequemlich zu leben."

[31] Samuel Pufendorf, *On the Duty of Man and Citizen* (1673), trans. Michael Silverthorne, ed. James Tully (Cambridge, 1991), bk. 2, chap. 5, par. 7, p. 133; also bk. 1, chap. 5, pp. 46–55, and bk. 2, chap. 7, par. 3, p. 139.

[32] *Von der Kunst Vernünftig und Tugendhaft zu lieben, Als dem eintzigen Mittel zu einem glückseeligen, galanten und vergnügten Leben zu gelangen; Oder Einleitung der Sitten-Lehre, Nebst einer Vorrede, In welcher unter andern der Verfertiger der curiösen Monatlichen Unterredung freundlich erinnert und gebeten wird, von Sachen, die er nicht verstehet, nicht zu ertheilen, und den Autoren dermalens in Ruhe zu lassen*, 8th

balance had shifted. Wolff's classic definition still recognized security, but could take it for granted—the Thirty Years' War had receded in memory and an optimistic future beckoned:

> Because individual houses could not by themselves create all the comforts of life [*alle Bequemlichkeiten des Lebens*] of which they were capable, nor could they alone secure life and limb, and consequently could not attain the highest good for which they are bound to strive, so it was necessary that as many should come together and with united energy promote their best, so that they would be able to create all the comforts of life and, in conformity with natural obligation, advance unhindered from one perfection to the next and protect themselves adequately against all injury. When this occurs, they form a society [*Gesellschaft*], and the untrammelled progress in encouraging the common best, which they may achieve with their united energy, is the welfare of this society. This society is called the common entity [*das gemeine Wesen*].[33]

After Wolff, most cameralists simply assumed that (especially material) happiness was the main purpose of the state/society.[34]

For the cameralists, then, civil society was the most organized, self-conscious form of human life. Government was an aspect of it, but one whose duties were measured entirely in relation to the goals of civil society itself. The cameralists, their administrative backgrounds, conceived of civil society on its own terms, separately from government—indeed, their use of *Regierung* makes this separation clear, however later generations have misunderstood their use of the word "state." Their preoccupation with materialism has also tempted some scholars to reduce the cameralist view of civil society to the sphere of economic activity.[35] This is far from accurate. Civil society for the cameralists was always society in its organized entirety, not just as a collection of economic relations. As one moves from the seventeenth to the eighteenth century, the cameralist understanding of civil society shifted subtly from a (somewhat abstracted) conception of a truly existing entity, whose needs gave moral guidance and legitimacy to government, to a label for a developing social order, organized according to new principles, whose outline was becoming progressively clearer. This future-oriented vision was never meant, however, to obliterate the old social order, but to improve it. The cameralists carefully balanced the new and potentially unruly principles with counterweights to achieve ordered moderation.

Since it was within this balance of energy and restraint that sexual behavior found its definition and place, we must now examine these balancing pairs of characteristics. For our purposes five qualities of civil society are salient.

---

ed. (Halle, 1726), part 9, par. 10, p. 360.

[33] *Vernünfftige Gedancken*, par. 213, pp. 161–62.

[34] Zincke, *Anfangsgründe*, 12; Justi, *Grundsätze der Policey-Wissenschaft*, sec. 308; Johann Heinrich Jung [Stilling], *Lehrbuch der Staats-Polizey-Wissenschaft* (Leipzig, 1788), par. 212, p. 85.

[35] As in Raupach, "Zum Verhältnis," 77; or Jürgen Habermas, *The Structural Transformation of the Public Sphere: An Inquiry into a Category of Bourgeois Society*, trans. Thomas Burger (Cambridge, Mass., 1991), 3, 14–15, 30.

Desire

Civil society was driven by desire. Freed from the dictates of necessity, its wheels were turned by the motor of pleasure. "There are only two main sources, or two great mainsprings [*Triebfedern*] from which all the genius, invention and industriousness of a people arise," wrote Justi. "These are the desires [*Begierden*], to make life comfortable and pleasant for oneself, and the desire [*Verlangen*] for advantage. Both are natural to people, and alike innate. They need not be planted in people. One need only guide them correctly and remove the hindrances that block their path. . . . This urge [*Trieb*] [to make life comfortable] is founded in love of self."[36]

"Love of self" was a principle diametrically opposed to the collective values of subsistence Europe, and insofar as the cameralists did not set out to shatter their own world, but to improve it, self-love was as dangerous as it was necessary. They countered the danger by two strategies designed to temper either the degree of desire or its relentless, autistic individualism. In the first strategy they embraced the self and immersed themselves in studying it, so that they might understand the wellsprings of desire. Thomasius engaged himself most energetically in this pursuit. In two large books dissecting the emotions, he explained to the reader how to recognze "his own" emotional constitution and guide it toward "reasonable love" and satisfaction.[37] He expected his readers to be shocked at the central importance of desire to emotional life: "How would it be, if we were to say: desire [*Verlangen*] (*desiderium*) or lust [*Begierde*] (*cupiditas*) was the single main emotion, which subsumed all others? That would seem paradoxical, and yet I believe one could well say this."[38] He went on to redefine desire more palatably as "love" and to offer lengthy advice on its proper uses. His advice hinged on two major assumptions. Moderation brought the greatest happiness: "All objects of the senses, which cause no extraordinary or very sensitive movement, but merely maintain one's natural movement in a calm condition, are good." "One's greatest happiness consists of calm and moderately changing thoughts [perceptions]."[39] All of the cameralists agreed that moderation was the key to the right use of pleasure.[40] Second, Thomasius followed Pufendorf's dictum that "the rule for passions is: however strong they may be, a man can rise superior to them by the due use of reason."[41] The ability to regulate

[36] *Grundfeste*, vol. 1, par. 786, p. 689. Justi thought one might subsume desire for comfort under desire for advantage. See ibid., 689 n.

[37] *Von der Kunst*, and *Von der Artzeney*. Thomasius's guides were written for a male reader, as his advice on courting women in *Von der Kunst*, par. 56, pp. 183–84, makes clear. See the excellent discussion in Werner Schneiders, *Naturrecht und Liebesethik. Zur Geschichte der praktischen Philosophie im Hinblick auf Christian Thomasius* (Hildesheim, 1971).

[38] Thomasius, *Von der Artzeney*, part 4, par. 4, pp. 108–9.

[39] Thomasius, *Von der Kunst*, part 1, par. 52, p. 21, and part 2, par. 62.

[40] Raupach, "Zum Verhältnis," 154.

[41] Pufendorf, *Duty of Man*, bk. 1, chap. 1, par. 14, p. 21. The genderized formula should be taken as intentional.

one's appetites was the hallmark of the rational man and, later, the sine qua non for admission to civil society.

But neither repression nor saintly transcendence was the method by which one arrived at moderate desire. Instead, one followed one's own self-interest, for self-love coincided with the moral duties one owed to oneself. "Thus, morality [*Sitten-Lehre*] is nothing but the teaching that instructs a person in what one's true and highest happiness consists, how to attain this, and how to remove and overcome the hindrances to this thrown up by oneself."[42]

The second strategy to protect against the ravages of self-love was to refocus and anchor it in another (human) object. This strategy interpreted self-love in a directly or indirectly sexual way. Thomasius's solution was to exalt heterosexual love and, thus, the couple: "Where two souls are united, two wills must become one, and each loving person lives more for the other than for him/herself." Self-love dissolves into other-love. But this can only occur on the foundation of total emotional transparency and mutual sexual pleasure. Thomasius continued, "This cannot happen, if they do not both give each other every conceivable pleasure [*alles er-denckliches Vergnügen*] that is not contrary to reason . . . and reciprocally discover all each other's secrets and weaknesses."[43] Thomasius developed here the Protestant positive valuation of sex. Far from being a necessary evil, sexual pleasure was a necessary good. Without it, true, self-transcending love could not exist.

> It cannot be denied that the union of human souls or of two wills cannot occur without the contribution of the body, such that two souls truly and indeed become one soul and one person; on the contrary, this state must always be sought for in nothing else but in the identity of the external acts and non-acts [*Thun und Lassen*] of the body directed by two wills. And thus one cannot conceive of either friendship or love without the identical working of the body; and if one looks for the union of souls in the identity of wills, why should one not also say that, on account of the identity of the external bodily movement in friendship and love, the bodies likewise become one, and thus from two friends, one body and one soul must emerge every time.[44]

Thomasius's enthusiasm for carnal pleasure was unusual, and one must remember the occasion for it was a treatise on love, not on police (*Polizey*). Nonetheless, it is surely significant that later cameralists typically redirected self-love not into the couple, but into the family, which then became the seat of selflessness and altruism. This strategy had many advantages, which we will examine presently, but chief among them was that it shifted the focus from sexual attraction to social reproduction, which gave society a firmer (theoretical) foundation.

Finally, there is a hint in the writings of the later cameralists, that desire might not only be susceptible to rational choice by the individual's will, but also to manipulation by the governing authorities. Justi's phrase, "One need only guide

[42] Thomasius, *Von der Kunst*, part 2, par. 1, p. 57.
[43] Ibid., part 3, par. 50, p. 180.
[44] Ibid., part 4, par. 33, p. 171.

them correctly" suggests this.[45] Justi later elaborated: "The government can direct [bilden] the genius of its subjects in the direction it wants. It is as if it possessed a creative power. It need only give its approbation to a certain manner of living [Lebensart] by rewarding those who accomplish something excellent in it, and this manner of living will then become popular."[46] Joachim Georg Darjes (1714–91) recommended something similar, if more negative, when he observed (1768) that "it is advisable to entice [locken] the inhabitants of a state to observe police commands more through consequences that are pleasant to them, than through punishments."[47] These common insights seem to have been limited to taking advantage of desires conceived of as natural, rather than actually forming those desires in the interests of easier administration.

Materialism

We have already seen the pronounced materialist bias inherent in cameralist theory. The cameralists' fixation on the Kammer (treasury) often led them to emphasize the economic aspects of civil society seemingly to the exclusion of all others. For instance, Darjes wrote that from the standpoint of "police," "a person [Mensch] is fitted to be useful to civil society if he possesses enough skill to feed himself and through his activities to give others the opportunity to earn something themselves." But that was not all there was to it. "The greatest skill proves in the final analysis to be unfruitful," he continued, "if the person's heart is not moral [moralisch]. . . . A person's heart is moral when he earnestly tries to measure the applications of his skill not according to his own use, but according to the welfare of the whole in which he lives."[48] Similar sentiments adorn virtually every cameralist tract. These epithets may be rhetorical insurance against charges of godlessness and impiety. Their ubiquity, however, demonstrates how nervous even cameralists felt about the new principles they were introducing into society.

But morality was a great deal more than just a guilty second thought; for the cameralists it was the true fundament of civil society. It grounded and held together civil society in a way no intertwining satisfaction of needs and desires ever could. This is why cameralists founded civil society on obligation, not rights. Obligation to the common good (Gemeinwohl) bound the ruler to his subjects, them to him (as the most efficient guarantor of the common good), and them to one another (in the subordination of individual to common interest). Civil society thus consisted in moral relations of mutual duty and consideration, not in abstract rights derived from natural law. For the cameralists, natural law brought with it merely another set of duties, those to oneself; these were not self-interest in the narrow sense—they

[45] Grundfeste, vol. 1, par. 786, p. 689.
[46] Ibid., par. 791, p. 695.
[47] Erste Gründe der Cameral-Wissenschaften darinnen die Haupttheile sowohl der Oeconomie als auch der Policey und besondern Cameral-Wissenschaft in ihrer natürlichen Verknüpfung zum Gebrauch seiner academischen Fürlesung entworfen, 2d ed. (Leipzig, 1768), par. 18, p. 371.
[48] Ibid., par. 59, p. 392, and par. 60, p. 393.

lay not on the immediate horizon of desire or comfort, but in the future of rational fulfillment of one's human potential. And to these duties some added the duty toward God as the source of natural law. When Wolff considered the nature of the commonwealth (*das gemeine Wesen*), he concluded that regarding its "common welfare [*Wohlfahrt*] one was responsible for everything to which the person [*Mensch*] is obligated by natural law, that is both the duties to himself, and to God and other people, as we [i.e. Wolff] have set out in our book on morality."[49] "Welfare" was thus more than material well-being. It was the right balance of mutual obligations among the constituents of civil society. Wilhelm Dilthey aptly summarized this cameralist view as follows: "Morality [is] the foundation of law and state."[50]

The cameralists have been soundly criticized for grounding civil society in moral obligation rather than in natural rights because of the deleterious consequences this had for political freedom. As Leonard Krieger puts it, "The individual [found] his freedom increasingly in conformity with rather than in resistance to the power of the state" and subordinated to "the prevailing system of law and custom."[51] Moral limits on the ruler were a conveniently weak substitute for constitutional guarantees,[52] and the cameralists' position as upper state bureaucrats may very well have made them more supine toward government power than was good, but this faith in the ruler was not the only, and was certainly not the main, reason why the cameralists fixed on morality. It was an overdetermined inheritance from many sources, some intellectual, others embedded in the life-world. Every post-Reformation German knew that God's order justified the state and that the ruler was the religious-moral leader of his territory and that his laws were supposed to be in conformity with Christian principles. Church observance and the regular taking of communion were closely observed signs of one's membership in the community.[53] State and community were suffused with moral meaning. Material relations were also simultaneously moral ones: from the territorial prince or the Prussian estate owner, both of whom owed their subjects sustenance in famine, to the guild members, whose ostentatious purity was the prerequisite to their economic existence, to the villagers who owed one another mutual support in time of need. Indeed, the Holy Roman Empire itself, with its criss-crossing lines of mutual obligation, was a living exemplar of practical morality. No wonder the cameralists could not conceive of order without morality.

The actual content of public moral obligation in the early cameralist writings was

---

[49] *Vernünfftige Gedancken*, par. 224, p. 167, also par. 252, p. 180.

[50] *Zur Preussischen Geschichte*, vol. 5 of *Gesammelte Schriften* (Stuttgart, 1985), 155.

[51] *The German Idea of Freedom: History of a Political Tradition. From the Reformation to 1871* (Chicago, 1957), 65, 55, on Thomasius and Pufendorf, respectively. Krieger's critique is true in many respects, but too forward-looking. It interprets the cameralists' use of "state" as (the modern) "state apparatus," rather than as the "entirety of organized society," and by focusing on the relation of individual to government, obscures that of the individual to the rest of society, which is, as in sexual matters, often a greater source of coercion.

[52] Ibid., 54.

[53] Sabean, *Power in the Blood*, 37–61.

strongly shaped by the Reformation. Seckendorff wrote in 1657: "As far as the subjects, or their persons and things are concerned, the first thing is this: [to lead] an honorable and virtuous life [*ein Erbar und züchtiges Leben und Wandel*]." Some deeds might be left to the church to admonish, but others provoking a public nuisance should be subject to law, including "an appropriate external celebration of Sundays and holidays, a sober and moderate life and avoidance of scandalous drunkenness. . . . Further, a proper job and occupation and avoidance of idleness, which ruins body and soul, wastes goods, and finally causes annoyance to other people . . . [and] the maintenance of the proper order and hierarchy among the estates [*Stände*] and subjects of the land according to their honor and office . . . including in clothing and other externa."[54] Sexual behavior was routinely embedded in the litany of social virtues and vices. In Becher's utopia "There should be much discussion of and admonitions to a good moral life, so that an honorable [*erbares*], quiet, virtuous [*züchtiges*], calm, satisfied life can be led in it, which is the main purpose of this commonwealth [*Gemeine*], such that all ill-will, hatred, envy, fighting, drinking, hitting, sexual misdeeds [*Unzucht*], will be completely expelled."[55] Lau included "a vicious life" (*lasterleben*) among the things undermining "good police."[56] Similarly, in the duties one had to oneself, to keep one's body healthy, Pufendorf advised, "we must avoid gluttony, drunkenness, excessive sex, and so on."[57]

Cameralists thus considered sexual disorder as one of the seven deadly social sins in an unreflective way, as part of the standard post-Reformation understanding of the morality relevant to public life. These associations still enjoyed a shadowy existence in the mid-eighteenth century, as Justi's admonitions attest:

> To the moral condition [*sittlichen Zustande*] of the subjects [*Unterthanen*] belongs, in addition to religion, the state of the customs [*Sitten*] themselves, and the police must pay special attention to upholding good discipline and order. It requires no great proof [to show] that the customs of a people and especially the reigning virtues or vices have a huge influence on the happiness of a people. History has all too many irrefutable examples of mighty empires and states finding their ruin through excesses and disorders [*Ausschweifungen und Unordnungen*] in their manner of living [*Lebensart*] and customs, and it is immediately obvious that increasing vices and excesses [*einreissenden Laster und Ausschweifungen*] make a people ever more incapable of the industry, capacities and skills necessary to furthering their happiness.

The phrases "excesses and disorders" and "increasing vices and excesses" the reader will recognize as standard bureaucratic jargon for sexual misdeeds and the vices associated with them. But the eighteenth century built upon these absolutist foundations. Not only did the personal, moral comportment of the subjects have direct consequences on the health of the commonwealth, which had been conceived

[54] Seckendorff, *Fürsten-Stat*, 90–92.
[55] *Psychosophia*, 119.
[56] Lau, *Entwurf*; cited in Zielenziger, *Kameralisten*, 401.
[57] *Duty of Man*, bk. 1, chap. 5, par. 3, p. 47.

in post-Reformation times in a largely negative way as a danger through sinfulness, but now virtue in the abstract had become the positive force moving the commonwealth forward. Justi continued,

> It is undeniable that the more perfect the moral condition [*sittliche Zustand*] of a people, the more it will be able to encourage its own happiness. It is therefore desirable for the government [*Regierung*] to hold its subjects to all kinds of virtue [*Tugend*], and it must indeed encourage all virtues as much as possible. . . . Virtue is the general mainspring [*Triebfeder*] of all states [*Staaten*], toward which their activity must be strained and directed, in order to encourage happiness.[58]

In mid-eighteenth-century cameralism, the content of public morality generally and the place of sexual behavior in it, although still built on post-Reformation, absolutist foundations, had begun to change. For now it is enough to observe that the moral foundation the cameralists gave to civil society continuously called attention to sexual behavior as a concern for the public welfare and encouraged the continued use of sexual (mis)behavior as a metaphor for social danger.

Externality

Civil society was only a partial aspect of social life; it was the sphere of external action in the here and now. Its standards were lower than those applying to the soul or to the more perfect future. "One must admit however," wrote Pufendorf, "that sometimes in civil life, where not every detail can be exactly as it should be, some things are said to be licit because they are not penalized in human courts, though in themselves they are repugnant to natural goodness."[59] This limitation produced both space for freedom of thought and danger for moral virtue. Justi regretted openly that the sheer size of modern territories made it impossible for them to mimic the ancients and make "these moral virtues [*moralischen Tugenden*] objects of civil law [*bürgerlichen Gesetze*]," thus making "the whole state [*Staat*] one, great family."[60] Wolff laid out the dilemma:

> Because penalties do not produce virtue, but only prevent one from committing the evil that one has in one's mind, they only uphold external discipline [*äusserliche Zucht*]. Namely, external discipline consists in the conformity of external actions with the laws of nature, but the desire [*Lust*] for repulsive actions can always remain. Therefore, because in the commonwealth [*gemeinen Wesen*] no one can be prevented from doing evil except through penalties, thus civil obligation [*bürgerliche Verbindlichkeit*] can go no further than external discipline. And this is why one says: thoughts are tax-free. And this is the difference between civil and natural obligation: the former pertains to the external, the latter also to the internal, and thus the former gives birth only to external discipline, and the latter, on the contrary, to true virtue [*Tugend*].[61]

[58] *Grundsätze der Policey-Wissenschaft*, par. 285, pp. 211–12, par. 286, and par. 286, pp. 212–13 n.
[59] *Duty of Man*, bk. 1, chap. 2, par. 11, p. 30.
[60] *Grundfeste*, vol. 2, par. 206, p. 250.
[61] *Vernünfftige Gedancken*, par. 355, p. 305, also par. 401, p. 416, and par. 434, p. 461.

The danger lay in the imperfection of government, which had already discovered that "it is not possible to proceed against all the errors of people with the sharpness of law,"[62] and in the damage done to the ultimate, moral goal of civil society, perfection (*Vollkommenheit*), by the evil example of those whom the law could not restrain. To counter these perils, the cameralists grasped at two remedies. The first was the temptation to ignore their own insights about the limits of law and instead to strengthen the content of positive law by including in it "inner" matters, that is natural law or even religious commandments. Wolff and Johann Heinrich Jung-Stilling (1740–1817) both did so when they proposed to outlaw atheism, for example.[63] The attraction of the idea is clear even for Justi, who rejected it. Although Justi pronounced it "always a mistake, when the laws of a state mix up moral virtue [*sittliche Tugend*] with civil," he was nonetheless convinced that only the "moral qualities of people" made them "skillful in the fulfillment of their civil duties," which influenced "the welfare of individual families and the common best."[64] Obviously, there was a visceral and indeed causal connection between moral virtues and the health and welfare of the commonwealth, even for cameralists like Justi, who struggled to separate them in positive law.

A less self-contradictory and thus more palatable solution to the dilemma was to strengthen the self-regulation of citizen/subjects. As Wolff observed, "Generally there is always more to be gained when one is disposed to something by an internal urge [*Trieb*], than when one is merely held to it against oneself by external coercion."[65] Fostering the correct internal urge might be accomplished by public moral (*sittliche*) education, which would produce "more honest and skillful people,"[66] and, the cameralists hoped, chaster ones: "Shame in girls and youths is an excellent dam against the growing passion of lust," Jung-Stilling remarked when writing on education.[67] Or one could promote religious faith, as virtually all cameralists did. The chief danger atheism posed to civil society was precisely that it destroyed self-regulation. Again, Jung-Stilling: "[The police] is too imperfect to observe [the atheist's] every move. Where he can satisfy his lusts [*Lüste*] unpunished, then no means is unacceptable to him, since he does not believe in sin. The thought, 'there is no God!' can arise as nothing but the long-nourished wish, 'I would that there were none.' Because the atheist is completely without credit in regard to political virtue [*politischen Tugend*], he can hardly be permitted in civil society [*bürgerlichen Gesellschaft*]."[68] Here, political virtue consists unabashedly in moral, indeed the words "lusts" and "sin" suggest especially sexual, virtue.

---

[62] Seckendorff, *Der Christenstat* (1685), cited in Unruh, "Polizei, Polizeiwissenschaft und Kameralistik," 413. We have seen that Seckendorff's insight was shared by upper-level bureaucrats by the mid-eighteenth century.

[63] Wolff, *Vernünfftige Gedancken*, par. 367, pp. 325–30; Jung, *Lehrbuch*, par. 286, p. 115.

[64] *Grundfeste*, vol. 1, par. 19, pp. 19–20.

[65] *Vernünfftige Gedancken*, par. 396, p. 403.

[66] Seckendorff, *Fürsten-Stat*, cited in Zielenziger, *Kameralisten*, 350.

[67] *Lehrbuch*, par. 141, p. 57.

[68] Ibid., par. 286, p. 115; also par. 293, pp. 118–19.

Finally, one could harness honor. That way, one mobilized the powerful internal mechanisms by which social groups already regulated themselves. In his section on the "establishment of the commonwealth," Wolff made upholding one's honor a civic obligation: "Everyone [*Jedermann*] is bound to do his utmost to make himself worthy of honor [*Ehre*], and to this end to undergo tests of goodness [*Proben des Guten*] and to seek everyone's friendship, so that he maintains the proper reputation [*Ruhm*]."[69] The phrase "everyone's friendship" underscores that honor was bestowed collectively; acting honorably meant acting in conformity with social expectations. It was another method of transcending divisive individualism and promoting harmony. But that harmony was not merely static but dynamically progressive. According to Jung-Stilling, one acquired the esteem of others, one was honored by them, because of one's excellence: "When we discover certain perfections in someone, we feel a kind of love [for him or her] which is called estimation. . . . This is the basic conception of honor [which perforce elicits imitation]. [F]rom this the urge to perfection [*Trieb der Vollkommenheit*], the rational love of honor, is created."[70] Pursuing honor therefore gradually produced perfection in individuals and also society.

Honor, like socially relevant morality, also came equipped with a traditional content in which sexual behavior was quite important, and gender-specific. Pufendorf explained that one could lose "simple reputation" (that conferred by public opinion) "when it is associated with vice or at least with a perception of vice" such as "with pimps and prostitutes and such like."[71] Women's honor consisted more exclusively in sexual virtue than men's. "No greater insult can be offered to a good woman than to attempt to take from her against her will that in whose integrity chiefly lies the reputation of her sex."[72] Several generations later, Justi made clear how much a man's honor was reflected in his virility.[73] By championing honor as a way to encourage the new civic individual to submit voluntarily to the collective good, the cameralists inherited previous cultural capital laden with sexual assumptions, some of which they welcomed and some of which they spurned as "superstitious." In order to remove the superstitious content of traditional notions of honor, Jung-Stilling therefore recommended that honor be removed from the purview of society and redefined by "police": "The basic concept of honor makes clear that only those actions can be dishonorable, which harm the state/society [*Staat*]."[74] He therefore proposed a much leaner concept of honor, stripped of the social particularities that had previously defined it: the honor of artisans, of peasant-owners, of nobles, and so on, was to be replaced by the honor of citizens,

---

[69] *Vernünfftige Gedancken*, par. 397, p. 404

[70] *Lehrbuch*, pars. 603–4, p. 252.

[71] *Duty of Man*, bk. 2, chap. 14, par. 8, p. 164.

[72] Ibid., bk. 1, chap. 5, par. 15, p. 52.

[73] *Rechtliche Abhandlung von denen Ehen, die an und vor sich selbst ungültig und nichtig sind; (de matrimonio putativo et illegitimo). Wobey zugleich von dem Wesen der Ehe und dem großen Einflusse der Ehegesetze in die Glückseligkeit des Staats gehandelt wird* (Leipzig, 1757), par. 75, pp. 128–29.

[74] *Lehrbuch*, par. 660, pp. 277–78.

defined solely in their relation to their common organization (*Staat*). His suggestion demonstrates two things. First, that society was not (yet) civil society; that is, that the opinions hallowed by (older) social usage were expected to give way to (newer) habits appropriate to a different kind of society, namely civil. Second, honor did not rest on the same secure foundations as morality, which was taken as the product of either natural law or God's law, or both. Honor was merely customary, and this raised the question of the relation between customary morality (*Sittlichkeit*) and absolute morality (*Moral*), though cameralists failed always to distinguish these two things semantically.[75]

Differentiation

The cameralists conceived of civil society as differentiated. Partly, they simply imposed the system of *Stände* (estates) onto the new civil order they were imagining. Partly, however, diversity was a necessary product of a growing economy. In Becher's dialogue between Philosophy and "Psychosophia," Philosophy asks how one should conceive of a utopia without hunger but also without a controlled economy (monopoly), so that one "could exist as a single producer [*in kleinen*] in peace and honest subsistence [*ehrlicher Nahrung*]?" Psychosophia replies, "It can't be done singly. Because, first, one hand must wash the other, and a community [*Gemeinschaft*] is made up of such members as can help themselves without outside assistance, which requires therefore different types of people and professions."[76] As Wolff carefully argued, different types of people have different types of needs and desires, the satisfaction of which inevitably lead one beyond subsistence into the new territory of civil society.[77] One example of this openness toward difference was the almost unanimous cameralist recommendation to import skilled foreigners into the various provincial backwaters they served. But this was not enough. Economic growth and moral perfection both required "police" to encourage potential diversity. Justi preached this gospel when writing on the growth of cities:

> One must especially underscore that a kind and mild government, a reasonable freedom allowed to citizens to engage in innocent actions irrelevant [to the good of civil society], and complete freedom of conscience must be made room for in a city, if one wants to encourage its expansion and growth. These are not just necessary means to encourage population, but are also necessary to accomplish a blooming manufacture. One can have little hope of growth for a city in which everybody [*jederman*] does not enjoy complete civil freedom and freedom of conscience.[78]

The multiplicity arising from this degree of freedom was a nerve-wracking prospect. Sonnenfels was unusual in thinking, like Adam Smith, that society's parts

[75] Hegel was the first to insist that *Moralität* and *Sittlichkeit* were different, in his critique of Kant's moral philosophy. See Wolfgang Kuhlmann, ed., *Moralität und Sittlichkeit. Das Problem Hegels und die Diskursethik* (Frankfurt, 1986). My usage of "morality" to cover both terms follows contemporary usage. Where the original German is important, it is given.

[76] *Psychosophia*, 114.

[77] Wolff, *Vernünfftige Gedancken*, pars. 210–12.

[78] *Grundfeste*, vol. 1, par. 387, pp. 330–31.

would regulate themselves.[79] Most other cameralists had a more traditional notion of social harmony, which they were anxious to secure against the whirlwind they were simultaneously sowing.[80] At the very least the corporate hierarchy of social authority had to be maintained. As Justi put it, "Every civil society [*bürgerliche Gesellschaft*] must have a good order and connection [*Zusammenhang*] in all its parts; namely, the different classes [*Classen*] of the people, the rulers and the ruled, must stand in a just relation to one another."[81]

But there were larger, philosophical reasons to strive toward a harmony transcending the contemporary social order. "Perfection consists in the harmonizing [*Zusammenstimmung*] of the diverse," wrote Wolff.[82] True to the cameralists' tendency to approach their subject from a socioeconomic rather than a political perspective, this problem appeared to them not as a question of how to determine the general will, but instead as a question of how to shape it, of how to educate people to will according to the consistent and harmonious laws of nature, in other words, to will one thing. Raupach sums up (a bit extremely) the cameralists' goals: "to diminish human spontaneity and fantasy in favor of a uniformity of thinking and a disciplined, reliable behavior, so that the order of social relations could be made independent of actual human nature, whether good or bad."[83] This would be achieved not so much by repression or drill, but by guidance toward the laws of nature, for that was a far deeper and more reliable source of conformity than social pressure or external force. The dream of natural uniformity included at its center sexual uniformity, as we shall see.

Dynamism

The cameralists proposed to open the floodgates of production, consumption, population, and wealth.[84] At the same time, they wanted these rivulets, streams and rivers to course through the absolutist landscape as they always had. In social terms, this meant upholding the estates (*Stände*) and their mutual, corporative relations, despite the influx of wealth that was bound to overturn them.[85] The cameralists expressed their utter ambivalence utterly clearly. As Sonnenfels puts it: "The wellspring of abundance will be led into the hut of the working peasant," yet "the unequal distribution of riches among the different *Stände*" would be maintained, because it "is one of the most important bonds of civil society [*bürgerliche Gesellschaft*]."[86] Or, as Jung-Stilling put it, who, in the interests of populationism, simultaneously favored equalization of wealth and the maintenance of separate

[79] "Der Stände," 100, 113.
[80] Raupach, "Zum Verhältnis," 164.
[81] *Grundfeste*, vol. 1, preface, [vii].
[82] *Vernünfftige Gedancken*, par. 224, p. 166.
[83] Raupach, "Zum Verhältnis," 360.
[84] As Justi put it: "A state can never achieve too much power and happiness. Each civil society does not set for itself regarding its great final goal of happiness a certain degree at which it wants to remain." *Grundfeste*, vol. 1, par. 209, pp. 174–75.
[85] Krieger, *Freedom*, 51, 56; Raupach, "Zum Verhältnis," 358.
[86] "Der Stände," 100, 101.

Stände: Since persons of wildly different wealth would not marry one another, "the police must know how to erect the cleverest institutions, so that at least the civil *Stände* do not permit rank or status hierarchy to arise." But he still saw one of the major duties of government as "the most exact determination of the boundaries of each *Stand;* each person must be able to inherit and possess all the happiness in his sphere, which is due to him in his nature, but only so that no other *Stand* is diminished."[87]

This solicitude for the *Stände* flowed partly from reverence for the social status quo, from the desire to placate potential royal or noble critics, and from the wish to keep intact the cameralists' own *ständisch* privileges as (often bourgeois) bureaucrats. But the *Stände* were also a comforting barrier against the dynamism loosed by cameralist economic theories. This taming and anchoring function was especially noticeable in the cameralists' use of two *Stände* whose foundational role in the estate system is so taken for granted that scholarship often ignores them, namely gender and the family. The cameralists did not ignore them; on the contrary, they considered them keystones to the stability and order of civil society. And since contemporaries held sexual behavior to be basic to both gender and family, they had to problematize sex in their reflections on social stability.

The pattern emerging from this analysis should be clear. With the exception of desire, in relation to which sexual desire served as an obvious analogy to individually directed pleasure-seeking and to productivity, the "place" of sex in the cameralists' thinking about civil society was overwhelmingly on the safety side of the ledger. That is, it occurred among the counterweights to the newly emerging principles that threatened to disrupt the old social order and its values. But it was not a counterweight in itself; rather, sexual behavior was exemplary for the possibility of controlling (re)productive urges altogether. If that problem could be solved, then, by analogy, the larger problem posed by the release of economic, intellectual, and (re)productive energy could be solved as well. Finally, one must underscore that cameralist thinking about sex occurred in relation to society, not in relation to the state (in the sense of government). This fact is sometimes obscured by their use of *Staat* to mean civil society. But it is important to understand that the first political theorists of Germany saw sexual behavior as a social issue, not a political one.

The Cameralists on Sexual Attraction and Its Place in Civil Society

Depending upon whether they were writing a moral textbook (*Sittenlehre*) or an administrative textbook (*Polizeywissenschaft*), the cameralists discussed sex in different connections. Insofar as their shared emphasis on morals permits one to distinguish the two genres, generally in the first, sexual considerations crop up in the duties to oneself, to God, and to the commonwealth. In the second, they occur

[87] *Lehrbuch*, par. 190, p. 76, and par. 574, p. 238.

in relation to the order necessary for civil life, the duties of police to regulate that order, the forms of social life (namely marriage), the moral virtues necessary to civil society, the promotion of population, and, as the eighteenth century developed, the sphere of freedom to be allowed to responsible citizens. Not surprisingly, marriage provided the opportunity for the cameralists' most extensive reflections on sex, since marriage continued to be primarily associated both with legitimate sexual expression and with social order and economic productivity. Many of the cameralists' basic assumptions about sex were entirely conventional. We turn to these first.

Sexual Conventions

To the end of the eighteenth century cameralists believed sexual attraction to be a natural, strong, God-given urge equally present in men and women.[88] "A female [*Weibsbild*] is easily seduced by a loose fellow [*leichtfertigen Kerl*], and a man as easily by a loose female," Becher observed.[89] It was a "weakness common to all people" (Thomasius),[90] "a sensitive lust which rouses both man and woman to intercourse" (Wolff).[91] Even Justi, whose peculiar ideas will occupy us presently, believed that "Nature has put in people a drive [*Trieb*] to reproduce the species, and both sexes feel this drive equally."[92] Sonnenfels, the ardent populationist, only regretted that "in every single person of both sexes there is a more active desire [*Begierde*] and capacity for reproduction than is usually acted upon."[93]

If everyone inherited a sexual drive, still, it could be manipulated within limits. Alas, most people apparently chose to arouse it, rather than dampen it. The preferred method in the earlier period was "all too tasty and diverse foods and drink, conversation with or the example of sensual people,"[94] or simply "many caresses."[95] Once the cameralists had redefined luxury as a good thing, exotic, rich or spicy foods, and drink were no longer mentioned as sources of sexual temptation. Instead, imagination[96] and bad example had become paramount.

The sex urge, however, was strong even without artificial stoking and consequently very difficult to stifle. Thomasius wrote that once lust had been awakened, a person "was powerless to withstand it, and even the wisest philosopher would not struggle against it."[97] That is why Justi and the others rejected celibacy. "Neither

---

[88] Pufendorf, *Duty of Man*, bk. 2, chap. 2, par. 2, p. 120.

[89] *Psychosophia*, 268.

[90] *Von der Kunst*, part 3, par. 58, p. 186.

[91] *Vernünfftige Gedancken*, 10.

[92] *Grundfeste*, vol. 1, par. 247, p. 210.

[93] "Bevölkerung," 232; similarly: Jung-Stilling, *Lehrbuch*, par. 141, p. 57.

[94] Thomasius, *Von der Artzeney*, part 8, par. 20, p. 194, and Thomasius, *Von der Kunst*, part 3, par. 48, p. 179, and par. 58, p. 186.

[95] Becher, *Psychosophia*, 267.

[96] Wolff, *Vernünfftige Gedancken*, 23; Justi, *Grundfeste*, vol. 2, par. 76, p. 61, and Jung-Stilling, *Lehrbuch*, par. 145, p. 58, on novel reading and female passion.

[97] *Von der Kunst*, part 3, par. 34, p. 172. Although he does not explicitly say so, the context makes clear that the person Thomasius has in mind is male.

nature nor reason," he concluded, "order us to abstain from the opposite sex, any more than they require us to abstain from food and drink. On the contrary, those are their first laws, and in both nature speaks all too clearly [*gar zu deutlich*]."[98] But for all its overpowering strength, however, the sexual urge was fleeting, capricious, and mercurial. "Love [*Liebe*] is blind," Becher observed. "It cannot govern itself; one thinks one can remain constant in it, but once one has tasted the fruit of love and become satiated, so it can easily happen that by chance one feels instead of love, hatred,"[99] or, as Thomasius put the same thing, "once the heat has blown over, one is overcome by real disgust."[100] Sexual lust "only lasts a moment and is shorter than all other sensual pleasures."[101] Clearly, nothing so fickle was fit to ground a social institution, and all the cameralists warned young people to choose their marriage partners on a less passionate basis.

Despite their belief that sexual desire was God-given, the cameralists still regarded it as of a lower order than other human qualities. Worse, sexual attraction often fixed itself to purely physical characteristics, which accounted for the evanescence of the attraction. This characteristic caused the cameralists, in good Christian and traditional fashion, to label sex under certain circumstances "brutish."[102]

What distinguished humans from animals was love. This delicate emotion sees beyond the merely physical to the beloved's character. To be used in this way, "love" needed to be redefined. When Becher used the word (1705), he meant a combination of emotional attraction and sexual desire that because it "judges according to the flesh and not the spirit," brought turmoil and unhappiness.[103] This was the usage common to the handbooks on love which Thomasius was determined to counter: "Yes, you say, I have heard that a real, rational love [*vernünftige Liebe*] cannot exist without disturbance, pain and then consequently heightened joy, and that jealousy and little fights are the test and tinder of rational love. All the books on love written by reasonable authors say this."[104] On the contrary, Thomasius described a "rational love" of an almost religious nature, of one soul, one will, total mutual respect, and complete equilibrium.[105] But unlike some earlier religious-inspired writers, Thomasius was equally intent to include sexual passion as the epitome of the lovers' oneness. Sexual desire was not less than or contrary to friendship, as many writers claimed; it was the highest form of friendship: "In true philosophy true friendship and love [the desire to join bodies] are one."[106] This

[98] *Grundfeste*, vol. 2, par. 200, p. 239.

[99] *Psychosophia*, 259.

[100] *Von der Kunst*, part 3, par. 47, pp. 178–79.

[101] Wolff, *Vernünfftige Gedancken*, 22.

[102] Becher, *Psychosophia*, 269, calls it "Ein viehisches Werck"; Thomasius, *Von der Kunst*, part 3, par. 30, pp. 169–70, also par. 129, p. 114, and indirectly, par. 46, p. 178, insists, "Denn auf diese Art lieben die Bestien"; Johann Heinrich Gottlob von Justi, *Natur und Wesen der Staaten als die Quelle aller Regierungswissenschaften und Gesezze* (Mitau, 1771), par. 196, p. 434 refers to the "an sich thierischen Handlung"; Jung-Stilling, *Lehrbuch*, par. 466, p. 191, decries "viehische Triebe."

[103] Becher, *Psychosophia*, 259.

[104] *Von der Kunst*, part 3, par. 61, p. 188.

[105] See above, p. 163: Thomasius *Von der Kunst*, part 3, par. 50, p. 180.

[106] Ibid., pars. 32–34, pp. 170–72, par. 49, pp. 179–80.

definition made sexual desire, under the right circumstances, fully compatible with dignified, nonanimalistic behavior, and with social stability, since it was anchored in the beloved's internal character, not adrift over her corruptible surface.

"Love" continued, and continues, to carry the double meaning of "mere" sexual infatuation versus clarified, mutual devotion. But Thomasius won at least a partial victory, insofar as his definition was the one that later writers used to make sexual desire safe for long-term social institutions. This was the conception of ideal monogamy that accompanied civil society from its inception and bound together the emotional fulfillment of the citizens with social stability. In 1788 Jung-Stilling summarized the idea:

> A man who guides his sensuality through reason and religion usually binds himself to one spouse, even where otherwise polygamy is permitted. He loves her alone, in the complete sense of the word; his interest is hers; they are one heart and one soul; they complete one another mutually. Their love becomes ever more moral [*moralischer*], and when the sexual drive [*Sexualtrieb*] is finally extinguished, then the highest bond of friendship has become so strong through the years, and the drive [*Trieb*] toward the common goal so regular, that the thought, to be joined in the hereafter for eternity, is the single calming consolation in death.[107]

With the exception of the ambivalent meaning of "love," which was debated in literate circles, the cameralists' positions were nothing other than what most early modern Germans "knew" about sex. Cameralist views on improper sexual acts were similarly conventional, though these may reflect literate more than popular opinion. The basic pattern according to which sexual behavior was divided into acceptable and not was set by marriage and its putative purposes. Pufendorf expressed this religious-based position pithily: God bestowed upon men and women "the burning attraction of the sexes," not for pleasure, but to cement their marriage and encourage child-bearing and -rearing. "It follows from this that any employment of the genital members which deviates from these purposes is repugnant to natural law. Under this heading come forbidden lust directed towards a different species or towards persons of the same sex; any kind of filthy impurity; and all extramarital intercourse, whether by mutual consent or against the woman's will."[108]

Pufendorf's was the standard Protestant view of skepticism toward sexual pleasure except for the sake of marital relations, combined with society's interest in stable child-bearing and -rearing. Positive law brought further restrictions, even for Thomasius who, despite his concern to diminish shame and enhance sexual expression within marriage, cautioned people not to contravene positive law in their erotic pursuits.[109] With the exception of Justi, about whom more shortly, later cameralists generally repeated the broad restrictions Pufendorf had enunciated. Their standard justifications were that deviant sex contravened natural law and harmed the ability to procreate, the institution of marriage, the health of the miscreant, and thus his [the male gender is usually assumed] ability to fulfill his civil duties. This litany

[107] *Lehrbuch*, par. 356, p. 145.
[108] *Duty of Man*, bk. 2, chap. 2, par. 2, p. 120.
[109] Thomasius, *Von der Kunst*, part 3, par. 57, p. 185.

appears in rough chronological order, the latter rationales coming later than the former, though often coexisting with them. This shift in the course of the eighteenth century describes the tendency to replace absolute prohibitions with instrumental ones, natural or religious law with the interests of the institutions of marriage or of civil society.

As one might expect, fears of institutional damage were speculative. Wolff opposed bestiality, homosexual relations, and nonmarital heterosexual relations because, in addition to their contravention of natural law and antiprocreative character, "many would rather have recourse to such a method [as bestiality] to soothe their carnal lusts than to enter matrimony because of the difficulties of the marital estate [*Ehestand*]."[110] Sonnenfels agreed that "a not inconsiderable hindrance to marriage is the ease of committing those excesses [*Ausschweifungen*] which dry up the source of procreation and satisfy the desire for the other sex without making it necessary to decide for the marital life."[111] Now, bestiality was an overwhelmingly male offense, and the phrase "dry up the source of procreation" [die Quelle der Erzeugung austrocknen] clearly refers to semen. The fear was thus that men, not women, would rather escape the burdens of marriage; male desire was construed as the problem, and reduced sexual scope was the solution.

Although the instrumental justifications for creating categories of deviant sexual behavior were speculative, often cameralists made do with simply apodictic judgments of disgust or repeating that an act was harmful, without explaining why. Sonnenfels could merely list "eunuchs; pederasty [*Knabenschänderey*], sodomy," "polyandry," "not to mention other evils [*Uebel*]" and be sure his audience would agree these were awful.[112] Jung-Stilling repeatedly fell back on the general rhetoric of harm: "Highly unnatural are the sins of sodomy, and an outrage against the creator and his creation. They also show a horrible and almost irremediable corruption of morals [*Sitten*], and their consequences for civil society are indescribably harmful. Therefore this crime must be horribly punished."[113] These and many other examples suggest that the catalog of bad sexual acts was a largely inherited one which the cameralists outfitted with new justifications when the older religious or sentimental justifications needed shoring up.

Polygamy: The Cameralist Thought Experiment

The cameralists' ideas about sex were largely but not entirely conventional. One of the more remarkable recurrent threads in cameralist discussions was their examination of whether polygamy, meaning polygyny, could be a useful or permissible institution. Virtually every major writer on law or government considered this

---

[110] Wolff, *Vernünfftige Gedancken*, 16.

[111] Sonnenfels, "Bevölkerung," 247.

[112] Ibid., 261. By "Knabenschänderey" and "Sodomie" Sonnenfels may have meant same-sex relations and bestiality respectively, which is how Wolff, *Vernünfftige Gedancken*, 16–17, used those terms.

[113] *Lehrbuch*, par. 531, p. 219; similar rhetorical examples are fornication (par. 466, p. 191) and birth control (par. 378, p. 155).

question. Debating polygamy had a long history among Western scholars. Natural law theorists used it to test and establish the difference between natural law (derived solely from reason) and divine moral law.[114] Cameralists welcomed the opportunity to reflect upon the social order and the rights of men in it.

Pufendorf considered polygamy in his section "On the duties of marriage":

> Though it is plainly against natural law that one woman should live at the same time with more than one man, it has been the custom among very many peoples, including formerly the Jewish people itself, that one man may have two or more wives at the same time. Nevertheless, even apart from the original institution of marriage as related in Holy Scripture, it is established on the basis of right reason itself that it is much more appropriate as well as more useful that one man be content with one woman. And this has been the custom approved among all the Christian nations that we know of these many centuries.[115]

This passage is remarkable for several reasons: for entertaining the proposition in the first place; for its asymmetry in rejecting polyandry, but not polygyny, out of hand; and for finding both religious and natural law arguments unsatisfying enough that usefulness needed to be adduced as a further argument against polygamy. Becher's contribution demonstrates better why this question arose in the first place.

> Polygamy . . . is in the Old Testament and also currently in practice in the Orient. Christians will hardly be able to convert Asian peoples if they do not permit polygamy, because the women in Asia and the Orient are very infertile and a man might have ten wives and not produce as many children as with a single woman in Germany. This proves that polygamy is a basic rule for maintaining population, and that it would be as scandalous [*schändlich*] to have only one wife there as it is criminal [*sträfflich*] to take many here.[116]

For bureaucrats like the cameralists, who were tinkering with fundamental principles of traditional economic, social, and political organization, cultural relativity was a strategically placed fulcrum helping them displace the old and engineer the future. Through Bible study, increased travel (and reading the ancients), the cameralists (and other exemplars of Enlightenment) had "discovered," or better, demonstrated, the peculiarity of their own customs. The short-lived Anabaptist experiment with polygamy in sixteenth-century Münster doubtless aided the relativist imagination. Even the most basic matters of social organization, like sexual customs, differed from place to place and time to time. This proved that much more was open to question, and thus also susceptible to rational manipulation, than anyone had hitherto dreamed.

But why polygamy? Because it was the most shocking, most radical example of cultural relativity one could adduce. It shook assumptions that most readers could

---

[114] Stephan Buchholz, "Erunt tres aut quattuor in carne una; Aspekte der neuzeitlichen Polygamiediskussion," in *Zur Geschichte des Familien- und Erbrechts: politische Implikationen und Perspektiven, Ius Commune* 32, ed. Heinz Mohnhaupt (Tübingen, 1987), 71–91.

[115] *Duty of Man*, bk. 2, chap. 2, par. 5, p. 122.

[116] *Psychosophia*, 272–73.

be expected to take as far more fundamental ("natural") and certainly more personally relevant, than principles relating to economy or government. Introducing polygamy would immediately have revolutionized the lives of all Germans, turned law, custom, inheritance, and economy (which was still tied to the couple-centered household) topsy-turvy in ways neither the introduction of capitalism nor republicanism would have done (or did, when they occurred). Even sodomy would not have had an equal effect, because it formed no permanent social bonds around which other institutions revolved, nor did it reproduce society, either physically or via socialization. Playing with polygamy, however, was truly playing with social fire.

Where others used polygamy's shock value implicitly, Lau shouted it from the rooftops. "To facilitate the populousness of a state [*Staat*], [I] would want to suggest using polygamy as is done in the Orient. Because such a suggestion like an alarm-signal would encourage the tremulous preachers and professors [*die schreckbaren Cantzeln*] in a dangerous tumult against me, I think it wiser to refrain."[117] Indeed, Thomasius attacked Lau the very year Lau's book appeared, and as his first and principle example of how dangerous Lau's entire approach was to the "commonwealth" (*gemeinen Wesen*), he cited—polygamy.[118]

After having compared polygamy favorably to the hypocritical and deleterious customs of Europe, Lau returned to anthropological arguments, using language that betrayed another, universally unacknowledged, reason polygamy was a favorite topic. "The Jews are able to marry many women and so amuse themselves as they want [*nach ihrem gusto sich divertiren*]. Why should a similar harmless licence be denied to Christians like a forbidden fruit? Especially since no irrefutable proof may be given that having intercourse with many wives is directly contrary to divine or natural law."[119] In short, polygamy was titillating for the male writers and readers of this genre. It was for cameralists what masturbation later became for Enlightened pedagogues, a thought experiment, a fantasy topic in which they might contemplate their own sexual powers and the extension of these at the expense of women. Montesquieu, writing in 1748 and widely read in Germany thereafter, made it clear that he considered polygamy an abuse of women.[120] German writers never made that point. And unlike Montesquieu, they never considered polyandry a possibility.[121] They simply rejected it out of hand, citing social reasons first, but always ending with the more basic sexual and moral reasons. "One would have to deny all healthy concepts [*alle gesunde Begriffe*] to maintain that different men, acting from

---

[117]Lau, *Entwurff* (1717); cited in Zielenziger, *Kameralisten*, 402.

[118]Christian Thomasius, ed., *D. Melchiors von Osse Testament gegen Hertzog Augusto Churfürsten zu Sachsen/Sr. Churfürstl. Gnaden Räthen und Landschafften 1556. Anitzo zum ersten mahl völlig gedruckt/ Auch hin und wieder durch nützliche Anmerckungen erläutert* (Halle, 1717), 505–6 n.

[119]Lau, *Entwurff*, cited in Zielenziger, *Kameralisten*, 402–3.

[120]Montesquieu, *Spirit of the Laws*, part 3, chap. 6, p. 268.

[121]Ibid., chap. 5, p. 267. Among Germans, only Thomasius considered polyandry on a par with polygyny.

economic motives, could be content with a single woman," wrote Justi.[122] Speculation about sexual power clearly had its limits.

In contrast to their gingerly handling of polyandry, the cameralists indulged in lengthy speculation about whether polygamy should or should not be introduced into Europe. Aside from populationist reasons, pro or con, the majority hinged on the putative ill effects of polygamy on men: too many children, jealous wives, household expenses, shortage of women available to other men.[123] The only argument the cameralists after Pufendorf did *not* employ against polygamy was natural law. Obviously, male sexual promiscuity (but not female) seemed natural to them. Only Justi, however, came right out and said so: "One thus sees nature's intent more than clearly, that man should have more than one wife. The legal scholars, who could not easily argue these clear grounds away, were obliged to postulate sexual satisfaction as among the main purposes of marriage, so that our customs and constitutions regarding monogamy might be upheld. However, that teaching does not even merit refutation."[124] Although Justi ultimately concluded that polygamy ought not be introduced into Germany (chiefly for reasons of domestic harmony), he stubbornly insisted that "polygamy by its nature has no harmful effects."[125]

Justi and the Sexual/Gender Outlines of Civil Society

It was typical of Justi to bring matters to hyperclarity and in doing so to break new ground. Justi was "the most important theoretician" of eighteenth-century cameralism.[126] This was so not only because of his categorical clarity in redefining the relation between cameralism, "police," and state security,[127] but more important, because he was the first to abandon the wishful thinking that had claimed the common good of civil society was identical with the government's interest. Justi thought they might differ, and if he did not develop this thought to its ultimate conclusion (namely, a constitution safeguarding the one from the other), he had nonetheless postulated a split between state (in the modern sense) and civil society and "laid the foundation for liberalism's understanding of state and society."[128] It was not merely the undertow of abstraction or the spur of Montesquieu that moved Justi in this direction, but commercial development and its social effects which he espoused even before he actually observed them in midcentury Prussia.[129] As

---

[122] *Rechtliche Abhandlung*, par. 5, p. 15. Also Jung-Stilling, *Lehrbuch*, par. 362, p. 148.

[123] Wolff, *Vernünfftige Gedancken*, 30; Jung-Stilling, *Lehrbuch*, par. 357, p. 146; Sonnenfels, "Bevölkerung," 261.

[124] *Rechtliche Abhandlung*, par. 9, p. 19.

[125] Ibid., par. 14, p. 28.

[126] Michael Stolleis, *Geschichte des öffentlichen Rechts in Deutschland* (Munich, 1988), 1:379; also see 376, n. 52.

[127] Maier, *Staats- und Verwaltungslehre*, 183–85.

[128] Unruh, "Polizei, Polizeiwissenschaft und Kameralistik," 417.

[129] Ursula A. J. Becher, *Politische Gesellschaft. Studien zur Genese bürgerlicher Öffentlichkeit in Deutschland* (Göttingen, 1978), 78–91, 217.

Michael Stolleis writes, "Where the [government's] fiscal interests collided with freedom of trade and manufacture, Justi decided in favor of developing liberalism." He did the same regarding religion, censorship and freedom of thought: "Everywhere he sought a middle way between anxious repression and limitless liberalization."[130]

Justi is therefore unique among eighteenth-century cameralists in his energetic (proto)liberalism and his self-conscious reflection on the relation between civil society and government, and therefore also on the exact duties of "police." From these vantage points Justi laid down the clay tablets containing his sexual pre- and proscriptions. These were just as startling and provocative as his administrative/ political ideas, and no wonder—they came from the same sources.

Since Saint Paul, stilling sexual desire had been a central justification for marriage. The Reformation had kept it as a ground, but stressed the mutual help and happiness of man and wife, which Thomasius also emphasized.[131] Everyone agreed that providing a suitable environment for children was a third reason. The cameralists' populationism encouraged a child-oriented view, though it seems that Wolff was the first to try to strip marriage of its other justifications: "Because intercourse is the means by which children are produced, and a means is how one reaches an intention, thus it is clear that one acts against nature, when one uses intercourse merely for one's pleasure [*Lust*]. Therefore one can also not reckon the satisfaction [*Büssung*] of carnal lust among the intentions of the marital estate."[132] Sexual pleasure was a means, not an end. Wolff continued immediately to catalog forbidden sexual acts, which he defined as all those, including heterosexual acts, not intending procreation.[133] This was a more extremely pleasure-denying position than Protestants had conventionally held in over two hundred years, and Wolff knew it. After announcing his logically consistent but fantastic conclusion that husbands who had sex with their pregnant wives were violating the laws of nature, he added: "I know perfectly well that generally the reverse is believed true, however, if we judge according to reason, we cannot say anything else but what the subject demands." (Thomasius, too, had proposed a procreative "drive" [*Trieb*] separate from that aiming at sexual pleasure, but for him, the desire for children followed from the mutual love of the spouses, which preceded procreation and made it possible;[134] his intent was never to forbid sexual pleasure.)

Justi made Wolff's unpopular interpretation of natural law categorical. His definition of marriage "holds only one single main purpose of the marital estate, namely creating children; and nature, healthy reason, and the intention of republics

---

[130] Stolleis, *Öffentlichen Rechts*, 381.

[131] Christian Thomasius, *Kurtzer Entwurff der Politischen Klugheit, sich selbst und andern in allen Menschlichen Gesellschafften wohlzurathen/ und zu einer gescheiden Conduite zu gelangen; Allen Menschen/ die sich klug seyn düncken/ oder die noch klug werden wollen/ zu höchst-nöthiger Bedürffnis und ungemeinem Nutzen* (Franckfurt, 1710), chap. 7, par. 2, p. 170.

[132] Wolff, *Vernünfftige Gedancken*, 15–16.

[133] Ibid., 16–19.

[134] Thomasius, *Von der Kunst*, part 3, par. 45, pp. 177–78.

regarding population can permit no other main purpose besides this." He argued, against "practically all" legal scholars, that neither mutual aid nor sexual satisfaction were main purposes of marriage. Sexual satisfaction as a purpose of marriage "ran against healthy reason because otherwise it would nonsensically follow that a true marriage could occur between man and man and woman and woman. There can after all be no doubt that persons of a single sex can give one another mutual aid and be in a permanent community of life together [*einer beständigen Gemeinschaft*]."[135] The context (sexual satisfaction) discloses the unspoken in this sentence: partners of a single sex could found long-standing relationships based on mutual sexual satisfaction.

Justi's sexual imagination was much better developed than those of his fellow cameralists, of whom none ever dreamed that marriage could be anything else but between a man and a woman, and apparently none had ever stopped to consider that single-sex attachments might be permanent. Therefore an argument like Justi's had never occurred to them. But precisely in relation to important social institutions Justi could imagine a spectrum of peculiar and possibly harmful individual desires. He therefore protected marriage against the vagaries of individual desire by removing desire from the constitution of marriage altogether. He reduced marriage to its populationist minimum and considered it wholly according to the commonwealth's interest, rather than the individual's. Where Thomasius had tried to make sexual desire safe for marriage and thus included it as the highest expression of true love, Justi expelled it again in order to make marriage safe for the republic.

Although Justi's sexual imagination was vivid and pliable in relation to civil society, it was rigid in regard to sexual expression. For where Justi had protected marriage from the wild growths of individual desire by an external definition simply banning sex from constituting marriage, he created a safety net of an internal sort to rescue heterosexual expression from the same danger. He postulated a rigid, gender-specific sexual nature, from which a clear sexual script followed, thus guarding people from sexual folly. Justi elevated to a natural principle the unreflected customary linkage of men with sexual power. In his words, "So nature had to ordain that one sex should bid and order while the other should defend itself. One sees that among all animals nature has allotted to the male sex attack, and to the female, defense."[136] Nature, as was only proper, left its imprint on customary honor, which held men and women to opposite standards of seemly sexual conduct. For a male to admit sexual impotence was "a very great self-debasement," indeed, impotence was a rare occurrence, according to Justi, who blamed female genital malformation for most sexual problems in marriage. In any case, it was shameless and dishonoring for a woman to complain of her spouse's impotence (for example at a divorce hearing), "because she makes through this complaint a free confession of her [sexual] inconti-

135 Justi, *Rechtliche Abhandlung*, par. 18, p. 31.
136 *Natur und Wesen*, par. 195, p. 431. The editor of the 1771 edition, Heinrich Godfried Scheidemantel, added the phrase "except for bees" (ausser bei den Bienen) after "all animals," par. 206, p. 343.

nence and immoderation."[137] Justi therefore anticipated nineteenth-century sexual prescriptions. After assuming male sexual aggressiveness and female passivity and ascribing them to the eternal natural order, Justi came close to advocating female passionlessness. At the least, he wanted sexual decorum to force women to dissemble about their own desires and to renounce their centuries-old right to the "marital duty."[138]

This was new territory for German thinkers. None of the preceding cameralists had thought that men and women were, or should be, so sexually different.[139] Justi had imported his new elaborations from France. Montesquieu, whom Justi copiously cites, had written that "all nations are equally agreed in attaching scorn to the incontinence of women; this is because nature has spoken to all nations. She has established defense, she has established attack; and, having put desires into both sides, she has placed temerity in the one and shame in the other."[140] Justi also cited the political philosopher Pierre Bayle and reports of French court proceedings on impotence in his treatment of "natural sex."[141] But discovering where Justi got his ideas does not explain why he adopted them. To do that, we must turn again to the context in which his new ideas about sexual nature occurred—namely, marriage.

Pufendorf had written that "without [marriage] a decent and well-ordered society among men and the development of civil life are inconceivable." From this he deduced without further justification, that marriage was a universal obligation.[142] Becher was more modest and less apodictic: "I recommend to civil society [*burgerliche Gesellschaft*] the marital estate, which a well set-up authority should above all maintain as the fundament of civil society. Because the unmarried estate [*ungeheuratete Stand*] hinders populousness, or introduces fornication [into the land], or carries with it other odd things."[143] Every cameralist agreed that "the marital society [*Societät*] is the first and the oldest, and from it all others flow."[144] For these two reasons then, anchoring everyone in "society" in its most ancient and "natural" form, and for ordered population increase, the cameralists pressed to expand access

---

[137] Justi, *Rechtliche Abhandlung*, par. 75, p. 129 ("self-debasement"); par. 71, p. 121 ("malformed genitals"); and par. 75, pp. 130–31 (incontinence).

[138] Justi's position is quite similar to J. G. Fichte's. See Chapter 8, pp. 319–20 and 322.

[139] See, for example, Becher's observations about the strength of female sexual desire, in *Psychosophia*, 267.

[140] Montesquieu, *Spirit of the Laws*, part 3, chap. 12, pp. 272–73.

[141] Justi, *Rechtliche Abhandlung*, par. 75, pp. 128, 130–31.

[142] *Duty of Man*, bk. 2, chap. 2, par. 3, pp. 120–21.

[143] Becher, *Psychosophia*, 258.

[144] Julius Bernhard Rohr, *Vollständiges Haußhaltungs-Recht, in welchem die nöthigsten und nützlichsten Rechts-Lehren, Welche so wohl bey den Land-Gütern überhaupt, derselben Kauffung, Verkauffung und Verpachtung, als insonderheit bey dem Acker-Bau, Gärtnerey, Viehzucht, Jagten, Wäldern, Fischereyn, Mühlen, Weinbergen, Bierbrauen, Bergwercken, Handel und Wandel und andern Oeconomischen Materien vorkommen, Der gesunden Vernunfft denen Römisch und Teutschen Gesetzen nach ordentlich und ausführlich abgehandelt werden, allen denenjenigen, so Land Güter besitzen oder dieselben zu administriren haben, höchstnützlich und ohnentbehrlich* (Leipzig, 1716), par. 5, p. 169. Also, Pufendorf, *Duty of Man*, bk. 2, chap. 2, par. 1, p. 120; Thomasius, *Kurtzer Entwurff*, chap. 7, par. 1, p. 170; Jung-Stilling, *Lehrbuch*, par. 354, p. 144.

to marriage. Both the inclusivity and the expansiveness of civil society dictated that even the poor be permitted to marry. All cameralists therefore dedicated page after page to clever schemes designed to remove legal, customary, and economic hindrances to marriage.[145] That was the first problem. The second was knottier. What if, even without hindrances, people did not choose to marry? They would then stand outside the bonds of civil society, unsocialized, lost or even dangerous to the commonwealth.

This second nightmare vexed the cameralists to an astonishing degree. It was an unrealistic fear, since most Germans of countryside and town in fact aspired to that estate which was synonymous with adulthood, independence, economic security, and social esteem. Nonetheless, the cameralists could imagine many reasons to avoid their favorite estate. As Becher put it:

> And one lives together like cats and dogs, but for reasons of external honor one must stay together and be forced into a single yoke; in the marital estate to see the object of one's unhappiness, hatred, and death constantly before one's eyes, and to have it at table and in bed, what a martyrdom and hellish pain that is! How is it? when thereafter moods change, and one is cheery and the other sad; How? when temperaments change and one is fat and the other skinny, one is fruitful, and the other sterile, one is healthy, the other sickly: How? when fortune and property change? How? when it goes so far that one wants to die together out of love, or despairs out of hatred and cannot bear to live together or even look at one another: when one has too many, or no children; when they die or turn out badly; when one has an evil father- or mother-in-law, disloyal brothers-in-law and loose servants; In a word, many thousand such inconveniences . . . easily make the marital estate an estate of pain [*Wehstand*].[146]

Becher's typical catalog of marital woes recalls the arguments Protestant Reformers refuted in their tracts advocating marriage over the Catholic Church's celebration of celibacy.[147] But that was 150 years earlier. Where Luther had been intent on persuading both women and men to marry, the cameralists only fretted about men.[148] In common parlance, a bachelor was single by choice, whereas a spinster was unfortunate; therefore, the cameralists commonly proposed to tax the one and dower the other, to improve her marriage prospects.[149] Justi concluded: "If the nonmarried estate is common in a state, that is usually because of the young men; the girls, as Montesquieu says, are always inclined of themselves to marry."[150]

The cameralists' anxieties about men and marriage were made possible by their own social position. Bureaucrats, *Bildungsbürger*, and the noninheriting male mem-

---

[145] Justi, *Grundfeste*, vol. 1, par. 249, pp. 211–12, pars. 252–54, pp. 217–20; Sonnenfels, "Bevölkerung," 240; Darjes, *Erste Gründe*, par. 44, pp. 385–87.

[146] Becher, *Psychosophia*, pp. 260–61. On problems in marriage, see Thomasius, *Von der Kunst*, part 9, par. 18, p. 365, and Jung-Stilling, *Lehrbuch*, pars. 379–80, p. 156.

[147] Luther, "Estate of Marriage (1522)," 39–40.

[148] Becher, *Psychosophia*, 256–57. See also page 174.

[149] Justi, *Grundfeste*, vol. 1, pars. 253, 257–59; Lau, *Entwurff*, chap. 1, par. 15, cited in Zielenziger, *Kameralisten*, 403–4; Sonnenfels, "Bevölkerung," 242–45, 252–53, 257; concerning the bachelor tax, see Jung-Stilling, *Lehrbuch*, par. 200, p. 80, and par. 194, p. 78.

[150] *Grundfeste*, vol. 1, par. 247, p. 210. Sonnenfels disagreed. See "Bevölkerung," 241.

bers of the noble strata were the only social groups that could indeed contemplate not marrying, for a wife was not a prerequisite to career, economic well-being, or, necessarily, happiness. Marriage had become for them a thinner institution; it was no longer buttressed by a thousand economic and social strands. If this social fact made marriage theoretically dispensable, the developing gender ideology of civil society made it downright problematic, as Justi's disquisition on why men shied away from marriage makes clear. The "difficult circumstances" hindering people from marrying, he wrote, "show themselves more on the side of the male sex, than the female. It is the men who, through their property, skills, or industry, must maintain the household and feed the families. And all business and provisioning falls mainly upon the men as heads of household and family."[151] This was untrue for the majority of the population, where women's work and the property they brought into the marriage were critical to family survival. But for men in the cameralists' social station, men's duties may indeed have seemed this one-sidedly onerous. The male's unique responsibility for household and family was in any event the necessary ideological pendant to the rights they received in civil society, for, once again, the cameralists postulated rights not of themselves, but only as the counterparts of obligations.

Adding to men's heavy domestic burden, according to Justi, was the weight of centuries of religious and legal maxims favoring women. This was why Justi was so keen to strip marriage of its religious aura and to proclaim it instead "a civil contract, not at all a clerical matter." Believing that marriage had religious content had misled generations of legal scholars into thinking that "our marriage laws all assume a complete equality [*Gleichheit*] of rights and authority [*Rechte und Befugnisse*] for the husband and for the wife, and that the domestic power and domination [*Gewalt und Herrschaft*] of the husband consist in almost nothing but mere words, without the least reality."[152] This was an appalling situation because "the most harmful effect of poorly made marriage laws on the welfare of the state/society [*Staat*] is that they place husbands . . . in fatal sorrow and listlessness, which robs them of all courage and desire [*Lust*] for useful works, and makes them useless for service to the commonwealth."[153] In the public interest, then, these laws had to be changed. "The best prescription is to restore completely the rights of the house-father and husband, namely the domination [*Herrschaft*] over his house and his wife, which are without doubt due him according to the rights of nature and of civil constitutions."[154]

Justi had indeed spotted a trend, though it was hardly as developed as he claimed. Church marriage law was nearly equally solicitous of men and women, and there are indications that women successfully used church marriage courts, for example in

---

[151] *Grundfeste*, vol. 1, par. 247, p. 210.

[152] Justi, *Rechtliche Abhandlung*, par. 20, p. 34; par. 21, p. 35.

[153] Ibid., par. 45, pp. 71–72.

[154] Justi, *Grundfeste*, vol. 1, par. 248, p. 211; cf. Justi, *Natur und Wesen*, pars. 230–31.

divorce cases, to advance their own interests.[155] The early Enlightened absolutist state was also not above intervening in family affairs on behalf of the wife, if the local authorities judged that tranquillity, productivity and the interests of subsistence [*Nahrung*] demanded it.[156] Furthermore, Enlightened absolutist legal principles tended increasingly to wipe out gender differences in favor of a kind of administrative equal treatment under the law, which we have seen in operation. But if Justi were intent on reversing these trends, he had other traditions at his disposal to build on and transform in ways appropriate to the new principles underlying civil society. For male domestic domination not only had a long tradition in fact and ideology, it was also viewed as a cornerstone of the commonwealth.

Pufendorf merely summed up what all early modern Germans knew when he wrote that "it is particularly in keeping with the natural condition of both sexes not only that the man's position should be superior, but also that the husband should be the head of the family which he has established." Furthermore, the duties of upholding the marriage, sexual fidelity, cohabitation, preserving "mutual harmony," all fell disproportionately upon the wife.[157] Thomasius, whose ideal of mutual love led him to the most egalitarian vision of domestic power in his time, still preserved male domination in larger matters by recognizing (consonant with actual social practice) a separate sphere where the wife ruled.[158] This common understanding of limited male domination began to need clarification as the legal/administrative tentacles of absolutist government brushed up against the household and as natural law and principles of Reason were being used to justify or criticize existing power relations and to lay the foundations for new ones. As Rohr remarked, "That a husband is authorized to direct the actions of his wife is beyond doubt, as both divine and human laws make clear. How far, however, this power of the husband goes, and which actions it pertains to, is not very clearly apparent in the laws."[159]

If the laws were not clear, neither were the general principles. Or rather, neither the principles of "society" nor those of Reason easily supported male domestic domination, as virtually all the cameralists wanted them to do. The resulting dilemma is wonderfully illustrated by the contortions Christian Wolff performed in his examination of power in marriage. The marital "society" meant that the peculiar interests of man and wife disappeared before the common interest. Reason therefore dictated that "whoever [man or wife] had more understanding of a subject should tell the other what was to be done, and the other should obey." This conclusion was impossible in practice, however,

> Because in most marriages, though not in all, it would be impossible to determine who knew best about a thing, and that would cause constant turmoil and strife. Since the man

---

[155] Safley, *Let No Man Put Asunder*, 170, 174, 177.
[156] Sabean, *Neckarhausen*, 134.
[157] *Duty of Man*, bk. 2, chap. 2, par. 4, pp. 121–22; par. 10, p. 123.
[158] *Von der Kunst*, part 9, par. 17, pp. 364–65.
[159] *Haußhaltungs-Recht*, par. 5, p. 169.

should in most cases understand the matter best, it is therefore reasonable that he should be permitted to say what is to be done. However, the husband is obligated to follow the good advice of his wife where she knows something better than he. Because domestic domination [*Herrschaft*] rests in the power to order what is to be done, it is thus clear that although the husband has dominion, this must be so limited that the husband must consult with the wife in matters she knows better. And then the wife is obligated to obey the husband as long as he orders nothing unfair.[160]

Resting the entire argument on the ungrounded assumption that the husband "should" simply know better was obviously unsatisfactory, so Wolff continued ostensibly from the woman's point of view, but actually from the standpoint of social honor (disgrace).

A reasonable [*verständiges*] wife will gladly leave domination to her husband, because it is a disgrace for her to have an ignorant [*unverständigen*] husband, and she gives everyone to understand that she has an ignorant husband, if she wants to have dominion herself. Thus, she would not demand to scold her husband. If it is necessary that things go her way, then, to save her husband's honor and to preserve his favor, she will use modest words and mien, as though her will were his and she were following him, when in fact he follows her.

But reasons of social honor seemed equally inadequate, so Wolff listed other "not petty reasons" why women should acquiesce in their own subordination. They should be "grateful" to their husbands for being in a position "to place them in happy circumstances," from which it followed that they "must make the man's pleasure [*Vergnügen*] their own and do what pleases him, that is, to submit [*unterwerffen*] her will to his." Besides, if she argues with him, she might ruin his health, which affects her, since "her external condition depends upon [his health]." She would also want to make sure she did not "push him to something adverse [*zu nichts wiedrigem*] against her," by which Wolff seems to mean physical violence. In the end, Wolff hoped it was obvious "that a reasonable man must be all the more sensitive [*empfindlicher*] to his wife, the more she overlooked peculiar circumstances [that is, his faults]; and he would be all the more ardent [*brünstiger*] in his love toward her, the more she paid him his due and showed in her actions, that she was doing so."

With the exception of the last, all of Wolff's arguments rested on a certain interpretation of the customary power discrepancy between men and women characteristic of early modern Germany. Men often did have greater economic resources and thus were able to "put women in happy circumstances," though Wolff ignores men's usual reciprocal reliance on women's work and property.[161] Women were dependent on the man's health for their material well-being, but the reverse was also true. Men did have the customary right to punish their wives physically, and they made use of that right. And honor and scandal did indeed reflect the

---

[160] Wolff, *Vernünfftige Gedancken*, 43–45.
[161] Which he examined in an earlier paragraph, ibid., 40–41.

collective expectations that formed from these social realities. Hence, Wolff's arguments for male domestic domination rested essentially on tradition and custom, from which he asserted tautologically that women's subordination was in her own interest. If this was so, of course, it was because the full weight of prior social structures formed her interest along these lines, not because these coincided with abstract Reason.

Only in his last, sexual argument, did Wolff begin to move onto new territory: a woman's erotic interests would be fulfilled to the measure in which she visibly subordinated them to her husband's will, even when he was incorrect (when she "knew a matter" better than he). But Wolff did not postulate subservience as part of a woman's sexual nature. Instead, he hoped that women would act according to rational choice based on (sexual) self-interest.

Justi was impatient with the weak philosophical grounding of male domination and the tortured and unconvincing arguments into which they had forced Wolff. He slashed the Gordian knot and declared that "marriage is an unequal society [*ungleiche Gesellschaft*]."[162] Its inequality was natural, based upon women's physical weakness relative to men.

> Equally indubitable is the power of the housefather over his wife. If it is appropriate to the nature of things that the weaker is dependent on the stronger, the protected on the protector, the nourished on the nourisher, then it follows inevitably that the wife must be subject to the domestic power of the man. The female sex is unarguably the weaker, if one looks at the matter in general, though many individual women can be stronger than their husbands.[163]

If physical strength were not a conclusive reason, then Justi anchored inequality more firmly into the reproductive organs:

> Nature has made the female sex, both in the condition of natural freedom as well as in the constitution of republics, unfit [*untüchtig*] for the performance of the most important business because of child-bearing and its associated illnesses and complaints, and because of other illnesses and weaknesses peculiar to the female sex. Nature speaks so clearly here than one must wonder why many legal scholars don't understand it and would rather be clever and strike down their own advantages [*Vorzüge*].[164]

Justi's opponents were not just "many legal scholars," but also, he suspected, the Enlightenment's postulate of a single human nature and a universal goal of happiness that clearly applied equally to both men and women. Things had gone far enough that Justi, like Wolff, had to defend himself against potential charges of misogyny.[165] "This right of men," he pleaded, discussing unequal chances to divorce, "is not unfair to the female sex and does not make it unhappy." His opponents' views would merit more consideration "if the female sex were actually

---

[162] Justi, *Rechtliche Abhandlung*, par. 29, p. 46.
[163] Justi, *Grundfeste*, vol. 2, par. 133, p. 132. Same argument: Justi, *Rechtliche Abhandlung*, par. 29, pp. 46–47.
[164] Justi, *Rechtliche Abhandlung*, par. 29, p. 47; also, Justi, *Grundfeste*, vol. 2, par. 133, pp. 132–33.
[165] See Jung-Stilling, *Lehrbuch*, par. 363, p. 148, and par. 379, p. 156, on women's rights.

made unhappy by a greater dependence and submission. However, that isn't so. The spirit of freedom and the independence of the female sex is merely a matter of habit and imagination [*Einbildung*]. If a woman [*Frauenzimmer*] sees others enjoying unlimited freedom, she can imagine herself terribly unhappy that she does not possess the same thing."[166]

Even if women were made unhappy by their subjection, their interests were subordinate to men's happiness because of the higher interest of the commonwealth. This was Justi's crowning argument, and it was meant to render all others superfluous.

> It is also more appropriate to the welfare and constitution of republics that laws [regulating domestic relations] must provide primarily for peace and quiet [*Ruhe*] for the husband. They are the actual members of the commonwealth [*gemeinen Wesens*] and on them rest the organization of all the business and the entire strength and welfare of the state [*Staates*]. It is without question disadvantageous to the republic for men to be hindered in [doing] the business of the state by domestic conflict, for them to be made unfit [*untüchtig*] for [state business] by consuming worries and depression and to be pushed prematurely into the grave.[167]

This melodramatic account elaborates the theme of the crushing burdens peculiar to men in civil society. More important, it explains, indeed it trumpets, the real consequences of the central assumption that all early modern political theorists made about civil society: that it was founded by male heads of households. This was so obvious to Pufendorf, that he only alluded to it, "But in states—and states have certainly been formed by men, not women— . . ."[168] Later writers, like Wolff, or even Justi, obscured this premise by referring to "single houses," or "many single families," as the units that agreed to establish civil society (or the "state").[169] Partly these phrases acknowledge the corporatist understanding that lurked in the cameralists' vision of harmonious civil society. But partly they were a kind of reverse synechdoche, where the whole actually stood for, and masked, the part, namely the householder/house-father/husband himself.[170] With his typical hyper-clarity Justi blurted the secret out and unabashedly concluded that since men were "the actual members" of civil society, its laws and arrangements should primarily benefit them.[171]

---

[166] *Rechtliche Abhandlung*, par. 55, pp. 93–94.

[167] Ibid.

[168] *Duty of Man*, bk. 2, chap. 3, par. 3, p. 125.

[169] Wolff, *Vernünfftige Gedancken*, par. 213, p. 161; Justi, *Grundfeste*, vol. 1, par. 1, p. 3. In the same paragraph Justi even refers to "einzelne Menschen," but this is unusual; thereafter it is "families."

[170] Later scholars have often ignored this usage and treated Justi's "individual family" as though it were interchangeable with universal, nongendered "individual." See, for example, Unruh, "Polizei, Polizeiwissenschaft und Kameralistik," 147, and Maier, *Staats- und Verwaltungslehre*, 183. Cf. Stolleis, *Öffentlichen Rechts*, 380.

[171] Few cameralists grounded male domestic domination in the manner of Archbishop Filmer: namely, that monarchical authority and male familial authority were mutually reinforcing analogies. Seckendorff and Justi explicitly denied the comparison: Seckendorff, *Fürsten-Stat*, 26–27; Justi, *Grundfeste*, vol. 2, par. 129, pp. 124–27, and *Natur und Wesen*, par. 230, pp. 519–27. See also Rohr,

Justi did not limit the principle of male domination to domestic legislation; he applied it to all laws regulating men's sexual relations to women. This at least was the function of his suggestions, though he justified them by reference not to male convenience, but to natural law, which he claimed ordered one sex to attack and the other to defend.

> All laws on this point must aim to hold the female sex to defense. It would be a very false principle, contrary to the wise mandates of nature, for one to hold the female as the weak sex and consequently to favor it. As soon as the female sex finds in the laws a sure route to reach marriage via unchastity, and of this sort is the well-known law that rules that a man must either marry or pay a women whom he has impregnated, even without a preceding promise of marriage; as soon as child support [for bastards] falls solely to the man, in short, as soon as the female finds protection in the law when she does not defend herself, but on the contrary acts as a seductress, then a great deal is lost in regard to good customs and decency [Erbarkeit].[172]

Such statements tempt one to dismiss Justi as an idiosyncratic misogynist on a quixotic mission to reestablish male domination wherever Enlightened absolutist principles or practices had let it slip. Two considerations warn against taking this path. First, the reforms in the Napoleonic period practiced what Justi had preached. The principles and suggestions he enunciated about domestic power and men's sexual and familial relations to women became law, though his name was rarely mentioned in the process. Second, the sexual and gender dimensions of Justi's thinking are not capricious, irrelevant appendages tacked on to an otherwise complete system of thought. They are consistent, and Justi thought central, aspects of his endeavor to systematize administration and its proper relation to society according to general principles. His starting point, especially in his later works, was civil society. His understanding of its origins as a creation of married men, its dynamics as an expanding but delicate mobile of individual families, its reproduction in marriage, and its protective mechanisms against its own dynamics (customary honor and binding morality) provided the contexts in which Justi developed, elaborated and justified his prescriptions on sexual behavior and gender. It was precisely his gropings toward the constitution of a liberal civil society that moved him to reestablish male domination at its core, to underscore the putative differences between men and women, and to rewrite sexual laws to reflect the new relation between government and the male-headed families he thought made up society. These gender and sexual principles were not necessary to the theoretical formation of liberal civil society. But they were not wholly unexpected either, because they built on earlier foundations, in the family, in customary conceptions of honor, and so on, whose reinvigoration promised stability, morality, and harmony to the new social edifice.

Haußhaltungs-Recht, par. 3. This argument was apparently so unpopular in Germany that when Wolff made it, in Vernünfftige Gedancken, par. 264; par. 266, pp. 203–5, he remarked that many people were sure to take umbrage at it.

[172] Justi, Natur und Wesen, par. 195, pp. 431–33.

Justi and the Sexual Foundations of the "Private Sphere"

A last, important example of the interrelation between gender and sexual principles and the constitution of civil society lies in Justi's formation of a nascent
"private sphere." Justi drew some limits to state interference in commerce and
trade, and some more in relation to freedom of thought.[173] But his most striking
delineation of where government stopped took place around the family.

> If the peace and quiet [*Ruhe und Ordnung*] that families require for their happiness is to
> take place, then neither the government [*Regierung*] nor especially the police must inter-
> fere with the government [*Regierung*] of the families. . . . Having the authorities govern
> the family could not occur without uncovering the inner affairs of every family, which is
> the worst of all despotisms and contradicts every reasonable concept of civil freedom
> [*bürgerlichen Freyheit*] . . . instead of peace and quiet [this interference] would always
> cause the opposite, because it would halt all subjection [*Unterwürfigkeit*], without which
> no peace and quiet is possible. Therefore the only thing that police and civil laws can and
> should do is to support and encourage domestic government.[174]

In case the reader should not have understood whose subjection Justi was talking
about, several paragraphs later he underscored the point. Borrowing an unacknowledged page from Locke, Justi described whatever authority a woman had in
her household (over children and servants) as

> only a mediate power, which is always subject to the power of the housefather. . . . There
> can never be two completely equal powers in a single government. . . . That the state
> [*Staat*] cannot decide the conflicts between both domestic powers follows from the same
> grounds I adduced earlier, where I proved that the state can neither stand itself at the head
> of domestic government nor is it permitted to see into and uncover family affairs.[175]

Thus, the first private sphere with an actual social location (as opposed to that
relating to exchange or thought) was established overtly as a sphere of male domination, primarily over women, secondarily over children and servants. It was not the
private sphere of the family, though it was located there. It was the private sphere of
the husband/father/housefather. And it derived from the interpretation that he
and his kind were the founders and chief upholders of civil society, and that laws
should therefore be primarily in his interest. His interest then described the limits
of government power, the line that in theory separated the state from civil society. It
was precisely this line that was inscribed in practice during the Napoleonic period
half a century later.

There can be no more striking example of the utter centrality of gender to the
constitution of the modern state and modern society. But this gender-determined

[173] Stolleis, *Öffentlichen Rechts*, 381.

[174] Justi, *Grundfeste*, vol. 2, par. 113, pp. 102–3.

[175] Ibid., par. 133, pp. 132–33. For Locke's argument about the impossibility of two domestic powers,
see John Locke, "Second Treatise of Government," in *Two Treatises of Government*, ed. Peter Laslett
(Cambridge, 1988), par. 82. Justi never mentions Locke as a source for any of his arguments about the
subjection of women.

private sphere had further effects, because marriage and household were simultaneously the (at least theoretically) exclusive locations of sexual expression. The internal family affairs that Justi was so intent on keeping secret from the prying eyes of government included as a main category, sex. That is why, though it pained him to do so, Justi was forced to permit married couples to misbehave sexually. Justi disapproved of the "all too frequent use of sexual desire" because

> it is harmful to our health, debilitates the body and even encourages premature death. This kind of unchastity can be practiced inside as well as outside of marriage. It can never become an object of civil laws because oversight is impossible. . . . Therefore the health of citizens, with its mediated influence on the common good, can never be a reason for civil laws against unchastity, because otherwise laws against this kind of unchastity would have to exist in relation to married people.[176]

Although Justi does not say so, the same lack of oversight protected far wider sorts of sexual adventurism in marriage. Of course, in practice absolutist government had never targeted marital sexual acts for regulation, but now Justi abstracted practice into principle. And he went further: by explicitly denying that health justified government interference, Justi countered, at least in this instance, the growing trend toward "medical police," which aimed to do just that.[177]

Justi had other unusual ideas about how closely government should regulate sexual behavior.[178] Although they did not derive as directly from his gendered conception of civil society, they still assumed and built on it. The putative demands of the common good, populationism, and the male sexual drive all combined to push Justi toward relaxing sex-crime laws. His stripped-down, populationist definition of marriage as a contract between a man and a women to enter a long-term relation for the sole purpose of producing and raising children made him incapable of distinguishing marriage from concubinage, or "wild marriage," so he favored decriminalization.[179] He also recommended lifting the penalties for fornication. Unlike most of his contemporaries, however, who advocated pardoning only the pregnant woman lest she be driven to infanticide, Justi included her impregnator, too, lest his apparently unstoppable sexual lust be diverted to more harmful pursuits, like "adulteries, insidious seductions, and even the most horrible crime against nature."[180] For the same reason Justi championed brothels and even sug-

---

[176] Justi, *Grundfeste*, vol. 2, par. 200, pp. 239–40.

[177] Johann Peter Süssmilch, *Die göttliche Ordnung in der Veränderung des menschlichen Geschlechts, aus der Geburt, dem Tode und der Fortpflanzung desselben erwiesen* (Berlin, 1742); Friedrich-Wilhelm Schwartz, "Idee und Konzeption der frühen territorial-staatlichen Gesundheitspflege in Deutschland ('Medizinische Polizei') in der ärtzlichen und staatswissenschaftlichen Fachliteratur des 16. -18. Jahrhunderts" (Ph.D. diss., Universität Frankfurt, 1973); George Rosen, "Cameralism and the Concept of Medical Police," *Bulletin of the History of Medicine* 27 (1953): 21–42; Gertrud Kroeger, *The Concept of Social Medicine as Presented by Physicians and Other Writers in Germany: 1779–1932* (Chicago, 1937).

[178] Justi's most developed conception of civil society occurs in his *Grundfeste*, which forms the basis of my discussion. As late as 1759 he still believed in much wider police powers, including suppression of fornication and prostitution. See his *Grundsätze der Policey-Wissenschaft*, par. 290, pp. 215–16.

[179] Justi, *Grundfeste*, vol. 2, par. 201, p. 242.

[180] Ibid., par. 204, p. 248.

gested that they be run by the police and their inmates regularly inspected for venereal disease, a position almost no one advocated until the French occupation of Napoleonic times.[181]

Obviously Justi believed that the male sexual drive required civil society's consideration and that the common good could not only tolerate a much wider range of sexual misbehavior than the early absolutist state thought possible, but it might even benefit from it, if populationism and child-rearing were served. Several other principles drove him farther down the path of official sexual leniency than he wanted to go. For one thing, Justi (like all cameralists) was enough in touch with real administration to know there were practical limits to what government could accomplish. Furthermore, "as I myself have often pointed out, an indubitably moral virtue must not necessarily be made into a civil virtue."[182] Justi here elaborated on the common distinction German natural law theorists made between complete (moral) duties, subject to state compulsion, and incomplete ones, which were voluntary. This distinction, however, was not rigorously developed to mean the separation of law (the rules governing state coercion) from morality (voluntary private behavior) until Kant and the late eighteenth century.[183] Nonetheless, Justi moved decisively in this direction by averring that not all moral acts should be inscribed in positive law. And finally, the common good was not obviously harmed by many sexual acts thought abhorrent, as Montesquieu had demonstrated with ancient Greek homosexual relations. All of these reasons should have suggested the decriminalization of sodomy, but Justi squirmed uneasily under this logic and produced instead a triple negative and a vague wish:

> I do not dare maintain that there could be no constitutions in a civil society in which this kind of unchastity would not cause the least disadvantage for the common best. [Still], nature itself abhors such a vice and every reasonable and moral people must observe the laws of nature. . . . I myself would not like to suggest how this unchastity might be made compatible [*verträglich*] with the common best, lest I attract the charge of encouraging this vice. In any case it would be desirable if it could be suppressed [*unterdrückt*] in states [*Staaten*], even though one would always work at this in vain.[184]

The reader will recognize in the tortured phrasing and pious defeatism the same sort of confusion contemporary central state bureaucrats were voicing about heterosexual misbehavior. It is not easy to tell whether Justi's unusual interest in homosexual relations (reflected in the length of this passage, its unexpected occurrence under the heading "promiscuous unchastity or whoring," and the unique argument he used to disqualify sexual satisfaction and mutual help from the definition of marriage) resulted from the increased sexual speculation characteristic of Enlightenment thinking, from Justi's compulsion to be systematically complete, or from private fascination. The resulting ambivalence, however, was typical of the

---

181 Ibid., pp. 247–49.
182 Ibid., par. 203, p. 244.
183 Schneiders, *Naturrecht und Liebesethik*, 306, 319, 321–26.
184 Justi, *Grundfeste*, vol. 2, par. 203, pp. 244, 247.

larger phenomenon we have already witnessed: governmental practice and theory were dragging the practioners and the theoreticians into new land where the boundaries distinguishing the permissible from the impermissible were not yet drawn.

Most other cameralists, not as theoretically consistent or forward-looking as Justi, were consequently less willing to pull government out of sexual regulation. Even Sonnenfels's extreme populationism, for example, did not move him to advocate decriminalizing fornication.[185] By the late 1780s, however, it had become harder to argue against the principles of civil society as Justi had sketched them. Jung-Stilling, whose romantic and populationist concept of marriage obliterated all other sexual possibilities, wanted government to punish those "who satisfied their merely animal desires" outside marriage. But even he had to nod in the direction of "civil freedom." "The police must be to the utmost degree watchful for this people-destroying horror. Admittedly, effective institutions against this are difficult without limiting civil freedom, but they are not impossible. If the police is truly concerned with the happiness of the subjects, it can achieve astoundingly much."[186]

Jung-Stilling's lingering faith in moral police brings us to a convenient conclusion to this discussion of the cameralists. For the nature of police was the problem the cameralists never solved, and when it had solved itself, in the early nineteenth century, cameralism died. The "well-ordered police state" of early modern times expressed the unity of administration and moral duty. "Police" *was* government, not just one of its administrative arms. Its goal, the common good (or "common best" as it was more accurately expressed by contemporaries), transcended mere order to encompass the prevention of future harm, and more, the constant improvement of conditions and of people toward perfection. There was therefore nothing that was not subject to "police." Even Justi, who rejected Wolff's eudaemonism, never wholly eradicated it from "police," because he and the other cameralists never rejected moral improvement as the goal of civil society, and that is what continued to give "police" its positive, expansionary role. Only Kant's (and Feuerbach's) argument, that moral behavior could occur only in the utter absence of coercion, preserved the moral element in civil society, while simultaneously capping police power.

Until that idea gained currency most cameralists allotted to "police" the minute regulation of everyday life (supervising weights and measures, sanitation, clothing codes, and so on) plus the entire panoply of negative and positive persuasion required by eudaemonism.[187] At most they might emphasize instruction rather than punishment as appropriate especially to moral matters and thus expand the

---

[185] Sonnenfels, "Bevölkerung," 247–48.

[186] Jung-Stilling, *Lehrbuch*, par. 466, p. 191.

[187] Concerning the persistence of eudaemonism, see Unruh, "Polizei, Polizeiwissenschaft und Kameralistik," 419–21; Stolleis, *Öffentlichen Rechts*, 384–85; and Maier, *Staats- und Verwaltungslehre*, 183–85. On the regulation of everyday life, see Wolff, *Vernünfftige Gedancken*, pars. 379–89, and Justi, *Grundsätze der Policey-Wissenschaft*, pars. 270–94, pp. 201–18.

church and school aspects of police at the expense of outright coercive intervention.[188] It was once again Justi who, without making a sharp break from this tradition, nonetheless pointed to the peculiar quasi-solution that emerged from the Napoleonic reforms.

Justi began from the familiar standpoint that moral virtues were necessary to the happiness and welfare of individual families and of civil society.[189] Because the moral condition of people exercised such a great influence on "the welfare of states [*Staaten*]" and the "common and particular well-being of the citizens [*Bürger*]," "the police cannot dispense with directing its attention to the moral virtues of subjects [*Unterthanen*]; not that it should order them or punish actions contrary [to moral virtue], but that it should try to encourage them in citizens [*Bürgern*]."[190] Nonetheless, sometimes the police would have to go beyond mere encouragement and apply correction. But under what circumstances? Justi tried to answer this question by mapping out a middle zone of police purview. There was a sphere of "free and irrelevant actions which have no influence on the common best" and which therefore should never be penalized and never subjected to police inspection. Justi seemed to conceive of these actions as primarily domestic, since in the following sentence he admonished the police (again) especially to avoid "interfering in family government."[191] At the other end of the spectrum was "harm to complete duties which belong to the actual administration of justice," that is, serious crimes to be handled by criminal courts.

> That leaves to the police in the narrow sense only the supervision and punishment of such vices and excesses [*Laster und Ausschweifungen*] which make people incapable of performing their civil duties and which disturb public quiet and security. But here also human weakness demands consideration; and supervision, especially in the first case, is so difficult, if one does not want to limit too much the freedom of irrelevant actions in the houses of private people [*Privatpersohnen*], that the police must rest content to root out only those vices and excesses that cause a public disturbance [*öffentliches Aergerniß*] or incite to seduction or imitation.[192]

Justi was thus the first cameralist to distinguish police from the administration of justice: "The actual crimes one leaves to police correction are never important [*wichtig*]; they are always only mistakes or flaws in the relation of the citizens [*Bürger*] to the common best" and they never require "hard punishments."[193] Justi was also the first to mark off, and label "private," a place ("in the houses of private people") where the police ought not tread. In between was the gray zone in which the police operated.

[188] Seckendorff, *Fürsten-Stat*, 91; Wolff, *Vernünfftige Gedancken*, par. 316, pp. 260–61.
[189] *Grundfeste*, vol. 1, par. 19, pp. 19–20.
[190] Ibid., vol. 2, 10th bk., "Einleitung," pp. 101–2.
[191] Ibid., par. 9, pp. 10–11.
[192] Justi, *Grundsätze der Policey-Wissenschaft*, par. 287, pp. 213–14.
[193] *Natur und Wesen*, par. 268, pp. 594–95.

The phrase "vices and excesses" betrays what sorts of activities Justi believed forfeited privacy, and therefore fell into police jurisdiction, even if they were practiced in private houses. Despite his reiteration that "the police should absolutely least of all hinder the innocent amusement in private houses [*Privat-Häusern*]," he rushed on to add that "as soon as things [in private houses] reach the point of public disturbance, seduction of young people and ruination of morals, then it is their duty to put a stop to these excesses. Thus they must not permit gambling in either private or public houses; and if music and dancing are used to offer the services of loose wenches [*liederlicher Dirnen*], or similar annoying things take place, then the police must destroy these houses of vice." Justi here repeated part of the standard, traditional catalog of moral vices that had always been subject to police control. In the next paragraph he made explicit how important sexual morality had become in this catalog and therefore in determining the extent of police power: "The main concern [*Vorsorge*] of the police in regard to morality [*Sitten*] must be to make sure that the vice of fornication [*Hurerey und Unzucht*] does not increase much."[194]

Therefore at the very moment when Justi tried to draw the first line between government and "private" social behavior, sexual misdeeds seemed to him exemplary of the continued need for police intervention, as they later seemed to Feuerbach exemplary of the whole problem of police intervention at a different stage in the same process of differentiation of state and society.

Besides the division of civil society into zones of more, less, or no government interference, Justi tackled a second major issue thrown up by the constitution of civil society, namely, its moral basis and goal. That civil society was founded upon, required, and aimed toward morality was an assumption all cameralists shared. But what determined the content of morality: God's law, natural law, positive law, or mere custom? The early cameralists, as we have seen, assumed a happy congruence among all four; if custom erred, then it could be set right by positive law, grounded in divine and natural law. Pufendorf foretold later developments by diminishing divine law into an indistinct foundation for the sharper etchings of natural law.[195] Natural law thereafter displaced divine law as the foundation for "the actual moral virtues" toward which civil society should move. Civil society's laws should never contradict the "actual moral virtues," but they need not contain all of them, since many referred to duties irrelevant to civil society.[196] Positive law, however, might balloon beyond natural law and proclaim all sorts of behavior civil virtues by simply making them law. Legislating "mere prejudices [into] moral virtues, which have no real basis in natural law," was a great infringement on freedom and therefore an enormous error, Justi felt.[197] This was the twilight realm of custom, which the German word *Sitten* expressed indistinguishably from "morality." The double

---

[194] *Grundsätze der Policey-Wissenschaft*, par. 289, and par. 290, p. 215.
[195] James Tully, "Introduction," to Pufendorf, *Duty of Man*, xxii–xxiv.
[196] Justi, *Grundfeste*, vol. 2, par. 9, p. 10.
[197] Ibid.

usage was a vestige of the pious hope that custom and morality based on religion or natural law would coincide. Montesquieu's *Spirit of the Laws* summed up the growing eighteenth-century conviction that this was not so, but the cameralists continued to use *Sitten* to mean both. That confusion perpetuated the danger that positive law would contain irrelevant moral injunctions permitting police interference at the cost of civil freedom.

Justi tried to define the problem away—and failed.

> One understands by *Sitten* the behavior and conduct of people in their irrelevant actions, which, in the condition of natural freedom have no immediate consequences for the duties stemming from natural law, or, if no societies exist, with the duties stemming from social life, or, in civil constitutions, with the final goals of the state or with civil duties. In short, one understands by *Sitten* more the actions of a person, than that of a member of society or of a citizen.[198]

Consequently, one would have expected *Sitten* to constitute a realm of nonsupervision. Far from it. Justi began back-tracking almost immediately, when he asserted that "*Sitten* must not be contrary to honor/decency [*Erbarkeit*]," the only examples of which he adduced were sexual and/or corporeal: female modesty and the necessity to perform "the necessary acts of nature" out of public view.[199] The crowning consideration that moved him to include *Sitten* in the purview of police was family and gender relations, for, as he had already written, "the domestic arrangement of families makes up a great part of the moral/*customary* [*sittlichen*] condition" of a people.[200]

> Domestic laws depend most greatly on *Sitten*. The freedom or confinement of women, the behavior of spouses to one another, the manner of raising children, the manners of servants, all this is directed by *Sitten*. Yes! even the domination of man over woman depends upon *Sitten*. We not only know that entire peoples have publicly left domination [*Herrschaft*] to the women, but that thanks to *Sitten*, women dominate in other countries where men publicly enjoy the name of lord.

From such historical examples Justi concluded, contrary to his previous definition, that

> *Sitten* have a large influence on the welfare of the state [*Staates*]. The state is made up of single families and the condition of the state, its power and strength, depends upon the qualities of the single families. Consequently, one is strengthened [in the opinion] that *Sitten* should never be left to themselves, but should be brought into the closest relation and conformity with civil laws.[201]

Justi had thus failed to limit positive law and therefore police intervention. And he had also skirted the problem of the relation between customary morality and absolute morality resting on divine and/or natural law. Instead, he had given

---

[198] *Natur und Wesen*, par. 221, p. 502.
[199] Ibid., par. 227, pp. 514–15.
[200] *Grundfeste*, vol. 2, par. 9, p. 11.
[201] *Natur und Wesen*, par. 229, pp. 517–19.

customary morality a different foundation: civil utility. The putative needs of civil society, especially the needs of its gender, familial, and therefore sexual organization, were now the adamantine basis upon which custom would be shaped and given the binding force of law.

This was the reverse of the tyranny of custom that later haunted J. S. Mill. In Justi this tyranny originated not with society and its habitual customs, but with the abstract requirements of its [re]organization into civil society. This was the old police state working to shape civil society and to make itself (potentially) superfluous:

> It is thus certain that police laws can never remain the same, but are much more subject to change than any other laws. As the condition of the commonwealth and of individual families changes, so must the other rules and means of enlarging the power and strength of the state/society [*Staat*]; and it is self-illuminating that those laws and institutions designed for the improvement of mistakes and ills must cease to exist as soon as their goal has truly been reached.[202]

As Justi wrestled unsuccessfully from the vantage point of bureaucratic theory to provide crystalline prescriptions for the journey into civil society, actual social changes were creating networks and institutions that increasingly thought of themselves as precisely the incarnation of the principles he and the other cameralists had been sketching.

---

[202] Justi, *Grundfeste*, vol. 2, par. 405, p. 473. See also Darjes, *Erste Gründe*, par. 27, p. 376, on the evanescence of police laws.

5

❧

The Practitioners
of Civil Society

German Civil Society in Practice and Scholarship

Germany's most recent history and historiography have thrown a great shadow over its eighteenth century; indeed, for a long time Enlightened Germany seemed to disappear altogether. Conservative historians were anxious to distance Germany from the intellectual "causes" of the French Revolution, whereas liberals lamented the seemingly late establishment of constitutions and political parties during the nineteenth century. Marxists measured Germany according to the development of capitalism and found it wanting. Non-German historians judged World War I and especially World War II incompatible with a past of vigorous Enlightenment and bourgeois culture. The modernization theorists of the 1960s applied their own version of socioeconomic determinism and pronounced Germany's development a deviation from the "Western model." These standpoints encouraged the impression, especially among nineteenth- and twentieth-century specialists, that the German Enlightenment was thin, derivative, apolitical, and overwhelmed by the conservative forces of court, state, nobility and peasantry.[1]

The last two decades of research into the eighteenth century have revealed, on the contrary, a native, robust, widespread, and active German Enlightenment. Its complexity has frustrated attempts at synthetic interpretation. Different historiographical interests emphasize different aspects of the German Enlightenment; the conventional phases of early, middle, and late Enlightenment occur at different

[1] For a clear, recent account of the older literature, see Elisabeth Fehrenbach, *Vom Ancien Régime zum Wiener Kongreß* (Munich, 1981), 51–65, 152–61, 212–19. Also see Wolfgang Ruppert, *Bürgerlicher Wandel. Die Geburt der modernen deutschen Gesellschaft im 18. Jahrhundert* (Frankfurt, 1983), 31–35. For a concise précis of literary/aesthetic argument, see Hans Jürgen Haferkorn, "Zur Entstehung der bürgerlich-literarischen Intelligenz und des Schriftstellers im Deutschland zwischen 1750 und 1800," in *Deutsches Bürgertum und literarische Intelligenz 1750–1800*, ed. Bernd Lutz (Stuttgart, 1974), 180–84, 190–95. Concerning Germany's defective modernization, see Gerhard A. Ritter and Jürgen Kocka, eds., *Deutsche Sozialgeschichte. Dokumente und Skizzen*, vol. 2, *1870–1914*, 3d ed. (Munich, 1982), 62–70, 322–24; Jürgen Kocka, "German History before Hitler: The Debate about the German 'Sonderweg,'" *Journal of Contemporary History* 23 (1988): 3–16; and Helga Grebing, *Der 'deutsche Sonderweg' in Europa, 1806–1945. Eine Kritik* (Stuttgart, 1986). For a critique of the modernization view, see David Blackbourn and Geoff Eley, *The Peculiarities of German History. Bourgeois Society and Politics in Nineteenth-Century Germany* (Oxford, 1984).

times, depending on whether one investigates belles lettres, philosophy, or political thought; the quality and preoccupations of Enlighteners look different if the focus is on Enlightened courts and courtiers, governmental reformers, the mercantile patriciate, academics, poets, or pastors; the sociology of Enlightened networks changes from east to west, north to south, Protestant to Catholic, and town to town. And, of course, Enlightenment was an ongoing argument among people who often disagreed.[2] The very variety of German Enlightenments reflects how far alternate social forms, discourses and visions of civil society had developed by the latter half of the eighteenth century. The existence of Enlightened civil society is critical to understanding what happened to the public interest in sexual behavior, for the late-eighteenth-century discussion of sexual behavior and its impact on state and society, the discussion that laid the foundation for the "modern" assumptions about "sexuality," was not only carried on by self-described Enlightened members of civil society, it was a public debate on the (sexual) ligaments holding that society together or threatening to pull it apart. Enlightened civil society *was* the framework within which the reorganization of thinking about sexual behavior took place. Post-Napoleonic Germany's undeniable political disasters have so focused historical attention on state and "politics" that society and culture in the anthropological sense have become virtually unrecognizable. Yet without civil society, both as a not-yet-realized project and as an actual sociocultural reality, the debate on "sexuality" would not have taken place—it would not even have been necessary.

I call the active subjects of civil society its "practitioners." By this term I wish to stress that they lived in and practiced the principles of civil society even as they were forming it. The practitioners of civil society were the overwhelmingly male members of the voluntary associations, the contributors to journals, and the deba-

---

[2] This is not the place for an exhaustive bibliography of newer works on the eighteenth century in Germany. Some books I have found helpful in examining Enlightened civil society are Rudolf Vierhaus, *Deutschland im 18. Jahrhundert. Politische Verfassung, soziales Gefüge, geistige Bewegungen* (Göttingen, 1987); Franklin Kopitzsch, ed., *Aufklärung, Absolutismus und Bürgertum in Deutschland* (Munich, 1976); Richard van Dülmen, *Die Gesellschaft der Aufklärer. Zur bürgerlichen Emanzipation und aufklärerischen Kultur in Deutschland* (Frankfurt, 1986); Rudolf Vierhaus, ed., *Bürger und Bürgerlichkeit im Zeitalter der Aufklärung* (Heidelberg, 1981); Otto Dann, ed., *Lesegesellschaften und bürgerliche Emanzipation: Ein europäischer Vergleich* (Munich, 1981); Ulrich Herrmann, ed., *"Die Bildung des Bürgers": Die Formierung der bürgerlichen Gesellschaft und die Gebildeten im 18. Jahrhundert* (Weinheim, 1989); Hans Erich Bödecker and Ulrich Herrmann, eds., *Über den Prozeß der Aufklärung in Deutschland im 18. Jahrhundert. Personen, Institutionen und Medien* (Göttingen, 1987); Ruppert, *Bürgerlicher Wandel;* Ulrich Im Hof, *Das gesellige Jahrhundert. Gesellschaft und Gesellschaften im Zeitalter der Aufklärung* (Munich, 1982); Horst Möller, *Vernunft und Kritik. Deutsche Aufklärung im 17. und 18. Jahrhundert* (Frankfurt, 1986), 346–54; Hans Erich Bödeker and Ulrich Herrmann, eds., *Aufklärung als Politisierung—Politisierung der Aufklärung* (Hamburg, 1987); Jonathan Knudsen, *Justus Möser and the German Enlightenment* (Cambridge, 1986); Horst Möller, *Aufklärung in Preußen: Der Verleger, Publizist und Geschichtsschreiber Friedrich Nicolai* (Berlin, 1974). Older, but still useful as introductions are Peter Gay, *The Enlightenment: An Interpretation*, 2 vols. (New York, 1966 and 1969), esp. the bibliographic essays at 1:423–555 and 2:570–705. Also, Norman Hampson, *The Enlightenment. An Evaluation of its Assumptions, Attitudes and Values*, rev. ed. (London, 1982). For Germany, see Horst Stuke, "Aufklärung," in Brunner, Conze, and Koselleck, *Geschichtliche Grundbegriffe*, 1:243–342, and Rudolf Vierhaus, *Zur historischen Deutung der Aufklärung. Probleme und Perspektiven* (Bremen, 1977), 39–54.

ters and discussants who considered themselves more than the sum of their individual selves, who created an integrated national discourse, who institutionalized Enlightenment thinking in functioning associations and journals, who really did provide state reformers with the goals, assumptions, and values guiding reform, and who furthermore did all of this expressly in the name of and from the vantage point of what they called "civil society." Insofar as civil society had begun to be actualized, to be lived, these men *were* civil society, and they thought of themselves as such. But they also recognized that civil society, like the Enlightenment it was supposed to embody, was not yet complete. In Kant's phrase, it was an age of Enlightenment, but not yet an Enlightened age.[3] Therefore, the Platonic vision of civil society still shone before them, within sight, but just out of reach. "Civil society in practice" existed, but it had not realized its perfection as civil society the project. Civil society in practice reformulated the sexual system as part of its preparation for ideal civil society.

Other scholars have used other terms to try and capture the essence of Enlightened civil society. I should briefly explain why I have not followed them in using terms like *Bürgertum* (bourgeois), "new *Bürgertum*," "public sphere," or *Öffentlichkeit*. By doing so, I shall also make clearer who the practitioners of civil society really were.

Bürgertum is too class-exclusive, too narrowly socioeconomic to grasp the reality of civil society in practice. The main creators and consumers of the Enlightened worldview were state and city officials (noble and non-noble); the *Bildungsbürgertum* (the non-noble, educated holders of official and non-state positions as scholars, educators [*Hofmeister*], doctors, lawyers, apothecaries, lease-holders on domain lands, independent writers, journalists, and so forth); and the bourgeoisie active in commerce, manufacture, or finance above the level of artisan or petty merchant.[4] The educated nobility, especially bureaucrats, contributed substantially to producing and consuming Enlightenment in Germany. For example, nobles made up 30 percent of the members of Bonn's reading association (*Lesegesellschaft*) and 15

---

[3] Immanuel Kant, "An Answer to the Question 'What is Enlightenment?'" (1784), in *Kant's Political Writing*, ed. Hans Reiss (Cambridge, 1970), 58.

[4] The classic study of the centrality of officials to Enlightenment is Hans Gerth, *Bürgerliche Intelligenz um 1800. Zur Soziologie des deutschen Frühliberalismus* (Göttingen, 1976), esp. 61–62, 72–77. On *Bildungsbürger*, see Ulrich Engelhardt, "*Bildungsbürgertum." Begriffs- und Dogmengeschichte eines Etiketts* (Stuttgart, 1986). For a list of typical occupations, see Wehler, *Deutsche Gesellschaftsgeschichte*, 1:204. Concerning commerce and finance, see Kopitzsch, "Die Sozialgeschichte der deutschen Aufklärung als Forschungsaufgabe," in Kopitzsch, *Aufklärung, Absolutismus und Bürgertum in Deutschland*, 36; Möller, *Vernunft und Kritik*, 293; Dülmen, *Gesellschaft der Aufklärer*, 59, 67–68, 87, 104; and Otto Dann, "Die Lesegesellschaften des 18. Jahrhunderts und der gesellschaftliche Aufbruch des deutschen Bürgertums," in Herrmann, *Bildung des Bürgers*, 105–7. Ruppert, *Bürgerlicher Wandel*, 57–102, leaves the impression that large merchants were more important to the process of Enlightenment than they probably were, except in cities like Hamburg. On the older, especially Marxist equation of bourgeoisie and Enlightenment, see Kopitzsch, "Sozialgeschichte der deutschen Aufklärung" (1976), 69; Möller, *Vernunft und Kritik*, 295–96; and Jürgen Kocka, "Bürgertum und bürgerliche Gesellschaft im 19. Jahrhundert. Europäische Entwicklungen und deutsche Eigenarten," in *Bürgertum im 19. Jahrhundert. Deutschland im europäischen Vergleich*, ed. Kocka, vol. 1 (Munich, 1988), 20 n. 16, 37.

percent of the contributors to the archetypical Enlightened journal, the *Berlinische Monatsschrift;* the latter figure Möller thinks representative of the noble presence in Enlightened organizations generally.[5] The Masonic lodges were so saturated with nobles that in them "the opposition of noble and bourgeois was largely eliminated."[6]

The Enlightened elite nonetheless made up only a small percentage of the total population. Through their writings, however, they may have reached a higher proportion of their social inferiors than was previously thought possible. The latest estimates of aggregate literacy west of the Elbe river range around 70 percent by 1800 (greater than in France). Although the effects of such widespread literacy are still uncertain,[7] the point is not that most Germans were "Enlightened," but that Enlightenment precepts dominated literate culture. Opponents were often reduced to arguing about who represented "real" as opposed to "false" Enlightenment.[8] The terms, forms, and categories of contest were set by the capacious bounds of "Enlightenment." Furthermore, adherents of Enlightenment were concentrated in the most strategic locations: in cities (especially trading and administrative centers)

[5] On Bonn, see Dann, "Lesegesellschaften," 106, and Möller, *Vernunft und Kritik,* 295–96.

[6] Dülmen, *Gesellschaft der Aufklärer,* 57–59. Of six lodges for which he gives membership information, the percentage of nobles ranges from 13 percent to 55 percent, the average being 38 percent.

[7] Etienne François, "Regionale Unterschiede der Lese- und Schreibfähigkeit in Deutschland im 18. und 19. Jahrhundert," *Jahrbuch für Regionalgeschichte und Landeskunde* (1990), 156–62; Etienne François, "Alphabetisierung und Lesefähigkeit in Frankreich und Deutschland," in *Deutschland und Frankreich im Zeitalter der Französischen Revolution,* ed. Helmut Berding, Etienne François, and Hans-Peter Ullmann (Frankfurt, 1989), 407–25; Reinhart Siegert, *Aufklärung und Volkslektüre. Exemplarisch dargestellt an Rudolf Zacharias Becker und seinem "Noth- und Hülfsbüchlein." Mit einer Bibliographie zum Gesamtthema,* which appeared in a special issue of *Archiv für Geschichte des Buchwesens* 19 (1978): cols. 566–1347, cols. 591–98; Reinhard Wittman, "Der lesende Landmann. Zur Rezeption aufklärerischer Bemühungen durch die bäuerliche Bevölkerung im 18. Jahrhundert," in *Der Bauer Mittel- und Osteuropas im sozio-ökonomischen Wandel des 18. und 19. Jahrhunderts,* ed. Dan Berindei (Cologne, 1973), 146–49. I thank Jonathan Knudsen for bringing these works to my attention. See also Jürgen Voss, "Der Gemeine Mann und die Volksaufklärung im späten 18. Jahrhundert," in *Vom Elend der Handarbeit: Probleme historischer Unterschichtenforschung,* ed. Hans Mommsen and Winfried Schulze (Stuttgart, 1981), 208–33, esp. 220–27. Older literacy estimates hovered around 25 percent: see Rudolf Schenda, *Volk ohne Buch. Studien zur Sozialgeschichte der populären Lesestoffe, 1770–1910* (Frankfurt, 1970); Rolf Engelsing, *Analphabetentum und Lektüre. Zur Sozialgeschichte des Lesens in Deutschland zwischen feudaler und industrieller Gesellschaft* (Stuttgart, 1973), 62; Ernst Hinrichs, *Einführung in die Geschichte der Frühen Neuzeit* (Munich, 1980), 100–106, 219–20, n. 20; and Helmuth Kiesel and Paul Münch, *Gesellschaft und Literatur im 18. Jahrhundert. Voraussetzungen und Entstehung des literarischen Markts in Deutschland* (Munich, 1977), 160–61. On the impact of popular Enlightenment, see Jonathan Knudsen, "On Enlightenment for the Common Man," in *"What Was Enlightenment?" Eighteenth-Century Answers and Twentieth-Century Questions,* ed. James Schmidt (Berkeley, 1994) and Franklin Kopitzsch, "Sozialgeschichte der Aufklärung in Deutschland" (1989), in Berding, François, and Ullmann, *Deutschland und Frankreich,* 373–91 and (on the underestimation of the successes of popular enlightenment) 379.

[8] Möller, *Vernunft und Kritik,* 36–41; Werner Schneiders, *Wahre Aufklärung. Zur Selbstverständnis der deutschen Aufklärung* (Freiburg, 1974). On opponents of the Enlightenment, see Klaus Epstein, *The Origins of German Conservatism* (Princeton, 1966), and Robert Berdahl, *The Politics of the Prussian Nobility: The Development of a Conservative Ideology, 1770–1848* (Princeton, 1988). On the ambivalent relation of pietism to Enlightenment, see Gerhard Kaiser, *Pietismus und Patriotismus im literarischen Deutschland: Ein Beitrag zum Problem der Säkularisation,* 2d ed. (Frankfurt, 1973).

and, more important, in the state apparatus. From these vantage points the enlightened elite began to reform the basic institutions of German life, in law, administrative practice, economy, and so forth. Their influence reached far beyond their actual accomplishments, for they provided the vision of the future, the guiding principles according to which the new formal and informal social order replaced the old. As Hans-Ulrich Wehler puts it, "No where else in the early modern societies of Europe and North America can one find a similar group [the 'bureaucratized intelligentsia'—*verstaatlichte Intelligenz*] with the same enduring influence, the same astonishing, long-term impact, even into the twentieth century."[9]

The term "new *Bürgertum*" has some advantages in describing the carriers of German Enlightenment.[10] First, it calls attention to the fact that educated nonnobles found in Enlightenment organizations the social grounding they had lost in society itself. The *Bildungsbürgertum* had literally fallen out of the *ständisch* order. Prussia, for instance, had exempted them from the usual *ständisch* courts,[11] and in the towns in which they lived, they were frequently without the citizens' rights (*Bürgerrechte*) of the old patriciate and/or artisanal *Bürgertum*. They were thus "new" in a concrete social sense. Second, they pointed to a new conception of *Bürgertum*, in the sense of *Staatsbürger*, or active, participating citizen-member of the new civil society. They were thus a class in becoming, not quite part of the traditional order, not yet at home in the future they were trying to create. The criterion for inclusion in this new group was not traditionally social, that is, it exactly coincided neither with status, profession, nor even directly with wealth. Instead, it was a quality to which all might theoretically aspire and even achieve: education, *Bildung*. Because it was transsocial, the claim that *Bildung* was the constituent principle of the new *Staatsbürger* was subversive of the old order; as Friedrich Nicolai remarked, "Reasonable and honorable people belong together *without regard* to *Stand*, religion, or other peripheral considerations."[12] Reason had replaced *Stand* as the "identity card of a new elite."[13] We should be careful, however, not to anticipate nineteenth-century developments and see this elite as more socially homogenous or class-like than it actually was. In order to preserve the social fluidity and future-orientedness characteristic of this elite, I avoid the term "new *Bürgertum*."[14]

---

[9] *Deutsche Gesellschaftsgeschichte* 1:211.

[10] Ruppert, *Bürgerlicher Wandel*, and Dülmen, *Gesellschaft der Aufklärer*, both use this term.

[11] Koselleck, *Preußen zwischen Reform und Revolution*, 89–104.

[12] Cited in Möller, *Vernunft und Kritik*, 290, emphasis in original.

[13] Thomas Nipperdey, "Verein als soziale Struktur in Deutschland im späten 18. und frühen 19. Jahrhundert," in *Gesellschaft, Kultur, Theorie. Gesammelte Aufsätze* (Göttingen, 1976), 174–205.

[14] On avoiding the sociological fallacy, see Möller, *Vernunft und Kritik*, 289–90, 293, 343 n. 35; Engelhardt, *Bildungsbürgertum*, 66, 84; and Kopitzsch, "Sozialgeschichte der Aufklärung" (1989), 378. Despite rehearsing its limitations, Kocka reverts to a firm sociological usage, "Bürgertum und bürgerliche Gesellschaft," cf. 13–17 with 36–39, 48. On the express intention of Enlighteners not to reflect particular interests of social groups or professions, see Dülmen, *Gesellschaft der Aufklärer*, 123, and Nipperdey, "Verein," 191.

Finally, there is the term *Öffentlichkeit* (public sphere). This is especially associated with Jürgen Habermas's famous 1962 study, *The Structural Transformation of the Public Sphere*. His functional account of civil society has been influential in political theory, in interpreting the relation between public and private, and has enjoyed renewed attention in the current debates about the nature of civil society. Habermas described "the public sphere of civil society" as "the abstract counterpart of public [state] authority," which finally developed "an awareness of itself as the [state's] opponent."[15] *Öffentlichkeit* was the forum in which the exercise of critical reason pointed the way toward an active, self-forming society, free of absolutist state tutelage and, potentially, toward political freedom.

Habermas's use of "public sphere" is in two respects a pithy formulation of how Enlightenment discourse actually functioned. He identified as the actually functioning agency organized associations and journals, which formed a national market of contested and contesting ideas. And he recognized that the content of its discussions became ever more critical and unruly, until by the 1780s and 1790s, voices within this "public sphere" claimed for it the right to bestow legitimation upon the state, or to revoke it and even perhaps to contemplate revolution.

But Habermas's work was not a historical study. It built on abstract and anachronistic foundations that make his concept of "public sphere" misleading for the late eighteenth century. Three problems are especially grave for our concerns: the too narrowly economic understanding of civil society, the mistaken notion of the (developing) conception of "private" and its relation to the state or common good, and the too idealized picture of the actual functioning of Enlightened discussion (*Öffentlichkeit*).

Habermas has subsequently seemed to acknowledge that his earlier identification of civil society with economic relations was inaccurate.[16] From the historian's perspective an economic definition is doubly problematic. On the one hand it is anachronistic, since neither capitalism nor capitalists characterized late-eighteenth-century Germany; on the other, it is reductionist. For such a narrow usage of "civil society" (*bürgerliche Gesellschaft*) was not at all what contemporaries meant by the term. As we have seen in the cameralists' writings, and the voices of late enlightened *Öffentlichkeit* were no different, "civil society" meant society in its organized aspect, society as it constituted a state apparatus to protect itself and to further the welfare of all its citizens. If earlier writers could more or less unproblematically equate civil society with the state, the late Enlightenment used "civil society" to mean the new social and political form(s) that would replace and were already replacing the *ständisch* order. Practitioners arrived at the new formulation of civil society in different ways. Some took advantage of the traditional legitimation of

---

[15] *Structural Transformation*, 23.

[16] Ibid., 3, 30; Jürgen Habermas, "Further Reflections on the Public Sphere," in *Habermas and the Public Sphere*, ed. Craig Calhoun (Cambridge, Mass., 1992), 421–61, esp. 438, 453–54. Nonetheless, Habermas still clings to the sociological expression of this economic definition, namely, that Öffentlichkeit was "an exclusively bourgeois affair." "Further Reflections," 423–24.

state authority via common welfare (*Gemeinwohl*) and made civil society its new arbiter and yardstick. Others rejected *Gemeinwohl* in favor of individual rights. Others developed the principle of rule of law (*Rechtsstaat*), which, accomplished through legal reforms, would newly define and circumscribe state power vis-à-vis the nonstate realm of civil society. Still others emphasized the moral aspect of civil society as the arena of self-development according to Reason. Finally, the sphere of economic production, unfettered by monopolies and undue state intervention, was another important aspect of civil society, but only one. Civil society in contemporary usage was thus much broader, more political (in the sense of being overtly connected to state power and to norm-setting), and more future-oriented (in the sense of a project to create a new order, rather than merely reflecting already existing [economic] needs) than Habermas's model allows. These three aspects of civil society must be acknowledged, not merely for the sake of historical accuracy, but more important, for the sake of conceptual acuity.

A second set of problems concerns the relation of public to private. Habermas writes that "the bourgeois public sphere may be conceived above all as the sphere of private people come together as a public."[17] Certainly many participants in *Öffentlichkeit* described themselves this way to distinguish their words from official pronouncements and to establish a realm of "public" judgment and activity separate from that of the state.[18] In this respect, Habermas's description is quite accurate. But one must take care not to infer more from the phrase "private people" than simply the subject position they assumed as writers. For at least half of those engaged in public discussion were servants of the state, and their expertise and state horizons strongly influenced their writings.[19] And the criteria forming their opinions, and those of their fellow *Bürger* not connected with the state as well, were not primarily those of home and hearth, but of *Gemeinwohl*, public usefulness (*Gemeinnützigkeit*), and the necessity to reform the social order as a whole. Contemporaries did not regard "private" and "public" as split.[20] Moreover, the content of their public orientation, the values of *Gemeinwohl*, systematic rationality, quiet productivity, moral honor, and so on, were values prized by the state, enunciated for decades by its servants in its interest (*vide* the cameralists), and generally associated with its welfare and its Enlightened, reforming activity. In short, the voices of *Öffentlichkeit* were generally not speaking from an idyll of private isolation; how much their experiences of home life shone through in their writings needs to be systematically researched. But it would be incorrect from the outset to maintain that a well-defined private sphere of the nineteenth-century sort was the basis for their published utterances. They were instead engaged in creating and legitimating

---

[17] *Structural Transformation*, 27.

[18] See the Hamburg activist J. Günther's telling phrase in Dülmen, *Gesellschaft der Aufklärer*, 72.

[19] Kopitzsch, "Sozialgeschichte der Aufklärung" (1989), 380–81.

[20] Lothar Pikulik, *Leistungsethik contra Gefühlskult* (Göttingen, 1984), 109–10; and Rudolf Vierhaus, "'Patriotismus'—Begriff und Realität einer moralisch-politischen Haltung," in Herrmann, *Bildung des Bürgers*, 119–32. Cf. the contrary view in Koselleck, *Kritik und Krise*.

that "private sphere," and they did so from foundations firmly set in state and community. Furthermore, they expected the state to play a major positive role in bringing about the revolutionary changes they favored, even when they criticized it for failing to do so.

There are further problems regarding the relation between *Öffentlichkeit* and that aspect of the private which, in *Structural Transformations*, Habermas calls the "intimate sphere." The "intimate sphere" he calls "the enclosed space of the patriarchal conjugal family," which is both the "scene of a psychological emancipation" from the stresses of economic competition (46), and the locus where "subjectivity" is created (29). The private experiences growing out of that subjectivity guide "the public's understanding of the public use of reason"; that is, Habermas believes the "intimate sphere" founded the "public sphere" and made it possible (28). Habermas goes on to say that despite the hypocritical fiction that the family was a realm of pure humanity and altruistic sentiment free of economic considerations (and therefore of competition and self-interest), the family nonetheless really did incorporate values, like "closeness . . . freedom, love, and cultivation of the person," "without whose subjective validity society would not have been able to reproduce itself" (47–48).

Habermas's view of the "intimate sphere" is thus perilously close to the domestic ideology that reached its hegemonic climax in the nineteenth century. No one would deny that their family lives must surely have affected the views of late-eighteenth-century discussants, or that families did provide their members with positive emotions. But the spectrum of family arrangements experienced by the socially, regionally, and religiously heterogeneous Enlighteners could hardly be reduced to a single model, and then hardly to one of unalloyed domestic harmony. "The family" Habermas describes is not the untidy, changing site of conflict and negotiation of late-eighteenth-century life-worlds, but a draft project legitimated, among other ways, by the claim that only such an arrangement guaranteed the continuance of civil society and economic productivity.

Habermas's term "patriarchal" to describe the family shows that he was aware that the "intimate sphere" had an ideological edge, namely, that it operated in the interest of the husband/householder. Recently, Habermas has reemphasized how important the subjection of women in this model has been to structuring civil society.[21] Nonetheless, his use of the term "intimate sphere" tends to obscure three important features of this Enlightened model. First, the subjection of women in the domestic sphere and their exclusion from participation in the "public sphere" were not peripheral or unintended consequences, but consciously pursued goals. In their public writings, Enlightened thinkers explicitly reserved the family-based "private experiences" leading to emancipatory "subjectivity" and ultimately to political participation to married males only. Second, the main argument they used to justify the shape they gave to the "public" (of civil society, the new state, and later politics)

---

[21] Habermas, "Further Reflections," 428–29.

was that this shape benefited the "private." The peculiar gender configuration of Habermas's "intimate sphere" was supposed to be the very basis of public reorganization. The "intimate sphere" tailored to the presumed needs of the new male citizen was one of the most successful ideological creations of late Enlightened discourse. It was a product, not a cause, of the larger project to redraft the "public" according to the requirements of civil society.

Finally, none of this struggle and argumentation would have been conceivable or necessary if the "public sphere" had not been run overwhelmingly by men. It was not an abstract market of ideas, and though women read, they did not publish, and their membership in associations was limited. Although Habermas considers women "active" in the public sphere by virtue of their reading, he does not claim that consumption was equivalent to production.[22] The producers of Enlightened discourse were men, and no other sociological observation is as important for our purposes as that one.

And it is for all of these reasons that the following discussion avoids the terms "*Bürgertum*," "new *Bürgertum*," and "public sphere"/*Öffentlichkeit* in favor of the "practitioners of civil society."

Association: The Quintessential Form of Practical Civil Society

The German Enlightenment did not take place inside the heads of isolated, unworldly individuals. More than in either England or France, the German Enlightenment and its practical civil society were organized in institutions, where its principles were made known, debated, and modified.[23] According to Otto Dann, "The reading societies were, in the Germany of the late eighteenth century, one of the most important crystallization points of social life, [they were] the form of civil society-building."[24] In the welter of associations, Nipperdey tells us, "the abstract concept 'citizen' [*Bürger*] became an unmediated, lively, concrete reality: here for the first time common civil forms of life [*gemeinbürgerliche Lebensformen*] created themselves."[25]

Association building began in the 1720s with the first moral-literary societies and continued in waves, changing form and widening constituency, throughout the century.[26] The moral-literary societies started in commercial centers such as Ham-

22 Habermas, *Structural Transformation*, 55.
23 On France, see Nipperdey, "Verein," 183.
24 "Lesegesellschaften," 101.
25 "Verein," 185.
26 The best single account is Dülmen, *Gesellschaft der Aufklärer*. See also Im Hof, *Das gesellige Jahrhundert;* Ruppert, *Bürgerlicher Wandel,* 104–54; Wolfgang Martens, *Die Botschaft der Tugend. Die Aufklärung im Spiegel der deutschen Moralischen Wochenschriften* (1971; rpt., Stuttgart, 1982); Rudolf Vierhaus, ed., *Deutsche patriotische und gemeinnützige Gesellschaften* (Munich, 1980); Dann, *Lesegesellschaften;* Marlies Prüsener, *Lesegesellschaften im 18. Jahrhundert* (Frankfurt, 1982); Nipperdey, "Verein"; and Wolfgang Hardtwig, "Strukturmerkmale und Entwicklungs-Tendenzen des Vereinswesens in Deutschland 1789–1948," in *Vereinswesen und bürgerliche Gesellschaft in Deutschland,* ed. Otto Dann, supplemental issue of *Historische Zeitschrift* (Munich) 9 (1984): 11–50.

burg and Leipzig and multiplied until there were about 230 of them, providing regular occasions for their members to meet, read, and discuss recent publications of general interest.[27] The most famous was the Moral-Patriotic Society of Hamburg, whose *Tatler*-like journal, *Der Patriot*, reached an estimated readership of twelve to fifteen thousand.[28] Moral-literary societies spread Enlightenment through "reflection about moral and even quotidian questions, apart from politics and theology. Professional and domestic activities became for the first time objects of public reflection."[29]

At midcentury two other types of assocation began to unseat the moral-literary societies as the most popular ways to practice Enlightenment. From 1750 to the mid 1780s perhaps as many as 350 secret Masonic lodges dotted the map, engaging the energies of fifteen to twenty thousand men.[30] Although the Rosicrucians's mystical obscurantism attests to the popularity of secret societies even among opponents of conventional Enlightenment, most Freemasonic lodges were devoted to Enlightened philosophy, which they read and discussed in their chambers, often guided by elaborate rules of civil comportment. The Patriotic-Beneficial (*gemeinnützig*) societies, on the contrary, were completely public. These locally active groups (of which there were fifty to sixty in the last third of the century) contained only five thousand members,[31] but they were typically the most respected and best-connected men of their communities and made up in purposeful activity what they lacked in numbers. These associations generally had libraries and meeting rooms for public discussions. They often organized prize campaigns devoted to the solution of social problems, such as poverty or infanticide. They published the details of technical inventions, sometimes the protocols of their own meetings, and they undertook actual projects designed to improve situations beyond the reach or, they thought, legitimate purposes of the state. Their activities pushed back the boundaries of government by expanding the competence of civil society to define and meet its own problems.[32]

Toward the end of the century, a third wave of self-organization produced reading associations ranging from informal groups sharing the cost of books or subscriptions to journals, through a series of intermediate forms, to the reading cabinet, which usually had its own library, silent reading and public discussion rooms, and statute of organization. These cabinets sponsored often weekly meetings with rotating, democratic leadership. By 1800 there were around 430 such groups incorporating fifteen to twenty thousand reader-discussants, and there would have been more, if governments, fearing the spread of revolution after 1789, had not begun to ban them.[33] Although official fears were probably misplaced, they

[27] Martens, *Botschaft der Tugend*, 162.
[28] Dülmen, *Gesellschaft der Aufklärer*, 45.
[29] Ibid., 44.
[30] Ibid., 57.
[31] Ibid., 69.
[32] Nipperdey, "Verein," 196.
[33] Dülmen, *Gesellschaft der Aufklärer*, 82, 84.

were not utterly groundless, since some reading cabinets had begun in the 1790s to spawn organizations, such as the Society of the Friends of Freedom and Equality in Mainz, devoted to the radical Enlightenment, specifically interested in political questions, and intent on spreading their message to social strata excluded by prior associations.[34]

Informal but regular social communication must have rivaled, if not outstripped, the formal organizations by century's end: popular coffeehouses, friendship networks, social visits, letter writing, and so forth made even denser the cultural networks of practical civil society.[35] Certainly, the exuberant newspaper and book markets are signs of an explosion in the passive consumption of written civil culture.[36] Between 1789 and 1806 there were 250 newspapers in Germany totaling 300,000 copies, each of course read by several people.[37] Still, the active, self-reflective shapers of practical civil society were primarily those who participated in the organized cycle of publication, reading, discussion, and publication again. And "there was no locality of any size in which the Enlightened-thinking citizens were not organized into societies."[38]

In these societies members literally practiced the basic principles of civil society and polished the virtues necessary to create and uphold it.[39] They came together voluntarily, as individuals. Out of the purview of state or church they organized themselves according to agreed-upon rules (statutes, constitutions). All members were equal, regardless of social rank outside the association. "Domination-free communication" was the goal,[40] but achieving it required members to agree upon and submit to rules of demeanor and judgment that ordered social intercourse in a new way. Members disciplined themselves corporeally and mentally. The statute of the *Deutsche Gesellschaft* in Göttingen (1738–55), for example, forbade members to interrupt one another or to use bad or sarcastic language in meetings. Drinking (alcohol), gambling, erotic "gallantries," excessive noise, and the like were expressly

---

[34] Ibid., 112–17.

[35] See the description of Wetzlar: Hans-Werther Hahn, "Von der 'Kultur der Bürger' zur 'bürgerlicher Kultur.' Veränderungen in der Lebenswelt des Wetzlarer Bürgertums zwischen 1700–1900," in *Armut, Liebe, Ehre. Studien zur historischen Kulturforschung,* ed. Richard van Dülmen (Frankfurt, 1988), 144–85, esp. 162. Also Ruppert, *Bürgerlicher Wandel,* 116–17.

[36] On the publishing industry, see Engelsing, *Analphabetentum,* 54–58; Kiesel and Münch, *Gesellschaft und Literatur,* 180–203; and Ruppert, *Bürgerlicher Wandel,* 123–26.

[37] Kopitzsch, "Sozialgeschichte der Aufklärung" (1989), 384. Estimates of how many readers might have shared a single copy fluctuated, then and now, between four or five to twenty. See Engelsing, *Analphabetentum,* 49–50, 57, 60.

[38] Dülmen, *Gesellschaft der Aufklärer,* 81. Protestant, northern Germany may have been more thoroughly organized than the more Catholic south, but the latter was nonetheless thickly covered by associations at the end of the century, and the journal subscribers' lists attest to as much Enlightened enthusiasm among Catholics as Protestants of the same social groups. For maps showing associations, see Dülmen, *Gesellschaft der Aufklärer,* 173–79; for lists of associations, see Ruppert, *Bürgerlicher Wandel,* 168, 214 n. 21. On geographical saturation, see Kopitzsch, "Sozialgeschichte der deutschen Aufklärung" (1976), 62.

[39] Dülmen, *Gesellschaft der Aufklärer,* 129–32; Nipperdey, "Verein," 177–82.

[40] Dülmen, *Gesellschaft der Aufklärer,* 113.

forbidden by most associations.[41] A sober, earnest, dispassionate atmosphere was also achieved by self-censorship. The Masonic lodge in Aachen declared, typically, that "in no lodge is it permitted to discuss subjects concerning the state, religion, family, and other matters that are of little interest or could give rise to arguments."[42] The exercise of Reason, then, took place under conditions of mental self-restraint. Nonetheless, state, religion, family, and other matters could not, by definition, remain untouched by a worldview so broad and interested in fundamentals as was the Enlightenment. But this list of taboos indicates that old pieties might swiftly be transformed into new ones for the sake of social order in the little societies, as well as the larger one.

The orderly use of Reason was not to be limited to mere discussion, but was meant to, and often did, lead to social action. The societies were supposed to have a useful, productive, ameliorative impact on the lives of their members and on society. But seriousness was not the only purpose they served. They also provided entertainment, social contact, and friendship. These psychological benefits, most historians believe, became generalized to encompass identity-formation on the part of those who participated in them. That is, the self-selection of the members, the mutual reinforcement they acquired from behaving alike under the aegis of Reason, their acceptance and mastery of a new set of social rules, and their growing sense of belonging to the elite that was creating the future led to a self-definition that transcended individualism in the direction of gender and class, while nonetheless being anchored in individualism and in individuals.[43]

Rules of Inclusion and Exclusion

The three waves of organizational activity, from the moral-literary societies of the 1720s through the 1760s, through the Freemasons and patriotic-beneficial associations of the 1750s through the 1790s, to the reading clubs of the 1770s to 1800, show a marked trend in membership. The moral-literary societies were the first to reach out beyond the narrow confines of scholars to tap a broader audience. The goal of social self-creation through morality determined who joined these societies and wrote for their journals. The nobility, secure in its own social position and worldview, contributed few authors dedicated to changing either. Literate peasant-owners and artisans were explicitly excluded from the new moral enterprise as prisoners of tradition, subsistence, and unrelenting labor. According to the weeklies, they allegedly lacked the interest or initiative, the material means, and the leisure time to devote to Enlightened self-improvement.[44] Among the middling

---

[41] Ibid., 50, 131. Pikulik *Leistungsethik*, 206–7, thinks of these rules in Elias's terms as the process of civilization of the bourgeoisie.

[42] Dülmen, *Gesellschaft der Aufklärer*, 62.

[43] Nipperdey, "Verein," 177, is especially sensitive to the possible psychological effects of association.

[44] Martens, *Botschaft der Tugend*, discusses nobility on 129–30, and artisans and peasant freeholders on 147, 383–404.

strata thus remaining, however, the moral-literary associations and publications specifically targeted women. They rejected the opinion that women were "incapable of reading and would be ruined by books, as though the female soul were of a lower nature than the male."[45] Still, although women might consume Enlightened wisdom, however, they were deemed unable to create it: they were to remain readers, not writers. And the goal of their Enlightenment was not self-fulfillment and the development of "personality," as it was for men, but "in order to became a better mother, wife, producer [*Wirthinn*], and friend, and to grasp more completely her duty to God and humankind [*Menschen*]."[46] Women's participation in the exercise of early civil society was therefore strictly instrumental and relational.

It was thus conceivable to include women in a limited way in a specifically moral endeavor. As the focus of associations shifted to individual development, concrete social activity, and the mobilization of broader social strata, such as artisans and even peasants,[47] women were barred. When a Masonic lodge in France proposed admitting women, it was banned.[48] The patriotic-beneficial societies were composed chiefly of patricians active in local government, a circumstance excluding women almost by definition. Even when such societies broadened to accept previously spurned religious minorities, as when the second Patriotic Society of Hamburg admitted Calvinists, Mennonites, Roman Catholics, and Jews, they still rejected women.[49] Similarly with the reading clubs, the first to extend a welcome to artisans: women were very seldom members.[50] And they were explicitly shut out of the Society of the Friends of Freedom and Equality in Mainz, the first expressly political association.[51] Dülmen cites the exclusion of women as one of the hallmarks of German society-building:

> This does not mean that here and there women did not find acceptance, mostly as wives of male members. There were many educated and even scholarly women—no one denied that—but apparently the male Enlighteners denied them the capacity to make decisions as free individuals and also to intervene publicly for knowledge, virtue, and Enlightenment. Not least of all granting women an autonomous role contradicted the earnest character of societies, free of games and eroticism. Above all the free Masons and reading clubs shut women out explicitly. This exclusion was so self-explanatory that a discussion of possibly including women never occurred, even though at the same time the first discourse about the emancipation of women was taking place. Mutual regard, uninhibited

[45] *Der Mahler der Sitten*, the journal of a moral society in Zurich; cited in Martens, *Botschaft der Tugend*, 523.

[46] From the *Greis*, in either 1763–65 or 1781 (this is not clear from Marten's discussion), cited in Martens, *Botschaft der Tugend*, 527; cf. similar sentiments cited on 528, 530.

[47] Karl-Heinz Ziessow, *Ländliche Lesekultur im 18. und 19. Jahrhundert. Das Kirchspiel Menslage und seine Lesegesellschaften* (Cloppenburg, 1988), 1:88–89. I thank Jonathan Knudsen for this citation.

[48] Im Hof, *Das gesellige Jahrhundert*, 224.

[49] Ibid., 140.

[50] An exception was Bremen, see Dann, "Lesegesellschaften," 106. Cf. Im Hof, *Das gesellige Jahrhundert*, 224 and Ruppert, *Bürgerlicher Wandel*, 153–54.

[51] Dülmen, *Gesellschaft der Aufklärer*, 116.

social intercourse, and Enlightened engagement were the business of men, since the goal of these men, who were mostly engaged in public life, was to wrest a new social position in the public [*in der Öffentlichkeit*] away from court and church.[52]

Although women were systematically excluded from public organizations, they were ubiquitous as the practitioners' friends, lovers, wives, and daughters. In these relationships the stark lines of gender conformity may have been considerably less evident than in associations and published tracts. Many of the practitioners self-consciously raised educated and ambitious daughters and sought as wives real companions rather than subordinates. Yet, where they consciously reflected upon the public, as in the literature on the public interest in sexual behavior, or on political rights, the practitioners tended to reason from a particularist and exclusively male standpoint. The relation between the practitioners' private lives and their public opinions on gender deserves further research.[53]

As characteristic of German associational life as the absence of women was the overwhelming presence of state officials. The radical Enlightener Adolph Freiherr von Knigge, casting an eye toward France in 1793, asked, "What does our 'third-estate' consist of, for the most part? Of servants of the prince, councillors, secretaries, officials, religious administrators, producers for the court [*Hof-Faktor*], uniformed servants, lawyers, doctors and such, who all more or less live from the crumbs that the masters [monarchs] let fall from their tables."[54] Knigge observed correctly. State servants of one sort or another normally dominated the associations.[55] Historians have long tended to lament this defining feature of the German Enlightenment, holding it responsible, as Knigge did, for lack of revolutionary fervor or even interpreting it as a sign of inauthentic or certainly apolitical Enlightenment. These views, which recognize the centrality of the state to German life, underestimate both the reforming zeal and potential of many late-eighteenth-century German states,[56] as well as the reciprocal relation between the state (as a reality and as an abstract idea) and its bureaucrats. For if their position within the state affected their ideas, their experiences in associations also affected their performance as state officials. Surely it was not negligible that "in the last third of the

---

[52] Ibid., 121. Earlier writers, Ruppert, *Bürgerlicher Wandel*, 149–50, 153–54 and Engelhardt, *Bildungsbürgertum*, 68, noted the exclusion of women, but did not comment on it further.

[53] See Anne-Charlott Trepp, "'Sanfte Männlichkeit und selbständige Weiblichkeit': Frauen und Männer im hamburgischen Bürgertum zwischen 1770 und 1840" (Ph.D. diss., University of Kiel, 1993).

[54] "Ueber die Ursachen, warum wir vorerst in Teutschland wohl keine gefährliche politische Haupt-Revolution zu erwarten haben," *Schleswigsches Journal*, 2 (1793), 293, cited in Kopitzsch, "Sozialgeschichte der deutschen Aufklärung" (1976), 39–40.

[55] See the figures in Dülmen, *Gesellschaft der Aufklärer*, 58–59, 87, 104; Dann, "Lesegesellschaften," 106; Martens, *Botschaft der Tugend*, 129–30; Kopitzsch, "Sozialgeschichte der Aufklärung" (1989), 380–81; and Wehler, *Deutsche Gesellschaftsgeschichte*, 1:210–11. On the preponderance of bureaucrats among early liberals, see Gerth, *Bürgerliche Intelligenz*, 72–77.

[56] See the studies by Eberhard Weis, *Deutschland und Frankreich um 1800. Aufklärung, Revolution, Reform* (Munich, 1990).

century a great part of the new administrative elite, that is the upper bureacrats, met together in Masonic lodges and had decisive experiences there with the new forms of Enlightened sociality,"[57] not to mention direct acquaintance with the most radical principles of Enlightenment. And far from being concentrated in a single administrative center, like Paris or London, German Enlightened bureaucrats were scattered throughout the land. The high percentage of bureaucrats involved in Enlightenment may account for the unusual number of journal contributors who lived in smaller towns or even in the countryside—two-thirds of all writers in the late eighteenth century.[58]

Although state servants often enjoyed the advantage of greater knowledge about other social strata and social problems than that held by the relatively isolated professional literati,[59] they nonetheless did not write simply *as* experts. A gradual double shift in their self-conception had taken place during the eighteenth century. Officials had first abandoned the notion that they were the prince's (personal, or indeed private) servants, and began to think of themselves as representatives of an abstraction, the state.[60] The higher, aggregated perspective they assumed was a sign of this long-term transformation. Toward the end of the century another dimension to their self-consciousness developed. When they joined associations or contributed to journals they did so as rational members of civil society, working toward its good, which they believed largely coincided with the good (and certainly with the legitimating end) of the state. In Prussia that presumed coincidence permitted the (mostly) state officials who made up the Wednesday Society to meet in secrecy to discuss Enlightened precepts and public policy as "well-meaning patriots," as the founder, a certain J.K.W. Moehsen, had declared in 1783.[61] In Hamburg, the accent was firmly on citizen; J. A. Günther described the (second) Hamburg Patriotic Society in 1792 as "an independent union of Enlightened citizens, many of whom take part themselves in the administration of state, who however appear here only as private men [*Privat-Männer*], bringing together civic-mindedly their multiple and various knowledge and experiences."[62] These government officials' subjective understanding of themselves as simultaneously, if not, primarily, members of civil society is crucial to the perspective the practitioners brought to their Enlightened activities.

---

[57] Dülmen, *Gesellschaft der Aufklärer*, 58.

[58] Kopitzsch, "Sozialgeschichte der deutschen Aufklärung" (1976), 61–62.

[59] On the social ignorance of independent writers, see Martens, *Botschaft der Tugend*, 330.

[60] Rosenberg, *Bureaucracy, Aristocracy, Autocracy*, 175–201.

[61] Ludwig Keller, "Die Berliner Mittwochs-Gesellschaft. Ein Beitrag zur Geschichte der Geistesentwicklung Preußens am Ausgang des 18. Jahrhunderts," *Monatshefte der Comenius-Gesellschaft* 5 (1896): 75; Günter Birtsch, "Die Berliner Mittwochsgesellschaft (1783–1798)," in Bödecker and Herrmann, *Über den Prozeß der Aufklärung*, 94–112.

[62] Cited in Dülmen, *Gesellschaft der Aufklärer*, 72; see also Kopitzsch, "Sozialgeschichte der deutschen Aufklärung" (1976), 73.

The Recognized Trustees of the Nation

Christoph M. Wieland may have waxed somewhat enthusiastic when, in 1791 he described publicists as "in a certain sense the actual *men of the nation,* because their immediate circle of activity is all of Germany."[63] Nonetheless, he summed up their self-interpretation in that phrase. In another pithy expression, Wieland captured the essence of how practical civil society viewed itself. He wrote,

> In the course of the existence for which nature determined it, humanity in several thousands of years has made marked progress. Ten, twenty or thirty million people *in a single* state will not let themselves be treated any longer as so and so many *moral ciphers.* Nonetheless, the larger part of these millions may be seen in a certain sense as immature [*unmündig*]; but they have *general reason* as their *trustee* [*Vormund*], and one may rest assured that in matters directly affecting the welfare or woe of the unending large majority, the *expression of this trustee* is *public opinion* [*öffentliche Meinung*].[64]

These "men of the nation," whom Wieland and his contemporaries thought of as expressing public opinion, but who can more accurately be described as shaping it, were by virtue of their education, wealth, and leisure, the exemplars of Reason in the real world. As such they were the trustees of all those less fortunate or less endowed; they held civil society in trust for the future, until that time when these groups might develop the qualities fitting them for active participation.

The trustee, or educator to patriotism,[65] thus assumed the old role of responsible *Hausvater,* but in a transformed setting. At the same time (the very end of the eighteenth century), the term *Staatsbürger* was similarly narrowed to mean not simply all those living under the laws of the land, but those participating in making those laws, that is, "active" citizens.[66] This, too, is a transformation of one of the older meanings of "Bürger," namely, those married, male heads of household who exercised political power in the community (*Gemeinde*). Through the process summed up in the idea of trustee, older notions of political propriety and legitimacy took on partially new social meanings; practical civil society endowed a wider group of men with (potentially) legitimate power, but the social characteristics of many of these men were still recognizably those traditionally associated with the *Hausvater* or *Nachbar* of the absolutist state.

Partly because the new conception of civil society retained elements of traditional legitimacy, and partly also because state officials played an active if not dominant role, in practical civil society, the self-understanding of the active Enlighteners as "trustees" and thus as the legitimate moral judges of politics as it pertained to the general good, was increasingly shared by government. The influen-

---

[63] Cited by Kiesel and Münch, *Gesellschaft und Literatur,* 174, emphasis in the original.
[64] Cited in Möller, *Vernunft und Kritik,* 288.
[65] Vierhaus, "Patriotismus," 124.
[66] Michael Stolleis, "Untertan-Bürger-Staatsbürger. Bemerkungen zur juristischen Terminologie im späten 18. Jahrhundert," in Vierhaus, *Bürger und Bürgerlichkeit,* 85.

tial judicial director Friedrich Leopold von Kircheisen was only stating a social fact when in 1792 he described to the Prussian crown prince the "civilized world [*gesittete Welt*]" as "a mighty tribunal," judging also the deeds of government.[67] When Frederick II decided in 1784 to reform the Prussian law code, and thus to redraw the relations among private persons as well as those between them and the state, he thought it necessary to permit "public opinion" to comment on the drafts. By "public opinion" he meant "legal scholars, 'men of practical wisdom,' and legal philosophers." This core of experts was later expanded to encompass more general commentators via a prize-contest, a method typical of the patriotic-beneficial societies.[68] In short, despite their unwillingness to submit to principled, constitutional limits to their powers, rulers were coming to accept the existence of a real entity called civil society, whose voice, public opinion, was in fact the voice of the minority of civilized, educated trustees, "men of the nation." And they were beginning to recognize that many of their officials already knew, that this practical expression of ideal civil society was critical to helping reshape political, that is, public relations.

The Project of the Practitioners of Civil Society

The late-eighteenth-century discussion of the relevance of sexual behavior to the "public" took place within the larger context of the establishment and definition of civil society and its relation to the state. Four characteristics of this larger framework are particularly relevant to interpreting that discussion: first, its orientation toward theory and the future, which encouraged radical speculation about (sexual) topics; second, its orientation toward the community, which, especially in discussions of sexual matters, provided an overarching framework of judgment; third, its relative acceptance of the state, which made *society* the focus of reflective attention; and fourth, its conception of politics as moral, which was the avenue through which sexual regulation ultimately was reintroduced in the name not of the state, but of civil society.

Project

The practitioners of civil society were engaged in a *project* aimed at "the complete overturning of culture in all areas of life."[69] They proposed to change the basis of social organization, the legitimate exercise of power (domination, or *Herr-*

---

[67] Kammergerichtsdirektor and legal reformer Kircheisen to the crown prince, 6 March 1792, cited in Kopitzsch, "Sozialgeschichte der deutschen Aufklärung" (1976), 53.

[68] Möller, *Vernunft und Kritik*, 303–4. The quotation is from 303; Möller is quoting Großkanzler von Carmer.

[69] Ernst Troeltsch, "Aufklärung," in *Realencyklopädie für protestantische Theologie und Kirche*, 3d ed. (Leipzig, 1897), 2:225, cited in Kopitzsch, "Sozialgeschichte der deutschen Aufklärung" (1976), 41.

schaft),[70] and the very people who made up the new order—its citizens. The nature of this endeavor meant that the discussions were future- and process-oriented, relatively nondogmatic, and radically contemplative, by which I mean that they might question the most basic pillars of the traditional order, at least theoretically.[71] Their questioning ran broad and deep: from the state to the secrets of the heart. In Kopitzsch's words: "Enlightenment as a process of the rational appropriation and shaping of the world [*Weltaneignung und Weltgestaltung*] was not only stamped by criticism and practicality, but also by a historical and political consciousness, by an interest in ways of living, forms of thought, events and happenings in the whole, ever developing world."[72] The members of associations engaged in "problematizing the self and the social foundations of life."[73] These preoccupations brought them to speculate on the nature of men versus women, on the passions, on the family, on sexual behavior, and on how all these issues might be linked together.

The designs that emerged from this discourse are more than mere wisps of intellectual history. They are the "new structure of thinking of a ruling class, or one potentially capable of ruling."[74] The practitioners of civil society were a new "*sinnvermittelnde Intelligenz*," an intelligentsia that laid down the values according to which social institutions and human action were to be measured and interpreted.[75] Guardians of knowledge and understanding wield tremendous social power, and it is a sign of the triumph of the new designs that one central group of old, official arbiters of sense-making, the clergy, joined the Enlightenment in large numbers;[76] so much so that, in fact, the sociology of discourse-formation retained something of its old outlines, even as it was being changed.

Finally, one must underscore the self-consciousness of this interpretive enterprise. Practical civil society attributed to correct ideas the power to transform the world and to incorrect ones the power to ruin it. Discourse in its widest sense, that is, structured debate leading to the discovery of ideas consonant with the principles of Reason, the communication network necessary to carry on debate and spread its results, the institutionalization of contact between scholars and practical people so that knowledge would be put to work, discourse in this sense was taken to be the motor of social change.[77] These discussions were therefore not trivial conversations; contemporaries meant them to be important contributions toward an immense project of social reconstruction.

---

[70] Habermas, *Structural Transformation*, 82–83.

[71] Lutz Niethammer, "Einführung: Bürgerliche Gesellschaft als Projekt," in *Bürgerliche Gesellschaft in Deutschland*, ed. Niethammer (Frankfurt, 1990), 17–38, esp. 17–19.

[72] "Sozialgeschichte der Aufklärung" (1989), 377.

[73] Dülmen, *Gesellschaft der Aufklärer*, 127.

[74] Niethammer, "Bürgerliche Gesellschaft als Projekt," 30.

[75] The phrase is Thomas Nipperdey's, cited in Engelhardt, '*Bildungsbürgertum*,' 85.

[76] Möller, *Vernunft und Kritik*, 296–97.

[77] Thus the observations in 1800 of Christian Jakob Kraus, the Königsberg professor of practical philosophy and cameralism who trained over a generation of bureaucrats. Cited in Ruppert, *Bürgerlicher Wandel*, 163.

Community

The Enlightenment project had a Janus face, whose most obvious side was individualism. Its practitioners explored the psychological wellsprings of the individual and made mostly his but sometimes her well-being the criterion of progress. The literary *Sturm and Drang* produced a hypertrophied, antisocial variant of this individualism, which some scholars have erroneously taken to characterize Enlightenment altogether.[78] Toward the century's end, practitioners like Kant or Wilhelm von Humboldt argued that the individual's welfare superseded the older claims of *Gemeinwohl* with their consequent state intervention.[79] Nonetheless, many other practitioners abandoned *Gemeinwohl;* instead they redefined it to mean specifically the good of the new civil society, rather than of the *ständisch* order. For them, lasting individual "happiness" was taken to be congruent with community welfare, a congruence underwritten by the silent equation of "individual" with male citizen/householder, so that relatively little discussion was devoted to possible clashes between these two principles. Much of the discourse of civil society was highly community-oriented; that is, its discourse revolved, not unexpectedly, around itself. As Zedler's *Universal-Lexikon* explained, *bürgerlich* itself "means so much as honorable [*ehrlich*], because it encourages a condition of a city or citizenry, in which everything is supposed to be related to usefulness [to the community] and to its welfare."[80] One observes the shaping power of community-usefulness in the lengthy disquisitions on civil (bourgeois) honor and virtue, in the pedagogical literature, and in the "patriotic-beneficial" and even the secret organizations, whose purpose was to improve the common life in which the individual shared. Arguments derived from the common good framed the practitioners' discussion of the public interest in sexual behavior.

The Role of the State

Frustrated by incomplete reforms, censorship, bans of secret societies and later of reading associations, and other manifestations of capricious state power, many practitioners of the 1780s and 1790s became increasingly critical of government and correspondingly eager to divest authority from it and bestow that authority on civil society instead. But civil society had begun to usurp the monopoly the state once

[78] On the community-orientation of civil society, see Martens, *Botschaft der Tugend*, 158, 296, 300–302, and Pikulik, *Leistungsethik*, 95–110; also Nipperdey, "Verein," 178, 182; Im Hof, *Das gesellige Jahrhundert*, 135–36; and Kopitzsch, "Sozialgeschichte der deutschen Aufklärung" (1976), 42.

[79] Immanuel Kant, "On the Common Saying: 'This may be true in theory, but it does not apply in practice,'" (1793) in Reiss, *Kant's Political Writings*, 73–75; Wilhelm von Humboldt, "Wie weit darf sich die Sorgfalt des Staats um das Wohl seiner Bürger erstrecken?" in *Wilhelm von Humboldts Gesammelte Werke* (Berlin, 1841), 2:242–63; Wilhelm von Humboldt, "Ueber die Sittenverbesserung durch Anstalten des Staats," in *Gesammelte Werke*, 1:318–35. On the practical, political limits of these insights, esp. for Kant, see Jonathan Knudsen, *Justus Möser and the German Enlightenment* (Cambridge, 1986), 174–86.

[80] Cited in Pikulik, *Leistungsethik*, 94.

held as simply the "public" (*öffentlich*) even among less critical spirits, but in a different way. Paradoxically, this usurpation could occur because of the indulgent attitude toward the state that most practitioners still harbored. For most writers at century's end still expected the state, especially through legal reform, to play a vital role in developing and guaranteeing an independent civil society. This positive expectation plus their familiarity with government (as officials themselves) meant that their writings left the state relatively undertheorized. They focused on the new and incalculable problems involved in forming civil society, instead. In their thinking the state became a backdrop to their attempts to draft civil society. The vantage point of civil society became an alternate way to think about what citizens had in common, about their mutual welfare and interdependence beyond their particular, and therefore private interests. This was "public" from a different angle than that of the state, without yet being wholly separate from it.

Morality Is Political

The project of civil society was political. This has been a controversial point because the form in which political aspirations were expressed was not that typical for later centuries. Most writers did not demand a constitution, set themselves against the state, or agitate expressly for the economic interests of their social group; nor did they form organized political clubs. Instead, they conceived of their task as moral reform. That has led some scholars to dismiss their efforts as quietistic, timid, relentlessly "private," and even defeatist;[81] others view them as simply not yet political.[82]

These judgments rest on sharp differentiations that had not yet come into existence, either in reality or in theory. As Kopitzsch argues, "In Hamburg . . . 'morality' and 'politics,' 'society' and 'state,' 'private sphere' and 'public' were inseparably bound together."[83] This was true not only in Hamburg, but generally, as we have seen in the common synonymous usage of "civil society" and "state," in the preponderance of bureaucrats in "private" associations, and in the legitimation of state policy (*Politik*) by reference to its moral duty toward the commonwealth (*Gemeinwohl*). It is also clear in the contemporaries' stubborn insistence that *Politik* should be consonant with *Moral*, long after the theorists of absolutism had dispensed with this quaint notion. The furthest acknowledgment granted to the likes of Hobbes or Macchiavelli by eighteenth-century German lexicographers was the admission that *Politik* had two definitions. The first described it as the science of how to "strengthen the basis of human societies and of a well conceived ruling . . . internally through salubrious laws, administration of justice, subsistence and

[81] Haferkorn, "Zur Entstehung der bürgerlich-literarischen Intelligenz," 182, 184, 190–95.

[82] Im Hof, *Das gesellige Jahrhundert*, 221. Concerning their striving to be political, see Koselleck, *Kritik und Krise*, 31, cited in Franklin Kopitzsch, *Grundzüge einer Sozialgeschichte der Aufklärung in Hamburg und Altona* (Hamburg, 1982), 598. Concerning "*Ersatzpolitik*," see Nipperdey, "Verein," 195. See also Becher, *Politische Gesellschaft*, 216.

[83] *Grundzüge*, 598.

industry, externally through the successful prosecution of wars and advantageous alliances." This stood in sharp contrast to the second or "usual modern usage" in which *Politik* was "the cleverness to interpret the advantage of a prince or state, to seek [it] in secret ways, and to achieve it using all possible means." Yet "a true politics takes care first of all to follow the general law of natural fairness, not to do to others what one would not wish to have done to oneself." This definition, first given in 1721 by Johann Theodor Jablonski, was repeated in Zedler's famous *Universal-Lexikon* (1741), which, after discussing *Politik* as cleverness, championed the first association of *Politik* and *Moral,* as Christian Wolff advised.[84] At century's end, Kant summed up the trend of German Enlightened thinking and "solved" the issue in favor of morality by granting politics a separate existence as the technical means to achieve an end, but subordinating it to morality, which set the goals of state. Johann Georg Krünitz's authoritative encyclopedia followed Kant: "*Politik* is only the handmaiden of constitutional law [*Staatsrecht*] [which, of course, follows natural law and is thus moral]. It should discover the means to achieve what constitutional law encourages or permits. Only that politics can be imagined as reasonable which upholds constitutional law and furthers its execution as far as possible."[85]

The inextricable link between politics and morality is clear from the other side of the ledger, too, that is, from morality, whose obligatory content was set by reference to the common social organization. Although the practitioners of civil society rarely cited the cameralists,[86] the conception of morality in the moral weeklies, and in the assocations' statutes and the journals thereafter, was virtually identical to theirs. The duties one owed to God [or Nature] and to oneself were to remain healthy and to expand one's natural capacities to their fullest extent. These duties were the physical and mental prerequisites for the duties one owed to society. The first flowed ineluctably into the second. An utterly typical expression of this law appeared in the premiere journal of Enlightenment, the *Berlinische Monatsschrift,* in 1783:

> *But the greatest possible development and practical use of the energies of a person [Menschen] can only occur in the best possible social union.* Without the latter the former cannot occur. *The truly best of a person requires the truly best of the social union.* . . . All actions and

---

[84] Johann Heinrich Zedler, *Grosses vollständiges Universal-Lexikon Aller Wissenschaften und Künste Welche bishero durch menschlichen Verstand und Witz erfunden worden* (Leipzig and Halle, 1741), vol. 27, cols. 1525–27. Jablonski cited by Volker Sellin, "Politik," in Brunner, Conze, and Koselleck, *Geschichtliche Grundbegriffe,* 4:834–35.

[85] *Oekonomisch-technologische Encyklopädie* (Berlin, 1810), 114:159–60, cited in Sellin, "Politik," 842. Sellin "Politik," 831–42, tends to stress the split of *Moral* from *Politik* but not the incompleteness of this split, though the latter is clear from his discussion. He also somewhat overemphasizes the cameralists' enthusiasm for pure state power (832), whose best exemplar, as his discussion shows, was Hobbes (833). Cf. Immanuel Kant, "Perpetual Peace: A Philosophical Sketch" (1795), in Reiss, *Kant's Political Writings,* 93–130

[86] Martens, *Botschaft der Tugend,* 331–32. The famous moralist Carl Friedrich Bahrdt was an exception; his handbook of 1789 was overtly moral and heavily influenced by Bahrdt's reverence for Justi. See Ulrich Herrmann, "Die Kodifizierung bürgerlichen Bewußtseins in der deutschen Spätaufklärung—Carl Friedrich Bahrdts 'Handbuch der Moral für den Bürgerstand' aus dem Jahre 1789," in Herrmann, *Bildung des Bürgers,* 155–57.

kinds of behavior of humankind, which relate to their social union are moral [*sittliche*]. Morality [*Moralität*] is consequently a product of social union; and the actions of a single person living for him or herself do not merit being called moral.[87]

In short, moral law was the expression of social life; moral law *was* social law.[88] It is therefore hardly surprising that since practical civil society aimed to explore, expand, and order itself, it would do so primarily in moral terms. And since the reformation of society into civil society was to be done in tandem with the state, and in any case would transform the relation between government and civil society, moral reordering was eminently political, in the sense of bearing a relation to government policy. Since moral reordering could hardly occur without affecting how those subject to it actually lived and interpreted their lives, the eighteenth-century moral debates were political in this wider, cultural sense, as well.

The high political stakes involved in moral reformation should become even clearer if we examine briefly how morality functioned in the late eighteenth century. We have already seen how the practitioners of civil society followed (often silently) state theorists in having adopted the common good as their moral measuring stick.[89] Doing so, in the early eighteenth century, meant placing "patriotism" alongside Christianity. The *Patriot* opined,

> We believe that true religious knowledge can stand to have an intelligent morality [*Sittenlehre*] flowing from healthy Reason standing beside it. The Christian does not end because the Patriot begins. I have never yet heard of a state in which Christianity fell because people acting with natural and reasonable grounds set about leading their fellow citizens from mistakes regarding social intercourse, householding, raising children, and common welfare and therefore needed to say to them things that either were so particular or so lively that the circumstances of a holy office or building would not permit it [to be said]. A thousand things occur which do not directly harm the soul, but do indeed harm health, prosperity, and wealth. And these things require their own cure. . . . The republic needs not only pious but at the same time smart and clever citizens.[90]

Although they doubtless did not intend it, and few lost their own faith, the early German Enlighteners ultimately replaced Christianity altogether with their vision of civil society as the fount of moral virtue. Society had become the new religion, and its priests were its articulate interpreters. In this fashion practical civil society usurped the monopoly on moral discourse previously exercised by the clergy.

[87] C. G. Selle, "Von der Moralität der menschlichen Handlungen," *Berlinische Monatsschrift* 2.6 (1783): 429–30.

[88] Habermas expresses this point: "In the eighteenth century the Aristotelian tradition of a philosophy of politics was reduced in a telling manner to moral philosophy, whereby the 'moral' (in any event thought as one with 'nature' and 'reason') also encompassed the emerging sphere of the 'social,' its connotation overlapping with those of the word 'social' given such peculiar emphasis at the time." *Structural Transformation*, 102–3.

[89] Martens, *Botschaft der Tugend*, 158; Wolfgang Martens, "Bürgerlichkeit in der frühen Aufklärung," in *Aufklärung, Absolutismus und Bürgertum in Deutschland*, ed. Franklin Kopitzsch (Munich, 1976), 356.

[90] Cited in Martens, *Botschaft der Tugend*, 173, also 174.

In the same way, civil society unseated the state as the arbiter of *Gemeinwohl*. This, too, was a gradual process, presaged by the traditional dictum that the common good was the purpose of government. Whereas previously the prince or perhaps his bureaucrats had decided what was in the collective interest, that was now more and more the prerogative of the articulate members of civil society. The associations "contested the interpretive monopoly of state and church insofar as they questioned things which were hitherto unquestionable. . . . They discussed public morality, institutions and fundamental principles of the common good, and thereby demanded of the official authorities that they legitimate themselves reasonably."[91] If this newfound authority over legitimation was not yet anchored in a (parliamentary) institution, it was nonetheless a sign of remarkable political power, for it created an Archimedean point outside church and state from which these could be lifted off their foundations. This moral arrogation was striking enough that when it was first expressed in the 1720s in the moral weekly the *Patriot*, a chorus of the astonished asked, "who appointed it master of morals [*Zuchtmeister*]?"[92] Self-appointment was, of course, the hallmark of patriotic activity.

By capturing the power to legitimate government via moral discourse, practical civil society set a new framework for politics. At the same time, the new moral discourse reorganized social groups and therefore reshuffled the lineaments of social power which a wider definition of "political" would surely include as fundamental to the political order. For in place of the older *ständisch* hierarchy, practical civil society proposed to sort out people according to their moral worth. A prominent Freemason put it thus in 1742 as he explained the three "basic pillars" of Masonry ("secrecy, morality and good company"):

> As great as is our consideration of people who have earned reputation in the world by their birth or high rank, still, among ourselves we actually judge a person only by how good he is by nature, and insofar as we only use the scale of nature to do this, we regard ourselves as brothers. Insofar as we follow the teachings of moral law, which primarily unites human society, we do not ask after the religious affiliation of our brothers when we elect them. We are satisfied if they are stamped by honesty. It is expressly forbidden to discuss religion in our meetings . . . in order to avoid the misunderstandings that commonly can come from such conversations. Loose speech [*Zuchtlose Reden*] is not less incompatible with morality; consequently, we refrain from every kind of loose [*leichtfertiger*] and immoral conversation which could offend chaste ears and never serve pure hearts.[93]

We need not believe that all Freemasons were angels to recognize that moral redefinition affected social behavior. Submission to visible standards of comportment (clothing, manners) may not have guaranteed a pure life, but for purposes of constituting a new social group, external demonstration was primary. Externally

---

[91] Nipperdey, "Verein," 195. Habermas, *Structural Transformation*, 36, and Becher, *Politische Gesellschaft*, 22–24.

[92] A pamphleteer cited in Martens, *Botschaft der Tugend*, 142.

[93] F. W. Steinheil, cited in Dülmen, *Gesellschaft der Aufklärer*, 63.

appropriate dress, manners, and taste and verbal agreement with deeper, internal values, in conversation or perhaps by agreeing with the chastisement of a moral offender, were sufficient to stamp one with the new imprimatur.[94]

Not only among Freemasons, but in the associations generally, moral rectitude as demonstrated by mannerly comportment and devotion to Reason dissolved the old social hierarchy and created the assumption of equality. Having dissolved the previous barriers of social status, the new moral standards then threw up new ones separating the new society of equals who submitted at least externally to the new standards from those who did not. Drunken or loose-tongued Freemasons were subject to fines or even exclusion,[95] just as "irregularities in lifestyle" could lead to dismissal from the other kinds of associations.[96] Moral virtue defined the new civil elite. It was the recognized prerequisite to being treated as an equal, and therefore to exercising freedom.

Like *Bildung*, morality was a quality potentially accessible to all; it was another expression of the expansionary, indeed, missionary quality of civil society. The General Report of the Illuminati of 1782 summed up the dynamism contemporaries expected from moral reform: "In a word, we must introduce a general moral regime [*Sittenregiment*], a form of government stretching generally over the whole world, without dissolving the civil bands in which all other governments continue their way; and we must do everything so as not to thwart the great goal, to make good victorious over evil."[97] This grandiose vision was thus explicitly imagined as both moral and political simultaneously.

There is yet another way in which the new morality functioned politically. It is undeniable that many of the concrete virtues championed by the associations and journals were an amalgam of traditional virtues associated with town dwellers, the old *Bürger*, and the Enlightened virtues esteemed by the *Bildungsbürger* and made possible by peculiarities of their social and work lives. That is, the new moral code that the practioners of civil society recommended for everybody was more consonant with the actual lives and aspirations of certain social groups than others. Insofar as these moral values became tests of active citizenship (which they did) and were inscribed into legal reform (which they were), they worked peculiarly in the (only now consolidating) interests of those favored groups and thus formed a powerful, but unacknowledged political support system for them. The very success of their moral endeavor in gaining hegemony has largely blinded scholarship to the tremendous subterranean political impact of the moral system and encouraged a scholarly bookkeeping that considers moral matters as rigorously separate from political ones.

Sociologists observe that as society becomes ever more complex and differenti-

---

[94] Dülmen, *Gesellschaft der Aufklärer*, 63–64, 80.
[95] Ibid., 65.
[96] Im Hof, *Das gesellige Jahrhundert*, 222.
[97] "Allgemeine Übersicht des ganzen Ordenssystem" (1782), cited in Dülmen, *Gesellschaft der Aufklärer*, 105.

ated, morality in the form of moral codes loses some of the power to structure social interaction that it exercises in simpler social configurations. It must compete against other "functional equivalents," like law, or love, or situational rationality.[98] Above all, complexity produces myriads of possible sources of moral precepts and situations where different obligations, goals, worldviews, and claims may arise and become expressed in moral subsystems.[99] Complexity therefore proliferates moral systems at the same time that it weakens their impact. The moral discussions of the late eighteenth century were in part reactions to this process; by expanding the ground of morality from religion to society, the practitioners of civil society significantly widened the criteria for moral behavior. If doing so in the long run undermined moral homogeneity and therefore the structuring power of morality, that was not their intent. They believed they were strengthening the moral order by becoming its overseers. The morality they chose to express a vision of correct social and political relations and ultimately to demand that institutions reflect that order was not formally different from the "moral economy of the lower orders."[100] From peasants defending customary rights to theorists of state, moral language, the political coin of the early modern realm, shaped the transition to the new sociopolitical order.

Characteristics of the New Morality

Before leaving this general examination of practical civil society and its relation to ideal civil society, it is necessary very briefly to sketch some of those characteristics of the moral discussion that are directly relevant to what was said about sexual behavior.

Civil Virtues

The concrete personal virtues touted by the practitioners of civil society came from two sources. The first and oldest was the catalog of virtues appropriate to the *Hausvater* or citizen of a town (*Bürger*). This list was virtually identical for cameralists and for civil moralists of the eighteenth century. Justi's litany contained bravery, "love of true honor,"[101] "love of diligence and skill," judiciousness, honesty,

---

[98] Niklas Luhmann, "Soziologie der Moral," in *Theorietechnik und Moral*, ed. Niklas Luhmann and Stephan H. Pfürtner (Frankfurt, 1978), 8–116, esp. 65–83.

[99] Steven Lukes, "Making Sense of Moral Conflict," in *Liberalism and the Moral Life*, ed. Nancy L. Rosenblum (Cambridge, Mass., 1989), 129–31.

[100] This is E. P. Thompson's phrase, which he uses in "The Moral Economy of the English Crowd in the Eighteenth Century," *Past and Present* 50 (1971): 76–136, and recently, in *Customs in Common: Studies in Traditional Popular Culture* (New York, 1991), esp. chaps. 3–5.

[101] Paul Münch, ed., *Ordnung, Fleiß und Sparsamkeit. Texte und Dokumente zur Entstehung der "bürgerlichen Tugenden"* (Munich, 1984), interprets these first two virtues as incongruously belonging to the nobility, 21–22. In fact, bravery was one of the defining cardinal virtues of Freemasonry, whereas love of honor (reputation) was held by almost all theorists of civil society as a prerequisite of moral behavior altogether. Concerning Masonic virtue, see Dülmen, *Gesellschaft der Aufklärer*, 62.

"civilized politeness," "love of equality," thrift, and moderation. To these he added, as personal virtues, sobriety and chastity.[102] In a separate passage, Justi summed up the virtues necessary to a "well-functioning household" as diligence, orderliness and thrift.[103] Finally, there was obedience and submission to authority, owed in the seventeenth century to one's superiors generally and in the eighteenth to the state-civil society.[104] This catalog, directly derived from church and state authorities but modified to make room for developing civil society ("love of equality," "civilized politeness"), formed the core, standard virtues for its members.[105]

Knowledge of nineteenth-century developments has misled some observers to reduce the rather extensive list above to the merely economic virtues: diligence, orderliness, and thrift. From here it is a small step to discover at the bottom of all three "control of emotions."[106] As with many stereotypes, there are some good reasons why the repressive hypothesis of bourgeois/civil virtue has attained such ubiquity. Self-control is certainly an important undercurrent in the moral discussions of the eighteenth century. Nonetheless, emphasizing the economic triad caricatures the moral code in at least two ways. First, it ignores the salience of citizen-virtues, both regarding the duties owed to society and the positive qualities needed for active participation in it. Second, it overlooks the second, new component of the moral code: the expansionary, dynamic vision of the future.[107] Preparing men for emerging civil society demanded more than anxious saving and routinized labor. Improvement and progress required openness to new challenges, risk-taking, investment (spending), energy, and, yes, desire, that is, higher aspirations to goad one to continuous activity and self-improvement. This side of the moral ledger was largely blank. Filling it in structured a large part of the eighteenth-century discussion, especially of sexual behavior, which provided a flexible metaphor to help examine the entire problematic of desire, energy, (re)productivity, control, social relations, and individual solipsism.[108]

Gender-Specificity

Morality expresses social expectations. It describes schematically the duties persons owe one another. Except under the assumption of absolute equality, these expectations will differ according to person and situation. Under the *ständisch* system, men and women, while sharing a number of Christian and economic virtues, nonetheless worked, were ruled, and acted socially according to schemas

---

[102] Justi, *Grundfeste* 2:211–50.

[103] Ibid., 2:135.

[104] Cf. Seckendorff, *Fürsten-Stat*, 96, and Justi, *Grundfeste*, 2:215.

[105] See the documents in Münch, *Ordnung, Fleiß und Sparsamkeit.*

[106] Pikulik, *Leistungsethik*, 153, and concerning the repressive hypothesis, 194–232. On overvaluation of economic virtues, see Münch, *Ordnung, Fleiß und Sparsamkeit*, 22–26.

[107] Ruppert, *Bürgerlicher Wandel*, 40.

[108] Isabel V. Hull, "'Sexualität' und bürgerliche Gesellschaft," in *Bürgerinnen und Bürger. Geschlechterverhältnisse im 19. Jahrhundert*, ed. Ute Frevert (Göttingen, 1988), 49–66.

appropriate to their gender. Traditional moral systems reflected these actual social differences, and the practitioners of civil society inherited from them a gender-specific catalog of virtues upon which they then elaborated.[109] In fact, the citizen-virtues listed above applied largely to married men; the economic virtues applied to everyone. The eighteenth century elaborated the moral code asymmetrically. Men's duties to society and most of all their duties to one another were the problem areas most discussed. Meanwhile, women's duties were conceived almost exclusively as duties to their husbands (and secondarily to their children). This tendency is clearly present in the traditional catalog, but its development, rather than possible reformulation, represents a cultural choice, and one with growing impact because of the political freight that moral argument bore.

The elaboration of the moral code shows that the practitioners of civil society sought primarily to recast relations among men. This explains the fiction common to all their associations that their members belonged to no *Stand* or religion; nor were they to discuss their profession or family.[110] They stood stripped of (almost) all their social markings. From this, as it was thought, natural foundation, one could build up a new system of social recognition based upon virtue. It is extremely important for the sexual discussion that came out of this endeavor, that the discussants thought of themselves in some important sense as naked. Having doffed the artificial signs of their previous social separation, they stood together as equals sharing the physical and mental attributes of men. It was critical to discover what this equality consisted of. What was a man? This question could not, by definition, be answered in any other way than by reference to what he was not, namely, a woman. The problem of discovering the nature of manhood largely organized the discussion of sexual behavior, but it was carried on in the guise of ratiocination about women, or "woman." It should be clear, however, that speculation about women was merely a function of the more fundamental task of defining men. Thus the identity-building in which the practitioners of civil society engaged was based more self-consciously on gender than on "class." Gender seemed a firmer foundation, because the new elite had not yet coalesced into a recognizable "class,"[111] and the fiction of natural universals (such as gender) seemed a logical extension of natural law and thus could both dissolve the old social status groups and ground the new in a single, efficient stroke. Gender was therefore a powerful tool in the self-creation made necessary by and contingent on the larger moral-political endeavor of creating civil society.[112]

---

[109] Pikulik, *Leistungsethik*, 152, 206.

[110] Dülmen, *Gesellschaft der Aufklärer*, 62.

[111] This never happened thoroughly, but the economic developments of the next century made it easier for the "bourgeoisie" (*Besitzbürgertum*) to propound its particular interests as those of the middling strata and of liberals altogether. See Lothar Gall, "Liberalismus und 'bürgerliche Gesellschaft.' Zu Charakter und Entwicklung der liberalen Bewegung in Deutschland," *Historische Zeitschrift* 220 (1975): 324–56.

[112] Hull, "'Sexualität' und bürgerliche Gesellschaft."

Morality and Freedom

It is no coincidence that the eighteenth century should have made both "moral-ity" and "freedom" such central themes.[113] They were both part of a mutually reinforcing relation. Following the Kantian dictum that only freedom from external (state) sanctions makes possible truly moral behavior, the duty of the state to provide the foundations for the moral improvement of its citizens leads paradox-ically to its own self-limitation, and thus to the expansion of the sphere of freedom for its citizens, a sphere of freedom coincident with (the legal foundation of) civil society. But the equation works in reverse, too. In order to exercise freedom of choice, one needs to know what the choices are; that is, one needs to know what the expectations are, before one can be in a position to choose to fulfill them or not. From this perspective, as Niklas Luhmann puts it, "Freedom is not a sign of behavior itself and certainly not a natural characteristic of mankind. It is an effect of the communication of expectations, norms, and predictions, it arises and passes away with communication."[114] Insofar as morality is the compact expression of these expectations, norms and predictions, freedom is an effect of morality. There-fore, a culture bent on expanding the sphere of freedom will perforce have to expand its moral expectations.[115] Or, put institutionally, a culture that expands its communication network, thereby bringing more citizens into (potential) contact with one another, also increases the mutual expectations they have of one another in the same measure as it enhances their freedom of action.

Despite this theoretical reciprocity, the symbiosis of freedom and morality ap-peared to many contemporaries as weighted on the side of morality, especially once the French Revolution illustrated where freedom might lead. In 1792 even C. M. Wieland, a fairly radical Enlightener,[116] compared the political freedom the French people had received from the first National Assembly to a "true Pandora's box, from which all kinds of evil passions, excesses, vices, and crimes, with all their very ruinous effects, spread like a poisonous fog." Typically, sexualized language (evil passion, excesses, vices) expressed the dangers to (and of!) civil freedom. National leaders had erred in believing "the people capable of bearing a constitution that can only come to pass and be maintained through a high degree of civil virtue [*bür-gerlichen Tugend*] on the part of all the constituent powers as well as of the entire people." [117] A year earlier he had listed the positive virtues necessary for political freedom: "True republican spirit demands habitual convictions and virtues . . . a

---

[113] Jürgen Schlumbohm, *Freiheitsbegriff und Emanzipationsprozeß. Zur Geschichte eines politischen Wortes* (Göttingen, 1973).

[114] Luhmann, "Soziologie der Moral," 60.

[115] Luhmann does not take this next step, but it follows both from his argument and from the development of civil society in history.

[116] Möller, *Vernunft und Kritik*, 306.

[117] Christoph M. Wieland, "Schreiben an einen Korrespondenten in Paris," *Neuer Teutscher Merkur,* October 1792, 197.

self-denial . . . a moderation . . . obedience toward the laws . . . because the entire existence of the republic depends upon this unlimited respect of every single citizen for the general will [*allgemeinen Willen*], that is for the law and its organs, the authority."[118]

For Wieland and for most practitioners of civil society, morality was a prerequisite of freedom. Moral deficiency was grounds for exclusion from the exercise of freedom and thus from practical participation in civil society, the sphere of freedom. This conviction was of course practiced in the rules governing membership in associations. Moral vetting was an inheritance from traditional practice, in which moral reputation was an important criterion for full social membership in the community. This is another example of the longevity of older social forms in the new civil society. But the meaning of inclusion and exclusion now carried broader and different significance, as civil society increasingly usurped previous government authority. The nineteenth century built on this foundation by raising the moral hurdle to full membership in civil society even higher.

Harmony versus Individuality

One of the paradoxes of the creation of civil society is that, at the same time that it prized individual creativity, tolerated differences, and promoted social differentiation, it longed for harmony. Martens describes the harmonious imperative in the early moral weeklies: "For this genre of the 1720s, as well as the 1760s, adaptation to society, harmonious adjustment to its directives, was the moral duty of every upstanding person."[119] Surprisingly, this yearning barely seems to have abated in the course of the century. Dülmen believes that the need to achieve "conflict free communication" among men of disparate backgrounds was the main impetus.[120] This was, of course on a larger scale, what creating civil society meant: producing and proliferating rules that the citizens accepted as binding for their mutual relations. The difference between a group of people forced to accede to state power and a civil society was the difference between depending on legal coercion or depending on morality to hold them together. Completely developed civil society was one where force gave way to conviction, and thus to freedom. But this would only occur upon achievement of a single, moral whole, as Kant declared in 1784 as he described the progress toward Enlightened civil society:

> There then occur the first true steps away from coarseness to culture, which consists actually in the social worth of mankind [*Menschen*]; all talents are gradually developed, taste is formed, and through continuous enlightenment the beginnings of the foundation of a way of thinking are made, which can in time transform the rough natural predilection

[118] Christoph M. Wieland, "Erklärung des Herausgebers über die im 6ten Monatsstück des T. Merk. 1791 auf der letzten Seite befindliche Note," *Neuer Teutscher Merkur*, October 1791, 132.
[119] *Botschaft der Tugend*, 296, also 299–300.
[120] *Gesellschaft der Aufklärer*, 123.

to make moral judgments into concrete, practical principles and thus transform a patho-logically forced agreement to [create] a society into a moral whole.[121]

Georg Chr. Wedekind, a member of the Society of the Friends of Freedom and Equality, explained the role of the practitioners of civil society (in their associations) and of discourse in this progress toward the moral whole: "There must be places where one can confer about public welfare, politics, law-making, morals, and so on; where one can without suffering any disadvantage, today pronounce a thing good and tomorrow after further reflection reject it; places where one can build the common spirit [*Gemeingeist*], where one can become of one opinion [*unter sich eins wird*] and thus prepare laws."[122] The practitioners of civil society were thus to discover (we would say create) the moral agreement underpinning not merely social norms, but also positive law.

The discussions about sexual behavior, to which we now turn, were part of this search for the moral harmony underlying civil society. They were also the products of the tensions in the enterprise of civil society itself: between the safe, core virtues and those more dangerous qualities appropriate to an expanding world; between the fascination with the nature of men and the actual discussion, which moved obliquely, upon the body of "woman"; between the pull of morality and the push of freedom; and between the dream of harmony and the dream of individuality.

---

[121] "Idee zu einer allgemeinen Geschichte . . . ," *Gesammelte Schriften* (Berlin, 1900–1955), 23:17–31, cited in Niethammer, "Bürgerliche Gesellschaft als Projekt," 19.
[122] Cited in Dülmen, *Gesellschaft der Aufklärer*, 113.

6

The Sexual Self-Image of Civil Society

The literary flood of the late eighteenth century carried in its swell an increasing number of books devoted to sexual subjects. At the very end of the century, the *Ehestandsalmanach* (Almanac of the Marital Estate) listed 1,201 titles on sexual themes, most in German; the editor claimed he knew of 3,000, while an acquaintance of his boasted of knowing twice as many.[1] Of course, a vastly greater number of works treated sexual subjects as part of a larger context. Statistics therefore cannot adequately reflect the level, much less the kind, of interest the eighteenth century paid to sexual behavior.

Much of the writing on sexual matters ignored society and focused instead on the individual, on his or her physical health, happiness, and personal development. Journals such as Carl Friedrich Pockels's *Magazin zur Erfahrungsseelenkunde* (Magazine for practical psychology) and Johann Samuel Fest's *Beiträge zur Beruhigung und Aufklärung* (Contributions toward reassurance and enlightenment)[2] functioned like early advice columns where (mostly male) readers shared their personal experiences and anxieties, including sexual ones. The cycle of mutual self-revelation eased the isolation that otherwise attended self-absorption. Journals became forums where carefully selected slices of intimate, "private" life were made "public," submitted to benevolent scrutiny, and ultimately refined into a system of norms and expectations according to which precisely those aspects of development and personality taken to be the innermost, most secret, most basic fundaments of individuality were in fact fashioned into a model for all to follow. Working out the contours of the (masculine) self was, of course, critical to the formation of civil society, because these were its citizens—and the female model was largely the negative of the male image. Nonetheless, exploring the byways of this process is beyond the purview of this book.[3]

---

[1] Dieter Hoof, *Pestalozzi und die Sexualität seines Zeitalters. Quellen, Texte und Untersuchungen zur Historischen Sexualwissenschaft* (Saint Augustin, 1987), 467–69. See also Hugo Hayn and Alfred N. Gotendorf, eds., *Bibliotheca Germanorum Erotica et Curiosa, Verzeichnis der gesamten deutschen erotischen Literatur mit Einschluß der Übersetzungen, nebst Beifügung der Originale*, 9 vols. (Munich, 1912–29).

[2] The full title was *Beiträge zur Beruhigung und Aufklärung über dieienigen Dinge, die dem Menschen unangenehm sind oder sein können, und zur nähern Kenntniß der leidenden Menschheit.*

[3] Doris Kaufmann's forthcoming study, "Aufklärung, bürgerliche Selbsterfahrung und der Anfang der Psychiatrie in Deutschland," addresses precisely these questions.

Instead, we turn to those writings which dealt more self-consciously with the relation of sexual themes to the organization of civil society. In particular we focus on the last quarter of the century, when the reality of civil society and the growing pressure for fundamental reform of public institutions to fit it made reflection about its principles a felt necessity. In these years the hegemony of mature, late-Enlightenment thinking and solidified self-confidence on the part of the practitioners of civil society made them chafe at the obstacles the states still threw up to the completion of the civil project. The French Revolution, before regicide and the Terror, seemed to confirm the inevitable triumph of civil society and Progress. The publications from the late 1770s to the early 1790s preserve a golden moment when the victory of the new principles was close at hand. These years were thus the last moment when the practitioners of civil society could contemplate the future they were dedicated to bringing into being. They rehearsed their last anxieties and corrected their blueprints.

Sexual images were a major aid to organizing the practitioners' reflections on drafting the future civil society. They were useful partly because sexual behavior had traditionally been a central marker of social order (most notably in the linkage: marriage/economic productivity/social status/*Bürgerrecht*); partly because hetero-sexual expression seemed an efficient epitome of the link between individual behavior and social consequences; and partly because sexual symbolism offered a pithy but also open-ended way to think about new constellations of problems. Seeing nonsexual or not necessarily sexual problems through a sexual lens influenced how these problems were interpreted and judged. At the same time, suffusing sexual expression, sexual acts, and sexual relations with new social meanings changed their significance and gave them a gravity they would otherwise have lacked. The sexualizing of social discourse laid the foundations for what the nineteenth century would call simply "sexuality."

The late-eighteenth-century literature discussing social issues in a sexual context emphasized four themes: the nature of the sexual drive, masturbation, infanticide, and marriage. The last three topics, the subjects of the next chapter, were discussed in the form of thought experiments which permitted practitioners to contemplate important issues raised by the principles of civil society (such as egotism versus altruism, or self-regulation versus government regulation, or the perils of expanded access to knowledge) in ways conducive to unfettered speculation. The first topic, the sexual drive, contained the essential assumptions about sexual energy upon which practitioners elaborated when they contemplated other sexual matters.

Aside from the themes around which it was organized, the late-eighteenth-century discussion of sexual behavior had two other important characteristics. One was the continuous reworking of traditional assumptions or associations into new constellations.[4] These "old saws" were recombined, elaborated, extended, or re-

---

[4] On continuity in sexual ideology, compare the common opinion in Kiesel and Münch, *Gesellschaft und Literatur*, 64, and Paul-Gabriel Boucé, "Some Sexual Beliefs and Myths in Eighteenth-Century

tracted; they were applied to select social groups or invoked under special circumstances. All this reworking succeeded in fashioning from this ideological raw material something new indeed.

The second characteristic is the salience of gender. For the late Enlightened period, gender was a more powerful organizer of ideas about sexual behavior than vice versa. Or perhaps one should say that gender posed the greater problem, and sex offered an ideal solution. That is, unlike the collective, *ständisch* order, civil society was to be based on a new unit, the individual citizen, who was presumed to be male and to share with his fellows characteristics more fundamental than those resulting from the chance of social status. Because the sexual model, as we shall see, was already highly genderized, it suggested almost ready-made, "natural" guidelines for defining the nascent, inchoate, universal (male) individual, for reformulating social and political relations between women and men, and thus for ordering the society-in-becoming. Gender differentiation based on sexual attraction was the pithiest analogue to the social differentiation already under way.

We turn now, first to the practitioners' reflection on the sexual characteristics of their age, and then to the knowledge they inherited and refashioned about the nature of the sexual drive.

The Self-Image of the Late Eighteenth Century as a Sexual Era

The practitioners of civil society were convinced that theirs was an age of increased sexual desire. They arrived at this conclusion in many ways, perhaps the most prevalent of these being the dual association of cultural refinement with sexual knowledge, leisure, and thus with excess, on the one hand, and with the sexual stimulants of wealth, exotic food and drink, and luxurious clothing and social amusements (especially French!), on the other.[5] Under absolutism, these seductions to vice had been limited to the nobility and courts. Now, as alarmed contemporaries such as Pastor Friedrich Traugott Schmidt were quite willing to point out, "Exactly that Enlightenment nowadays, exactly that development of all arts and sciences, that extended training of all intellectual energies, that refinement of customs [*Sitten*], in which all estates [*Stände*] more or less take part, that more elevated containment [*aufgehobene Gefangenschaft*] of human intellectual energy, in combination with the very much increased population and opulence of our times, has led almost inevitably to this ruin [*Verderben*]."[6] It was simply a commonplace

---

Britain," in *Sexuality in Eighteenth-Century Britain,* ed. Boucé (Manchester, 1982), 28–46, with the subtler formulations of Michel Foucault, *The Use of Pleasure,* trans. Robert Hurley (New York, 1986) and *The Care of the Self,* trans. Robert Hurley (New York, 1988).

[5] I discuss this association of refinement, wealth and leisure with the sex drive in greater detail later.

[6] Friedrich Traugott Schmidt (pastor in Wahren, Mecklenburg-Schwerin), "Preisschrift über das Sittenverderben der Bedienten," in *Verhandlungen und Schriften der Hamburgischen Gesellschaft zur Beförderung der Künste und nützlichen Gewerbe* (Hamburg, 1793), 70–71. Schmidt wrote here of the ruined manners and customs of servants, but he targeted specifically the "unfortunate disrupted balance between reason and sensuality" (70), that is, sexual behavior.

that the eighteenth century's "exagerrated culture" brought with it a "strengthening of the sexual drive."[7]

In addition to the undoubted material improvements of the age, which were sometimes still ignominiously styled "luxury," eighteenth-century observers cited the effects of education designed to bring boys and girls together. Some contemporaries greeted this new, purposive heterosociality as an enrichment for both sexes; others granted that it was an "in itself agreeable education," but worried that bringing the sexes together "makes each one much more important in the other's eyes," which might lead to sexual disorder.[8] Cynics rejected the whole pedagogical drift: "Our entire education is directed to making love-lorn weaklings who are a burden to themselves and to the state."[9] Whether one hailed the new developments or cursed them, clearly the spokesmen of Enlightenment perceived the late eighteenth century as having inaugurated much closer social relations between men and women. Early acquaintance, the much vaunted rise in the position of women,[10] the education of males to sensitivity (*Empfindsamkeit*), mixed social events, even the stereotypical plague of novel-reading, were all taken as signs of the attempt to encourage mutual understanding and interest between men and women and thus to create the foundations for solid marriages based on something other than economic necessity. These activities were the necessary counterweight to the equally intense striving to engender enormous differences between men and women. Nonetheless, the practitioners of civil society understood the legendary sociability of their century as outspokenly heterosocial and thus, potentially, heterosexual.[11]

The century's reputation for sexual mischief was further enhanced by its skepticism. Contemporaries experienced their age as relentless in its destruction of taboos, including sexual ones, as this anonymous contributor to the *Deutsches Magazin* put it in 1798:

It was to be expected in a time like the present one, when all the usual principles, institutions, customs and opinions have been subjected to scrutiny, that those principles would not be neglected according to which the satisfaction of the sexual drive is only permitted in marriage, appropriate to the order of reason according to the laws of humankind [*des Menschen*]; and that therefore all satisfaction outside of marriage is regarded as against the order of reason. And this has indeed happened, and happened in such a way that some have tried to maintain that according to the principles of natural law

[7] Thus the anonymous reviewer of Karl Gottfried Bauer's *Über die Mittel dem Geschlechtstriebe eine unschädliche Richtung zu geben*, in *Beitr.z.B.* 3.2 (1792): 523–24.

[8] Cf. anon., "Auch ein Wort über Priesterehe und Cölibat," *Dt. Mon.* 1 (1792): 78–90, esp. 88, with Peter Villaume, "Ueber die Unzuchtssünden in der Jugend. Eine gekrönte Preisschrift," in Joachim Heinrich Campe, *Allgemeine Revision des gesammten Schul- und Erziehungswesens von einer Gesellschaft practischer Erzieher*, ed. (Wolfenbüttel, 1787), 7:103.

[9] Anon., "Galanterien mit dem medicinischen Fernglase betrachtet," *Alm. f. Ä.* (1783): 195.

[10] Advancing civilization was generally taken to have elevated the status of women and improved their treatment. Claudia Honegger, *Die Ordnung der Geschlechter. Die Wissenschaften vom Menschen und das Weib* (Frankfurt, 1991), 52–54.

[11] It was precisely this feature that drove Ernst Brandes to pen his mysogynist classic, *Ueber die Weiber* (Leipzig, 1787).

humankind has a right to the unlimited freedom to satisfy his/her sexual drive, and that consequently it is an unnatural [*widernatürliche*] limitation of and offense against human rights if civil laws forbid anything more than the use of violence to force the satisfaction of the sexual drive.[12]

Although the defenders of marriage and therefore of the traditional limits placed on sexual expression overwhelmed the free spirits, still, the perception that it was necessary to defend marriage at all testifies to how far Enlightened questioning had run. The cameralists' polygamy debate was just as vigorously entertained among nonstate theorists, and concubinage, state-run brothels, and the decriminalization of fornication all found their articulate defenders. Even radical practices like infibulation (the insertion of a ring in the prepuce to prevent erection) were seriously discussed, though not championed.[13] The famous pedagogue Joachim Heinrich Campe informed readers that Enlightenment had advanced so much, "especially in the last decade," that is, the 1780s, that introducing Roman togas for youths (as a masturbation-preventative) could not simply be dismissed as an impossibly utopian scheme.[14] Clearly brainstorming about sexual matters might favor either more sex or less; the point is that brainstorming occurred to such a degree that many contemporaries felt disoriented. Karl Gottfried Bauer, winner of a prize contest for the best essay on how to control the sexual drive (1791), found the eternal questioning and justifying annoying. He labeled it all "unfruitful uses of skepticism that only confuse the issue" and thereby hoped to dismiss the uncertainty without having addressed the questions.[15]

[12] Anon., "Ist wohl nur die erzwungene Befriedigung des Geschlechtstriebes als Unzucht und widernatürlich zu betrachten?" *Dt. Mag.* 16 (1798): 459–60.

[13] Christian Salzmann, the pedagogue, credited Dr. Börner of Leipzig with having suggested this procedure. Salzmann shied away from recommending it for fear it could not easily be undone and might leave lasting damage: Christian Gotthilf Salzmann, *Ueber die heimlichen Sünden der Jugend*, 4th "unveränderte Auflage" (Leipzig, 1819), 204–9. Dr. Vogel, author of an antimasturbation text for parents, was not at ease about the procedure either, though he was willing to take a chance on it as a last resort. See Samuel Gottlieb Vogel, *Unterricht für Eltern, Erzieher und Kinderaufseher: wie das unglaublich gemeine Laster der zerstörenden Selbstbefleckung am sichersten zu entdecken, zu verhüten und zu heilen* (Stendahl, 1786), 132–37. J. S. Fest, "Ein vielleicht nicht unnöthiger Wink zur Verhütung ungünstiger und unrichtiger Urtheile über zween aus diesen Beiträgen bekannte iunge Männer," *Beitr.z.B.* 2 (1790): 484–88, esp. 486–87, reported the method did not work. Campe mostly repeated Salzmann's information. See his editorial addition to J. F. Oest, "Versuch einer Beantwortung der pädagogischen Frage: wie man Kinder und junge Leute vor dem Leib und Seele verwüstenden Laster der Unzucht überhaupt, und der Selbstschwächung insonderheit verwahren, oder, wofern die schon davon angesteckt waren, wie man sie davon heilen könne?" in Campe, *Revision*, 6: 218–25. Modern observers, such as Hoof, *Pestalozzi*, 517–19; and Paul Derks, *Die Schande der heiligen Päderastie; Homosexualität und Öffentlichkeit in der deutschen Literatur, 1750–1850* (Berlin, 1990), 127, have overrated the pedagogues' enthusiasm for infibulation. Hilke Hentze, *Sexualität in der Pädagogik des späten 18. Jahrhunderts* (Frankfurt, 1979), 85 (on Salzmann), is more cautious.

[14] Campe's introduction to Dr. Bernhard Christian Faust, *Wie der Geschlechtstrieb der Menschen in Ordnung zu bringen und wie die Menschen besser und glücklicher zu machen* (Braunschweig, 1791), ix. F. J. Bertuch, "Ueber Kinder-Kleidung," *JdL* 6 (1791): 571–74, politely disagreed.

[15] Karl Gottfried Bauer, *Über die Mittel dem Geschlechtstriebe eine unschädliche Richtung zu geben. Eine durch die Erziehungsanstalt zu Schnepfenthal gekrönte Preisschrift. Mit einer Vorrede und Anmerkungen von C. G. Salzmann* (Leipzig, 1791), 61. See also 284.

But the questions remained.[16] Fortunately, Enlightenment was perceived not only to cause increasing sexual desire and moral confusion, but to cure them, too. Let us return to Pastor Schmidt, who identified Enlightenment as the culprit in sensual ruin. He also warned against the impulse simply to quash the new principles and return to the darkness of absolutism and mere subsistence: "If one took the sun from the sky, one would remove the light and warmth from the earth, and soon no more weeds would sprout from its soil; but neither would healthy and wholesome fruits spring any more from its womb [*Schooß*]. In short, if we want the good of Enlightenment, then we cannot entirely prevent the bad that comes in its wake." However, all was not lost. "The higher true Enlightenment rises, the easier one can discover the means and the stronger becomes the drive [*Trieb*] in the hearts of [Enlightenment's] true admirers, to work against all excrescences of moral ruination."[17] Discovering the means, widening the knowledge about sexual behavior, became the method to extend Enlightenment and preserve it from its own negative tendencies. In this way and for this reason, what was presumed to be the "nature" of the sexual drive became an object of systematic scrutiny. This marked a new departure. The scrutinizers had to struggle to establish sexual behavior as a legitimate object of Enlightened debate. Bauer complained that the conflation of sexual misbehavior with luxury and fashion had festooned the subject in frivolity. "The air of flightiness, the veneer of ridiculousness, with which people [*man*] have gradually come to regard all objects connected with sexual pleasure have repressed [*verdrängt*] all thoughts of the serious relationships, of the connection of these things to morality [*Sittlichkeit*]."[18] Almost all the writers on masturbation began their tracts with defensive hyperbole about the seriousness of the problem. Placing the sexual drive at the center of one's intellectual inquiry remained a risky business, however, as Schiller's (and Goethe's) response to Friedrich von Ramdohr's examination of the nature of love proved. Ramdohr discovered sexual attraction as the hidden and usually oblique force behind emotions and even behind social interaction. Schiller scoffed at the very notion: "He [Ramdohr] gets his ideas about beauty from pretty low down, since he appeals to the sexual drive for help."[19]

Despite such discouragements, enough writers persisted in their efforts to make sexual behavior a serious object of study that they produced a substantial body of essays and books. Most of these arose in the usual pattern of essay-response-essay-response, clustered around particular themes. But that favorite Enlightened institution, the essay prize contest, encouraged adumbration on such topics as masturbation in youth (1785), nature and control of the sexual drive (1788), the moral ruination of servants (1790) (which was a popular screen for discussing untram-

---

[16] See Cella's eloquent paragraph on confusing moral messages, in *Über Verbrechen und Strafe*, 10–11.
[17] Schmidt, "Preisschrift," 70–71.
[18] Bauer, *Über die Mittel*, 160–61.
[19] Schiller to Goethe on 12 November 1794, Friedrich Schiller and Johann Wolfgang v. Goethe, *Der Briefwechsel zwischen Schiller und Goethe*, ed. Paul Stapf (Berlin, 1970), 21, cited in Derks, *Die Schande*, 379. Cf. Friedrich Wilhelm Basilius von Ramdohr, *Venus Urania. Ueber die Natur der Liebe, über ihre Veredlung und Verschönerung*, 3 parts (Leipzig, 1798).

meled sensuality), and celibacy (1791). In the nineteenth century, such subjects would have been the prerogative of doctors. In the eighteenth, interest (and competence) were much broader. The king of England apparently donated the prize money for the inquiry on celibacy; the prestigious Patriotische Gesellschaft in Hamburg was behind the investigation of servants' morals.[20] Pedagogues played a leading part in encouraging and structuring the discussion of sexual behavior. Campe's question, "How can one save children and young people from the body- and soul-destroying vice [*Laster*] of sexual misbehavior [*Unzucht*] and particularly of masturbation [*Selbstschändung*], or, if they have already been infected [*angesteckt*], how can one cure them?" was set out in the first volume of the authoritative sixteen-volume pedagogical compendium, the so-called *General Revision*.[21] It produced three prize winners and one runner-up, whose book-length essays appeared in the *Revision*, but were also issued in less expensive separate editions, making them accessible to more readers.[22] Three years later, Campe's colleague Salzmann published two broader prize questions. For the first, one could win thirty French gold sovereigns: "What are causes in our legislation, social constitution [*Staatsverfassung*], manner of living, reading and education for the fact that the sexual drive [*Zeugungstrieb*] is *earlier* awakened and *stronger* than it should be according to the powers of nature? What influence does this have on the character of the nation [*Nation*]? What must the state authority, teacher, writer, and pastor do to return this drive to the limits of nature?" Salzmann thus wrote the universal assumption that the eighteenth century was peculiarly sexual into his problem. The second question focused on what was presumably believed to be the most common expression of this putative problem. The prize was divided according to gender— fifteen sovereigns each for the best book for men and the best for women "in which the great and diverse danger is most clearly described to which both sexes expose themselves under current circumstances when they satisfy their sexual drive outside marriage; and which give the best means of moderating the urgency of the sexual drive and of avoiding the temptations to excess."[23] Whether the smaller prizes were ever awarded is unclear. The first, however, produced a number of responses, of which the winner, by Bauer, is an invaluable compendium of sexual common sense in late-eighteenth-century Germany. As one reviewer described it, it contained "for the most part no new ideas about this important subject, but these had perhaps never before been so well put."[24] The earnestness with which the subject was treated and the broad social implications it was thought to possess

---

[20] Anon., "Vorbereitung zu den künftigen Preisschriften über den Cölibat," *NTM*, October 1791, 149. The Hamburg Patriotic Society's prize contest asked: "Which are the main sources of the moral ruin of servants of both sexes and how can these best be defended against, without legal coercion, for the best of the servants and their masters?" *Verhandlungen und Schriften*, 2:61.

[21] Cited in full at note 8.

[22] Campe, *Allgemeine Revision*, 1:xxxv–xli and 6:iv–vii.

[23] Published in the *Braun. J.* 2 (1788): 255–56, emphasis in original. Salzmann launched the project with his son-in-law Lenz.

[24] Anonymous review of Bauer's, *Über die Mittel*, 518.

(placing it therefore beyond the purview of mere doctors) are indicated by the three prize judges: J.G.H. Feder (1740–1821, privy councillor and professor of philosophy at Göttingen), Ernst Platner (professor of medicine at Leipzig and anthropologist), and Professor Adam Friedrich Christian Reinhard (1747–1808, professor of law and mathematics at Erfurt).[25]

All the diverse writing on sexual behavior built on assumptions about the nature of the sexual drive and its amenability to control.

The Sexual Drive

Virtually all eighteenth-century writers believed that a strong, natural, God-given sexual drive existed in both men and women. This opinion stood at the end of a long development; where the official Roman Catholic view had been (and still was) that complete sexual continence was quite possible, and the Reformation had thought it highly unusual, the eighteenth century considered it almost impossible and the very attempt harmful. Of all the "drives and desires of humankind, the procreative drive [*Zeugungstrieb*] is the most sensitive, the strongest, and most irresistible of all."[26] The Catholic founder of the discipline "medical police," Johann Peter Frank, struggled with his faith for chapter after chapter, before capitulating before the hegemonic wisdom of medicine and learned opinion: "I know of no means reliably capable of withstanding this physical mechanism," "so mighty are the motors which nature has devoted to propagating progeny."[27] This standard conviction was repeated in essay after essay, book after book, regardless of subject,[28] whether morality, health, law, education, personal reminiscence, and so on. It even appeared in doggerel:

> The drive after this thing gnaws
> At every human heart, 'til the gods it still;

---

[25] Ibid. On Platner, see Honegger, *Ordnung der Geschlechter*, 117–20. Reinhard[t] (Salzmann misspelled his name, adding a "t") in addition to his professorship at Erfurt, was actively involved in church and school matters; see *Deutsches Biographisches Archiv*, ed. Bernard Fabian (Munich, 1982), fiche no. 1015, frames 282–87.

[26] Vogel, *Unterricht für Eltern*, 39.

[27] Johann Peter Frank, *System einer vollständigen medicinischen Polizey*, 2d ed. (Mannheim, 1784), 1:104.

[28] For example, from law, see Krünitz, *Oekonomisch-technologische Encyklopädie*, s.v. "Hure," part 26, pp. 635–41, 694–97, and Globig and Huster, *Abhandlung von der Criminal-Gesetzgebung*, 228; from medicine, see Vogel, *Unterricht für Eltern*, and Frank, *System* (for the long history of the medical assumption of strong sexual desire in both sexes, see Danielle Jacquart and Claude Thomasset, *Sexuality and Medicine in the Middle Ages*, trans. Matthew Adamson [Princeton, N.J., 1988], 78–86); from education, the clearest examples are found in the antimasturbation literature (discussed below); from morality, see Carl Friedrich Bahrdt, *System der moralischen Religion zur endlichen Beruhigung für Zweifler und Denker, allen Christen und Nichtchristen lesbar* (Berlin, 1787), 370–72, and Christian Fürchtegott Gellert, *Moralische Vorlesungen*, ed. Johann Adolf Schlegel and Gottlieb Leberecht Heyern (Leipzig, 1770), 2:408–9, 548; and from personal reminiscence, see anon., "Fragmente aus dem Tagebuch des verstorbenen R***," *Mag. z. Er.* 4 (1785): 41.

Otherwise, it eats against our will
'Til everything is consumed.[29]

If left to itself, the sexual urge appeared first at puberty, earlier for girls than for boys, and disappeared or greatly slackened at menopause for women and slightly thereafter for men. Procreation was thus still taken to set the natural parameters of the sexual drive—though not to dictate how often sexual activity should occur in the procreative years; as one doctor noted (1787), "The 'too much' in sex [*Liebeswerk*] is of course always a very relative concept."[30] If nature set the general sexual framework, nature was still susceptible to cultural intervention. The literate eighteenth-century's at once worried and boastful self-image as hypersexual came, as we have seen, from its conviction that imagination and a refined or luxurious material environment strengthened the sexual urge. That held potential dangers that in particular the antimasturbation campaign explored.

But the dangers were only half the story. It is as important to recall that as a "natural" drive, sexual activity was considered necessary to health. Here general opinion followed centuries-old medical teaching: total continence was harmful. "Such attacks [as clerical celibacy] on the rights of nature never occur without [natural] punishment. . . . *The cosmopolitan [Weltbürger] is destined without any disadvantage [to himself] to make his kind eternal through procreation. He cannot, he should not, even [if he lives] in the most exemplary fashion, suffocate a part of his animal nature without penalty, without making an adverse disruption in the law of circulation and secretion."*[31] The latter meant that retaining sexual fluids poisoned the body, injured the genitals, and triggered "hidden illnesses."[32] It is noteworthy that descriptions of male sufferers usually stressed, along with genital deformity, mental impairment: that is, "crazy brains" or "at least an imagination which exhausts the ligaments of the body [and makes the sufferer useless] for all the more serious and useful work of the soul."[33] Meanwhile, continent women made themselves vulnerable to almost any sickness. Such thinking was consonant with a long medical tradition that prescribed marriage (that is, sex) to cure the ills of any woman of marriageable age. This conviction was still lively in late-eighteenth-century Germany. Sexual activity was not thought quite as unreservedly healthy for men as for women. Still, moderate sexual indulgence was plainly considered the physical prerequisite for a normal, healthy life for both sexes.[34]

[29] Anon. ["Sch-p"], "Der Ursprung der Liebe. Nach dem Plato," *TM* 7 (1774): 260–61.

[30] Ernst Schwabe, *Anweisung zu den Pflichten und Geschäften eines Stadt- oder Land-Physikus* (Erfurth, 1786–87), part 2, 254. The very different recommendations in both medical and nonmedical literature concerning how often to engage in sex testify to the correctness of Schwabe's observation. My thanks to Barbara Happe for bringing Schwabe's book to my attention.

[31] Anon., "Ehelosigkeit der Geistlichen," *Alm.f.Ä.* (1793): 244, emphasis in original.

[32] Ibid., 249.

[33] Anon., "Soll man ihnen Weiber geben? Eine Antwort aus der Erfahrung," *Chronologen* 8 (1780): 204. See Frank's compendium of the ailments due to sexual continence in *System*, 1:128–40.

[34] Salzmann, citing Dr. Peter Kamper, in Bauer, *Über die Mittel*, 51; anon., "Sachen, welche gesucht werden," *Alm.f.Ä.* (1791): 77–94; anon., "Rettung unschuldiger Kinder weiblichen Geschlechts von

Sexual activity was more than just a physical necessity, an unfortunate reminder of humans' animal inheritance. The sexual drive was celebrated as the motor of society and the mark of the independent, adult, productive citizen. Self-preservation and the sexual drive (*Trieb*) were the two most basic urges motivating human activity. Precisely because it was held to be universal, basic and irrepressible, the sexual drive became exemplary of drive altogether, and it thus became enmeshed in the eighteenth century's heated anthropological and philosophical dispute over the distinction between drive, instinct, and desire and the relation these held to freedom, reason, and morality. These were issues of the greatest importance to the founding of civil society, for they determined how one judged the nature of the new basic unit of that society, the individual. How far was he (or she) a creature of preexisting instincts and thus "unfree?" If instincts revolved only around the self and its gratification, how was society possible? How far were instincts susceptible to the will, and thus capable of being subordinated to reason, and thus "moral?" What was the relation between morality and happiness, or to put it another way, would socially useful, moral behavior happen "naturally" as a result of the uncoordinated striving of individuals toward what they imagined would make them happy, or must moral action instead be enforced? The answers carried high political and social stakes. Therefore it is not surprising that a cacaphony of voices arose in debate and the very words, stretched to suit polemical purposes, became ill-defined. As one of the many writers on this subject complained,

> The word "drives" is ambiguous. In the strictest sense it means those lower energies of the soul which *spur* people to activity, such as taste, tendency toward pleasure, love, etc. 2) It encompasses also higher and more noble feelings [*Gefühle*], which one might call emotions [*Empfindungen*] or virtues [*Tugenden*], like philanthropy, religiosity, etc. 3) Those feelings are also called drives, which hold people back, like modesty [*Schaam*], etc., though this usage is very inappropriate. 4) An habitual activity directed to certain objects, which has become a skill, also can become a drive, and occasionally receives that name . . . like the drive to read, and so forth.[35]

Such definitional confusion indicates precisely how central the notion of drive was to the eighteenth century, for more meanings were attached to the word than it could bear. Even so normally precise a thinker as Kant entangled himself in contradictions on this subject.[36]

This analogic slippage affected the conception of the sexual drive as well, which attracted in this period a cluster of socially relevant associations. Primary among

---

fälschlich beschuldigter Selbstbefleckung gegen den Herrn Leibarzt Zimmermann," *Bald. Mag.* 1 (1779): 52–60, esp. 59; Karl Friedrich Burdach, *Eugon, oder über Impotenz und Schwäche der Zeugungskraft und die sicherste Methode, sie zu heilen* (Leipzig, 1804), 28–29.

[35] Peter Villaume, *Allgemeine Theorie, wie gute Triebe und Fertigkeiten durch die Erziehung erwekt, gestärkt und gelenkt werden müssen*, in Campe, *Allgemeine Revision*, 4: 6–7.

[36] Wilhelm G. Jacobs, *Trieb als sittliches Phänomen. Eine Untersuchung zur Grundlegung der Philosophie nach Kant und Fichte* (Bonn, 1967), esp. 13–21.

these were original sociability (the result of sexual attraction), energy resulting in productivity and creativity (partly an analogy to reproduction, partly an extension of the drive for pleasure, for which sexual pleasure stood as the first and most basic example), and independence and freedom (an at once biological and social analogy: sexual capacity occurred only with biological maturity and legitimate sexual relations, that is, marriage, emancipated one from the tutelage of childhood).

Wrapped in its cluster of associations, the sexual drive recapitulated the movement from nature to culture. Everyone agreed that the sexual drive was "natural," in the sense of physically implanted, and thus prior to society and to culture.[37] Cesare Beccaria described it as "an eternal need common to all of nature; a need that existed before society," but one whose trajectory overcame this starting point; thus it "existed before society, for which it in fact laid the foundation."[38] It did so immediately by creating the couple, which most commentators hurried to conflate with marriage and the family. From there it was a small step to social altruism, a step that the anonymous writer of "Whether a wise man must marry" (1753) accomplished in a single sentence: "The wise intention of the creator implanted in us the drive to social life, so that each should encourage the happiness of the other, which happens when we try to encourage the welfare of our own [family], share with a friend [meaning wife] fortune and misfortune, help the oppressed, and via a quiet life not die out from the world." [39]

Sexual attraction as the spur to domesticity was thought especially necessary to attract men to that institution. Just like the cameralists, other observers also worried that men would reject marriage, were it not for the compensation of sexual pleasure they found there.[40] That explained why nature (or God) had made the sexual urge so strong, wrote Bauer. Only the expectation of sexual satisfaction spurred a man "to sacrifice a part of his complete freedom and independence, and to increase his subsistence concerns from a point when they have been little pressing to where they become truly worrisome."[41]

It is typical of late Enlightened writings that the very strength of a drive should lead in the same breath to the thought of its modification in an institution, in this case the domestication of the sexual drive into marriage. That same thought was behind the criticism a reviewer leveled at Thomas Abbt's praise of passion in his "On the determination of the youth as a future useful member of human society" (1794): "Abbt should not have said, nor should the editor have agreed with him, that passions [*Leidenschaften*] are our benefactors and protectors. One can say that correctly of drives [*Triebe*], but not of the blind outbreak of drives, which is pas-

[37] Hence the word "animalistic" (*thierisch*) frequently used to describe it. See Chap. 4, note 102. Also, Immanuel Kant, *Anthropologie in pragmatischer Hinsicht*, in *Kant's gesammelte Schriften* (Berlin, 1917), 7:276, cited in Jacobs, *Trieb als sittliches Phänomen*, 14.
[38] Beccaria as cited on the title page of Cella, *Über Verbrechen und Strafen*.
[39] Anon., "Ob ein Weiser heyrathen müsse," *Hann. G.A.* 3 (1753), col. 504.
[40] See pp. 183 and 285–93.
[41] Bauer, *Über die Mittel*, 48–49.

sion."[42] In short, it was the guided harnessing of drives that made society possible; it was the very development of the sexual drive from nature to society that made it positive. For once confined in marriage, it turned into love, which preserved and ennobled its useful qualities and protected against its destructive potential. As Villaume explained it, "Love should provide the preservative [*Präservativ*] against excesses; it should be the spur that drives [*antreibt*] a young person to useful striving and noble deeds. But love has even further uses. Strengthening the soul, lifting the heart, directing the drives, education for society, for philanthropy, for courteousness and flexibility—it can do all these things, if one knows how to use it." [43]

A man without love was a menace to himself and to society. He "knew no greatness of spirit or excellence [*Vollkommenheiten*], nor had he ever felt either the inner worth of such qualities, nor externally [experienced them] for the good of mankind."[44] In a world in which "everyone breathes love and sexual attraction [*Wollust*]" such a person remained "alone and isolated."[45] Isolation was not only a personal tragedy, but a social one: "The single man lives for himself; the married man drags throughout his life the heavy burden of being yoked [*Gespannschaft*]."[46] This burden was, however, his stake in society and society's very lifeblood. In a comparison with the celibate priesthood, one contemporary wrote that "the citizen [*Bürger*] is tied by marriage to the state [*Staat*] as the clergyman is by celibacy to the church; for the one supports everything concerning the welfare of the state, in which and through which his children find their own welfare, and the other everything concerning the power and majesty of the church."[47]

This exploration of the sexual drive passed through marriage, love, and altruism to arrive, finally, at the state/society. This analogic slide was something the practitioners of civil society commonly tried in vain to interrupt by distinguishing the sexual drive from love.[48] They never succeeded. The dual usage of "love" (*Liebe*) to mean both the tender emotion and physical desire was common throughout the period.[49] Even a writer like Villaume, who was intent on distinguishing physical desire from love, nevertheless found himself using a sexual term, "preservative" or condom, to describe love's function. The point is not that the practitioners of civil

---

[42] Anon., ["Je"], review of Thomas Abbt's, *Über innere und äussere Bestimmung des Jünglings zum künftigen nützlichen Mitgliede der menschlichen Gesellschaft. Nebst einer Abhandlung über die Bestimmung des Mädchens* (Halberstadt, 1794), in *NADB* 19.2 (1795): 549.

[43] Villaume, *Allgemeine Theorie*, 556.

[44] "N," "Ueber das Wort und Begrif Liebe," *Hann. Mag.* 18.62 (4 August 1780): col. 991.

[45] Anon., "Nachrichten von einer seltsamen Irrung eines menschlichen Triebes," *Beitr.z.B.* 2 (1789): 329.

[46] Anon., "Gedanken über den Ehestand," *JaJ* 11.2 (1788): 101.

[47] Anon., "Vorbereitung zu den künftigen Preisschriften," 164.

[48] See Hoof, *Pestalozzi*, 442–47, on their efforts to achieve a dichotomy between love and sexual desire.

[49] "N" devoted an entire essay, "Ueber das Wort and Begrif Liebe," to clearing up this problem. Some random examples of using *Liebe* to mean the sexual drive: Johann G. Herder, "Liebe und Selbstheit," *TM* 4 (1781): 219; anon., "Ehelosigkeit der Geistlichen," 242–54; anon., "Ueber die politische Räthlichkeit des geistlichen Zölibats," *TM* 1 (1783): 243; "Rs," review of *Liebe. Was sie ist und seyn sollte* (Gotha, 1790), *ADB* 98.2 (1791): 599. These examples could be endlessly multiplied.

society worshiped at the altar of sex, but that, even if they did not want to, they intuited a deep connection between the sexual drive and the foundation of society through the ties it might form via emotional love, marriage, and children.

More than this, however, the mature sexual drive was seen as crucial to the development of the useful citizen. Sexual maturity not only marked the completion of the individual, it actually caused it. The energy the individual inherited through this process was the very motor of productivity and of public life. This argument appeared again and again in the discussion of celibacy; as a contributor to the *Deutsche Monatsschrift* put it:

> The creator of nature has not laid this love [*Liebe,* referring to sexual desire] in our hearts for nothing! It is the sun which ripens the fruits of the man! It helps that deeply buried seed of good develop in us; and the unfortunate one whom the law [of celibacy] orders to flee this all-warming sun as if from the very light of day, must not only renounce the most beautiful pleasure of life, but also the great mainspring [*Triebfeder*] of his social perfection/destiny [*gesellschaftlichen Vervollkommnung*].[50]

And this argument was repeated again and again in the antimasturbation tracts, for this was the physiological heart of their message. If one squandered sexual energy prematurely, then "the sexual drive cannot be to people what it is supposed to be," namely, the finishing school of body and mind: "All ideas, emotions and desires [*Neigungen*] of people receive [at puberty], if [the sexual drive] ripens at the right time and in the right way, a higher degree of consistency . . . it is a certain feeling of inner power and—I would say masculinity, if the observation did not concern both sexes—that fills him." Those who have interfered with their sexual development "can never achieve this feeling of a real superfluity of energies"; in Bauer's terms, "his character can never receive [*empfangen*] solidity through the sexual drive."[51]

This conviction was a modern restatement of the venerable medical view of sperm as the magic elixir and quintessence of bodily energy, addition of which made "all the functions of the body go better."[52] The energy flowing from sexual potency completed the individual, and only on this miniature completion could the larger completion (*Vervollkommnung*) of society be based. Dr. Karl Friedrich Burdach, an expert on impotence and the medical authority on whom the canonical nineteenth-century liberal theorist Carl Theodor Welcker relied for his appeals to (sexual) nature,[53] stated the matter succinctly:

> Love of humankind and obedience to moral laws are virtues whose practice demands a pure and strong soul, which is supported by a healthy [physical] organization equipped with the necessary degree of energy. Weakness and bodily disabilities are the major causes

---

[50] Anon., "Auch ein Wort über Priesterehe," 82.

[51] Bauer, *Über die Mittel,* 266, 267, 268.

[52] Georg Sarganeck, *Ueberzeugende und bewegliche Warnung vor allen Sünden der Unreinigkeit und Heimlichen Unzucht: darinnen aus Medicinischen u. Theologischen Gründen vernünftig vorgestellt wird,* 2d ed. (Züllichau, 1746), 41.

[53] Carl Theodor Welcker, "Geschlechtverhältnisse," in *Staats-Lexikon, oder Encyklopädie der Staatswissenschaften,* ed. Carl Theodor Welcker and Karl Rotteck (Altona, 1836), 6:642.

of that mad self-love by which one regards oneself as the center of creation and in the end loses all feeling for the joys and sorrows of other beings. Of all the bodily disabilities, however, none produces more hard egoism than impotence.[54]

The association of sexual maturity, sexual potency, solidity of character, citizenship, marriage, and social stability formed a tightly wound tautology, in which each term flowed ineluctably into the other. Indeed, the very condition of being human was defined in this constellation in which the sexual component was absolutely necessary. Hence, the common descriptions of nuns and monks as "these unfortunate middle things [*unseeligen Mitteldinger*]," "these hermaphroditic creatures [*Zwittergeschöpfe*]," or of bachelors as "sick souls."[55] The free-thinking mayor of Königsberg, Theodor von Hippel, champion of early liberalism and female civil emancipation, made a characteristically pithy summary of this linked chain: "The word 'father' is a great word, the greatest that exists in a state [*Staat*]. Whoever is not [a father] does not deserve the name citizen! and, even being generous, only half deserves the name human!"[56]

The tautology we have been examining shows that the traditional association of sexual maturity, sufficient subsistence, marriage, and citizen rights had been elaborated upon and consequently transformed. The old entry to this sequence had been "sufficient subsistence"; whoever could show economic adequacy had the privilege of legitimate sexual expression (marriage) and the subsequent social, economic, and perhaps political rights that accrued to it. Now, this entry occurred earlier, at "sexual maturity." This move reflected the underlying assumption of civil society: that the operative principle was not an economically threatened social order, but the individual, stripped of his social differences, reduced to a common body governed by universal, natural laws. When one threw off the "fashion that had strictly separated" and thus, in the absence of social distinction, made "all people brothers," as Schiller wrote, one was left with the naked body.[57] This body's sexual characteristics then became central to defining its essence. The putatively natural sexual characteristics were filled with content not much different for the practitioners of civil society than it had been for the absolutists and before: timely, procreative heterosexual drive. It was comforting to hang onto this older vision, because according to it, the sexual drive was naturally self-limiting, produced a stable social form (marriage), and encouraged economic productivity. On this rock one could build civil society.

But the traditional sequence of associations was being extended at the other end as well: citizenship meant more. This was true in two respects. First, the passive subject was changing into the active citizen. At least potentially, he would shape the positive laws governing his own life. Since the practitioners of civil society envi-

---

[54] Burdach, *Eugon*, 29–30.

[55] Anon., "Soll man ihnen Weiber geben?" 203–4; anon., "Ehelosigkeit der Geistlichen," 253; anon., "Eheglück," *Schl. Prov. Bl.* 11 (1790): 519.

[56] Theodor Gottlieb von Hippel, *Ueber die Ehe*, 2d ed. (Berlin, 1776), 5.

[57] In his "Ode to Joy."

sioned themselves (tacitly and unconsciously perhaps) as the model of the universal citizen, by the 1780s and 1790s they had little trouble imagining that their exemplary rationality entitled them to share, if modestly, in the process of bringing the state's positive law into congruence with natural law. At the very least, they certainly viewed themselves as shapers of civil society. Second, as civil society developed, citizenship would expand to include more and more people. For "citizen" meant more than the organized, legal, and potentially political aspect of a person's life. It was the crowning title for a process of development, the fulfillment of one's destiny as a free human being, the sign one had reached one's full potential as a rational creature. Hence its normativity. The citizen was what all human beings *should* become. Following the sexual script was as necessary to this fulfillment as following the rational script, for both followed natural law and both participated in defining the human. And both were the attributes of true freedom, which entailed discovering the laws of nature, willing them, and acting them. Therefore, it is hardly surprising to find contemporaries thinking of the impetus to freedom in sexual terms. The reviewer in the *Allgemeine Deutsche Bibliothek* could be sure his audience would understand perfectly when he compared the "drive to freedom as a necessary result of the true culture of reason" to "the sexual drive [*Begattungstrieb*] as the result of the use of bodily energies."[58] He could depend on the widespread resonance of the sequence of associations we have been examining. Which returns us to Hippel's formulation. The legitimate expression of the sexual drive (timely, procreative heterosexual acts within marriage) had been a limited privilege under absolutist circumstances, and had become a virtual right and duty under civil society. The reader will recall the symbiotic, indivisible reciprocity in cameralist thinking between rights and duties. This feature of German social thinking reappears here in a sexual aspect. The right was an expression of biological necessity (Beccaria), of the fulfillment of human nature, energy, and freedom. The duty was to an orderly and institutionalized expansion of society (a secular reworking of God's admonition to be fruitful and multiply). Evading one's sexual duties, as Hippel wrote, meant one was not a citizen—and hardly a human being.

It has been necessary to describe in some detail the positive views the practitioners of civil society held about the sexual drive in order to counter the widespread belief that the advent of civil society, or bourgeois morality, which is often presented as the shorthand formula for it, inaugurated a regime of sexual repression. After reading umpteen antimasturbation tracts it is in fact easy to forget that it was precisely their almost worshipful attitude toward sexual energy and heterosexual maturity that moved the pamphleteers to such paroxysms of repressive-seeming concern.[59] In fact, the late-eighteenth-century pamphleteers aimed not at repres-

[58] In the *ADB* 109.2 (1792): 606, cited in Johanna Schultze, *Die Auseinandersetzung zwischen Adel und Bürgertum in den deutschen Zeitschriften der letzten drei Jahrzehnte des 18. Jahrhunderts 1773–1806* (Berlin, 1925), 112 n. 4.

[59] Cf. Hoof, *Pestalozzi*, 447, but cf. 449 and 453.

sion, but at an ideal of moderate, sensible sexual pleasure. Here the doctors, moralists, pedagogues, state theorists, and philosophers were all of one mind. Furthermore, they applied no different standard to sexual enjoyment than they did to other sorts of consumption (such as food and drink, reading, or emotional indulgence).[60] The moralist Carl Friedrich Bahrdt received a good review in the *Allgemeine Deutsche Bibliothek* for his rules of sexual moderation:

> The sexual drive should be satisfied (1) never to the point of destruction, but instead to aid bodily health, and only under conditions of a completely mature body, by means of natural coitus [i.e. man with woman, procreatively], with a naturally aroused drive [i.e., not "artificially" stimulated], a healthy body and not during digestion or other activities, without vehement passions, but calmly; (2) in marriage . . . ,[61] that is, no promiscuous sexual contacts; (3) moderately. Energy determines the amount, of which the sign is that no exhaustion should follow; (4) modestly and cleanly; (5) quietly with the spouse.[62]

The reviewer of Bauer's book counted fewer rules, but the message was identical.[63]

As we saw in the last chapter, the exercise of freedom, as the practitioners conceived it, brought with it by definition the demand for self-control; otherwise, one was enslaved to one's passions or desires, and slavery was, of course, the very opposite of freedom. This insight was the framework within which sexual moderation was understood. As a last example let us cite the preeminent moralist of his day, Gellert, who, with his unerring instinct for the mainstream, gave this excellent summary of "the duties regarding the capacities of the heart, and particularly of the domination [*Herrschaft*] over its desires [*Begierden*] and passions":

> This duty consists in the soul's ability carefully and wisely to rule [*regieren*] and apply our natural desires consonant with their intentions and objects—to weaken them, when they are stronger and more continuous than their object demands; to awaken them, if they are weaker than the fulfillment of their intention requires; in short, so to arrange each of these desires [*Neigungen*] so that they do not harm but rather help the system of our other drives, which affect our own and other's welfare. . . . Without this domination [*Herrschaft*] the natural drives, which affect the maintenance of our life and external welfare, degenerate into destructive passions.[64]

Sexual desire was subject to the same rules of moderation as the other sensual drives:

---

[60]"I do not say *avoid emotions* [*Empfindungen*]; that would be neither possible nor advisable." Villaume, "Über die Unzuchtssünden," 146. On diet, see ibid., 95. On reading, see Bauer, *Über die Mittel*, 198n; on moderate, but not repressed emotion, see anon., "Anzeige der Geburts- und Todten-Listen aus verschiedenen Orten von Franken. Vom Jahr 1760," *Fränkischen Sammlungen von Anmerkungen aus der Naturlehre, Arzneygelahrheit, Oekonomie und den damit verwandten Wissenschaften* (1761): 188–89.

[61]Here Bahrdt outlined his latitudinarian understanding of marriage, meaning any regulated, consensual intercourse, including prostitution. This idiosyncratic view would have been highly debatable.

[62]"Rr," review of Carl Friedrich Bahrdt's, *System der moralischen Religion* (1787), *ADB* 85.2 (1789): 372–73.

[63]Anon., review of Bauer's, *Über die Mittel*, 520–21.

[64]Gellert, *Moralische Vorlesungen*, 2, 398, 403–4.

The desire [*Verlangen*] for sensual pleasure and the love that both sexes feel for each other according to divine arrangement are within certain bounds innocent. The continuous striving to contain this natural desire, consonant with its intention, within the bounds of reason and conscience as set by God, is the control [*Beherrschung*] of the same. Outside these bounds it becomes a dishonoring, furious, and animalistic passion, and thus the control [*Herrschaft*] over it is a good of great worth, and a continuing human duty.[65]

Other writers put the matter more positively, for example, in terms of the greater, longer-lasting pleasure or happiness one achieved by expressing one's sexual capacities in a moderate fashion, but the virtually unanimous opinion was that the sexual drive was a kind of raw energy whose physical, moral, and social beneficence was only truly realized when it was domesticated.[66] Once again we are returned to the sequence of associations, in which sexual drive moved from nature, through reason, to culture.

The Male Sexual Model

No doubt the reader will have already noticed from the language of the eighteenth-century pamphleteers that their discussion of the sexual drive related almost solely to men. This long-standing cultural conflation, so deep an assumption that it often seems to have been unconscious, was especially useful as a metaphor for a similar, usually unspoken conflation, namely that of the universal individual, citizen and the male.

The male sexual model had a long history. The ancients bequeathed to Europeans competing theories of semen and conception, with different consequences for interpreting sexual physiology and pleasure.[67] Broadly, Aristotle and his followers considered male sexual physiology perfect; semen caused conception by itself (the one-seed theory). The sexual desire and functioning of women were therefore irrelevant. Galen, whose teachings exercised great influence on medieval and early modern doctors, believed that both men and women contributed to conception through the seed each expelled during coitus (the two-seed theory). Male and female sexual desire was equally important to conception. Galen further expressed the analogous contributions of male and female by conceiving of the female genitalia as internal versions of the male: the vagina was an inverted penis, the clitoris a miniature echo of the penis, and the ovaries were testicles inside the body, rather than outside. At different times, Galen's or Aristotle's theories were more or less dominant among European doctors and sages. But both theories

---

[65] Ibid., 408–9.

[66] Some further examples illustrating the aim of moderation, not repression: anon. ["K-f-d"], "Ueber das Verhältniß beyder Geschlechter," *TM* 1 (1781): 106–34, esp. 111; anon., "Milet. An den Herrn Verfasser der Abhandlung über die heimlichen Sünde der Jugend," *Hyp. Br.* 3 (1788): 201–7, esp. 204; anon., "Etwas zur Erziehung der Mägden," *Hann.Mag.* 1.39 (16 May 1763): cols. 609–16, esp. 612–13; anon., "Fragmente"; Christian Salzmann's "Vorrede" to Bauer, *Über die Mittel*, vii-viii.

[67] My discussion is indebted to Jacquart and Thomasset, *Sexuality and Medicine*, and Thomas Laqueur, *Making Sex: Body and Gender from the Greeks to Freud* (Cambridge, Mass., 1990). Laqueur stresses, perhaps too much, the hegemony of the two-seed theory down to the eighteenth century.

reckoned sexual desire and sexual physiology according to the male model. This is obvious in the Aristotelian teachings, where women's sexual imperfection relative to man's is so complete that she is barely required for reproducing the species. Aristotle did not deny that women experienced sexual pleasure, but, significantly, he attributed it to their ejaculation of a nonseminal fluid; that is, the physiology of sexual pleasure was so supremely male that it demanded analogous functioning in the female. Although Galen took female sexual pleasure more seriously, his two-seed theory and his notion of female genital inversion makes it plain that he considered female sexual economy an analogue of the male. Furthermore, his theory of humors, which dominated Western medicine into the early modern period and beyond, allotted to males the dominant characteristic of heat which was synonymous with sexual desire and successful sexual activity.[68]

The male sexual model in all its variants made men the peculiarly sexual sex— their nature was primed for it and congruent with it,[69] their bodies were the measure of it, their desire for it was natural and expected. The medieval inheritance of early modern medicine in no way denied the woman's sexual desire or pleasure, but the supposed analogous quality of her sex organs and her colder humors created an unacknowledged linkage between men and sexual activity. One sees this linkage at work even in the writings of the famous baroque authority on sex, Dr. Nicolas Venette, whose awareness and indeed awe of female sexual capacity was both beyond question and emblematic of medieval and early modern opinion. Venette's immense, learned but also sprightly volume on generation (1696) spread throughout Europe in translation, retranslation, and pirated copy. It appeared in German in 1711 and remained the most popular compendium of sexual knowledge of the entire century.[70] Venette provided detailed information on sexual physiology, but more important from our perspective, on sexual desire and pleasure. Although he acknowledged women's greater sexual capacity, he could not believe that women experienced greater desire or pleasure than men. He ended his long discussion of this subject with a qualitative assertion: "Because nature made our [men's] lust

---

[68] Jacquart and Thomasset, *Sexuality and Medicine,* 141–43, 49.

[69] The association of women with sexual *sin* was a product of religious, not medical theory. Similarly, the religious association of women with uncontrolled sexual desire emphasized the woman's putative lack of self-control, not necessarily her stronger sexual drive.

[70] See the enthusiastic review in the *ADB:* anon. ["Hf"] review of Dr. Niklas Venette's, *Geheimnisse keuscher Liebeswerke, mit Einschaltungen aus den neuesten Naturforschern und Aerzten* (Dresden, 1785), *ADB* 91.2 (1790): 412. It is uncertain whether Venette actually wrote all the editions and translations attributed to him. I have used the 1711 translation, which is unquestionably his: Nicolai Venette, *Abhandlung von Erzeugung der Menschen* (Leipzig, 1711). A popularized, possibly spurious Cologne edition of 1724, *Tableau de l'Amour: Die Geheimnisse keuscher Liebes-Wercke, In gesegnetem Kinder-Zeugen Zu Fortpflanzung des Menschlichen Geschlechts und Erhaltung der Familien,* went through many editions. On authenticity and dating, see Hoof, *Pestalozzi,* 563 n. 342, also 478–84; Roy Porter, "'The Secrets of Generation Display'd': *Aristotle's Master-Piece* in Eighteenth-Century England," in *'Tis Nature's Fault: Unauthorized Sexuality during the Enlightenment,* ed. Robert P. Maccubbin (Cambridge, 1987), 1–21, 1; Roy Porter, "Spreading Carnal Knowledge or Selling Dirt Cheap? Nicholas Venette's *Tableau de l'Amour Conjugal* in Eighteenth-Century England," *Journal of European Studies* 14 (1984): 233–55; and Peter Wagner, *Eros Revived. Erotica of the Enlightenment in England and America* (London, 1990), 11.

[*Wollust*] of shorter duration, nature also ordained that it be greater, and since women's enjoyment is less, nature made it longer."[71]

The peril in such argumentation was that men's putatively stronger sexual pleasure/desire might harm their elevated image relative to women by connecting them with the negative association of sex as animalistic rather than rational-human. Venette closed off this possibility with an old piece of sophistry that found new life in the eighteenth century. Although men were indeed hotter than women and went about their sexual business with more energy, still, "because the man has a much stronger mind [*geist*] than the woman has, he is not so subject to haste and disorderly [sexual] impulse. It appears that his passion is somewhat moderated by reason, whereas the desire [*neigung*] of a woman is without order and moderation."[72]

Reason, the single most powerful organizing idea of the eighteenth century, thus vouchsafed to men the positive associations of sexual energy while protecting them from the negative ones. This happy solution was another example of the movement from nature to culture: raw male sexual drive was theoretically subject to cultural taming within the individual male himself. In this way drive, whose undomesticated urgency threatened to enslave the individual to his irrational passions and was thus the very exemplar of slavery/unfreedom, became instead tempered into desire, subject to will, and thus "free." This transformation of drive into willed desire is the key to the eighteenth-century's thinking about sexual behavior in relation to society.

And, once again, this transformation occurred solely for males. In the realm of sexual moderation the formal analogue to reason in males was modesty in females. Modesty, insofar as it was more than a mere character attribute, was the product of education, not a basic faculty. Unlike reason, it was hardly the principle differentiating humans from other creatures, nor could it be used to discover the knowledge or generate the progress on which society, economy, and politics rested. In short, modesty was not analogous to reason in any other connection; it was a metaphoric dead end, whereas reason led on to freedom. This elementary connection between the possession of greater reason and the enjoyment of greater freedom is fully reflected in eighteenth-century sexual stereotypes. Central among these was the assertion that sexual desire and activity was more tangential to the male than to the female, thus "freeing" the male for his public duties.[73] Bauer's literal-mindedness understood this popular idea physically: for men "the desire for purely sexual satisfaction [*Geilheit*] *expresses itself almost exclusively in those parts which, according to their position and nature, are not essential or indispensible to life*," whereas for women, the physical and emotional consequences of sexual activity were almost life determining.[74] Venette discussed the same phenomenon from a more psychological

[71] Venette, *Abhandlung*, 207, also 145–48, 175.

[72] Ibid., 145.

[73] Jean-Jacques Rousseau put this most cogently in his *Emile, or On Education* (1762), trans. Allan Bloom (New York, 1979), esp. 361.

[74] Bauer, *Über die Mittel*, 75, 88, emphasis in original.

perspective. "Love [meaning sexual desire] is such a crazy and powerful emotion," he wrote, "that one usually finds it in its extreme forms more among the lower than among the higher spirits [gemüthern]. . . . The weakest of all, among whose number are women, are much more entangled in it than we are." By this he meant that their lives were much more devoted to it and that sexual attachments meant much more to them, from which principle he derived the old stereotype of male sexual (and emotional) promiscuity. Venette's language, however, was political: "Our spirit is always too free [frey] to subject us to a tyrannical constancy [tyrannischen beständigkeit]."[75]

The male sexual model thus assigned to men powerful, but self-controlled sexual desire whose qualities of egotistic energy, self-willing, and rational self-limitation were metaphorical rehearsals of the arguments for political freedom. The elaboration of this model by Kant and Fichte in helping to determine political freedom and subjection will concern us shortly. At the moment we must turn to another important cluster of associations contained by the male sexual model. These were vitalism or life force, mental energy, and creativity.

These associations were accomplished in a single figure: semen. According to Danielle Jacquart and Claude Thomasset, "The connection between brain, spinal cord, and semen (and its affinities with the cosmos) seems to have originated in the beliefs of ancient Persia."[76] Supported by the notion of the fungibility of bodily fluids, this connection remained lively throughout the eighteenth century.[77] Semen was the most precious distillation of, depending on one's viewpoint, blood, (nervous) spinal fluid, or energy-giving food. The Swiss doctor Tissot called it "the Essential Oil" to "all the functions that are any wise important, of the animal machine." According to Dr. J. P. Frank, it "contributes a useful and spiritual [geistigen] part to the blood from which strength and health are increased." According to Villaume, those lacking semen (women, eunuchs, sexually profligate males) remained "well below the activity, the energies, and all qualities of body and soul characteristic of the complete [male]."[78]

More than physical energy, semen was "pure life force" (Lebenskraft),[79] the seed of mental creativity. This association easily derived from the ancient belief that semen was a product of or related to the brain and nervous system. "We notice," Karl Friedrich Burdach wrote, "a wonderful harmony between the productive energy of the soul and that of the body; these energies mutually support one

---

[75] Venette, Abhandlung, 238, 240. These pages also contain Venette's discussion of female modesty.

[76] Jacquart and Thomasset, Sexuality and Medicine, 53; also concerning theories of male semen, see 52–60, and female semen, 61–70.

[77] Barbara Duden, Geschichte unter der Haut. Ein Eisenacher Arzt und seine Patientinnen um 1730 (Stuttgart, 1987), chap. 4, parts 5–6.

[78] Samuel Auguste André David Tissot, Onanism: Or, a Treatise Upon the Disorders Produced by Masturbation: Or, the Dangerous Effects of Secret and Excessive Venery, trans. A. Hume (New York, 1985), 52, 51; Frank, System, 1:106 (also see Venette, Abhandlung, 318–20; Burdach, Eugon, 38–39; Vogel, Unterricht für Eltern, 141–43; among others); Villaume, "Über die Unzuchtssünden," 44.

[79] Faust, Geschlechtstrieb, 3.

another, rising and sinking together. Therefore all the greatest geniuses of all centuries have shown a lively desire [*Hang*] for the pleasures of love."[80] Georg Sarganeck, among the first German writers to discuss masturbation (1746), made clear the double connection between semen and intellectual power: "*Semen is the most powerful, highly spiritual and most noble fluid of the human body, which is made of identical or related material as the nervous fluid.*" He insisted not only that semen was fundamentally related to nervous energy and thus to movement altogether, but also that the testes, which produced semen, were highly analogous to the brain, which produced thoughts:

> From anatomy it is common knowledge and undeniable that the fabrication of the testes is extremely close to the structure of the brain and the *medullae spinalis* in subtlety and kind. Now, God has made it such in all of nature, that where there are similar organs, there are also similar structures and similar products; therefore we can say that the testes as well as the brain produce a fluid which is of the highest degree of strength compared to the other fluids of the body, a *fluidum activissimum et movendi potens.*[81]

Semen was therefore the metaphoric link between brain and nerves, whence arose male creativity, that is intelligent, innovative action upon the world. Thus male creativity, in silent analogy to female procreativity, was represented as also somehow genital. The equation of (male) idea with (female) conception, literally in the case of Aristotle or even in William Harvey (who thought of conception as the womb having an idea sparked by sperm), is too well known to need lengthy demonstration.[82] The important point is that in the eighteenth century as creativity came to be reinterpreted as overwhelmingly rational-intellectual, as occurring in science, institution-building, and manufacturing, it could be ascribed exclusively to males with the help of a model that had long since associated brainpower, life force, and male sexual apparatus. As that recondite Enlightener Johann Georg Hamann admitted to Herder, "My coarse imagination has never been able to envision a creative spirit without genitalia."[83]

Another aspect of the male sexual model was the (limited) definition of the sexual act. The pan-sexual assumptions of the twentieth century permit the imagining of all kinds of acts and relations as sexual or quasi-sexual; these are then endlessly categorized along different axes: according to object choice (hetero- or homosexual), degree of pleasure (orgasmic or non-), putative physical or psychological origin of pleasure (expressed in preferences for different orifices and/or for equal or unequal power relations); and so on. The sexual act for the eighteenth century was

---

[80] Burdach, *Eugon*, 27. The interaction of body and mind was generally assumed by eighteenth-century science and philosophy; the rigorous split between them is only characteristic of later times. Ludmilla Jordanova, *Sexual Visions: Images of Gender in Science and Medicine between the Eighteenth and Twentieth Centuries* (Madison, Wis., 1989), 26.

[81] Sarganeck, *Warnung*, 36–37 (Sarganeck's emphasis), 38.

[82] Laqueur, *Making Sex*, discusses the relation of males to conception in Western thinking from antiquity to the present. For his discussion of Harvey, see 142.

[83] Johann Georg Hamann to Johann Gottfried Herder, 23 May 1768, *Briefwechsel*, ed. Walther Ziesemer and Arthur Henkel (Wiesbaden, 1955—), 2: 415, cited in Derks, *Die Schande*, 64.

simpler. Its parameters were set by male sexual organization and by the exclusively male viewpoint of the writers who discussed it. Consequently, real sex demanded penetration and, because pleasure was understood to be caused by expelling the seed, ejaculation. Without penetration and ejaculation, acts might be thought harmful, dishonorable, or sinful, but they were not considered truly sexual. This, from the perspective of later times, narrow construal of real sex survived longest in the institutionalized form of legal precedent, where both penetration and ejaculation were for a long time required to define rape and continued to be necessary throughout the nineteenth century to define (illegal) homosexual acts.[84]

The second quality of sexual acts according to the male model was their violence, both physical and social. The physical violence (and thus danger) pertained to men: they were considered to be the active agent, and thus they lost energy; but more important, they lost semen, the elixir of life. Ejaculation appears in the literature as a "violent ejection" "which looks like a certain convulsion of the entire body," making men afterward exhausted and vulnerable in ways women were not.[85] The socially violent effects of sexual activity concerned women, however, for it was their social status which abruptly changed according to their sexual status—and they were not active in determining this, as they were not considered to be active in the sexual act itself. Law recognized rape as a double example where violence and sexually determined social status coincided: the forced ruination of the woman's chances for a secure social life (via marriage) was the specific grounds for criminalization. But even voluntary extramarital relations were held to destroy the woman's social standing, as the infanticide debate made clear. The literature routinely represented such consummated sexual relations as a "triumph" over the woman's "honor,"[86] suggesting that a battle had occurred. The power of men's sexual potency to transform the social standing of women was just as true on the positive, legitimate side of the ledger as on the illegitimate. Only through marriage, sealed by sex, could women be "manumitted," as Hippel put it. Therefore they owed gratitude to the man "who freed you from the slavery you experienced in your parents' house."[87] One reviewer understood Hippel's social point sexually, as a violent emancipation from enforced sexual continence: "The woman who is ripped [entrissen] by a man from her virginal estate [Stand], in which perhaps she would against her will and desire have had to remain longer, possibly for her whole life, owes thanks to the man who chose her from among so many and who nourishes her and often her relatives and maintains her at the level of her estate [standesmäßig]."[88] According to the male sexual model, then, the sexual act was perilous because of the

---

[84] See Derks's interesting discussion in Die Schande, 40–42.

[85] Sarganeck, Warnung, 35. Also, Tissot, Onanism, 57–69; Venette, Abhandlung, 117–18; on the resulting sexual danger to men, McLaren, Contraception, 55, 112; on the violence of the sexual act, see Laqueur, Making Sex, 45–46.

[86] For example, anon., "Die vernünftige Frau (Eine wahre Geschichte, aus dem Englischen)," N. Mannig. 2.1 (1779): 295.

[87] Hippel, Ueber die Ehe, 116.

[88] Anon., review of Theodor Gottlieb Hippel's Ueber die Ehe, in Hann.Mag. (1777): col. 700.

power it unleashed. Since that power was identified as male and since it was actively unleashed by the male, he stood to suffer the direct physical consequences of it. But he also enjoyed the enhanced social stature that accrued from wielding it. His sexual activity was able to a certain degree to define social relations, to make or destroy the social standing of women, to free them from parental tutelage or consign them to social dishonor and oblivion.

Women's Place in the Male Sexual Model

As sexual derivatives of men, women willy-nilly shared in a number of the qualities the male sexual model postulated as human. Foremost among these were the existence of an equally urgent sexual drive and the ability to achieve pleasure through ejaculation of the female seed. But we have seen subtle differences as well. Women were thought to need sexual intercourse more for their health,[89] and they were less harmed by it because they lost less vital energy. The latter was true because women here held to be passive during intercourse, they received men's seed, whereas their own seed was less perfect and therefore less precious than the male's.[90] Women were thus the less perfect example of the male sexual model.

These subtle discrepancies between male and female sexual nature had been long discussed. More important from our perspective was another, subtler difference that began to take shape in the early modern and Enlightened periods. This concerned sexual desire as a willed activity, as opposed to a mere animal-like drive. Women's greater need for sex (for health reasons), their putatively passive sexual role, the lack of identification of their gender with energy and (sexual) violence, all subtly undermined the idea of autonomous female desire. This lack of willed desire was often expressed as lack of control due to a weaker mind or body, or to a greater sexual capacity and thus insatiability, which translated into a lack of internal limits.

The discussion of women's willed sexual desire was overtly social: that is, its function was to establish gender relations on firm, hierarchical grounds. Since the starting point was, once again, the man and his needs and desires, whereas the woman was for the most part conceived entirely in relation to him, the discussion easily slipped from sexual matters to the entire panoply of gendered social relations, especially to marriage and family. The sexual content is often present as a shadow in discussions of pedagogy, women's virtue, or literature. It is therefore impossible to separate the sexual aspects from the social and would be distorting to try, since they were mutually determining.

The main argument one encounters in the late eighteenth century was not that women did not or could not experience sexual desire or set about achieving sexual

[89] Venette, *Abhandlung,* 330; Bauer, *Über die Mittel,* 49–50; Jacquart and Thomasset, *Sexuality and Medicine,* 152–54; Boucé, "Some Sexual Beliefs," 44. Tissot, *Onanism,* 160, thought this widespread opinion exaggerated.

[90] On female seed, see Jacquart and Thomasset, *Sexuality and Medicine,* 61–70, and Laqueur, *Making Sex,* 35–52.

satisfaction, but that they *should* not. It was an entirely secular moral argument. Its contours recall Rousseau: although the woman has "unlimited desires," she contains these through modesty and taste, and ultimately receives her sexual satisfaction by subordinating herself completely to her husband's sexual wishes. Female sexual satisfaction thus became entirely indirect and relational; contingent upon male desire, it lost its own autonomy. Rousseau, especially his *Emile* (which contains the most thorough account of the author's sexual views), was very popular in Germany.[91] *Emile* was indisputably the central pedagogical text in Germany; Campe reissued it (in translation) in his *General Revision*, and citing it was simply obligatory for everyone writing on education, women, and social-sexual topics like male-female relations and even masturbation. But like most icons of cultural opinion, Rousseau was probably less influential in terms of setting a trend, than he was in marking views that had been current for some time: "What oft was thought, but ne'er so well expressed."[92] Rousseau's ideas of female subordination and their sexual foundation and elaboration at most sorted, coordinated, and extended hoary notions of female sexual danger and male superiority. His real innovation, embedded in his subtle and often contradictory sexual-psychological musings, was rarely picked up by German writers.[93] What interested them was rather the context in which Rousseau placed the old notions of male dominance and female subordination: the education of people to become citizens of a new civil society. Rousseau placed great weight on the importance of the individual and his or her sexual constitution to the social order;[94] the linking of the sexual/gender foundation of individualism and society was new, because both individualism and civil society were new.

Turning to the German writings, we see a flatter picture of female sexual desire, stripped of the psychological conundrums Rousseau had assigned it. Instead, we find a simple condemnation of sexually desirous young women, as in Christoph M. Wieland's offhand remark about the possibly ill effects of racy literature on "precocious boys and ardent [male] youths (ardent girls don't exist, because for those

---

[91] Rousseau, *Emile*, esp. 357–65. Also see the excellent discussion of Susan M. Okin, *Women in Western Political Thought* (Princeton, 1979), 99–194. For an uncritical and idiosyncratic discussion of Rousseau, see Joel Schwarz, *The Sexual Politics of Jean-Jacques Rousseau* (Chicago, 1984). I also—very briefly—touch on the reception given Rousseau's sexual ideas in Germany in "Sexualität," 57–60. On German reception of Rousseau in general, see Claus Süßenberger, *Rousseau im Urteil der deutschen Publizistik bis zum Ende der Französischen Revolution. Ein Beitrag zur Rezeptionsgeschichte* (Frankfurt, 1974); and Bernhard Weissel, *Von wem die Gewalt in den Staaten herrührt. Beiträge zu den Auswirkungen der Staats- und Gesellschaftsauffassungen Rousseaus auf Deutschland im letzten Viertel des 18. Jahrhunderts* (Berlin, 1963). *Emile* was translated immediately into German under the title *Aemile, oder von der Erziehung*, by Johann Joachim Schwabe.

[92] See Hentze, *Sexualität in der Pädagogik*, 17–46, esp. 41–44, on Rousseau's influence on eighteenth-century German sexual theories.

[93] I have briefly outlined these in "Sexualität," 58–59.

[94] This explains Rousseau's enthusiastic adoption of Tissot's concern about youthful masturbation, as well as the fact that Rousseau begins his discussion of Sophie's education, indeed grounds it, on her putative sexual nature.

that do, there is nothing further that can be ruined)."[95] Most of the writing on female sexual desire in fact focused on unmarried women, underscoring that autonomy was the real problem; once married, the woman's sexual expression was in any event subject to her husband's rule and was thus less threatening and even positive. Bauer made the autonomy issue clear in his discussion of "fallen" women. He pointed out that women often became sexually profligate [*Wollüstlinge*] for different reasons than men, who, he assumed, were ruthlessly pursuing their pleasure. Some women, of whom Bauer wrote sympathetically, "fell because of their good naturedness . . . ; the drive of hot desire [*Geilheit*] was not so urgent, was less the cause of their trespass than weakness in withstanding temptation. In them there is more of a passive feeling of comfort about sensual pleasure, which of course can spill over into dark longing, rather than a vehement, actively expressed desire [*ein heftiges, thätig geäußertes, Begehren*]." It was an entirely different matter with women whose motives were as sexual as men's. "But the [sexual] attention [to men] of those women in whom brutality [*Brutalität*] has spread, in whom an uncontrolled desire [*zügellosen Hang*] for lascivious excesses forms the foundation of their character, and who therefore know no limit, the attention of these women is always highly ambivalent, highly egotistical, and often makes way for the blackest malice and meanness."[96] Bauer here loads women's autonomous sexual desire with the usual negative associations of the sexual drive generally: animal-like violence (brutality), lack of control, insatiability. He warns men of the dangerous egotism at this sexual base, and it is clearly that quality which is most threatening.

A psychologically oriented interpretation of this material would doubtless stress the male fear of female sexual power or expression. Such speculation, in any case beyond my competence and inclination, is less relevant to a dissection of the social uses of sexual themes than is another fear, which is easily demonstrated. Bauer (and Wieland) both came to express their views on independent female sexual desire in a comparative context, in which men (married or not) were granted the right to posit their own desire, whereas (especially unmarried) women were not. Whatever ancient sexual fears may or may not have been at play, clearly gender differentiation played a central role. Women were not supposed to behave like men; they were not to appropriate characteristics now more and more associated with basic male identity, to which the sexual drive could not have been more fundamental. As the expression of active sexual desire came to be considered increasingly a male attribute, it became more and more socially dangerous for women to exhibit it.

This lesson is well illustrated by a typical, and therefore otherwise unremarkable, little story by J. F. Engelschall, which appeared in Wieland's journal in 1791.[97] It told of a spoiled, romantic young girl, Kordelia, whose French (of course!) gov-

---

[95] Christoph Martin Wieland, "Unterredung zwischen W** und dem Pfarrer zu ***," *TM* 1 (1775): 90.

[96] Bauer, *Über die Mittel*, 303–4n.

[97] J. F. Engelschall, "Kordelia," *NTM* 2 (1791), 26–27.

erness [*Hofmeisterin*] had filled her head with visions of fulfilling one's romantic desires. One such tale concerned a young nobleman who threw social convention to the winds and married a beautiful, but impoverished young woman, whom he once had found sleeping in a field and whose bosom had filled him with delight. His daring was rewarded (in the story) with a happy end. After hearing this tale, Kordelia falls asleep and dreams that she does exactly the same. She discovers an enchanting young man in a strange castle; after he has been absent for some time, she searches for him and finds him asleep on his bed. She is sexually aroused: "Charm suffused his manly-beautiful face, to which slumber had given new appeal. The half-visible breast with each breath lifted the cover of silver gauze decorated with real flowers, which lightly covered the beautiful limbs without hiding them." When he speaks Kordelia's name, "no moderation anymore! She was about to sink into [his] arms" when a servant youth interrupts and hands her a cup of wine. Just as "she lusted [*lüstern*] to taste it, . . . an icy shudder ran through her limbs. The cup had become a horrible skull; the roses surrounding it were sprayed with greenish moss and the wine had turned to blood, foaming and bubbling." Needless to say, this dreadful vision crushed her sexual desire; she awoke from her troubled sleep a chastened and more realistic young girl. The author's artistic inexpertise makes all too plain that Kordelia's transgression was to entertain a male dream of sexual self-determination independent of social convention.

The sexual metaphor was useful as a more powerful and compact expression for independent wishes altogether. The elision from one to the other is clear in the pedagogue Campe's *Fatherly Advice to My Daughter.* He began his list of specifically female virtues with "purity of heart," which consisted of "being aware of no evil thoughts or feelings, of no unpermitted intentions or wishes, no disorderly, impure and scandalous desires and passions [*Begierden und Leidenschaften*]." From this moral alpha of sexual commandments, Campe moved through other positive qualities (including chastity and modesty) to the omega; "and lastly a loving submission of her own will to the will of her husband, whence will gradually arise a completely sweet melting together of her own existence with his."[98] Suppressing sexual desire led ultimately to suppressing one's independence. The path connecting renunciation of independent sexual desire with subjection generally was becoming well trodden. When another pedagogue, Johann Daniel Hensel, neglected it in his description of the education of women to become good wives, the reviewer in the *Allgemeine Deutsche Bibliothek* curtly showed him the way: "We would have thought that a number of other highly necessary qualities for a future wife should have been added: modesty [*Verschämtheit*], habituation to limiting her own wishes and to obedience toward her parents, because a daughter who is used to having her own will and dominating over her parents, will never become a good

---

[98] Joachim Heinrich Campe, *Väterlicher Rath für meine Tochter* (Braunschweig, 1788), 134–35, cited in Pikulik, *Leistungsethik,* 154 and 152.

wife."[99] Modesty, which for women was always primarily sexual, ushered in the other renunciations of willing.

The purpose was not to make women passionless, but to redirect their desire from self-fulfillment to pleasure in serving others. Bauer expressed this typical idea in its social form: "Wife, mother, and overseer of the house is the purpose [*Bestimmung*] of the woman for the world; and also her absolute purpose, even for herself as an individual can never be achieved except via the capacity to fulfill these relative purposes; she will always be less, if she tries to be more, or different."[100] Although society gained from such wifely self-renunciation, the chief direct beneficiary was the husband. It was a small step from social altruism to complete sexual self-abnegation. The misogynist Brandes took that step. He suspected that even behind the Rousseauist reduction of women's desire to the mere desire to please men there might still lurk the rudiments of female sexual egoism. "The desire [*Begierde*] to please our sex, this . . . in and of itself natural desire, only deserves censure if it sinks to merely feeding [the woman's] self-centered pleasure."[101]

Although a strong trend, these were still ideas under construction.[102] Persons less committed to gender differentiation, or more committed to a truly genderless conception of individualism were relatively unimpressed with these sorts of arguments. It is not an accident that precisely someone like the freethinking nobleman, Ramdohr, held a less drastic view. Ramdohr believed that sexual characteristics of passivity and/or activity generally, but not always, correlated with gender; nonetheless, all persons were to some degree mixtures of sexual qualities. He therefore was not troubled by the vision of a somewhat independent woman. "She must have sufficient energy of character and independence to determine for herself the principles of her desire [*Wollen*] and action in those areas where, despite her union with a man, she can be judged as an individual person, an individual woman."[103] This conviction did not stop Ramdohr from subscribing to limited male domestic domination.[104] Yet Ramdohr's belief in the nondeterminate connection between the sexual drive and gender meant he had little need for the metaphorical associations that other writers found so compelling to ground social and domestic hierarchy.

The same was true for "Hr," the male censor of the *Neues Hannoversches Magazin* (1795). He took issue with an article (purportedly written by a woman) in extreme praise of female self-sacrifice. Writing modestly in the third person, he opined, "it also seemed to him that she regarded her sex too much as a mere means and too little as an end and to assume that we men, who are in any event arrogant

---

[99] Anon., review of Johann Daniel Hensel's, *System der weiblichen Erziehung, besonders für den mittlern und höhern Stand,* part 1 (Halle, 1787), *ADB* 79.2 (1788): 562.

[100] Bauer, *Über die Mittel,* 152.

[101] Brandes, *Ueber die Weiber,* 196.

[102] Brandes's book, for example, received a very mixed review in the *ADB* 101.1 (1791): 133–36.

[103] Ramdohr, *Venus Urania,* 2: 410–11.

[104] Ibid.

enough, were the main purpose of creation. Wife, mother, companion—and all that for the man! What if there were no men? Would women then have no worth, doesn't their existence have a purpose independent of men?"[105] From this Kantian perspective, too, the relation between sexual nature and gender is simply irrelevant, since the author views women as things in themselves, independently of their relation to men and hence as both sexless and genderless. Thus, the whole associational complex we have been examining operated most strongly when a practitioner was trying to establish or clarify relations between men and women or to ground or justify institutions on that analogy. When gender did not matter, or when no necessary connection between sexual nature and gender was postulated, then the chain of associations lost its argumentative power.

The argument denying independent, willed sexual desire to women tended also to cut women off from the rest of the chain of associations: lacking desire suggested they lacked energy, which suggested they were incapable of creativity and generally lacked the attributes required of full citizens. Not surprisingly, Brandes did not shrink from explicitly making these points in a long discussion of female sexual nature and its connection to civilized society. He admitted that "in single moments they perhaps surpass us in vehemence of sensual fury. They can enjoy longer than we are able to give." But, he asked rhetorically,

> Does one find among them the consuming desire [*Begierde*], the restless tumult that troubles the greatest, liveliest brains of those with sanguine temperament? . . .
>
> The high fire of enthusiasm, this product of energy, which fathers [*zeugen*] immortal works, cannot be theirs, because they lack energy. . . .
>
> Doesn't the very strength of male nerves prove the longer constancy of [men's] desires? Woman lacks firmness of character. She only follows [male] strength. Nature did not want to create in woman an independent being.[106]

Not everyone was as vociferous as Brandes. But the associations were all there; it was not necessary to shout them from the rooftops—they came to mind whenever any element in the chain was invoked.

---

[105] Anon. ["Hr"] "Note des Censors," *N. Hann. Mag.* 5.14 (1795): cols. 223–24. This was in reference to anon. ["K"], "Warum werden so viele Mädchen alte Jungfern?" *N. Hann. Mag.*, 4.102 (1794): cols. 1617–30; 4.103 (1794): cols. 1633–36.

[106] Brandes, *Ueber die Weiber*, 44, 41, 46.

7

❖

Thought Experiments

In the twenty or so years from the mid 1770s to the early 1790s, that open moment when the triumph of late Enlightened principles and the successful, legal consolidation of civil society seemed immediate, the practitioners of civil society entertained a series of thought experiments in which they explored their fears about this brave new world and the people in it. Their ruminations about the interior life of the individual, the psychosexual shadowlands, the delicate contrariness of emotions, and the nondeterminacy of gender are fascinating pieces in their mosaic of sexual self-construction. Alas, they are not directly related to our theme of the public interest in sexual behavior, so we must neglect them in favor of other discussions more overtly aimed at a public effect. The public nature of this debate often meant that these discussions were less nuanced and more stereotypical than the private ones. Particularity can afford eccentricity. Generality cannot. If we were to attempt to piece together a full view of the sexual self-images of the practitioners of civil society, we would have to examine all their writings, especially their unpublished correspondence and diaries.

The practitioners' public thoughts on the interrelations between society and sexual behavior are organized under three themes: masturbation, infanticide, and marriage. The first weighed in obsessive form the dangers of the Enlightenment against the proved limitations of absolutism. Since this problematic was the central issue in the transition from the traditional world to the modern and is thus also the analytic kernel of this book, we will devote considerable attention to interpreting this fascination with masturbation. Infanticide we have met before as the delict progressive officials used to propel legal reform. Infanticide as a theme also masked explorations of the nature of gender and class relations in the new bourgeois world of masculine power and female vulnerability. Meanwhile, marriage remained what it had been for Reformationists and cameralists, the major rubric for legitimate as opposed to illegitimate sexual behavior.[1] From the vantage point of civil society, marriage acquired new valence as the arena where the emotional tangle of love versus sex versus friendship was sorted out anew. Given the ever higher esteem in which marriage was publicly held, however, it is remarkable how often the discussion of marriage centered around its failures. Marriage had come to embody the widely recognized and lamented counterexample to Christian Wolff's confident, early Enlightenment assertion that moral behavior and happiness were congruent.

---

[1] See Hoof, *Pestalozzi*, 475, on the titles listed in the *Ehestandsalmanach*.

Before examining these three themes, we must observe what the eighteenth-century Enlighteners did not discuss. Missing are the classic themes of nineteenth-century sexual discourse: prostitution, (male) homosexuality, and venereal disease. None of these seem to have fit the social concerns of the late Enlightenment. One might say that the practitioners of late-eighteenth-century civil society were preoccupied with laying down the principles of "normality." Their eyes were fixed on the reestablishment or regrounding of the gender system, the production of the male individual as citizen, and the reproduction of the new society. They aimed to discover universally binding laws of human behavior, and even when they scrutinized infanticide and masturbation, they did so in the conviction that these practices were widespread and, given unfortunate circumstances, many otherwise good and innocent people might be liable to them. That is, the practitioners did not usually try to solve their problems of definition by resort to deviance; their intentions were formally inclusive, not exclusive. The nineteenth-century discourse ran according to opposite principles (and faced different problems) and so it produced a very different set of sexual-social preoccupations. To late-eighteenth-century Germany, for example, women did not pose the same kind or degree of symbolic threat that they would later in the nineteenth century (or did in France of the French Revolution). Neither female independence, represented symbolically by commercialism, nor female misbehavior, meriting the dishonor attendant upon prostitution, seemed to describe the actual or symbolic role of women in late-eighteenth-century Germany, and thus prostitution was a useless metaphor. Similarly, male (sexual) desire menaced the late Enlightenment by virtue of its antisociality: its self-devouring egoism (masturbation) or its ruthless victimization of unmarried women (driven to infanticide after abandonment by the seducer), rather than by counter-sociality, that is by the putative building of networks of like-minded men, dedicated conspiratorially to principles contrary to those of robust heterosexuality. That late-nineteenth-century nightmare is faintly visible in the eighteenth, but remained without importance as an organizer of discourse. The same is true for venereal disease. Although fairly widespread and of occasional concern to officials worried about infected soldiers loose in the countryside, it simply lacked symbolic resonance. The imaginary ailments of masturbation seemed more devastating. In any event, two prerequisites for a veneral-disease mania, the absorption with personal health and the (semi)deification of doctors were not yet features of civil life.

The Antimasturbation Campaign

Before the eighteenth century, masturbation may have been a sin, but it was neither a disease nor a focus of public attention. Here and there a Protestant pastor would condemn it, but these isolated products found little echo.[2] The European interest in

[2] Karl-Felix Jacobs, "Die Entstehung der Onanie-Literatur im 17. und 18. Jahrhundert" (Med. diss., Munich, 1963), sees a continuity between these writings and the later antimasturbation wave, but the

masturbation is generally dated to the publication of *Onania, or the Heinous Sin of Self-Pollution*, which appeared anonymously, either in Amsterdam around 1700, or in London in 1710.[3] *Onania* raced through numerous editions in various languages, appearing in German for the first time in 1736.[4] But even its idiosyncratic success would have remained a curiosity had not the Swiss doctor Samuel Auguste André David Tissot given medical respectability to it in 1758.[5] Under Tissot's imprimatur masturbation became touted as the secret cause of a legion of ailments. Broadly, masturbation's career as a "great anxiety"[6] seems to have had three phases. Eighteenth-century Europeans feared its deleterious physical effects. Their nineteenth-century counterparts, during the presumed crest of the masturbation mania,[7] linked it more to mental illness, though doctors did not shrink from physical intervention to halt it.[8] While doctors disputed among themselves, popular literature kept the anxiety alive in a third form, at least among readers of the middling classes, who may have clung to their fear of physical and mental disease after the medical experts dropped the subject in the early twentieth century.[9]

Characteristics of the Antimasturbation Literature in Germany

The German antimasturbation campaign is obviously part of this larger history, but it is also different in at least three important ways. First, the German literature was not primarily medical, but pedagogic.[10] It was Rousseau who, in his *Emile, or on*

---

sixty-seven years elapsing between Richard Capel, *Tentations, their Nature, Danger, Cure* (London, 1640), and the next treatise, by Johann Friedrich Osterwald, *Traité contre l'Impureté* (Amsterdam, 1707), cast doubt upon this reading.

[3] See René A. Spitz, "Authority and Masturbation. Some Remarks on a Bibliographical Investigation," *Yearbook of Psychoanalysis* 9 (1953): 116; H. Tristram Engelhardt Jr., "The Disease of Masturbation: Values and the Concept of Disease," *Bulletin of the History of Medicine* 48 (1974): 235 n. 4; and Robert H. MacDonald, "The Frightful Consequences of Onanism: Notes on the History of a Delusion," *Journal of the History of Ideas* 28 (1967): 424 n. 4. See also E. H. Hare, "Masturbatory Insanity: The History of an Idea," *Journal of Mental Science* 108 (January 1962): 19 n. 3.

[4] Franz X. Thalhofer, *Die Sexualpädagogik bei den Philanthropen* (Kempten, 1907), 6. The *Gesamtverzeichnis des deutschsprachigen Schrifttums, 1700–1910* (Munich, 1985), lists 1757 as the first German translation (followed by others in 1758 and 1765).

[5] Samuel Auguste André David Tissot, *Tentamen de morbis ex manustrupratione* (Lausanne, 1758), and *L'Onanisme, ou Dissertation physique sur les maladie produites par la masturbation* (Lausanne, 1760).

[6] The phrase comes from Jean Stengers and Anne van Neck, *Histoire d'une Grande Peur: La Masturbation* (Brussels, 1984).

[7] Most scholarly attention to masturbation, especially earlier work, has focused on the nineteenth century (and particularly on Britain and the United States): G. J. Barker-Benfield, *The Horrors of the Half-Known Life* (New York, 1976); Peter T. Cominos, "Late Victorian Sexual Respectability and the Social System," *International Review of Social History* 8 (1963), 18–48; Steven Marcus, *The Other Victorians* (New York, 1964); Hare, "Masturbatory Insanity,"; and Engelhardt, "Disease of Masturbation."

[8] This description follows Hare, "Masturbatory Insanity."

[9] Lesley A. Hall, "Forbidden by God, Despised by Men: Masturbation, Medical Warnings, Moral Panic, and Manhood in Great Britain, 1850–1950," in *Forbidden History. The State, Society, and the Regulation of Sexuality in Modern Europe*, ed. John C. Fout (Chicago, 1992), 293–316.

[10] Thalhofer, *Sexualpädagogik*; Hentze, *Sexualität in der Pädagogik*; Hoof, *Pestalozzi*, 456–67.

Education, had praised and popularized Tissot's views; the eighteenth-century masturbation discussion in Germany never really left the twin contexts of education and youth.[11] Armed with their citations from Tissot (and Rousseau),[12] pedagogues like Campe and Salzmann raised the battle flag. These men, the so-called Philanthropinists, were Germany's first professional educators. Their boarding schools, an eighteenth-century invention, were designed to prepare a broader section of male youth for *Bildung*, the prerequisite for true humanity and citizenship. Through their own publications, but more important via prize contests, which produced the bulk of the writings on the subject in the 1780s and 1790s, the pedagogues dominated the German discussion of masturbation.[13] The petulant tone of the physician Johann Georg Zimmermann's assertion that "no one can fill some of the holes in the moralist's knowledge and warnings [about masturbation] like the doctor" testifies to how keenly the doctors felt a need to clear a place for themselves in the great public debate.[14]

Second, in keeping with the pedagogical orientation the German discussion was much more concerned about the social effects and social context of masturbation than seems to have been true elsewhere. Even among German writers, the more medical the text, the more devoted it was to the health of the individual and the less it tended to say about the social etiology and broader consequences of widespread onanism. The more pedagogical German writings were especially concerned to locate the cultural and economic reasons for what they took to be a growing phenomenon, though they shrank from suggesting broad, social cures.

Third, the German masturbation discussion was essentially a phenomenon of the 1780s; doubts about the scare were being expressed by the early 1790s, and after mid-decade, few new works appeared on the subject.[15] A decade of crying wolf may

[11] Thalhofer, *Sexualpädagogik*, 6.

[12] Tissot appeared in numerous German translations, the first in 1760 from the original Latin edition, *Versuch von denen Krankheiten, welche aus der Selbstbestekung entstehen; aus dem Lateinischen übersetzt* (Frankfurt, 1760), and again in 1797 and 1800, and thereafter from the French (1767, 1770, 1771, 1782, 1785, 1791, 1792 [twice], 1798, 1802). Cf. Thalhofer, *Sexualpädagogik*, 4 n. 1.

[13] Significantly, infibulation was contemplated only in relation to boys, never girls. Hentze, *Sexualität in der Pädagogik*; Thalhofer, *Sexualpädagogik*; *Studien über den Philanthropinismus und die Dessauer Aufklärung. Vorträge zur Geistesgeschichte des Dessau-Wörlitzer Kulturkreises* (Halle, 1970); Günter Ulbricht, "Der Philanthropinismus—eine fortschrittliche pädagogische Reformbewegung der deutschen Aufklärung" *Pädagogik*, 20 (1955): 750–64; Reinhold Schumann, "Die Auffassung des Philanthropinismus von Gesellschaft und Staat" (Ph.D. diss., Universität Leipzig, 1905); Albert Pinloche, *Geschichte des Philanthropinismus*, 2d ed. (Leipzig, 1914). For an introduction to German educational systems, see Peter Lundgreen, *Sozialgeschichte der deutschen Schule im Überblick, 1770–1918* (Göttingen, 1980). Concerning the domination of the topic by pedagogues, see anon., ["Qw"], review of J.F. Oest, *Für Eltern, Erzieher und Jugendfreunde*, *ADB* 82.2 (1788): 572. Also, Oest, "Versuch einer Beantwortung."

[14] Johann Georg Zimmermann, "Warnung an Eltern, Erzieher und Kinderfreunde wegen der Selbstbefleckung, zumal bei ganz jungen Mädchen," *Dt. Mus.* 1 (1778): 460. Also see Vogel, *Unterricht für Eltern*, vii.

[15] Of the twenty-six articles on masturbation cited in the *Index deutschsprachiger Zeitschriften* (which catalogs articles from 250 German journals published between 1750 and 1800), 92 percent appeared between 1777 and 1792. The most cited books on the subject were, in chronological order, Sarganeck, *Warnung* (1746); various editions of Tissot from 1760 on; Christian Friedrich Börner, *Werk von der Onanie* (Leipzig, 1776); Johann Georg Zimmermann, *Warnung an Eltern, Erzieher und Kinderfreunde*

have made Germans so skeptical about the dangers of masturbation that they remained relatively unimpressed by the ensuing nineteenth-century uproar over masturbatory insanity. Hare reports that German medical writers then "seem to have taken a much more moderate view than the French or English."[16] The seeming rise in medical interest in masturbation at the fin de siècle, exemplified by Richard von Krafft-Ebing, is probably a separate event. At any rate, the antimasturbation campaign of the late eighteenth century was clearly a product of its own, peculiar social circumstances.

Turning to the content and form of the late-eighteenth-century tracts, one becomes engulfed by solipsism. The antimasturbation literature lived off itself; it recycled descriptions and "case studies" especially from Tissot, the anonymous *Onania*, Salzmann, and then from each successive work, until later volumes were often cut-and-paste compendiums of earlier ones.[17] It is a literature of which it can truly be said that you do not have to have read it all, to have read it all.

The antimasturbation literature also helped define the self-help genre characteristic of later civil society. That is, sound advice was interspersed with putative letters from sufferers describing their temptations, torments, and (sometimes) triumph over their "disease." This epistolary form reflected the Enlightenment's project of self-education, in which regular citizens helped shape the improvement

wegen der Selbstbefleckung (Leipzig, 1779); Johann Stuve, *Über die körperliche Erziehung* (Berlin, 1779); Wilhelm Heinrich Friedrich Seehase, *Soll man junge Leute über die eigentliche Art der Erzeugung des Menschen belehren?* (Stendal, 1784); Johannes Kämpf, *Für Aerzte und Kranke bestimmte Abhandlung von einer neuen Methode, die hartnäckigsten Krankheiten, die ihren Sitz im Unterleibe haben, besonders die Hypochondrie, sicher und gründlich zu heilen* (Dessau, 1784); Christoph Gotthilf Salzmann, *Ist es Recht über die heimlichen Sünden der Jugend öffentlich zu schreiben?* (Schnepfenthal, 1785); Salzmann, *Über die heimlichen Sünden der Jugend* (orig. 1785); Vogel, *Unterricht für Eltern* (1786); Villaume, "Über die Unzuchtssünden" (1787); Oest, "Versuch einer Beantwortung"; J. F. Oest, "Versuch einer Belehrung für die männliche und weibliche Jugend über die Laster der Unkeuschheit überhaupt und über die Selbstschwächung insonderheit, nebst einem kurzen Vortrage der Erzeugungslehre," in Campe, *Allgemeine Revision*, 6:287–506; M. A. Winterfeld, "Über die heimlichen Sünden der Jugend," in Campe, *Allgemeine Revision*, 6:507–609; Gotthilf Sebastian Rötger, *Über Kinderzucht und Selbstbefleckung, ein Buch bloß für Aeltern, Erzieher und Jugendfreunde von einem Schulmanne* (Züllichau, 1787); Christian August Peschek, *Versuch über die Ausartung des Begattungstriebes unter den Menschen. Ein Beytrag zur Sittenlehre und Erziehungskunde* (Breslau, 1790); Faust, *Geschlechtstrieb* (1791); Jakob Gottlieb Boetticher, *Winke für Eltern, Erzieher und Jünglinge die Selbstbefleckung betr.* (Königsberg, 1791); Christian Gotthilf Salzmann, *Paedagogisches Bedenken über eine Schrift des Herrn Hofraths Faust, wie der Geschlechtstrieb der Menschen in Ordnung zu Bringen, und wie die Menschen besser und glücklicher zu Machen* (Schnepfenthal, 1791). Medical dissertations on masturbation also appeared with some frequency during this time, among them: Christian Gottfried Gruner, "De masturbatione peste iuventutis longe perniciosissima" (Med. diss., Jena, 1784); Wilhelm Ernst Christian Huschke, "De masturbatione" (Med. diss., Jena, 1788); and Johann Wilhelm Friedrich Weise, "De signis mastuprationis certioribus" (Med. diss., Erfurt, 1792).

[16] Hare, "Masturbatory Insanity," 5. For an excellent study of the clinical application of the "masturbation" diagnosis to actual patients in early- to mid-nineteenth-century Germany, see Anne Goldberg, "A Social Analysis of Insanity in Nineteenth-Century Germany: Sexuality, Delinquency, and Anti-Semitism in the Records of the Eberbach Asylum" (Ph.D. diss., University of California, Los Angeles, 1992), chap. 4.

[17] For examples of this cut-and-paste effect, see Oest, "Versuch einer Beantwortung," 7,8; Zimmermann, "Warnung," 453; Winterfeld, "Heimlichen Sünden," 535–36, 540–49, 566, 570; Salzmann, *Ueber die heimlichen Sünden*, 51, 54, 205, 227–28; and Vogel, *Unterricht für Eltern*, ix-xii.

(norms) of their fellow citizens through active participation in the public sphere, in this case, through published self-revelation of their darkest sexual secrets. Personal testimony was surely more convincing than the admonitions of experts and laid a much firmer basis for self-identification and thus for voluntary change. The antimasturbation genre was therefore quite modern in its educational and psychological presumptions and in its almost democratic pretensions, given the participatory aspect of its efforts.

We have already examined the central physiological assumption behind the antimasturbation literature: that of semen as the most precious, strength-giving fluid of the body, whose premature or inordinate loss leads to physical and mental weakness. Indeed, these tracts are the last and best expression of that earlier sexual model.[18] Just as that model was male-oriented, so was the antimasturbation literature. Women were usually included as afterthoughts and in any event as a weak elaboration upon the male analogy.[19] Tissot, for example, devoted just eight pages to women out of 184, and explained that

> the accidents [that is, the ill effects of masturbation] to which women are liable are accounted for upon the same principles as those of men. The humour which they lose being of more or less value, and not so elaborate as the sperm of man, its loss does not perhaps weaken so soon; but when they are guilty of excesses, their nervous system being weaker than ours, and naturally more subject to spasms, the accidents which arise therefore are more violent. Sudden excesses bring on disorders analogous to those of the young man.[20]

German writers generally followed Tissot's line, though they tended to be somewhat more attentive to women than he had been. Oest wrote an entire book (in female persona) designed for young girls, but typically, it was only half the length of the one he wrote for boys.[21] Although Salzmann opined that "even more girls" than

---

[18] For example, Sarganeck, *Warnung*, 36; Faust, *Geschlechtstrieb*, 4–11, 17–18; Tissot, *Onanism*, 52–57; Vogel, *Unterricht für Eltern*, 141–43; Winterfeld, "Heimlichen Sünden," 511–13; and Salzmann, *Ueber die heimlichen Sünden*, 32–36. Villaume, "Über die Unzuchtssünden," 44–45, 281, did not believe that women and children had seed, but he thought they nonetheless lost a precious fluid.

[19] Margita Lipping overemphasizes the prominence of women in the German antimasturbation literature, though she admits that women make up only 20 percent of the case studies: Lipping, "Bürgerliche Konzepte zur weiblichen Sexualität in der zweiten Hälfte des 18. Jahrhunderts. Rekonstruktionsversuche am Material medizinischer und pädagogischer Texte," in *Frauenkörper. Medizin. Sexualität. Auf dem Wege zu einer neuen Sexualmoral*, ed. Johanna Geyer-Kordesch and Annette Kuhn (Düsseldorf, 1986), 32. This figure may indeed be higher in Germany than elsewhere, but if it is, that reflects the greater endurance in Germany than in England, France, or Holland of the Galenic sexual model, whereby women were construed as sexually inverted men and thus shared male's sexual characteristics, if to a slightly lesser degree; it does not show any especial interest in women or in interpreting female sexual nature via the subject of masturbation. Goldberg has found that in early-nineteenth-century German clinics, "masturbatory insanity" was a virtually all-male classification. Goldberg, "Social Analysis," chap. 4.

[20] Tissot, *Onanism*, 71.

[21] J.F. Oest, "Nöthige Belehrung und Warnung für Jünglinge und solche Knaben, die schon zu einigem Nachdenken gewöhnt sind," in Campe, *Allgemeine Revision*, 6:293; and Oest, "Nöthige Belehrung und Warnung für junge Mädchen, zur allerfrühesten Bewahrung ihrer Unschuld, von einer erfahrnen Jugendfreundin," in Campe, *Allgemeine Revision*, 6:435–506.

boys had fallen prey to the practice, nonetheless, he sighed, "I cannot do much to prevent this, and must limit myself only to the excesses of the male sex."[22] Campe, whose prize contest and *General Revision* did more to produce book-length works on masturbation than anybody else, was similarly negligent when it came to women. Contemporaries found it puzzling that Campe had neglected even to mention the subject in his celebrated *Fatherly Advice to My Daughter*.[23] And, finally, the two writers of journal articles in this period devoted exclusively to female masturbation struggled against what they felt was widespread ignorance and denial.[24] Apparently they were correct, for Dr. Zimmermann's article on the subject elicited a savage reply from an anonymous fellow doctor, "Rescue of innocent children of the female sex from the false accusation of masturbation by Dr. Zimmermann."[25] All of these examples indicate that the concern about masturbation centered around males and their putative sexual constitution.

The antimasturbation crusaders believed that this habit had vastly increased "in the last two generations, or, since that time when refined opulence, lasciviousness, weakness, effemininity, poverty and multiple misery has overwhelmed mankind and discipline and order have been lost," as Faust pessimistically put it.[26] That is, masturbation was a product of vast material, social, and cultural changes. These changes caused "the seeds of desire to develop prematurely in children" and thus predisposed them to danger from previously harmless accidental sources, such as boredom, tree-climbing, bad acquaintances, tight clothing, and the like.[27] All writers, pedagogues, doctors, and reviewers alike, saw masturbation therefore as a problem of children and youth, who ignorantly robbed themselves of the quintessence of bodily energy they needed for physical and mental development.

---

[22] Presumably Salzmann was referring to his expertise as head of a famous boys' school, though it is hard to see why this would have prevented him writing a book for girls: Salzmann, *Ueber die heimlichen Sünden*, 10–11. Vogel, *Unterricht für Eltern*, 23, also thought girls were perhaps more tempted to masturbation than boys.

[23] J. S. Fest, "Einige Anmerkungen und Zusätze des Herausgebers zu dem vorstehenden Aufsatze," *Beitr.z.B.* 2 (1790): 427, and anon. ["Nm"], review of Joachim Heinrich Campe, *Väterlicher Rat für meine Tochter, ADB* 91.2 (1790): 311–12.

[24] The most cited expert on female masturbation was Dr. Zimmermann, author of "Warnung an Eltern, Erzieher und Kinderfreunde wegen der Selbstbefleckung, zumal bei ganz jungen Mädchen," in which he opined that this practice among girls was "less well known" (454) than among boys, and thus "people can be unbelievably indifferent" about it (455). The anonymous author of "Was ist weibliche Onanie? Eine Frage der Menschheit wichtig," *Alm.f.Ä.* (1782): 264, expressed outrage that "people still want to doubt this fact." A possible third work on this subject listed in the *Index deutschsprachiger Zeitschriften*, concerned the suicide of a woman, allegedly as the result of masturbation: Samuel Gottlieb Vogel, "Weiblicher Selbstmord als eine Folge eines geheimen Lasters. (Aus dem Briefe des Arztes der Unglücklichen)," *Berl. Mon.* 10.5 (1787): 172–76.

[25] Anon., "Rettung," 52–60; Zimmermann's reply: "Anmerkungen über eine Schrift zur Rettung unschuldiger Kinder . . . ," *Bald. Mag.* 1 (1779): 60–63.

[26] Faust, *Geschlechtstrieb*, 1. Concerning the recentness of the phenomenon, see Villaume, "Über die Unzuchtssünden," 114; Salzmann, *Ueber die heimlichen Sünden*, 69–72; and anon., "Onanie," *Alm. f. Ä* (1785): 239; see also below, on masturbation as a disease of civilization.

[27] Salzmann, *Ueber die heimlichen Sünden*, 110, and the discussion on 82–121. On immediate causes, see Villaume, "Über die Unzuchtssünden," 50–66, 81–113; Winterfeld, "Heimlichen Sünden," 530–40; and Oest, "Versuch einer Beantwortung," 50–85.

The longevity in popular culture of the mythical ill-effects of masturbation may make a rehearsal of these seem superfluous, nonetheless, the catalog of symptoms provides one key to the meaning masturbation held for developing civil society. The anonymous author of the article "Onanie" in the *Almanac for Doctors and Non-Doctors* (*Almanach für Ärzte und Nichtärzte*) (1785) gave a comparatively short but typical rendition of the fate awaiting sufferers:

> The face becomes pale, the body tired and sluggish, the step dragging, the appetite weak, the eye stupid, the gaze dull, and the cheek fallen. In addition come other symptoms: transitory pain in different parts, alternating chill and fever, especially in the loins, pimples in the face, unpleasant sensations in the genitals, shriveling of the genitals [in males], involuntary emission of seed, spit, and fluid, and ugly white discharge [in females], prolapse of the uterus, lengthening of the clitoris [*Ruthe*], and nymphomania [*Manntolheit*] in girls, difficulty swallowing, deterioration of mental energies and of the so-called external and internal senses, anxiety and oppression, trembling and heart palpatations, tendency to fainting and cramps, including epilepsy. . . . Finally the consumption [*Auszehrung*] hastens death, which the sufferers no longer feel, since they have long since gone numb to themselves and to the world. Some experience a continuous aversion to marriage, insanity, depression, hypochondria and hysteria, stiffness of the neck, epilepsy, along with other unfortunate, untreatable complaints."[28]

A much more thorough account appeared in Dr. Samuel Gottlieb Vogel's book (1786), from which, with the reader's indulgence, I would like to choose several significant examples, which Vogel helpfully arranged according to gender:

> *Male sufferers experienced:* "stinking breath and foul-smelling white, thick urine"; "inability to contain urine"; "sleeplessness, narcolepsy or disturbed sleep"; "all the ailments and weaknesses of the most frail kind of old age in the bloom of youth"; "masculine inability [to engage in sex]"; "constipation, or diarrhea"; "lack of appetite, or disorderly cravings or gluttony"; "atrophy of the male organ, which, together with the scrotum, hangs down withered and limp"; and so on.
>
> *For female sufferers:* "illnesses of the bladder and clitoris, which becomes bigger and more sensitive"; "inability to contain urine"; "hysteria, which consists of an irresistible desire for sexual intercourse"; "horrible anxiety; miscarriages; sterility"; "loss of rosiness in the cheeks and lips"; and so on.[29]

All writings combating masturbation contained similar lists.[30] At first glance, it appears that nothing was missing from the litany of complaints; masturbation could cause every dysfunction conceivable. In a sense this observation is true. Masturbation was a catchall explanation, because it was a catchall symbolic category. But if one delves a bit below the surface of the symptom catalog, a number of interesting peculiarities appear. Masturbation could produce almost any ailment because its essence was *immoderation*. Thus, one suffered either constipation or diarrhea,

---

[28] Anon., "Onanie," 244–45.

[29] Vogel, *Unterricht für Eltern*, 19–21 (males), 23–24 (females).

[30] Tissot, *Onanism*, 4–47; Oest, "Versuch einer Beantwortung," 16–50; Villaume, "Über die Unzuchtssünden," 13–47; Salzmann, *Ueber die heimlichen Sünden*, 21–60; anon., "Galanterien," 199–202; Winterfeld, "Heimlichen Sünden," 515–26 (men); 527–29 (women).

anorexia or gluttony, stupor or insomnia, and so on. Neither the organ nor the bodily process was important; the inappropriateness and immoderation of masturbation was the problem, or as one anonymous reviewer put it, "it appears as if nature wanted to avenge itself in this awful fashion for the transgressions against its laws."[31] If one recalls that both medicine and moral philosophy had long held the moderate, balanced life as the correct model for health and happiness, then this fundamental association between excess and generalized indisposition becomes even clearer.

A further reason for the unending litany of harm was the peculiarly liminal property of sexual desire and energy, existing, as it was thought to do, at the very point where corporeal stuff (blood or nourishment) transformed itself into life force (semen), expressing its overabundance in desire (a quality of the will or mind), culminating in pleasure (ejaculation), that is, in an emotional experience. The economy that masturbatory immoderation upset was therefore not limited to the material body, but was equally damaging to the nervous system, the emotions, and the brain. Therefore, it was hardly surprising to learn that squandering the emblem of this complex nexus, namely semen, should lead to "a certain disability in thinking and acting," to a "high degree of weakness of mind," to "melancholy, depression," or to "hypochondria that is in our days epidemic."[32]

It was logical that masturbation should lead to genital infirmities, but the reader will have noticed that these expressed themselves as gender confusion. Men suffered an inability to consummate sexual intercourse, they remained unanimated by stories of "lusty maidens,"[33] their very genitals shriveled. Thus men lost the physical and social markers of their ascribed masculine sexual nature and women gained them.[34] Women's clitorises swelled simultaneously with their immoderate and unseemly sexual desire. Whereas masturbation caused men and women to trade sexual/gender places, this criss-cross, far from increasing their desire for one another, caused "aversion to marriage" and the whole business of procreation, if they were not already physically incapable of it.[35] By mixing up the primary building blocks of society (the gendered individual) and then sundering their link with one another by preventing the formation of the original social institution (marriage), masturbation threatened society at its very root.

---

[31] Anon., review of anon. ["Schl"], *Ueber Kinderunzucht und Selbstbefleckung* (1787), in *Braun.J.* 2 (1788): 100.

[32] Salzmann, *Ueber die heimlichen Sünden,* 33, 37, 38.

[33] Anon., "Galanterien," 199.

[34] Goldberg, "Social Analysis," 226, found the same pattern in the Eberbach clinic.

[35] On aversion to marriage, see Cella, *Über Verbrechen und Strafen,* 65; anon., "Onanie," 244–45; that masturbation leads to "Hurerey" instead of marriage, see Zimmermann, "Warnung," 460. Also see Villaume, "Über die Unzuchtssünden," 284 and Oest, "Versuch einer Beantwortung," 23. The belief that masturbation caused general weakness and genital damage indicates that most authors thought habitual masturbators unfit for marriage. Vogel, *Unterricht für Eltern,* 20, 24, explicitly cites sterility or weak or defective progeny (*jämmerliche Früchte*) as consequences. Also see Salzmann, *Ueber die heimlichen Sünden,* 10.

The fact that the masturbation literature overwhelmingly presented children and youths as threatened also indicates the social framework in which it occurred. For the age-inappropriateness of masturbation consisted of the premature enjoyment of pleasures reserved for adults (citizens). Legitimate sexual expression, traditionally a mark of adulthood and of some degree of wealth, had developed at the end of the eighteenth and beginning of the nineteenth centuries more broadly into a sign of the citizen's coming of age. As, at least in theory, the importance of *Stand* and wealth as preconditions for legitimate sexual expression waned, the age criteria, buttressed by reference to natural biological development, became more salient. Sexual expression was part of the panoply of civilized activities reserved for those rational and controlled enough to enjoy them without harm to themselves or others. The capacity to enjoy other civilized, social amusements, which not incidentally were thought to heighten sexual pleasure, was part of functioning as a rational adult in civil society. But this was not for children (nor was it for the impoverished, for countryfolk, or for other groups of questionable rationality). Salzmann explained that "early cultivation [*Cultur*] which one tries to impart to children, increases even more the evil [of the temptation to masturbation]. . . . . One refines their feeling so much . . . , that they become prematurely sensitized, that temptations touch them, whose enjoyment was intended for them many years hence." Such enjoyments, which led to masturbation, were "love songs, plays, poems, novels," in short, the defining icons of civilized public life.[36] The penalty for premature pleasure, which amounted to pleasure without the social exchange involved in participating and sacrificing as a full member of civil society, was the pain of myriad ills making pleasure impossible for ever after.

The Antimasturbation Campaign in the Context of Civil Society

Given the exhaustive litany of putative ills following masturbation and the often shrill tone of the antimasturbation tracts, it is easy to see why most secondary works have interpreted the antimasturbation campaign as "repressive." Scholars of pedagogy see in them an attempt to "desexualize" childhood.[37] Others view the campaign as a sign of and contributor to "early bourgeois repression,"[38] with "bourgeois" understood either as a class and its ideology,[39] as an economy,[40] or as a shorthand

---

[36] Salzmann, *Ueber die heimlichen Sünden*, 86. On the same theme, see Winterfeld, "Heimlichen Sünden," 550–51; Oest, "Versuch einer Beantwortung," 76, 81; Faust, *Geschlechtstrieb*, 1; Vogel, *Unterricht für Eltern*, 51; Villaume, "Über die Unzuchtssünden," 114–15; and anon., review of anon. ["Schl"], *Ueber Kinderunzucht*, 100.

[37] Thalhofer, *Sexualpädagogik*, 45–46, and Ingrid Peikert, "Zur Geschichte der Kindheit im 18. und 19. Jahrhundert. Einige Entwicklungstendenzen," in *Die Familie in der Geschichte*, ed. Heinz Reif (Göttingen, 1982), 114–36, esp. 122.

[38] Hoof, *Pestalozzi*, 449.

[39] Jos van Ussel, *Sexualunterdrückung. Geschichte der Sexualfeindschaft*, 2d ed. (Giessen, 1977), 148.

[40] Ben Barker-Benfield, "The Spermatic Economy: A Nineteenth-Century View of Sexuality," *Feminist Studies* 1.1 (1972): 45–74, who emphasizes the capitalist stress on saving, as opposed to spending; and Thomas Laqueur, "The Social Evil, the Solitary Vice and Pouring Tea," in *Fragments for a History*

for the modern *Zeitgeist* and its new conception of regulation.[41] Scholars observing the phenomenon from the medical point of view attribute the antimasturbation campaign to shifts within the medical profession and to its growing importance in diagnosing disorders in society.[42] Most interpreters in fact advance a number of causal hypotheses, since the curious features of the antimasturbation excitement defy simple explanations. Given the contemporary judgment that the sexual drive was both natural and beneficent, "repression" is a misleading label; nonetheless, the brief burst of public interest in masturbation can surely be characterized as anxious.[43] In the following discussion I explore the social component of that anxiety. I do not seek to explain the antimasturbation campaign itself, but rather how it functioned in the context of civil society. In the process a number of the puzzling qualities of the antimasturbation craze also become clearer.

Seen from the vantage point of civil society, the masturbation scare functioned as an inventory list where the advantages and disadvantages of the social principles of the Enlightenment were weighed against the advantages and disadvantages of the social principles of absolutism. Here, as if in the laboratory, one rehearsed for a last time the pros and cons of the larger experiment that was the Enlightenment.

For the same reasons that the practitioners of civil society found their age more sexual than previous ones, they found it perforce encouraged masturbation. The rise in the material standard of living meant that presumably more people consumed rich, spicy foods and alcohol, they had more leisure and less hard work, more comfort and less hardship. The old theories of sexual energy all associated these former luxuries, which once only the putatively dissolute nobility had enjoyed, with a rise in sexual desire and capacity.[44] And it was precisely the old theories of sexual energy that still determined the sexual interpretations of the German Enlightenment. Dr. Vogel's book on masturbation contained the typical list of physical causes of masturbation. The reviewer in the *Allgemeine Deutsche Bibliothek* deemed this list canonical enough to cite verbatim. One needed above all to avoid "spoiled mother's milk, swaddling, infrequent washing of children; spirits of all kinds; frequent [meals of] meat and rich or hard-to-digest meals; spices; too warm rooms, beds and clothing; becoming overheated too often; too much sleep, too little exercise."[45] Apart from the child-rearing maxims, all the other dangers resulted from material progress, formerly unattainable for most people.

As absolutist luxuries turned into Enlightenment necessities,[46] the physical

---

of the Human Body, vol. 3, ed. Michel Feher (New York, 1987), 334–343, on the anxiety raised by the new market economy.

[41] Spitz, "Authority and Masturbation."

[42] Hare, "Masturbatory Insanity," 11–12; Engelhardt, "Disease of Masturbation," 239.

[43] As Stengers and Neck have chosen for their title: *Histoire d'une Grande Peur.* See Chapter 6, pp. 236–45, on the contemporaries' positive judgment of the sexual drive.

[44] Karl Leonhard Reinhold, "Die Drey Stände. Ein Dialog," *NTM*, March 1792, 238–39.

[45] Anon. ["Dt"] review of D. Samuel Gottlieb Vogel, *Unterricht für Eltern* (1786), *ADB* 82.2 (1788): 568.

[46] In a section on luxury, Salzmann, *Ueber die heimlichen Sünden*, 71, declared in agreement with many

foundations for increased sexual activity were thought to have been set. To these physical predispositions the institutions and values of civil life added the mental and social stimuli on which masturbation thrived: books, plays, poems, paintings, social gatherings, and civilized habits (of kissing acquaintances, of debonair conversation), all of which inflamed the imagination.

Masturbation was so firmly associated with civilized living that everyone assumed it to be a plague of the cities. According to Villaume,

> The atmosphere of the city, the luxury [*Pracht*], the food, the privacy [*Eingezogenheit*], the idleness, the early efforts at education, the refined upbringing, the early gallantry, reading, the societies, dancing, these are the causes of this difference [between the predisposition to masturbation in the city and the countryside]. In the countryside the fresh air, the moderate nourishment of poverty, physical labor, the simplicity of the style of living, and the strength and health which flow from all these sources, all these causes, I tell you, protect [country] youth from the ruinous sins of sexual profligacy.[47]

Rural youth were protected from masturbation by their very isolation from the sources of Enlightenment and progress. That was the reason that, "this sin is extremely rare in villages."[48] If village youths indeed became "infected (*angesteckt*)"[49] then it was from sources in contact with cities or with Enlightened ideas or styles of living, usually soldiers returning from urban garrisons, servants who had picked up bad habits from their more refined masters and mistresses, or boys in private schools, which a generation earlier had not even existed.[50]

Traditional society, therefore, was not to blame. The nouns writers used to describe their times referred unmistakably to the modern age. "Lust and overblown sensitivity [*Empfindelei*] are the hallmarks of our decade," sighed the anonymous writer of the article "Onanie" in 1785.[51] Another opined that "effeminateness, luxury [*Ueppigkeit*], unnatural styles of living and the bodily weakness and ruined fluids they produce . . . are the main cause of this sad occurrence [masturbation] and its awful consequences."[52] These typical writers described an interesting movement of sexual reproach from its earlier stereotypical location at the doorstep of the allegedly sybaritic nobility into the heart of the process of civilization itself. As Enlightenment reformers sought to make material comfort, leisure, and refined manners accessible to more social groups, indeed, as they tried to represent them-

---

writers, that luxury caused (men) to avoid marriage: "One now has so many needs [*Bedürfnisse*], that in order to satisfy them, one is prevented from satisfying one of the very first." This single sentence subsumes three typical contemporary assumptions: luxuries have become necessities; marriage is a euphemism for sexual activity; sexual expression is itself a necessity and, if dammed up by lack of marriage, it will spill over into other channels, such as masturbation.

[47] Villaume, "Über die Unzuchtssünden," 114–15.

[48] Salzmann, *Ueber die heimlichen Sünden*, 64; also Bertuch, "Ueber Kinder-Kleidung," 572.

[49] Salzmann, *Ueber die heimlichen Sünden*, 66; Fest, "Einige Anmerkungen," 425.

[50] Salzmann, *Ueber die heimlichen Sünden*, 66; Fest, "Einige Anmerkungen," 425; Vogel, *Unterricht für Eltern*, 53–54; Oest, "Versuch einer Beantwortung," 78–79; Zimmermann, "Warnung," 253; anon., "Galanterien," 202.

[51] Anon., "Onanie," 240.

[52] Anon., review of anon. ["Schl"], *Ueber Kinderunzucht*, 100.

selves as the motors of cultivation, they fell heir to the same criticisms they had once directed at the nobles. This was an uncomfortable position, but not an illogical one, since refinement and "civilization" in that sense had always stood for, among other things, sexual libertinage. The problem was how to have one without the other.

Although writers acknowledged that some children discovered masturbation on their own, their basic model explaining the spread of masturbation was educational. Children learned the desire and the technique from written material or from the already knowledgeable. Masturbation was therefore, literally, the negative exemplar of Enlightenment. It proved that the very mechanisms that disseminated progress also disseminated destruction. These mechanisms were, broadly, two: expanded social contact through institutions, conviviality, and mobility; and reading.

The two most often cited sources of "contagion" through social contact were servants and other children, particularly fellow schoolchildren.[53] The danger represented here thus lay in the two institutions most fundamental to bourgeois and civil life: the family and school. There had always been servants; if they were suddenly considered sources of moral ruin, then what had changed was the idea of the family. Once the seat of economic production, the family was now the sphere of privacy and intimacy dedicated to individual (male) emotional development and to the preparation of the next generation for personal fulfillment and citizenship. Suspicion of servants regarding masturbation was merely a subset of the wider association at this time of servants with sexual-moral ruin. Historians have explained the capacious literature on this topic precisely as the result of the efforts of the master and mistress to differentiate themselves from their servants, which effort included assuming sexual virtue for themselves and postulating sexual vice for their class underlings.[54] This is a reasonable, functionalist explanation, but it is not how contemporaries analyzed it.[55] When the Hamburg Patriotic Society inquired in 1790 into the reasons for servants' putative moral failings, it was especially interested to hear from servants themselves how their masters contributed to this, since the Society was convinced that "*the moral ruination of the lower orders [Stände] must be trickling down from the upper ones.*"[56] The inclusion of this assumption in the prize question itself indicates how common this belief was. Respondents (none of whom appear in fact to have been servants) did not disappoint the expectation either, but duly reported how masters and mistresses cultivated immorality in their servants. Aside from outright seduction (a reason more commonly found in the infanticide than in the servant literature), the "trickle-down" effects concerned the

[53] See above, note 50.
[54] Engelsing, "Zur Stellung der Dienstboten," 413–24; Dagmar Müller-Staats, *Klagen über Dienstboten. Eine Untersuchung über Dienstboten und ihre Herrschaften* (Frankfurt, 1987), 78–82, 185–202; cf. for England, Lawrence Stone, *The Family, Sex and Marriage in England, 1500–1800* (New York, 1977), 255.
[55] Although contemporaries saw the class division between servants and their employers, they were unconscious of the ideological function that presumed moral differences between classes played.
[56] Announcement of the prize contest, in *Verhandlungen und Schriften*, 2:63, emphasis in original.

new style of living thought to characterize the carriers of civil society. The new private life was having its public effect. Dr. Peter Otto Kürn believed that masters and mistresses were too familiar with their servants, were too dependent upon them for running the household, employed too many, fed them too little (an idiosyncratic opinion—most writers believed the opposite),[57] clothed them too extravagantly, mocked religion in their presence, and absented themselves too often from the house.[58] Luxury (too many servants, extravagant clothing), skepticism (mocking religion) and mobility, three archetypical characteristics of the Enlightenment, were to blame. Even members of the lower orders not directly in contact with their social betters became "entangled in their moral notions," a slightly later observer remarked.[59] The reason was, of course, that the private habits of householders were part of the larger, public changes Pastor Schmidt had labeled Enlightenment.[60] With Enlightenment, he thought, came increased opportunities even for servants to indulge in luxury, attend the theater, and read books, to search for "love stories" and urban novelties, to "fill one's head with dreams of fantasy, and so on, all of which work to make morals worse."[61] Enlightened tolerance and the legal reforms we have already examined were said to have further loosened general moral attitudes.[62]

The practitioners' fear that servants introduced children to masturbation was part of a tautology; for the servants were themselves "infected" by their masters and, indirectly, by the vast social changes creating civil society. The new ideal family, epitomized by its sexually innocent children, could hardly be isolated from these larger forces, because it was both the product and the producer of them.

The same was true for the other major source of "infection": schools. The reference was not to (theoretically) mandatory popular education, but to boarding schools. Many of these were run by the very pedagogues who campaigned most vociferously against masturbation. That their schools were reproached as places where "children are educated to become masturbators, pederasts, and sodomites" is more than ironic; it illustrates how inescapable was the self-critical tautology in which the masturbation discussion was enmeshed.[63]

---

[57] Carl Friedrich Wiesiger recommended frugal food and drink, in his "Preisschrift," in *Verhandlungen und Schriften*, 2:169–70.

[58] Kürn, "Preisschrift," in *Verhandlungen und Schriften*, 2:119–22. Similarly, J. G. Büsch, *Zwei kleine Schriften die im Werk begriffene Verbesserung des Armenwesens in dieser Stadt Hamburg betreffend* (Hamburg, 1786), vorbericht A 3 b, cited in Möller, *Kleinbürgerliche Familie*, 297.

[59] H. Koenig (1790–1869), *Aus einer Jugend* (Leipzig, 1852), 40, cited in Möller, *Kleinbürgerliche Familie*, 297.

[60] See Chapter 6, p. 231.

[61] Schmidt, "Preisschrift," 74–77, citation, 77.

[62] Wiesiger, "Preisschrift," in *Verhandlungen und Schriften*, 2:165, emphasis in original. Also, Carl Hübbe, "Preisschrift," in *Verhandlungen und Schriften*, 2:144.

[63] Winterfeld, "Heimlichen Sünden," 540, also 534–36, 572–79; Ussel, *Sexualunterdrückung*, 144; anon. ["F"], "Brief, das Erziehungswesen betreffend," *TM* 4 (1779): 67–78 (on suppressing masturbation at Basedow's model school in Dessau). Also, Vogel, *Unterricht für Eltern*, 4; Frank, *System*, 2:599; Zimmermann, "Warnung," 453; anon., "Galanterien," 202; and anon., *Wie die großen und kleinern Schul- und Erziehungsanstalten gegen das Laster der Selbstbefleckung am ersten gesichert, und wie die davon angesteckten Zöglinge gerettet und vor den Folgen desselben bewahret werden können* (Halle, 1791).

The pedagogues were involved in an even greater tautology through their anti-masturbation publications, for, as even Tissot had said of his own book, critics might believe that it "tends more to promote vice than to suppress it."[64] Enlightened campaigners faced the dilemma of knowledge versus censorship, publicity versus secrecy. Before publishing his influential tract "Secret Sins of Youth," Salzmann issued a justification called "Is it right to write openly about the secret sins of youth?" in which he answered the question affirmatively.[65] His reason, which others in his position echoed, was that masturbation was a hitherto unknown, unappreciated danger, "which had attacked almost the entire world of youth." Only an avalanche of information could counteract this passive ignorance.[66] Even the careful J. S. Fest, who believed that exposure to Tissot probably harmed some readers, still concluded that more people had been helped than hurt by antimasturbation tracts, and judging by the generally positive reviews they received, more practitioners of civil society agreed with him than disagreed.[67] In short, when the campaigners were directly confronted with the dilemma that the principles of, the changes promoted by, and the institutions that embodied the Enlightenment might actually cause vice, they called for more Enlightenment, not less.[68]

Masturbation was immoderation. The prevailing model of the sexual drive discovered the source of immoderation in the artificial stimulation of the mind. The direct connection the model postulated among the brain, nervous system, and semen underscored the central role that imagination played in sexual desire. As Salzmann put it, "Although the natural sexual drive [*Trieb zur Wollust*] is already strong, experience shows that it receives its greatest strength through the imagination."[69] Hence, the ubiquitous warnings especially against novels, which, "heated the imagination."[70] The awe with which contemporaries regarded imagination is difficult to grasp nowadays, unless one recalls that imagination's companion, Reason, had been crowned the motor of human progress, and that the practitioners of civil society were engaged in a process of building a future whose outlines had been

---

[64] Tissot, *Onanism*, viii.

[65] For the pedagogues' views on luxury and needs see note 46.

[66] Salzmann, *Ueber die heimlichen Sünden*, 1, whole discussion from 1–21. Also see Fest, "Einige Anmerkungen," 421; Villaume, "Über die Unzuchtssünden," 4; Zimmermann, "Warnung," 455; Oest, "Versuch einer Beantwortung," 7–8, 230–47; Vogel, *Unterricht für Eltern*, x, 91–102; anon. ["Schl"], *Ueber Kinderunzucht und Selbstbefleckung. Ein Buch bloß für Aeltern, Erzieher und Jugendfreunde, von einem Schulmanne* (Züllichau, 1787), part 1; Thalhofer, *Sexualpädagogik*, 31 (on Rötger); and Seehase, *Soll man junge Leute?*

[67] Fest, "Einige Anmerkungen," 419–22; anon. ["Dt"], review of Vogel *Unterricht für Eltern* 567–71; anon. ["Qw"], review of Oest, *Für Eltern*, 571–75; anon., review of Wolke, *An die von ihm geliebten Kinder, welche gern Rath und Warnung annehmen, um gesund und glücklich zu bleiben, ADB* 95.1 (1789): 268.

[68] This unshakable enthusiasm for Enlightenment among the antimasturbationists makes clear that anti-onanism was a discussion among progressives, not an attack on Enlightenment by critics of it. Cf. Ussel, *Sexualunterdrückung*, 144.

[69] Salzmann, *Ueber die heimlichen Sünden*, 81–82. Similarly, Bauer, *Über die Mittel*, 77–79.

[70] *Der Gesindefreund* (Liegnitz, 1803), 66, cited in Dagmar Müller-Staats, "Klagen über Dienstboten," (Ph.D. diss., Universität Hamburg, 1983), 99 (I was unable to find this passage in the published version); Vogel, *Unterricht für Eltern*, 51. Also see Villaume, "Über die Unzuchtssünden," 96.

sketched, they felt, inside their own minds. That is, the power of the mind to change the material world was thought to be almost unlimited. Imagination, the creative mental faculty, was accorded almost magical power. Salzmann cited an anonymous correspondent to the effect that "as soon as one lets the imagination run for only one moment, and does not force it at the first thought, then afterwards everything is lost for ideas of reason or religion."[71]

The terror of imagination and the terror of desire operated in tandem. Salzmann wrote that "all desires [Begierden], all wishes must be repressed, each act broken off, each business given up, which harms duty. We must reach the point that everything we think, speak, and do aims at the fulfillment of duty."[72] This extreme Kantian, or Rousseauian, position held no place for imagination. One historian of the Philanthropinists has described how the "anxiety about losing themselves in fantasy" led them to espouse "thought control" or a "ban on the imagination."[73] Imagination was dangerous because it epitomized self-centered desire, immoderation, unreality, passion, and greed; in short, it was associated with the extremes of qualities purposely set loose by Enlightenment reforms. The ineluctable slide from material improvement and expanded consumer desire, through imagination, to moral and social ruin was pithily expressed by Dr. Kürn in his prize essay on the moral corruption of servants. His starting point was luxury, some degree of which was useful to the progress of society, as his fellow Hamburger Georg Sieveking had shown in the paradigmatic essay on the subject.[74] But luxury was a peril if "it entirely rules people; when the sum of sensual pleasures surpasses the sum of more noble and more useful pursuits, when the natural needs can no longer be distinguished from the crowd of *imagined* and *fantastic* ones, when reason does not choose, but only sensuality, and especially when all of this occurs among people who have become used to consumption [Aufwand] that outstrips their wealth; this lays the foundation for their ruin."[75] Dr. Kürn here expressed in a single sentence the classic fear of his age, that when the securing fetters of absolutism, religion, and subsistence were sprung, nothing would be able to restrain the energies thus set loose. This fear appeared in different guises in the arguments surrounding the relaxation of laws against fornication,[76] the partial lifting of censorship,[77] the

[71] Salzmann, *Ueber die heimlichen Sünden,* 25. Also, Kaufmann, "Aufklärung," chap. 1.

[72] Salzmann, *Über die heimlichen Sünden der Jugend,* 3d ed. (Leipzig, 1799), 31, cited in Hentze, *Sexualität in der Pädagogik,* 90. All other references in this book to Salzmann's work are to the 1819 edition.

[73] Hentze, *Sexualität in der Pädagogik,* 165.

[74] Georg Heinrich Sieveking, "Fragmente über Luxus, Bürgertugend, und Bürgerwohl," in *Verhandlungen und Schriften,* 4:163–82.

[75] Kürn, "Preisschrift," 2:116.

[76] See Chapter 3.

[77] As the great Bavarian reformer, *Illuminat,* and censor, Count Montgelas, explained to his royal master about censorship, "The great problem of where freedom ends and licentiousness [Zügellosigkeit] begins, has never been well solved in any state." Max Josef, count von Montgelas, memoire to the duke of Bavaria, 30 September 1796, cited in Eberhard Weis, "Montgelas' innenpolitisches Reformprogramm: Das Ansbacher Mémoire für den Herzog vom 30.9.1796," *Zeitschrift für bayerische Landesgeschichte* 33.1 (1970):238; Kiesel and Münch, *Gesellschaft und Literatur,* 104–23.

permitting of associations,[78] the lifting of clothing regulations and other sumptuary legislation,[79] the undermining of guild monopolies over production,[80] the extension of literacy to a wider population,[81] and more.[82]

The antimasturbation campaign expressed this same fear in a remarkably similar way. It, too, began on the presumed foundation of material excess, which encouraged a physical predisposition to premature sexual activity, which was, in turn, enhanced by the cultural/educational/imaginative impetuses of Enlightenment, which the censorship, literacy, and association discussions had debated in their own fashion. In the masturbation model, the chain of associations ended in the imagination; that is, it was the sufferer's fantasy that held him in thrall, and it was paradoxically his most exalted capacities of mind and will that the habit, in turn, dissolved. Masturbation was a perfect illustration of the negative movement from matter to mind, of the possible ill effects of material progress on rationality.

The problem with the solution of "thought control" or the "ban on the imagination" was that imagination was as necessary to civil society as luxury was, and for the same reasons.[83] J. G. Schlosser, in a work on economics, called imagination "the mainspring [*Triebfeder*] of human enterprise" (just as Sieveking had called luxury, "the mighty drive [*Trieb*] to useful activity," and the cameralist Johann Justi had called it, "the warmth of the body politic, which maintains prosperity and circula-

---

[78] The two most famous examples of ambivalence connected with associations were the banning of the Bavarian Illuminati and the crackdown against the reading associations after the French Revolution. Dann, "Lesegesellschaften," 112–13; Dülmen, *Gesellschaft der Aufklärer*, 84; Richard van Dülmen, *Der Geheimbund der Illuminaten. Darstellung, Analyse, Dokumentation* (Stuttgart, 1975).

[79] Raeff, *Well-Ordered Police State*, 84–85; Christian Garve, *Über die Moden* (1792), ed. by Thomas Pittrof (Frankfurt, 1987); F. J. Bertuch, "An das Publicum, zum Schlusse des Jahres," *JdL*, 1 (1786): 449–63; see also *Index deutschsprachiger Zeitschriften*, under rubric "Luxus."

[80] Raeff, *Well-Ordered Police State*, 103–6; Walker, *German Home Towns*, 145–84; Stürmer, *Herbst des alten Handwerks*, 225–39, 278–80.

[81] On hopes and fears concerning popular education: see Knudsen, "On Enlightenment for the Common Man."

[82] The cameralist and social critic Jung-Stilling summed up the entire danger in the "revolutionary spirit," which he located (as a reviewer summarized) in "the *pride* produced by misunderstood Enlightenment and the *luxury* that comes from it, to which he reckons the moral [grounds] such as the *addiction to reading*, which is so hard to satisfy, and *freedom of the press*, when it is left to its own delights. Further [he finds] the *immorality* [*Sittenlosigkeit*] that is no less terrible, and the rejection of religion, which is connected with it, and which leads to the dissolution of all the other *bonds* of civil society." Anon. ["Ea"], review of Johann Heinrich Jung[-Stilling], *Über den Revolutionsgeist unsrer Zeit, zur Belehrung der bürgerlichen Stände* (Marburg, 1794), *NADB* 14.2 (1795): 377.

[83] The cameralist Johann Heinrich Jung[-Stilling] expressed the close connection between luxury and imagination and the emblematic role they played in fear of revolution in his memorable label for imagination: "moral luxury." As a "mainspring [*Triebfeder*]" of revolution "moral luxury works almost stronger, but surely as strongly as [material luxury]: everybody reads novels and dramas. . . . In this wide field of the imagination the spirit of our times creates nothing but ideals expressing its notion of the beautiful and good, ideals which at base are beings which do not exist and in our world cannot exist. . . . How can this have any other effect than that we transfer these exaggerated ideals into the real world, and make them the measuring stick of mankind and of human action?" Johann Heinrich Jung-[Stilling], *Über den Revolutions-Geist unserer Zeit zur Belehrung der bürgerlichen Stände* (Marburg, 1793), 7–8.

tion in their vitality and fluidity").[84] As Schlosser (and others) linked imagination and economic progress, Bauer explained the connection among economic progress (luxury), imaginative desire, free will, and indirectly (since his work was about the sexual drive) sexual desire:

> Luxury, understood subjectively, is a work of whim, and when it remains in the bounds set for it by nature, one cannot have anything against it—whimsy is the highest degree of freedom of the will. I need this or that—I could do this or that—I like this or that—this feeling of completely unrestricted self-determination, to be allowed to want, because one wants, or to want because one is permitted to want, has something so sweet about it, that one can grant this to people occasionally. It is a matter of the health of the mind [*Seele*], of the abundance of inner energy, and mostly an aggregate of refinement. Intelligence, sharpness, creativity, artistry, often large projects and sprawling enterprises are the fruits of this happy whimsy.

Typically, Bauer warned, however, against the "tyranny" that could result from following whimsy, which must "never suppress the respect for basic principles of reason and morality."[85]

Whereas a Schlosser, or to a lesser extent a Bauer, believed that imagination must not be stifled for economic reasons, there were equally excellent political grounds arguing against a "ban on imagination." Insofar as civil society was an abstraction, it was created and recreated through an act of imagination on the part of each individual who considered himself part of it. The anonymous author of "In Praise of Imagination" (1801) explained how this process worked, and simultaneously defended freedom of the press and the much maligned "reading mania": "The kind of happiness that many newspaper readers enjoy has only been available to Europeans in the past century. [It consists of] sailing on the wings of fantasy out of their small bourgeois and domestic sphere and into the great theater, and there playing in their minds the roles of a main actor, a public speaker, a statesman, a legislator, a hero."[86] The breakdown of the particular, concrete worlds of *Stand* and locality meant that only imaginative self-identification with the "statemen" and "legislators" would guarantee the congruence of self-interest with public interest; or as the anonymous author put it, the actual, smaller world in which the newspaper reader lived profited from his imaginative flights, for they moved him to action in the sphere he actually inhabited.[87] Moses Mendelssohn recognized the same principle, though he termed it "enthusiasm." This was a practical virtue, "the ability to give to distant relations of moral life definition and strength, to hear like Socrates the voice of the fatherland and of law, when love of life, the pleading of friends, or the

---

[84] Johann G. Schlosser, *Xenocrates oder Über die Abgaben* (Basel, 1784), 128–30, cited in Helen P. Liebel, *Enlightened Bureaucracy versus Enlightened Despotism in Baden, 1750–1792*, (Philadelphia, 1965), 87; Sieveking, "Fragmente über Luxus," 164; Justi, *Grundfeste*, 1:67. Consequently, luxury "could not be completely eliminated." *Grundfeste*, vol. 2, par. 258, p. 334.

[85] Bauer, *Über die Mittel*, 168, 169.

[86] Anon., "Lob der Einbildungskraft," *Hamburg und Altona* 1.3 (1801): 269.

[87] Ibid., 272.

tears of family rob him of his senses."[88] Mendelssohn here describes the same quality of mind that Jung-Stilling feared as "moral luxury," namely, the capacity to substitute for the really existing world imaginary ideals. This process of mind need not be ruinous; on the contrary, it might encourage the subordination of concrete self-interest to the abstractions of civil society. This ability of imagination, far from being against morality, actually founded the new morality, for it made possible the republican virtue at the base of the new, abstract, principled form of society and government.

These were excellent reasons why the crusade to stamp out imagination could never succeed, even theoretically. Nonetheless, mind was a dangerous thing. The antimasturbation campaign, along with the fulminations against "reading mania" (whose evil was epitomized by sexual misconduct, in any case), were perhaps the two strongest expressions of the fear of the chaos of imagination.

Masturbation was well suited as an emblem for the perils both of privacy and of solipsistic, egoistic individualism, for it was by definition a form of sex without society; it created no social relations. It was pure pleasure, without consequence. Therefore, the campaigners hastened to give it both personal and social consequences, so that it might be brought under moral law (via the duty to maintain one's health) and of society (via the duty to keep oneself fit enough to fulfill social obligations).[89]

Although the individual was isolated, he was also ubiquitous, both in the sense that this new type of person/citizen was destined everywhere to replace the older subject, and in the sense that the new individual was more mobile and less restricted than his absolutist predecessor. Masturbation was thus also the perfect emblem for this ubiquity, for it could be practiced anywhere the individual was "hidden," "undisturbed[,] and by himself."[90] "The school, church, bed, the toilet, every corner of the house and garden, the sunny field, the shady valley, these are all altars upon which this debilitating lust is offered up, and every chair, stool, chair arm or similar object becomes the tool by which this sacrifice is made."[91] Masturbation was everywhere, a kind of original sin of the privacy wrought by civil society. It appeared to be as liberal or as "democratic" a disease as the social aspirations that spawned it—yet another reason the epistolary form of sufferers' testimonials was so well suited to express it.

Because it might be ubiquitous, because privacy cloaked it, because even the campaigners admitted its debilities took some time to leave their physical traces,[92] masturbation seemed impossible to control.[93] It rehearsed in condensed form the

[88] Moses Mendelssohn, "Giebt es natürliche Anlagen zum Laster?" *Berl.Mon.* 7.3 (1786): 202.

[89] As in the letter Salzmann, *Ueber die heimlichen Sünden*, 55, 53 n. 148, cited from the anonymous sufferer, who had become a burden to his family. Also see Bauer, *Über die Mittel*, 258–62.

[90] Cella, *Über Verbrechen und Strafe*, 46.

[91] Anon., "Onanie," 243. Vogel, *Unterricht*, 5, claimed that this article was written by Gruner. "The opportunity to sin is never lacking." Anon., "Onanie," 245.

[92] If they left them at all: Winterfeld, "Heimlichen Sünden," 595.

[93] Ussel, *Sexualunterdrückung*, 147–48.

old absolutist dilemma: should one attempt to eradicate this habit by externally applied sanctions, or should one trust to education and the voluntary self-control of the citizen motivated by self-interest? In a sense, the whole antimasturbation literature chose the second option, insofar as it claimed to educate parents and youth about the alleged harms the indulgence caused. The aesthetic judgments that masturbation "erases all charm, grace, and beauty from each male and female face, kills the fire and life of the eyes" and "gives the entire face a horrible, disgusting and repulsive aspect"[94] were surely designed to appeal to the *amour propre* of youth and convince them to act in their own behalf.

But the enduring temptation to revive methods of absolutist control surfaces again and again in the literature. The Philanthropinists' main educational method was absolutist: deterrence through fright. The relentless and plastic description of bodily harm was meant to be as vivid and therefore as repellent as the public, theatrical executions of the old regime. The same is true for their recommended sexual education for children, which consisted, variously, of dreadful descriptions of the pain of childbirth, observations of birth among animals, or dissection of a female animal cadaver with fetus.[95] That is, the lessons never dealt with the pleasures of sexual intercourse, but only with its graver consequences.

Perhaps the most absolutistic "solution" the campaigners promoted to end the masturbation problem was the complete censorship and surveillance of the school children they proposed to protect. Just as Rousseau never let Emile alone: "One is never to let the little ones out of one's sight, in order to remove all the opportunities for sin." "One should prevent the tendency to be alone and to play in isolated corners." "One should listen after them and surprise them when they are alone." "One should remove all dissolute pictures, all novels and all love poems."[96] Most educational works on the subject carried advice on how to extract confessions from the little sinners. The antimasturbation vision was clearly patterned after the absolutist *Polizey* system of tutelage, censorship, and theoretical transparency, that is, the lack of a private sphere. The educators had become the absolutists, and the children, their subjects. Which, of course, raised serious questions about how citizens were ever to emerge from such total control.

Absolutist prevention of masturbation took its most obvious, physical form in infibulation. This possibility was not, in fact, an enthusiasm of the Philanthropinists, as too many later observers have suggested,[97] but an antimasturbationist did revive the idea, and others publicized information about it and gingerly weighed its propriety and utility. Such a crass use of force, applied directly to the offending body part, is testimony to the vivid legacy of absolutist solutions.

---

[94] Vogel, *Unterricht für Eltern*, 18. Also Oest, "Nöthige Belehrung und Warnung für junge Mädchen," 472–73.

[95] Salzmann, *Ueber die heimlichen Sünden*, 181–85, 193; Villaume, "Über die Unzuchtssünden," 236–66, esp. 255–59.

[96] These suggestions from anon., "Onanie," 245, 246, 247, 246, 239–50, 245–48.

[97] See Chapter 6, note 13.

Masturbation was heir to the panoply of associations that had traditionally been thought to link different kinds of immorality, on the one hand, and immoral behavior with health and social consequences, on the other. The capacious absolutist definition of *Unsittlichkeit,* which meant luxury, excessive drinking, gluttony, sexual excess, laziness, and so on, was now (with the exception of swearing) associated with masturbation. All these vices culminated in onanism. These old examples of immorality laid the foundation for a single manifestation of evil, which, for the symbolic reasons we have examined, was sexual, individual, and private. Just as immoral behavior was previously taken to injure health, so it still was. That is why the moralist Christian Gellert, writing in 1770 before the wave of masturbation consciousness, could prescribe a list of habits to improve moral and physical health that coincides exactly with the later recommendations of the Philanthropinists for preventing masturbation: simple foods, avoiding softness or effeminacy (*Verweichlichung*), physical exercise, hard beds, cleanliness, light clothing, moderation in passions, avoiding bad companions and tempting situations, avoiding overstimulation of the imagination, and so on.[98] That is also why the populationist and early public health statistician Süßmilch, writing in 1756, could list, in addition to death, the "completely terrible army of imperfections [*Unvollkommenheiten*]" resulting from "sexual excess and overdrinking" and come very close to the effects later ascribed to the secret habit: "Lack of virtue, laziness, poverty, weakening of the body, inability to work, fraud, thievery, persecution, burdening of the state and the poor chest, ruination of families. . . ."[99] This old chain of associations further explains the repeated, fantastic assertion that masturbation could lead to death—after all, death had always been the final fruit of immorality.

A final sign that masturbation was a pastiche of old-fashioned ideas is given by the sexual acts actually grouped under its umbrella. For contemporaries did not consider rubbing one's own genitals to have exhausted the definition of masturbation. They used it also to label mutual genital touching (for instance among school comrades of the same sex, or between girls and boys, but also between adults, such as wet nurses or servants, and children of either sex, or, another example, between a seventeen-year-old male youth and a six-year-old girl) and even for the case of a boy who had taught his dog to lick him.[100] Clearly, masturbation was a name given to a multitude of sexual sins that the careful nineteenth and twentieth centuries would sort into their own categories. For the late eighteenth century, however, masturbation summed up pure, objectless sexual pleasure, where neither penetration nor social relation occurred. It was not used to define social groups (like "homosexuals") or to categorize sexual knowledge; on the contrary, masturbation was ubiq-

[98] Gellert, *Moralische Vorlesungen,* 1:294–95, 2:513–14.

[99] Johann Peter Süßmilch, *Die Göttliche Ordnung in den Veränderungen des menschlichen Geschlechts, besonders im Tode. Durch einige neue Beweißthümer bestätiget, und gegen des Königl. Groß-Brittanischen Berg-Raths Herrn von Justi Erinnerungen und Muthmaaßungen in zweyen Send-Schreiben an selbigen gerettet* (Berlin, 1756), 50.

[100] See examples in Villaume, "Über die Unzuchtssünden," 7; anon., "Was ist weibliche Onanie?" 262–70; anon., "Onanie," 247; anon. ["Qw"], review of Oest, *Für Eltern,* 573.

uitous and democratic, and came prepackaged from the old, absolutist moral mill. Its causes and remedies were well known and were now simply attached to a single phenomenon.

The one innovation that the antimasturbation campaign did accomplish was to focus attention on childhood sexual pleasure. Far from desexualizing childhood, as some later observers have thought, the campaigners turned activities that parents, teachers, and children had thought unremarkable into sexual events.[101] In doing so, they spread sexual meaning into more social arenas and onto more people, sooner, than had been true before. If we can believe the authenticity of the letters the campaigners printed, then some people suddenly discovered they had been having sex all their lives (and that it was dangerous).[102] The practitioners of civil society self-consciously discussed an aspect of this problem, by asking if writing about masturbation did not promote it? As we have seen, the antimasturbationists answered that question head on and chose to spread that knowledge after all (by publicizing the existence of masturbation and its putative harm, and in some cases, even by describing how it was done). Their choice to publish sexual information was entirely consonant with the gradual upward valuation of (especially male) sexual expression and the expanded use of things sexual as symbolic interpreters of social facts. But although the antimasturbationists were Germany's first sexual educators, it is doubtful whether they understood that they were contributing to the increased *sexualization* of their society. They believed they were merely responding to a preexisting condition.

As all these facets of the topic show, the antimasturbation campaign permitted the practitioners of civil society to express the ambivalence or anxiety they felt about their own project, which they not surprisingly did in absolutist terms. The quick demise of the campaign, as well as its overt message, both testify to the realization that there was no return to absolutism.

By the late 1780s voices were being raised against what one reviewer called "the fashionable question of the pedagogues."[103] Readers yawned at the latest tract festooned with "the usual declamations about the ubiquity and horror of this evil, whose exaggeration, particularly regarding its widespreadness, one is beginning to understand."[104] After all, as one anonymous commentator noted, masturbation was only "a small physical evil"; if it were truly as destructive as the campaigners claimed, "then the whole human race would long since have died out."[105] Even

---

[101] For the focus on childhood, see the works listed in note 15. For the paradoxical effect of attempted repression as successful sexualization, see Foucault, *History of Sexuality,* 104.

[102] For some excellent examples, see Salzmann, *Ueber die heimlichen Sünden,* 11, 14, and anon., "Fragmente aus dem Tagebuch," 42.

[103] Anon. ["Dt"], review of anon. ["Schl"], *Über Kinderzucht und Selbstbefleckung, ADB,* vol. 3 of the supplement to vols. 53–86, p. 1262.

[104] Anon. ["Tb"], review of anon., *Wie die großen und kleinern Schul- und Erziehungsanstalten . . . , ADB* 107.1 (1792): 283.

[105] Anon., "Etwas über Onanie. Zur endlichen Beruhigung der Pädagogen," *Alm. f. Ä* (1790): 159, 161.

reviewers who thought there was some merit in the pedagogues' crusade could be heard sighing at the end of yet another contribution: "Finally, we would like to express the wish that, after so many writings on this sorry matter, one will stop delivering general treatises that only repeat what we already know."[106]

Exaggeration and repetition were not necessarily successful in combating skepticism about the extent and danger of masturbation, and there is much evidence of skepticism in the pedagogues' and doctors' own complaints about willful ignorance, as well as in reviews and other publications.[107] Many readers also rejected the absolutist-like notion of transparency, that is, the claim that the habit left physical marks allowing one to identify masturbators. The possibilities for misplaced social opprobrium moved several authors to deny this assertion point-blank and to return the presumption of civic equality and usefulness to the pale and tired.[108] And the absolutist undertones of the campaign did not escape censure, either. One anonymous interlocutor of Salzmann's complained that "the police, which suffers anyway from addiction to expansion, hears you shout your masturbatory Kyrie. Under the welcome pretext of protecting the health of its future citizens [*Bürger*], it will erect a pious chastity commission and this monster will send observers into houses and schools in order to search through beds and shirts."[109]

In fact, the pedagogues did not want any such thing. First, it was not the government they had appointed to watch after children, but themselves and parents. They explicitly understood themselves as leaders of civil society, whose mere servants were the bureaucrats and the prince. Campe wrote, in much the same way he wrote about good students, about "good princes, who want of themselves, what bad ones must want in the future, namely, that which the nation wants; and the nation wants what its teachers and leaders—in schools, [Masonic] temples and publications—make it want."[110] It was thus pedagogues and writers who led the nation, not the government. Second, Campe's phrase about making persons want the right thing, about shaping desire, sums up not only his and the other pedagogues' view of their own task, but also that of civil society at large. And this conviction weakened and ultimately canceled the absolutist temptation so evident in the antimasturbation campaign. After having rehearsed the dangers of sexual immorality, pondered the control mechanisms, weighed surveillance, punishment, and external force, in short, after having traversed the same territory as the Enlightened reform bureaucrats before them, the pedagogues came to the same conclusion: "In the end, I find it necessary to warn about capricious punishments [for masturbating youngsters]," Winterfeld wrote on the last page of his prize contribution, "because they aren't useful, and they can only harm. The criminal [*Verbrecher*]

---

106 Anon., review of anon. ["Schl"], *Ueber Kinderunzucht,* 100.

107 See pages 260–61 and 271; Hentze, *Sexualität in der Pädagogik,* 80–81; and Cella, *Über Verbrechen und Strafen,* 44.

108 Fest, "Ein vielleicht nicht unnöthiger Wink"; anon ["Tb"], review of *Wie die großen . . . ,* 284–85.

109 Anon., "Milet," 206.

110 J. H. Campe's introduction to Faust, *Geschlechtstrieb,* xv.

is improved neither morally nor physically. The will to sin remains; and his power of invention will give him sure means and ways to achieve his end, indeed [he will do so] even more carefully, the more he fears you."[111] In the end, only the education to self-control remained effective. The form of the antimasturbation campaign, that is, relentless publicity, rather than its actual, old-fashioned content, was its fundamental message. Its writers had dived back into the conundrums of absolutism and surfaced again, where they had begun, in civil society. The thought experiment had ended, and its thinkers fell silent.[112]

Infanticide

In Chapter 3 I explored the role infanticide played as the "key delict" in eighteenth-century German legal reform. The extraordinary position of infanticide in German public discourse, unparalleled in neighboring countries, was also evident in the over four hundred responses to the famous prize contest of 1780 on the subject.[113] The prize contest of 1780 occasioned the first popular, systematic writings by the practitioners of civil society on sexual behavior. The infanticide question posed sexual behavior as a problem because in the eyes of the law only an unwed mother could commit the act; therefore out-of-wedlock heterosexual relations, which practitioners thought the most widespread form of illegitimate sexual expression, were thus the very heart of the matter. Infanticide, then, was a central organizer of late-eighteenth-century German sexual discourse. The prize contest of 1780 on infanticide was the model and impetus for the contest on the sexual drive that Salzmann announced in 1787. He wanted "the investigation to be continued, which many excellent contributions to the essay contest *on infanticide* have already begun."[114]

Whereas the prize-contest essays tended to focus on legal reform, belles lettres used infanticide to explore gender relations. Beginning in 1775 and following in close succession thereafter until the early 1790s, infanticide figured as a main or exclusive theme in works by virtually all the "Sturm und Drang" authors, and by others besides.[115] In 1927 J. M. Rameckers subjected the German fiction on this

---

[111] Winterfeld, "Heimlichen Sünden," 609.

[112] Foucault is mistaken. "The war against onanism" did not last "two centuries," for it was not one war, but several different ones, with different meanings; the eighteenth century was not the nineteenth. Still, the eighteenth-century tales of the horrors of masturbation were a ready resource for other campaigners fighting other campaigns. Foucault, *History of Sexuality*, 104.

[113] The best account is by Ulbricht, *Kindsmord*, 217–328. See also the literature cited in Chap. 3, notes 18–24, and in Ulbricht's bibliography.

[114] Salzmann, preface to Bauer, *Über die Mittel*, ix.

[115] Rameckers, *Kindermord*, 4–5. Among these works were Heinrich Leopold Wagner, *Die Kindermörderin*, a tragedy in 6 acts (1775); Jakob Michael Reinhold Lenz, "Zerbin, oder die neuere Philosophie," short story (1775); Johann Wolfgang von Goethe, *Urfaust*, Gretchen scene (1775); Maler Müller, "Das Nußkernen," poem (1776); Anton Matthias Sprickmann, "Ida," poem (1777); Christian Friedrich Daniel Schubart, "Das schwangere Mädchen," poem (date?); Friedrich Schiller, "Die Kindesmörderin," poem (1781); Otto Heinrich Reichsfreiherr von Gemmingen, *Der deutsche Hausvater*, drama

topic to a close and sensitive analysis, which forms the basis of the following discussion.[116]

The infanticide literature was as fictional as the masturbation tracts. The social portrait it drew bore little relation to reality. Historical research has shown that infanticide was not a widespread practice, most illegitimate mothers and illegitimate fathers were of the same age and social origins, few were bourgeois, and the mother's motive to kill her baby was more likely to be economic and generally social, than to save her (sexual) honor.[117] Against this historical record, which was available to contemporaries, the infanticide literature assumed the crime was rampant and increasing and committed by a young, otherwise sexually inexperienced girl, often bourgeois, who had been seduced and cruelly abandoned by a more experienced male of a superior class (often a noble). Her motive was sexual shame, hatred of the living memory of her seducer (in the face of his child), and temporary insanity induced by emotional turmoil, but especially by the physical/emotional "illness" of childbirth.

The discrepancy between these two stories shows again that public discussion of fashionable topics does not primarily aim at a painstaking analysis of actual practices, but serves to organize cultural preoccupations in an efficient and symbolically resonant manner. In some respects belles lettres are more suited to this task than essays, and so we now turn to the patterns in the overtly fictional literature on infanticide.

Although sexual contact between the unwed woman and her lover forms the necessary basis for the infanticide dramas, the writings were not "about" sex. They did not dwell on the sexual act or even on the sexual attraction that preceded it, but on the gender and class relations that were expressed through sex. The reader is presented with a power relation that is asymmetrical in two ways, by gender, and by class. The rules governing these power relations are social, but the results are "natural," that is, pregnancy and childbirth, and then "unnatural," infanticide, as the biological facts become subject to social forces. The classic civil solution to this problem, marriage, does not occur, which sets the stage for the tragedy. No marriage occurs because the man chooses, or his parents pressure him, not to marry, and no law forces him to own up to his responsibilities. The infanticide theme thus rehearses the man's greater freedom, (as irresponsibility) against the woman's dependence.

In the dramas the origin of the man's greater (sexual) freedom is his superior social status. Since the authors were bourgeois, their aristocratic villains may be

---

(1782); Friedrich Maximilian Klinger, *Fausts Leben, Thaten und Höllenfahrt*, novel (1791). For further works, see Rameckers, *Kindermord*, 227–68.

[116] Manfred Schwarz's justified criticism of Rameckers's insistence that the Stürmer and Dränger aimed at milder, legal reform takes nothing away from the care and insight of Rameckers's literary analysis. See Schwarz, *Kindestötung*.

[117] Ulbricht, *Kindsmord*, 25–216; Schwarz, *Kindestötung*, 146–50; Richard van Dülmen, *Frauen vor Gericht. Kindsmord in der Frühen Neuzeit* (Frankfurt, 1991), 58–108.

read as instruments of class criticism. But this aristocratic freedom to avoid forced marriage, to express one's manhood sexually without entangling social results, to engage in "gallantry" (the mark of the knowledgeable and civilized man of the world), were rights the practitioners of civil society, including the bourgeois Stürmer and Dränger, were asserting for themselves. Freedom to marry, increasingly touted as a right of all citizens, meant not only that the poor might wed, but that the state no longer had the right to force marriage on fornicants, as it had done under absolutism. An anonymous reviewer of yet another book on infanticide took the author to task for favoring forced marriage and then making an exception in cases where the *Stand* difference was very great. The reviewer immediately leapt to the stereotypical conclusion: "That simply means [an exception] when a nobleman has been involved with a bourgeois lowling [*Kanalje*]. Hm! No other exceptions to the rule? Hm!"[118] The widespread fear that men would not marry, which we have seen in the cameralists' and in other writings, was another expression of the movement toward a time when men would indeed be free not to. The infanticide literature is a harbinger, a rehearsal of the potential consequences of this development in civil society, a development which reached its logical conclusion in section 340 of the Code Napoléon, forbidding state inquiry into out-of-wedlock paternity.[119]

If the noble seducer had stood, against his will as it were, for what would become bourgeois male freedoms, aspects of his character already epitomized the characterological dangers that observers saw hidden in the development toward a society of individuals motivated by personal desire. Rameckers describes the typical seducer as "a pleasure-seeking materialist: egotistical, calculating, cold and educated in the arts of disguise and seduction"; "a sensual egotist."[120] This was the new individual taken to extremes. There was another quality linking the noble seducer to the future citizen. For it is not only the noble's *Stand*, but also his superior education and knowledge (which he demonstrates as sexual knowledge, the art of seduction) which give him, he believes, the right to behave as he pleases. And knowledge was the basis for the new hierarchy of rights and privileges characteristic of civil society. The licentious, cultivated noble seducer was therefore a conveniently ambivalent symbol. Writers could take advantage of the stereotype identifying the entire noble *Stand* with civilized luxury and the whole train of associations from dissolute idleness to sexual hyperactivity and irresponsibility that luxury pulled in its wake; however, because civil society aimed to spread luxury and cultivation, and potentially its dangers as well, the figure of the noble seducer could belong to both past and future. That is, the negative qualities of the seducer were

---

[118] Anon. ["Wu"], review of *Der Kindermord. Zur Beherzigung an alle meine Mitmenschen* (Rostock, 1792), *NADB* 8.1 (1794): 45. Cf. anon. ["Im"], review of *Vom Kindermord und dessen Verhütung* (Frankfurt, 1787), *ADB* 79.2 (1788): 407, who thought that forced marriage for fornicants was among the suggestions that were "partly unenforceable and partly politically not good."

[119] See Chapter 10.

[120] Rameckers, *Kindermord*, 151, 185.

liminal, they were a characteristic of the (noble) past that was being (perhaps) projected into the future.

It would be unwise simply to equate the noble sexual villain with the new male individual of civil society. After all, his noble status conflicted with that and in any event his character was much less clearly drawn than that of his victim, the real object of the writers' imagination. But despite their criticism of him, the bourgeois writers did not totally vilify the noble seducer. In most works, he comes to rue his conduct and even to commit suicide out of remorse.[121] Clearly his creators were not devoid of sympathy for him. They may have even identified with him. The parallels to the sexual freedoms all men would soon enjoy, the seducer as embodiment of egoistic, sensual individualism and the flourish of sympathy the bourgeois writers paid to him, make one suspect that these figures were indeed meant to function as the male social analogue to the much more clearly profiled modern woman, whom the writers made the victim/child-murderess.

The female victim of the male's seduction is the epitome of modern femininity as its content was being developed in the 1770s and 1780s. She is innocent, pious, credulous, self-sacrificing, and devoted to the love of a single man. Rameckers describes one such example (in Lenz's "Zerbin") as "a young, slim, light-footed, always happy and joyful maiden. Her good-heartedness is unlimited. . . . This honesty, this carefree endlessly cheering quality of her eyes spreads consolation and joy to all who see her. . . . She is entirely love and self-sacrifice. . . . She trusts him [the seducer] completely, believes everything he says." Or, his summary of Gretchen's character in Goethe's *Faust*: "her unusual simplicity, her childlike trust and belief, her healthy sensuality and self-sacrificing love, in short, her wonderful naturalness."[122] There was nothing "natural" about this model of femininity at all, of course. These qualities were worked out in great and repetitious detail in the prescriptive and pedagogical literature of the late Enlightenment. Campe's *Fatherly Advice to My Daughter* (1789) is the most famous German example of the genre, but Rousseau had already perfected the type by 1762.[123] These works set out to produce exactly the girl who figured in the infanticide literature. "Modesty, lack of vanity . . . friendliness and an always constant goodness of heart, to which belong a disposition lightly inclined to cheerfulness and joy, patience, gentleness, pliability and self-denial," these were the qualities that education should produce in women, summarized the approving reviewer of Campe's book.[124] This was such a dominant

[121] Only the writers forced by the Faust theme to keep the seducer unrepentant, on the one hand, and Schiller, on the other, resisted this display of sympathy.

[122] Rameckers, *Kindermord*, 184, 191, also 152.

[123] In the person of Sophie, a character in *Emile*. On the larger context, see Peter Petschauer, "Eighteenth-Century German Opinions about Education for Women," *Central European History* 19 (1986): 262–92. Christine Garbe, "Sophie oder die heimliche Macht der Frauen. Zur Konzeption des Weiblichen bei Jean-Jacques Rousseau," in *Frauen in der Geschichte*, ed. Ilse Brehmer et al., vol. 4, "*Wissen heißt leben . . .*" *Beiträge zur Bildungsgeschichte von Frauen im 18. und 19. Jahrhundert* (Düsseldorf, 1983), 65–87.

[124] "Nm," review of Campe, *Väterlicher Rat*, 312. Also, Rückert, "Über die Kunst zu gefallen. Zur Bildung des schönen Geschlechts," *NTM*, September 1796, 46–60.

view that even those willing to grant that "the encouragement of her own happiness" was the first goal of female education, still held that "the satisfaction of the husband" was "without doubt" the other "main goal."[125] Although the actual education the future wives of the practitioners of civil society received never reached the perfection of the blueprint, the agreement among male writers that women's education should occur entirely in reference to themselves is nonetheless remarkable; this sentiment was shared equally by liberal supporters of the early French Revolution, like Campe, and by implacable conservative foes of the Revolution like Brandes.[126]

We are already acquainted with the sexual side of this prescription, which discouraged active sexual desire on the part of women. Not surprisingly, the infanticide stories are true to this part of the model, too. The woman never chooses her seducer, she is chosen. Although he may awaken her slumbering sexual drive, generally she agrees to consummate sexual relations not for this reason, but out of pity or sympathy for him, and "always in order to submit to his will and in the rock-hard trust that he will keep his word."[127] These tales efface autonomous female sexual desire and replace it with emotional attachment and utter subordination. The desire for pleasure has been turned inside out; it has become instead the desire to please.[128]

The infanticide tales, like the prescriptive literature, occur in a world of pure fantasy, where the man is the only active subject. He determines everything and fashions, or finds fashioned for him, women who exist only for his pleasure. Nothing limits the unfolding of his desire, because nothing protects her or posits an interest other than his own. The social ligaments that used to perform these functions are either missing or too weak (in these stories her father is often dead, or her parents are flighty, superstitious, and ineffectual), the legal sanctions (to marry or provide child support) have apparently dropped away, and the customary expectations of moral behavior that guide the woman's behavior ("the rock-hard trust that he will keep his word") no longer guide him.[129] In short, the woman is completely at the man's mercy. His power is unlimited and it is played out, significantly, on the sexual plane, because on any other, his interests would conflict with those of other men—his freedom of action would be limited.

The literary contemplation of infanticide was thus the place to try out for size the fantasy of pure, unlimited (male) desire. This thought experiment required that

---

[125] Anon. ["Rc"] review of *Bildungsjournal für Frauenzimmer, zur Beförderung des Guten für beyde Geschlechter* (Zittau, 1787), *ADB*, vol. 3 of the supplement to vols. 53–86, p. 1585.

[126] Concerning actual women's education, see Ute Frevert, *Frauen-Geschichte. Zwischen bürgerlicher Verbesserung und neuer Weiblichkeit* (Frankfurt, 1986), 33–40. Concerning conservatives on women's education, see Brandes, *Über die Weiber*, 57, 68–69, 71, and passim, and (the not-so-misogynistic) August von Kotzebue, *Vom Adel. Bruchstück eines größeren historisch-philosophischen Werkes über Ehre und Schande, Ruhm und Nachruhm, aller Völker, aller Jahrhunderte* (Leipzig, 1792), 187–88.

[127] Rameckers, *Kindermord*, 152.

[128] Rameckers, *Kindermord*, 191, 198–99, points out that only Goethe escaped this ironclad rule. Gretchen is much less passive than her counterparts.

[129] Contract (marriage) no longer follows upon oath.

social, legal, and customary limits be cleared away, changes that were already under way. In the meantime, before these changes were complete, the status superiority of the noble man against the bourgeois woman created similarly unequal power conditions. The resulting fantasy, however, turned from (male) dream to nightmare. The infanticide scenario sketched the awful results when complete female (sexual) subjection met boundless male (sexual) power. The writers' empathetic imaginations recall Rousseau, whose own imaginary experiments in the new gender order, Emile, Sophie, and Julie, ended badly, too. For the Stürmer und Dränger, the victim becomes the most awful criminal, a murderer. Yet because the fantasy so strongly required her to be passive and willess she remains so even as she murders—she kills her baby in a fever, without knowing what she is doing. This is the basis for "the *motif of guiltlessness by reason of insanity* which the authors never tire of rehearsing."[130] Thus even in their expressions of empathy, the writers remained true to the gender pattern they were exploring.

The infanticide tales imagine the dark side of the emerging gender order, and it was dark, indeed. The complete realization of men's desire created only female victims. In the stories, the victims "rarely forgive the seducer. Usually they curse him and see in every man a hypocrite and traitor."[131] Worse, the gender system seems literally incapable of reproducing itself; it creates no lasting social institutions (marriage) and it murders its own fruit. If this were truly the future, then coming civil society would be in great peril. But what happened when one tried to combine the dynamic of (male) sexual desire with the stability, protection, and limits of marriage? That was the subject of the last popular thought experiment we will examine.

Marriage

Marriage was still the center point around which all discussion of sexual behavior revolved. Despite the upsurge in writing about sexual matters at the end of the eighteenth century, "practically all writings share the feature that they are written either from the standpoint of marriage or are about it."[132] The practitioners of civil society assumed that marital sex was the only legitimate form of sexual expression, indeed, in what might be taken as a harbinger of future troubles, they were becoming more and more insistent on this point. Masturbation, for example, was considered harmful because it was *premature* and usurped an adult, married prerogative; still, at the same time the discovery of masturbation in younger and younger children undercut the easy identification of sexual pleasure with married life.

The late eighteenth century in Germany, like the Reformation, was another period when (especially male) sexual expression was relatively upgraded, this time as an attribute of natural health and a sign of robust civic participation. But, as in

---

[130] Rameckers, *Kindermord*, 150, emphasis in the original.
[131] Ibid., 153.
[132] Hoof, *Pestalozzi*, 475.

the Reformation, sexual expression was expected to be contained within marriage. That meant that both sexual expression and marriage were thought more important to society than before, which led to a postulated right to marriage for the poor as well as the propertied. Actually, given the assumption of universal heterosexual drive, the right had become a duty: "The marital estate belongs among the privileged human and civil rights. The natural drive forces the healthy adult to sex [*Begattung*] and according to law one has the obligation [*Obliegenheit*] to marry, and not live and die as a bachelor or old maid."[133] The aggressiveness with which marriage was championed as the only legitimate form of adult life is clear in the attacks on bachelors as immoral and on clerical celibates as either immoral or unnatural.[134] Nonsexual, that is, nonmarried adults, were stigmatized as at worst "half human" (as Hippel had put it), at best unemancipated and therefore not fully members of civil society. The single estate "is civic death," summarized one observer in 1793.[135]

Given the strident, universal normativity the practitioners of civil society had granted to marriage, it is surprising how fragile and unsatisfactory their essays make marriage seem. "Unhappy marriage" was a favorite theme. Contemporaries seem generally to have assumed that "happy marriages are becoming ever rarer in many *Ständen*," which piqued their curiosity to explore the reasons "why in our days there are so many unhappy marriages."[136] Cynics claimed a happy marriage was simply not to be found.[137] This absorption with marital disaster was not a German phenomenon; the English were similarly convinced that all was not well at home.[138] Apparently, aside from the usual temperamental and accidental reasons for marital dissatisfaction, the larger changes the institution of marriage was undergoing in the late eighteenth century were creating real or imagined problems common to civil society across national boundaries. Among these changes were its very normativity (there were fewer honorable alternatives to marriage), the heightened emotional expectations made of it, its lessened importance to direct economic production (at least for the practitioners of civil society), greater mobility tending to undercut it, and not least, changes in sexual assumptions. Whereas most of these changes in marriage as an institution are beyond the scope of this book, the sexual context is central. And, according to contemporary observers, the sexual aspects of marital failure were among the most important. This was a logical assumption so long as marriage still held the monopoly on legitimate sexual expression and "married"

[133] Anon., "Dinge, die gesucht werden," *Alm.f.Ä.* (1796): 93.
[134] See Chapter 6, p. 242, on celibacy.
[135] Anon., "Ehelosigkeit der Geistlichen," 254.
[136] Anon., review of C.S. von Zigesar, *Winke . . .* (Stuttgart, 1796), *Beitr.z.B.* 5 (1797): 243; K. G. Horstig, "Einige Ursachen über die Unzufriedenheit in der Ehe," *Schlesw.J.* 3 (1792): 431. See the articles listed in the *Index deutschsprachiger Zeitschriften* under "Ehe, unglückliche." Considerably more articles than these few touch on the theme.
[137] "Sch" [W. F. Graf von Schmettau], "Nicht jeder unbeweibte verdient den Namen *Hagestolz* noch den Spott seiner Mitbürger," *Schlesw.J.* 1 (1793): 279–313.
[138] Norah Smith, "Sexual Mores in the Eighteenth Century: Robert Wallace's 'Of Venery,'" *Journal of the History of Ideas* 39 (1978): 420.

continued to be synonymous with "sexually experienced." But there was a second reason contemporaries were so taken with the sexual causes of marital unhappiness. Their analysis reflected two major changes in what one might call the sexual economy: (1) the heightened identification of the "individual" with his or her putative sexual character, and (2) the upward valuation of sexual expression, both of which were putting added strain onto an institution already burdened, ideologically and legally, with the duty of forming society, ordering it, reproducing it, and determining the line between it and state power (since "private" related to those acts occurring within the house). We turn now to how the practitioners of civil society analyzed the role of sexual expression within marriage.

Unsteady, evanescent, and capricious, sexual attraction had never been thought an adequate foundation for a satisfying and stable marriage.[139] The incompatibility of sexual passion and marriage was not a problem, so long as sexual expression was not considered a constituent of personal identity, a prerequisite of productive citizenship, or a right; however, once these assumptions were even partly in force, then mere marital duty became transformed into something much more demanding. Sexual passion, once the epitome of transience, became increasingly expected to characterize enduring marriage.[140] As long as the model of sexual passion remained unchanged, it was difficult to see how the two could be reconciled, since they followed contrary principles. More than that, because the sexual model was basically male, his sexual satisfaction seemed less reconcilable with marriage than hers. The reader will recall that men's sexual desire was thought to be peculiarly transitory in three respects: regarding capacity ("she can enjoy longer than we can give"—Brandes), preoccupation ("his passion is somewhat moderated by reason"—Venette, whereas women were said to be perpetually consumed with thoughts of love) and, more important, object choice. But although the polygamy discussion ultimately chose monogamy as best suited to Europeans, it did so despite the conviction that promiscuous sexual desire was "natural" to men, but not to women.[141] So, although everyone recognized that ardor faded for both sexes, that "the tenderness of newlyweds gradually becomes indifference," this process was logically more costly for husbands than for wives.[142] Few writers even bothered to consider how marriage affected women sexually.

In 1792 K. G. Horstig analyzed the process by which the male sexual drive overwhelmed the modern woman's feminine passivity and thereby ruined marriage. According to this stereotypical scenario, "the wife behaves passively, she lets it

---

[139] See the cameralists' views, in Chapter 4, pp. 162–64.

[140] This new expectation, which partly parallels and partly expresses the concomitant expectation of greater emotional intimacy, is widely taken as one of the hallmarks of the new "modern" family. See Rosenbaum, *Formen der Familie*, 263–67, 285–88; Shorter, *Modern Family*, 245–68; and Habermas, *Structural Transformation*, 43–51.

[141] See Chapter 4, pp. 176–79.

[142] Anon., "Gedanken über den Ehestand," *JaJ* 11.2 (1788): 102. Also, Christoph Martin Wieland, "An Psyche," *TM* 7 (1774): 14–33, esp. 31; anon. ["J. G. St."] and J. S. Fest, "An einen mißvergnügten iungen Prediger," *Beitr.z.B.* 3 (1793): 163–88, esp. 169, 179–80.

happen, that the husband rules over her inclinations and wishes according to his own lights." He presses for sex too frequently. In Horstig's words,

> Whoever sees in his wife a mere tool through whose use he wants to recompense himself for his earlier [sexual] abstinence . . . whoever imagines that every satisfaction of our often only accidentally awakened needs is permitted in a union, which would be dishonoring were it to occur without the civic stamp of legality under which the lowest feelings pass toll free—whoever thinks and acts like this must pay early enough for his folly with saturation, disgust [*Ekel*], and nausea [*Überdruß*].[143]

Horstig's was a warning against the dangers in the lopsided gender system currently under formation, which accorded the husband too much freedom to indulge his sexual nature, which revenged itself physically and emotionally. The second and third points were rephrasings of common wisdom; we have seen how Christian Thomasius wrote of the "justifiable disgust [*Ekel*] that overcomes" the husband after "the heat has somewhat dissipated," how Johann Joachim Becher described love turning to hate, how Venette declared that "[sexual] love was not created such, that we [men] would be long satisfied" in a single sexual relation.[144] Thomasius and Becher were merely giving the time-honored warning against marrying for motives of sexual attraction; Venette merely repeated what everyone knew about the nature of male sexual desire. Horstig, however, had introduced a new consideration by claiming that power relations inside marriage could contribute to the dilemma created by the mismatch between the sexual model and marriage.

The dilemma itself remained, however, putting every marriage at risk of falling prey to too much sexual passion, producing "disgust [*Ekel*] and disdain of both spouses for one another."[145] Although everyone knew that there are many reasons marriages go sour,[146] still, the (male) practitioners of civil society were generally convinced that they paid the greater sexual price, assumed the greater burden (of maintaining the wife and children), and lost the greater portion of freedom, or, as Bauer put it, the husband "sacrifice[d] a part of his complete freedom and independence."[147] This is the reason for the ubiquitous fear that men (not women) would simply stop wanting to marry altogether.[148] How were men to be enticed into this fundamental institution of civil society?

The journalistic writings make clear that enticement was not to occur at the cost of men's putative sexual nature. This decision was hardly unexpected, since the characteristics of the new male citizen were to a large extent a distillation of his sexual nature. The qualities of energy, self-actualization, self-assuredness, independence, decisiveness, aggressiveness, and so forth were civil translations of analogous

[143] "Einige Ursachen," 438, 439–40.
[144] Thomasius, *Von der Kunst*, part 3, par. 47, pp. 178–79; Becher, *Psychosophia*, par. 138, p. 259; Venette, *Abhandlung*, 202.
[145] Bauer, *Über die Mittel*, 312–13, 302.
[146] As Salzmann noted as a corrective to Bauer's one-sided sexual emphasis: see Salzmann's note *q* at Bauer, *Über die Mittel*, 316.
[147] Bauer, *Über die Mittel*, 48–49.
[148] See Chapter 4, pp. 183–84.

sexual qualities deemed so important to the functioning of the new society that even their negative expression, such as in "egoism," "impertinence" (*Dreistigkeit*), or "impetuosity" (*Ungestümes*) were preferable to undermining masculinity at its base.[149] Hence the frequent praise for a "manly" style of writing and the ubiquitous warnings against "effeminization" (*Verweichlichung*) and false cultivation "inconsistent with a manly German character."[150]

The inviolability of masculine nature undermined the traditional calls for male self-restraint, since restraint now would have meant doing violence to the essential male self. Since the male sexual essence must remain intact, reconciling male sexual demands with marriage tended to produce two sorts of solutions: internal control motivated by sexual self-interest, and external accommodation either by changing how marriage functioned or by changing women. Both of these solutions compensated men for what they were perceived to have lost by agreeing to marry. I discuss the solutions based on external accommodation first.

The reader will recall the cameralist Justi's bitter complaints at the loss of paternal power in marriage through the extension of the absolutist reformed police (*Polizey*) state. The more it legislated, the less discretionary power remained with the husband and head of household. This trend, which Justi had sensed in 1760, reached its actual apex in the Prussian legal reform of 1794 (*Allgemeines Landrecht*). The Allgemeines Landrecht trimmed the father's disciplinary powers, arrogated to the state the right to intervene in the family on behalf of children, and granted to illegitimate mothers and their children increased rights.[151] It had been a long time in the making; by the time it was published, it was already obsolete. Its interventions into "family happiness" were widely criticized as old-fashioned, absolutist limits to the individual freedom civil society was aiming to produce. The "individual freedom" in question, later secured under the Code Napoléon, meant the individual freedom of the individual male citizen. The sphere in which this freedom was granted was the "private" sphere of his household. In short, his freedom meant in practice the establishment or reestablishment of male domestic domination. Whereas some conservatively inclined writers used the word "patriarchal" to describe male domestic domination and explicitly equated it with the "happy mar-

---

[149] Concerning male characteristics, see Ch. 6, pp. 245–51, and Salzmann, *Ueber die heimlichen Sünden*, 34–36; Brandes, *Über die Weiber*, 54–56; and Hippel, *Ueber die Ehe*, 242. Concerning "Muth und Entschlossenheit," see Bauer, *Über die Mittel*, 299–300, and anon. ["K—f—d"], "Ueber das Verhältniß," 113. Concerning "Dreistigkeit" and Ungestümes," see anon. ["K—f—d"], "Ueber das Verhältniß," 126.

[150] On "manly" style, see anon. ["Dk"], review of *Zeichen und Werth des verletzten und unverletzten jungfräulichen Zustandes nach Nationalbegriffen, Physiologie, Moral und Politik* (Berlin, 1795), *NADB* 16.2 (1795): 404; and anon., review of *Ueber die Ehe* (1796), *Beitr.z.B.* 5 (1797): 232. Also, anon. ["Zw"], review of C. Meiners, *Geschichte des Verfalls der Sitten, der Wissenschaften und Sprache der Römer in den ersten Jahrhunderten nach Christi Geburt. Als Einleitung zu Gibbons Geschichte der Abnahme und des Falls des römischen Reichs* (Vienna, 1791), *ADB* 113.1 (1793): 199. Concerning "manly" German character, see T. Stille, "Ueber den Mißbrauch des Freundschafts-Kusses und der Umarmungen," *NTM*, Nov. 1790, 295, and anon. ["Gr."], "Vertheidigung meiner Landsleute gegen einen Aufsatz im *Teutschen Merkur* No. III, Stück 7, 1793," *NTM*, October 1793, 214.

[151] Koselleck, *Preußen zwischen Reform und Revolution*, 62–68.

riages" of the past and with good morals and clean living,[152] more practitioners defended the reemergence of male domestic dominion as a progressive reflection of natural law and thus as the literal foundation of civil society. The liberal Hippel, later a champion of women's civil rights, summed up this position succinctly, if extremely, in his 1776 treatise on marriage: "Men receive the government [of the house], and each husband is the legislator in his house. The laws he makes there are house laws. House law breaks city law, city law breaks territorial law and territorial law breaks imperial law."[153] This was a polemical, legalistic restatement of Justi's formulation that families were the original units of society from which all higher political forms flowed. A less perverse and more common late-eighteenth-century rendering of Hippel's observation equated "the most pleasant social enjoyment" with male domestic domination and derived both from

> the mutual dependence of both sexes . . . each according to its own nature [*Anlage*]. In this [nature] lies also the social subordination of both sexes, and the distribution of their duties and privileges. The wife bears enough [duties] that the husband is bound to relieve her as much as possible. The husband must do the heavier, the wife the lighter matters. If they lead a domiciled life, . . . the man must take care of business outside the house, the wife within. The man must subject himself to all public offices where mind and body work more strictly and continuously and take over everything which the wife could not do without neglecting the birth, nourishment, and upbringing of her children and the maintenance and economy of the house and without overstraining herself. In such a distribution of duties one of the two must have the leading word, since they are a pair and have the say in common deliberations.[154]

That one was, of course, the husband, and should there be occasional instances where the wife ruled, the state should in any event not recognize or encourage such exceptions, but maintain a discreet distance from family matters.[155] This viewpoint is significant both because it occurs in an essay (in the *Teutscher Merkur* of 1781) containing the strongest arguments for women's civic equality I have been able to find in the late-eighteenth-century German literature, and because it makes explicit the connection among putative natural character, civic and domestic gender arrangements, and pleasure (expressed in the quaint phrase "the most pleasant social enjoyment"). In short, the principles of gender difference and male pleasure underlying male domestic domination were thought to be rooted in nature and expressed in civil society and the state.

Guaranteeing male domestic domination from state interference was one way to make marriage more palatable to men. Encouraging wifely submission was its counterpart. That was the overt goal of countless pedagogical handbooks on

[152] "Sch," "Nicht jeder unbeweibte . . . ," 312–13.

[153] Hippel, *Ueber die Ehe,* 139.

[154] Anon. ["K—f—d"], "Ueber das Verhältniß," 127.

[155] Ibid., 129. See also Hans Ernst von Globig, *Über die Gründe und Gränzen der Väterlichen Gewalt. Beantwortung einer, im Jahr 1786 von der Akademie der Wissenschaften zu Berlin ausgeschriebenen Preisausgabe* (Dresden, 1789), and anon. ["Zm"], review of Hans Ernst v. Globig, *Ueber die Gründe und Gränzen der Vaterlichen Gewalt, ADB* 94.2 (1790): 324–33, which discusses this whole issue at length.

women's education and the dream picture that men drew for themselves: "if only I could have the feminine devotion, which I could almost call submissiveness, the whole tone, which you enjoy in your domestic arrangements," one letter writer is made to sigh.[156] The dangers of the dream, as K. G. Horstig pointed out, were that it produced male sexual tyranny and self-destruction. The solution lay with the properly educated wife. She needed not knowledge, in the usual sense of *Bildung* for citizenship, but "the art of loving, the difficult knowledge of how to win human hearts":

> The wife has without question the most unerring means in her hands, via the wise and careful use of tenderness, for nature has not given her in vain so many instincts [*Anlagen*], to secure for herself forever the love of her husband. The wife has the means at hand, both through her sweet [sexual] obligingness as well as her charming refusal, to spice the life of her spouse with such grace that she binds her spouse indissolubly to her with a tie of eternal thankfulness. . . . But who teaches the wife how to increase for her husband the enjoyment of love, to sweeten, lengthen, and multiply it? Who teaches her how to spare her husband with delicate forebearance every bitter feeling of [sexual] obtrusiveness [*Zudringlichkeit*] without ever becoming a burden to him with her own love, or transforming the sweetness of his emotions into indifference by untimeliness.[157]

Horstig here merely makes explicit the sexual side of what the prescriptive literature preached generally. The properly educated woman was not a passive slave, because, as everyone knew, "bliss [*Wonne*] cannot exist between a tyrant and a slave."[158] She was both more and less: she was to study men to divine their real needs and orchestrate their desires accordingly. Doing so required, however, entirely subsuming her own desire in that orchestration. Rather than passively suffer effacement, women were actively to achieve self-effacement. Women were thus supposed at their own cost to save men from themselves. Horstig's perfect wife follows the same principles as Rousseau's Sophie, whose entire being was designed to fit Emile's needs. And even Mary Wollstonecraft's woman, whose moral perfection would redeem civil society if it were released from its domestic bondage, operated after the same pattern of redemption through self-sacrifice. This figure of the redemptive woman went on to a long career in the next century. The only curious part of Horstig's scenario for the eighteenth century is that it denied men the capacity of sexual self-control that the rest of gender ideology hailed as their very definition. This curiosity is, I believe, merely an effect of the clashing principles of the sexual drive and marriage and of the attempt to bind them together for social reasons.

The only vestige of the earlier demand that men exercise (sexual) self-control came packaged in the argument that some marital restraint was in his own sexual self-interest. This argument was two steps removed from the traditional moral position that sexual pleasure was animalistic and ought to be avoided as much as

---

[156] Anon., "Eheglück," *Schl. Prov. Bl.* 11 (1790): 546.
[157] "Einige Ursachen," 437, 438.
[158] Anon. ["K—f—d"], "Ueber das Verhältniß," 132.

possible for that reason; and one step removed from the argument from negative self-interest, which had emphasized the physical danger to men from excessive sex. Both of these older positions were losing ground to a new formulation according to which sexual pleasure itself had two grades. The lower was animalistic, merely physical, short term, and comparatively unsatisfying. The higher was sublime. Emotional attachment made pleasure more intense, reciprocity made it longer lasting, mutual regard made it sweeter and undiminished by regret or self-reproach, and physical moderation, enlivening the imagination and thus renewing the well-springs of pleasure, made it inexhaustible. The true connoisseur of sexual pleasure was no longer the roué, but the husband. An anonymous analyzer of "marital pleasure" has a young man, who had hesitated to wed, put it this way: "I was never able to fill the emptiness of my heart when I enjoyed commercial love; I always felt an indescribable disgust [*Eckel*] when I only satisfied the animal need but could not enjoy love, love of the soul. Ah, friend! I truly believe, 'virtue is the only thing that satisfies all the desires of the soul and the purest, highest lust [*Wollust*] is only achieved in the chaste marital bed.'" Now that he has traded a mistress for a wife, he not only can live more economically, "but I also have more *pleasure. . . .* For the first time I feel that the corporeality of the enjoyment of love has been spiced and made delicious through harmony of the soul."[159] For Herder, the entire foundation of the "ecstasy of pleasure" was laid by emotional attachment. Its sweetest moment was "the instant of that mental recognition, that revelation of the soul through a look which sets us back . . . into the joys of paradise. . . . The future can only develop, but rarely add to" that foundation.[160] The spouses' mutual regard, the product of love, was also the basis of their mutual moral improvement, of course. For "solely among virtuous people is [social] intercourse of any duration possible; and only duration brings endless pleasure, pleasure that has as its basis the [spouses'] recognition of mutual moral advantage."[161] In short, the vice-ridden person "will never share the wise man's happiness created by his enjoyment of life." "Countless sources of even sensual lust will dry up" for such a person.[162]

Such widespread sentiments moved Christian Wolff's old equation between happiness and morality to an explicitly sexual plane. Sexual self-interest did, after all, coincide with marriage, only if one appreciated sex as something more than mere irresponsible ejaculation. This reinterpretation of sexual pleasure as something potentially higher than mere animal drive, more durable than an instant, and more sublime than a mere physical "convulsion,"[163] was related to, but still

[159] Anon., "Eheglück," 535, 545.

[160] Herder, "Liebe und Selbstheit," 222. Herder thought sex threatened to undermine the pure heights of emotion (222–23).

[161] Anon. ["D. S."], "Haben Ehegatten gegen einander Pflichten in Ansehung des Umganges, und welches sind sie?" *Hann.Mag.* 24 (1786): cols. 1083–84.

[162] Bauer, *Über die Mittel*, 302; also anon., "Betrachtungen über das menschliche Leben, dessen Zweck und Werth," *Hann.Mag.* 19 (1781): col. 1675.

[163] Sarganeck, *Warnung*, 35.

different from Thomasius's sex-sympathetic early modern formulation.[164] Thomasius had understood marital sexual acts as ways to express one's love and to give love a firm, physical foundation; his stress was on the relationship, and sex was a means of elaborating that relationship. The practitioners of civil society pushed Thomasius's beginning further down the path toward making sexual expression an end in itself, which could only be achieved in its most intense and enjoyable form within marriage grounded in mutual love. They had not completed the journey, but they had moved in that direction. Their drift was accelerated by the Enlightenment's more exalted notion of mankind, which tended to upgrade his "natural drives" from the mere animalistic, and by the cultural discovery that the sexual drive was analogous to positive qualities necessary to individuals and to society, and not merely symbolic of negative forces bent on destruction. That sexual passion might under circumstances be similarly positive or exalted was a logical reflection of these other trends, and it was a new idea.

The positive revaluation of sexual pleasure along the model sketched above was also peculiarly well suited to the idea of the citizen-individual, for it respected, indeed required individuality, rehearsed restraint and practiced reciprocity, while retaining the pleasure principle. As Emilie von Berlepsch put it, "Where reciprocal love exists, says Plato, there also is stringent observation of oneself, because each one is trying to please the other; and so both parties carefully avoid indecency and humiliation, so that they never disdain one another; they strive to attain the uplifting and beautiful, so that they may be ever more worthy of the other's love."[165] The "spiral of love" begins with the individual who, aspiring to be loved, engages in self-surveillance, the effect of which, however, is not repression, but the attainment of more and more love (and pleasure) as one becomes worthier and worthier. The reader will recognize this as the same theoretical model as that of the progress of civil society itself. Herder underscored the individualism at the base of this process: "We are individual beings, and must be so, if we are not to lose the foundation of all pleasure, that is, our own consciousness, for the sake of pleasure, and thus lose ourselves, in order to find ourselves in another being, who cannot be ourselves."[166] In less sybilline prose: experiencing pleasure can only occur through the consciousness of an individual who has not abandoned himself completely either to the idea of love or to a loved one; if he did seek pleasure without bounds, love without limits, he would destroy his selfhood by giving up the consciousness of himself, and thus he would destroy his very capacity to experience pleasure. Herder postulated here a self-limitation of the pleasure principle that coincided perfectly both with the ideology of individualism and, as we shall see, with gender differentiation.

---

[164] See Chapter 4, pp. 174–75.

[165] Emilie von Berlepsch, "Ueber Liebe als Leidenschaft, und den Grundsatz zur Beurtheilung ihrer Dignität," *NTM* 3 (1790): 432.

[166] Herder, "Liebe und Selbstheit," 229.

Sex, Gender and Civil Society

The contemporaries' discussions of the sexual drive, masturbation, infanticide, and marriage are subject to many possible interpretations. From our standpoint, the relation of sexual behavior to civil society, these discussions aimed to produce an economy of sexual pleasure commensurate as far as possible with social solidity and individual male freedom. Marriage was the key institution (as it had been since at least the Reformation), mediating between individual desire and the public interest. In these writings, marriage served as a model of civil society. Accordingly, the male subject appeared to relinquish some of his sexual freedom to join a relation limited by contract. But he actually received more than he gave up, for in addition to the domestic dominion he kept over persons not yet (or never) ready for independence, he acquired in marriage the possibility of truly sublime happiness in a heightened form of sexual and emotional pleasure unattainable elsewhere. Just as civil society was the prerequisite for progress toward the perfection and therefore the happiness of mankind, marriage was the same for individuals in their private lives.

Tyranny was unacceptable in both private and public spheres. Those writers aiming to revivify male domestic domination were careful to deny that they were laying the foundations for male tyranny. As "K—f—d" put it, "Anyone who stretches subordination farther [than what the natural difference between the sexes required] until it become tyranny or rule by force, delivers the other party from the duty of obedience. And this order nature must perforce have laid upon that party which, in general, more often has his head and body under his own control [that is, the man]."[167] Hippel declaimed that "where male tyranny has made the wife a rebel everyone must wish to come to the wife's aid,"[168] and Herder felt that tyranny was, in the end, simply impossible. "A tyrant, who can be everything himself, who wishes to swallow everything . . . is capable neither of friendship nor love, nor even of parental tenderness. He presses and oppresses; next to him nothing can grow, not to speak of growing with him into a common crown [community]."[169] Incapable of love, he does not receive pleasure, either. The domestic tyrant, wrote "K—f—d," "robs himself of all the bliss [*Wonne*] of marital society. Because bliss cannot exist between a tyrant and a slave."[170]

Yet the practitioners of civil society championed male dominion and domestic hierarchy. Like the most Enlightened reform bureaucrats, however, they preferred *douce violence* to absolutist force; they aimed for domestic government that ran like civil society was supposed to, according to desire and pleasure. Returning to Hippel, he made clear that the principle of this domestic government was different from other forms of domination: "The domination [*Herrschaft*] of the husband over the wife must not be like that of the master over his household, or like the manager

---

167 Anon. ["K—f—d"], "Ueber das Verhältniß," 128.
168 Hippel, *Ueber die Ehe*, 145.
169 Herder, "Liebe und Selbstheit," 230.
170 Anon. ["K—f—d"], "Ueber das Verhältniß," 132.

over his fields, but, as the ancient saying has it, like the soul over the body. Or like a pair of harmonious tones, would be better, because very often the soul must give way. Like a pair of harmonious tones, I say, from which, when one is played, the other plays along."[171] The little society of marriage was therefore founded on difference, the difference between men and women, which an unseen hand orchestrated into pleasure and into the pleasures of community. Herder uses precisely the same metaphor: "Unison [*Einklang*] is neither pleasant, useful nor possible in this marriage of souls. There must be consonant tones to produce the melody of life and of pleasure, not unison."[172]

Like Rousseau, the practitioners of civil society believed that gender difference was the basis of sexual attraction, which, in turn, produced the first protosociety (marriage) and thus by extension the larger society. Gender differentiation was thus the motor of the entire process of civilization. The anonymous "K—f—d" authored a remarkably progressive piece on women's equality in civil society in which he described that motor as follows:

> Because nature intended that difference [between men and women] in order to produce that much greater a union for the purpose of common happiness, so nature also has taken care to create equal dignity and happiness for both halves. The seeming weaknesses of the wife give her through the power of charm, flattery, and obligingness, such a superiority that the strengths of the husband seem to be only a weak pleasure [*Vergnügen*], in order to hold both halves in equilibrium.[173]

But this reassuring portrait of "seeming" equality, as the author lets slip, is based upon an ironclad distinction between men and women.

> Never must equality [the product of advancing civilization] extend to the qualities of the sexes. The exchange of these [qualities] through a misunderstood accommodation causes distance and degeneration [*Ausartung*], through which both sexes become contemptuous of and unbearable to one another. I feel sorry for sweet little men [*süßen Männchen*] and amazons.[174]

The devotion "K—f—d" felt for absolute gender distinction thus moved him to express disdain for effeminate men and masculine women. Here he anticipates the nineteenth-century fixation on homosexuality and thereby makes explicit how gender anxiety, the proximate cause of antihomosexuality, stood for much greater fears about social cohesion and integration generally. Both explicit antihomosexuality and extreme gender rigidity are paradoxical markers of "K—f—d"'s progressiveness, since precisely his liberalism and his firm standpoint within civil society made both subjects so important. After all, state coercion would no longer hold the fragile edifice together. But "K—f—d" shows the other face of civil society, too, by revealing ten pages earlier the obvious criticism of gender rigidity. There he has a

---

[171] Hippel, *Ueber die Ehe*, 144–46, metaphor repeated on 164.
[172] Herder, "Liebe und Selbstheit," 213
[173] Anon. ["K—f—d"], "Ueber das Verhältniß," 131.
[174] Ibid., 132–33.

female interlocutor exclaim, "I reckon this [fear of losing gender difference] to the petty modes of thinking common to your sex: that you, out of fear of losing your usurped superiority, hold on so jealously to the exact boundary marks between both sexes, in clothing, games and practices."

"K—f—d"'s piece laid out the gender assumptions that organized nature and society, according to the practitioners of civil society. "As God placed two lights in heaven, he placed two sexes on earth, who, in the movement of emotions, hold each other in equilibrium. Each complements the other, giving what one lacks in tenderness, what the other lacks in strength, and in the empire of love tenderness is mightier than strength."[175] This is Herder, but it could have been almost anyone, so obviously true did it seem.[176] Herder's invocation of the image of the sun and moon ("two lights") recalls the hoary tradition of gender difference in the European cultural imagination.[177] But now the appeal to nature, and even the appeal to tradition, meant something different. For now society was made to bear more weight in the anticipated weakening of external support and guidelines from the state (and from religion). The natural principles thought to give society order and stability seemed to stand almost alone against the threat of chaos. Where once gender differentiation had ordered the private, nonstate world and created at most symbolic echoes in the public, it was now supposed to organize both. Thus, as society swelled in importance, so did gender differentiation.

As in all fundamental reorganizations, the one that created civil society was centrally concerned with reallocating power, not just among classes or *Stände*, but also between men and women. Contemporaries knew this, as their references to "usurped superiority," "male egotism," and their feverish demonstrations of women's subordination prove. But the principle of civil society, that it rest on an unforced revelation of natural law, that its participants should desire the order in which they acted, meant that coercion should be replaced by "the empire of love."

The institutionalized form of the empire of love was marriage, where gender differentiation and sexual nature were both reconciled and tempered to fit civil society. Whereas marriage had for a very long time been held to be synonymous with sexual expression altogether, it was now held to be synonymous with a particular kind of sexual expression befitting civilization, as opposed to raw nature. Marriage and sexual expression had both changed in order to make them characteristic and defining of the civilized. As the masturbation literature made clear, real sex was the prerogative of adults, that is, of persons mature biologically, and rationally. For this same reason the cultivated and gallant literature discussing sexual topics was harmless and possibly even beneficial to the Enlightened, but harmful when it fell

[175] Herder, "Liebe und Selbstheit," 213.
[176] See Honegger, *Ordnung der Geschlechter*, 46–71; Barbara Duden, "Das schöne Eigentum. Zur Herausbildung des bürgerlichen Frauenbildes an der Wende vom 18. zum 19. Jahrhundert," *Kursbuch* 47 (1977), 125–40; Frevert, *Frauen-Geschichte*, 15–25; and Hausen, "Family and Role-Division."
[177] Wunder, *Er ist die Sonn'*.

into the hands of others. An anonymous reviewer of the apparently prurient work *On Intercourse* explained the principle:

> One will concede to us, that *truly enlightened people*, even when they are spoiled regarding their drives and daily transgress the bounds of chastity, nonetheless may bear a shameless and immoderate discussion of this point [sexual intercourse] and pay attention with silent phantasy and concentration. One may expect and even demand [such behavior] from them. But, what about even young citizens and subjects [*Landleuten*], school-children, soldiers, artisans and young servants?[178]

He answered a ringing "no" for these members of the "great sensual mass."[179] His silence on women did not indicate that he included them among the truly enlightened; on the contrary, women did not even come into question. Female credulity regarding romantic novels and the delicate sensibilities that ought to characterize them increasingly seemed to require shielding them from sexual writings and expressions.[180] Those who did not partake fully in civil society, did not share fully in the sexual knowledge it produced.

The same principle applied to sexual education, an invention of the Philanthropinists, who reserved it for the future citizens, the young members [virtually all male] of the "educated estates" (*gesittete Stände*). Their cultivation put them at sexual risk, and therefore sexual knowledge must save them. In his convoluted way, Villaume explained:

> It is among the educated estates, for whom alone one writes, since other estates neither read nor buy books, that it is simply impossible to leave children in complete naïvete, ignorance, and innocence, because education, nourishment, new customs, early [social] intercourse, premature education, and the reigning errors of this estate makes this impossible. Consequently one must preempt the knowledge and temptation pressing in from all sides. That is the reason one must teach; one must lend to the ideas that cannot with certainty be avoided, a certain touch of dignity which might turn aside possible harm.[181]

Knowledge and cultivation therefore brought more sexual knowledge in their train.

The sexual knowledge propagated by the practitioners of civil society had subtly changed the received picture of sexual expression. There was now a higher form of

---

[178] Anon. ["Lb"], review of anon., *Ueber den Beyschlaf*, *NADB* 10.1 (1794): 171, emphasis in original.
[179] Ibid.
[180] Worries about women and romantic novels were ubiquitous throughout the period; Möller lists some of these typical polemics in *Kleinbürgerliche Familie*, 266. Goethe wrote the following poem to his publisher, thanking him for removing drastic phrases from Goethe's works and making them acceptable to "the little women":
Und bring', da hast du meinen Danck,
Mich vor die Weiblein ohn' Gestanck.
Musst alle garst'gen Worte lindern,
Aus Scheiskerl Schurken, aus Arsch mach' Hintern,
Und gleich' das Alles so fortan,
Wie du's wohl ehmals schon gethan."
Goethe to F. W. Gotter (1773), in *Der Junge Goethe*, ed. Hanna Fischer-Lamberg, 3:39, cited in Kiesel and Münch, *Gesellschaft und Literatur*, 120–21.
[181] Villaume, "Über die Unzuchtssünden," 145–46.

sex, suitable to the higher sort of people who practiced it. Tempered by emotional attachment and the desire for self-control, it became better, not just morally or socially, but qualitatively; it was longer lasting, sweeter, more meaningful, and above all free of disgust, remorse, regret, or shame at having indulged in animalistic display, and thus no negative psychological aftertaste sullied the pure experience. This was the sex characteristic of citizens, and it divided citizens from the "great sensual mass" as surely as literacy, taste, wealth, and occupation did. In this way the sexual experience itself, not just its sociological characteristics, was made into a definition of class.

Enjoying this new experience of sex was a mark of the citizen; it was made possible by the cultivation carried and developed by civil society, and it was at the same time a reward for participating fully in that society, with all its stresses and strain. As Cella put it, "It is this *love*, this nobler passion of the more educated [*gesittetern*] youth and of the better girl . . . , it is this love that spurs the youth more than any other reward and passion to make himself [*sich bilden*] into a moral, pliable and useful man, which steels the man's courage to use up his best energies for business of the state and fatherland, so that he may unreservedly enjoy the joys of life in the arms of a loyal wife." This, according to Cella, was the "main goal of marriage on the man's part."[182]

These were the rewards that would entice the man into the fundamental private institution of civil society: marriage. Marriage was thus the man's social purpose (*soziale Bestimmung*). As the infanticide literature made clear, he was bound to it by his word, by his sense of honor, perhaps by social pressure. But where the man was bound by his word, "the wife is bound by nature."[183] As the prescriptive and theoretical literature never tired of pointing out, while the man's *social* purpose was marriage, it was woman's *natural* purpose. This was the distinction that made all the difference as we move out of the mere founding of civil society and into the realm of its actual functioning, into politics.

[182] Cella, *Über Verbrechen und Strafen*, 82, 122, emphasis in original. This common view of marriage/ sex as the recompense for the man's putatively harder lot in civil society we have already examined amongst the cameralists; see Chapter 4, pp. 183–89. See also, as typical examples, J. G. Jacobi, "Von der Schaamhaftigkeit," *Iris* 5 (1776): 138–44, esp. 142; anon., review of *Ueber die Ehe, Hann.Mag.* (1777), cols. 695–702, esp. 700.
[183] Hippel, *Ueber die Ehe*, 120.

8

Pre-Napoleonic Liberals and the Sexual Determination of Rights

The sexual views we have been examining were formulated primarily by Enlightened progressives in the course of their efforts to define civil society and
reform the late absolutist state. In the 1780s, as Enlightenment became politicized,
liberalism became its political expression, which called into being the opposing
political formation of conservatism.[1] The most influential exponent of this pre-
Napoleonic, or early, liberalism was Immanuel Kant. For all his unwillingness to
oppose Frederick the Great's absolutism openly, Kant nonetheless had laid bare the
critical principles that, when applied to politics, demanded the establishment of the
rule of law (*Rechtsstaat*), which guaranteed civil society just as it defined and
circumscribed state power. I discuss the legal reforms themselves in the next two
chapters. In this chapter I examine how legal reform was to determine the distribution of rights and duties in the new civil society/state. How did the early liberals'
reflections on sexual nature, worked out in relation to society, affect their views of
the rights and protection guaranteed by government? How did the sexual characteristics imputed (often unconsciously) to the citizen help determine how political
rights (*Bürgerrechte*) should be distributed?

Kant, his friend, fellow bachelor, and frequent dinner companion Theodor von
Hippel, and Kant's most famous pupil, J. G. Fichte, succinctly demonstrated the
developmental possibilities within early liberalism at the end of the eighteenth
century. Each man drew different conclusions about the relation of rights and
justice to the sexual order, depending especially upon his starting point, that is,
whether he reasoned from society or state (law). Social reckoning significantly
thwarted egalitarianism. And, though none is known primarily for his contributions
to sexual theory, the writings of each reveal how the assumptions the practitioners
of civil society made about sex could have real civil and political consequences.

[1] Hans Erich Bödeker and Ulrich Herrmann, eds., *Aufklärung als Politisierung—Politisierung der
Aufklärung* (Hamburg, 1987); Fritz Valjavec, *Die Entstehung der politischen Strömungen in Deutschland,
1770–1815* (1951; Kronberg, 1978); Zwi Batscha, *Studien zur politischen Theorie des deutschen
Frühliberalismus* (Frankfurt, 1981).

Rights

Contemporaries sometimes distinguished "human rights" (*Menschenrechte*) from political, or citizens', rights (*Bürgerrechte*). The former adhered to all persons by virtue of being human; human rights were the presumption of freedom, that is, the right to dispose over oneself and to determine one's own happiness, and the right to equal treatment before the law.[2] Citizens' rights pertained to those rights exercised in civil society understood in its broad sense, as the organized aspect of society-at-large (*Staatsbürgergesellschaft*). Rights exercised in civil society in this sense had two aspects: political and economic. Immanuel Kant referred to these rights as "the *independence* (*sibisufficientia*) of a member of the commonwealth as a *citizen*, i.e. as a co-legislator," which meant "the right to vote," to participate generally in affairs of state (and presumably also the right to hold public office); these political rights assumed economic independence ["a citizen . . . must be his *own master*"], which in turn assumed the right to hold and dispose of property, to conclude (business) contracts, and to engage in trade or manufacture.[3]

Hammering out the catalog of rights based on natural law was perhaps the Enlightenment Liberals' greatest achievement. Not all of them, however, distinguished the two categories of rights, human and citizen, as cleanly as I have done. Kant, for example, described the three "*a priori* principles" of the "civil state" as "the *freedom* of every member of society as a *human being;* the *equality* of each with all the others as a *subject;* and the *independence* of each member of a common-wealth as a *citizen.*"[4] Though all human beings were probably also subjects, Kant did not consider them all citizens, and thus the rights they enjoyed were unequal. Later observers have also tended to speak simply of "rights" or "fundamental rights" as though these were universal.[5] Dieter Grimm, in an excellent article on how the Enlightenment-liberal conception of rights fundamentally transformed power relations with the advent of civil society, lists four groups of fundamental rights: (1) "freedom of person and private sphere. To this group belong personal freedom created by the abolition of every private relation of domination, freedom from capricious arrest and punishment, as well as protection of the private living

---

[2] Kant, "On the Common Saying," 74–75. See Krünitz's article, "Bürger" (1776), in his *Ökonomisch-technologische Encyklopädie,* part 7, pp. 376–78, for the distinction between human and citizens' rights. Krünitz's later article "Naturrecht" (1806), in part 101, pp. 630–47, barely addresses this issue. The full-blown nineteenth-century statement of this difference is made by Wilhelm Traugott Krug, *Allgemeines Handwörterbuch der philosophischen Wissenschaft, nebst ihrer Literatur und Geschichte* (Leipzig, 1827), 2:61, cited in Ursula Pia Jauch, *Immanuel Kant zur Geschlechterdifferenz. Aufklärerische Vorurteilskritik und bürgerliche Geschlechtsvormundschaft* (Vienna, 1988), 20.

[3] Kant, "On the Common Saying," 77–78.

[4] Ibid., 74.

[5] For instance, Richard Dagger, "Rights," in *Political Innovation and Conceptual Change,* ed. Terence Ball, James Farr, and Russell L. Hanson (Cambridge, 1989), 292–308. For the Anglo-Saxon literature on rights see his bibliography. Fritz Loos and Hans-Ludwig Schreiber, "Recht, Gerechtigkeit," in Brunner, Conze, and Koselleck, *Geschichtliche Grundbegriffe,* 5:231–311, does not discuss human versus citizen's rights, or their peculiar, gendered application.

space"; (2) freedom of communication (freedom of the press and opinion); (3) economic freedom (freedom of property, trade, and contract); and (4) equality before the law.[6] Because this list omits the rights of political participation, it appears to name the human rights applicable to all persons. Yet, in neither theory nor practice in the late eighteenth century and on into the nineteenth did Grimm's list actually cover human beings equally.

Children, the mentally impaired, the poor or economically dependent, and women did not enjoy the full complement of rights.[7] The exclusion of the last two groups from human and political rights does not follow from natural-rights principles. Other considerations, especially social ones, were at work here. Among these "other considerations" were Enlightened sexual views not only about sexual behavior directly but, more important, about the sexual nature of men and women, about the sexual aspects of civil morality, and so on. These sexual views contributed to the actual, skewed distribution of rights by helping to form the social norms and expectations organizing civil society, which in turn became partly institutionalized in law. In the nineteenth century especially, sexual judgments were instrumental in defining the "lower classes" as less worthy of the rights of citizens.[8] In the late eighteenth century, however, liberal sexual views worked primarily to discriminate against women.

There seem to have been three broad ways in which Enlightened progressives', or early liberals', sexual assumptions shaped their conception of how rights ought to be distributed. These were implicitly, as in the case of Kant; explicitly, as with Johann Gottlieb Fichte, who actually grounded rights in sexual behavior; and not at all, as with Theodor Gottlieb von Hippel.

The Implicit Sexual Model (Immanuel Kant)

Kant exemplifies what was probably the most common habit among late-eighteenth-century liberals. When he thought about sexual behavior explicitly, he tended to follow the male sexual model and thus to conclude that men and women were more alike than different. Society, however, required different sexual conduct

[6] Dieter Grimm, "Die Grundrechte im Entstehungszusammenhang der bürgerlichen Gesellschaft," in *Die Zukunft der Verfassung* (Frankfurt, 1991), 70.

[7] Marxist critics began to write the history of the exclusion of the poor and workers from civil rights, but it took longer for historians to recognize the exclusion of women. See, for Germany, Ute Gerhard, *Gleichheit ohne Angleichung. Frauen im Recht* (Munich, 1990), and Ute Gerhard et al., eds., *Differenz und Gleichheit. Menschen Rechte haben (k)ein Geschlecht* (Frankfurt, 1990), esp. 188–267. On the mentally ill, see Dirk Blasius, *Der verwaltete Wahnsinn. Eine Sozialgeschichte des Irrenhauses* (Frankfurt, 1980). I am unaware of a history of the legal rights of children under German law.

[8] See Lipp, "Reproduktion," on how marriage restrictions and resulting illegitimacy restructured rural society in Württemberg. On sexual behavior and its misinterpretation by "respectable" observers and how both helped shape a new class of workers in proto-industry, see Braun, *Industrialisation*, 41–46. For the later industrial working class, see Carola Lipp, "Die Innenseite der Arbeiterkultur. Sexualität im Arbeitermilieu des 19. und frühen 20. Jahrhunderts," in *Arbeit, Frömmigkeit und Eigensinn. Studien zur historischen Kulturforschung*, ed. Richard van Dülmen (Frankfurt, 1990), 214–59.

from men and women for its own purposes. Therefore, Kant was tugged in two contrary directions. When he thought about sexual ethics as derived from the nature of sexual relations, he arrived at remarkably egalitarian standards for both men and women, as he outlined in his *Lectures on Ethics* (1775–80).[9] When he thought about how society functioned and how sexual attraction caused different roles for men and women, he derived different duties and different rights for each gender. One finds this kind of thinking in his early *Observations on the Feeling of the Beautiful and the Sublime* (1764), his unpublished *Remarks* on the *Observations*, which he penned over the years, and in his *Pragmatic Anthropology*, which set down in published form in 1796–97 lectures he had delivered almost yearly since 1772–73.[10] Finally, when Kant thought about politics and the organization of the state, he assumed a male citizen-individual whose rational, energetic, and physical characteristics had been previously defined by the male sexual model, which now sank, unnoticed, into the background.[11] Hence, the rights enjoyed by this figure were indeed grounded on his sexual nature, but only implicitly. It was precisely the implicit nature of the grounding that permitted Kant to leave the egalitarian insights of the *Ethics* unintegrated with his other writings.

In most respects, Kant's beliefs about sexual nature were conventional. Consonant with the male sexual model, he too believed that "in the primitive condition, there is a mutual need" for sex in both women and men (*Bemerkungen*, 188, 96).[12] Typically, however, when Kant came to imagine the consequences of sexual abstinence, he revealed the subterranean identification of sexual activity with maleness. Without sex, he wrote, "a human would be incomplete; one would rightly believe that one lacked the necessary organs, and this would make one imperfect as a human being" (*Lectures on Ethics*, 164). Although he referred to the ungendered human (*der Mensch*), it seems clear that the "necessary tools [*Werkzeuge*]" he had in mind are the male genitalia—contemporaries never used that phrase to describe female sex organs.

Again typically, Kant clearly associated (the sexual) drive with the impulse to independence, autonomy, and freedom. The drive to freedom and the sexual drive were the two, basic, innate passions (*Leidenschaften*) defining mankind (*An-*

[9] Immanuel Kant, *Lectures on Ethics*, trans. Louis Infield (New York, 1963). Wherever feasible Kant's *Lectures on Ethics* is hereafter cited parenthetically in the text. Jauch, *Immanuel Kant zur Geschlechterdifferenz*, is the first person to explore in depth Kant's views on gender and, to some degree, sex, using this source together with Kant's other writings. Robin Schott, *Cognition and Eros: A Critique of the Kantian Paradigm* (University Park, Pa., 1993), examines Kant's sexual views strictly regarding their function in his philosophical writings.

[10] Immanuel Kant, *Bemerkungen zu den Beobachtungen über das Gefühl des Schönen und Erhabenen*, vol. 22 of *Kant's gesammelte Schriften*, ed. Preußische Akademie der Wissenschaften (Berlin, 1942), 1–192, which also contains the *Beobachtungen* themselves in notes at the bottom of each page. Immanuel Kant, *Anthropologie in pragmatischer Hinsicht* (1798), 7th ed. (Hamburg, 1980). Wherever feasible, Kant's *Anthropologie* and *Bernerkungen* are hereafter cited parenthetically in the text.

[11] See the collection of essays edited by Hans Reiss, *Kant's Political Writings* (Cambridge, 1970).

[12] Kant apparently omitted most punctuation in his *Bemerkungen;* I have therefore supplied the punctuation as necessary.

thropologie, par. 81, pp. 205–6). And desire, generally, drove the independent action of the free subject: "Desire [*Begierde*] (appetitio) is the self-determination of the energy of a subject through the imagination of a future condition as an effect [caused by] the subject" (par. 73, p. 183). As in philosophy, so in society, for it was in the moment of his sexual activation, the moment when he acquired a wife, that a man became emancipated and entered into the state of natural freedom: "The man who has a wife is complete; he separates himself from his parents and is alone in the state of nature" (*Bemerkungen* 74, also 28).

But the consummated sexual relation of man and woman did not create a static world of autonomous monads. Like most observers of his time, Kant was acutely aware of what he saw as the historical development of the species, in which the social physics of sexual attraction played a paradigmatic role. For sexual attraction was based on the two contradictory movements that caused progress: the friction of difference and the reconciliation of opposites. Kant described the "character of the [human] species" as that of

> an animal with the capacity for reason through which it can make itself a rational animal. Whereby it, first, maintains itself [that is, through mere reproduction]; second, practices and prepares itself for domestic society; and third, rules itself as a whole, which is destined, systematically and rationally ordered, for society. . . . Nature has laid the seed of discord [*Zwietracht*] in the species, and wants that [the species's] own reason should make harmony [*Eintracht*] out of it. . . . In nature's plan, [Harmony] is thus the goal and [discord] the means of the highest, most ineffable wisdom, which is: the perfectibility of mankind through progressive culture. (*Anthropologie,* part 2, p. 275)

The sexual attraction that men feel for women, which Kant conflated with the role of women altogether, played a central role in the movement through the stages of progress from mere species maintenance to culture. For two dangers threatened to prevent men from traveling the road to moral culture. One was their very autonomy. What other eighteenth-century observers commonly referred to as male "egotism" was merely the unlimited aspect of the male individual's prime virtue: independence. Rather than arguing, as others did, that men became "domesticated," or linked to others, through tender concern for wife and especially children, Kant argued instead that the characterological peculiarities of the wife gradually subjected the husband to social dictates and processes. Women were a kind of luxury; satisfying them created needs that men in the state of nature did not know: "The greatest obstacle preventing the male sex from returning to a state of happy simplicity is the female sex" (*Bemerkungen*, 108). Women, therefore, launched men on the spiral of desire-need-activity-fulfillment and then more desire, which characterized cultural progress. Women's very dependence entangled her mate in society. Whereas "a man's honor lies in his own self-judgment, a woman's lies in the judgment of others" (86). At the mercy of society, a woman, Kant believed, paid much closer attention to its opinions. Although this might open her to mere superstition, as other writers noted, it also had positive effects, since society was the only repository of the collected, critical wisdom of the species, and it was only through society that individual progress was possible (*Anthropologie,* part 2, p. 279). The respect that women paid to society's views made them agents of society's morality.

As women overcame men's egotism in favor of social norms, they also guarded them against a second hindrance to their social progress: sensual excess. In his "summary of the pragmatic anthropology," Kant identifies the human "inclination [*Hang*] *passively* to give oneself over to the charms of leisure and luxury [*Wohlleben*], which one calls happiness, instead of *actively* making oneself worthy of mankind by fighting . . . the coarseness of one's nature" as the chief barrier to the duties "to *cultivate,* to *civilize,* and to make oneself *moral.*" (279) Although it is sensual delight that first moves a man to female companionship, her character and natural circumstances tend to prevent his sexual drive from overwhelming him (and her). Nature has given her "artifice" to counter his strength, thus allowing her to manipulate his sexual desire, making it compatible with a "continuing domestic union" (250), since "when [his] last desire [*Begierde*] is satisfied, the desire, at least regarding the same person, immediately is sated and ceases," and thus "at least regarding the object cannot be a *continuous* principle" (203, emphasis original). Therefore, women developed sexual modesty, which was the chief content of their honor (310; *Bemerkungen,* 131, 165). Female modesty tames male desire and fits it for domesticity. Modesty is not the product of female self-reflection or rational struggle and therefore does not qualify in Kant's view as moral; it flows instead from the natural circumstances of women, if not from their actual, unmediated nature. "The girl [*Frauenzimmer*] is not so much virtuous as she has the capacity to make men virtuous. Although it may seem paradoxical, women are the greatest means of [producing] chastity in men, because an otherwise fickle person [*Menschen*] is made through nothing more chaste than through his love of a girl" (*Bemerkungen,* 109).

As civilization progressed, the almost natural modesty of women gave rise to new sexual customs that magically combined greater sensual pleasure with moral taste. Kant thus subscribed to a (heavily Rousseauian) version of the phenomenon of cultivated sexual desire that we met in the last chapter, in which her restraint saves him from excess and "exhaustion": "In cultivated times . . . the female sex assumes the appearance of not needing [sex] . . . so that the infatuation with the ideal pleasure remains tied to moral taste." Consequently, "female surrender [*Ergebungen*] seems either forced [*erzwungen*] or a sign of favor" (*Bemerkungen,* 189).

By disguising their own, equal desire for sexual satisfaction, women subject men's sexual desire to social necessity. It is necessary to repeat that in Kant's view, women do not engage in this civilizing process out of their own virtue or moral superiority. They do not discover or postulate this law for themselves and then actively set out to follow it. They suffer it to happen as passive instruments of nature. "The *purpose of nature* in setting up femininity" was "the maintenance of the species, and . . . the culture of society and the refinement of the same through femininity" (*Anthropologie*, part 2, 253). Femininity, then, is a product of nature in the service of culture.

Kant's notion of the paradoxical movement of progress via the friction of difference and the reconciliation of opposites encouraged him to cling to a dichotomous view of gender difference that he had first worked out (under the immediate influence of Rousseau) in 1764 with the publication of the *Observations*. That these views still saturated the *Anthropology*, published in 1798, is probably due to a number of factors. First, the *Anthropology* was not a work of critical philosophy; it was the product of a double social tautology. It was meant to reflect the world as it was, and thus its sources were "world history, biographies, even plays and novels," which is to say, it incorporated unabashedly both the existing inequalities in current society, as well as their ideological reinforcement in the intellectual products on which society was based.[13] Another, perhaps stronger social tautology was the *Anthropology*'s moral framework. As Kant explained in its preface (*Vorrede*), the *Anthropology* was "pragmatic" in that it took as its object "what the human being as a free-acting being makes of him/herself or could or should make" (3). It was the "should," the social-moral perfectibilism, which determined how he evaluated especially women. "One cannot take what we [men] *make* as our goal, but rather what the *goal of nature* was when it set up femininity, as the principle according to which we arrive at the characteristics of this sex" (253). Thus, the social embeddedness of the *Anthropology* reinforces the gender dichotomous and goal-oriented view of women.[14] Second, the same forces, namely, regard for society as it partially was and as it should become, had meanwhile encouraged dichotomous ideas about men and women to flourish among late Enlightened and early liberal writers surrounding Kant. He had even less reason in 1798 to doubt his views than he had had in 1764. Finally, the fact that Kant's intervening critical philosophy, which conceivably might have encouraged him to adopt a more equal view of women by virtue of their shared rational qualities, did not do so, strongly suggests that Kant assumed that *der Mensch* about whom he wrote, was really *der Mann*.

Kant's dichotomous views about men and women were entirely conventional. "The woman is *defensive* [in sexual comportment], the man *offensive* [*bewerbend*]." Whereas a woman's honor is her "chastity," a man's is his "courage." "The female sex is closer to nature than the male." Whereas men are more naturally promiscuous, women have more innate sexual capacity. Laughing is a male quality; crying a female one. Women are especially patient.[15] Because the progress of civilization depended precisely on the chemistry created by these differences between men and women, Kant felt it was imperative that advancing refinement enhance, not obliter-

[13] Kant, *Anthropologie*, 5; also par. 79, p. 199, where he adds *Ritterbücher* as a further source.
[14] As Kant had noted in the *Bemerkungen*, 62: "If you reflect that man and wife are meant to be a moral whole, then [it is clear] that they must not receive the same qualities, but instead one receives what the other lacks."
[15] Kant, *Anthropologie*, 254, 258, 310, 189, 191; Kant, *Bemerkungen*, 89, 131, 165, 103, 50, 124.

ate them: "It is most important that the man becomes more complete as a husband, and the woman as a wife, that is, that the mainsprings [*Triebfeder*] of sexual attraction work according to the guidelines of nature."[16]

If social-evolutionary concerns made Kant emphasize gender difference, sexual danger moved him to imagine utter gender equality. For despite the important place Kant granted to sexual attraction as a spur to civilization, he also shared the fear that sexual desire imperiled freedom. The dilemma posed by passion, including sexual passion, was that it "surrenders [freedom and domination over oneself] and finds its appetite and satisfaction in slavery" (*Anthropologie*, par. 81, p. 204). Freedom, for Kant, meant self-determination, not permitting oneself to be led by desires determined by nature or by others, and it meant discovering and willing the laws of morality. (Sexual) passion dimmed the desire to do either. In his *Lectures on Ethics*, Kant judged sexual desire always along this axis of freedom and morality. Only free acts could be moral, but they could only be moral if they were freely obedient to law. And the version of the law, the categorical imperative, which provides the measuring stick for moral acts in the *Ethics*, is to treat persons never as means, but always as ends in themselves (120). Kant found it difficult to reconcile this principle with what he took to be the dynamics of sexual attraction. Kant's solution to the sexual-moral dilemma postulated a relation between man and woman (marriage) characterized by utter equality.

Under the rubric of "duties to oneself," Kant first comes to discuss sex. Treating oneself as an end means the following:

> Neither can we without destroying our person abandon ourselves to others in order to satisfy their desires. . . . If done in order to satisfy one's own desires, it is very immodest and immoral, but yet not so unnatural; but if it be done for money, or for some other reason, a person allows him or herself to be treated as a thing, and so throws away the worth of his or her humanity. Vices of the flesh (*crimina carnis*) are also crimes against the self, which for that reason are not spoken of. They do not harm anyone, but they dishonor one in one's person and this harms the value of humanity in one's own person. (119)

Kant branded as immoral both acting as an object of someone else's sexual pleasure and using someone else as the object of one's own. Kant could not conceive of sexual pleasure as anything other than objectification. Whereas love was a sentiment, sex was always an appetite, and thus "sexual love makes of the loved person an object of appetite; as soon as one has the person and the appetite has been stilled, the person is cast aside as one casts away a lemon which has been sucked dry" (163). Although sexual appetite might combine with the nobler sentiment of love, "taken by itself it is a degradation of human nature," precisely because it objectifies and cannot treat a human as an end in itself (163).

Actually, Kant believed the necessary objectification that sexual attraction accomplished was even worse, since it did not desire a specific person, but any person with the proper physical characteristics, or more abominable still, simply the proper

[16] Kant, *Beobachtungen*, 76. Also see Kant, *Lectures on Ethics*, 168.

sex organs. Thus "sexual desire [*Geschlechtsneigung*] is not an inclination which one human being has for another as such, but is an inclination for the sex [*Geschlecht*] of another" (164), or, as in concubinage, it establishes a relation in which one person received the "right of disposal over only a part of the whole person, namely the *organa sexualia*" (166). Either alternative clashed with the moral principle of means and ends. The second was also pernicious because it suggested that the body was disposable property which the "owner" might alienate, in whole or in part. But "a human being cannot dispose over oneself, because the human being is not a thing. The human being is not one's own property," since one could not be a (willing) subject and an object, a person and a thing at the same time.[17]

Since sexual engagement inevitably meant objectification, and since using another sexually inevitably meant using their entire person, not just a part, then only a relation in which this occurred mutually and completely could be considered moral. "The sole condition on which we are free to make use of our sexual desire depends upon the right to dispose over the person as a whole—over the welfare and happiness and generally over all the circumstances of that person. . . . But how am I to obtain these rights over the whole person? Only by giving that person the same rights over the whole of myself. This happens only in marriage." And therefore "matrimony is the only condition in which use can [morally] by made of one's sexual desire" (166–67).

In marriage

> one devotes one's person to another, one devotes not only sex but the whole person. . . . [O]ne yields ones person, body and soul, for good and ill and in every respect. . . . But if I yield myself completely to another and obtain the person of the other in return, I win myself back; I have given myself up as the property of another, but in turn I take that other as my property, and so win myself back again in winning the person whose property I have become. In this way the two persons become a unity of will. . . . Thus sexual desire leads to a union of human beings, and in that union alone its exercise is possible. (167)

All other possible sexual arrangements Kant condemned as immoral, "for the end of humanity in respect of sexual attraction is to preserve the species without debasing the person" (170). He specifically named concubinage, prostitution, polygamy, incest between parents and children, masturbation, homosexual relations, and bestiality. The first four were immoral because either the exchange between sexual partners was unequal, or, as in parent-child incest, their hierarchical relation made an equal exchange impossible, and thus debased the persons. The last three did not preserve the species. Kant censured the last group, the "crimes against nature," as "the most despicable [*Verächtlichste*] a person can commit" and wondered whether they should even be discussed publicly (169–71).

By fixing all sexual expression inside marriage, Kant simply upheld the dominant

---

[17] Immanuel Kant, *Eine Vorlesung über Ethik*, ed. Gerd Gerhardt (Frankfort, 1990), 178–79. The English translation is less clear and complete than the German.

opinions of his day. But what of the other sexual assumptions contained in the *Ethics*? Here, perhaps befitting an ethical treatise, Kant was less "modern" than many of his contemporaries. It is striking how much he distrusts pleasure, how impossible he finds it to imagine that one might give and take sexual pleasure simultaneously. Instead, his model of mutual objectification portrays two solipsistic egotists using each other; it is the model of cold property exchange; it is a model of masturbation in which one uses the organs of another instead of one's own, which partly explains why Kant had to go to such lengths to enforce mutuality and relationship in marriage. Kant's basically nonemotional and nonrelational under-standing of sexual relations recalls two older cultural models: first, the widespread assumption that men's sexual desire was unproblematic and unconnected to the partner's response (hence, Kant's remark that pursuing one's own pleasure, while immoral, was less "unnatural" than putting oneself passively at the pleasure of another) (119); and second, the pure egotism of pleasure as an animal drive.

Both Kant's rejection of pleasure as a reliable motive for moral action (against Christian Wolff) and his identification of sexual desire with animalism make his stance almost religious in its dourness. Indeed, Kant understands well why "all strict moralists and those who wanted to be considered saints have sought to suppress and do without this desire" (163–64). Kant's sexual standards were so high that, like the church, they would seem to condemn all nonmarital sex equally; his exclamation that acts "against nature" were worse than others had no founda-tion in his sexual-moral precepts.

Kant's conviction that the sexual act by itself was automatically debasing (163) is also remarkable because it tended to extend to men a judgment more often reserved for women. This, too, is reminiscent of religious doctrine, as is the utter equality of sexual relations between men and women that Kant prescribes. In his discussion of why parents and children are forbidden to engage in intercourse, Kant refers to the "equality" (*Gleichheit*) established between lovers.[18] As sexual abstinence was equally sanctifying for men and for women, and as the "marital duty" applied equally to both spouses in Christian dogma, moral sexual relations in Kant's view created an equality of condition, of mutual objectification and "submission" (*Un-terwürfigkeit*),[19] that his contemporaries imagined as a result of love, not sex.

In Kant, this almost religious formulation of the importance and role of sexual desire occurs in the absence of an interest either in psychology or in the actual workings of society, two topics that Kant's fellow Enlighteners reflected on at length. It is noteworthy that Kant did not speculate about how desire worked in the human psyche or, more important, about possible differences in how it might work in men and women. And (again, like the church) he did not derive moral duty, at least regarding sexual desire, from social obligation. Missing, therefore, was the

[18] Kant, *Lectures on Ethics*, 168.

[19] Ibid., translated as "each person submits to the other in the highest degree." Recall that Kant (and other writers) use *Unterwerfung* to describe the woman's agreeing to sexual intercourse: Kant, *An-thropologie*, 254.

temptation to tailor duty to existing social roles, a temptation that caused the Kant of the *Anthropology* to postulate radical gender difference. Instead, if duties were defined in reference to the self, and the self were considered independent of social relations, a radical asocialism that extended even to sexual relations (hence the masturbatory model), then there was no opportunity for gender differentiation to develop. Equality, even if it were merely the equality of objectification and submission, was then possible.

There are two places where Kant's ideas about gender and sex should have had consequences for the distribution of rights: within the household and in the person's relation to the state. Both are political in the broad sense, because both were the objects of conscious reflection about how relations within them ought to be ordered, and because both were objects of legal regulation. The surprising thing about Kant's discussion is its inconsequentiality; he makes no attempt to integrate his sexual ethics with his pronouncements about domestic relations or political participation, nor does he explain or legitimate the subterranean connection between his assumptions about gender and their consequences for citizens' rights.[20]

Kant appears to have thought about the domestic relations of man and wife in three different, almost hermetically sealed, ways. The first way focuses on marriage as an emotional arrangement. Because inclination (*Neigung*) by definition cannot be forced, the emotional aspect of marriage underscores its potential reciprocity and limits to domination. As he wrote in 1764, "If it comes to the point that one adduces the rights of the commander, then the matter is already extremely ruined. For when a whole relation is actually set up according to inclination, then it is already half torn apart as soon as 'ought' lets itself be heard. It is extremely ugly when the woman arrogates this hard tone to herself, and ignoble and despicable when the man does so" (*Beobachtungen*, 80). The last sentence shows that Kant thought either party might be tempted to dominate. The actual play of emotional power between the spouses Kant continued to visualize in Rousseauian terms as a wifely manipulation of the husband's sexual-emotional attachment: "It is not good for the wife to offer herself to her husband or anticipate his declarations of love. Because the one who alone has power [*Macht*] must necessarily be dependent upon the one who has charms and the latter must be aware of the value of her charms because otherwise there would be no equality [*Gleichheit*], only slavery" (*Bemerkungen*, 187).[21] The "equality" Kant had in mind was not a static balance of two equal parts, however, because marriage is an indivisible unity, not a summation. As he noted some time after 1764: "Agreement [*Einigkeit*] can always occur in equality, but unity [*Einheit*] never. Because marriage must be a unity, everything must be ruled either by the husband or the wife. Now, it is inclination rather than reason [*Verstand*] that rules [*regiert*]. Thus, either the husband's or the wife's inclination will rule; the latter is the best" (76). This shorthand note, with its suggestion that wives should rule at

---

[20] Jauch, *Immanuel Kant zur Geschlechterdifferenz*, 144–47, 156–202, 224–29.
[21] Cf. Rousseau, *Emile*, 358, 364–65.

home, discusses only half of the situation, however. By 1798 Kant had clarified how he believed emotional domestic power relations functioned.

> For the unity and indivisibility of a union the mere coming together of two people is not enough. One partner must be *subject* to the other, and reciprocally one must be superior to the other in some respects, in order to be able to dominate [*beherrschen*] or rule [*regieren*]. For, in the *equality* of the demands of two people who cannot do without each other, self-love will simply lead to arguments. One partner must be superior in a heterogeneous way for *the progress of culture:* the man [superior] to the wife by virtue of his bodily strength and courage, the wife [superior] to the man through her natural gift of mastering his inclination [*Neigung*] for her. (*Anthropologie,* part 2, 250–51; emphasis in original)

To the question, "who should have the upper command in the house?" Kant answered "in the language of gallantry (but not without truth), that the wife should *dominate* [*herrschen*] and the husband *rule* [*regieren*], because inclination dominates and reason rules" (259; emphasis in original). In short, the alleged sexual power of women over men, which drives "the progress of culture," gave women domestic influence without undermining men's power, which is based on reason. Kant could avoid the question of how to reconcile the two principles by referring to the "unity," as opposed to mere agreement, that characterizes marriage. Of course, if unity actually exists, then reciprocity can hardly occur, since reciprocity requires two forces to constitute itself. In any event, even though the "process of culture" is to be served by this dyadic arrangement, Kant made sure to describe it as "natural" (her "natural gift" and his biological strength). And, finally, Kant's bipartite interpretation of domestic power relations rested on the convenient allotment to women of inclination (which, the reader will recall, Kant identified as an inborn drive) and to men of reason.

One might summarize Kant's thinking about emotional domestic relations as reciprocal, but unequal, and saturated with gender-specific, allegedly natural characterizations of the spouses.

The second aspect of domestic relations was purely sexual. We have seen that in the *Lectures on Ethics,* this viewpoint led Kant to postulate a radically reciprocal, and thus equal, relation between husband and wife. He repeated this conclusion in the *Metaphysics of Morals,* written in the first half of the 1790s: "The relation of the spouses is a relation of *equality* of possession, both of the[ir] persons . . . and also of the possessions relating to their happiness."[22] The importance of the sexual relation for Kant can hardly be overestimated. It accounts for his blunt definition, harshly criticized by many contemporaries, of marriage as "the union of two persons of different sexes for the lifelong reciprocal possession of their sexual qualities." Whereas procreation and child-rearing might very well be a "goal of nature," only the sexual intention and consummation actually constituted marriage.[23] Kant

---

[22] Immanuel Kant, *Metaphysik der Sitten,* ed. Karl Vorländer (Hamburg, 1966), 1. Teil, 2. Hauptstück, 3. Abschnitt, Paragraph 26, Seiten 92–93; emphasis in original. Concerning the dating of *Metaphysik der Sitten;* see the introduction, xi-xiii, of this edition.

[23] Ibid., 1. Teil, 2. Hauptstück, 3. Abschnitt, Paragraph 24, Seiten 91–92.

therefore moved in exactly the opposite direction from the cameralist Johann von Justi and instead, like his mentor in such matters, Rousseau, conceived of marriage strictly as a sexual relation between the members of a couple. The accent was not on the socially sustaining possibilities of sexual congress (procreation), but on inevitable, natural heterosexual attraction and how that was to be made ethically acceptable.

The third aspect of domestic relations was legal, and suddenly Kant's argument changed. Here the husband received the power to rule; the incompatibility of this legal maxim with the reciprocity or outright equality postulated in the foregoing seems to have embarrassed Kant, given the defensive tone of the following:

> If therefore the question is: whether the equality of the spouses is contradicted when the law says of the husband regarding his wife: he should be your master (he the commanding, she the obeying part), then this cannot be seen as contradicting the natural equality of the human couple, if this domination [*Herrschaft*] is based on the natural superiority of the husband's capacity over that of the woman in achieving the common interest of the household and of the rights based on this, which therefore themselves can be deduced from the duty of unity [*Einheit*] and equality regarding the *goal*.[24]

When it comes down to the real institutionalization of domestic power relations by public action, then Kant retreats to the usual assumptions: the marital relation and the household it founds are a single-interest unit; the husband is naturally more fit to define and defend that interest; therefore, he rules. This way of thinking justifies the preexisting legal situation as a reflection of natural necessity, and unlike either the emotional or sexual arguments, it proceeds in its investigation from the outside in, by imagining the institution, rather than the people who make it up, as the singular starting point from which rights and duties can be "deduced." The only reason to set the rights of an institution above those of the persons within it is the importance of its social function; thus Kant silently adopts the social framework of judgment that led his contemporaries to similar conclusions about domestic rights.

If Kant was inconsequential about domestic power, he at least discussed it in some detail; his opinions on political participation are scanty and underargued. We have already cited the pithy statement: "The only qualification required by a citizen (apart, of course, from being an adult male) is that he must be his *own master*."[25] The "of course" testifies to an assumption so powerful that it arrests thinking. In the *Metaphysics of Morals,* under "public law," Kant elaborated the point.

> Only the capacity to vote defines the qualification as citizen [*Staatsbürger*]. Voting assumes independence characteristic of those who are not merely a part of the commonwealth, but actually members of it, that is, who want to be voluntarily in the community as an active part [*handelnder Teil*]. This last quality necessitates the differentiation of *active* from *passive* citizens, although the latter concept appears to contradict the explanation of the concept of citizen.

---

24 Ibid., Paragraph 26, Seiten 93–94; emphasis in original.
25 Kant, "On the Common Saying," 78.

Instead of explaining "independence," Kant gave examples "to remove this uncertainty":

> The journeyman of a merchant or artisan; the servant (though not civil servants); the person under natural or civil tutelage [*Unmündige*]; all women [*alles Frauenzimmer*], and generally everyone, who does not maintain his own workshop, but instead is forced to maintain his existence (sustenance and protection) by being at the disposition of another, and thus loses civil personality, and his existence is thus only inherent.[26]

The "of course" in the first citation and the "all women" in the second were inaccurate abstractions from general sociolegal reality. In fact, most women were under the tutelage of father or husband, and most did not run their own businesses; however, there were exceptions. Propertied widows and spinsters fit Kant's criterion of independence and did sometimes actually participate in local government. If Kant wished to make of the civil immaturity of most women a general principle applicable to all women, then he did this not according to the criterion of material independence, but according to some innate quality peculiar to their gender. Kant's method, then, was to deduce a universal (and thus natural) principle from a simplified view of existing social reality. He was helped along in this process by the same chain of associations we examined in the preceding chapter.

The chain of associations was built into Kant's identification of the terms freedom, self-determination, independence, rationality, and activity. These were equally the qualities of the human subject and of the *Staatsbürger*, and they were quintessentially male. As for most German thinkers of the eighteeenth century, so also for Kant, the principles of natural law thought to define the individual led directly to the unfolding of principles of government. Kant expressed this direct link time and again as the balance between freedom and law. For the individual: "The fundamental rule, in terms of which I ought to restrain my freedom, is the conformity of free behaviour to the essential ends of humanity," that is, "one should not follow one's inclinations" (*Lectures on Ethics*, 122). For the commonwealth: "Freedom and law (through which the former is limited) are the two anchor points around which civil legislation turns" (*Anthropologie*, part 2, 286). Kant repeatedly wrote of the duties to oneself in political terms: "There is in man a certain rabble of acts of sensuality [*Sinnlichkeit*] which has to be vigilantly disciplined, and kept under strict rule, even to the point of applying force to make it submit to the ordinances of government" (*Lectures on Ethics*, 138).[27] Or, again, "Just as law restricts our freedom in our relations with other men, so do our duties to ourselves restrict our freedom in dealing with ourselves" (125), or "The mind must therefore ensure that it establishes an autocracy over the body so that the latter cannot change the mind's condition," and so that "it can guide and direct [the body] in accordance with moral and pragmatic principles and maxims" (157). Self-mastery and political

---

[26] Kant, *Metaphysik der Sitten*, 2. Teil, 1. Abschnitt, Paragraph 46, Seite 137; emphasis in original.
[27] Kant repeats this metaphor on 139, 140, and 158.

rule were two sides of the same coin. Kant's identification of the wife with inclination (that is, natural emotion) and the husband with reason and his oft expressed observations about the limits of women's reason[28] clearly indicate that his dichotomous assumptions about gender would almost inevitably make women less free, from the philosophical and social perspectives, and thus make them the object, rather than the subject, of law.

Was there an underlying sexual content to these gender assumptions? In general, Kant's rather traditional understanding of sexual desire affected his gender prescriptions not by imagining natural differences in the sexual makeup of men and women, but rather (like Rousseau) in deducing gender differences from the putative demands of heterosexual attraction, namely, that only opposites attracted. The requirement that women attract men demanded and produced gender difference. The nature of sexual determinism for Kant was therefore relational rather than original or biological. And yet Kant presents women's perpetual civil immaturity as so universal, that is, as applying to all women without exception, that it suggests a more originary or categorical source. Kant never properly analyzed the submerged sexual content behind his notion of gender dichotomy; he remained unaware and uncritical of the extent to which his sexual assumptions, whether relational or biological, shaped his political-philosophical maxims. His lack of critical self-awareness on these matters struck some of the most prominent readers of his *Anthropology* as old-fashioned. Goethe criticized one of Kant's remarks on women as "typical of such an old bachelor" and found the *Anthropology* "in many places narrow-minded and in more, illiberal."[29] Friedrich Daniel Schleiermacher similarly condemned Kant's "handling of the female sex as an abnormality, and completely as a means," rather than an end, as Kant's general philosophical maxim should have demanded.[30]

There were three ways that the murky and, by the end of the eighteenth century, old-fashioned, implicit sexual model might be clarified. One, as Schleiermacher suggested, was to see women as ends in themselves, nonrelationally—a viewpoint we will examine presently with Hippel. A second was the route the nineteenth century followed, of reducing women to a putatively biological-sexual essence that disqualified them from participation in civil society.[31] The third possibility was to examine openly the relational-sexual assumptions issuing from the male sexual model and simply accept them. It was Fichte who boldly seized this alternative.

---

[28] See the careful analysis of Sylvia Bovenschen, *Die imaginierte Weiblichkeit. Exemplarische Untersuchungen zu kulturgeschichtlichen und literarischen Präsentationsformen des Weiblichen* (Frankfurt, 1979), 225–39.

[29] Johann Wolfgang von Goethe to C. G. Voigt, Weimar, 19 December 1798, in *Goethes Werke* (Weimar edition), (Weimar, 1893), 13:347–48; reprinted in the appendix to Kant, *Anthropologie*, 337.

[30] Friedrich Daniel Schleiermacher, review of the *Anthropologie* in *Athenaeum* 2.2 (1799): 300–306; reprinted in Kant, *Anthropologie*, 338–43, here 343.

[31] Esther Fischer-Homberger, *Krankheit Frau und andere Arbeiten zur Medizingeschichte der Frau* (Bern, 1979), and Honegger, *Ordnung der Geschlechter.*

The Explicit Sexual Model (Johann Gottlieb Fichte)

Where Kant left unspoken and unreconciled the interplay of sexual ethics with political rights, Fichte attempted to knit both into a single system. By boldly reformulating the silent assumptions of many of his contemporaries into a system of logical determinism, Fichte became a lightning rod for later critics of these assumptions, who found Fichte's work outlandish, which it may be, and idiosyncratic or reactionary, which it was not.[32]

As to his politics: Fichte's liberal credentials are unassailable. Nervous conservatives labeled him (incorrectly) a Jacobin, because he greeted the French Revolution as a sign of progress, opposed noble privilege, and sought fundamental political reform according to the principle of freedom grounded in natural law.[33] If Fichte "no longer counts as part of the Enlightenment," it was because he was emblematic of the transition into the nineteenth century; under the impact of the French revolutionary wars, he did not move backward, however, but forward toward more democratic (and therefore nationalist) participation in public affairs, toward more reform, not less.[34]

As to Fichte's sexual theories: these are only shocking for the same reason they are useful—they make completely explicit the sexual (not gender) ground for political rights. The actual content of these sexual ideas was not remarkable. Indeed, they were quite representative of the assumptions of liberal-progressives of his day, which is why the rights and legal maxims that Fichte derived from (or legitimated through) these ideas remained so constant into the twentieth century. Ute Gerhard is quite right to call Fichte the "chief ideologue of bourgeois patriarchalism," whose achievement it was to have anticipated and clearly expressed the founding opinions of liberal civil society and its "family fathers."[35]

---

[32] Gertrud Bäumer, *Fichte und sein Werk*, 57–58, cited in Ute Gerhard, *Verhältnisse und Verhinderungen. Frauenarbeit, Familie und Rechte der Frauen im 19. Jahrhundert* (Frankfurt, 1981), 144; Gerhard's own characterization of Fichte's "reactionary marriage law," 145; Honegger, *Ordnung der Geschlechter*, 71, 187, on Fichte's "idiosyncratic" sexual theories. Also, Hannelore Schröder, *Die Rechtlosigkeit der Frau im Rechtsstaat, dargestellt am Allgemeinen Preußischen Landrecht, am Bürgerlichen Gesetzbuch und an J. G. Fichtes Grundlage des Naturrechts* (Frankfurt, 1979), 19, 26–28. Despite its vehemence and its materialist slant, Schröder's study was instrumental in recalling Fichte's importance to the study of gender relations.

[33] Anthony J. La Vopa, "The Revelatory Moment: Fichte and the French Revolution," *Central European History* 22 (June 1989): 130–50, esp. 132. Also, Zwi Batscha, *Gesellschaft und Staat in der politischen Philosophie Fichtes* (Frankfurt, 1970), and Bernhard Willms, *Die totale Freiheit: Fichtes politische Philosophie* (Cologne, 1967).

[34] Möller, *Vernunft und Kritik*, 306; Engelhardt, *Bildungsbürgertum*, 80–83.

[35] Gerhard, *Verhältnisse und Verhinderungen*, 143, 144; also cited by Honegger, *Ordnung der Geschlechter*, 252 n. 331. Gerhard describes these opinions as "reactionary," which may refer to our present-day judgment of them, but does not describe them accurately in their own political context. Schröder, *Rechtlosigkeit*, 150, also refers to Fichte as a "petty bourgeois patriarch."

Fichte's Sexual Theory

The beginning and basis of Fichte's philosophy and his sexual theory was the self-activating individual, the subject of history. Its freedom was expressed in self-determining activity, a Kantian postulate on which Fichte elaborated.[36] This was, once again, the philosophical expression of the idea of the rational, male citizen-individual.

Fichte began from the standpoint that this actual human being possessed the natural drive to sexual satisfaction, "itself a goal of our nature."[37] Thus, Fichte agreed with Kant that procreation was not the goal for humans, though it might have been for nature. This assumption enabled Fichte to attach such importance to sex per se and to make the relation between the man and the woman, rather than their duties to their children, the focal point of his investigation.

Fichte next made two assumptions from which everything else followed logically. The first being, since nature had divided the species into male and female, it decreed that "one sex keeps purely active, and the other purely passive," and these were "throughout all nature" the male and female respectively. The only ground Fichte adduced for this statement was the suggestion that passive substance and motion might thus be united dynamically (393). This dichotomy of the passive and the active is, of course, one of the oldest European sexual tropes. The second assumption resembled the first: "The character of reason is absolute self-activity; pure passivity for the sake of passivity contradicts reason and utterly cancels it" (394). This maxim, too, rested upon the long-standing chain of association linking males to active sexual expression to superior rational faculty. But Fichte reckoned reason as the defining quality of all humans, male and female.

For women, the problem now arose in the clash between the first and second assumptions, for women were at once (as humans) rational beings and thus active, yet their sexual nature was passive.

> Hence, it is not against reason that the first sex [the male] should propose to itself the satisfaction of its sexual impulse as an end in itself, since it can be satisfied through activity; but it is absolutely against reason that the second sex should propose to itself the satisfaction of its sexual impulse as an end, because in that case it would make a pure passivity its end. Hence, the female sex is either not rational even in its tendencies, which contradicts our presupposition that they are human [and thus rational], or this tendency cannot be developed in that sex in consequence of its peculiar nature, which is a self-contradiction, since it assumes a tendency in nature which nature does not accept; or,

---

[36] Frederick Neuhouser, *Fichte's Theory of Subjectivity* (Cambridge, 1990).

[37] Johann Gottlieb Fichte, *Grundlage des Naturrechts nach Prinzipien der Wissenschaftslehre* (1796) (Hamburg, 1979), appendix 1, par 1, p. 299, and Johann Gottlieb Fichte, *The Science of Rights*, trans. A. E. Kroeger (London, 1889), 391. My translations usually follow Kroeger, except where gender-blind nineteenth-century usage obscures Fichte's point. Hereafter cited parenthetically in the text by the English edition page numbers. All emphases are in the original.

finally, that sex can never propose to itself the satisfaction of its sexual impulse as its end. Such an end and rationality utterly cancel each other in that sex.(394)

Obviously, the answer must be the third: women cannot posit their own sexual satisfaction. Here Fichte merely concluded what Enlightenment thought had been suggesting for some time, namely, that there was something disturbing about women's pursuing the satisfaction of their own sexual desire.[38]

Fichte then elaborated. It was, of course, physically possible for a woman to take her own sexual satisfaction as an end in itself, but this "degrades her to irrationality," that is, to a subhuman or animal status. Or she might actively use her sexual capacity to pursue another, active end, such as getting married or having children, which Fichte also criticized, because she could achieve it with any man, and Fichte assumes that her "self-respect" would forbid her from wishing to appear as though she had simply chosen the first man to come along (395–96). The first reason is a restatement of the old association of the sexual drive with animalistic nature; the second is a weakly argued identification of a woman's honor with sexual monogamy and another attempt to establish monogamous marriage on putative female nature. Both are transparent; neither is at all peculiar to Fichte.

Just as Kant and many other practitioners of civil society had identified women peculiarly with the moral progress of civilization, so did Fichte, and he did using almost the same steps as Kant had used in his *Anthropology* lectures. He postulated moral superiority from natural inferiority and identified the moral superiority as specifically sexual in nature:

> The second sex stands one step lower in the arrangement of nature than the first sex; it is the object of a power of the first sex, and no other arrangement was possible if both sexes were to be connected. But at the same time both sexes, as moral beings, ought to be equal. To make this possible, a new faculty, utterly wanting in the first sex, had to be given to the second. This faculty is the form in which the sexual impulse appears to woman, whereas to man it appears in its true form. [Whereas] the male can, without giving up his dignity, confess to himself the sexual drive and seek its satisfaction. . . . The female cannot admit to this drive. The male can court; the female cannot. It would be the highest self-contempt for her to do so. . . .
> This one distinction constitutes, indeed, the whole difference between the sexes. It is this natural constitution of woman which gives rise to female modesty, which in this degree is inappropriate to the male sex. (396–98)

Modesty was the first step in the civilizing process. A more important one, however, was the actual form that female sexual desire, incapable of positing or fulfilling itself, took.

Fichte had women escape from the dilemma of having a sexual drive (active) whose nature was contrary (passive) by changing the object of their desire from themselves (passive) to their male sexual partner (active).

---

[38] See Chapter 6, pp. 251–56.

Woman cannot confess to herself that she gives herself up—and since, in a rational being, every thing is only in so far as it arises in consciousness—woman cannot give herself up to sexual pleasure [*Geschlechtslust*] merely to satisfy her own drive [*Trieb*]. But since she can give herself up only in obedience to a drive, this drive must assume in woman the character of a drive to satisfy the man. Woman becomes, in this act, the means for the end of another, because she cannot be her own end without renouncing her ultimate end—the dignity of reason! This dignity she maintains, although she becomes means, because she voluntarily makes herself means in virtue of a noble natural drive—*love*! (398)

Fichte's reasoning was tortured, but it was not idiosyncratic. He merely expressed in sexual terms what most Enlightened advice and educational literature had been recommending for several decades, namely, that women should be raised to please men. All of the stages of Fichte's argument had been long prepared: the interpretation of women's sexual activity as a "giving up," the imperative to direct her actions to "satisfy the man," the appeal to her dignity (honor), the hope that her sacrifice would happen voluntarily (a critical consideration to which we shall return), the appellation "love" as the shorthand for this process,[39] and, finally, the assertion that the process was "natural."

Through "love" women brought men into society and made both civilization and moral progress possible. "The moral law demands that one forget oneself for others; love sacrifices itself for others." But "love" was peculiar to women. "Love, the noblest of all natural drives, is only innate to woman; only through her does [love] become the common property of mankind, as with other social drives, as well" (398–99). For Fichte, as for Kant, the woman's role in the civilizing process was therefore both necessary and involuntary; "love" was natural, "innate," as was her other civilizing virtue, modesty (405). Women did not achieve civilization through rational, conscious activity; they were an inert means through which men achieved it.

Fichte emphasized, as others had before him, that the sexual drive was the original motor powering this process. "In the union of both sexes, and . . . *only* in this union, is there to be found an *external* impulse to virtue." Sexual attraction, according to the rational principles of active/passive as Fichte had sketched them, was thus the guarantor of moral progress. "Thus the problem is solved: How can the human race be led to virtue through nature? I answer: this can be done only by restoring the natural relation between the sexes" (405). Just as the man's "mere natural [sexual] drive" would become "purified" when he observed the unqualified self-abnegation of his wife, so would his individualistic egoism become tempered in the interest of society and his "social drives" become "the common property of mankind" (421).

It is important to emphasize that Fichte never denied that women possessed a natural sexual drive. Fichte did not make women passionless, he made them

---

[39] On "love" as the umbrella term for female self-sacrifice, see Gisela Bock and Barbara Duden, "Arbeit aus Liebe—Liebe als Arbeit: Zur Entstehung der Hausarbeit im Kapitalismus," in *Frauen und Wissenschaft. Beiträge zur Berliner Sommeruniversität für Frauen, Juli 1976* (Berlin, 1977), 118–99.

un[self]conscious. He refashioned and redirected their passion. Fichte's discussion of corrupted women, including those who engaged in sex to satisfy their own sexual desire, shows clearly that he admitted women did indeed have sexual desire (395–96). The conclusion he tried to prevent was that female sexual desire should be raised to the level of independence from male subjectivity. "Or does one want to promote [*fördern*] the basic drive of feminine nature to a *thing in itself?*" he asked rhetorically.[40] Fichte was thus, in this context, trying to prevent a female drive from limiting the male subject (the ease with which philosophical language might express this goal indicates again the close identification of subjectivity with maleness). The upshot was that since self-denying "*love*, therefore, is the form in which the sexual drive appears to women" (398), women must remain unconscious of their sexual drive, and unconsciousness assured they would never act on it for its own sake (398, 406).

Fichte's was a fundamentally moral argument in two senses.[41] Its framework was the moral perfection of society, and its agent, woman, acted from a natural moral sense. Admitting her own sexual desire was a "dishonoring thought" for a woman, making her "contemptible in her own eyes" (401). The content of morality was entirely gender-specific: "As the moral impulse of the woman manifests itself as love, so in man that impulse manifests itself as *generosity*" (403). Elsewhere, Fichte makes female "dignity" the counterpart to male generosity (407). Everywhere, however, it is a sexual morality peculiar to herself. And from this sexual morality followed female social and political status, "The conception of marriage involves the most unlimited subjection of the woman to the will of the husband; not from legal, but from moral reasons. She must subject herself for the sake of her own honor" (417).

Domestic Consequences (Marriage)

Marriage was the institution in which the complete civil erasure of women occurred. Marriage was a total, natural, and necessary institution, one that went beyond the purely sexual definition Kant had given it. Fichte's definition was better suited to the social purposes the institution fulfilled in civil society. Fichte wrote, "Marriage is a *complete union* of persons of both sexes, based upon the sexual drive and having its end in itself" (405–06). That meant that though sexual attraction grounded it, neither sexual satisfaction, nor procreation, nor child-raising, nor mutual help, nor even indirect social utility was its reason. Instead, "The marriage relation is the true mode of existence of grown persons of both sexes, required even by nature. Only in this relation do all their faculties develop; outside of it, very

[40] This sentence was omitted in the English translation. See Fichte, *Naturrecht*, appendix 1, par. 4, p. 305, emphasis in original. On things-in-themselves, see Neuhouser, *Fichte's Theory of Subjectivity*, 48–49, 54–55, 102–6. The thing-in-itself existed independently from the self-actuating, free subject, and thus might be construed as a limit on it.

[41] Gerhard, *Verhältnisse und Verhinderungen*, 144–45.

many, indeed the most remarkable sides of humanity remain undeveloped" (406). The reader will recognize in this sentiment the widespread ideas that moral sexual relations were necessary to complete a human being and that therefore marriage was a prerequisite to the moral, social life.

The classical Enlightenment had often defined marriage as a contract, Fichte moved solidly into the nineteenth century by denying precisely this. "Marriage is . . . no invented custom, nor an arbitrary institution, but a relation necessarily and perfectly determined through nature and reason in their union" (407). The error in thinking it might be a contract led to "improper and immoral" imaginings (408). Not being contractual, neither did marriage assume "a living together of free beings" (408), nor did it tempt the state to intervene in it to enforce the terms of any contract. Fichte's definition made marriage much more compatible with both inequality inside it and with the expansion of the "private sphere" around it to protect that inequality from state intervention.

Because women were, after all, human beings and therefore rational and active, and because marriage erased them entirely as civil beings, Fichte went to extraordinary pains to ensure that their decision to enter marriage be made freely. Again, he argued from morality (honor). "It is the duty of the state to protect the *honor* of the female sex; that is, to see that women are not compelled to give themselves up to men they do not love; for this honor is a part, nay, the noblest part, of their personality" (424–25). Fichte's vehemence (on page 409 of the *Science of Rights* he calls this the "absolute duty of the state") is due partly to the need to legitimate women's annihilation by making it a willed activity; partly, however, to Fichte's need to mask a fundamental contradiction in his system. For insofar as female morality is "natural," as Fichte insisted it was, it is also perforce determined, unfree, and therefore not moral at all, since only free acts are truly moral. The strong undertow in Fichte's system pulling women into will-less inactivity needs to be overcome if women are to be the exemplars of moral behavior, and, indeed, if they are to be considered human. Therefore it was supremely important for Fichte (and others) to represent women's civil status as not merely natural, but also voluntary, as "love" was voluntary.

Once the woman freely entered marriage and thus "subjected" herself sexually to her husband exclusively out of love for him, her civil status fitted itself to her passive sexual condition. As Fichte put it:

> The wife, in making herself the means to satisfy the husband, gives up her personality. . . .
> The wife who thus surrenders her personality, and yet retains her full dignity in so doing, necessarily gives up to her lover all that she has . . .
> Her own dignity requires that she should give herself up entirely as she is and lives to him and should utterly lose herself in him. The least that follows from this is that she should renounce to him all her property and all her rights. Henceforth she has life and activity only under his eyes and in his business. She has ceased to lead the life of an individual; her life has become a part of the life of her lover. (This is aptly characterized by her assuming his name.) (401–2)

For Fichte, it was exactly the moral quality of the relation that brought with it the woman's civil annihilation, for if the woman reserved anything (property, emotion, and so on), then, Fichte argued, "she would thereby confess that it had a higher value for her than her own person; and this undoubtedly would be a deep devaluing of her person" (402). Having surrendered her self, her "dignity" required that she surrender everything.

Fichte's seemingly brutal civil annulment of married women in fact merely spoke out loud the consequences inherent, but rarely acknowledged, in the sentimental notion of "one heart, one soul," in which the couple was considered a unit for which the husband spoke and in which he retained chief domestic authority. The many early liberal voices favoring restoration of the husband's domestic authority were the springboard from which Fichte catapulted to his logical conclusion.

Furthermore, one of the lasting theoretical and actual effects of this entire train of thought was the establishment of the private sphere. In Fichte's words, "Man and wife are intimately united. Their union is a union of hearts and wills. Hence, it is not to be assumed at all that a legal dispute can arise between them. The state, therefore, passes no laws regulating the relation of husband and wife, their whole relation being of a natural and moral, but not of a legal character" (417). The presumption of unity under the husband's leadership, a condition reflecting the "natural" sexual and therefore moral relations between men and women, made marriage an institution outside the purview of the state. It was lawless: "The state . . . passes no laws regulating the relation of husband and wife, their whole relation being of a natural and moral, but not of a legal character" (417). The state had only two functions regarding marriage, one at the beginning and one at the end: to ensure that the woman entered it freely (412–17) and to investigate those cases where one party, but not the other, wanted a divorce (430–33). Otherwise, because Fichte took literally the view of marriage as a purely emotional-sexual relation it made no sense to apply external sanction to it. The spouses were free to tie or untie the knot depending on their feelings. Neither social responsibilities (children) nor individual rights (even to sexual intercourse—the marital "duty") determined the fate of a marriage (434). The only vestige of state tutelage adhered to the wife's request for divorce, where Fichte recommended that the state hesitate until it was certain the woman knew her own mind (435–36).

Fichte's Romantic (male) individualism thus resulted in a radical clipping of the state's wings and the establishment of a private sphere coterminous with marriage. But Fichte's liberalism pulled him further. Although the state had the duty to make possible a moral life, which Fichte expresses as the duty "to protect the *honor* of the female sex," it did not have the duty to enforce this (424). Since "giving in" to sex for a woman destroyed her "personality" (either in the moral case, by annulling it in favor of her husband, or in the immoral, by exposing herself as below human standards), the proper analogy for female sexual expression was suicide.

Every person has the right to sacrifice one's personality, that is, there is no *external* legal ground against doing so. Precisely as each person has an unlimited external—not internal, or moral—right to take one's own life, the state having no right to make laws against suicide, so also has woman unlimited external right over her own honor. . . . If therefore, a woman chooses to give herself up from mere voluptuousness or from other motives, and if a man can be found who is willing to dispense with [his wife's] love, the state has no right to prevent it. (425)

That is, both men and women were free to engage in sexual relations outside marriage. Moral freedom demanded also the freedom to act immorally.

Moral freedom required the state to refrain from punishing immoral consensual sexual acts. At most Fichte felt the police might be "watchful" over immoral relationships that became public knowledge (426). Fichte specifically discussed prostitution, fornication, concubinage and adultery (424–30). About the last, Fichte declared,

> The state can no more prohibit it or punish it by law than any other illegitimate satisfaction of the sexual impulse. For, let me ask, whose rights are violated by this offense? . . . Is conjugal fidelity an object of penal legislation? Or has it not, in fact, its ground in a connection of hearts? But such a connection of hearts is free, and cannot be compelled by penal laws; and if *it* ceases, the compulsion of *external fidelity*—which compulsion alone is physically possible—is both illegal and impossible. (430)

Fichte assumed that no husband and few wives would forgive adultery, so he expected her adultery automatically and his probably would lead to divorce. But that was the only civil consequence.[42] In the absence of all criminal penalties, then, Fichte's private sphere de facto extended to include consensual sexual expression altogether, equally for men and for women. His reasons were identical to those of Anselm Feuerbach—the state had no right to impinge on moral freedom or to interfere, in the absence of harm to the rights of third parties.

Political Consequences (Citizens' Rights)

"Has woman the same rights in the state which man has? This question may appear ridiculous to many. For if the only ground of all legal rights is reason and freedom, how can a distinction exist between two sexes which possess both the same reason and the same freedom?" Fichte asked (438). And yet, he observed that everywhere women in fact enjoyed fewer rights. This was certainly not because they possessed "less mental or physical energy" (as Kant had suggested), for such differences among men did not erase their equal rights (439–40). Above all, it was not because women were not human or were less human than men.[43] No, Fichte began his justification for women's lack of citizen rights from a much more liberal-progressive standpoint than many of his contemporaries.

[42] Property would be divided in the same proportion in which the spouses had brought it into their marriage, regardless of who had committed the adultery: Fichte, *Science of Rights*, 436–38.

[43] Ibid., 440. Schröder, *Rechtlosigkeit*, 148, and passim, is mistaken in her repeated insistence that Fichte believed women were inferior as human beings.

It was neither women's sexual nature, nor their gender, but their civil-sexual status alone that determined their (lack of) political rights.[44] Rightlessness came from marriage. As we have seen, entertaining moral sexual relations, such as marrying, meant for a woman giving up her "personality," "all her property and all her rights," her "life as an individual," and her very name (402). To complete the quotation cited partially before:

> The conception of marriage involves the most unlimited subjection of the woman to the will of the husband; not from legal, but from moral reasons. She must subject herself for the sake of her own honor. The woman does not belong to herself, but to the man. The state, by recognizing marriage as a relation based upon something far higher than itself [that is, on natural law], abandons all claims to consider the woman as a legal person. The husband occupies her place; her marriage utterly annuls her, so far as the state is concerned, by virtue of her own necessary will, which the state has guaranteed. The husband is her guarantee before the state; he becomes her legal guardian; he lives in all her public life, and she retains for herself only a house life. (417–18)

Fichte is adamant that this situation is not compelled, but desired. "Woman is not subjected to her husband, so that her husband should have a *right of compulsion* over her; she is subjected through her own continuous necessary wish—a wish which is the condition of her morality" (441). The moment a women chooses to lead a moral life, she has also chosen to disappear from society. The wife's alienation from her rights and her property comes from her civil-sexual status.[45]

Fichte granted the wife limited rights, "for she is a citizen." But these turn out to be the right to influence her husband politically and to vote his wish in his absence (442). Consistent with the wife's civil disappearance into her husband and his responsibility for her and the children, Fichte favored granting the "family father" "greater influence and a more decisive voice in public affairs" than the unmarried exercised (442). This suggestion, again, merely spoke out loud the assumption that most practitioners of civil society shared, namely, that the ideal member of civil society was the married father.[46] Fichte contemptuously dismissed the call for greater civil rights for women (Hippel) as the product of mere immodest vanity (443–44).

Unlike Kant, Fichte was carefully consistent in limiting civil annihilation to married women only. Unmarried women without fathers, and widows might enjoy citizens' rights, both political and economic, as "actually happens in our states."[47] Since mere sexual activity brought with it no necessary civil or criminal consequences,[48] and thus no change in civil status, "immoral" sexual behavior should

---

[44] This is why Fichte, *Science of Rights*, 440–41, immediately turned to consider sexual status (virgin versus married) after he had laid out his principal foundations.

[45] Lack of rights does not come from lack of property, as Schröder argues; both together are the products of sexual condition. Schröder, *Rechtlosigkeit*, 126–38.

[46] For this assumption in the actual legal reforms, see Chapter 10.

[47] Fichte, *Naturrecht*, appendix 1, par. 36, p. 344; omitted in Fichte, *Science of Rights*, 445.

[48] For example, Fichte, *Science of Rights*, 426, says of concubinage: "It lacks the legal consequences of marriage."

have caused no loss of citizens' rights in Fichte's system. In fact, criminal prosecution in nonsexual matters might even be interpreted paradoxically as restoring the woman's citizen rights to her, because Fichte interpreted a guilty verdict as an insertion of the state between the husband and his wife, which disrupted the privileged relation. By being treated as a direct subject of the state under criminal law, the wife "receives her self-sufficiency [*Selbständigkeit*], and is thus divorced,"[49] if her husband so wishes. This was, of course, Fichte's reinterpretation of the older legal custom whereby dishonoring penalties were grounds for divorce (for both men and women). It is illustrative of how the hermetically sealed private sphere operated, that in this interpretation, only the wife might be divorced; the husband's public status was unchanged by criminal proceedings. As odd as Fichte's interpretation may seem, it anticipated a nineteenth-century truth: the reformed criminal law of civil society did tend to treat women more equally than was true in civil law or in many other regards.[50] A direct relation to the state was a relation of equality.

Fichte's observation that mature, non-, or no longer married women "actually" did participate fully in public life shows once more how closely he had tailored his sexual theory to explain civil society as it either already worked or was being shaped to work. Consonant with this principle, the one civil right Fichte refused to grant otherwise free women was a right they had rarely enjoyed in Germany anyway, the right to hold office. Officials embodied even more strongly than citizens the necessary virtues of independence and intellectual freedom. To ensure those qualities, a woman would have to promise not to marry, a promise Fichte imagined she could not give, "For woman is destined to love and love comes to women of itself—it does not depend upon her free will" (446). Here Fichte comes closest to undermining his repeated contention that a woman's civil condition was the result of her free moral choice and maintaining instead that it was determined by her sexual constitution. This contradiction testifies to the strong undertow in the direction of sexual-biological determination running through Fichte's work, despite himself. In just a few years male commentators upon women's civil rights would be even less inclined to struggle against that undertow than Fichte had been in 1796.

The Model of Sexual Irrelevancy (Theodor Gottlieb von Hippel)

Four years earlier, in exactly the same months as Mary Wollstonecraft was working at her *Vindication of the Rights of Woman*, the mayor and former police director of Königsberg, the freethinking writer and friend of Kant, Theodor Gottlieb von Hippel, penned the only appeal for unlimited civil and economic rights for women to emerge in the German states in the eighteenth century. In *On Improving the Civil [bürgerliche] Status of Women*, Hippel made the sexual nature, activity, and status of women as irrelevant to their receiving rights as all other writers had made these

---

[49] Fichte, *Naturrecht*, appendix 1, par. 29, p. 335; omitted in Fichte, *Science of Rights*, 436.
[50] See Chaps. 9 and 10.

matters irrelevant for men.[51] As we saw in the last chapter, many of Hippel's ideas about gender and sexual nature were typical of the late Enlightenment; yet, clearly others must have made Hippel's unusual appeal intellectually conceivable for him. What factors might cancel the ever stronger tendency to advocate the total alienation of civil rights from women? We turn now to these two sides of Hippel's argument, the usual and the unusual.

Hippel's conception of women and of sexual nature were entirely unremarkable. He believed in the male sexual model and its corollaries and in the active-male/passive-female dichotomy, which he held necessary for grounding society.[52] Hippel considered some (but not all) of women's particular qualities "inherent" and insisted that his own ideas were designed to cause "both men and women to make the effort to become *true* men and women."[53] Exactly like Kant, and later Fichte, Hippel also believed that women were the natural motor of civilization because they made men moral. Women transformed male (sexual) egotism into lasting, socially anchored altruism.[54] Like most other civil practitioners, Hippel therefore deemed marriage the key institution in the moral completion of citizens and the civil advancement of society.

Hippel busied himself for over twenty years with this theme, publishing anonymously and thrice revising his popular book, *On Marriage.* In the first two editions (1774 and 1776), Hippel had been more concerned to anchor the husband's domestic power than to explore the impetuses for equality inside marriage. By the third edition (1792), however, Hippel piped a different, more egalitarian tune. In place of the flip aphorisms of the cavalier, one discovers a more rigorous evaluation of marriage according to both legal, liberal principles and to tolerance as the foundation of civil society. Hippel seemed intent on defining the purpose of marriage in the widest possible way, in order to fit it to as many different private lifestyles as possible. Flexibility would enable marriage truly to become the basic institution organizing civil society, because it would fulfill the needs and aspirations of different kinds of people. Hippel's definition had nothing to do with sex; it was mutual aid. "*The most exact union of life, mutual support,* I say—whoever reckons procreation [to this], may do so; whoever accepts other limits, may do that: this concept is so full of tolerance, that not only all—*ists,* but even all—*ians,* and these are much worse than those, can hereby exercise their free marital gymnastics [*freie Eheübungen*]."[55] Hippel's reference to marital gymnastics meant not merely polemicists' argumentative acrobatics, but their private sexual conduct as well. Preserving

[51] Theodor Gottlieb von Hippel, *On Improving the Status of Women* (1792), trans. Timothy F. Sellner (Detroit, 1979).

[52] Theodor Gottlieb von Hippel, *Über die Ehe,* 4th ed. (Berlin, 1793), active/passive: 423, women's gender-specific qualities: 249–50, 423, 426–27, men's promiscuity: 178, 205; sexual drive: 113, 134–38, 185–86, 208–9, 304–5, 479.

[53] Hippel, *Improving,* 189, 128, 62, emphasis in original. On his interesting views on the social causes of women's different development from men, see 126–28, 136–49, 161–63, 168–69, 180.

[54] Ibid., 105, 140, 152.

[55] Theodor Gottlieb von Hippel, *Über die Ehe,* 3d ed. (Berlin, 1792), 95–96.

the latter from state scrutiny, and thus guaranteeing a private sphere, was an important reason for Hippel's nonsexual, latitudinarian definition of marriage. This stance followed logically from liberal legal principles: "According to strict natural law, everything—if God will!—is permitted which does not injure [*zu nahe treten*] third parties and those persons who have bound themselves to one another. Here the satisfaction of the natural drive is the end of the song."[56]

Hippel's new view of domestic relations in 1792 had become equally tolerant. Standing Kant on his head, Hippel opined in a legal-political metaphor, that "if men have the right to *domination* [*Herrschaft*] in the household, then women get the right of *government* [*Regierung*]; if the husband is president of house-justice, she is the police-president."[57] In the fourth edition of *On Marriage* (1793), Hippel made even plainer that neither should permanently dominate the other. Instead, he envisioned a continuous flux of reciprocal, situational domination, in which that spouse would temporarily rule according to whichever of them was more competent in the issue at hand. Equality was thus the summation of years of alternating power.[58] Hippel's pragmatic vision of domestic relations avoided the straitjacket of dogmatic roles and simply left the whole matter to the negotiation of the partners. His stringent application of hands-off liberalism to marriage prevented the state from first setting a skewed rights framework for marriage before retiring from the scene, as Fichte shortly outlined and the nineteenth century actually accomplished. Instead, Hippel made marriage an ill-defined, capacious institution beyond state purview from the very beginning.

The most remarkable thing about Hippel's new domestic egalitarianism is that it had nothing to do with his assumptions about either sexual nature or gender. For even in the fourth edition of *On Marriage* (1793), the sections on those two subjects remained substantially unchanged.[59] But none of the old clichés seemed to matter. Hippel obviously did not reason from the putative nature of the sexual drive or gender to domestic arrangement. Deriving the latter from the former was such a common form of argument in the late eighteenth century and became so hegemonic thereafter, that even modern observers are troubled by Hippel's ability to compartmentalize them. Hippel seems inconsistent to them.[60] But Hippel's "inconsistency" contains more than one element of design. First, the pragmatic mayor rejected dogmatic systems on principle;[61] they ill-suited his playful and speculative

---

[56] Ibid., 96. The last sentence suggests that Hippel may have restricted private sexual freedom to heterosexual acts.

[57] Ibid., 202, emphasis in original.

[58] Hippel, *Über die Ehe*, 4th ed., 244, 248–49.

[59] See note 52.

[60] Ruth P. Dawson, "The Feminist Manifesto of Theodor Gottlieb von Hippel (1741–96)," in *Gestaltet und Gestaltend. Frauen in der deutschen Literatur*, ed. Marianne Burkhard (Amsterdam, 1980), 29–30. In his introduction to Hippel, *Improving*, 25, Timothy Sellner sees Hippel's inconsistency more in his simultaneous belief in Enlightenment and in religion, but that combination was common, indeed, the rule in Germany.

[61] Joseph Kohnen, *Theodor Gottlieb von Hippel. Eine zentrale Persönlichkeit der Königsberger Geistesgeschichte. Biographie und Bibliographie* (Lüneburg, 1987), 33.

imagination and clashed with his programmatic tolerance. Hippel was an Enlightener of the skeptical stripe, who knew that not all things were dreamt of in
anyone's philosophy. Second, Hippel's experience as a lawyer and administrator
encouraged him to view men and women as equal objects of a uniform system of
law. Ascriptive characteristics, whether of *Stand,* gender, or putative sexual biology,
were largely irrelevant from this viewpoint. Both of these convictions undercut the
easy deduction of domestic power from sexual or gender stereotypes.

It is possible, as some have suggested, that Hippel may have derived his argument
for equality for women in the "public" spheres of politics and economy from his
new egalitarian views of domestic power.[62] But then it is hard to explain why Hippel
barely mentions marriage in *On Improving the Civil Status of Women* and never
invokes an idealized version of it as a public guideline. It seems more likely that
Hippel's new, egalitarian interpretation of marriage and his argument for civic
equality were both products of the maturation of his enlightened Weltanschauung.

Scholars have suspected that unknown personal reasons might have spurred
Hippel's change of heart regarding marital domination,[63] but everyone agrees, and
the texts confirm, that the French Revolution and the promulgation of the Prussian
Reform Code (*Allgemeines Landrecht*) were decisive as the imaginary interlocutors
against which Hippel argued.[64] Both events were major decisions about how to
organize civil society and distribute rights. Hippel was deeply disappointed with
both—with the Revolution for not fulfilling the emancipatory promises with which
German Enlighteners had invested it, and with the *Allgemeines Landrecht* for its
fussy tutelage and Roman-legal hangovers. Hippel may have nursed his views on
domestic and civic equality during the 1780s, before these events then forced him to
crystallize and perfect his ideas in opposition to the trends of the 1790s.

What made it possible for Hippel, whose basic assumptions were the same
liberal, progressive, Enlightened views as those of his contemporaries, to adopt a
much more radical vision of equality than that which emerged in fact or in most
other writings in the 1790s? One might say that Hippel had a more unmediated
understanding of Enlightenment principles that made it easier for him to apply
these in an abstract, universalistic fashion.[65] Judging from how he argued in *On
Improving the Civil Status of Women,* two main sources encouraged his universalism:
religious conviction and legal-bureaucratic principle.

Hippel returned again and again to the equality of men and women in divine
creation as the fundamental proof of his argument. As with most German En-

---

[62] Jauch, *Immanuel Kant zur Geschlechterdifferenz,* 222.

[63] Dawson, "Feminist Manifesto," 30–31; Kohnen, *Theodor Gottlieb von Hippel,* 77–79. Kohnen's
careful work unearthed no biographical reasons for Hippel's new views, though he discovered potential
reasons for the relative misogyny of the first editions of *Über die Ehe.* The destruction of much of
Hippel's personal correspondence for the last years dims hope of further discovery. Ibid., 184, 240–41 n.
456.

[64] Dawson, "Feminist Manifesto," 30; Sellner's introduction to Hippel, *Improving,* 39, 43–45.

[65] Jauch expresses what I am calling Hippel's universalism as his greater consistency in applying
Kantian principles than Kant himself. Jauch, *Immanuel Kant zur Geschlechterdifferenz,* 209–14.

lighteners, Hippel had no trouble reconciling religion and Reason; on the contrary, God appeared as the foundation of natural law and rationality as a manifestation of the divine. The equality of male and female souls in the sight of God passed effortlessly for Hippel into their equality before the law and in all aspects of social organization.

> Man can renounce the image of God for a moment, but not forever. Is Reason not greater than all else? . . . Wherever *it* is to be found, there resides humanity, and to undervalue this dignity in the other sex deliberately, amidst the radiance of her divinity, is equivalent to leaving no stone unturned in the determination of our own [men's] importance. Not a mere code of laws written on clay tablets would be shattered here; rather, we could be sinning against the divine spirit which resides within ourselves. Can anything be an affair of God which contradicts Reason?[66]

Even Hippel's legal reasoning was at base religious. "Can it be denied that in every code of laws one can and must proceed from the basic premise of a natural equality and begin with the Garden of Eden?" (122). Religious conviction saturates Hippel's book; he begins his argument for equality with Genesis (64), he adduces throughout religious examples, but more important, the tone and rhetoric of the piece, for all its secular wit and worldly erudition, come from the pulpit. *On Improving the Civil Status of Women* is, in form and content, a sermon (64).

We have seen other practitioners of civil society use the secularized remnant of religious argumentation, in the form of appeals to morality, as their chief weapon to deprive women of equal domestic and civil rights. Hippel, again sharing many common moral suppositions, nonetheless showed how one could build a different house on the same foundations. And he used a quintessentially religious story to make his point. Hippel, too, believed that Enlightenment and the progress of civil society were works of moral reform. But far from arguing that women's moral duty removed them from active inclusion, Hippel asked, "And do not the obstacles to a moral reform of the human race . . . arise chiefly from the fact that we have desired to erect this temple of reform from our own sex alone, while the fair sex has been left to lie in ruins? Is it not inexcusable to leave half of the resources of mankind unknown, unassessed, and unused?" (62). For, as Fichte in response to Hippel had been forced specifically to grant, women were equally human and therefore equally intelligent, rational, and endowed with subjective will (76). Hippel responded to the undercurrent of sentiment linking women with irrationality and immorality (present even in those who protested to the contrary) in a typically playful but also sharp-sighted way. He reinterpreted the powerful religious symbol of female im-morality, Eve and the Fall, as the paradigm of Enlightened emancipation. He chose that story because it illustrated three conflations that still figured strongly in

---

[66] Hippel, *Improving*, 68. I have changed Sellner's translation to omit gender attributions based on accidents of German grammar. *Die Vernunft* (reason), for example, is feminine, which Sellner retained in the English. On page 167 Hippel does in fact ask, "Is reason not of the feminine gender?" but it is unclear if he always had this double sense in mind. Henceforth, references to *Improving* will appear parenthetically in the text. All emphases in original.

arguments making women rightless. It identified Eve as especially immoral, especially sexual, and therefore as especially deserving of punishment (subjection and physical suffering due to sexual intercourse). Nonsense, he countered. Eve's "sin" was in fact the introduction of Enlightenment, the first step on the road to civilized advancement via free thinking and individual autonomy. "It was she who shattered the bonds of instinct which had prevented human reason from rising up. . . . In memory of her the words *Eve* and *Reason* ought to be regarded as synonymous" (65). Far from impiety, Hippel here illustrated his peculiar brand of Enlightened-reinterpreted religion.[67]

The second major impetus to Hippel's universalistic application of the principles of equality was law. Law was Hippel's training and profession. His successful career from poverty, through the legal bureaucracy of the city of Königsberg, to mayor, testifies to his legal and bureaucratic aptitude. Law remained a continuing intellectual interest of his, especially in his last years, as he wrote his revised treatises on marriage and on civic betterment.[68] The legal-bureaucratic mind tended to regard subjects as equally and interchangeably liable to systematic, bureaucratic procedure as justified by written law. Both bureaucracy and law thus carried with them the habit of equality. This habit was, of course, much more self-reflexive in Hippel's case, for he believed that the content of law should reflect divine, natural equality (122); that "the customs of nations are attributable for the most part to the effect of their laws" (159); and that therefore, law was the major instrument for moral, Enlightened reform; and that legal equality demanded more than equal subjection to law; it demanded equal legislation (Kant's *Bürgerrechte*) and equal participation in the administration of justice. This last opinion was radical, indeed: "Already the idea is beginning to make itself felt that only equals can pass judgment on equals if the law is to be a living entity instead of a lifeless one. Would it not meanwhile be a monstrous injustice to exclude women from judge's benches and the jury room before that glowing ember bursts into flame?" he asked (158–59). Nowhere in Germany had women ever served in such a capacity, yet Hippel did not shrink from recommending that they do so now.

Late-eighteenth-century law (and legal reform drafts) held up stricter standards of equality, in actual fact, than existed elsewhere. There is no question that Hippel used these standards to judge history and his own times. His biting critique of the French Revolution stemmed from the discrepancy between its rhetorical principles and its legal constitution, which denied civic equality to women (57, 120–21). He blasted Roman law for the misogynist inheritance it bequeathed to Germans, visible even in the 1794 Prussian legal reform (100–109). It was especially galling that the very instrument of justice should dispense injustice. At the end of his book on civic

---

[67] Hippel had originally trained to become a Protestant minister, like his father, and only later switched to law. He remained devout, in his own freethinking fashion, his whole life. His tolerance extended to Roman Catholicism, whose services he occasionally attended. Kohnen, *Theodor Gottlieb von Hippel*, 32–35, 171–72.

[68] Ibid., 182–83.

betterment, Hippel enters an imagined dialogue with his critics. "Why start with the state" in improving the status of women, Hippel imagines they will ask. "Because we do not need to grasp at twigs and even leaves when the trunk is so close at hand" (184). His answer pithily expressed the common opinion of reform bureaucrats, that the state, as the organized aspect of society, was responsible for setting the framework within which society flourished. Legal reform created social reform; indeed, it was the prerequisite for it. That is why the jurist and bureaucrat Hippel was so intent to make sure that positive law and legal procedure be consonant with natural (divine) law.

By "starting with the state," Hippel did not start with society. And this is the main difference between him and his opponents on the issue of the civil equality of women. The Kant of the *Anthropology*, Fichte, the Philanthropinists, many others writing in the 1790s, and most others writing thereafter took (civil) society as their starting point. They either imported its actual discriminatory practices into their principles (as we saw Fichte doing), or they understood their task as the fleshing out and institutionalization of what they took to be its principles via the guarantee of law (that is, they began from what they took to be society's vantage point and sought to create a state that would support such a society). Hippel was slightly more old-fashioned; he began from abstract principles, whose formal structure was identical to the bureaucratic ideal of equal interchangeability, and sought to incorporate those principles into positive law, out of which a society would form, whose operation and structure were uncertain. All he could say was that "society as a concept presupposes equality among its members," including women (62). Exactly what that society would look like, was as yet, unclear.

By "starting with the state," Hippel remained critical of society as it actually was (without at all suggesting that society had been corrupted by Enlightenment, as conservatives or Rousseauists sometimes argued). Unquestionably the French Revolution had confirmed Hippel in his belief that human institutions were transient; imperfect, often unjust, they were doomed to be swept away and replaced by others.[69] Therefore, society, as the agglomerate of human institutions, should not be taken as an infallible guideline for law. Quite the contrary, for society itself might foster injustice. Hippel produced a subtly speculative anthropology according to which social progress, not the least caused by the female inventions of agriculture and domesticity, nonetheless had gradually turned against its co-inventors. "The development of human society, which gave the human race as a whole such an astounding impetus, was nevertheless so disadvantageous to one half of this same race" (86, 92). Civil society, not nature, had caused female subjection:

> Then, while understanding and the powers of judgment in the man began to increase through his enlarged sphere of influence; while his dealings with bourgeois society took on a higher form through the generalization of his concepts, the soul of the woman shrank more and more into the limits of her household. (92)

[69] Hippel, *Über die Ehe*, 4th ed., 240, 261, 371, 379–80.

By and by the vigor of the female sex disappeared entirely. Because the business of the state was taken away from the women, and because upon the foundation of bourgeois society they were banished to the household, they failed to become true citizens of the state, and remained simply aliens enjoying certain citizen's rights. (92–93)

These peculiar dynamics of civil society Hippel wished to undo by legal reform because he interpreted them as chance, not reflective of eternal laws. Like other bureaucrats we have encountered (for instance J. N. Brauer in Baden), Hippel was sharply critical of male egoism and its pretense to knowledge of nature. "Above all else in the world, we [men] would like to convince the other half of the human race that it was not *we* but *nature* who pushed them into the background and subjected their will to ours" (93–94). Thus, Hippel's capacity for social criticism quickened also his criticism of knowledge and made him skeptical of self-serving male arguments.

Hippel's social skepticism had another fruit, too. Because he did not apotheosize civil society, he was less inclined to judge women strictly according to their putative relation to it, which generally meant according to their relation to their husband.

Are the women never to attain an absolute value *in* and *for* the state, but always to possess mere relative worth? Are they never to take a direct part in the founding and preservation of the state? Are they never to think and act *for* and *by* themselves? (116)

As long as women have only *privileges* and not *rights;* as long as the state treats them as mere parasitic plants, which are indebted for their existence and worth as citizens only to that man with whom they have been united by fate, will not the woman fulfill only very incompletely (and the longer it takes, the more incompletely) that great calling of her nature: to be the wife of her husband, the mother of her children, and, by virtue of these noble designations, a member, a citizen—and not merely a denizen—of the state? (80)

By calling for an "absolute value," Hippel in effect called for the removal of all mediating moments between the woman and the state/civil society. She was to take "a direct part," unmediated by institutions (marriage) or personal relations (to her husband or father). This notion of a direct relationship between subject and state was quintessentially reform bureaucratic; formally speaking, the whole reform project consisted in removing from legal/administrative influence the ascriptive, corporatist, and/or personal structures that had limited state power under absolutism by inserting themselves between the central government and the governed.[70] It was doubtless more likely for a practicing bureaucrat to imagine the application of this principle of equality (by virtue of a direct relation to the state) to both halves of the population. Furthermore, as the second quotation above proves, such a notion was entirely compatible with the continued existence (and even praise) of precisely those mediating institutions. That is, social forms like marriage and the family would not be obliterated by Enlightened bureaucratic reform; they merely became irrelevant to legal and civic status. Or, more accurately and more remarkably, Hippel was obviously able to conceive of a differentiated society composed of incommensu-

---

[70] Willoweit, "Struktur und Funktion intermediärer Gewalten."

rate contributions by different kinds of people, all equally deserving the title and rights of the active citizen.[71]

From our perspective, the greatest silence in Hippel's tract on civic improvement concerns sexual nature. From his writings *On Marriage*, we know that his ideas on this subject were unremarkable. These same ideas led others to derive or to justify the distribution of rights and privileges accordingly. Yet Hippel, just as he concluded nothing from women's physical weakness, concluded nothing from their putative sexual nature (69–76). We have already examined the positive principles (of religion, law, and bureaucratic practice) that worked to counteract sexually based thinking. Perhaps these are sufficient to account for its irrelevancy in Hippel's eyes. Four further observations deserve mention, however. First, though Hippel believed as did everyone else, that sexual desire required self-regulation lest it get out of hand, he does not appear to have shared the moralistic repugnance (Kant, Gellert), or the physical fear (Rousseau, the masturbation literature) that haunted some of his contemporaries. His attitude was, rather, interested and humorous, but not obsessed. Second, Hippel did not lose sight of sexual attraction's positive qualities, which he characteristically expressed in religious language: "This harmony [between men and women] is a result of the sex drive, that secret inner feeling which confirms the divine words: 'It is not good that the man should be alone'" (168). Sexual attraction was thus primarily benevolent, which is why it was divinely ordained. Third, Hippel distrusted doctors and thought medicine a far more dubious guide for social life than law: "We jurists write [*schreiben*], while doctors prescribe [*verschreiben*], indeed they often do so in the sense of the words 'mislearn,' 'disdain,' and 'cause pain' ['*verlernen, verachten und verschmerzen*']."[72] For Hippel, the arguments of the doctors, which were becoming more prominent in interpreting sexual matters socially, did not stand a chance against legal principle. Finally, because Hippel did not worship society and therefore did not try to justify its peculiarities by claiming they were based in nature, the main reason to argue from sexual nature simply disappeared. Hippel apparently was not even interested in deriving equality by reference to sexual nature (as he could have done using the male model, or as Kant did in his lectures on *Ethics*), because Hippel preferred to argue directly from divine creation and desirable legal principle. By the end of the eighteenth century, these were surely stronger arguments, in any case, because they lacked the chain of associations pulling sexual argument in predetermined directions.

Therefore, Hippel was free to recommend "the state [should] open to women its council chambers, its courts, lecture halls, commercial establishments, and its places of employment" and should "not draw a distinction between the sexes, [but]

---

[71] Recall Kant's distinction between these two categories. Hippel also believed that the production of complete scientific knowledge equally called for different abilities, and he happily turned around the old criticism that "the nerves of the female are more pliant, irritable, and sensitive than our own" into a female advantage for scientific inquiry. Hippel, *Improving*, 168.

[72] Hippel, *Über die Ehe*, 4th ed., 105; emphasis in original.

choose rather to follow the wishes of nature and what ought to be the desires of civil society as well" (165, also 191).

The progressive Enlightenment, which by the 1790s had crystallized into recognizable early liberalism, thus contained several different developmental potentials for the relation among sexual nature, gender, and civil rights. But even in the early years of the decade, the assumed social imperatives of emerging civil society were already eclipsing the possibilities that adhered to purer, more abstract bureaucratic-legal reformism. Hippel was the exception, Fichte was becoming the rule. The actual legal reforms of the Napoleonic period built on both inheritances. Anselm Feuerbach's Bavarian criminal code was heir to the abstract egalitarianism that could be equally derived from a certain interpretation of natural law and from principles inherent in administrative practice.[73] Like Hippel, Feuerbach began with the state. The civil code reform in Baden, however, sought to redraft *society*, and not surprisingly its principles were closer to Fichte's. We leave the drafts and thought experiments of civil society-in-becoming and turn, finally, to the realization of civil society in law.

---

[73] Feuerbach applied Kant's natural law principles more rigorously and with less regard for society than his mentor had done.

9

Morality and Law: Feuerbach's Reformed Criminal Code in Bavaria

The Napoleonic Reforms

The French revolutionary wars changed the German social, political, economic, and legal landscape in fundamental ways. The French were largely successful in defeating their sluggish and fragmented German opponents. French armies occupied the area west of the Rhine in October 1792, consolidated their hold there in late 1794, and secured international recognition for a fait accompli in 1797. The armies of the Directory and, after 1799, those of Napoléon continued the successes. French influence ranged from outright occupation and direct responsibility for all policies west of the Rhine, through government by French-appointed proxy in the new model states of Westphalia and Berg (established in 1807 and 1806), through government by indigenous collaborators of varying degrees of reforming enthusiasm (the Rhenish Confederation [*Rheinbund*] founded on 8 August 1806), to enforced but sullen allegiance (Prussia, after its catastrophic defeats in 1806).

Napoléon simplified the German chessboard. On 25 February 1803 hundreds of sovereign German mini-states disappeared from the map. Except for the archbishopric of Mainz, all ecclesiastical states were secularized and handed over to larger territorial states, whose lands swelled further with the addition of all save the very largest imperial cities, and contiguous enclaves cut off geographically from their home governments, as well as bits and pieces of territories whose princes had, alas, hesitated to join the Napoleonic bandwagon in time. In southern Germany the hundreds of imperial knights, who had actually governed their tiny holdings, were left their land, but stripped of their rule, which passed over to the territorial states. The big winners were Baden, Württemberg, and Bavaria, and in the north, the entirely new creation, Westphalia. This geographical upheaval smashed the traditional, legal entities that had made up the Holy Roman Empire, which died quietly in 1806 and was replaced by the Rhenish Confederation consisting at first of sixteen German states, but later of all of them except Prussia and Austria.

The reforms that reorganized the German states in the Napoleonic period resulted from a complex interaction between French imperial and German state interests. On the one hand, the Rhenish Confederation allowed Napoléon to coordinate the foreign, military, and fiscal policies of the German states in his own interests. The internal reforms that he pressed upon the members of the Confederation were designed to create efficient states along the French model. Sharing in the benefits of French revolutionary principles (as interpreted and modified by Napoléon), the states would become more and more willing junior partners whose enhanced extractive capacities would, in turn, benefit imperial France.[1] Still, Napoléon did not want the reforms to be too radical, lest they create social turmoil, or too successful, lest they make the German governments powerful enough to overthrow French hegemony.

On the other hand, Napoléon's victories provided indigenous German reformers with the golden opportunity to achieve the agenda of late Enlightened reform absolutism. The French helpfully crushed the thousand hindrances to full-scale reform in the eighteenth century: the Holy Roman Empire and its courts, the temporal power of the Roman Catholic Church, the *Standesherren*, the inherited rights and privileges of myriad families, corporations, and other institutions—all these could now be disregarded. The situation was at hand "of which the eighteenth-century theorists of political reform had dreamed, a situation in which reason, freed of the chains of tradition, could prove its creative power."[2] The way was clear to a far-reaching reform of administration (the creation from the top down of streamlined bureaucracies with clear jurisdictions), politics (the creation of constitutions), and society (the creation of a postrevolutionary, modern society and economy). The goal was a strong state *and* a vibrant, productive society independent of it. The triumph of absolutism would consist in its own curtailment at the borders of a society of citizens protected from absolutist interference.[3] This central paradox of German reform grew difficult to negotiate when Napoleon's interests and those of the reformers no longer complemented each other and when fiscal collapse threatened the new governments.[4] Nonetheless, for a brief moment, *raison d'état*, late Enlightened absolutist/early liberal reform ideology, German idealism, and geopolitics pulled in the same direction.[5]

---

[1] Lothar Gall, *Der Liberalismus als regierende Partei. Das Grossherzogtum Baden zwischen Restauration und Reichsgründung* (Wiesbaden, 1968), 1–6.

[2] Ibid., 5; Helmut Berding and Hans-Peter Ullmann, "Veränderungen in Deutschland an der Wende vom 18. zum 19. Jahrhundert," in Berding and Ullmann, *Deutschland zwischen Revolution und Restauration*, 11–42, esp. 11–12.

[3] This is the paradox that Reinhard Koselleck explores at length in his famous study, *Preußen zwischen Reform und Revolution*.

[4] Walter Demel analyzes the tangled nexus of motives, ideology, necessity, and external conditions for Bavaria in his excellent book *Der bayerische Staatsabsolutismus 1806/08–1817. Staats- und gesellschaftspolitische Motivationen und Hintergründe der Reformära in der ersten Phase des Königreichs Bayern* (Munich, 1983).

[5] See Demel's summary of the motives behind Montgelas's constitution of 1808, no one of which should be regarded as "the" fundamental motive. Ibid., 334.

❖ Feuerbach's Reformed Criminal Code in Bavaria ❖

The paradox of the strong state creating and guaranteeing the non-state (society) was largely to be solved by law. The strengths of absolutism were to be retained and disciplined in the new *Rechtsstaat*, the state subordinated to law. Constitutions set down basic political principles; civil codes redrew the relations among individuals and inside families within civil society; criminal codes sharply delineated the circumstances under which the state might use its monopoly of violence against individuals. Laws drew the line between state and society and ordered their mutual relation. Sexual crimes, as they had been previously organized under absolutism, fell messily on both sides of this line. It was therefore in the context of the civil and criminal codes that the central bureaucratic reformers and their provincial-level allies discussed how sexual behavior fit into the new world they were creating. Finally the whole matter of sexual regulation had to be addressed in a systematic way. What danger did which sexual acts pose to the state or to society or to individuals? How important was sexual expression to the sphere of freedom granted to the citizen? Did the real or putative differences between men and women in the sexual sphere undermine the principle of equality under the law? Should the principle of separation of the judiciary from the police be applied to sexual offenses? In clashes between the *Gemeinwohl* and the individual in sexual matters, whose interest should be more protected by the state?

The experiences of Baden and Bavaria permit us to examine both sides of the reform ledger, civil and criminal. Baden introduced a lightly modified version of the Code Napoléon, but kept its criminal code virtually intact. Bavaria retained its civil code, but reformed its criminal code. For several reasons we begin with Anselm Feuerbach's reformed criminal code for Bavaria. As the historian of reform Bavaria, Walter Demel, notes, "If one views the securing of an individual sphere of freedom against state and private arbitrary [interference] as the center of all considerations of the legal order [*aller rechtsstaatlichen Überlegungen*], then one must view the protection of the person and of human dignity as the foundation of all guarantees of civil rights, and in this the police and criminal practice—thus, the criminal code— doubtless sooner plays a key role than the more 'inter-private' civil law."[6] Thus the criminal code is more likely to answer fundamental questions about the border between the individual and the state than the civil code is. Feuerbach's own rigor brings the principles behind the formation of civil society into sharp focus, making the inconsistencies in the sections of his reformed criminal code dealing with sexual crimes much easier to see. These inconsistencies map the ideological limits beyond which progressive contemporaries could not go in granting to citizens the right to consensual sexual expression protected from the interference of authorities.

Where Feuerbach's code marks the limits negatively, from the standpoint of the state, Baden's experience with the Code Napoléon does so positively, from the standpoint of civil principles. That is, in Baden the principles of liberal (male) civil society came thundering down with the suddenness of the Ten Commandments on

---

[6] Ibid., 347–48.

a traditional set of actual social relations and an unreformed criminal code and police system. The incongruities concerning illegitimate paternity and adultery illustrate the cleft not just between traditional and "advanced" civil society, but more important, between late Enlightened absolutist reform principles and those of postrevolutionary liberalism.

The reforms of the Napoleonic period permit us to distinguish among three closely related reform varieties of the late eighteenth and early nineteenth centuries. The first, late Enlightened absolutist reformism, characterized central state bureaucracies and often regents in the last third of the eighteenth century. We have observed their continuous, but ambivalent and usually incomplete reform efforts, which headed toward systematizing the rule of law according to principles of natural law and bureaucratic uniformity, but which did not dare relinquish the reassuring tutelage of *Polizey*. The Prussian *Allgemeines Landrecht* and the partial legal reforms in Baden and Bavaria of the 1780s and early 1790s are typical examples. While late Enlightened absolutist reformers were inching their way toward the de facto creation of a limited state and guaranteed civil society, other reform-minded persons by the 1780s and 1790s had grown weary of hesitation and were prepared to move quickly and radically in the same direction. The two varieties of pre-Napoleonic early liberalism we examined in the last chapter are characteristic of this impatience. The French victories permitted German reformers to realize reforms according to one or the other tendency in pre-Napoleonic early liberalism. Thus, the second variety of reform is that epitomized by Hippel or by Feuerbach. It proceeded according to principles deduced abstractly from natural law and simply issued by fiat from the state authority with little or no regard for whatever (moral) principles should guide civil society. This pristine legalism was thus comparatively state-oriented, rather than society-oriented; yet paradoxically it created more rigid limits to state intervention into society than did the third variety. Once civil society had been in fact legally guaranteed (by a constitution or simply by other legal reforms) the way was free for the third variety to blossom. This was post-[French] revolutionary liberalism, which deduced its guidelines, especially regarding gender and, later, nonmarital sexual behavior, from the principles it conceived as governing and maintaining civil society. These guidelines were both more differentiated (for example, along gender or sexual lines) and more redolent of morality than the sharper, more abstract principles of liberal-statist reformers, who worried less about upholding civil society and more about creating a protected space for it in the first place.

Because the period of reform was so brief, these three varieties of reform coexisted. Sometimes they were even embodied—sequentially—in a single person. It is often hard to distinguish a late Enlightened reform absolutist from a postrevolutionary liberal, since both felt the law should promote moral behavior and both supported some state intervention into "private" behavior to effect that end. Furthermore, even a stringent and abstract legalist like Feuerbach left surprising room for ill-defined *Polizey* intervention. Nonetheless, the three varieties of reform are useful as ideal types to help sort out the different principles animating actual reform, which produced very different effects in defining the line between state and civil society and the role sexual behavior played in defining that line.

The Bavarian Reform Administration of Montgelas

The French Revolution reached Bavaria in 1796 during a brief French occupation. The French returned three years later and remained this time until 1801. This second occupation coincided with the accession to the throne of Maximilian IV Joseph (1799–1825), whom Napoleon shortly elevated to King Maximilian I. Maximilian favored reform in any event, but under the circumstances reform offered the only hope of uniting the territories to which Bavaria had recently fallen heir, completing long overdue reforms in many areas, and most important, mollifying Napoleon sufficiently to escape further occupation.

Maximilian's architect for reform was Maximilian Joseph Freiherr (later Count) von Montgelas, a radical bureaucrat whose activities in the conspiratorial Illuminati in the 1790s had caused Elector Karl Theodor to suspend him from office.[7] French power and Bavarian weakness gave Montgelas a laboratory opportunity to enact the perfect late Enlightened absolutist reforms. Montgelas was a bureaucratic Joseph II, but unlike the unfortunate Austrian monarch, Montgelas was arguably the most successful exemplar of that breed of planner in all of Europe. In his seventeen years of influence he transformed virtually all of Bavaria's institutions according to the late Enlightened absolutist agenda.[8] Under Montgelas Bavaria secularized church land and broke the aristocrats' monopoly on offices and subjected them to equal taxation and equal treatment under the law. They were still strong enough, however, as they were everywhere in central Europe, to prevent abolition of all of their quasi-feudal property rights and their right to dispense justice on their estates (patrimonial jurisdiction). Still, limited land reform did occur, and noble justices, although they still existed, were redefined as state servants and thus subjected to state supervision. Censorship gave way to freedom of the press (until Napoleon intervened to quell it); the Tolerance Edict lifted religious barriers; and schools and public medicine were encouraged, even thrust upon the populace. These measures were designed both to foster an active, healthy civil society and to enhance the power of the central state. Its bureaucracy became a professional *Stand*, with regulated pay scales, entrance exams, protection from arbitrary dismissal, and pensions.[9] Administrative reforms streamlined government to provide for the smooth transmission of orders from the center down.[10] Therefore, municipal re-

---

[7] Eberhard Weis, *Montgelas, 1759–1799: Zwischen Revolution und Reform* (Munich, 1971).

[8] Eberhard Weis, "Die Begründung des modernen bayerischen Staates unter König Max I," in *Handbuch der bayerischen Geschichte,* vol. 4.1, ed. M. Spindler (Munich 1974), 3–86.

[9] Bernd Wunder, *Privilegierung und Disziplinierung. Die Entstehung des Berufsbeamtentums in Bayern und Württemberg (1780–1825)* (Munich, 1978).

[10] Demel, *Staatsabsolutismus,* 116–24.

forms removed self-government and self-policing from the localities (*Städte, Märkte, Gemeinden*) to the 8 provincial governments (*Kreisregierungen*). The constitution of 1808, the first such granted in central Europe, was carefully circumscribed so that it would replace the troublesome Estates, without creating a parliament powerful enough to challenge the government.[11] Thus the parliament enjoyed no legislative initiative, no veto power, and no general freedom of speech (criticism) for its members. It was indirectly elected by assemblages of wealthy landowners. Even the financial reforms the parliament made possible enhanced central state power by eliminating state debts and making the state that much more independent. Still, the constitution of 1808 also guaranteed civil freedoms and rights to individuals. As this brief summary makes clear, Montgelas aimed institutionally to complete that paradoxical, late-absolutist ambition to use the perfection of state structures to lay the groundwork for the development of a society independent of the state.[12]

More than anything else, law was key to providing the ground rules by which the delicate new balance between state and society would be established.[13] Legal reform was therefore of critical importance to Montgelas's endeavor. As he did for all the territories under his influence, Napoléon insisted that Bavaria adopt "his" civil code. Anselm Feuerbach, a young Turk from the university of Jena, recently hired by Bavaria to reform the criminal code, and Nikolaus Thaddäus Gönner, an experienced Bavarian jurist, swiftly produced a lightly modified version of the Napoleonic code. Despite their personal squabbling, both men were convinced that the code's principles, which they identified with enlightenment and progress, required adoption in its entirety.[14] Feuerbach's official defense of the new code summarized its "main ideas" and "main foundations" as "personal freedom," equality under the law, freedom of property, and separation of church and state:

> Even this [brief summary] is sufficient to indicate the powerful new spirit in this law code, which permits nothing or very little to be stripped away; to the contrary, which extends itself imperially [*weitherrschend*] to all relations of political life and saturates the innermost being not only of the constitution, but also of the state administration in all directions. Even the immediate results, the direct effects of each principle, how important and far ranging [they are]! And then the indirect effects, the results of results in their long series, which must develop completely only in time, and now only partly imagined or

[11] Karl Möckl, *Der moderne bayerische Staat. Eine Verfassungsgeschichte vom Aufgeklärten Absolutismus bis zum Ende der Reformepoche* (Munich, 1979).

[12] On Montgelas's goals, see Weis, *Montgelas*, 188–92, 266–87, and Demel, *Staatsabsolutismus*, 98–163. After Montgelas's dismissal in 1817, several of his reforms were partly undone: the *Konkordat* restored some of the Roman Catholic Church's power; the Constitution of 1818 inched toward greater parliamentary power, and the *Gemeindeedikt* of 1818 returned self-government to the localities.

[13] See the discussion in Walker, *German Home Towns*, 194–205.

[14] Feuerbach and Gönner were quite similar politically, though Gönner's views tended to be more congruent with nineteenth-century trends than Feuerbach's. On their political agreement, see Fritz Eduard Rosenberger, "Das Sexualstrafrecht in Bayern von 1813 bis 1871" (J.S.D. diss., Universität Marburg, 1973), 81.

suspected, may not yet certainly be grasped, reckoned, or counted! Wherever Napoleon's law code comes, there arises a new time, a new world, a new state.[15]

No clearer statement of the anticipatory, prescriptive quality of law reform for state and society could be made. Feuerbach granted to law the same guiding function that other bureaucrats had located in state administration.

Alas for these sentiments, dissension inside the central government sabotaged the adoption of the Code Napoléon and even doomed a second reform draft based on Bavarian precedents. No uniform civil code existed in Bavaria until 1900, when the all-German *Bürgerliches Gesetzbuch* took effect.[16]

The failure of civil code reform redoubled the importance of the criminal code to defining the relation between state and society. This was only appropriate, since criminal code reform had been so well prepared by the debates and even attempts of the 1780s and 1790s. Even then sexual delicts had been the vanguard of reform. In the few intervening years pressure from the lower courts toward leniency in consensual sexual acts had not abated. Privy Councillor Johann Adam von Aretin remarked in 1801 that "practically every lower court, without having so much as asked [the higher administration], has permitted itself an arbitrary modification of the penalty for first-time adultery."[17] Appellate courts seem to have followed the same drummer. A mere three years after an edict ended punishment for fornicants, the appeals court in Munich extended "by analogy" this principle to *Konkubinat*.[18] More important for legislative reform, the central administration seemed after Maximilian's ascension to be less frightened of lightening penalties for consensual heterosexual acts. In 1808 it finally took the plunge and decriminalized by edict "extramarital impregnations,"[19] completing in a single stroke the long, tortuous process that had been under way for a century.

Some fainthearted central bureaucrats had stalled sexual crime reform in the 1790s by claiming that fixing one section of the criminal code would only distort the rest; after 1800 they were robbed of this excuse. On 2 February 1800 Maximilian ordered a complete overhaul of the criminal code, trial procedure, and the police code.[20] They were to be redesigned according to the "proper principles of reason and of civil life [*des bürgerlichen Lebens*]." The reform of sex-crime laws therefore would occur within the context of all laws and ordinances and explicitly according to Enlightened principles of natural law (reason) and concern for the development

[15] Paul Johann Anselm Feuerbach, "Betrachtungen über den Geist des Code Napoléon, und dessen Verhältniß zur Gesezgebung und Verfassung teutscher Staaten überhaupt, und Baierns insbesondere," in *Themis, oder Beiträge zur Gesezgebung* (Landshut, 1812), 61. "Political life" refers to social relations among the inhabitants of the state, not to their political activities in the modern sense. This follows Austrian legal usage as embedded in Joseph II's law code of 1787.

[16] See Gustav Radbruch, *Paul Johann Anselm Feuerbach. Ein Juristenleben* (Vienna, 1934), 68–82.

[17] General-Landesdirektion, Conclusum, signed von Aretin, 1 April 1801, Bay HStA, GR 322/8.

[18] Copy of decision of Appellationsgericht, Munich, 31 May 1811, Bay HStA, MInn 72654.

[19] Organisches Edikt über Patrimonial Gerichtsbarkeit, 10 September 1808, *Königlich-Baierisches Regierungsblatt* (Munich, 1808), 2254.

[20] Verordnung of 2 February 1800, Bay HStA, GR 969/35.

of civil society. This clear aim required the reformers to assess the relative importance of sexual crimes to other delicts, to the state, and to society.

The first reform draft was entrusted to the Bavarian jurist Gallus Alois Kleinschrod, who produced in 1802 a code that met with universal dissatisfaction. Kleinschrod had not understood the revolutionary social task that the reform criminal code was supposed to attempt. Instead of finding a clean way to organize the relation between state and society, he built on and refined the practice of the reform absolutist police state. Like his counterparts E. F. Klein and C. G. Svarez who had authored the Prussian *Allgemeines Landrecht* of 1794, he produced an ungainly compendium of detailed legislation that assumed police tutelage over childlike subjects.[21] But also like late reform absolutist bureaucrats, Kleinschrod favored mild penalties, nowhere more strikingly so than in sexual delicts.

Kleinschrod's section on "carnal [*fleischlichen*] crimes" penalized two kinds of infractions: those outside of marriage and those "against the order of nature," both of which justified state intervention.[22] Kleinschrod, however, removed consensual extramarital heterosexual acts (fornication, *Konkubinat, Kuppelei*, and even pimping [*Hurenwirthschaft*]) from the criminal code altogether and consigned them to the police for arbitrary punishment. He ordered the police punishment to be as secret as the commission of acts themselves, in order to avoid unnecessary public outcry. Kleinschrod explicitly departed from earlier Bavarian laws in handling adultery in a gender-neutral manner. That, the lightened penalty,[23] and the recognition of unsatisfied sexual desire inside the marriage (due to absence, illness, or refusal) as a mitigating circumstance all are characteristic of late Enlightened absolutist reformers. But Kleinschrod kept the old moral distinctions according to which rape was more severely punished, the more "honorable" the victim's *Stand* or the more important her relation to men; the female pyramid of sexual honor peaked in the wife, and descended through nuns, brides, widows and "honorable" maidens, fallen but not yet disreputable women, and ended with "loose women" (*liederliche Weibspersonen*), or, astonishingly, women "whom [the rapist] for good reasons held to be a loose person."[24] A similar moral pyramid prioritized sodomy, with bestiality meriting a harder punishment (three to four years hard labor in the *Zuchthaus*) than same-sex relations between men, which earned only eight to thirty-two months hard labor. Although Kleinschrod retained the old practice of destroying the animal involved in bestiality, his penalty for same-sex relations between men was remarkably light, considering that previous codes had demanded the death penalty. Apparently the two other offenses comprising "sodomy," same-sex relations between

[21] For the Allgemeines Landrecht, see Koselleck, *Preußen zwischen Reform und Revolution.*

[22] Gallus Alois Kleinschrod, *Entwurf eines peinlichen Gesetzbuchs für die kurpfalzbaierischen Staaten* (Munich, 1802), part 2, sec. 2, chap. 12, pars. 1428–1563, pp. 230–48.

[23] Four to six months in jail (*Gefängnis*) for double adultery (when both partners were married), two to three months in jail for single adultery. Ibid., pars. 1460–61.

[24] Ibid., par. 1520. Kleinschrod also contemplated the possibility that a woman might force a man to intercourse through cunning or power, for which she would be punished as a man who raped a fallen but not yet disreputable woman, that is, by four to six months in the work house. Par. 1521.

women and nonprocreative sex between men and women, were too unimportant to merit specific punishment, though he still listed these acts as criminal.[25] In a modern departure reflecting the antimasturbation campaign, Kleinschrod criminalized that act, if it were performed in public. Otherwise, his list of criminal acts was standard: bigamy, incest, intercourse with minors or persons who could not consent, and contributing to the seduction of a minor under one's tutelage.

Kleinschrod's draft illustrates contradictory possibilities inside the reform police state framework. On the one hand, utilitarianism, practical experience, the desire for enforceable laws, and a down-to-earth, literal-minded brand of Enlightenment encouraged lighter penalties for consensual heterosexual acts, gender-neutral treatment of miscreants, and an openness to psychological, pedagogical and/or sexual theories said to reveal the laws of nature. (This latter characteristic might, of course, counter other principles, as we have seen "liberal" sexual theory do in the case of gender equal treatment in the preceding chapter.)[26] Nonetheless, these police-state principles encouraged reform in the direction of lessened state intervention in some forms of sexual behavior. On the other hand, the police state was also encumbered with numberless old ordinances proscribing and prescribing according to moral, customary, and other types of injunctions. It was difficult for the police state to emancipate itself from these temptations to interfere, particularly given the educative function ascribed to the police. That is, since the police was supposed to teach subjects how to behave correctly, the enforcement of moral, customary, and, latterly, scientific injunctions seemed quite proper to its social function.

Kleinschrod's critics fastened on this paradox of the police-state viewpoint, which they interpreted as chaos.[27] They found "that Kleinschrod could not have proceeded from a common principle";[28] even the representative of the state police delegation to the Bavarian state council found the draft "too broad, too complicated."[29] Further, the critics decried the leniency of his proposed punishments,[30] thus signaling the end to the gradualist reform approach of the eighteenth century. The gap between the draconian written common law of the Reformation era (the Carolina) and actual social custom and judicial practice had been by 1800 largely closed by milder penalties. The danger now seemed to lurk in continuing the

[25] Ibid., pars. 1538–45.

[26] See also Kleinschrod's own ambivalence, following current theories about the biological differences between men and women, in Gallus Aloys [sic] Kleinschrod, *Systematische Entwickelung der Grundbegriffe und Grundwahrheiten des peinlichen Rechts nach der Natur der Sache und der positiven Gesetzgebung,* (Erlangen, 1794), 1:142–48.

[27] See the comparative table of Kleinschrod's punishments in Paul Johann Anselm Feuerbach, *Kritik des Kleinschrodischen Entwurfs zu einem peinlichen Gesetzbuche für die Chur-Pfalz-Bayrischen Staaten* (Giesen [sic], 1804), 124–25.

[28] "Erstes schriftliches Votum über die Prüfung des von Kleinschrod gemachten Entwurfs eines peinlichen Gesetzbuches für Baiern," signed Heller von Hellerberg, Munich, 27 July 1803, Bay HStA, GR 969/36.

[29] J. von Obernberg, "Über den Entwurf einer peinlichen Gesetzbuches für die pfalzbaierischen Staaten von Kleinschrod" (1802), Bay HStA, GR 969/36.

[30] The critics rarely specify which crimes they think Kleinschrod punished too leniently, so it is impossible to say how great a role sex crimes may have played in their criticism.

Enlightenment trend toward milder punishments, possibly fostering anarchic individualism against the needs of nascent civil society. State Councillor Karl Heller von Hellersberg, commenting during the first vote on Kleinschrod's draft in the Bavarian Law Commission, summarized the task of criminal law code revision:

> Kleinschrod's draft left the criminal better off than the state. . . . Our goal is to counter those acts of citizens [*Staatsbürger*], which, were they to become common modes of behavior, would render impossible the maintenance or establishment of a legal state-society [*rechtliche Staatsgesellschaft*]. The regent must therefore exactly determine these acts and explicitly forbid them. One cannot leave the determination of these [acts] to the caprice of the state subjects [*Staatsunterthanen*].[31]

The task was to discover the principles that would identify criminal acts, assess their magnitude, and punish them justly, without violating individual liberty. The clearest and most principled of Kleinschrod's critics was Anselm Feuerbach, and it was he whom Maximilian appointed in August 1804 to produce a new criminal law reform.

Feuerbach's Political, Philosophical, and Legal Principles

Feuerbach, a lawyer's son from Frankfurt, was headed toward a career in philosophy when the second extramarital pregnancy of his fiancée forced him to switch suddenly to law, a quicker, more practical path to earnings and marriage.[32] While a philosophy student at Jena, Feuerbach had become a thoroughgoing Kantian liberal. Indeed, Kant's philosophy was the explicit basis for Feuerbach's later politics and for his conception of law. Liberal legal historians prize Feuerbach as "a liberal, moderate constitutionalist,"[33] and as "the most authentic enlightened philosopher, the most authentic natural law jurist, who not only believe[d] a strictly objective discovery of truth is possible in the realm of the natural, causally explicable world, but moreover in the same way believe[d] that one must search for and can find final, objective truths also in the realm of cultural values."[34] These descriptions are accurate: Feuerbach was a late Enlightened state reformer informed, better, galvanized, by the early liberal critique of Enlightened absolutism. He shared with late Enlightened reform absolutism its confidence in *applied* Enlightenment, that following the principles of natural law, one can deduce institutions that will permit and encourage human progress. Indeed, only the state might guarantee the conditions of progress and freedom. As Feuerbach put it, "outside civil society [*der bürgerlichen Gesellschaft*, here a synonym for 'state'] there is no freedom . . . we lose nothing through the state, except the freedom to injure without being punished. . . . [T]he state fills the rank of the most honorable and holiest of all human

[31] "Erstes schriftliches Votum," 27 July 1803, Bay HStA, GR 969/36.
[32] Radbruch, *Feuerbach*, 37–38.
[33] Ibid., 188–89.
[34] Schmidt, *Strafrechtspflege*, 237.

institutions [standing] before Reason."[35] But by the 1790s, many Enlightened reformers had begun to see the state not as the solution, but as part of the problem. These early liberals, Feuerbach among them, were convinced that state institutions could not force progress on their own. They believed that progress could only come through legal, constitutional limits to monarchical power. Kant had come this far; Feuerbach went further. Arguing strict contractarianism and citing Rousseau, in *Anti-Hobbes* (1797), Feuerbach explicitly granted subjects the right to rebel against an unjust, tyrannical monarch.[36] This was a much more radical step than most German lawyers were prepared to take at the time.

Feuerbach's statism, his readiness to sanction abrupt, even violent political change, plus his belief in objectively correct natural principles according to which laws and societies should be grounded, led him to support Napoléon and the emperor's civil code.[37] It also caused him later to reject Napoléon himself for his despotism.

Feuerbach's brand of early liberalism marks the consummation of Enlightened absolutist reform. It contained the dynamic elements and philosophical foundation of Enlightened state reform, but criticized the very role of the state in bringing those reforms about. It looked forward to securing a civil society beyond the state that would bloom in its absence and fulfill the progressive Enlightened agenda in the lives of individual citizens. To some extent, such a civil society, in the form of educated, public opinion knit together by books, journals, and associations, already existed. Feuerbach and the early liberals were partly products of this society. But neither it, nor the social relations governing the lives of most Germans, nor those new social relations that liberal reform would shortly introduce were what early liberals of Feuerbach's stripe understood by "civil society." Theirs was a Platonic, prospective vision.[38] Certainly Feuerbach did not understand until later, when he left academia and government for the judge's bench, how the world of liberal "civil society" actually operated, or what it demanded, or why. This ignorance accounts for the principled clarity of his legal vision, as well as its much-criticized practical shortcomings, and finally and for our theme most important, its blindness to the principles that were said to bind civil society together.

For Feuerbach, correct legal principles demanded and established the division between state and society. The proper relations of law, state, and society all derived from Kant's understanding of morality, which could be deduced from Reason. Therefore, Feuerbach's conception of law was idealist;[39] it began with a deduction of the moral nature of the individual and reasoned from there to the institutions necessary to fulfill that nature.

[35] Paul Johann Anselm Feuerbach, *Anti-Hobbes* (Giessen, 1797; rpt., Darmstadt, 1967), 46.

[36] *Ibid.*, 80–148. Cf. Kant, "On the Common Saying," 79–81.

[37] See p. 338–39 for Feuerbach's encomium to the civil code.

[38] Gall, "Liberalismus und 'bürgerliche Gesellschaft'"; Batscha, *Studien.*

[39] Feuerbach is sometimes viewed as a positivist, primarily because of his fanatical devotion to the dictatorship of the letter of the law, but he derived his laws not from legal history or custom, but from abstract principles. Radbruch, *Feuerbach,* 182–83.

The Separation of Law and Morality

"Morality is the final purpose of the world," Feuerbach wrote.[40] The moral law (*Sittengesetz*) was Kant's categorical imperative, which Feuerbach summarized as the duty to use neither yourself nor any other sentient being as a mere means to an end and "to use your freedom to further the use of freedom in other sentient beings . . . and in yourself."[41] Freedom, that is, the unhindered use of free will, was crucial to moral behavior, because moral acts were only those acts in conformity with the fundamental law of Reason, freely taken for their own sake, as duties, without regard to self-interest.[42] Even doing a good act, or refraining from doing a bad one, did not qualify as moral, if the actor were motivated by gain, pleasure, pride, or the desire to avoid pain, harm, or punishment. This stricture was Kant's effort to separate morality from eighteenth-century utilitarianism, which had tended to equate moral acts with happiness. Kant removed morality into the realm of the autonomous activity of free will independent of external influences.

This move demanded a wide sphere of personal autonomy for each individual; it should have been the death knell to moral interference from the state. For the state was incapable of causing or enjoining moral behavior. Neither by reward (a fond scheme of Enlighteners), nor by punishment, could the state produce morality, since both appealed to individual self-interest, which could never be the fount of moral behavior. Therefore, morality ceased to be the state's business. As Feuerbach summarized this line of reasoning, "The fulfillment of the moral order lies entirely outside the boundaries of the law; to encourage or establish this moral order is neither the goal of the state (which consists merely in the legal order, the legal condition), nor is it even a means to this end."[43]

For the sake of morality, Feuerbach wanted morality expunged from law root and branch: "Juridical Reason must clear away the hindrances that block the fulfillment of the highest purpose. *Freely* following the moral law is a precondition for fulfilling the highest purpose. . . . Therefore juridical Reason must also sanction the sphere of unmoral actions, that is, it must declare these actions to be undamaging [*unverletzlich*] and permit the use of force against persons who would hinder me from committing them." Therefore, the state must permit even suicide, lest its prohibitions cause citizens "to have fulfilled the[ir] duty not through freedom, but necessity. But Reason must want freedom in the fulfillment of duties. Consequently, it [Reason] must give me the right not to be forced to fulfill my duties; it must give me the *right* to take my own life."[44]

---

[40] Paul Johann Anselm Feuerbach, *Kritik des natürlichen Rechts als Propädeutik zu einer Wissenschaft der natürlichen Rechte* (Altona, 1796; rpt., Hildesheim, 1963), 276.

[41] Ibid., 269–73.

[42] Ibid., 275.

[43] Paul Johann Anselm von [*sic*] Feuerbach, *Revision der Grundsätze und Grundbegriffe des positiven peinlichen Rechts* (Erfurt, 1799; rpt., Aalen, 1966), 1:31–32.

[44] Feuerbach, *Kritik des natürlichen Rechts*, 290–91. Cf. Fichte's agreement, in Chapter 8, p. 320–21.

Exactly the same logic would wipe the law books clean of consensual sexual acts. Insofar as sodomy is "merely immorality," Feuerbach insists in his *Revision der Grundsätze*, it is not criminal (1:312). Feuerbach's moral vendetta against morality in law destroyed both the historical and the philosophical justifications for most sex-crime legislation, since the legal prohibitions had largely originated in canon law and were defended in the late eighteenth century as still necessary for popular moral education. Although Feuerbach, reasoning idealistically, did not justify his call for decriminalization by claiming that (Enlightened) attitudes toward the seriousness of these acts had changed and that law should reflect modern opinion, nonetheless, that change made Feuerbach's idealist claim possible. For he could cite legal scholars, like Cella, who had demonstrated by other methods the inequities of old legislation. And the uncharacteristically strong language he used to describe the old laws indicates that Feuerbach expected educated opinion to agree, generally, with his view. Thus, he calls the old punishment for sodomy "from the standpoint of objective judgment thoroughly inappropriate, completely counterproductive, and highly barbaric" (1:312).

The Dogma of Rights

Feuerbach replaced morality as the foundation of criminal law with the single, stringent standard of harm to fundamental rights (*Rechtsverletzung*). These rights flowed from Reason and from the purpose of the state, which was "the mutual freedom of all citizens [*Bürger*], in other words, the condition in which each can fully exercise his rights, and is secure from injuries" (*Revision*, 1:39). Therefore, "the state can only punish injuries to rights [*Rechtsverletzungen*]. . . . It is not the transgressions against duties, and sins, but only the *danger* and *damage* of the deed (for the condition of rights) which the state punishes" (1:65, 66). This high standard, too, excluded many current sexual delicts from a future law code. According to Feuerbach, rights accrued either to the state or to individuals. The state's rights were either absolute (existence, use of executive power, external representation, and honor) or contingent (*bedingt-nothwendig*) (2:219–20). The private rights of individuals derived either from Reason itself or were acquired (2:228–38). Consensual sexual acts were not easy to subsume under these categories; it seems clear that Feuerbach's stringent legal logic led ineluctably to their entire decriminalization. As we shall see, however, the doctrine of the contingent rights of the state might provide a back door by which these acts could silently be drawn back under surveillance and punishment.

The Dictatorship of Law

There is one further principle that affected how sexual delicts would be handled in Feuerbach's code: the utter primacy of laws. Positive laws were the only guarantors of freedom (*Revision*, 1:54–56). They established the border beyond which the state could not exercise its power (*Gewalt*) (1:63–66). Feuerbach established Beccaria's maxim, "no crime, no punishment, without law," as the foundation of the legal system (1:148). Therefore positive laws had to be complete, explicit, and watertight; they had to describe exactly the possible injuries to real rights and establish fitting punishments, but include nothing further. They had to stand on their own as the bulwark between state power and civic freedom, and therefore they had to be "absolute." In order to revolutionize the world Marx wanted to establish the dictatorship of the proletariat; in order to do the same thing Feuerbach tried to establish the dictatorship of positive law.

The dictatorship of positive law, in other words, its utter independence from corrupting influence, demanded that it apply to everyone without exception and without regard to social station, including gender and sexual reputation; that is, it required absolute equality before the law. It required that the crime itself, the harm done to rights, not the subjective characteristics of the criminal or his or her motivation or mental state, determine punishment. This meant the sphere of judicial discretion was drastically curtailed. Judges were to be chained to the letter of the law, divested of their role as mediators between social opinion and legislation. Feuerbach went even further. He wanted commentaries to his legal code of 1813 forbidden, lest legal opinion confuse the clarity of the word of law itself. As it was, Feuerbach had to put up with one commentary drafted by his personal enemy Gönner and published with the code in 1813. All others, however, were forbidden by law.[45]

The Greatest Danger to Rights

Finally, Feuerbach's legal absolutism and his mechanical understanding of criminal psychology encouraged relatively stiff punishments designed to deter, not by cruel, public example, as under absolutism, but by virtue of the rational calculation of the potential criminal. Punishments were calculated to offset the pleasure or gain of the crime.[46] Knowing that the exact letter of the law, unmitigated by judicial discretion, would always be enforced, the rational citizen would refrain from crime. Feuerbach's project, to establish the civil sphere of freedom in which citizens might fulfill their human potential by freely acting according to the laws of Reason, predisposed him to conceive of punishment according to an equally rational schema. It also meant that the greatest potential threat to civil order was not the rational criminal, that is, the one acting within a greater sphere of moral freedom and thus more immorally, whom Enlightened legal reformers proposed to punish

[45] Rosenberger, "Sexualstrafrecht," 49–50.
[46] For Feuerbach's refutation of the doctrine of "special prevention" and his adumbration of "general prevention," see Feuerbach, *Revision,* 1:114–20; Feuerbach, *Kritik des Kleinschrodischen Entwurfs,* 140; Schmidt, *Strafrechtspflege,* 238–39; Radbruch, *Feuerbach,* 44–46; and Rosenberger, "Sexualstrafrecht," 51–60.

the hardest, but on the contrary, citizens so enthralled to "sensual drives" originating in nature that they disregarded the careful calculation of crime/pleasure and punishment/displeasure, and proceeded with their foolish acts anyway. These criminals deserved harsher punishment, because their peculiar nature predisposed them to repeat their criminal acts.[47] Feuerbach's belief in the principle of rationality grounding civil society had thus led him from eighteenth-century, Enlightened leniency to nineteenth-century severity, and from compassion for the passionate, intemperate, and irrational to fear of them. The nineteenth-century myth of rational civil society justified the punishment and exclusion from it of individuals and groups labeled irrational. Feuerbach's thinking foreshadows those later social practices without being identical with them. For Feuerbach arrived at his theory of punishment not to protect an existing civil society, but to create one, and not by embedding moral considerations in the law, but by trying to ban them from it. That he should sound so "advanced" attests to how powerfully "rationality" and the viewpoint of civil society (as opposed to that of the state) operated together to recreate a control agenda in theory and in practice.

Feuerbach on State and Civil Society

Before examining Feuerbach's 1813 code, we should pause to analyze his views on state and civil society, for these confirm his liminal place at the apex of Enlightenment state reform before the emergence of full-blown, nineteenth-century liberalism. As we have seen, the split between law and morality, which Radbruch claims was Feuerbach's most important contribution to legal theory,[48] also described the future split between state and civil society. That is, law, dedicated purely to safeguarding rights, relegated morality to civil society and erected the barrier behind which civil society was free to develop and in which individuals exercised moral (or immoral) behavior. Sequestering civil society behind the law diminished the extent of the state. But Feuerbach had gone even further; following contract theory, he had subordinated the state to the service of civil society. As he put it in *Anti-Hobbes*, "Constituting the regent is not the goal, but only a means of society—a means can never contradict the goal" (96). Therefore, neither the regent nor the administrative apparatus (*Staatsverwaltung, Regierung*) was independent of the goal of civil society, which was "the complete security of mutual freedom" (35). Indeed, "an act [by state officials] that harms the purpose of society, is no act of government" (156). The state was therefore the *Rechtsstaat* dedicated to civil freedom.

Although Feuerbach's intent was clearly to create an independent civil society, his language betrays the prospective quality of his endeavor. He vacillates between speaking of civil society as something truly separate from the state and speaking of the state as a (higher) aspect of civil society, in the manner of all previous German

---

[47] Feuerbach, *Revision*, 2:335–36, 374–75, 388, 405.
[48] Radbruch, *Feuerbach*, 25.

political theorists.[49] For example, when Feuerbach explains the foundation of the state, he writes, "Through the contract of subjection and the constitution, civil society [*bürgerliche Gesellschaft*] becomes the *state,* that is, becomes an *organized civil society,* and thus becomes an institution [*Anstalt*] in which the sought-for legal condition, the complete security of mutual freedom, is at hand."[50] Usually, Feuerbach seems to use "state" and "civil society" interchangeably, rhetorically repeating one and then the other to strengthen a point.[51] But sometimes he obviously regards them as quite separate, such as when he discusses the situation after a successful revolt against a tyrant when government (*Regierung*) has ceased: "The people would then find themselves in the pure condition of a mere civil society and thus the complete fulfillment of the purpose of society [*Gesellschaftszweck*] would be simply impossible."[52]

Feuerbach wrote little about how he thought civil society operated or what principles of behavior held it together. He believed mere society, the agglomeration of people for the purpose of satisfying (material) needs, was plagued by disharmony and friction. The regent, he wrote, focuses and makes possible the articulation of the "general will."[53] How this operates was left entirely obscure. So were the guidelines for determining the state's right "to force its subjects [*Unterthanen*] to subject their private interests to the public interest and to fashion their acts according to the declared general will."[54] It may be that in the two years separating Feuerbach's ruminations on the state (*Anti-Hobbes,* 1797) and his major statement of legal principles (*Revision,* 1799), he had warmed to the task of reining in Leviathan. But the fact remains that Feuerbach's starting point in thinking about civil society was the state, as it was and had to be for most Germans before the nineteenth century. This is why so many of them used the word "state-society" (*Staatsgesellschaft*) in the period from 1790 to 1820 to describe the organism they were trying to cleave. Feuerbach's most articulate supporter in the Bavarian Council of State, Heller von Hellersberg, who had thoroughly studied Feuerbach's theoretical writings, explained during the discussion of Kleinschrod's draft code in 1803 that positive law had to be absolute because civil society did not yet exist and citizens had yet to be created: "In our states as they are now the majority of people have absolutely no conception of a state-society [*Staatsgesellschaft*], or a work of state [*Staatswerk*], and they act merely according to sensual drives. It even costs the greatest energy to move the more educated estates [*gebildetern Stände*], so that they will fulfill their natural obligation by limiting sensual caprice for the merely pleasant and useful and approach the goal of state [*Staatszweck*]!!"[55]

---

[49] Manfred Riedel, "Gesellschaft, bürgerliche," in Brunner, Conze, and Koselleck, *Geschichtliche Grundbegriffe,* 2:739–41.

[50] Feuerbach, *Anti-Hobbes,* 34–35, emphases in original.

[51] For example, ibid., 46, 47, 74, 258; Feuerbach, *Revision,* 1:39, and passim.

[52] Feuerbach, *Anti-Hobbes,* 57.

[53] Ibid., 11 n, 26–29, 32–33.

[54] Ibid., 45.

[55] "Erstes schriftliches Votum," 27 July 1803, Bay HStA, GR 969/36.

The Bavarian Criminal Code of 1813

Feuerbach finished the second draft of his code in 1810.[56] Two different, law commissions discussed it, the second of which approved a somewhat modified version in 1813. None of the modifications, however, significantly diluted Feuerbach's principles, which determined the code's conception, arrangement, hierarchy of delicts, and punishments. The 1813 code was unmistakably Feuerbach's work.

Feuerbach restricted his code stringently to injuries to real rights. These could be suffered by either the state or private persons and, befitting the attempt to secure civil society, Feuerbach listed the private ones first. Under each category, two types of acts were punished. Crimes (*Verbrechen*) were serious injuries to fundamental rights committed through malicious plan. Lesser crimes (*Vergehen*) injured real rights, perhaps even intentionally, but more often through negligence.[57] The gray, transitional area between them was not always easy to determine. Nonetheless, both encompassed acts which "are not allowed through *purely juridical* reasons, always and under all circumstances; their prohibition is indelibly inscribed in the heart of every reasonable person" (*Strafgesetzbuch*, 1:24). Both were therefore the only proper concern of a criminal code. A third kind of act was a matter of "judicial indifference" (*rechtlich gleichgültig*). "These are forbidden from *purely political* reasons, and are contingent upon the time, circumstances, character and customs/ morals [*Sitten*] of nations, peculiar institutions, and other accidental circumstances." These acts belonged in a separate police code, so as not "to mix different things and confuse the moral judgment of the people" (1:24). Feuerbach refused to write a police code and thus escaped responsibility for what happened to these acts.

The Decriminalization of Consensual Sexual Acts

The most striking and most controversial aspect of the 1813 code was the disappearance from it of virtually all consensual sexual acts. Fornication, *Konkubinat*, "sodomy" (that is, homosexuality, bestiality, and nonprocreative acts between men and women), commercial prostitution and *Kuppelei*, and masturbation had all been decriminalized. Incest was only included in the code over Feuerbach's objections.[58] Indeed, there was no section for "carnal delicts" at all, because morality no longer grounded law and because Feuerbach did not deem injuries to moral precepts worthy of legal protection—they were not *Rechtsgüter*. As he put it in the *Strafgesetzbuch*: "As long as a person only harms the internal duties toward himself by unchaste deeds, only contravenes the commandments of morality without harming the rights of another person, then those deeds are not included in the present law code. Masturbation, sodomy, bestiality, extramarital consensual inter-

---

[56] On the earlier draft, see Rosenberger, "Sexualstrafrecht," 44.

[57] Paul Johann Anselm Feuerbach, *Strafgesetzbuch für das Königreich Bayern* (Munich, 1813), 3:207–12.

[58] Rosenberger, "Sexualstrafrecht," 166–67, 187–88, 212.

course are serious contraventions against moral commandments, but, as sins [*Sünde*], they do not belong to the domain of external law codes" (vol. 2, art. 186, pp. 59–60). Following a single principle, Feuerbach, it seems, had managed to complete the long process of gradual, lenient reform that had been proceeding since the early eighteenth century. Whereas the eighteenth-century reformers had concentrated on single offenses, especially fornication, and had reasoned, variously, from utility, forgiveness, and pragmatism, Feuerbach, by applying the underlying principle of *Rechtsverletzung*, had consolidated and regularized that reform process and extended it from consensual heterosexual, procreative acts to all others, too. Yet, as we shall see, the perfection of this schema proved impossible to maintain. Nonetheless, it is noteworthy that the law commissioners of Montgelas's reform state offered no criticism of the decriminalization of homosexual acts, sodomy, or masturbation; they accepted Feuerbach's arguments without demur.[59] Apparently, they saw no social harm in the acts themselves or in the fact that morality was unprotected by law.

Remaining Sex Crimes: The Transformational Results of Feuerbach's Principles

Sexual acts involving force, threat, or fraud or with persons deemed unable to consent remained crimes. But these acts were not lumped together under the rubric "sexual crimes." Their sexual aspect was not their defining characteristic. Feuerbach's is the only nineteenth-century German law code that lacks a category for sexual crime. Feuerbach's stringent secularism (the split of law and morality) is the main reason for this, since the sexual crime rubric was originally religious; however, this omission also suggests that Feuerbach did not feel it necessary, as other nineteenth-century codifiers did, to reconstruct the moral category of sexual crime in secular terms as a profound organizing principle of either society or individuals. For him criminal sexual behavior was merely a mode of committing fraud, violence, or achieving pleasure at someone else's expense. It carried no peculiar legal weight by virtue of being sexual. Rosenberger chides Feuerbach for his "narrow" view of injury that neglected the importance of early sexual experiences in psychological development, the "right to sexual self-determination," and the right to be undisturbed by the intrusion of sexual images.[60] But these are all "rights" that can only be conceived if one has attributed to sexual matters distinctive importance per se. That attribution is characteristic of the nineteenth and twentieth centuries, but not necessarily of the eighteenth, which was only in the process of contemplating a revaluation of the sexual. It was clearly possible for a mind trained in the late eighteenth century, like Feuerbach's, to be unconvinced of this revaluation and to

[59] Ibid., 209.
[60] Ibid., 126, 167, 168.

retain instead a worldview in which, for the purposes of criminal law at least, the sexual was merely another aspect of human behavior.

As radical as the elimination of the rubric "sexual crimes" and the decriminalization of consensual sexual acts were several innovations produced by Feuerbach's consistent application of his legal principles to the sexual acts that remained criminal. The statutes on rape and misuse of others for sexual purposes contained three remarkable examples. The first is gender equality. Males could for the first time be victims of rape, and women could now be the perpetrators of misuse for sexual purposes [*Mißbrauch zur Unzucht*].[61] The possibility that males might be sexual victims and women sexual threats was a new constellation that, as we shall see in the example of Baden, might justify discriminatory treatment of women in the sphere of rights. But Feuerbach derived his innovation not from fear *for* men or fear *of* women, but from the formal necessity for completeness, uniformity, and symmetry in the law, if it is to be the dictator holding state and society in their respective places. It is merely conceivable that such acts could occur and the law should therefore provide for them. The impetus for gender symmetry came from the imperialism of absolute law and its imperative, equality before the law.

It was inconceivable to Feuerbach and the legal commissioners, however, that women could commit rape: "In nonconsensual sexual intercourse, the code takes the difference of sex into special consideration."[62] It seems that penetration was so identified with rape that they could not imagine a woman forcing either a man or woman to perform an act ending in the female perpetrator's sexual satisfaction. Biology, having been used to define the act in the first place, then set the limit for gender symmetry in this one instance.

Although the penetration model still defined rape from the perpetrator's point of view, the victim's injury was differently conceived. Old rape laws had often contained a mixed view; on the one hand, rape was an injury to the property interests a man held in his victimized wife, or a father, in his victimized daughter. On the other hand, the victim herself had increasingly been recognized as aggrieved against, insofar as she was finally permitted to bring rape charges herself, rather than only through the male whose responsibility she was. The triumph of property as a protected right, indeed as a basis for citizenship and individual self-fulfillment, reorganized how rape was thought to injure. In his criticism of Kleinschrod's draft, Feuerbach had written that "forcible rape injures directly in the [female] rape victim [*in der Genothzüchtigten*] the holy right to her personality and to the property of her body. She is used as a mere object and demeaned as a means for animal lusts."[63] Contractarians, like Locke, had conceived of the body as personal property, and that view was consistent with Kant's location of moral activity in the individual, beginning with the duties to oneself, which included duties to one's

---

[61] Feuerbach, *Strafgesetzbuch*, vol. 2, arts. 186–91, pp. 58–68.
[62] Ibid., vol. 2, art. 189, p. 60.
[63] Feuerbach, *Kritik des Kleinschrodischen Entwurfs*, 105.

body.[64] In short, the body as property was a foundation for civil rights in the liberal schema, but it was not always consistently granted to women, especially regarding pregnancy and abortion. Feuerbach assigned all such property interests to the female as part of her natural rights.[65]

Gönner's notes to the 1813 code also speak to the injury to the "personality," but typically he added a moral note more characteristic of the nineteenth century: rape "is a double assault on the personality [*Persönlichkeit*] of a person [*eines Menschen*], it is an attack on the physical person and simultaneously on his or her moral integrity [*moralische Integrität*]."[66] This went beyond Feuerbach's modest, civil-rights oriented property claim and inserted moral integrity as a good that should be protected by law.

The third innovation caused by Feuerbach's principles illustrates how Gönner, by going "beyond" Feuerbach in including morality, had actually lost ground. At least three of Feuerbach's principles led ineluctably to the conclusion that a "morally disreputable" woman could also be a victim of rape. Older laws had usually excepted "whores" from legal protection on the implicit grounds that no male lost property value as a consequence of the act and that the woman herself had not lost anything, since in a manner of speaking, she had nothing to lose. But Feuerbach assigned absolute rights derived from Reason, to all regardless of subsequent social category. Among these was the absolute right to bodily integrity and self-determination of action.[67] Second, transgression of this right must be punished under the provisions of positive law. This law was "a *categorical* (that is, unlimited and valid in itself) *declaration*"; it was "*valid by itself for all cases.*"[68] In other words, it was the act that determined the illegality and the punishment, not the status of the victim. Third, neither the status of the perpetrator (as male) nor the relation or lack of one that the victim might enjoy to other males was relevant to the operation of law. Considerations of status, previous customary rights and privilege disfigured the pure form of Reason and were to be swept away.[69] The law was valid "for all who stand under its power. . . . Everyone, who commits this act, will suffer the legal punishment for it."[70] Applying Gönner's principle of moral integrity would have withheld the protection of law from women deemed disreputable. Feuerbach's principles, however, were so compelling that Gönner was forced to return in his annotations on rape to the first of them and silently abandon the moral appendage

---

[64] Locke, "Second Treatise of Government," 28; Kant, *Lectures on Ethics*, 157 (where he clearly conceives of the body as property), and 166 (where he does not); in general, 148–71.

[65] Feuerbach, *Revision*, 2:236, which lists as the fundamental private rights of individuals: "The right to the free use of the body, which consists of (1) the right to the *possession of [the body] altogether*—the right to life. (2) The right to the undisturbed possession [*Besitz*] of *the energies thereof,* the right to *health*. (3) The right to the undisturbed use of these energies for self-chosen ends, the right to *bodily, physical freedom*."

[66] Feuerbach, *Strafgesetzbuch*, vol. 2, art. 189, p. 59 (Gönner's annotation).

[67] Feuerbach, *Revision*, 2:236.

[68] Ibid., 1:146–47, emphasis in original.

[69] Feuerbach, "Betrachtungen über den Geist des Code Napoléon," 24–25.

[70] Feuerbach, *Revision*, 1:149.

he had previously added: "No difference shall be made between reputable and disreputable persons [as victims], because even a disreputable person has not lost [the right of] disposition over her body."[71]

The tendency in Feuerbach's principled innovations should be clear from these examples. Gender, status, and moral reputation were declared irrelevant to law, whereas rights and the property model were held equally applicable to all citizens under the law. The inherited differentials inside sex-crime law were eliminated. Such a profound reformation could only occur by ignoring the social practices that created and maintained gender, status, and moral reputation. Feuerbach could ignore society because his Enlightened convictions made the principles of Reason superior to actual social practice in two ways: theoretically, by founding fundamental institutions according to Reason's principles rather than according to tradition, and chronologically, by imagining that social practices would change under the salutory influence of reasonable institutions. This latter vision was produced by the presocial aspect of state-based early liberalism, whose task was to (re)form society, not to be guided by it.

The easy disregard of existing social convention is nowhere more clearly evident than in Feuerbach's attempt to remove incest from the criminal code. Radical Enlightened reformers, like Cella, Hommel and Gmelin, had lumped incest with other consensual acts and recommended decriminalization.[72] Feuerbach agreed, eliminated incest from his draft codes, but was pushed by the legal commissioners to restore it.[73] But Feuerbach strove to reinterpret incest such that the crime was not moral/religious (much less biological, which subject was unmentioned in the discussions), but rather a subspecies of misuse of "private power [*Privatgewalt*]."[74] This redefinition put family relations on a par with other unequal relations produced by contract, tutelage, or institution (for example, the relation between teacher and pupil). Focusing on the power relations inside the family, rather than on the "natural" relations among its members, meant denying the family a privileged place as a *Rechtsgut*. Thus, one sought to protect individual family members, but not the moral integrity of the family as an institution. This was counterintuitive to the legal commissioners, who continued to speak of "incest" in their discussions, rather than of "misuse of private power."[75] Gönner even smuggled incest between siblings back into the law, ruining the coherent model of "private power."[76]

---

[71] Feuerbach, *Strafgesetzbuch*, vol. 2, art. 186, p. 62, Gönner's annotation. Strictly speaking, Gönner did not genderize this sentence. He used "*Person*," which might refer to either men or women, but the entire legal history of the problem of the victim's reputation in rape cases referred exclusively to women, and it is this history on which Gönner is commenting. Hence the translation of "*ihre Körper*" as "her body" seems justified.

[72] Rosenberger, "Sexualstrafrecht," 151 n. 2.

[73] See the excellent discussion in ibid., 179–88.

[74] Feuerbach, *Strafgesetzbuch*, vol. 2, arts. 204–7, pp. 86–92.

[75] Rosenberger, "Sexualstrafrecht," 179–80.

[76] Feuerbach, *Strafgesetzbuch*, vol. 2, art. 207, pp. 89–92 and Gönner's notes, ibid.

Internal Contradictions in Feuerbach's Code

Although Feuerbach's position on incest was internally consistent and thwarted by the intervention of the legal commissioners, his law code did contain internal self-contradictions. When a thinker as rigorously logical as Feuerbach overlooks contradictions, these surely indicate areas of deep resistance against the radical reforms he overtly championed. The most glaring inconsistency concerned gender: female adulterers were imprisoned for up to three months, male adulterers from eight days to a month.[77] Feuerbach was so convinced of the justice of this provision that he prevailed over the objections of the legal commissioners and he even kept the inequality when he revised his own draft in 1824. Feuerbach argued that "the woman injures the family more than the man."[78] Gönner interpreted this to mean that "the woman's adultery puts the family in danger, by [potentially] bringing foreign children into it."[79] If Gönner correctly interpreted Feuerbach's reasoning, then both men were following the Code Napoléon and both were disrupting Feuerbach's grid of rights by suddenly introducing the family as a *Rechtsgut*, an institution demanding legal protection. Feuerbach had gone to great lengths to avoid precisely this elsewhere in the code, especially in relation to incest.

A second inconsistency concerned adultery, which, as a consensual act, should have been absent from the criminal code. If the spouse's rights were harmed, then he or she should have had recourse to civil courts for redress on grounds of breach of contract.[80] One of the legal commissioners, Carl Count Arco, pushed for complete decriminalization, and the very low penalty, even for women, indicates that adultery was indeed slipping out of the criminal sphere. Yet Feuerbach held on to it. His explicit reason was not "the family," as it was for Gönner,[81] but "marriage," that is the contract between man and woman. Like Kant, Feuerbach believed marriage to be a sexual contract guaranteeing exclusive sexual rights in the partner, "marital fidelity."[82] Apparently he felt this right to legitimate, sanctioned (hetero)sexual expression was so fundamental that the state was duty bound to protect it by pressing criminal charges if the injured party complained.

It is significant that in the few cases where Feuerbach was inconsistent, these should involve the discriminatory treatment of sexually profligate married women and the (re)anchoring of legitimate, moral heterosexual expression in marriage. These two slips are also two main axes along which uneven treatment of sexual

[77] Ibid., vol. 3, art. 401, p. 268.

[78] Rosenberger, "Sexualstrafrecht," 205.

[79] Feuerbach, *Strafgesetzbuch*, vol. 3, art. 401, p. 269, Gönner's annotation.

[80] Rosenberger, "Sexualstrafrecht," 112–19, contains an excellent discussion of the legal arguments about adultery.

[81] Feuerbach, *Strafgesetzbuch*, vol. 3, art. 401, p. 268, Gönner's notes to arts. 401–3, pp. 268–69: "Adultery often undermines the happiness of families."

[82] Immanuel Kant, *The Philosophy of Law. An Exposition of the Fundamental Principles of Jurisprudence as the Science of Right*, trans. W. Hastie (Edinburgh, 1887), 110. Feuerbach, *Strafgesetzbuch*, vol. 3, art. 401: "The injury to marital fidelty via adultery" (268).

behavior in law developed in the nineteenth century. The new *Rechtsgüter* Feuerbach adduced that surreptitiously opened the way for these developments were the family (wielded against women), marriage as a sexual contract, and, possibly, marriage as an institution generally.[83] These institutions were deemed worthy of legal protection at the expense of individuals or their consensual sexual behavior.

Inconsistencies Introduced by Gönner

Gönner, the author of the code's annotations, went much further in contradicting Feuerbach's principles. For him, marriage as an institution (not merely a sexual contract) was unequivocally a *Rechtsgut:* "It lay far outside the intention of the lawgiver to regard marriage as less worthy of protection than property. Marriage interests the state in itself; on it often depends the entire happiness [*Lebensglück*] of persons and their property [*sic*]; it is entered into with a religious ceremony; it is thus an institution which, according to the number and importance of the rights depending on it, has a very well grounded right [*Anspruch*] to protection of the laws."[84] So, too, did the "welfare of families," Gönner wrote.[85] Although Feuerbach had adduced protecting the family once in the state council, he never mentioned it in the actual code book.[86] Most strikingly of all, Gönner could barely contain himself from including morality (*Sittlichkeit*) and *bürgerliche Ordnung* as *Rechtsgüter.* "The necessary consideration for purity of morals [*Reinigkeit der Sitten*] in the families" demanded that sibling incest be criminalized.[87] Danger to *Sittlichkeit* also partly justified criminalizing the male who seduced, made pregnant, and then abandoned a girl after promising her marriage.[88] Although Gönner had to admit that certain acts "only contravene civil order [*bürgerliche Ordnung*], but do not injure rights," he nonetheless mentions the injury to civil order, usually coupled with remarks concerning a danger to *Sittlichkeit*, as a consideration in criminalizing the misuse of private rights through seduction and *Kuppelei.*[89] Finally, the concept of "public indignation" (*öffentliches Aergerniß*) justified police intervention in adultery cases, and therefore into the secrets of the marriage, even if the offended spouse had not complained.[90] The specific example Gönner mentions is the removal of the mistress from the marital home. Once again, this innovation follows the Code Napoléon.

[83] It is unclear if article 374 punishing the single man or woman who knowingly marries a married man or woman was meant to protect sexual fidelity or marriage as an institution.

[84] Feuerbach, *Strafgesetzbuch*, vol. 2, art. 281, pp. 285–86, Gönner's annotation.

[85] Ibid., vol. 3, art. 372, p. 220, Gönner's annotation on penalizing forced marriage.

[86] Both Feuerbach and Gönner grant *Familienstand* (and *Bürgerstand*) protection of the laws, but this refers to the private rights and privileges accruing to these as estates or status groups in society. It does not refer to the family as an institution.

[87] Feuerbach, *Strafgesetzbuch*, vol. 2, art. 207, p. 91, Gönner's annotation.

[88] Ibid., vol. 3, art. 376, p. 226, Gönner's annotation.

[89] Ibid., vol. 2, art. 207–8, pp. 90, 92, Gönner's annotation.

[90] Ibid., vol. 3, art. 403, p. 269, Gönner's annotation.

Gönner's departures from Feuerbach's principles virtually sum up the categories under which nineteenth-century laws and police practice would systematically encroach on the sphere Feuerbach intended to set apart from state intervention. Family welfare, civil order defined as synonymous with moral respectability, morality, and social opinion (expressed negatively as "public indignation") deserved legal protection over and above the consensual sexual behavior of citizens. These collective, social goods outweighed individual rights. Yet none could be derived from the principles of Reason Feuerbach identified as being expressed through the individual. On the contrary, these new *Rechtsgüter* were products or foundations of society. These became paramount at the moment the lawmaker had assumed the viewpoint of an already-existing society. From this perspective, Gönner was more "progressive" than Feuerbach, for he inhabited a mental world that was already suffused with the reality of "civil society." Gönner's liberalism, and Gönner was most assuredly a liberal, was more mature than Feuerbach's. And less "enlightened."

The Achievement and Contemporary Criticism of Feuerbach's Code

The second law commission[91] that discussed and modified Feuerbach's draft contained representatives from the full spectrum of Bavarian political opinion, from the reforming Napoleonic enthusiasts like Feuerbach and Gönner, to the "old Bavarian" conservatives, like Carl Count Arco. It was the conservative Arco who generally favored lighter penalties and less state intervention in sexual matters, whereas the liberal Gönner strove to include more acts (sibling incest), to extend state tutelage and protection over children (especially girls) and over those in dependent relationships, and to allow police to investigate adultery without the spouse's complaint. Aretin weighed in, unsuccessfully, for equal treatment of women in adultery.[92] Although the legal commissioners often pushed for higher punishments for sexual crimes,[93] they left Feuerbach's concepts and schema intact. The Bavarian criminal code of 1813 faithfully reflected Feuerbach's principles and the government was proud of the reform work it had sponsored.

Legal scholars call Feuerbach's work "the first modern German criminal code."[94] In it, according to Eberhard Schmidt, he successfully realized the principle that "law [must] introduce into the unsteadiness of a criminal system tending to arbitrariness complete legal [*rechtsstaatliche*] steadiness, security, and predictability." In doing so, the political meaning of Feuerbach's theory and the main reason for its effectiveness in this period are revealed. [Feuerbach's theory] is the complete fulfillment of the political longing of German liberalism of the early nineteenth

[91] Consisting of the chairman Justice Minister Heinrich Aloys von Reigersberg, Feuerbach, Johann Nepomuk von Effner, Friedrich von Zentner, Carl Graf Arco, Johann Adam Freiherr von Aretin, Franz von Krenner, Johann Nepomuk Graf von Welsberg, and Gönner. Rosenberger, "Sexualstrafrecht," 47.
[92] Rosenberger, "Sexualstrafrecht," 46–49, 187–88, 204–13, and elsewhere, contains the best discussion of the commissioners' deliberations.
[93] Ibid., 173, 174, 175, 178, 179.
[94] Hippel, *Deutsches Strafrecht*, 1:295.

century."[95] In the words of Gustav Radbruch, "Saturated . . . with the Weltanschauung . . . of liberalism," the Bavarian code of 1813 was "great, pathbreaking, and a model."[96]

It was indeed a model, but one whose innovations in sex-crime law were never followed. Oldenburg, the states of Thuringia, Württemberg, Hannover, Braunschweig, and Saxony all patterned their criminal law reforms after Feuerbach.[97] All, however, insisted on including a section for "crimes against *Sittlichkeit*"; all punished delicts Feuerbach had dropped from his code (especially "unnatural sexual acts"); and usually they called for higher punishments.[98] Although many of these states enacted their reforms from 1839 to 1852, when opinions on the danger arising from sexual behavior and the duty of the state to intervene had crystallized in a controlling/regulatory direction, it is significant that even Oldenburg, whose code appeared in 1814, abandoned Feuerbach's lead on sexual crime, but followed him in virtually every other respect.[99]

Clearly, the sexual provisions of the 1813 code were the most immediately controversial. The liberal jurist Anton Thibaut, in fact, criticized them before they even appeared, insofar as he recognized the logical results of Feuerbach's narrow construction of *Rechtsverletzung*. "There are acts," he wrote in 1802, "that do not harm rights, but could occasion such harm directly or indirectly, like smoking on the street, sodomy, and so on—Since such acts are in general incompatible with the purpose of the state [*Staatszweck*], they should be forbidden by law."[100] The rejection of *Rechtsverletzung* as a principle, so as to permit the criminalization of consensual sexual acts, was a common refrain thereafter.[101] Once the code had appeared, the liberal jurist C.J.A. Mittermaier established himself early as one of its chief critics.[102] He devoted considerable attention to the shortcomings of the sexual

---

[95] Schmidt, *Strafrechtspflege*, 239.

[96] Radbruch, *Feuerbach*, 85–86.

[97] So did Basel, Zurich, and Saint Gall in Switzerland; see Hippel, *Deutsches Strafrecht*, 1:300, 302, 304. The Thuringian law code of 1852 was valid for the territories of Saxe-Weimar-Eisenach, Saxe-Meiningen, Saxe-Coburg-Gotha, Anhalt-Dessau and Köthen, Schwarzburg-Rudolstadt, Schwarzburg-Sondershausen, and Reuß, younger line.

[98] Some codes punished "unnatural sexual acts" only if they occasioned public indignation (*öffentliches Ärgerniß*); the Thuringian code of 1852 is the only one not to criminalize unnatural acts at all.

[99] Rosenberger, "Sexualstrafrecht," 239 n. 1; Radbruch, *Feuerbach*, 162, does not mention that the sections on sexual crimes did not follow Feuerbach.

[100] Anton Friedrich Justus Thibaut, *Beyträge zur Critik der Feuerbachischen Theorie über die Grundbegriffe des peinlichen Rechts* (Hamburg, 1802), 32–33.

[101] Rosenberger, "Sexualstrafrecht," 239, remarks on the swift waning of *Rechtsverletzung* after the late Enlightenment. Berner lists as a "mistake" of the code its "identification of crime and *Rechtsverletzung*, which leads to an unsatisfactory handling of crimes against *Sittlichkeit*." See also Gernot Schubert, *Feuerbachs Entwurf zu einem Strafgesetzbuch für das Königreich Bayern aus dem Jahre 1824* (Berlin, 1978), 35, and Albert Friedrich Berner, *Die Strafgesetzgebung in Deutschland vom Jahre 1751 bis zur Gegenwart* (Leipzig, 1867), 91.

[102] Radbruch, *Feuerbach*, 162, identifies him as the anonymous author of "Ueber die Einführung des Baierischen Strafgesetzbuches in Weimar mit Betrachtungen über den Werth dieses Gesetzbuches," *Neues Archiv des Criminalrechts*, 2 (Halle, 1818): 54–64. Also Carl Joseph Anton Mittermaier, "Über den neuesten Zustand der Criminalrechtswissenschaft in Deutschland," *Neues Archiv des Criminalrechts* 4.1

provisions. Rosenberger sums up Mittermaier's objections as having centered on 1) noncriminalization of seduction of housemates (that is, master's children by servants); (2) noncriminalization of homosexuality and bestiality; (3) noncriminalization of *Kuppelei;* (4) incomplete criminalization of incest; and 5) too light a punishment for adultery.[103] In short, even after the legal commissioners had successfully raised some penalties and included more delicts, liberal legal opinion was unsatisfied and wished to move even further in that direction.

Feuerbach acknowledged the widespread criticisms of the sexual provisions by incorporating many of them into his own revision of the 1813 code, which he was commissioned to undertake in 1824. The new draft collected sexual delicts together under a single heading. Male homosexuality and bestiality appeared as crimes. The adultery punishments were doubled, with their gender unfairness to women retained. Further protection for the marriage contract, from the specifically male point of view, was provided by making it a crime for a single man to seduce a married woman to infidelity.[104] Feuerbach's revisions contradicted his earlier principles by introducing (sexual) morality as a rubric of legal organization and, more important, as a *Rechtsgut,* by expanding legal protection for the marriage contract, and by specifically focusing on the interests of men: in punishing adulterous women more harshly, in creating legal barriers against single men seducing other men's wives, and in focusing on male (but not female) homosexuality. In the interests of all of these items, the occasions for state intervention were expanded. Both the univocal criticisms (of the sexual provisions) and Feuerbach's intervening experience as a judge doubtless made him more sensitive to the demands of "society" as opposed to philosophical perfection.[105] Feuerbach's renunciation of the theory of *Rechtsverletzung* was also hastened, as Schubert remarks, by the fact that "the necessity of delimiting the legal encroachments of state authorities into the sphere of citizens via dogmatic criminal law could not be seen as so pressing in Bavaria around 1825. Liberal political precepts had largely triumphed in the area of criminal law," and the constitution of 1818 firmly guaranteed property.[106] I would go further and say that it was precisely the triumph of liberal principles in having created civil society in Bavaria that encouraged greater state intervention, especially into the lives of those often marginal or less powerful persons identified as (symbolic) dangers to society, in order to protect the institutions and values on which civil society was thought to rest.

(Halle, 1820): 76–107, 157–93, and 400–428; Carl Joseph Anton Mittermaier, "Der neue Entwurf des Strafgesetzbuchs für das Königreich Bayern," *Neues Archiv des Criminalrechts* (Halle) 6.2 (1823): 173–227, 351–77. Mittermaier had been Feuerbach's private secretary. He served on the Badenese Law Revision Committee in 1839, was a "moderate liberal" associated with the "Württemberg Hof" political club, and served as president of the national *Vorparlament* during the Revolution of 1848.

[103] Rosenberger, "Sexualstrafrecht," 238–39.

[104] Schubert, *Feuerbachs Entwurf,* 280–83.

[105] Radbruch, *Feuerbach,* 112, 167, 178, following C.J.A. Mittermaier, "Ueber den gegenwärtigen Zustand der Strafgesetzgebung, die Gebrechen derselben und die Gesichtspunkte ihrer Verbesserung," *Archiv des Criminalrechts* (Halle), n.s., 4 (1847):586.

[106] Schubert, *Feuerbachs Entwurf,* 43–44.

In fact Feuerbach's 1813 code was not replaced in 1824, or indeed until 1862. It remained in force, a monument to late Enlightened-early liberal reform, frozen at the moment of its philosophical perfection, outdated the moment it took effect. Its rigorous provisions were undercut by 151 rescripts in the first three years.[107] A more serious and more systematic practical undermining, however, was built into the code itself. This was the police code, which covered many of the delicts Feuerbach had expunged from the criminal code. Precisely where Feuerbach had banished the state, the police restored it.

The Bavarian Police Code and State Intervention into Sexual Behavior

For all the attention late Enlightened reformers devoted to criminal law reform, they neglected administrative, or police law, almost entirely.[108] Police law consisted of the mass of ordinances, rescripts, edicts, instructions, and so on, that poured out from the organs of government regulating everything from correct bread weights, to bathing in rivers, to assault, to various sexual acts. By 1800 most territorial governments had amassed thousands of these regulations, which if actually applied, would have saturated every facet of everyday life. Their sheer number and detail made codification, much less reform, a daunting task. In most territories, no one had ever attempted it, and so Bavaria was hardly alone in having reached the nineteenth century without a single, written, publicly accessible police code. That lack was a serious hindrance to the secure delineation of civil society. Not only was the police the most intrusive tentacle of the state in practice, it was difficult, indeed ultimately impossible,[109] to decide where police jurisdiction in crimes should leave off and criminal jurisdiction begin. Furthermore, police hearings were summary; they lacked the judicial safeguards that reformers carefully built into court procedures, and police sentences could not be appealed to a court, but only further up the administrative ladder. And the police meted out real punishment. Offenders could be sent to jail for up to a month and fines were unlimited. Repeat offenders were even liable to receive punishments comparable in severity with those meted out in the criminal code.[110]

Nonetheless, late Enlightened reformers and early liberals alike were content to leave police laws unexamined. They imagined that their government experience and education gave them a panoramic view of the distance between the eudaemonistic goals of German early liberalism and the actual backwardness of "the people." This prospective view yielded three important tasks remaining for the police. One was the harmonious and regular coordination of relations among private persons generally. The second, especially held by late Enlightened reformers and moderate

---

[107] Radbruch, *Feuerbach*, 163.
[108] Rosenberger, "Sexualstrafrecht," 61–78, 216–81, gives an excellent account of Bavarian police law and practice in this period. My discussion owes much to his account.
[109] Hippel, *Deutsches Strafrecht*, 1:36–37.
[110] Rosenberger, "Sexualstrafrecht," 65 n. 2.

skeptics (like Brauer in Baden), conceived of the police not primarily as a repressive mechanism, though it could be that if need be, but as a school to instruct via admonishment the populace in its civic duties.[111] Police regulations were a catechism of proper conduct. Police chastisement was educational; it did not carry the stigma attached to criminal punishment, and thus did not isolate the miscreant permanently from society, but rather returned him or her to it a wiser, more useful person.[112] The third, particularly attractive to early liberals, likewise began with the judgment that not everyone was yet ready for civil society. Where the absolute legal equality characteristic of criminal law treated "the day laborer equally with the minister," as the legal reformer Cella observed (1787), "the caprice of the police did not have such narrow limits. . . . Neither [the police's] reputation nor order suffered because they took account of each class of citizen in determining punishment."[113] That is, police factored in social reality in ways early (and later) liberals approved of. In fact, police mostly regulated exactly those lower social strata whom the practitioners of civil society least trusted to be good citizens.[114] Unreformed police codes helped create a dual order: a legally protected civil society for some, and a continuation of absolutist caprice for others.

Typically comprehensive, Montgelas wanted Bavarian legal reform to include the police law code. Feuerbach refused. It is not merely that he failed to understand how an unreformed police code might sabotage his own, but that his very position on the police was ambivalent.[115] Feuerbach justified police law singularly; the rights that were here violated and therefore deserving of punishment were not absolute rights, as they were in every other case, but merely contingent (*bedingt-nothwendig*) (*Revision*, 2:219–20, 228–30). These contingent rights "are also based in the social contract [*Staatsvertrag*], but require for their actual existence an act of state power, *as such*" (2:221). And furthermore, "Police power has as its object the fulfillment of *auxiliary state goals* [*Hülfszwecke des Staats*]. Therefore all acts to the commission or omission of which the citizen is not directly obliged can only be forbidden because they are a means to the fulfillment of an auxiliary state goal" (2:223).

Feuerbach never had any trouble assigning acts to this spongy category. In his criticism of Kleinschrod's draft in 1802, he listed examples of "so-called police delicts [as] usury, false trading [*Dardanariat*], whoring, sexual violation [*Schändung*], sodomy and such things"; or, later, "for example, incest, sexual violation, sodomy, whoring."[116] Elsewhere, his examples were "witchcraft, sodomy, fornication, irreligion, heresy, blasphemy, and so on."[117] With the exception of false

---

[111] Feuerbach, *Kritik des Kleinschrodischen Entwurfs*, 67.
[112] For example, Gönner, "Motive zur Revision des königlich baierischen Straf-Gesetz-Buches über Verbrechen und Vergehen," 29 January 1820, Bay HStA, MInn 54148.
[113] Cella, *Über Verbrechen und Strafen*, 58–59.
[114] Concerning actual police practice, see, pp. 367–68.
[115] Rosenberger, "Sexualstrafrecht," 65–67.
[116] Feuerbach, *Kritik des Kleinschrodischen Entwurfs*, 16–17.
[117] Feuerbach, *Strafgesetzbuch*, 1:25.

trading, which was acknowledged for centuries as a proper object of police regulation, these delicts' common denominator is their historic criminalization in canon law. Indeed, it was on that very account that Feuerbach was trying to remove them from criminal law; one suspects that he had added witchcraft and heresy to the list to make the whole group seem too antiquated for a modern law code.

Nonetheless, the prominence of sexual acts in Feuerbach's lists is remarkable. Even more remarkable is the fact that sodomy is the only act to appear in every one.[118] Sodomy was Feuerbach's archetypical example of the liminal delict, the one that defined the line between two categories. He used it to illustrate the different workings of arbitrary (that is, discretionary) versus set punishments,[119] and to explain the difference between setting punishments according to moral or to civil rights criteria.[120] As he put it in his *Revision der Grundsätze:*

> The contingent rights of the state come after all private rights. Because these [contingent rights] stem from police instructions of the state; the citizens' acts contained in these instructions are only forbidden by the state because, if these acts occur, the purpose of the state cannot be reached so surely or so easily, although fulfilling the purpose of the state, and the existence of the state itself, is still possible without [these prohibitions]. Sodomy does not directly contradict the purpose of the state; the purpose of the state is not even limited or suspended. One can imagine a whole state of sodomites without being obliged to alter anything in the most stringent conception of the state. Omitting this act merely removes a hindrance to the more comfortable fulfillment of the purpose of the state, namely, the physical and mental weakness the vice causes the perpetrator and the diminution in population that arises from this [weakness]. Only that act which directly contravenes a private right contradicts the purpose of the state directly. Because it is only in the protection of these rights that the purpose of the civil union [*des bürgerlichen Vereins*] consists, and only for the sake of the protection of these rights are other acts forbidden that are in themselves legally indifferent.[121]

Feuerbach here opens a breach in his otherwise tight system of *Rechtsverletzung* that would be impossible to close again, since virtually anything might be construed as hindering the "comfortable fulfillment" of some purpose of state. It is unlikely he opened this breach simply to accommodate offensive sexual activities. First, Kantian moral precepts showed how vain it was to enjoin individual moral behavior by external pressure. Second, it is clear that Feuerbach knew most police regulations concerned other matters (like false trading), and therefore justification for these would be required in any case. Why, then, did Feuerbach use sodomy to make his case (and the other two distinctions, above)? It seems to me he did so for a double purpose, based on a double agreement he was sure existed in Enlightened public opinion. The first agreement concerned the outrageous penalty for sodomy in written common law: death by fire. Feuerbach felt that Enlightened thinkers had

---

[118] Including the only other such list in ibid., vol. 2, art. 186, pp. 59–60, quoted on page 349–50.
[119] Feuerbach, *Revision*, 1:312–14.
[120] Feuerbach, *Kritik des Kleinschrodischen Entwurfs*, 58–59.
[121] Feuerbach, *Revision*, 2:22. Partly cited in Rosenberger, "Sexualstrafrecht," 70.

long since established that sentence as "thoroughly inappropriate, completely counterproductive, and highly barbaric."[122] That discrepancy offered Feuerbach the best means to argue for the removal of sodomy and other consensual sexual acts from the criminal code, which was farther, in fact, than most public or legal opinion was willing to go, as the Oldenburg and subsequent law books otherwise based on the 1813 code proved. The second agreement on which Feuerbach could count was the opinion that sodomy was harmful and should not be countenanced by the authorities, even though it did not merit the death penalty. This made it the perfect illustration for an appropriate police delict and a useful mollification for those who were unsure whether it should truly be removed from the criminal code.

In his critical writings, Feuerbach judged sodomy dangerous strictly because of its alleged harm to others, which he construed in terms of harm to the state and harm to the individual. The harm to the state, population decline, was an old-fashioned, cameralist imperative that was swiftly being eclipsed by fears of over-population.[123] The harm to the individual, however, Feuerbach conceived in a more modern way, following the contours of the antimasturbation literature: "The ped-erast, while dishonoring and enervating himself, harms at the same time the health of another person. He is usually the seducer and murders the honor [*mordet Ehre*], innocence, and morality of another, perhaps of a hopeful boy or youth. The man who commits sodomy with an animal dishonors only himself and in civil terms is not more dangerous than the one who wastes his energy by masturbation."[124] These assumptions and elisions were products of Feuerbach's appreciation of the modern, scientific literature on masturbation. They became the stock litany of the nineteenth century and the main justification for criminalizing male homosexuality: the assumption that the person committing the act was male,[125] that the act was "enervating," that the act usually involved seduction, generally of younger, inexpe-rienced boys or adolescents. These assumptions also account for the harsher penalty Feuerbach assigned to persons engaging in "unnatural" sex with children under twelve, rather than when men engaged in intercourse with girls under twelve.[126] It seems reasonable to conclude, with Rosenberger, that Feuerbach feared the developmental consequences of "unnatural sex" for children much more than he did those of premature "natural" intercourse.[127]

Feuerbach's textbook (*Lehrbuch*), which like all compendia blurs the line between

---

[122] Feuerbach, *Revision*, 1:312.

[123] Bavaria was for many years less frightened of overpopulation than the southwestern German states, however.

[124] Feuerbach, *Kritik des Kleinschrodischen Entwurfs*, 58–59.

[125] Kleinschrod's text reads, "when sodomy is completed between two persons [*Menschen*]," not "men." Kleinschrod, *Entwurf,* art. 1543, p. 245. It is also noteworthy that Feuerbach personifies the person as a "pederast," rather than imagining him as merely the occasional or even one-time perpetrator of an act.

[126] Feuerbach, *Strafgesetzbuch*, vol. 2, art. 191, p. 65, and vol. 3, art. 378, p. 227.

[127] Rosenberger, "Sexualstrafrecht," 126–29, 213.

the received opinions the scholar is obliged to relate and his own, is even more (and differently) crass about why the police are justified in prosecuting sodomy.

> The high degree of depravity [*Verworfenheit*], which this vice [*Laster*] requires; the disdain for marriage that it causes, which must have as a consequence the depopulation, weakening [*Schwächung*], and finally the dissolution of the state; finally, the physical and mental enervation, which makes the degenerate [*einen so Entarteten*] useless [*unfähig*] for the purposes of the state, [these] are the reasons that demand the police to forbid and punish these acts [that is, same-sex relations and bestiality].[128]

This collection of hoary and new arguments is noteworthy for averring that moral depravity justifies state intervention; including harm the actor does to himself as further grounds for state intervention; identifying marriage as the institution directly harmed by sodomy; and equating marriage with the practical foundations of the state. These dominoes are not necessarily all Feuerbach's own, since the purpose of the textbook was to present the history of legal opinion, not to criticize it. The textbook is also not remotely on an intellectual level with Feuerbach's other writings.[129] Nonetheless, these are his words, and they are remarkable for the emotional and judgmental force they bring to bear. The choice of *Schwächung* is especially revealing, since it means not only "weakening," but also "fornication" (*stuprum*),[130] and "pregnancy." The reader can hardly avoid imagining that some-how, through the homosexual act, the state itself has become female; by permitting sodomy, it has become the illicit sexual partner of a male and has found itself "weakened/pregnant."[131] No wonder sodomy was so dangerous, if it could doubly dishonor the state by rendering it female and sexually subject.

The linguistic and logical elisions operating in all of Feuerbach's passages on sodomy show that they are being made to bear more weight than their superficial message would first indicate. In retrospect it seems clear that Feuerbach did associate police power with checking consensual sexual acts. That is, when he ruminated on the duty of police, his thoughts fell not to the myriad mundane tasks that no one questioned as appropriate to the police, but to the new ones whose objects were being gathered together under the umbrella of "morality" and shunted out of the criminal code, and whose consequences were likely to become ever more severe in a thriving civil society, where free will and individualism loosened the customary restraints on behavior. This is why consensual sexual acts appear so prominently in Feuerbach's listings of the proper objects of police. Sodomy then functioned as the archetypal example of these delicts because it was socially "simpler" than the others. Unlike other undesirable consensual acts, it produced no children, so it did

---

[128] Feuerbach, *Lehrbuch*, par. 467, p. 392.

[129] As Rosenberger, "Sexualstrafrecht," 107–9, points out.

[130] Feuerbach, *Lehrbuch*, par. 452, p. 380.

[131] Feuerbach focuses his attention on the male actor. He explicitly says that criminalizing same-sex relations between women was literally a mistake; it was based on a misreading of *Romans*. Ibid., par. 468, p. 393, note b.

not involve sticky questions of inheritance or social obligation. It was not entangled in commerce or in issues of public health. Narrowly redefined as male homosexuality, it focused on active males, the quintessence of civil subjecthood, and further redefined as pederasty, it focused on male children and the vulnerability of the future (citizens) to misuse by untrammeled freedom. Best of all, however, sodomy was unpopular in two senses. It inherited a legacy of opprobrium useful to marking it an epitome of social danger. And it seemed considerably less widespread than other consensual sexual acts, less truly connected to actual social issues, and less likely to be an object of identification. Therefore, its consensus-creating possibilities were greater at a moment when self-conscious heterosexuality was being elevated to a modern social principle. In short, sodomy was, while not quite an empty signifier, still a relatively open one that could be more easily shaped to guide the discussion of how state and society should relate to one another. Hence its appearance in Feuerbach's argumentation at the border where state and society should have separated, but did not.

The Police Law Code and Police Practice

After Feuerbach refused Montgelas's request to draft a police law code, this task fell to Privy Councillor Franz Joseph Wigand von Stichaner, the provincial president (*Generalkreiskommissar*) of the Illerkreis.[132] The blindness of reformers to the civil and judicial consequences of the police law code is clear in the choice of Stichaner's assistants, who all came from the Ministry of the Interior, whereas the advisers for the criminal code included Justice Ministry officials as well. Stichaner's draft, completed in 1812, seems to have reflected current police practice. Although it was more expansive and moralizing than the criminal code, it nonetheless was true to the conviction of Montgelas's administration that the police's main function was supervision and surveillance, not repression.

Stichaner's draft, unlike the criminal code, collected sexually related delicts under one rubric, "offenses against public decency."[133] These offenses included, however, nonsexual acts like gambling and drunkenness, testimony to the traditional structure of all police codes, whose conception of proper, moral behavior was inherited from absolutism and which therefore did not disproportionately emphasize sexual offenses. Most of the sentences called for imprisonment for eight to fourteen days.

One might analyze the draft's sexual provisions according to three categories. The first contained the standard procreative offenses, or preparations for them, that were the real targets of actual police activity: "repeated extramarital pregnancy," *Konkubinat, Kuppelei* pursued as a business [*gewerbsmäßige Kuppelei*], *Hurerei* and "illegal amusements" (i.e., dancing, which most officials were convinced led to fornication). The reader will recognize in "repeated extra-marital pregnancy" the

---

[132] My discussion of Stichaner's draft follows Rosenberger, "Sexualstrafrecht," 70–73, 277–81.
[133] Ibid., 277.

last gasp of the fornication ordinances, now *de jure* what they had always been *de facto:* a prohibition on unwed pregnancy. Only now, all semblance of punishing the male had vanished, making the rule more gender discriminatory than past Bavarian practice. *Hurerei* was only punished if it produced public indignation or involved the seduction of youth, which gave the police discretionary power, but in practice made the act tolerated. The *Konkubinat* provision was important because marriage restrictions produced an ever larger number of such liaisons and later police practice focused especially sharply on them. This draft, however, only called for the couple to be separated, or punished only if they resisted, which was milder than what the future would bring.

The second category of sexual offense in Stichaner's draft directly assumed acts pushed out of the criminal code: incest among siblings (which Gönner had managed to smuggle into the notes but not into the code's articles), seduction by servants, and voluntary kidnapping (that is, elopement to circumvent parental disapproval of a marriage).

The third category was also a catch-basin for acts washed out of the criminal code, but it operated by the accordion method of potentially expansive vagueness. "Public shamelessness" (*öffentliche Schamlosigkeit*), intentionally ill-defined, was now the only way sodomy or lesser sexual offenses could be punished. The term "public," however, was a major barrier to untrammelled police investigation and set down inside the police code a spatial elaboration of the same split between public and private that Feuerbach had erected in the criminal code. An entirely new measure outlawed "immoral writings," specifying sexual content in censorship for the first time. This responded to the new threat to the moral order posed by widespread literacy and cheaper publications; it might be seen as a specifically sexually informed continuation of "public enlightenment" (*Volksaufklärung*) by negative, preemptive means.[134] The last measure was as old as police regulation, but unfolded to new heights of practice in the *Vormärz* period, that is, the decades leading up to the revolutions of March 1848. It forbade "bad and loose living" (*schlechter und liederlicher Lebenswandel*). Its targets were "immoral people" (*unsittliche Menschen*), "disorderly, excessive, and wasteful manners of living," "behavior contrary to police ordinances, *Liederlichkeit*, disobedience against parents," and so on. This absolutist conflation of poverty, idleness, sexual incontinence, and social disorder took on new meaning during the economic dislocation and demographic upheavals of the *Vormärz* and provided new and widespread targets for police repression.

Despite its shortcomings, Stichaner's draft would have promoted uniform police procedure throughout Bavaria and would have tended to freeze police power at a point in its development where it was relatively less repressive than it had been earlier, or would shortly become. In this respect, Stichaner's draft was an appropriate complement to Feuerbach's code. But neither Stichaner's draft nor any other

---

[134] Knudsen, "On Enlightenment for the Common Man."

was adopted; Bavaria therefore limped along until 1862 with no police code other than the tattered collection of ordinances, modified and expanded piecemeal. One suspects that the government preferred this chaotic situation, especially after Montgelas's departure in 1817, because it made the police that much more flexible an instrument of state control. For one thing, one might continue to govern many matters by ordinance, without having to consult the parliament to pass an appropriate law.

The lengthy memorandum (1814) that seems to have been mainly responsible for the decision to abandon a written police law code expressed the government's dilemma in fitting police practice to the new conditions being created by all the other Napoleonic transformations.[135] On the one hand, the author, W. Butte, recognized that the police law code "collides countless times with what the civil law says are the rights and privileges of private persons." On the other, two main changes attendant on the development of civil society seemed to demand greater, not less, police intervention. The first was the fact "that important support for public life that formerly consisted in the stricter attitude of people through the bond of custom regarded as holy, has become ever more rotten [*morscher*], the more individuality and egoism [*Individualität und Egoismus*] of the single person have developed, a necessary result of developing culture. Many matters that one used comfortably to leave to custom, need now to be resolved legally." At the same time these mediating structures of social control were dissolving, civil society was setting higher standards of activity, energy, education, and independence appropriate to citizens, as opposed to mere subjects. But many individuals were unable to meet these standards and were left vulnerable by the new state of affairs: "For the sake of the child, dying persons, idiots, the propertyless, and foreigners, the police must forbid many things they would otherwise gladly permit if the population really consisted only of individuals to whom the concept of citizen fitted to its complete extent." The trick, Butte opined, was to find the right balance. "If the government chooses too distant a standpoint, then it easily drops the reins, and the people's lack of restraint engenders great disorders. If it chooses too close a standpoint, then all free life stops, and in the end the government must pull the wagon all by itself, so to speak." Pulling the wagon by itself was, of course, exactly what all the reforms were designed to overcome. Finally, a combination of allegiance to the old, educational duties of the police plus sensitivity to the discrepancy between the prospective vision of civil society and the actual condition of society encouraged Butte to hang onto the police as they were. He declared that uniform written rules made it impossible for the police to tailor their chastisement to individuals or to individual regions.[136] The harmony of custom and spirit that civil society would sooner or later produce lay in the future. The real-life transition to that goal

---

[135] "Einige Ideen, kritische Bemerkungen und Literatur-Notizzen betreffend die Polizey-Gesetzgebung," W. Butte, Munich, 7 February 1814, Bay HStA, MInn 31385. Rosenberger, "Sexualstrafrecht," 71–72.

[136] Rosenberger, "Sexualstrafrecht," 72 n. 2.

required the utmost flexibility, and that could only be achieved by postponing codification.

The result was that, in the absence of a single, written code and despite Montgelas's attempts to impose organizational conformity onto local police, actual practice remained disparate. Sometimes difference resulted from legal peculiarities; for example, the 1808 ordinance removing punishment for fornication was in effect earlier, later, or not at all, depending on the legal status of a district in the turbulent year 1808.[137] Local demographic, economic, inheritance, and other customs were important variables; so were the energy, moral conviction, ambition, and other peculiar characteristics of the particular police official in a given area. In the absence of detailed social histories comparing several districts, it is not possible to describe actual police practice with assurance. Rosenberger's study is useful, but it was not guided by a social historical research agenda, nor is it complete enough. Nonetheless, it did compare the archives of several cities and towns in Bavaria. Rosenberger concluded that, although police practice was uneven, in the Montgelas period the police only occasionally hounded people for sexual misdemeanors and generally did not pursue fornication or *Konkubinat* cases.[138] Montgelas, following late enlightened suggestions, experimented in Munich first with state-tolerated and then with state-regulated brothels, but this experiment was swiftly abandoned.[139] Otherwise, in the reform years, Bavarian police limited themselves more to surveillance than to outright intervention. In the Restoration/*Vormärz* period, however, benign neglect turned to active interference.

Thanks to Montgelas's assiduousness, from 1809 to 1817, and occasionally thereafter, the provincial governments (*Kreise*) forwarded to Munich lists of the cases their police underlings had investigated/punished for every quarter.[140] These data are not as complete as Montgelas, or a historian, would have liked, nor as exact. It is not always crystal clear, for example, if a category like "nighttime excess" (*nächtliche Excesse*) (usually alcohol-induced disturbance) or "vagrancy," when the vagrant is referred to as a *Dirne*, might not occasionally have covered a sexual offense. The term *Liederlichkeit* covers a multitude of acts. The real meaning of the data lies locked in the context of the localities that produced them. Still, they tell what the central government "knew" was happening with police practice and they do give a rough suggestion of the trends for the reform period.

Keeping these caveats in mind, one can hazard some tentative conclusions. The data indicate that the police spent most of their time chasing beggars, vagabonds, and persons without passes; keeping order in the streets; and intervening in trade matters. Sexually related offenses accounted for about 7 percent of the cases pur-

---

[137] Ibid., 220–21.

[138] Ibid., 236, 242, 247.

[139] Ibid., 225–31, 249.

[140] Polizei Geschäftsberichte for each of the *Kreise*, Bay HStA, MInn 15244–254. I have tabulated all the crimes and collated the sexual offenses, their punishments, and the gender and social backgrounds of the accused.

sued.[141] The data are not good enough to indicate if this percentage was rising, falling, or staying steady. Altogether there is enormous variation across Bavaria in percentage, types of cases, and punishments meted out. There are, however, several constants. First, the offenses were overwhelmingly, almost exclusively heterosexual. Second, the accused tended far more often to be women than men, and women seem to have received marginally harsher penalties than men, though only marginally. Moreover, when women and men were caught together (in *Konkubinat*, for example), their punishments were equal. Although some localities sent persons to the workhouse for six months, most of the punishments were much more lenient: one day's arrest on bread and water, or a fine, or a corporal punishment. Whether pregnancy caused the gender inequality in arrest, as it used to, only detailed study will reveal.[142] Women were more likely to receive dishonoring punishments, where those still survived, than were men, and were far more likely to be sent to workhouses (*Zwangsarbeitshäuser*) by the few communities that used this harsh punishment. In both cases, it was likely that the female victims of this special treatment were, or were labeled as, prostitutes, since Rosenberger reports that almost all persons serving time in the workhouses for sexual offenses were there for prostitution or *Kuppelei*.[143] It is not possible to tell whether the unequal treatment of women was simply a continuation of older Bavarian practice (which was more discriminatory than, say, in Baden), or whether these figures indicate the beginning of the discriminatory wave characteristic of the nineteenth century and its obsession with prostitution. Still, the language of the reports accompanying the statistics was fairly old-fashioned and does not hint that sexual delicts were being newly interpreted. Finally, all the persons who felt the hand of the police and whose occupations were given were rural day laborers, servants, or artisans or their family members. The educated, wealthy, and titled do not appear in these records.

These data and Rosenberger's comparison indicate that Bavarian police practice during the reform period tolerated consensual sexual behavior to a greater extent than at any previous time. Police performance seems roughly congruent with the tendencies of the 1813 criminal code. Its watchfulness was still directed toward heterosexual, procreative acts, and the old axes of gender and class unfairness still marked its efforts, but there was greater room for nonmarital sexual behavior. Nonetheless, the potential for greater interference lay ready to be activated, since the only police reform to have occurred had been designed to increase police efficiency, not to question or curb its controlling duties.

[141] Two tabulations of the cases handled by the *Hofgerichte* in 1804 and 1805, before consensual sexual crimes were removed from their jurisdiction, list 4.5 percent of their total caseload as sexual. Demel, *Staatsabsolutismus*, 349.

[142] Pregnancy, because visible, had been considered "public"; that classification still left it open to prosecution under the new, reform rubric "public indignation": as in the phrase, "if the female is pregnant, and therefore the indignation [*Aergerniß*] has already become public [*öffentlich*]." Bishop von Fraunberg to king, 30 June 1824, no. 3666, Bay HStA, MInn 72654.

[143] Rosenberger, "Sexualstrafrecht," 237, 237 n. 4, reports that 12.5 percent of the inmates were there for sexual offenses. Rosenberger's data, however, come from the period 1818–22.

The Ambivalent Official Encouragement of Marriage

Most of our discussion has concerned negative regulation or neutral tolerance. The Montgelas administration took one positive police step to encourage sexual behavior of which it approved: it loosened the restrictions on marriage.[144] Still, the imprint of absolutist police thinking and the distrust of untrammeled freedom operated as strongly here as they did in the reform of the criminal and police codes.

Secular restrictions against free marriage had begun in Bavaria in 1553, when the "thoughtless marriage of servants" was forbidden.[145] Subsequent mandates had given the *Gemeinde* power to forbid the marriage of residents on grounds of poverty or reputation.[146] Enlightened reformers, following the cameralists, had virtually unanimously recommended easing marriage in order to channel the "irresistible" sex drive into legal and socially responsible channels, and to produce more children, who would be raised and educated under better circumstances. To counteract local intransigence Montgelas in 1808 stripped the *Gemeinden* altogether of their power to grant permission to marry and gave it to the police, instead.[147] Nevertheless, the central government was still too anxious to give up regulation altogether and was especially fearful of being swamped by indigent foreigners. Therefore, "unknown, foreign, nonresident persons" who probably would not be able to feed their families, could not marry; the official who granted such people permission to marry was liable for their upkeep (art. 3). As though this were not disheartening enough, the ordinance gave three other grounds for refusing permission: (1) inability to consummate the marriage as attested to by a doctor; (2) commission of crimes, which suggested "danger to the family status [*Familienstand*] or civil society"; or (3) if "one of the partners had shown him/herself through unsteady living, *Liederlichkeit*, and idleness to be a useless member of the state."

Clearly, the mental universe of the ordinance of 1808 was still the Enlightened police state. Not surprisingly, the reform was too timid to counteract the restrictive tendencies of local officials. One bureaucrat reported in the early 1820s that "this ordinance has not had the desired effect of encouraging marriage in the countryside because cautious officials, on account of the responsibility anchored in article 3, go to work dispensing marriage licenses extremely sparingly and carefully."[148] The

---

[144] Matz, *Pauperismus und Bevölkerung,* 33, 34–35.

[145] *Bairische Lanndtsordnung,* 1553 (Ingolstadt, 1553), fol. 158, art. 5, tit. 12.

[146] For example, Bettel Mandat, 27 July 1770, art. 13, in Mayr, *Sammlung der neuest . . . Landes-verordnungen,* 421. Repeated on 3 March 1780, Mayr, *Sammlung der . . . allgemeinen und besondern Landes-Verordnungen,* 2:948. Matz, *Pauperismus und Bevölkerung,* 33, incorrectly suggests this is the first such mandate. The marriage of "non-resident, loose [*liederlicher*] people" was forbidden again in the ordinance of 11 October 1788, ibid., 5:163.

[147] Ordinance of 12 July 1808, *Regierungsblatt,* 1808, 1505. Matz, *Pauperismus und Bevölkerung,* 34, erroneously 12 June 1808. Police power was wielded, in towns, by the elected mayor or local superintendant (in his capacity as the executive of the lower court), in the countryside by the appointed police director or commissar. Demel, *Staatsabsolutismus,* 275.

[148] "Vortrag über die Revision der Verordnung über Ansässigmachung und Heurathen auf dem

structural effects of continuing prohibitions on marriage were widespread, the reporter continued. Discouraging new families also hindered the completion of land reform, since the "demand" for land made available from the break-up of larger estates was diminished, and land freed up in this way went to older, established families, not to the creation of a new class of independent landowners. From the sexual standpoint, the failed reform condemned a growing class of citizens to celibacy or police offenses. The bureaucrat described the result in old-fashioned language: "the overwhelming immorality [*überhandnehmende Unsittlichkeit*] of the country people." By this, he meant the steep growth in illegitimacy, for which the provincial governments had been compiling statistics since 1809.[149]

Reforms like Feuerbach's and the introduction of constitutions, especially in south Germany, successfully guaranteed a place for important aspects of civil society to develop shielded from capricious state interference. Nevertheless, neither the momentary banishment of morality from criminal law nor the limitation of state power were permanent accomplishments. The failure to make marital heterosexual activity available to the poor, the reform of the criminal code that stopped short of limiting police power, official anxiety about possible (sexual and other) disorderliness during the transformation to civil society, and the anxiety of the liberal spokesmen of civil society about the moral ties that should bind it together, all set the stage for the reemergence of moral politics and state intervention in the restoration/*Vormärz* period.

Lande betrf." appended to the report of the Regierung des Regenkreises to Interior Minister, Regensburg, no. 1294, 8 February 1822, Bay HStA, MInn 52132.

[149] Polizei Geschäftsberichte for each of the *Kreise,* Bay HStA, MInn 15244–254. There has been much historical work on the demographics and politics of illegitimacy especially in southern Germany in the early nineteenth century. For our purposes, which are not primarily social-historical, that material properly belongs in a discussion of the restoration/*Vormärz* period, because only then did governments use illegitimacy statistics to ground public *Moralpolitik.* See Matz, *Pauperismus und Bevölkerung,* and, generally, Michael Mitterauer, *Ledige Mütter. Zur Geschichte unehelicher Geburten in Europa* (Munich, 1983).

IO

Public and Private: The Code Napoléon in Baden

Criminal law reform drew the line between state and society, but civil code reform rearranged relations within society according to the model of the new civil society. The legal birth of this "private" zone out of the newly reformed "public" took place not just at the moment when the law reforms were announced, but also during the following years when state officials struggled to determine in practice the contours of privacy and the rights and obligations derived from it. Not surprisingly, sexual behavior and the relations between men and women played a central part in determining the line between public and private. The private sphere that actually emerged in the reform period incorporated revolutionary changes in principle from those that had previously characterized government and the governed. Official concern about women had driven criminal law reform in the eighteenth century; official concern about and for men drove civil code reform in the nineteenth century. Just as cameralists and civil practitioners had identified men as the defining element of civil society but also its weakest link (they might refuse to marry, they were peculiarly at risk of becoming exhausted by their greater civic and economic burdens, or of becoming depleted by indulgence), so the civil code especially protected the married, propertied, male citizen. His private social status as presumptive family father and producer of wealth became the basis for his greater, state-guaranteed rights. The entire framework of rights became thus redefined: social rights, that is, the rights calculated according to one's private status, now superseded natural rights, derived from one's presocial condition as human. Community rights (*Gemeinwohl*) now weakened before those of the (male) individual. Family status carried almost opposite consequences in rights for the husband and the wife. These changes had enormous impact on the lives of real people, on government finances, and on administrative practice. The contours and internal principles of civil society were very much as Fichte had outlined them and postrevolutionary liberals had envisioned them. But this accomplishment required doing battle with those late Enlightened reform absolutist officials who still adhered to principles of *Gemeinwohl*, state protectionary tutelage, and state economic interests, and with those early liberals whose commitment to natural rights and abstract justice contradicted the social engineering principles of the civil code. Baden's experience with the Code Napoléon illustrates especially well the battle among these principles and the ultimate practical triumph of a particular vision of civil society and the "private" sphere.

The Code Napoléon

The most revolutionary instrument of social reform was the model *civil code*, or Code Napoléon (1804). It aimed to reorganize social relations according to the liberal principles of legal equality and property ownership. It destroyed feudal relations of subservience, restrictions on property holding and disposal, and on commerce. Status privilege in law and politics disappeared. Church and state were separated. Marital and extramarital relations were recodified. Together with the administrative institutions designed to execute it, especially separation of the judiciary from administration, the Code Napoléon destroyed the traditional bases of society and relaid its foundations according to the liberal vision.

On the west bank of the Rhine, where they exercised direct control, the French introduced the Code Napoléon without modification. At the height of his power, in October 1807, Napoléon ordered it to be introduced into the Hansa cities, Bavaria, Baden, and Hessen-Darmstadt, as it had already been in the model states of Berg and Westphalia.[1] Everyone knew the high stakes involved in reforming civil law. On the one hand, the German states had no uniform civil code: each territory used a pastiche of modified Roman, Holy Roman, canon, and local law.[2] The Code Napoléon was a unitary, modern model, which, if adopted wholesale, provided instant reform and immediate integration of the disparate lands newly thrown together in the upheaval of 1803. Indeed, if all states had adopted it, it would have been the legal precursor to a united Germany. On the other hand, caution seemed necessary because, as the conservative Prussian jurist Karl von Kamptz wrote, "Each change in the civil legal condition of a people is a very important matter, each

---

[1] In addition to Baden, the grand duchy of Frankfurt, Aremberg, and Anhalt-Köthen all introduced some version of the Code. Nowhere except the west bank, however, did the Code result in the complete reordering of property or social relations. The interests of princes, nobles, and Napoléon himself conspired to prevent complete social transformation. The best study is Werner Schubert, *Französisches Recht in Deutschland zu Beginn des 19. Jahrhunderts. Zivilrecht, Gerichtsverfassungsrecht und Zivilprozeßrecht* (Cologne, 1977). For the political context, see Elisabeth Fehrenbach, *Traditionale Gesellschaft und revolutionäres Recht. Die Einführung des Code Napoléon in den Rheinbundstaaten* (Göttingen, 1974), and Helmut Berding, *Napoleonische Herrschafts- und Gesellschaftspolitik im Königreich Westfalen 1807–1813* (Göttingen, 1973). On civil code reform, see Barbara Dölemeyer, "Kodifikationsbewegung" and "Kodifikationen und Projekte," in *Handbuch der Quellen und Literatur der neueren europäischen Privatrechtsgeschichte*, ed. Helmut Coing (Munich, 1982), vol. 3, part 2, pp. 1421–1611, esp. 1421–78, 1504–18.

[2] G. D. Arnold and F. Lassaulx, "Ansichten über die Einführung des Codex Napoleon in teutschen Staaten, veranlaßt durch eine von Hrn. von Almendingen in gegenwärtiger Zeitschrift (36tes Heft S. 46 u.f.) an die Unterzeichneten gerichtete Aufforderung," in *Der Rheinische Bund* 16 (1818): 3–21, esp. 5; F. Lassaulx, "Einige Gedanken über die Einführungen des Codex Napoleon in die Staaten der Rheinischen Conföderation," *Annalen der Gesetzgebung Napoleons*, 1.1 (1808): 169–74, esp. 169. See also Ulrich Eisenhardt, *Deutsche Rechtsgeschichte* (Munich, 1984), 187–92.

citizen has a lively interest in it [because he or she is touched by it] in [his/her] holiest relations."[3]

Even progressive opinion differed over how far these holiest, private relations could or should be recast. The most radical voices inside bureaucracies argued that the Code Napoléon embodied the laws of reason, and these "do not proceed from the experience of a single nation, but from the cooperation of all mankind."[4] Most bureaucrats in charge of adopting the Code Napoléon remained more guarded. They had been active in the late absolutist reform period and recognized the opportunity the Code Napoléon presented to realize stalled Enlightened and rational reforms and to administer efficiently newly acquired, disparate territories. Like Montesquieu, however, moderate reformers believed that law could not usefully rush too far ahead of social developments, nor contravene too shockingly the existing customs of a people.[5] Therefore, most of them wanted to modify the Code Napoléon. In no area touched by the Code were these considerations more important than in those dealing with the intimate relations between men and women.

The socioeconomic focus of most recent historiography has made it appear that the debate over adopting the Code Napoléon revolved exclusively around dissolving feudal property relations, introducing French administrative institutions, and establishing constitutions for the individual states.[6] These problems were indeed of major importance and attracted considerable attention; however, contemporaries discussing the actual provisions of the Code concentrated overwhelmingly on three issues: feudal property relations, civil marriage, and the intimate relations between men and women (family law, marriage, divorce, the consequences of illegitimacy, and so on).[7] Opponents of the Code realized its provisions on men and women were its Achilles heel and thus the best place to attack it. The conservative August Rehberg found that the Code was most internally inconsistent and most contrary to German custom and religious-based morality on questions of marriage and divorce.[8] Karl Albert von Kamptz agreed that the articles on marriage required a

---

[3] Karl Albert von Kamptz, "Gedanken über die Einführung des Code Napoleon in den Staaten des Rheinbundes," *Der Rheinische Bund* 3 (1807): 475.

[4] Privy Council Report in Berg, printed in *Der Rheinische Bund* 10 (1809): 147–48, cited in Fehrenbach, *Traditionale Gesellschaft*, 71. Conservative critic August Rehberg expressed this position pithily: enthusiasts saw the Code Napoléon as "the pure expression of all that . . . which the law of reason prescribed for human social [*bürgerlichen*] relations." August Wilhelm Rehberg, *Ueber den Code Napoleon und dessen Einführung in Deutschland* (Hannover, 1814), 3.

[5] Fehrenbach, *Traditionale Gesellschaft*, 71–73, 109.

[6] Ibid., 36–78; Wehler, *Deutsche Gesellschaftsgeschichte*, 1:377–78; Hans Berding and Hans-Peter Ullmann, "Introduction," in Berding and Ullmann, *Deutschland zwischen Revolution und Restauration*, 11–40.

[7] Earlier, non-socioeconomically directed historiography realized how important other social issues were to the contemporaries: Willy Andreas (1913), for example, devoted exactly as much space to matters pertaining to men and women as he did to the debates over defeudalization and administrative changes. See Willy Andreas, "Die Einführung des Code Napoléon in Baden," *Zeitschrift der Savigny-Stiftung für Rechtsgeschichte*, Germanische Abteilung 31 (1910): 182–234, esp. 218–24.

[8] Rehberg, *Ueber den Code Napoléon*, 124–25, in general 114–61.

complete suspension of German (Protestant) custom.[9] But even moderate critics like Anton Bauer, professor of law at Marburg, were scathing in their judgments of these provisions.[10] Laymen recognized immediately how far the Code diverged from previous German marriage law.[11] D. Grolman was forced to devote the second volume of his popular handbook on the Code entirely to marriage and divorce.[12]

The public discussion among jurists echoed the debates inside government. According to Willy Andreas, describing the situation in Baden, along with "a few mitigating changes in a couple of articles which to German sensibilities appeared oppressive to women, marriage law occupied the special attention of [Grand Duke] Karl Friedrich's [legal] advisers. The only conflict of serious importance occurred on this point."[13] Like their colleagues in Baden, the law commissioners in the grand duchy of Frankfurt spent much energy debating the articles discriminating against women, though, in the end, they let these provisions stand.[14] Even N. T. Gönner, the Bavarian expert who advocated unmodified acceptance, had to admit that Bavaria had changed the sections on adultery and divorce, to make them fairer to women.[15] The criticism of these provisions was loud enough that even Napoléon himself became defensive. In a letter designed to persuade the Dutch king to adopt the unmodified Code, Napoléon wrote, "You are still quite young in dealing with administrative matters, if you believe that the creation of a uniform law code could disturb family life and plunge the land into dangerous confusion. What people are telling you about this is a fairy tale."[16]

Why were the gender, family, and sexual provisions of the Code Napoléon so controversial? Part of the answer lies in the Code itself. Rehberg was absolutely right and the first of many to recognize that in these articles the Code contradicts its basic principles, if these are taken to be equality before the law, an end to ascriptive privilege, and the triumph of contract and individualism.[17] The Code energetically disadvantaged married women economically, legally, politically, and in terms of their power inside the family; it reduced the freedom of young persons to marry, of

[9] Kamptz, "Gedanken über die Einführung," 476–77.

[10] Anton Bauer, *Beiträge zur Charakteristik und Critik des Code Napoléon* (Marburg, 1810), 52–54, 105–9, 143–51, 173–76, 180–85.

[11] A. G. Eberhard, "Einige wesentliche Hinweisungen auf Abweichungen der neuen französischen Civilgesetze von den sonst in Deutschland geltend gewesenen Gesetzen und Gebräuchen," *Allgemeiner Anzeiger der Deutschen*, no. 272 (October 1807): cols. 2825–28.

[12] D. Grolman, *Ausführliches Handbuch über den Code Napoleon. Zum Gebrauche wissenschaftlich gebildeter deutschen Geschäftsmänner*, 2 vols. (Giessen, 1811).

[13] Andreas, "Einführung des Code Napoléon," 221 n. 1.

[14] Ibid.

[15] Nikolaus Thaddäus Gönner, "Mein letztes Wort über die Reception des Code Napoleon in den Staaten der rheinischen Conföderation, als Antwort auf den Aufsatz des Herrn v. Almendingen im Rh.B., Heft 29, S. 306–17," *Der Rheinische Bund* 12 (July 1809): 47–61, esp. 59–60.

[16] Napoléon to the king of Holland, 13 November 1807, cited in Andreas, "Einführung des Code Napoleon," 225.

[17] Fehrenbach, *Traditionale Gesellschaft*, 23–24; Dieter Grimm, "Die verfassungsrechtlichen Grundlagen der Privatrechtsgesetzgebung," in *Handbuch der Quellen und Literatur der neueren europäischen Privatrechtsgeschichte*, ed. Coing (Munich, 1982), vol. 3, part 1, p. 32; Dölemeyer, "Kodifikation und Projekte," 1448.

all people to divorce, of illegitimate children to economic and social claims on their fathers. Upon marriage, women lost their legal and economic personhood; they were forbidden to represent themselves in court or do business without their husband's permission, or a judge's, if the husband refused (pars. 214–26).[18] Fathers suddenly came into possession of all the parental power over children, which they had once shared equally with wives (art. 373). Widows were disadvantaged, relative to legitimate children, when their husbands died intestate. The Code also construed common marital property in a way more advantageous to the husband than was the case in Germany. The three most discriminatory provisions were also the ones that caused the greatest furor in Germany: paragraphs 229–30, which permitted men to divorce adulterous wives, but women to divorce adulterous husbands only if the latter moved the other woman into the house; paragraph 298, which punished only the adulterous woman, but not the adulterous man;[19] and paragraphs 340–41, which forbade officials from inquiring after the fathers, but not the mothers, of illegitimate children. There were other astonishing sections in the same vein, spelling out how fathers could question the legitimacy of children borne to their wives, or deny paternity altogether (pars. 312–13, 319–30).

Clearly these provisions all but made maleness a privileged *Stand*. The principle of contract was also breached since marriage was defined as a contract that mutual consent could not easily annul, as it could every other sort of contract (pars. 275–94). Finally, the fetters on married women and the extension of parents' and relatives' rights to hinder or prevent both the marriages and divorces of persons in whom they had an "interest," clearly limited individual freedom of choice.

Commentators have often explained these articles as products of the Napoleonic reaction against the purest expression of revolutionary principle. This is misleading, for it assumes that revolutionary legislation was gender equal. Prior to the Terror, it is true, the triumph of the Enlightened concepts of equality before the law, anticlericalism, and progressive human (not merely male) reason did level some of the legal inequities of the ancien régime.[20] Female adultery was (briefly) as immune to punishment as male adultery had been; divorce was easier and equally available to husbands or wives. But these fragile gains were more than offset by other legislation (concerning political rights, common marital property, and so forth) favoring males and by vocal opposition from within the revolutionaries' own camps, particularly from the Jacobins. For example, paragraph 340 of the Code Napoléon forbidding paternity searches was a Jacobin law of 1793.[21] Claudia Opitz

---

[18] A woman owning in her own name a business having no connection whatsoever with her husband's property, could enter business obligations by herself, but her husband's property was also bound by these obligations, which increased his interest in controlling his wife's actions (art. 220).

[19] The punishment was three to twenty-four months in prison for the woman, but articles 308–9 suspended the prison sentence if her husband agreed to take her back.

[20] James F. Traer, *Marriage and the Family in Eighteenth-Century France* (Ithaca, N.Y., 1980), 105–36.

[21] Ute Gerhard, "Menschenrechte-Frauenrechte 1789," in *Sklavin oder Bürgerin? Französische Revolution und Neue Weiblichkeit 1760–1830*, ed. Viktoria Schmidt-Linsenhoff (Frankfurt, 1989), 55–72, esp. 65.

sums up the revolutionaries' accomplishments before the Directory assumed power: "The balance of revolutionary changes in civil law from the standpoint of the interests of women and the realization of freedom and equality is negative and highly unsatisfactory. Far from actually permitting women the enjoyment of equal principles, the reformers decided fundamentally in favor of the interests of domestic domination—in each case of conflict preferring the man over the woman."[22] The Directory and Napoléon simply continued this trend.[23]

Historians have identified a number of dynamics within the revolution undercutting and ultimately negating the gender egalitarian tendencies of prerevolutionary Enlightenment thought. Among these was the fear of female revolutionaries, who were becoming more active and better organized throughout 1793. Especially worrisome to the Jacobins was their identification of female revolutionaries, often from the popular classes, with the sansculottes, whom they were moving to exclude from power.[24] Other historians have emphasized the cult of revolutionary-republican virtue, which reformulated national political symbolism around the specifically male citizen.[25] That project of reformation and legitimation dovetailed with the requirements of creating and maintaining the new revolutionary society. The figure of public versus private spheres, the complete separation and complementarity of male and female duties, the solidity of the French family as the locus of stability in political storm, and the nursery of republican virtue and patriotism operated not merely as powerful organizing symbols, but as the guidelines for laws and institutions. The Jacobins at the end of 1793, the Directory, and the Consulate all sought to impose the same, new social order in which female subordination to men inside the family and out, female political rightlessness, gender conformity (for both men and women), and (especially female) sexual continence would guarantee the social foundations of national politics.[26] These were the principles informing the Code Napoléon.[27] Although they were at odds with those of German late Enlightened reform absolutism and they contradicted many of the customs and social assump-

---

[22] Claudia Opitz, "'Die vergessenen Töchter der Revolution'—Frauen und Frauenrechte im revolutionären Frankreich von 1789–1795," in *Grenzgängerinnen. Revolutionären Frauen im 18. und 19. Jahrhundert. Weibliche Wirklichkeit und männliche Phantasien,* ed. Helga Grubitzsch, Hannelore Cyrus, and Elke Haarbusch (Düsseldorf, 1985), 287–312, 298.

[23] Gerhard, "Menschenrechte-Frauenrechte," 65, sees the Directory as the "turning point," yet she cites several examples herself that contradict her view. See also Opitz, "Die vergessenen Töchter," 292, 293, 294, 303, 304, and Joan B. Landes, *Women and the Public Sphere in the Age of the French Revolution* (Ithaca, N.Y., 1988), 106–46, on the revolutionaries' views on women.

[24] Harriet B. Applewhite and Darline Gay Levy, "Reaktionen auf den politischen Aktivismus der Frauen des Volkes im revolutionären Paris von 1789 bis 1793," in *Frauen im Frankreich des 18. Jahrhunderts: Amazonen, Mütter, Revolutionärinnen,* ed. Jutta Held (Frankfurt, 1989), 67–91; Inge Baxmann, "Von der Egalité im Salon zur Citoyenne—Einige Aspekte der Genese des bürgerlichen Frauenbildes," in *Frauen in der Geschichte,* ed. Annette Kuhn and Jörn Rüsen (Düsseldorf, 1983), 3:109–37, esp. 129–36.

[25] Landes, *Women and the Public Sphere,* 152–68; Dorinda Outram, *The Body and the French Revolution: Sex, Class and Political Culture* (New Haven, Conn., 1989).

[26] Opitz, "Die vergessenen Töchter," 303–7; Applewhite and Levy, "Reaktionen," 85–90; and Baxmann, "Von der Egalité," 131–35.

[27] Traer, *Marriage and the Family,* 166–91.

tions of individual German lands, they were congruent with that variant of early liberalism which steered its course by the beacon of civil society.

The Struggle in Baden over Paragraph 340

The new archduchy of Baden owed its elevation in stature, its enormous expansion in size, and its political security to Napoléon. For these reasons, to integrate its legally disparate acquisitions, and not least out of reforming zeal, the Conference of Privy Councillors recommended in May 1806 that the Code Napoléon be adopted with modifications. Two years later Grand Duke Karl Friedrich agreed, and a law commission headed by the moderate reformer J. N. Brauer produced the modified code in 1809.[28] It retained all of the French provisions, but added others to make the code conform somewhat better to the conditions and customs of Baden. Since one of the major disagreements concerned the code's harsh and relatively unfair treatment of women, it is not surprising that many of these provisions were subject to "additions," including paragraphs 340 and 230 (adultery as a ground for divorce). According to paragraph 340, "it is forbidden to investigate who is the father of a[n illegitimate] child"; however, according to paragraph 340a, a man *could* "be declared a father, who had been shown to have supported a woman with him as a sexual partner or who had voluntarily admitted, or by accident been shown, to have slept with her at the time of conception" or if he had purposely rendered her unconscious before the act.[29]

Although paragraph 229 permitted men to divorce adulterous wives, paragraph 230 permitted a woman to divorce her adulterous husband only if he brought his mistress into the marital house. Brauer explained French thinking as having followed the assumption that

> nature itself had given the female sex through its bodily and mental creation both stronger ability and stricter necessity to be sexually continent, that the disadvantage to the family good occasioned by her infidelity was much greater than that of her husband's, because it surreptitiously burdened the man with foreign fruits [illegitimate children], and that according to older laws, and not merely heathen ones, but Christian customs, too, male infidelity was regarded as mere fornication, while female infidelity was adultery.

Only the additional insult to the domestic home justified her claim to divorce. We have already seen how strongly Brauer opposed such arguments in the 1790s, when he labeled them mere "male egotism." Nonetheless, probably in order to hasten the general law reform, he now let them stand and restricted himself to a small modification to lessen the law's inequity:

---

[28] Which went into effect in 1810.

[29] Heinrich Gottfried Wilhelm Daniels, trans., *Code Napoléon. Gesetzbuch Napoleons, nach dem officiellen Texte übersetzt* (Cologne, 1808), 133; Johann Niclas Friedrich Brauer, *Erläuterungen über den Code Napoleon und die Großherzoglich Badische bürgerliche Gesetzgebung*, 6 vols. (Karlsruhe, 1809–1812), 1:199–200, 243–49.

Such a narrow limitation on the right of woman, who has hitherto in our laws been used to equality, would have seemed so much the harsher for the female sex, since the stricter police regulation of extramarital relations [*Konkubinat*] that is possible and actually exists in the grand duchy would have made it difficult for this ground for divorce to occur. That would have left the woman with virtually no rights in the case of her husband's adultery. Therefore, in order to bring this outspoken inequality, since it has been uttered by the law, into greater conformity with our customs and usages, the additional paragraph [230a] has widened the divorce grounds open to women to include those cases where husbands practice infidelity in the hometown [*Heimat*] or in such proximity that the intimate relation [*Zuwandel*] occurs at slightly greater remove.[30]

It may be that paragraph 230a actually did nullify the effect of paragraph 230, but only a detailed search of the divorce records could establish this. Clearly, however, paragraph 340a had no such effect on paternity searches, though its intention was, as one bureaucrat noted, "virtually to reintroduce the old proceedings."[31]

Precisely the failure of paragraph 340a to modify the Code Napoleon in practice riveted the bureaucrats' attention to paragraph 340 and refocused the debate in government circles over state regulation of sexual behavior from infanticide to paternity. The shift did not obliterate the old issues, which continued to vex administrators. Instead, infanticide, decriminalization of fornication, gender equality of punishment for sexual offences, and the proper role of government in the enforcement of morality continued to be hotly debated, but this debate now occurred inside the framework of paternity, which shifted the focus from mother's duties or behavior (or children's rights) to men's rights. Furthermore, the French understood paternity as primarily a property issue,[32] an interpretation that introduced a hitherto alien principle into the government discussion of sexual regulation and which utterly changed the parameters of that discussion. In order to make this transformation clear, we must briefly untangle the legal maneuvering down to the early 1820s, before turning to what these maneuverings reveal about the government's changing interest in sexual behavior.

The Administrative Struggle over Legal Principles, 1804–1820

We know from the events of the 1790s that government officials had intended to reform Badenese law by beginning with the criminal code. As luck would have it, the French civil code was finished (1804) before the penal code (1810). The latter was both deficient in conception and appeared after French hegemony had ended. Thus the French civil code served as a model for German legal reform, but its penal code did not. For Baden, and for other German states, this meant that although the modified or unmodified Code Napoléon revolutionized civil law, criminal, admin-

[30] Brauer, *Erläuterungen*, 1:199–200.
[31] Roggenbach (Directorium of the Dreysam Kreis) to Justice Ministry, 14 January 1811, GLA 234/3546.
[32] Traer, *Marriage and the Family*, 154–55.

istrative, and police law all remained intact and unreformed. The resulting clash of principles, jurisdictions, and institutions created a jagged legal landscape in which wary bureaucrats gingerly tinkered with the resulting, embarrassing paradoxes. Paragraph 340 raised three particularly knotty problems. First was gender inequality, a crass difference between French code and Badenese custom and law. This would perhaps have been less troublesome had Baden followed France in decriminalizing fornication, the proximate cause of illegitimacy. But in the Eighth Organizational Edict of 4 April 1803 Brauer had provided Baden's new territories with a uniform, but unreformed, criminal code based on the customary legislation slightly modified to reflect the actual judicial trend toward more lenient punishments. Fornication, *Verküppelung* and promoting prostitution, "unnatural fornication" (sodomy, bestiality, same-sex relations), incest, kidnapping with sexual intent, adultery, and bigamy, along with nonconsensual acts (rape and statutory rape), all remained crimes. The criminal prosecution of men for fornication was now, however, materially hampered by the civil injunction not to question them about paternity, since extramarital paternity was a subcategory of fornication. It was also unclear who should be posing the questions: the (civil) judge, or the magistrate, who had first jurisdiction over police and criminal matters. Finally, depending upon jurisdiction, the procedures and forms of oaths were different as well. Thus the second problem was legal and administrative. The third was fiscal. Paragraph 340 made paternity more difficult to establish at just the moment when, for other reasons, the illegitimacy rate began to climb. If the father could not be identified, he escaped contributing to his offspring's support, a burden that fell increasingly on truly impoverished localities. The fiscal interests of everyone except the male miscreant dictated circumvention of paragraph 340.

To solve the problems raised by paragraph 340, the government immediately began tinkering. An administrative ordinance of 10 June 1809 reiterated that police were not to question single mothers about the father of their children, and even should a woman volunteer the man's name, no investigation was to begin unless her testimony were easily corroborated independently. If neither the mother nor her parents could pay child support, the local government (*Gemeinde*) had to split the cost with the central state; if it could not, then the central state would assume the entire burden.[33] Bureaucratic reaction took three forms. First, by either (deliberately?) misunderstanding paragaph 340's allusion to civil instead of criminal penalties for fornication, or reasoning that since women not only could not sue for support from the father, but were by law required themselves to support their children and even possibly to suffer criminal penalties for fornication while the father got off, some bureaucrats concluded either that fornication had been erased from the criminal code and demoted to a civil offense or that women were being

---

[33] Ordinance of 10 June 1809, in *Vollständige Sammlung der Großherzoglich Badischen Regierungsblätter von deren Entstehung 1803 bis Ende 1825,* 4 vols. (Karlsruhe, 1826–43), *Regierungsblatt* (1809): 233–39.

punished enough and should be simply exempt from all fornication penalties.[34] Second, others simply protested the enormous expense being shouldered by innocent government institutions, local and central.[35] Third, some, and they were not few, quietly circumvented the regulations.

This situation produced the ordinance of 27 June 1812, which tried to dun the father by permitting state and *Gemeinde* to sue a man, not for being the father, but for being the sexual partner of the woman at the legally recognized time of conception.[36] Even so-called "suspicious carriage" (*verdächtiger Zuwandel*) was sufficient to wrest one-third of the support costs from the man.[37] Should the woman have voluntarily mentioned the man's name and the court have good, independent reason to believe he might be guilty, then the criminal investigation was to proceed, carefully avoiding, however, the use of the word "paternity" (*Vaterschaft*) or any mention of support costs, since these were civil matters.

Having addressed the fiscal and administrative problems in some detail, the government next tried to remedy the gender inequality. It ordered on 16 February 1813 that unwed pregnant women who either reported their pregnancy or who simply bore a live child would be free of all punishment for fornication.[38] This ordinance thus moved one step further in the long evolution begun in the early eighteenth century toward decriminalization of nonmarital heterosexual intercourse among single people. The legacy of the infanticide debate strongly influenced the bureaucrats. The Justice Ministry explained its motives for supporting decriminalization for single mothers at this time: "The old question, 'how does one prevent infanticide' has been raised anew by two recent cases of infanticide coming one after the other at a time when the new civil code generally removes from the unwed pregnant woman all legal rights to a support suit against her impregnator, and at a time when food is expensive, taxes have risen and the means of subsistence are more difficult [to find]."[39] Besides, they added, the French, from whom the civil code came, also let such women go unpunished. The Justice Ministry's words reflect the new element in the debate, namely the outrage many bureaucrats felt about the unequal treatment of women under the new code.[40] They bludgeoned the

---

[34] Großherzoglich Badisches Hofgericht (Freiburg) to Justice Ministry, Freiburg, 23 October 1810, no. 2424, GLA 234/602; and Carl Friedrich Wielandt's memorandum of 30 May 1812, no. 2424, GLA 234/3546.

[35] See the heated exchange between the Justice and Interior Ministries, the former of which favored having the central state bear the costs, the latter of which did not: Ministry of Interior, General Directorium, to Justice Ministry, Karlsruhe, 22 August 1811, no. 3017, and the Justice Ministry's draft reply, in GLA 234/3546.

[36] Ordinance of 27 June 1812, *Regierungsblatt* (1812): 117–20.

[37] *Verdächtiger Zuwandel* was defined as "numerous meetings taking place outside the usual and customarily permitted social times, either in a forbidden fashion, or such as to awaken decided judicial suspicions of immoral intentions." Ibid., 118.

[38] Ordinance of 16 February 1813, *Regierungsblatt* (1813):29–30.

[39] Justice Ministry to Interior Ministry, Karlsruhe, 11 October 1812, GLA 236/8479.

[40] One of the most eloquent and vociferous calls for gender equality is in Wielandt's memorandum of

gender inequality French law had introduced with the old trope of infanticide, as in a report (1810) from the Directorium of the Neckarkreis in Mannheim, which found that it was all very well and good to ensure state support for illegitimate children, "but this doesn't remove them from the danger that threatens them through the embarrassment of their usually impoverished mothers, who are struggling bravely against a tremendous burden, who have usually been seduced, and who are now punished with a double shame, whereby the law does not even regard their acknowledgment and report of their guilty partners as libel any more, indeed, it doesn't even think it worthy of investigation."[41] The very language of the ordinance made clear that although preventing infanticide was the ostensible goal of the law, its real impetus was to remedy gender inequality. After the preamble mentioned the need to avoid infanticide and to punish women who succumbed to that temptation, it continued, "finally, in consideration that We must also punish female weakness, foolhardiness and looseness leniently because our new law code generally removes from pregnant women that right to legal recourse against the impregnator for paternity-recognition, and therefore in order to establish equal harmony [zu Herstellung ebenmäßigen Einklangs] with [that code] We order . . ."[42]

Since after the 1813 ordinance most pregnant unwed women went unpunished, many localities halted all questioning. As one official put it, "There is no reason to investigate a single woman as soon as one suspects she is pregnant, and the good deed that the law of 16 February 1813 wants to do for such girls would be halfway taken back if one should subject them to an investigation, since many would feel that far worse than a punishment itself."[43]

By discouraging an initial investigation, of course, the 1813 ordinance blocked the occasion provided in 1809 and 1812 for inquiring after the woman's sexual partner and thus further hindered the state's efforts to collect money from the fathers. In short, tinkering had solved nothing.

The next years brought a continuing rise in illegitimacy rates and a flood of complaints from bureaucrats and church authorities protesting the moral, fiscal, criminal, police, and administrative consequences of paragraph 340 and its ragtag amendments. By 1818 the matter had come once again to a head. The Interior Ministry, its eye on the poor chest, wanted to replace paragraph 340 with swift police procedures aimed at recovering child support from the putative father. The Justice Ministry wanted to abolish it and permit the mother, child, and/or guardian to bring civil suit against the father. That would keep the matter in the civil courts,

---

31 May 1812, GLA 234/3546. Wielandt's later report on the same subject is cited by the Justice Ministry as a reason for its recommendation to change the fornication law: Justice Ministry to Interior Ministry, Karlsruhe, 11 October 1812, GLA 236/8479.

[41] Friedrich von Manger, Directorium of the Neckarkreis to Justice Ministry, Mannheim, 4 December 1810, 7 pages, GLA 234/3546.

[42] Ordinance of 16 February 1813, Regierungsblatt (1813):29–30.

[43] Report of the Bezirksamt Mosbach, 21 October 1833, no. 15609, GLA 236/8479.

safe from arbitrary police acts.[44] The Ministry of State (*Staatsministerium*), loath to upset the interlocking Napoleonic civil system, won time by polling the upper courts, who in turn polled lower authorities. A majority of those questioned wanted to rescind the controversial paragraph and return to the earlier system of investigations or permit the woman recourse to civil action. But a sizable minority were satisfied to retain it—for a variety of reasons.[45] Presumably as a result of this division of opinion, the Justice officials in 1822 suggested a precarious compromise.[46] Paragraphs 340 and 340a would remain on the books, and no police inquiry into fatherhood would be permitted. But "fallen women" of good reputation, that is, who could show they were not promiscuous, might sue their sexual partner for child support in civil proceedings. So might interested third parties. These suits would not establish or even mention fatherhood, but would aim strictly to recover support payments. Of course, the man and woman might always settle out of court, which ended the suit. Mere suspicious carriage (*verdächtiger Zuwandel*) no longer would suffice to force support payments. Finally, the justice officials gently hinted that reducing fornication from a criminal to a mere civil offense for both men and women would improve the situation, but barring that, pregnant women should continue to go unpunished.

Despite the urgings of the Justice and Interior ministries and the outcry from lower authorities, the Ministry of State left the legal tangle as it was. Not surprisingly the same evasions, confusions, and pleas recurred throughout the 1820s, 1830s, and 1840s, punctuated by intermittent government and parliamentary efforts to remedy matters. Finally, an 1850 law ended the struggles with a compromise that left the mother unprotected, shielded the father from the inheritance consequences of his act, but enabled the government to collect some child support from the "sexual partner"—the term father was carefully avoided.[47] We restrict our analysis to the period ending in 1820, when the documentation shows the private sphere in the process of formation.

The Code Napoléon changed the framework within which the nexus of sexual behavior and public control was conceived in Baden. Above all, introducing the yardstick of private property had the greatest transformative impact of any principle.[48] For it was the French concern about inheritance that placed fatherhood at the center of legislation on illegitimacy and fornication. As Brauer noted in his legal

[44] Justice Ministry to Ministry of State, Karlsruhe, 24 November 1818, no. 965, 8 pages, GLA 233/27494. This document also sums up the Interior Ministry's position.

[45] The results of the questionnaire tabulated and summarized in "Akten-Auszug, die Aufhebung des Landrecht-Satzes 340. betrf.," 20 March 1822, 34 pages, GLA 234/3546.

[46] Justice Ministry report (*Vortrag*), 8 April 1822, no. 962, 25 pages, GLA 234/3546.

[47] Law of 14 December 1850, GLA 233/27494. Instead of the mother, her guardian and/or the community received the right to resort to civil suit.

[48] On the influential contention that the institution of private property "causes" gender discrimination, see Friedrich Engels, *The Origin of the Family, Private Property, and the State* (1884), trans. Ernest Untermann (Chicago, 1902). Schröder, *Rechtlosigkeit*, 126–38, interprets the Napoleonic period similarly. This is an unproven and unnecessary conclusion that I do not share and the examination of which is impossible here. The following discussion handles these questions separately.

commentary on paragraph 340: "The question of nonmarital intercourse was handled in earlier times mainly as a criminal matter, while the fact of fatherhood was regarded and decided as an appendix [to this]. [The Napoleonic code] turned this around, and handled fatherhood as the main issue and the criminal aspect as peripheral."[49] For the French, fatherhood was the main issue because it safeguarded the regular transmission of property from the [male] citizen to his legitimate heirs and, by maintaining property across generations, stabilized the distribution of wealth and the contours of the established civil order.[50] As the French and their German supporters never tired of pointing out, biological paternity was impossible to prove legally. Therefore, they simply redefined fatherhood as a social construction: fathers were men whose offspring were born inside their legal marriage (unless the man himself contested this fact, claiming for example that he had been absent for over nine months), or who admitted to fathering a child out of wedlock. Anchoring paternity in the social order rather than the biological or "natural" one was fully consistent with the French task (which the German reform states partly assumed, as well) of constructing a new society of contractually linked males.

The property principle with its emphasis on fatherhood caused the discussion of sexual behavior and social control to shift in several ways: (1) from criminal to civil law; (2) consequently from state initiative to civil initiative, that is, from theoretically unlimited state intervention and tutelage to limits thereon—therefore, the creation of "privacy"; (3) from the community interest to that of the individual, in this case, the putative father; (4) since the father was also a male, the shift away from the community interest occurred at the expense of women and their children; (5) rights came to be construed in terms of property and one's location in the emerging public/private nexus, rather than other, earlier criteria, such as (passive) citizenship in the community, Christian obligation, or, especially, natural rights.

The Criminal/Civil Balance

Brauer's observation that paragraph 340 redirected legal scrutiny in fornication cases from criminal penalties to civil issues was quite right and accounts for the administrators' inability to prosecute men for fornication thereafter. We have already seen the legal reasoning the bureaucrats followed: if women bore the shame and costs of childbirth and childrearing, but men could not be touched because of the interdiction on questioning paternity, then it seemed unfair to continue to burden women with criminal penalties as well (Ordinance of 1813). Once (pregnant) women were no longer punished, then the investigative opportunity to target men disappeared. Although some Ämter continued to press pregnant women to name the fathers of their children, but left this information out of the protocol,[51] in

[49] Brauer, *Erläuterungen*, 1:243.
[50] Traer, *Marriage and the Family*, 154–55.
[51] Report of Bezirksamt Mosbach, no. 1560, Mosbach, 21 October 1833, GLA 236/8479.

fact, few men after 1813 not voluntarily named by pregnant women were successfully prosecuted for fornication,[52] despite widespread administrative desire to the contrary.[53] In short, fornication was decriminalized de facto. The Ministry of State helped this process along in 1820 when it ended by fiat corporal punishment for fornication, making it henceforth punishable only by civil (*bürgerlich*) means.[54] Adultery also was escaping the criminal camp, first by being punished without loss of civil honor,[55] second by being prosecuted only upon the complaint of the spouse, not by state initiative.[56]

The widening scope of civil law is also made clear in the remedies bureaucrats recommended for the injustices toward women contained in paragraph 340. Except for the Interior Ministry, which favored quick police procedures to recover child support from putative fathers, even outspoken bureaucratic critics of paragraph 340 tended to favor simply extending the benefits of civil law to women.[57] This would have permitted them to bring civil suit for child support from the alleged father. Even those who proposed abolishing paragraph 340 hastened to aver "that we are far removed from the opinion, that pregnancy and paternity should be investigated according to the old rules by police or inquisitorial methods at the local level [*von Amtswegen*]. In place of paragraph 340 we consider appropriate only the legal admission of civil suit according to the law against every impregnator."[58] When the Justice Ministry in 1822 backed down from its original proposal (1818) to abolish paragraph 340, it, too, took the route of opening up civil remedies to women and third parties, rather than diminishing the newly acquired male right to sexual secrecy.[59] Thus the handling of fornication cases from both the criminal and civil sides acknowledged the greater salience of civil over criminal or police considerations.

The shifting balance between the criminal and civil codes had another important aspect, too. It determined which official had jurisdiction over which matters: the "police," which in a town meant the elected mayor or superintendant

---

[52] Reports of Amt Gerlachsheim, no. 7567, Gerlachsheim, 4 November 1833; Oberamt Heidelberg, Heidelberg, 7 November 1833; Oberamt Durlach, no. 15825, Durlach, 29 October 1833; and Oberamt Pforzheim, no. 21286, Pforzheim, 4 November 1833, all in GLA 236/8479.

[53] "Akten-Auszug die Aufhebung des Landrecht-Satzes 340 betrf," 20 March 1822, GLA 234/3546, in which relatively few of the surveyed bureaucrats recommended decriminalization of fornication for male offenders.

[54] Ministry of State Rescript, no. 942, 23 March 1820, GLA 234/602. Typically, this step occurred with insufficient publicity to reach all the local authorities, some of whom had not heard of the decision a decade later. The "civil punishment" in Baden would have been the equivalent in Bavaria of a police offense.

[55] This tendency, already visible in late absolutist practice, was encouraged further by the practice in the former Austrian territories Baden had annexed, whereby adultery was a mere "political misdemeanor." See Hofgericht Freiburg to Justice Ministry, 13 September 1811, GLA 234/602.

[56] Hofgericht of the See-Provinz to Justice Ministry, Meersburg, 31 January 1815, GLA 234/602.

[57] Justice Ministry to Ministry of State, Karlsruhe, 24 November 1818, GLA 233/27494, which argues against the Interior Ministry's position.

[58] Hofgericht of the See-Provinz, Meersburg, no. 727, 11 February 1819, GLA 234/3546.

[59] Baumüller report for Justice Ministry, no. 962, 8 April 1822, GLA 234/3546. This report claimed that civil procedures avoided the "scandalous investigations" typical of criminal or police processes.

(*Ortsvorsteher*) and in the countryside meant the appointed administrative head of the local *Gemeinde* (the Amtsmann), who also functioned as the lowest level court was empowered to hand down light civil sentences of up to four weeks in jail,[60] or the higher court judges (*Hofgericht*) empowered to inflict more serious, corporal punishment.[61] The elaboration of civil law and the concomitant development of something conceived of as civil society demanded a much stricter delineation among these jurisdictions. It especially demanded the restriction of potentially arbitrary police power in favor of the regularized judicial process of the courts. As the Justice Ministry declared, "Since, as is well known, after life itself, honor and freedom is [*sic*] the most precious possession [*Gut*] which can be removed from a citizen [*Staatsbürger*], therefore a more than four-week sentence to a correctional facility cannot be handed down in a mere summary police trial, or by a police authority, but must instead occur through a judge in a legal court proceeding."[62] Hence, the two contrary movements in sexually related cases. Those construed as having to do primarily with property were reclassified upward as civil cases and went to the courts. Thus Brauer (1812) and all succeeding justice ministry officials redefined the establishment of paternity as a civil proceeding to be conducted before a judge and removed the issue from police jurisdiction.[63] As Brauer's successor in the Justice Ministry explained (1818): "Paternity and child support cases belong according to their inmost nature, not to the police, but to the courts, since these cases are strictly based on the first and important rights of mine and thine, and thus even conceptually cannot be placed among the objects of police, which in any event lacks the necessary limitation and which, alas, experience has only too often shown is prey to caprice and prejudice."[64] Divorce, with its implications for property settlement, also became a civil matter. The Marriage Regulations of 1807 had decreed divorce a police matter. Two years later it was moved to the jurisdiction of the higher courts (*Hofgerichte*).[65]

Although property issues were pulling some cases up into the courts, the trend toward decriminalization of sexual delicts was tugging in the opposite direction. The local police dealt with the unwed mother when she reported her pregnancy; they also investigated cases of hidden pregnancy and were in charge of the initial investigation of more serious but related offenses, such as infanticide.[66] First-time adultery, if it did not involve divorce, was also a matter for the police, not the

[60] Directorium of the Dreysam-Kreis (Freiburg) to Justice Ministry, 1 June 1813, GLA 236/2207.

[61] Willy Andreas, *Geschichte der badischen Verwaltungsorganisation und Verfassung in den Jahren 1802–1818* (Leipzig, 1913), 1:216.

[62] Justice Ministry to Directorium of the Dreysam-Kreis, Karlsruhe, 23 June 1813, GLA 236/2207.

[63] Brauer, "Entwurf einer Verordnung das Verhalten in Vertheilung der UnzuchtsSachen betreffend," 1812, GLA 234/3546.

[64] Justice Ministry, Karlsruhe, no. 965, 24 November 1818, GLA 233/27494.

[65] Justice Ministry, no. 4410, 23 September 1828, GLA 233/30794.

[66] Brauer, "Entwurf einer Verordnung," 1812, GLA 234/3546. Again, it is noteworthy that the experienced Brauer, typical of reform absolutist administrators, still regarded paternity and support costs for illegitimate children as subcategories of fornication (*Unzucht*).

courts.[67] Although some transgressions gravitated toward the police, others fell from the higher to lower courts. The first two fornication charges involving men or nonpregnant women had dropped out of the *Hofgericht* jurisdiction into the local courts after 1812 when the penalties were reduced.[68] Later, this practice was extended to third-time offenders.

Clearly, common heterosexual delicts had become less important to the civil order than property matters. One of the perhaps unintended consequences of this development was that increasingly such cases landed (or stayed) with the police, which many bureaucrats acknowledged to be a less capable,[69] more prejudiced venue than the courts and one that afforded the accused fewer rights. The scope for capricious discretion and local peculiarity thus became wider for the handling of sexual delicts. In Baden as in Bavaria, the police became more and more a buffer between the state and emerging civil society. The gray zone of police surveillance expanded to catch especially sexual delicts, but others as well, before they achieved the zone of legal protection afforded by the right to "privacy." In Baden, especially, one might describe the police buffer zone as a survival of absolutist regulatory practices and assumptions. Institutionally, of course, one would be right to do so. But police had a more complicated meaning, which Hegel, the first theorist to distinguish between state and civil society, described in 1820. He situated police squarely within civil society.[70] For Hegel, the police was a necessary function of civil society, not only to safeguard against crime, regulate trade, provide public education, and dampen poverty and thus the threat of revolution, that is, in general to ensure the smooth running of clashing interests in a system of property, but for other, more nebulous reasons as well. It might intervene even where no injury (crime) had occurred because

> there is no inherent line of distinction between what is and what is not injurious, even where crime is concerned, or between what is and what is not suspicious, or between what is to be forbidden or subjected to supervision and what is to be exempt from prohibition, from surveillance and suspicion, from inquiry and the demand to render an account of itself. These details are determined by custom, the spirit of the rest of the constitution, contemporary conditions, the crisis of the hour, and so forth.[71]

Understood in this way, the police becomes the agent of society's self-regulation, reflective of its customary opinions, those very notions that many Enlightened

[67] Justice Ministry to Directorium of the Dreysam-Kreis (Freiburg), Karlsruhe, 29 April 1812, GLA 234/3546.

[68] Ministry of State, no. 942, Karlsruhe, 23 March 1820, GLA 234/602; Ministry of the Interior, Karlsruhe, 17 November 1837, GLA 236/8479.

[69] For example, the remarks of the Oberamt Pforzheim on "how little the local police officials can be trusted, [who are] mostly elderly people, who through fecklessness [*Leichtsinn*] failed at their original profession and then volunteered [for the police] to help earn their living." Report of Oberamt Pforzheim, no. 21286, 4 November 1833, GLA 236/8479.

[70] Georg Wilhelm Friedrich Hegel, *Philosophy of Right*, (1820), trans. T.M. Knox (London, 1952), 145–52.

[71] Ibid., 146.

thinkers and early liberals like Feueurbach had tried to ban from positive law and legitimate state action. As always, Hegel's Janus-faced dialectic looked backward and forward at the same time; the police was both a remembrance of absolutist tutelage and an agent of civil-social moral opinion. The efflorescence of the police as medium of approved social custom, rather than strictly as tool of state intervention, occurred in the Vormärz, but the foundations for the police's transformation along these lines were laid in the Napoleonic period.

The Peculiar Development of the "Private Sphere"

The most striking features of the new "private sphere" were its limitation to males, its unspoken class bias, its partial displacement of the older notion of the "public good" (Gemeinwohl), and the function that marriage played in legitimating it.

The peculiar contours of "privacy" inscribed in the Code Napoléon had long been anticipated and desired by some German officials. Palatine Privy Councillor Weiler had argued at great length in 1783 that sexual privacy for extramarital male dalliance should be protected against the fiscal claims of the state or the potential private claims of women.[72] Furthermore, the French discussions of paragraph 340 were well known to German observers, who understood that the narrow legal issue of the undemonstrable nature of biological paternity was not the heart of the matter. Instead, as von Roggenbach, director of Baden's Dreysam province, noted, it was "the secret [geheimen] stories of human strayings [menschlichen Verirrungen], which the French law wanted to keep veiled."[73] "Secret" here is being used in the old sense of not publicly known; however, in this context "secret" is also being made to mean not subject to public (state) investigation and intervention. (In other words, "secret" is being used to mean "private.") But, of course, it was not "human strayings" the French were reserving to the private sphere, for pregnancy could not be hidden, and paragraph 341 explicitly permitted investigation into the names of mothers of illegitimate children. It was men's strayings.

The male-centeredness in the establishment of a legal "private sphere" was explicit. The state was forbidden to pry into questions of out-of-wedlock paternity, and forbidden to overlook out-of-wedlock maternity. Indeed, the burden of reporting a pregnancy was on the woman. Official knowledge of her pregnancy (and therefore of her sexual transgression) was the price she paid to escape punishment for "hidden pregnancy." In addition, birth registries of illegitimate children carefully listed the mother's name. So, despite the fervid discussion of female modesty, whose contours were paradigmatically set by the infanticide debate, indeed as part of it, since the "hidden pregnancy" legislation was designed to prevent

---

[72] Weiler's report of 12 June 1783, GLA 77/4677.

[73] Adam Franz Xaver von Roggenbach of Directorium of Dreysam-Kreis, Freyburg, 14 January 1811, 23 pages, GLA 234/3546. Baumüller in the Justice Ministry described French intentions as "wanting to keep the secret sins cloaked in a dark veil," no. 962, 8 April 1822, GLA 234/3546.

infanticide, disclosure of female "straying" was mandated by law. Illegitimate pregnancy, and therefore the female fornicant, remained "public."

From what, exactly, were French legislators and the German bureaucrats who adopted their thinking, shielding men by cloaking them in privacy? Roggenbach explained further:

> The [French] negotiations on this part of the law book [par. 340] show us that by forbidding investigations into paternity they wanted to diminish the disgusting investigations [*eckelhaften Untersuchungen*], the indecent details [*unanständigen Particularitäten*], which the courts on such occasions usually in the clumsiest manner inscribe in the files; [they wanted] to avoid conflict in the families of the accused; and they created through experience the principle that many a whore [*Dirne*] made a business out of accusing one or more often innocent persons [*oft unschuldige Personen*] of being the fathers of their children, who then pay something to avoid trouble.[74]

The "disgusting investigations" and "indecent details" were anatomically exact descriptions of sexual congress necessary to establish the possibility of paternity. During the infanticide debate, eighteenth-century commentators worried about the effects on young mothers of giving such testimony before male witnesses.[75] Now, during the "paternity" debate, nineteenth-century commentators focus their concern on the male. Affronts to female modesty are no longer the issue. Instead, it is the male reputation, which must be safeguarded, since the female's has already been damaged by the mere fact of pregnancy.[76] Enlightened doctors had already in the 1790s protested against the occasional court practice in divorce cases of ordering manipulation of the defendant's penis to test the wife's allegation of her husband's impotence.[77] Such protests, along with the contemporaneous antimasturbation publicity, are signs of the growing interest in male sexual functioning and its use generally as a metaphor for male power, individualism, and creative productivity in society. As a consequence of this social revaluation, the penis and its use became "secret," that is, "private," and no longer subject to defilement by public (state) scrutiny. Hence the banishment of "disgusting investigations."

It is perhaps also noteworthy that Roggenbach identifies as the object of particular distaste the inscription of these details in the files.[78] This concern recalls Privy Councillor Weiler's repulsion at the idea that father's names might be entered into registry books of illegitimate births. Such bureaucratic acts occurred on the educated male terrain of the official, written document, as opposed to that alternative "public" locus, traditional oral scolding or slander, which was accessible to (if not in

---

[74] Roggenbach, Directorium of the Dreysam-Kreis, Freyburg, 14 January 1811, GLA 234/3546. On the French discussions, see Traer, *Marriage and the Family*, 173–74.

[75] Ulbricht, *Kindsmord*, 288–89.

[76] For example, Justice Ministry report no. 962, 8 April 1822, GLA 234/3546.

[77] See the controversy between Dr. Franz Mai and the Heidelberg medical faculty in the Palatinate, 15 September 1798 to December 1799, in GLA 77/4631a.

[78] In his own words, " . . . welche von den Gerichten . . . gewöhnlich auf ungeschickte Weise den Acten einverleibt wurden."

fact dominated by) women and the illiterate.[79] Government documentation was clearly a far greater threat to those bureacrats who identified with the male transgressor. And, besides, documentation made eternal an act that many males, since they could not become pregnant, must have experienced as inherently transient and without consequence.

Although it is necessary to point out the coarse gender divide in operation, in fact paragraph 340 and the limited privacy it offered were also predicated on distinctions among males. The French deliberations on paragraph 340 justified this discrimination by claiming to protect "family happiness" from disharmony caused by indecent paternity trials and to protect the right of legitimate children over illegitimate ones to their father's estate. Obviously, French revolutionary legislators envisioned the accused male as married and/or propertied,[80] and thus a target for the schemes of "loose women." The protection of "privacy" was therefore targeted specifically to heterosexually active, married, propertied men. Without speculating whether French men of this description actually needed or deserved this protection, one must note that this assumption fit perfectly the model of illegitimacy that late Enlightened belles lettres had developed in Germany. That is, the novelists who wrote about illegitimacy and infanticide in the 1770s to 1790s imagined the seducer as socially superior to his victim, who was usually a poor servant girl. Late-eighteenth-century German bureaucrats knew better. Most cases of illegitimacy in Germany involved single people of the same age and low social circumstance. The French and German literary model, which was the unspoken basis of paragraph 340, therefore clashed with German social reality.

The new climate of the French civil code encouraged some German bureaucrats to forget what they knew about social reality. Thus an official in Mannheim, discussing the fact that even before paragraph 340 the city had rarely collected money from the fathers of illegitimate children, decided that this proved that women were protecting the wealthy fathers in return for secret payments, which they kept for themselves, while forcing the city to support their children. "Experience seems to show this, since how else can you explain . . . why normally [these women] name poor [men as] fathers of their illegitimate children? Are rich or propertied males less likely to indulge lust than poor ones?"[81]

Nonetheless, the discrepancy between the ideal, married beneficiary of paragraph 340 and the actual German pattern of illegitimacy caused most officials in

---

[79] Regina Schulte, "Bevor das Gerede zum Tratsch wird," in Hausen and Wunder, *Frauengeschichte-Geschlechtergeschichte*, 67–73; Carola Lipp, "Katzenmusiken, Krawalle und 'Weiberrevolution,'" in *Schimpfende Weiber und patriotische Jungfrauen. Frauen im Vormärz und in der Revolution 1848/49*, ed. Lipp (Moos, 1986), 112–30, esp. 116–17, 124–27; Norton, "Gender and Defamation in Seventeenth-Century Maryland."

[80] Since most German states forbad marriage to those without property or income, and since marriage was still generally the prerequisite for full citizenship for males, "propertied" (not wealthy) and "married" were conflated for good social reason by most German bureaucrats.

[81] Stengel's report, no. 3223, "Über die Aufhebung des Bastardfalls," part 3, Mannheim, January 1809, GLA 77/415.

Baden to focus on the single man. Not surprisingly bureaucratic opponents of paragraph 340 made this point one of the centerpieces of their criticism. Thus, they consistently argued that paragraph 340 encouraged (single) men to shun marriage, since they could get sexual satisfaction, as it were, for free. "Lust and seduction will be encouraged by the new law and the nonmarital state will become more attractive to male youth."[82] "[Paragraph 340] must be very favorable to the unmarried estate, since under its protection the sexual drive can be satisfied without danger or disadvantage." "Why should a sensual person [*Mensch*], who can so easily reach his goal without danger of being held accountable for his act, why should he trouble himself to curb his natural sexual instinct, or seek to satisfy it in marital society [which is hedged around with] so many hindering circumstances?"[83] This argument was so convincing to contemporaries that even proponents of paragraph 340 felt forced to acknowledge its truth before they went on to considerations they argued outweighed it.[84]

The bureaucrats' reluctance to permit single men to enjoy the protection of "privacy" should not be interpreted to mean they opposed creating such a protected place, or that they opposed limiting it to a certain class of men, or that they necessarily favored untrammeled state investigations into sexual matters. It may instead signify the bureaucrats' view that the law was unsuited to Baden's more rural circumstances. The position the Justice Ministry took in 1822 underscores this view. On the one hand, it proposed permitting greater access to the putative father's money via civil suit, averring that civil process injured the man's privacy less than criminal trials or police investigations might. On the other hand, it carefully and specifically addressed the problem of the married transgressor. "But no longer would the husband, who has forgotten himself once, be publicly pilloried, because not only have we provided for [private, that is, outside of court] child-support negotiations, but any third party may declare himself prepared to pay the child's support and thus in advance make any civil suit impossible."[85] As the *Vormärz* period developed, the solicitude for the married, cross-class male heterosexual offender, who is so crassly championed in paragraph 340, became more widespread in Baden and elsewhere. In the Napoleonic period, however, when the rough outlines of the protection of "privacy" were being sketched, the particularity of this protection by gender and *Stand* clearly troubled many contemporaries.

Finally, two other aspects of the peculiar privacy inherent in paragraph 340 need

---

[82] Directorium of the Neckar-Kreis to Justice Ministry, Mannheim, 4 December 1810, GLA 234/3546.

[83] Hofgericht of the See-Provinz, Meersburg, no. 727, 11 February 1819, GLA 234/3546.

[84] Thus in the summary of arguments made in 1819 to keep paragraph 340, the admission that "men are encouraged to remain single" figured prominently at the beginning of the list. "Akten-Auszug," 20 March 1822, GLA 234/3546.

[85] Justice Ministry, no. 962, 8 April 1822, GLA 234/3546. This echoes the sentiment in Klüser's anti-Napoleonic diatribe, Hofgericht of the See-Provinz, Meersburg, no. 727, 11 February 1819, which, despite its vitriol, ultimately opined that private deals between women and the (propertied or sufficiently wealthy) fathers were the best solution.

to be addressed. The first is the importance of marriage in defining it. The married man, or the man wealthy enough to be expected to marry some day, was the unspoken beneficiary of paragraph 340. And upholding the institution of marriage and the inheritance lines it laid down were two of the main reasons given to justify it. But we have also seen that opponents of the paragraph adduced essentially the same arguments for their side: paragraph 340 contravened "family rights," "family happiness," "domestic order";[86] it discouraged men from marrying at all. In fact one of the most striking things about the 1822 summary of the views of thirty-nine different bureaucrats or institutions on this issue is precisely that they are all at least partly framed around the same icon: the sanctity of marriage.[87] Marriage was the magnetic center around which not social reality, but social theory and therefore bureaucratic argument revolved. Marriage could function as a versatile guideline for state policy because it justified the discrete extension of privacy, that is, the partial limiting of state intervention, but did so explicitly in the public interest, since "the family bond [is that] in whose strengthening the happy duration of the state-society [*Staatsgesellschaft*] consists."[88]

The second noteworthy peculiarity of the privacy granted by paragraph 340 is that, just as it was unevenly extended to some men, it was expressly denied to some women, who were reclassified as "public," and on that account made rightless. The right in question was the ability to bring civil suit for child support against the putative father. Bureaucrats favoring reform of paragraph 340 wanted to widen the access of unwed mothers to civil remedies, but they also wanted to protect men from the fear of false accusation that had haunted the original French deliberations of the paragraph. Therefore, the Justice Ministry in 1818 suggested allowing judges summarily to throw out suits brought by "a whore [*Dirne*] who can be shown to have had sexual relations with several men, made money from her body, or had resided in a public brothel."[89] In 1822 justice officials explained that "a whore [*Dirne*] who makes a living doing this deserves such a declaration of rightlessness [*Recht-loserklärung*], but not a fallen maiden." They went on to extend the rightless category to include vagrant women, that is, women who should have been in domestic service but were not.[90] The judicial officials of the Hofgericht in Meersburg wanted to encompass in addition foreign women traveling through the country and "those females who follow after the markets by themselves, even if she should claim to be pursuing an insignificant trade in small commodities."[91] These rightless groups shared two attributes in common: they were not circumscribed within an easily recognizable domestic environment, and they were economically independent, either making money themselves or subsisting in some manner not

---

[86] Hofgericht of the See-Provinz, Meersburg, no. 727, 11 February 1819, GLA 234/3546.
[87] "Akten-Auszug," 20 March 1822, GLA 234/3546.
[88] Hofgericht of the See-Provinz, Meersburg, no. 727, 11 February 1819, GLA 234/3546.
[89] Justice Ministry, no. 965, 24 November 1818, GLA 233/27494.
[90] Justice Ministry, no. 962, 8 April 1822, GLA 234/3546.
[91] Hofgericht of the See-Provinz, Meersburg, no. 727, 11 February 1819, GLA 234/3546.

easily ascertained by government officials. In short, they were "public," in several of its senses: they did not keep the secret of their sexual intimacy, or they engaged in commerce (including nonsexual commerce), or they were not domestic (attached to their home or to someone else's, as servants—indeed, some were allegedly living in "public" houses, that is, brothels). The condition of being "public" in any of its guises condemned them to rightlessness on an axis that appeared increasingly to identify rights with private condition. Of course, the Ministry of State's reluctance to change paragraph 340 at all meant that these suggestions were not adopted in these years. But the current and direction of opinion on the subject of "public" versus "private" for women and men should be clear from these deliberations.

The Displacement of Community and Natural Rights

Paragraph 340 made it impossible, despite the amendments added to it in 1812 and 1813, to identify most fathers of illegitimate children or to extract child-support payments from them. Because most mothers were poor, communities (*Gemeinden*) shouldered most of the cost, aided by the state, when community resources were insufficient. Even before the great wave of illegitimacy and pauperism of the 1820s to 1840s, some communities were sorely taxed by this new drain on their meager funds. One bureaucrat reported a village in one of the high illegitimacy areas of Baden where twelve citizens had to support fourteen illegitimate children.[92] There could hardly be a clearer case of the rights to privacy and property of a (male) individual superseding the fiscal and property interests of the community.[93] This fundamental shift of rights from the community to a specific group of individuals did not go unnoticed or unchallenged. But insofar as paragraph 340 was not reformed, it did go unchanged.

Not surprisingly, bureaucrats who supported paragraph 340 kept silent about the loss of community rights that it caused.[94] Opponents, however, waxed eloquent on the subject, obviously one of their strongest arguments, because the *Gemeinde* was the most concrete unit of sociopolitical organization and the good of the community in the abstract (*Gemeinwohl*) had been the major legitimating theory of (absolutist) government. Abandoning either of these principles demanded a mental revolution that needed to be accompanied by tangible gains that paragraph 340 did not seem to provide.

Opponents of paragraph 340 argued on three levels. First, state welfare and therefore state law superseded the rights of individuals, as the general superseded the particular, or the public the private. Second, in any case, the state had two compelling interests overriding those of unwed fathers, the education of its future

[92] Ibid.

[93] In 1820 the central government spent 12,020 gulden supporting illegitimate children for communities too poor to do so themselves. By 1850, this sum had risen to 95,523 gulden. Justice Ministry report no. 6525, Karlsruhe, 10 June 1850, GLA 233/27494.

[94] The argument is not broached by the thirteen official writers who felt paragraph 340 should be retained: "Akten-Auszug," 20 March 1822, GLA 234/3546.

citizens, including illegitimate ones, and the maintenance of public morality. And third, since in a well-governed state, positive law reflected natural law, state interests also coincided with the natural rights of biological relatives: of mothers against the fathers of their children, of children against their fathers, of grandparents against the fathers, if the grandparents were forced by law to pay upkeep for illegitimate grandchildren (as was the case).

The Hofgericht of Meersburg (1819), the judicial seat in the area with the highest illegitimacy rate in Baden, expounded on these themes:

> Positive laws [*bürgerliche Geseze*] may limit the natural rights of individual people and individual families, where the state order and the welfare of all demands it. It cannot be doubted that according to the laws of nature each child may cry for its father and use his name; that each mother may demand of her lover, sexual partner, or seducer either that he save her honor through marriage or alternatively pay for the upkeep of her child, and that she has the right to achieve this last through all permissible means, including a suit before a judge; that each father, each mother, to whom falls the burden of supporting an illegitimate grandchild, must be permitted to search for the impregnator or seducer of their daughter with or without a court, in order to make him accept responsibility for his deed and to demand what he owes to the maintenance of his child. A law that limits without sufficient motive these primary family rights, much less which does so against the purposes of the state, distorts the holy laws of nature, is unjust, tends toward the dissolution of family bonds, in the strengthening of which the fortunate continuance of the state-society [*Staatsgesellschaft*] consists. . . .
> . . . The state must be interested . . . [in the fact] that each newborn member of the greater society has a father and a name.[95]

The "father and name" were to guarantee a proper upbringing as a useful and productive citizen: "the child requires education as a human and as a citizen, and the duty to provide this rests with the parents."[96]

The reader will recognize these arguments as "old-fashioned," that is, as typical of the late Enlightened absolutist bureaucracy. The heart of their argument was that "the state must precisely protect natural rights, which the *Landrecht* [in paragraph 340] does not do."[97] The residual weight of appeals to natural law and *Gemeinwohl* was still strong enough in 1819 that even proponents of paragraph 340 had to admit "that [under its provisions] the woman and the child lose their *natural right* of information about the father, that the *Gemeinwohl* is threatened, (a) because men are encouraged not to marry, (b) infanticide can be caused, and (c) bastards are neglected and become morally ruined."[98] But they claimed that "these grounds [for reforming it] are nonetheless outweighed by others," which they went on to adduce.[99]

[95] Hofgericht of the See-Provinz, Meersburg, no. 727, 11 February 1819, GLA 234/3546.
[96] "Akten-Auszug," citing the Justice Ministry and four other respondents of 1819, 20 March 1822, GLA 234/3546.
[97] Amtmann Merk of Stühlingen, cited in ibid.
[98] Hofgerichtsrat Schachleiter of Mannheim, summarized in ibid.
[99] Ibid.

The insufficiency of natural rights as a conclusive argument robbed women and illegitimate children of their traditionally unquestioned call on the father's resources. The Directory of the Neckar province made the natural rights argument succinctly:

> The bond between father and mother, whether it is sanctioned by religion and state law [marriage], or whether it is joined without these, belongs to the more intimate bonds of nature; in the natural relations between father and mother lies a natural right, which gives both the duty to nourish and raise their children. A positive law may append additions to this duty, but it must never destroy the natural law itself, or forbid the judicial guarantee of the natural law.[100]

But that was precisely what this law did: it elevated social bonds (such as those established in legal marriage) above what the eighteenth century had regarded as "natural," presocial ones, based on sexual intimacy and procreation. In doing so, it refounded society on different principles.

By 1822 the Justice Ministry, after a long struggle, silently admitted that natural rights could no longer function as the theory regulating the relations between men and women, parents and children, or the state and individuals. It had to abandon eighteenth-century precepts. Even practical ones, like the concern to hinder infanticide, now were "less relevant than the civil-legal relations [*Privatrechtsverhältniße*] of the persons, who must enjoy equal state protection, and the consideration of third parties, who have been drawn into the matter [*ins Mitleid gezogen worden*]."[101] The justice officials consequently reconstrued mothers', grandparents', and Gemeinde rights as property rights that the father had injured by committing a crime (fornication). Civil suits for child support were permissible, where paternity suits were not, "because fornication [*Unzucht*] is immoral and harmful to the social union of state [*gesellschaftlichen StaatsVerein*]; therefore the lawmaker has the right [*Befugnis*] to hold liable to those concerned him who has caused damage to the community [*Gemeinwesen*]."

This roundabout method of avoiding a natural rights argument had interesting potential consequences, because it forced the continued criminalization of consensual heterosexual intercourse in order to derive damage compensation. Justice officials were even driven to claim that unwed mothers must be given the right to civil suit because even criminals had a right to their day in court! "Taking away the right of the mother to civil complaint would mean declaring her *rightless* [*rechtlos*], not even allowing her that step into the courtroom that is owed to two thieves who share together the punishment, costs and damages."[102] This form of argument kept the state involved in the business of regulating consensual heterosexual conduct, which, in fact, the justice officials did not desire.[103] The displacement of natural

---

[100] Directorium of the Neckar-Kreis to Justice Ministry, Mannheim, 4 December 1810, GLA 234/3546.

[101] Justice Ministry report no. 962, 8 April 1822, GLA 234/3546.

[102] Ibid., emphasis in original.

[103] Ibid.

rights by arguments based on property thus distorted the framework within which laws on sexual conduct operated and bureaucrats reasoned.

Without natural rights, the most efficient foundation for a claim to legal rights, bureaucrats scrambled for other reasons of equal moral force to order the relations between citizens and their state. It is not immediately clear why the common good (*Gemeinwohl*) could not serve this purpose, but in practice, as we have seen, the emerging rights of the propertied male to (sexual) privacy outweighed this. Whereas in the late eighteenth century, moral arguments based on natural rights had been used to ground equal legal rights, at the beginning of the nineteenth century moral arguments operated to undermine that principle and to reintroduce differential treatment according to the moral worth of the delinquent. The content of moral evaluations had always been to a degree gender specific: "immoral" sexual conduct damaged a woman's moral reputation more than it did a man's. From 1800 to 1820, the gender differential became much more pronounced than it had been earlier as morality became more closely identified with sexual conduct and as sexual conduct became, in turn, more central to the moral evaluation of women. These glacial shifts fit changing social opinion far better than they did legal principle, for, although bureaucrats moved in this direction, they did so not only grudgingly, but seemingly unconsciously. Their language and their silence[104] reveal their dilemma even more clearly than tortured argument.

We have already examined a crass example of how moral argument reconstructed an economy of rights in the exclusion of "public" women from the right to civil suit for child support. Since this exclusion was the brainchild of officials who sought to redress the gender imbalance in paragraph 340, one might interpret this new form of gender unfairness as a compensation they felt compelled to offer proponents of paragraph 340 in return for reforming it. If men sacrificed their complete invulnerability from fiscal responsibility for their extramarital affairs, at least they were protected from classes of women deemed morally suspect and thus likely to bring false suit. Such an acquiescence to gender inequality seemed almost a consequence of the logic of bureaucratic argument.

A more striking example of how morally charged, gender-specific sexual considerations moved bureaucrats almost unconsciously toward an unequal reformulation of rights exists in the vocabulary officials used to discuss an unwed mother's claim against her impregnator. Again, the examples come from critics of paragraph 340. Without reflecting on their words or using them as technical legal terms, officials wrote of "mothers," when they discussed an unwed pregnant woman's right to child support or legal redress, and "wench" (*Dirne*), with its connotation of whore or loose woman, when they discussed the same woman's rightlessness or criminal status. Wielandt (1812) began a memorandum critical of paragraph 340 by discussing the fact that "the mother has a more direct interest [than state or *Ge-*

---

[104] Cf. Brauer's silent acceptance of the principles justifying the prejudicial treatment of women in paragraph 340, principles he had earlier labeled "male egotism," above, p. 377, and Chapter 3, p. 149.

meinde]. . . . Why should she have no right to [the father's financial] contribution?" After a break, he continued: "I had written this down and let it sit a long time while I reflected on the matter. Then I was admittedly convinced that the *Dirne* who agrees to sexual intercourse does an equally bad deed as her partner [*Beischläfer*] and that she has no right recognized by law to demand support for her child from the impregnator [*Stuprator*]." Wielandt found this legal situation intolerable and called in impassioned language for change, but continued throughout the next paragraphs, which emphasized the woman's rightlessness, to refer to her as *Dirne*.[105] Roggenbach's lengthy memorandum of 1811 criticizing paragraph 340 and the current operation of sexual laws in Baden began by putting "*Dirne*" in quotation marks, to underscore its old-fashioned, moralistic ring.[106] He then discussed "the right [*Ansprache*] of the mother for compensation for birthing costs," and continued to use "mother" to describe the woman heroically fighting poverty to feed her child, to plead for her freedom from punishment for fornication, and for "giving to mothers the pursuance of this right [to child support] via civil law and with all civil means." Remarkably, Roggenbach himself then reverted to *Dirne*, without quotation marks, to refer to women of "ruined spirit" or who made money by sex, who then regarded the fornication fine as a "tax," and later he referred to "many a *Dirne* who makes a living from sex and who then accuses one or more innocent persons [*Personen*] as fathers . . . ," and to "shameless *Dirnen*." And he used the term again to underscore the fact that the burden of proof in paternity or child-support suits lay with her: "According to the previous constitution, the *Dirne* in any event had to produce proof." Twice Roggenbach used *Dirne* in a relatively neutral way, but that usage was quite overwhelmed by the use of Dirne in an explicitly negative sense.

The official, printed government ordinances speak the same language as the bureaucrats' internal memorandums. Even the ordinance of 13 February 1813, which explicitly sought to reestablish some semblance of gender equality after paragraph 340 by exempting unwed pregnant women from fornication fines, refers to the women as *Dirnen* in connection with their out-of-wedlock pregnancies, or their temptation to commit infanticide. It reverts to the earlier, neutral language of absolutist rescripts, "pregnant female persons" (*Weibspersonen*), when it discusses their freedom from punishment, or the equality of their treatment (should they not be pregnant) with "male persons" (*Mannspersonen*.)[107]

The two long justice ministry reform drafts of 1818 and 1822 adopted the identical vocabulary. Here we find "ruthless *Dirnen*, who greatly embarrass innocents [men] by their impudent accusations [of paternity]," and who have "been

---

[105] Wielandt memorandum of 30 May 1812, GLA 234/3546. At the beginning of the memo, it is true, Wielandt had referred once to his support for granting the *Dirne* the right to child support. Otherwise, his usage is consistent with the *Mutter/Dirne* split.

[106] Roggenbach, Directorium of the Dreysam-Kreis to Justice Ministry, 14 January 1811, GLA 234/3546.

[107] Ordinance of 16 February 1813, *Regierungsblatt*, 3 March 1813, 29–30.

shown to have had sex with numerous [men]" set off against the "mother, who has an interest in bringing a support suit against the natural father of her child."[108] In the later draft the "*Dirne*, deeply sunken, who impudently calls her [community-donated] child support sum her 'pension,'" the "*Dirne*, who makes a living at it [sex]," the "cheap *Dirne*, who heaps good men with accusation and scandal," is cleanly separated from the "kidnapped or defrauded mother," the "mother [who has] a right to support," the women whose "motherly feelings" move her to sue for support. Indeed, the phrase "the mother's right to sue" becomes almost epithetic.[109] Between the two, the officials introduced a transition category, the "fallen maiden," "the good maiden, who has fallen," the maiden who has a "weak moment," who is, of course, the future mother, but considered at the moment of sexual temptation, not pregnancy.

The moral triage being accomplished here is in sharp contradistinction to absolutist and late reform absolutist usage, which tended to refer to men and women fornicants equally as *Weibspersonen* and *Mannspersonen*. If absolutist officials wanted to make a moral statement, then they set off *Dirne* against "loose boy" (*liederliche Bursche*). That latter phrase, however, is virtually nonexistent in these later documents. When they are not victims of false accusations ("good men," "innocent persons," "married men"), men show up as "impregnator" (*Schwängerer, Stuprator*), "seducer" (*Verführer*), boy (*Bursche*, unmodified), and more often as "person," man, or occasionally even as "citizen" (*Bürger*). Only rarely are they called "father," since that word was taboo under paragraph 340, but was occasionally used to invoke responsibility. The closest to moral opprobrium the officials came was "seducer," which at least carried with it the connotation of clever activity, or "bachelor" (*Hagestolze*), imputing lack of civic responsibility. No term describing the male sexual partner approached the censure of *Dirne*.

By using this terminology, officials shifted the focus of law from "the fate of the innocent child . . . which was the standpoint from which most older and recent legislators viewed the subject,"[110] to the putative moral standing of the woman, measured by the danger she posed to men and her active sexual engagement. For the good mother is portrayed as a victim of men's seduction and a self-sacrificing provider for her children, whereas the *Dirne* is portrayed as a victimizer of men, robbing them of their money and their reputations. This is the axis along which the right to civil suit for child support was to be determined.

Beyond this, however, lies a deeper sexual and gender reconstruction of rights. For the mother did not have a right by virtue of herself or her own condition as a person/citizen or the results of her sexual relation to a man, but only by virtue of her obligation to her child. It was only the woman's dutiful relation to a child, and by extension her obligation to the community to nourish and bring up the child properly, that gave her the right to civil suit. In short, it was her relation to others in

---

[108] Justice Ministry, no. 965, 24 November 1818, GLA 233/27494.
[109] Justice Ministry, no. 962, 8 April 1822, GLA 234/3546.
[110] Hofgericht of the See-Provinz, Meersburg, 11 February 1819, GLA 234/3546.

the form of duty to others that provided rights. The *Dirne*, stripped of her mother-ness and standing in direct relation to the man as sexual partner, had no rights, either to civil suit, or even to being heard in court. No rights accrued to her sexual relation to the man, because she did not owe it to him; their sexual relation was in the nature of a short-term commercial contract that expired upon ejaculation. The state of owing sexual service (in marriage) did bring specific rights to support. Sexual independence, indeed independence of any kind for a woman, was tanta-mount to rightlessness. And sexual independence was the most perfect metaphor for independence in other spheres, as the suggestion to include market women, transients, and unemployed domestic servants in the category of sexually suspect and therefore rightless persons demonstrates. For men, of course, the construction of rights worked differently. Economic independence was silently equated with married status, and therefore with the man's duty to his family, summed up in the phrase "family happiness" (*Familienglück*). Preserving the latter and guaranteeing future economic independence via legitimate inheritance secured for men the pre-sumptive right of sexual privacy and sexual irresponsibility. Thus, family status worked oppositely for men and women in the realm of rights. Furthermore, whereas duty (to family) helped ground men's legal rights to sexual privacy and irresponsibility, that duty was strictly theoretical, insofar as these rights were en-joyed by all men whether propertied or married or not. Finally, the rights men enjoyed by virtue of only theoretical family duties were stronger than the actual "family" obligation (to her child) incurred by the unwed mother.

Morality, Nationalism, and Xenophobia

Our discussion of the property principle has led us from the focus on fatherhood to the expansion of the civil sphere and from there to the peculiar, gendered construc-tion of "privacy" from state investigation of consensual heterosexual acts, behind which operated highly gendered reconceptions of rights structured according to moral assumptions that functioned differently, indeed almost oppositely, for men and women. Still, more was being rearranged and justified by moral percepts strongly rounded in, among other things, sexual considerations, than only civil society, the relations inside it between men and women, and the relations between both and the state. For the new conception of German national identity also received some of its contours from a sexual-moral dichotomy drawn between itself and France. Baden was one of the most pro-French territories in central Europe, but even before Napoléon's defeat, bureaucrats in Baden articulated their sense of being German according to the difference in sexual customs they found separating "Germany" and France. German nationalism found one of its earliest and most vehement expressions, in Baden at least, in the sexual arena.

Even a liberally inclined official like Roggenbach, writing in 1811 at the height of French influence, distanced himself from the moral stance of paragraph 340. "The responsibility to support a being, whom one has caused to exist, lies so grounded in the nature of the thing, coincides so exactly with the philosophical doctrine of justice, that one must be truly astonished at how French law could sanction the substantial departure [from this] that paragraph 340 of the Code Napoléon contains."[111] After detailing French motives as they were revealed in the National Assembly debates, Roggenbach continued:

It may well be that in France, where there are so many big cities, where refinement has risen so far in all areas of activity and ended up in such countless byways, where fraud and swindle appear in so many forms, that paternity suits are more often misused as a business by shameless wenches and their helpers. It may well be that so many disruptions of domestic harmony have thus arisen that the government felt obliged to be watchful. However here [*bei uns*] morality [*die Sitten*] is not yet so generally ruined. We don't even have big cities, those seats of luxurious excess, and here a wench is not so easily inclined to accuse a man with whom she was not in fact intimate.

Roggenbach's tactic combined anthropological observation of cultural and developmental difference with a call to the principles of natural rights that progressive Germans associated with French philosophy. In short, Roggenbach flattered France while he criticized it. Eight years later the justice ministry officials followed virtually the identical path. They branded paragraph 340

against the demands of nature and against the rights of mankind [*Rechte der Menschheit*] which flowed from it [nature]. . . . How the French could come to pass such an unnatural law is hard to understand. Of course one reads a great deal about the great ruination of morality [*Verdorbenheit der Sitten*] which is supposed to reign in France. However, this is limited largely to the capital, and even there to a certain class [*Claße*] of people, who certainly do not deserve on their account to have the laws of humanity [*Gesetze der Humanität*] so degraded.

Such laws could not be justified "before the judgment seat of reason" (*vor dem Richterstuhl der Vernunft*).[112]

Such statements, couched as they were in the language of the philosophes, were mild in comparison to the diatribes offered by other officials. "Only out of love for paradox and prejudice in favor of everything not homegrown [*nicht vaterländisch*] and new can one explain how this law [paragraph 340] was accepted and found defenders in Germany," wrote Klüser of the Hofgericht in Meersburg (1819). He continued, "One can recognize in this law the times and the land in which it originated—one can recognize the goals of the French legislator and his belittlement of all considerations of morality [*Sitten*], and family rights, and family happiness." Paragraph 340 was the product of a "ruined nation" (*verdorbenen Nation*); Klüser found it impossible to imagine "how this law should flourish on German soil, where morality [*Sitten*] is still worth something."[113]

[111] Directorium of the Dreysam-Kreis, Freyburg, 14 January 1811, GLA 234/3546.
[112] Justice Ministry, no. 965, 24 November 1818, GLA 233/27494.
[113] Hofgericht of the See-Provinz, Meersburg, 11 February 1819, GLA 234/3546.

Klüser's opinion, was by far the most widespread, especially after Napoléon's fall. The official who compiled the responses of the bureaucrats to the Justice Ministry's reform draft in 1819 summarized those of the majority who opposed paragraph 340 as follows: "This law does not fit at all the character of the German people. Practically every respondent agreed with this viewpoint." He then cited typical remarks, such as "'our morality [*Sitten*] is still much better than the French,'" or "'paragraph 340 is French in origin and purpose, and therefore dishonoring [*schmachvoll*] and unfitting for Germany [*Teutschland*]'" and "'this law is harmful to religion, morality [*Moral*], good customs [*den guten Sitten*], and social bonds.'"[114]

It is a commonplace that early German nationalism formed in opposition to France and French values, which historians mostly sum up as progressive and forward-looking.[115] Less widely understood is the importance of morality as an organizing principle for nationalism, or the complex valences it contained. The case of Baden makes clear, on the one hand, that opposition to French law crystallized around the real fiscal and social havoc it caused and, most tellingly, around issues where French law deviated most spectacularly from the principles of natural law, state and social responsibility, and above all reform common to many, if not most, middle-, and upper-level German bureaucrats. Opposition to Napoléon was therefore not uniformly emotion-laden. Furthermore, it was not simply the product of the overheated imaginations of unworldly scribblers; it arose also in response to real problems and survived because it proved useful to bureaucrats as they interpreted the new situations they faced.

On the other hand, it is true that professions of moral and sexual superiority helped cement an idea of "us" against "them," much as the *Bürgertum* had used sexual morality to define and elevate itself above the nobility. The gender discrimination in paragraph 340, which seemed to encourage men to sexual irresponsibility, suited it for use as an epitome of the negative possibilities of the new age and therefore as a rallying point for nascent conservative politics. In the citations above one can already discern the constellation of conservative values typical, of the *Vormärz*. "Germany's" relative backwardness is prized as a virtue: its morality "is not *yet* ruined," its moral customs "*still* count for something," its morality "is *still* much better than the French." The future was a world of big cities, widespread fraud, immoral women, threatened families, impiety, dissolved social bonds. None of these conditions *yet* obtained in Germany and the duty of government was to prevent their occurring. By describing what French government did not do, Klüser clarified the proper role of German government(s): "Whether children have parents, or parents have children, whether marriages or immoral bach-

---

[114] "Akten-Auszug," 20 March 1822, GLA 234/3546. See also Evangelical Section of the Ministry of Interior, Karlsruhe, 6 July 1818, GLA 236/8479, which sums up the opinions of various diocese, synods, and so on, from 1816 to 1817, which all agree that paragraph 340 should be made "more fitting to the character of the land and people."

[115] Wehler, *Deutsche Gesellschaftsgeschichte*, 1:521–25.

elordom are encouraged or hindered, whether domestic order, family rights, and honor are protected—this was not a concern of government in those times."[116] This is not a call to return to the police system of absolutism, though it preserves some of the communitarian sentiments peculiar to it. The focus on sexual conduct, bachelors, families, and honor is new; the morality Klüser peddles is not the externally imposed Christian piety of a subsistence society, but a more dynamic and all-inclusive agreement among citizens to hold society together through ties of mutual obligation. It is a blueprint for an alternative, new society based on "natural" ties made social, hence the emphasis on sexual-procreative bonds within marriage, rather than on social ties declared natural, as the paternity sections of the Code Napoléon prescribed. Nonetheless, this understanding of society and government gave the latter a mandate for (re)interference in the lives of its citizens after a fashion that reform absolutism and state-based early liberalism had begun to abandon.

The Bureaucrats' Changing Views on the Public Relevance of Sexual Behavior

The basic framework within which bureaucrats in the Napoleonic period viewed sexual behavior remained what it had been in the eighteenth century: consensual, heterosexual, procreative sex. This was still the source of the fiscal and social problems they faced. But the role of the state in regulating this had become much more difficult and confusing. On the one hand, presistent, yet somewhat less insistent, fears of infanticide had been joined by anger at the unfairness to women caused by paragraph 340 to underscore calls for complete freedom from penalty for pregnant women. Virtually no one recommended resuming punishment for pregnant women.[117] On the other hand, anger at the newly created ability of men to escape economic responsibility encouraged officials to hang onto fornication fines for men, as the last weapon one could use against them. These unintended consequences of paragraph 340 probably explain the results of the poll conducted in 1819–1820 by the Ministry of State in Baden in which three proponents of paragraph 340 favored decriminalizing fornication altogether and none spoke out strongly for keeping penalties, but only two opponents of paragraph 340 favored abolishing these penalties and seven explicitly called for retaining them. These last justified continued state regulation on moral grounds, for example: "According to our religion fornication is a vice [Laster], our state must protect religion, therefore vice must be punished"; "the rural people don't think fornication is a sin [Sünde] any more."[118] We are probably not wrong in reading the moral grounds as cover for financial worries, since these seven bureaucrats came from areas with fairly high

[116] Hofgericht of the See-Provinz, Meersburg, 11 February 1819, GLA 234/3546.
[117] Except occasionally for third- or fourth-time fornicants. The Justice Ministry rejected this suggestion, fearing infanticide. Justice Ministry, no. 962, 8 April 1822, GLA 234/3546.
[118] See the discussion on pp. 381–82. "Akten-Auszug," 20 March 1822, GLA 234/3546.

illegitimacy rates. The growing number of illegitimate births in Baden (and else-where) was obviously another damper on the earlier trend toward decriminalizing fornication.

The upshot of these criss-crossing tendencies were mixed opinions on state regulation via criminal law. One can discover bureaucrats citing Feuerbach for decriminalization: "Fornication should not be punished at all, since it is merely a sin, but does not harm legal rights [of third parties]" (*keine Rechts-Verletzung*), alongside others who adduced religious and social reasons to intervene.[119] The alleged prevalence of fornication was variously interpreted to support retention or decriminalization.[120] If there is a pattern, it is that central state bureaucrats, for example in the Justice Ministry and the Ministry of State, were more favorably inclined toward decriminalization or lessened criminalization than were their colleagues at the local level. Their lenient inclinations were checked by the growing resort to moral arguments to reform paragraph 340 and by extension to interpret sexual-social conditions, which worked against decriminalization and for state intervention. This is one reason that officials favoring paragraph 340, which contravened moral-communitarian assumptions, were more comfortable with dropping fornication penalties altogether than were others.

The bureaucratic argument over paragraph 340 revealed a number of slow changes in official attitudes toward sexual behavior. Foremost among these was the gradual weakening of the late Enlightenment topoi of the overwhelming, natural sex drive, equal in men and women, that demanded satisfaction; the scenario depicting the seduction of the less experienced woman by the more experienced man and the sequential unfolding of female emotions from love (leading to first-time sex), to shock and confusion (at abandonment by her lover), shame and fear of social and parental disapproval (at her pregnancy), and desperation (in reclaiming her honor via infanticide). This constellation survived in the Napoleonic period primarily because of its usefulness to bureaucrats trying to explain rural sexual practices and the harm done by paragraph 340. Officials interested in placing sexual behavior in a social, legal, and economic nexus invariably used eighteenth-century categories for their analysis. In 1812 Roggenbach, director of the Dreysam province with its seat in Freiburg, explained the higher illegitimacy rates of the Black Forest as the result of nonpartible inheritance, which meant that all the younger siblings, having no inheritance, were too poor to marry.

> Just because fortune has closed the entrance to marriage does not mean that nature retracts its rights; it [nature] affects the sex drive of these unfortunates in the same way as it does that of the more fortunate [inheriting] brother, even if only the latter can satisfy it legally. The same conditions obtain for the daughters. . . . Is it a wonder, when this large number of unmarried, healthy, strong natural people [*Naturmenschen*] frequently suc-

---

[119] Ibid. Fornication cases fell to the *Amt*, operating as the court of lowest jurisdiction.

[120] Ibid. for retention; Justice Ministry, 11 October 1812, GLA 236/8479, for timid suggestion to lighten the burden on *Ämter* by dropping fornication from the crime books.

cumb in the battle between human law and natural desire [*zwischen Menschengesetz und Naturtrieb*], and, inexperienced in the finer arts of immorality, indulge it such that it betrays the forbidden pleasure [that is, without birth control, ending in visible pregnancy]?[121]

Roggenbach went on to recite the infanticide litany and, finally, to plead for social, but not criminal intervention against unwed pregnant women. In a previous memo, he had made clear how very widespread he thought fornication was, how seldom it was discovered, and how inadequate a tool the law was to handle such matters.[122]

Even a bureaucrat given to moralistic hyperbole, like Klüser, reverted to eighteenth-century topoi when he explained the social circumstances militating against a law like paragraph 340, which was a disaster "in times, when conscience is a weak restraint against the eruption of the passionate sex drive, when luxury and public debt increase the difficulties of getting married. . . . In times when a long war and the mixing together with a ruined and loose people [the French!] have undermined also among the common people moral custom together with discipline, shame, and a feeling of honor and honesty."[123] Klüser accepted the fact of a "natural sex drive," which, together with the economic and moral conse-quences of the war now combined with paragraph 340 which "increased the artistry and means of seduction, and the girl [*Mädchen*], usually the weaker party, will be brought to her fall." Given this foundation, it is no surprise that Klüser also subscribed to the infanticide script, nor that he, like Roggenbach, was predisposed toward easing or even abolishing fornication penalties for men and women.

But Roggenbach's and Klüser's position was becoming marginalized. The "natu-ral sex drive," a ubiquitous feature of late eighteenth-century government discus-sions of sex-crime law, is notably absent in the 1800s and 1810s. It was no longer the beginning of the story bureaucrats told, because the new narrative did not demand it. The old narrative had begun with a natural, unalterable, human characteristic (sex drive) that artificial, positive law could either handle well, by encouraging its expression in socially useful ways (via marriage), or badly (by discouraging mar-riage, or, worse, by encouraging infanticide). The new narrative did not begin with "nature," but with social arrangements, namely with property and its ordered transmission via inheritance. "Natural" exigencies, insofar as it admitted of them, were irrelevant. Furthermore, the viewpoint of government itself had shifted. In the late eighteenth century, pursuing *Gemeinwohl* had been interpreted by bu-reaucrats to mean protecting the unwed mother and her child; they were the weakest link in the social chain. After the Napoleonic rearrangement, the law mandated protecting the male, his sexual privacy and his ability to carry on a domestic life, or to begin one if he were not already married, and to dispose of his property within marriage, not to illegitimate children. The male had become the weakest link in the social chain. Ironically, the recurrent fear that men would not

---

[121] Roggenbach, Directorium of the Dreysam-Kreis, Freyburg, 14 October 1812, GLA 236/8479.
[122] Roggenbach, Directorium of the Dreysam-Kreis, Freyburg, 14 January 1811, GLA 234/3546.
[123] Hofgericht of the See-Provinz, Meersburg, 11 February 1819, GLA 234/3546.

marry and thus would selfishly remain outside the social network, expresses the weak-link perception in another, almost opposite, way.[124]

This shift in perspective is clear in the transformation of the "mother" into the *Dirne*. Where late-eighteenth-century bureaucrats saw a mother, a victim of seduction and betrayal, Napoleonic bureaucrats increasingly suspected a *Dirne*, a victimizer of innocent men. Sexual power in the eighteenth century had been wielded by the male seducer. Now, "one cannot any longer assume, that the *woman* has been seduced";[125] "the older laws assume that the woman has always been seduced, but this is now doubtless never [*niemals*] claimed."[126] The man had become the victim: "It is *the mother's* fault that the child has no certain father. . . . No man can have a child thrust upon him which is not certainly his own."[127] The wielder of sexual power, the sexual criminal, had become the woman. As in the eighteenth-century model, where the victim had received legal protection, legal rights, so in the nineteenth, only now this protection and these rights accrued to the new victim, the man, not the woman.

According to the new narrative, the woman's motive for engaging in illicit sexual activity was no longer "natural sex drive" (the mechanistic view), or love (the romantic, psychological view), but gain (the commercial view). It is hardly surprising that a new model based on property and on reversing the pattern of victim/ victimizer should have encouraged the specter of the prostitute, for the prostitute was a sexual/economic entrepreneur. The repeated fear that the *Dirne* used procreative sex as a "trade" (*Gewerbe*) or "source of income" (*Erwerbsmittel*), the use of *Dirne* interchangeably with "whore,"[128] and the suggestion to presume that women engaged in petty trade were sexually unreliable and therefore not permitted to bring civil suits, all demonstrate how strongly the property/commerce principle had penetrated bureaucrats' thinking on sexual relations. Whereas late-eighteenth-century bureaucrats had gone out of their way to interpret *Hure* widely, so as to include the "fallen (honest) maiden" in its possibilities,[129] early nineteenth-century bureaucrats tended to push *Dirne* in the opposite direction, so its negative sexual connotations obliterated its innocent usage.[130] This ineluctable slippage toward the presumption of prostitution caused Klüser, who himself used *Dirne* in this way, to

---

[124] Cf. Chapter 4, pp. 183–85, and Chapter 7, pp. 286–88.

[125] "Akten-Auszug," 20 March 1822, GLA 234/3546, emphasis in the original.

[126] Justice Ministry, no. 962, 8 April 1822, GLA 234/3546.

[127] "Akten-Auszug," 20 March 1822, citing Schachleiter, and for the second sentence Reichard and Wolff. GLA 234/3546. Emphasis in original.

[128] Justice Ministry, no. 965, 24 November 1818, GLA 233/27494.

[129] See Chapter 3, pp. 116–19.

[130] Although *Dirne* could mean a sexually loose woman, the innocent meaning "maiden" predominated in earlier usage. In the eighteenth century, northern German vernacular retained the innocent meaning, but educated, high German began to emphasize its negative connotation, though usually by adding an adjective like "loose" or "shameless." Cf. S.J.E. Stosch, *Versuch in richtiger Bestimmung einiger gleichbedeutender Wörter der deutschen Sprache*, 2d part (Berlin, 1780), 325–27; Grimm, *Deutsches Wörterbuch*, vol. 4, part 2 (Leipzig, 1877), 1185–88; and Johann Chr. Aug. Heyse, *Handwörterbuch der deutschen Sprache mit Hinsicht auf Rechtschreibung, Abstammung und Bildung . . .* , 2 vols. in 3 (Magdeburg, 1833–49), part 1, 263.

warn his overzealous colleagues that they must not misinterpret the customary exchange of gifts between rural lovers as "payment" in the commercial sense.[131]

Klüser's admonition reminds us that the bureaucrats' new mental categories fit theoretical civil society, or slivers of actual educated society, much better than they did the actual living conditions or sexual relations of most Germans. Although eighteenth-century bureaucrats projected psychological motives onto the subjects they administered and probably misunderstood much of what they saw of these subjects, they still seem to have been closer to social reality, or at least more flexible in interpretion, than the post-Napoleonic bureaucracy was. The anthropological impetus to interpret sexual behavior in a broad socioeconomic, customary, and legal nexus seems to have been largely displaced by apodictic judgments about fallen morality and ruined morals. If individual or collective (class) moral failure were the main cause of sexual disorder, then it was not necessary to inquire further. The Napoleonic period marks a turn in this direction, though hardly the full development of it.

Finally, the dogmatic split of fatherhood from motherhood encouraged by paragraph 340 further removed the sexual act from its social moorings and even fragmented it in its own terms. Fatherhood (paternity) became completely social, not sexual at all, since it was marriage, not coitus, that created the condition of being a father. This principle drove one exasperated bureaucrat to exclaim, "If conception did not occur after each act of coitus, still conception *had* to have occurred after some act of coitus."[132] Fatherhood as a social, not sexual fact effectively split male sexual experience from procreation and rang the death knell, from the male point of view, to centuries of religious and cultural effort to equate the two.[133] The emphasis on social fatherhood also had the curious effect of erasing mention of male sexual activity. This, too, was an effect of the "privacy" accorded to their sexual experiences. Silence, in turn, backhandedly encouraged the double standard, whereby women's sexual activity was marked as immoral and men's went simply unremarked, or at most became a "forgetting."[134] In the sexual realm men's and women's experiences moved farther apart, followed different trajectories, had different meanings and consequences, at least as they were interpreted in government circles. And moral opprobrium, which eighteenth-century bureaucrats had striven to minimize in relation to consensual sexual acts, now reappeared in language and interpretation and cleaved disproportionately to women.

The dwindling curiosity about the "natural sex drive," the waning of interest in the socioeconomic nexus in which sexual activity took place, the transformation of men from seducers to victims, the countertransformation of women from victims to

---

[131] Hofgericht of the See-Provinz, Meersburg, 11 February 1819, GLA 234/3546.

[132] Bordollo in "Akten-Auszug," 3 March 1822, GLA 234/3546.

[133] This step also inadvertently helped set the groundwork for the coming nineteenth-century obsession with nonprocreative male sexual expression, especially male homosexuality.

[134] As in the phrase "the husband, who has forgotten himself once." Justice Ministry, no. 962, 8 April 1822, GLA 234/3546.

threats, the construal of nonmarital female sexuality in terms of commerce (prostitution), the reappearance of a moral explanatory framework for popular sexual activity, the redefinition of fatherhood as a social but not a sexual phenomenon, and the bestowal of silence on men and of moral judgment on women in matters sexual are major changes in outlook to have occurred in such a short time. They had been long prepared for, but crystallized only when civil society had replaced government as the fount of public values. Only the tremendous upheavals in state and social organization could have produced, permitted, and demanded such conceptual somersaults.

I I

The Sexual Foundations of the Nineteenth Century

The reforms of the Napoleonic period inaugurated the principles of the new age, but they did not develop them. That was for the nineteenth century to do. Although few reformed German states ceded much overt political ground to civil society, they yielded their previous moral monopoly almost entirely. Absolutist states had claimed the theoretical duty to police their subjects' sexual behavior by virtue of authority derived from God; thus they claimed to base law on universal, Christian principles. Enlightened critics revised this system in two ways. First, they argued that the authority for moral policing must shift from state to civil society. The clearest proponent of this position was Anselm Feuerbach, who denied the state any right, much less obligation, to "force" good behavior on its "citizens"; that task must be voluntary and thus rested with civil society alone. Feuerbach therefore enjoined on state authority a position of moral agnosticism. Although this first Enlightened criticism removed the state from the business of sexual-moral regulation, a second critique prepared the way for a new brand of moral politics in which the state played an important, but subsidiary role. For critics less stringently philosophical than Feuerbach, it was primarily the justification for moral law that had shifted: the purpose was no longer to realize universal (religious) ethics, but to achieve salutary, practical social effects. Furthermore, the "society" in question was not the extant society of orders (*Ständegesellschaft*), which Enlighteners sought to reform, but its successor, civil society. The reformed, nineteenth-century states emerging from this Enlightened critique therefore conceived of criminal and civil law as derived from principles upholding civil society (such as private property and "normal" heterosexual relations, for example). These civil-social principles might indeed be moral, not in the sense of universally ethical, but in the sense of *sittlich*, customarily desirable. If the purpose of the state was to guarantee civil society, then it was appropriate for state law to contain moral injunctions helpful to it. None of the reformed, nineteenth–century states therefore dared follow Feuerbach's model of state moral agnosticism.

In a way, this second Enlightened criticism had attacked a straw man, for we know that absolutist claims to uphold universal moral standards were false; in fact, both the content of the repeated moral edicts and state enforcement practices

407

largely reflected the concrete interests of the established and successful members of traditional society (male heads of household, guilds, those enjoying citizen rights in the village, and so on). Nonetheless, the successful Enlightened critique was enormously important. For one thing, the content of moral legislation now increasingly reflected not the actual needs of a *Ständegesellschaft* that largely still existed, but the anticipated needs of civil society, which ran on very different principles. More important, by renouncing moral stewardship, however theoretical, the modern states explicitly recognized civil society as the defining force, the moral arbiter, in their mutual relationship. Reformers had transformed the state from moral monopolist to guarantor of the moral principles acknowledged as emanating from and necessary for the maintenance and reproduction of civil society. This was one of the biggest shifts occasioned by the change in the public sphere itself.

But a second change in the states' interest in sexual behavior, together with a continuity in administrative practice, worked against the complete triumph of civil-social moral policy. Whereas absolutist mandates had conceived of sexual-moral transgressions as harms to duties, the reformed states tended to see harms to rights: thus, for example, they decriminalized many consensual sexual acts and defended the right of illegitimate children to sustenance from the father. This tendency to think in terms of rights was not fully developed theoretically, but it is intermittently visible in administrative practice. Much better developed was the old bureaucratic habit of regarding the objects of administration as interchangeable units. This attitude had tended to produce fairly evenhanded treatment of men and women, and, in a framework of rights, it encouraged a tendency toward equal rights. Together, these two administrative inclinations ran against the moral politics emanating from civil society, first, by tending to restrict the scope of moral legislation to offenses harmful to rights, and second, by contradicting the programmatic gender bias promoted ever more strongly by nineteenth-century spokesmen of civil society. It is likely that as the nineteenth century wore on, state administration became less effective against the moral pull of civil society, but one cannot understand the vectors of nineteenth-century moral policy without recognizing that the active agent was civil society, not state administration.

If we turn, then, to civil society's interest in sexual behavior, we must confront the double discrepancy in definition: first, between civil society as an incomplete but adequate description of the actual lives of its practitioners (especially the *Bildungsbürger*) and civil society as the future project encompassing ever larger strata of active citizens; and, second, between civil society, in either of these senses, and the actual practices of the families, strata, and *Stände* that made up "society" in the social-historical sense at the turn of the nineteenth century. There were, of course, enormous continuities in the latter. The calculations of families and individuals about marriage, honor, economic well-being, and so on changed slowly in ways accessible only to micro-historians.[1] The calculations of the community (*Gemeinde*)

---

[1] David Sabean has found an increasing tendency toward endogamy in the marital practices of wider

are easier to see; these remained in the first half of the nineteenth century almost identical to the nervous, restrictive policies of bygone absolutism. Overpopulation, economic instability, and streams of vagabonds reinforced the old subsistence fears of local worthies and kept their eyes glued to extramarital, especially premarital, procreative sexual (mis)behavior.

Meanwhile, the practitioners of civil society who spoke on behalf of its realization, however, had reoriented the gaze of the new public from the old regulatory concerns. The new order retained the familiar axes of judgment which ran along heterosexual, marital, procreative, and gender-differentiated lines but changed their emphasis and contextual meaning. The traditional assumption that most sexual behavior was heterosexual, and that legitimate sexual behavior should occur solely within marriage, had now become a positive injunction for all citizens to be (hetero)sexually active and to marry. Early moderns had restricted legitimate sexual expression to those who could demonstrate economic self-sufficiency; hence, legitimate sexual activity had marked a man's accession to economic independence through land inheritance or guild mastership, for example, and potentially to active citizen's rights in the community, and it had marked a woman's emancipation from her family and the assumption of rule over her new household. The coincidence in traditional society of legitimate sexual expression with independence and emancipation meant that civil society (which its eighteenth-century practitioners assumed would one day include almost all males as independent, emancipated, active citizens) considered sexual expression virtually a male right.[2] Sexual self-determination thus expanded to apply to more males exactly as, and because, self-determination generally had expanded. Only those unfortunates deemed incapable of participating in civil society would remain sexually non-self-determining: the celibate and those stigmatized as either sexually criminal or sexually subordinate (women). Harnessing this newly released (sexual) energy, as the practitioners thought of it, for social order required making marriage a universal institution, widely accessible and also buttressed legally as a fundamental *Rechtsgut*.

Whereas civil society's elision of sexual maturity with citizenship promoted both the assumption of universal heterosexual orientation and the institution of marriage, it diminished the previous concentration on procreation. This may seem paradoxical, given how strongly communities from 1820 to 1848 fixated on solving the bastardy problem as they actually created it via marriage restrictions. But that fixation was the product of the convergence of two quite different vectors: the continuity of the narrow, absolutist horizon in the communities, noted above, and the shrinking of the universalist project of civil society to fit the reduced, chastened

---

and wider social circles in Germany from the eighteenth century onward. What effects, if any, such developments had on sexual behavior remain to be demonstrated. David Sabean, *Kinship in Neckarhausen* (forthcoming).

[2] On the inclusive-emancipatory quality of late-eighteenth-century German conception of civil society, see Niethammer, "Bürgerliche Gesellschaft als Projekt," and Gall, "Liberalismus und 'bürgerliche Gesellschaft.'"

politics and self-centered interests of well-off bourgeois. For after the reform period, from 1815 to 1848, economic disruption, social dislocation, and the sociological shift in the carriers and spokesmen of civil society from *Bildungsbürger* to property owners meant that the late-eighteenth-century project of increasingly inclusionary reform had given way to the meaner goal of upholding the status quo. The meaning of "civil society" had changed. The poor were considered less and less fit to participate in it. The bourgeois underscored the marginality of the poor by relegating them to illegitimate sexual expression and upheld the virtues of (bourgeois) marriage in a negative way by discriminating against illegitimate children. These later developments, however, should not blind us to the fact that, at the end of the eighteenth century, the absolutist identification of the public interest with regulated procreation had significantly paled. Economic optimism (soon dashed by Napoléon) encouraged the practitioners of civil society to believe that illegitimate children could easily be transformed into productive members of society. Further, the interest in sexual energy per se meant that the "goal" of sexual expression seemed more internal, directed more to the development of one's own body and character and less toward reproduction. This reorientation opened the path for new ruminations on the public and private significance of nonprocreative sexual acts. Although the eighteenth century barely engaged in such rumination, it had created the framework that made such speculation possible.

The most fascinating reorientation concerned gender. Here, the practitioners of civil society took the gendered sexual assumptions of traditional society, detached them from their social context, developed and reified them, and then used them to define the essence of males and females in civil society. Whereas early moderns were in awe of women's putative sexual *capacity,* they nonetheless identified males with sexual *energy* and *desire*—hence the assumption that young males more often seduced innocent maidens than vice versa; hence the strongly gender-specific traditional views of sexual honor: fidelity for women versus sexual potency for men. The strong social embeddedness of sexual behavior kept these differentials in check in early modern practice. But the practitioners of civil society were out to change the world, so to speak, and at least conceptually, they released the foundation of their new society, the male individual, from his social "fetters" and reconceived him according to dynamics they understood as "natural." Not surprisingly, they built upon the traditional sexual associations, and their creation became the sexually potent, desiring, self-determining individual fit for active citizenship. With women, the practitioners' thought process was reversed. Her they put in social fetters. Her they reconceived according to dynamics they understood as social and relational. Her they considered only as wife and mother, that is, as defined from the standpoints of the husband and of civil society's reproduction. Her derivative social status was mirrored in her derivative sexual nature: not independent, emancipated, or a citizen, she could not be sexually self-determining, she could not "posit" her own desire, will it, and act upon it (in Fichte's phrase). The resulting schematic dichotomy of male-active/female-passive is familiar to any observer of the nineteenth century. The ideological expression of this dichotomy as male/public versus female/private reversed its actual intellectual foundation, however. Men's autonomy (and therefore fitness for the new public of civil society) rested upon their presocial, private individuality, reckoned independently of society, whereas women's dependence derived precisely from the social, "public" reckoning used to define their "nature." From the standpoint of determination, men were private, women, public.

The institutional location of this intellectual dichotomy was the family, which reformed civil law constituted as the sphere of male domination over women, beyond the purview of state intervention. The family mediated the contradictions of the new split between public and private. Its privacy, which consisted in being beyond public scrutiny, was publicly guaranteed (upheld by state law). Inside that sphere of privacy, the state, by refusing to extend there the equal protection of law, created more complete male domination than had been true under late Enlightened absolutism. This negative act of creation, undertaken to achieve the conditions necessary for civil society, emancipated the man (husband) from subjection (to his father and to state scrutiny) at the same moment that it made him the subjugator of his wife. Her unfreedom created his freedom; his position as private dominator qualified him to participate in the wider, public sphere of equals, in civil society. The key relation that qualified a citizen was therefore a sexual relation of domination, for, let us repeat, the family was the product of a publicly defined and privately consummated *sexual* relation.[3] The civic and the sexual mutually constituted each other.

This book has examined civil society at the moment of its legal crystallization in the German states. Almost immediately thereafter, great social, economic, and political shock waves rippled across the new creation, making the axes of wealth, class, and even religion and politics seem far more fundamental to its constitution than sexual or gender considerations. Appearances deceived. The sexual and gender definitions that founded civil society remained archetypal, surviving revolution (1848), unification (1871), and capitalist development largely untouched and unquestioned. To the end of the nineteenth century and beyond they continued to permeate official and unofficial institutions and ideologies (liberal, conservative, even socialist and national-socialist), as well as the everyday expectations of the people who inhabited the new order.

[3] As Carole Pateman has argued in *The Sexual Contract* (Stanford, 1988).

Bibliography

Unpublished Primary Sources

Badisches Generallandesarchiv Karlsruhe (GLA)

Abteilung 61: Protokolle
  61/1806: Minutes of the *Geheimer Rath*, April-May 1799
  61/1807: Minutes of the *Geheimer Rath*, May-June 1799
  61/3322: Minutes of the *Hofrath*, March-April, 1799
  61/3323: Minutes of the *Hofrath*, April-May, 1799
Abteilung 74: Akten Baden Generalia
  74/3457: Marriage regulations (1678–1702)
  74/3460: Marriage regulations (1678)
  74/3902: Infanticide (1779–81)
  74/3903: Infanticide (1781)
  74/3919: Fornication and adultery (1613–1801)
  74/3920: Fornication and adultery (1613–1802)
  74/3921: Fornication and adultery (1624)
  74/3923: Fornication and hiding pregnancy (1713–68)
  74/3924: Premature coitus (1714, 1784)
  74/3925: Fornication, adultery, and curfew violations (1716–48)
  74/3926: Fornication of single women and soldiers (1721–1806)
  74/3929: Fornication and pregnancy (1749, 1766)
  74/3931: Incest (1768)
  74/3932: Fornication, adultery, and premature coitus (1773, 1804)
  74/4521: Mixed-sex sleeping quarters (1743)
  74/6354: Profligate householders and idleness (1682)
  74/6361: *Sittenpolizei* (1712–45)
Abteilung 77: Akten Pfalz Generalia
  77/415: Legitimizing out-of-wedlock children
  77/4631a: Prof. Dr. Franz Mai (1798–1801)
  77/4677: Recording out-of-wedlock fathers' names (1783)
  77/5075: Trysting spots, cursing, drinking, and so on (1592–1678)
  77/6491: Infanticide (1726–1802)
Abteilung 233: Staatsministerium
  233/27494: Paternity suits (1818–56)
  233/30794: Marriage regulations (1807–68)
Abteilung 234: Justizministerium
  234/602: Eighth Organizational Edict: Crimes of the flesh (1803–34)

234/3546: Paternity suits (1808–1933)
234/7580: Reform of the criminal code (1813–46)
Abteilung 236: Innenministerium
  236/2207: Punishment of *liederliche* persons (1813)
  236/3155–57: Ordinances on local disciplinary courts (*Vogt-*, *Rug-*, and *Freuelgerichte*)
    (1758–1851)
  236/8479: Fornication (1809–56)
Abteilung 313: Kreis regierungen
  313/2793: Local disciplinary courts (*Rug-* and *Vogtgerichte*) (1773–1808)

Bayerisches Hauptstaatsarchiv München (Bay HStA)

General-Registratur (GR)
  Faszikel 321, Nr. 7: Fornication (1629–1725)
  Fasz. 322, Nr. 8: Fornication (1726–1808)
  Fasz. 969, Nr. 35: Reform of the criminal code (1800–1802)
  Fasz. 969, Nr. 36: Discussion of Kleinschrod's penal draft (1800–1803)
  Fasz. 1187, Nr. 55: Marriage restrictions (1590–1773)
  Fasz. 1187, Nr. 58: Infanticide (1493–1806)
Repertorium Innenministerium (MInn)
  Nrs. 15244–15254: Local police reports (1809–22)
  Nr. 31385: Stichaner's draft penal code (1813)
  Nr. 52132: Citizenship rights and marriage (1822–26)
  Nr. 54148: Penal code revision (1820–32)
  Nr. 72654: *Konkubinat* (1811–82)

Published Primary Sources

Allgemeines Landrecht für die Preussischen Staaten. Berlin, 1804.
Anon. "Anzeige der Geburts- und Todten-Listen aus verschiedenen Orten von Franken. Vom Jahr 1760." *Fränkischen Sammlungen von Anmerkungen aus der Naturlehre, Arzneygelahrheit, Oekonomie und den damit verwandten Wissenschaften* (1761): 176–91.
Anon. "Auch ein Wort über Priesterehe und Cölibat." *Deutsche Monatsschrift* 1 (1792): 78–90.
Anon. "Betrachtungen über das menschliche Leben, dessen Zweck und Werth." *Hannoversches Magazin* 19 (1781): cols. 1671–78.
Anon. "Dinge, die gesucht werden." *Almanach für Ärzte und Nichtärzte* (1796): 79–95.
Anon. "Eheglück." *Schlesische Provinzial-Blätter* 11 (1790): 519–50.
Anon. "Ehelosigkeit der Geistlichen." *Almanach für Ärzte und Nichtärzte* (1793): 242–54.
Anon. "Etwas über Onanie. Zur endlichen Beruhigung der Pädagogen." *Almanach für Ärzte und Nichtärzte* (1790): 158–63.
Anon. "Etwas zur Erziehung der Mägden." *Hannoversches Magazin* 1 (1763): cols. 609–16.
Anon. "Fragmente aus dem Tagebuch des verstorbenen R***." *Magazin zur Erfahrungsseelenkunde* 4 (1785): 33–42; 5 (1787): 65–69.
Anon. "Galanterien mit dem medicinischen Fernglase betrachtet." *Almanach für Ärzte und Nichtärzte* (1783): 195–204.
Anon. "Gedanken über den Ehestand." *Journal aller Journale* 11:2 (1788): 100–103.

❧ Bibliography ❧

Anon. "Ist wohl nur die erzwungene Befriedigung des Geschlechtstriebes als Unzucht und widernatürlich zu betrachten?" *Deutsches Magazin* 16 (1798): 459–76.

Anon. "Lob der Einbildungskraft." *Hamburg und Altona* 1.3 (1801): 268–72.

Anon. "Milet. An den Herrn Verfasser der Abhandlung über die heimlichen Sünde der Jugend." *Hyperboreïsche Briefe* 3 (1788): 201–7.

Anon. "Nachrichten von einer seltsamen Irrung eines menschlichen Triebes." *Beiträge zur Beruhigung und Aufklärung* 1 (1789): 327–49.

Anon. "Ob ein Weiser heyrathen müsse." *Hannoverische Gelehrter Anzeiger* 3 (1753): cols. 499–504.

Anon. "Onanie." *Almanach für Ärzte und Nichtärzte* (1785): 239–50.

Anon. "Rettung unschuldiger Kinder weiblichen Geschlechts von fälschlich beschuldigter Selbstbefleckung gegen den Herrn Leibarzt Zimmermann." *Baldingers Neues Magazin für Aerzte* 1 (1779): 52–60.

Anon. Review of anon. ["Schl"], *Ueber Kinderunzucht und Selbstbefleckung* (1787). *Braunschweigisches Journal* 2 (1788): 95–101.

Anon. Review of C. S. von Zigesar, *Winke . . .* (Stuttgart, 1796). *Beiträge zur Beruhigung und Aufklärung* 5 (1797): 243–45.

Anon. Review of Ernst Brandes, *Ueber die Weiber. Allgemeine Deutsche Bibliothek* 101.1 (1791): 133–36.

Anon. Review of J. F. Oest, "Für Eltern, Erzieher und Jugendfreunde . . . " (1787). *Allgemeine Deutsche Bibliothek* 82.2 (1788): 571–75.

Anon. Review of Johann Daniel Hensel, *System der weiblichen Erziehung, besonders für den mittlern und höhern Stand,* part 1 (Halle, 1787). *Allgemeine Deutsche Bibliothek* 79.2 (1788): 560–63.

Anon. Review of Karl Gottfried Bauer, *Über die Mittel dem Geschlechtstriebe eine unschädliche Richtung zu geben. . . . Beiträge zur Beruhigung und Aufklärung* 3 (1792): 518–25.

Anon. Review of Theodor Gottlieb Hippel, *Ueber die Ehe. Hannoversches Magazin* 15 (1777): cols. 695–702.

Anon. Review of *Ueber die Ehe* (1796). *Beiträge zur Beruhigung und Aufklärung* 5.2 (1797): 231–35.

Anon. Review of Wolke, *An die von ihm geliebten Kinder, welche gern Rath und Warnung annehmen, um gesund und glücklich zu bleiben. Allgemeine Deutsche Bibliothek* 95.1 (1789): 268.

Anon. "Sachen, welche gesucht werden." *Almanach für Ärzte und Nichtärzte* (1791): 77–94.

Anon. "Soll man ihnen Weiber geben? Eine Antwort aus der Erfahrung." *Chronologen* 8 (1780): 195–206.

Anon. "Ueber die politische Räthlichkeit des geistlichen Zölibats." *Teutscher Merkur* 1 (1783): 240–47.

Anon. "Die vernünftige Frau (Eine wahre Geschichte, aus dem Englischen)." *Neueste Mannigfaltigkeiten* 2.1 (1779): 289–301.

Anon. "Vorbereitung zu den künftigen Preisschriften über den Cölibat." *Neuer Teutscher Merkur,* (Oct. 1791): 149–72.

Anon. "Was ist weibliche Onanie? Eine Frage der Menschheit wichtig." *Almanach für Ärzte und Nichtärzte* (1782): 262–72.

Anon. *Wie die großen und kleinern Schul- und Erziehungsanstalten gegen das Laster der Selbstbefleckung am ersten gesichert, und wie die davon angesteckten Zöglinge gerettet und vor den Folgen desselben bewahret werden können?.* Halle, 1791.

Anon. ["Dk"]. Review of *Zeichen und Werth des verletzten und unverletzten jungfräulichen Zustandes nach Nationalbegriffen, Physiologie, Moral und Politik* (Berlin, 1795). *Neue Allgemeine Deutsche Bibliothek* 16.2 (1795): 404–5.

Anon. ["D.S."]. "Haben Ehegatten gegen einander Pflichten in Ansehung des Umganges, und welches sind sie?" *Hannoverisches Magazin* 24 (1786): cols. 1073–86.

Anon. ["Dt"]. Review of anon. ["Schl"], *Über Kinderzucht und Selbstbefleckung*. In *Allgemeine Deutsche Bibliothek*, vol. 3 of supplement to vols. 53–86, p. 1262.

Anon. ["Dt"]. Review of D. Samuel Gottlieb Vogel, *Unterricht für Eltern* (1786). *Allgemeine Deutsche Bibliothek* 82.2 (1788): 567–71.

Anon. ["Ea"]. Review of Johann Heinrich Jung[-Stilling], *Über den Revolutionsgeist unsrer Zeit, zur Belehrung der bürgerlichen Stände* (Marburg, 1794). *Neue Allgemeine Deutsche Bibliothek* 14.2 (1795): 377–78.

Anon. ["F"]. "Brief, das Erziehungswesen betreffend." *Teutscher Merkur* 4 (1779): 67–78.

Anon. ["Gr"]. "Vertheidigung meiner Landsleute gegen einen Aufsatz im *Teutschen Merkur* No. III, Stück 7, 1793." *Neuer Teutscher Merkur*, October 1793: 212–15.

Anon. ["Hf"]. Review of Dr. Niklas Venette, *Geheimnisse keuscher Liebeswerke, mit Einschaltungen aus den neuesten Naturforschern und Aerzten* (Dresden, 1785). *Allgemeine Deutsche Bibliothek* 91.2 (1790): 412–13.

Anon. ["Hr"]. "Note des Censors." *Neues Hannoversches Magazin* 5 (1795): cols. 223–24.

Anon. ["Im"]. Review of *Vom Kindermord und dessen Verhütung* (Frankfurt, 1787). *Allgemeine Deutsche Bibliothek* 79.2 (1788): 406–7.

Anon. ["J. G. St"]. and J. S. Fest. "An einen mißvergnügten iungen Prediger." *Beiträge zur Beruhigung und Aufklärung* 3 (1793): 163–88.

Anon. ["Je"]. Review of Thomas Abbt, *Über innere und äussere Bestimmung des Jünglings zum künftigen nützlichen Mitgliede der menschlichen Gesellschaft. Nebst einer Abhandlung über die Bestimmung des Mädchens* (Halberstadt, 1794). *Neue Allgemeine Deutsche Bibliothek* 19.2 (1795): 549.

Anon. ["K"]. "Warum werden so viele Mädchen alte Jungfern?" *Neues Hannoversches Magazin* 4 (1794): cols. 1617–30; no. 103 (1794): cols. 1633–36.

Anon. ["K-f-d"]. "Ueber das Verhältniß beyder Geschlechter." *Teutscher Merkur* 1 (1781): 106–34.

Anon. ["Lb"]. Review of anon., *Ueber den Beyschlaf*. *Neue Allgemeine Deutsche Bibliothek* 10.1 (1794): 169–72.

Anon. ["N"]. "Ueber das Wort und Begrif Liebe." *Hannoversches Magazin* 18 (1780): cols. 977–92.

Anon. ["Nm"]. Review of Joachim Heinrich Campe, *Väterlicher Rath für meine Tochter* (Braunschweig, 1789). *Allgemeine Deutsche Bibliothek* 91.2 (1790): 307–20.

Anon. ["Qw"]. Review of J. F. Oest, *Für Eltern, Erzieher und Jugendfreunde* (1787). *Allgemeine Deutsche Bibliothek* 82.2 (1788): 571–75.

Anon. ["Rc"]. Review of *Bildungsjournal für Frauenzimmer, zur Beförderung des Guten für beyde Geschlechter* (Zittau, 1787). *Allgemeine Deutsche Bibliothek*, vol. 3 of the supplement to vols. 53–86, pp. 1585–87.

Anon. ["Rr"]. Review of Carl Friedrich Bahrdt, *System der moralischen Religion* (1787). *Allgemeine Deutsche Bibliothek* 85.2 (1789): 366–74.

Anon. ["Rs"]. Review of *Liebe. Was sie ist und seyn sollte* (Gotha, 1790). *Allgemeine Deutsche Bibliothek* 98.2 (1791): 599–601.

❧ Bibliography ❧

Anon. ["Schl"]. *Ueber Kinderunzucht und Selbstbefleckung. Ein Buch bloß für Aeltern, Erzieher und Jugendfreunde, von einem Schulmanne.* Züllichau, 1787.

Anon. ["Sch-p"]. "Der Ursprung der Liebe. Nach dem Plato." *Teutscher Merkur* 7 (1774): 259–66.

Anon. ["Tb"]. Review of anon., *Wie die großen und kleinern Schul- und Erziehungsanstalten. . . . Allgemeine Deutsche Bibliothek* 107.1 (1792): 283–87.

Anon. ["Wu"]. Review of *Der Kindermord. Zur Beherzigung an alle meine Mitmenschen* (Rostock, 1792). *Neue Allgemeine Deutsche Bibliothek* 8:1 (1794): 40–46.

Anon. ["Zm"]. Review of Hans Ernst v. Globig, *Ueber die Gründe und Gränzen der Vaterlichen Gewalt. Allgemeine Deutsche Bibliothek* 94.2 (1790): 324–33.

Anon. ["Zw"]. Review of C. Meiners, *Geschichte des Verfalls der Sitten, der Wissenschaften und Sprache der Römer in den ersten Jahrhunderten nach Christi Geburt. Als Einleitung zu Gibbons Geschichte der Abnahme und des Falls des römischen Reichs* (Vienna, 1791). *Allgemeine Deutsche Bibliothek* 113.1 (1793): 197–200.

Arnold, G. D., and F. Lassaulx. "Ansichten über die Einführung des Codex Napoleon in teutschen Staaten, veranlaßt durch eine von Hrn. von Almendingen in gegenwärtiger Zeitschrift (36tes Heft S. 46 u.f.) an die Unterzeichneten gerichtete Aufforderung." *Der Rheinische Bund* 16 (1818): 3–21.

Bahrdt, Carl Friedrich. *System der moralischen Religion zur endlichen Beruhigung für Zweifler und Denker, allen Christen und Nichtchristen lesbar.* Berlin, 1787.

Bairische Lanndtsordnung, 1553. Ingolstadt, 1553.

Bartz. "Ueber die Strafbarkeit der verheimlichten Schwangerschaft und Geburt." *Archiv des Criminalrechts* (Halle) vol. 6.2 (1805): 63–84.

Bauer, Anton. *Beiträge zur Charakteristik und Critik des Code Napoléon.* Marburg, 1810.

Bauer, Karl Gottfried. *Über die Mittel dem Geschlechtstriebe eine unschädliche Richtung zu geben. Eine durch die Erziehungsanstalt zu Schnepfenthal gekrönte Preisschrift. Mit einer Vorrede und Anmerkungen von C. G. Salzmann.* Leipzig, 1791.

Beccaria, Cesare. *Des Herrn Marquis von Beccaria unsterbliches Werk von Verbrechen und Strafen. Auf das Neue selbst aus dem Italiänischen übersetzt mit durchgängigen Anmerkungen des Ordinarius zu Leipzig Herrn Hofrath Hommels.* Breslau, 1778.

Becher, Johann Joachim. *Psychosophia oder Seelen-Weißheit / Wie nemlich ein jeder Mensch auß Betrachtung seiner Seelen selbst allein alle Wissenschafft und Weißheit gründlich und beständig erlangen könne.* 2d ed. Hamburg, 1705.

Berlepsch, Emilie von. "Ueber Liebe als Leidenschaft, und den Grundsatz zur Beurtheilung ihrer Dignität." In *Neuer Teutscher Merkur* 3 (1790): 411–38.

Bertuch, F. J. "An das Publicum, zum Schlusse des Jahres." *Journal des Luxus und der Moden* 1 (1786): 449–63.

——. "Ueber Kinder-Kleidung." *Journal des Luxus und der Moden* 6 (1791): 571–74.

Boetticher, Jakob Gottlieb. *Winke für Eltern, Erzieher und Jünglinge die Selbstbefleckung betr.* Königsberg, 1791.

Bopp, Philipp. "Kindermord. Verheimlichung der Schwangerschaft und Geburt. Abtreibung der Leibesfrucht. Kinderaussetzung." In Rotteck and Welcker, *Staats-Lexikon,* 9:253–55.

Börner, Christian Friedrich. *Werk von der Onanie.* Leipzig, 1776.

Brandes, Ernst. *Ueber die Weiber.* Leipzig, 1787.

Brauer, Johann Niclas Friedrich. *Erläuterungen über den Code Napoleon und die Großherzoglich Badische bürgerliche Gesetzgebung.* 6 vols. Karlsruhe, 1809–12.

❧ Bibliography ❧

Burdach, Karl Friedrich. *Eugon, oder über Impotenz und Schwäche der Zeugungskraft und die sicherste Methode, sie zu heilen.* Leipzig, 1804.

Calvin, Jean. *Institutes of the Christian Religion.* 2 vols. Trans. Henry Beveridge. Grand Rapids, Mich., 1957.

Campe, Joachim Heinrich. *Väterlicher Rath für meine Tochter.* Braunschweig, 1788.

——, ed. *Allgemeine Revision des gesammten Schul- und Erziehungswesens von einer Gesellschaft practischer Erzieher.* 16 vols. Vols. 1–16. Hamburg, 1785–92. Vols. 5–9. Wolfenbüttel, 1786–87. Vols. 8–16. Vienna, 1787–92. Vols. 10–16. Braunschweig, 1788–92.

Cella, Johann Jakob. *Über Verbrechen und Strafe in Unzuchtsfällen.* Saarbrücken, 1787.

——. *Von Strafen unehelicher Schwängerungen, besondern von den diessfalls gebräuchlichen Zwangskopulationen.* Erlangen, 1783.

Daniels, Heinrich Gottfried Wilhelm, trans. *Code Napoléon. Gesetzbuch Napoleons, nach dem officiellen Texte übersetzt.* Cologne, 1808.

Darjes, Joachim Georg. *Erste Gründe der Cameral-Wissenschaften darinnen die Haupttheile sowohl der Oeconomie als auch der Policey und besondern Cameral-Wissenschaft in ihrer natürlichen Verknüpfung zum Gebrauch seiner academischen Fürlesung entworfen.* 2d ed. Leipzig, 1768.

Ebel, Wilhelm, ed. *Friedrich Esajas Pufendorfs Entwurf eines hannoverschen Landrechts (vom Jahre 1772).* Hildesheim, 1970.

Eberhard, A. G. "Einige wesentliche Hinweisungen auf Abweichungen der neuen französischen Civilgesetze von den sonst in Deutschland geltend gewesenen Gesetzen und Gebräuchen." *Allgemeiner Anzeiger der Deutschen* no. 272 (October 1807): cols. 2825–28.

Engelschall, J. F. "Kordelia." *Der Neue Teutsche Merkur,* May 1791, 3–29.

Faust, Dr. Bernhard Christian. *Wie der Geschlechtstrieb der Menschen in Ordnung zu bringen und wie die Menschen besser und glücklicher zu machen.* Braunschweig, 1791.

Fest, J. S. "Einige Anmerkungen und Zusätze des Herausgebers zu dem vorstehenden Aufsatze." *Beiträge zur Beruhigung und Aufklärung* 2 (1790): 418–35.

——. "Ein vielleicht nicht unnöthiger Wink zur Verhütung ungünstiger und unrichtiger Urtheile über zween aus diesen Beiträgen bekannte iunge Männer." *Beiträge zur Beruhigung und Aufklärung* 2 (1790): 484–88.

Feuerbach, Paul Johann Anselm. *Anti-Hobbes.* Giessen, 1797. Reprint. Darmstadt, 1967.

——. "Betrachtungen über den Geist des Code Napoléon, und dessen Verhältniß zur Gesezgebung und Verfassung teutscher Staaten überhaupt, und Baierns insbesondere." In *Themis, oder Beiträge zur Gesetzgebung.* Landshut, 1812.

——. *Kritik des Kleinschrodischen Entwurfs zu einem peinlichen Gesetzbuche für die Chur-Pfalz-Bayrischen Staaten.* Giesen [sic], 1804.

——. *Kritik des natürlichen Rechts als Propädeutik zu einer Wissenschaft der natürlichen Rechte.* Altona, 1796. Reprint. Hildesheim, 1963.

——. *Lehrbuch des gemeinen in Deutschland gültigen peinlichen Rechts.* 9th ed. Giessen, 1826.

——. *Revision der Grundsätze und Grundbegriffe des positiven peinlichen Rechts,* 2 vols. Erfurt, 1799; reprint Aalen, 1966.

——. *Strafgesetzbuch für das Königreich Bayern.* 3 vols. Munich, 1813.

Fichte, Johann Gottlieb. *Grundlage des Naturrechts nach Prinzipien der Wissenschaftslehre* (1796). Hamburg, 1979.

——. *The Science of Rights.* Trans. A. E. Kroeger. London, 1889.

❧ Bibliography ❧

Frank, Johann Peter. *System einer vollständigen medicinischen Polizey* 2d ed. 2 vols. Mannheim, 1784.

Friedrich Esajas Pufendorfs Entwurf eines hannoverschen Landrechts (vom Jahre 1772). Ed. Wilhelm Ebel. Hildesheim, 1970.

Garve, Christian. *Über die Moden* (1792). Ed. Thomas Pittrof. Frankfurt, 1987.

Gellert, Christian Fürchtegott. *Moralische Vorlesungen*. 2 vols. Ed. Johann Adolf Schlegeln, and Gottlieb Leberecht Heyern. Leipzig, 1770.

Globig, Hans Ernst von. *Über die Gründe und Gränzen der Väterlichen Gewalt. Beantwortung einer, im Jahr 1786 von der Akademie der Wissenschaften zu Berlin ausgeschriebenen Preisausgabe*. Dresden, 1789.

Globig, Hans Ernst von, and Johann Georg Huster. *Abhandlungen von der Criminal-Gesetzgebung*. Zurich, 1783.

Gönner, Nikolaus Thaddäus. "Mein letztes Wort über die Reception des Code Napoleon in den Staaten der rheinischen Conföderation, als Antwort auf den Aufsatz des Herrn v. Almendingen im Rh.B., Heft 29, S. 306–17." *Der Rheinische Bund* 12 (1809): 47–61.

Grolman, D. *Ausführliches Handbuch über den Code Napoleon. Zum Gebrauche wissenschaftlich gebildeter deutscher Geschäftsmänner*. 2 vols. Giessen, 1811.

Gruner, Christian Gottfried. "De masturbatione peste iuventutis longe perniciosissima." Med. diss., Jena, 1784.

Hegel, Georg Wilhelm Friedrich. *Philosophy of Right* (1820). Trans. T. M. Knox. London, 1952.

Herder, Johann G. "Liebe und Selbstheit." *Teutscher Merkur* 4 (1781): 211–35.

Hermann, Johann Hieronymus. *Sammlung allerhand auserlesener Responsorum*, 3 parts. Jena, 1733–34.

Heß, Ludwig von. *Eine Antwort auf die Preisfrage: Welches sind die beßten ausfürbaren Mittel dem Kindermorde Einhalt zu thun?* Hamburg, 1780.

Heyse, Joh[ann] Christ[ian] Aug[ust]. *Handwörterbuch der deutschen Sprache mit Hinsicht auf Rechtschreibung, Abstammung und Bildung . . .* 2 vols. in 3. Magdeburg, 1833–49.

Hippel, Theodor Gottlieb von. *On Improving the Status of Women* (1792). Trans. Timothy F. Sellner. Detroit, 1979.

———. *Über die Ehe*. 4th ed. Berlin, 1793.

———. *Über die Ehe*. 3d ed. Berlin, 1792.

———. *Ueber die Ehe*. 2d ed. Berlin, 1776.

Hommel, Karl Ferdinand, trans. and ed. *Cesare Beccaria, Vom Verbrechen und Strafen*. Breslau, 1778.

Hörnigk, Philipp Wilhelm von. *Österreich über alles, wenn es nur will* (1684). Ed. Gustav Otruba. Vienna, 1964.

Horstig, K. G. "Einige Ursachen über die Unzufriedenheit in der Ehe." *Schleswigisches Journal* 3 (1792): 430–43.

Hübbe, Carl. "Preisschrift." In *Verhandlungen und Schriften*, 2:142–62.

Humboldt, Wilhelm von. "Ueber die Sittenverbesserung durch Anstalten des Staats." In *Wilhelm von Humboldts Gesammelte Werke*. Vol. 1. Berlin, 1841.

———. "Wie weit darf sich die Sorgfalt des Staats um das Wohl seiner Bürger erstrecken?" In *Wilhelm von Humboldts Gesammelte Werke*. Vol. 2. Berlin, 1841.

Huschke, Wilhelm Ernst Christian. "De masturbatione." Med. diss., Jena, 1788.

Jacobi, J. G. "Von der Schaamhaftigkeit." *Iris* 5 (1776): 138–44.

Jung [-Stilling], Johann Heinrich. *Lehrbuch der Staats-Polizey-Wissenschaft*. Leipzig, 1788.

——. *Über den Revolutions-Geist unserer Zeit zur Belehrung der bürgerlichen Stände.* Marburg, 1793.

Justi, Johann Heinrich Gottlob von. *Die Grundfeste zu der Macht und Glückseeligkeiten der Staaten; oder ausführliche Vorstellung der gesamten Policey-Wissenschaft.* 2 vols. Königsberg, 1760.

——. *Grundsätze der Policey-Wissenschaft in einem vernünftigen, auf den Endzweck der Policey gegründeten, Zusammenhange und zum Gebrauch academischer Vorlesungen abgefasset.* 2d ed. Göttingen, 1759.

——. *Natur und Wesen der Staaten als die Quelle aller Regierungswissenschaften und Gesezze.* Mitau, 1771.

——. *Rechtliche Abhandlung von denen Ehen, die an und vor sich selbst ungültig und nichtig sind; (de matrimonio putativo et illegitimo). Wobey zugleich von dem Wesen der Ehe und dem großen Einflusse der Ehegesetze in die Glückseligkeit des Staats gehandelt wird.* Leipzig, 1757.

Kämpf, Johannes. *Für Aerzte und Kranke bestimmte Abhandlung von einer neuen Methode, die hartnäckigsten Krankheiten, die ihren Sitz im Unterleibe haben, besonders die Hypochondrie, sicher und gründlich zu heilen.* Dessau, 1784.

Kamptz, Karl Albert von. "Gedanken über die Einführung des Code Napoleon in den Staaten des Rheinbundes." *Der Rheinische Bund* 3 (1807): 474–79.

Kant, Immanuel. "An Answer to the Question 'What is Enlightenment?'" (1784). In *Kant's Political Writing,* ed. Han Reiss. Cambridge, 1970.

——. *Anthropologie in pragmatischer Hinsicht* (1798). 7th ed. Philosophische Bibliothek, vol. 44. Hamburg, 1980.

——. *Bemerkungen zu den Beobachtungen über das Gefühl des Schönen und Erhabenen.* Vol. 22 of *Kants gesammelte Schriften.* Ed. Preußische Akademie der Wissenschaften. Berlin, 1942.

——. *Eine Vorlesung über Ethik.* Ed. Gerd Gerhardt. Frankfurt, 1990.

——. *Lectures on Ethics.* Trans. Louis Infield. New York, 1963.

——. *Metaphysik der Sitten* (1797). Ed. Karl Vorländer. Hamburg, 1966.

——. "On the Common Saying: 'This may be true in theory, but it does not apply in practice'" (1793). In *Kant's Political Writings,* ed. Hans Reiss. Cambridge, 1970.

——. "Perpetual Peace: A Philosophical Sketch." In *Kant's Political Writings,* ed. Hans Reiss. Cambridge, 1970.

——. *The Philosophy of Law. An Exposition of the Fundamental Principles of Jurisprudence as the Science of Right.* Trans. W. Hastie. Edinburgh, 1887.

Klefeker, J. *Sammlung der Hamburgische Gesetze und Verfassungen in Bürger- und kirchlichen, auch Cammer-, Handlungs- und übrigen Policey-Angelegenheiten und Geschäften somit historischen Einleitungen.* Hamburg, 1765–73.

Kleinschrod, Gallus Alois. *Entwurf eines peinlichen Gesetzbuchs für die kurpfalzbaierischen Staaten.* Munich, 1802.

——. *Systematische Entwickelung der Grundbegriffe und Grundwahrheiten des peinlichen Rechts nach der Natur der Sache und der positiven Gesetzgebung,* 3 parts. Erlangen, 1794.

Königlich-Baierisches Regierungsblatt, 40 vols. in 38. Munich, 1802–73.

Kotzebue, August von. *Vom Adel. Bruchstück eines größeren historisch-philosophischen Werkes über Ehre und Schande, Ruhm und Nachruhm, aller Völker, aller Jahrhunderte.* Leipzig, 1792.

Kreittmayr, Wiguleus Xaver Alois, Freiherr von. *Codex Juris Bavarici Criminalis de anno 1751, 1753 [nebst] Anmerckungen.* Munich, 1751–54.

❦ Bibliography ❦

Krünitz, Johann Georg. *Oekonomisch-technologische Encyklopädie, oder Allgemeines System der Staats-, Stadt-, Haus- und Landwirthschaft, in alphabetischer Ordnung.* 242 vols. Berlin, 1773–1858.

Kürn, Dr. Peter Otto. "Preisschrift über das Sittenverderben des Gesindes." In *Verhandlungen und Schriften,* 2:101–39.

Landrecht und Ordnung der Fürstenthumben der Marggraveschafften Baden und Hochberg. Durlach, 1622.

Lassaulx, F. "Einige Gedanken über die Einführungen des Codex Napoleon in die Staaten der Rheinischen Conföderation." *Annalen der Gesetzgebung Napoleons* 1.1 (1808): 169–74.

Locke, John. "Second Treatise of Government." In *Two Treatises of Government,* ed. Peter Laslett. Cambridge, 1988.

Luther, Martin. *D. Martin Luther's Werke. Kritische Gesammtausgabe,* ed. J.K.F. Knaake et al. Vol. 1. Weimar, 1883. Reprint. Graz, 1966.

———. "The Estate of Marriage (1522)." Trans. Walther I. Brandt. In *Luther's Works,* ed. Helmut T. Lehmann. Vol. 45, *The Christian in Society II,* ed. Walther I. Brandt. Philadelphia, 1962.

———. "Der große Katechismus (1529)." In *Dr. Martin Luther's sämmtliche Werke.* Vol. 21, *Dr. Martin Luther's katechetische deutsche Schriften.* Erlangen, 1932.

———. "A Sermon on the Estate of Marriage (1519)." Trans. James Atkinson. In *Luther's Works,* ed. Helmut T. Lehmann. Vol. 44., *The Christian in Society I,* ed. James Atkinson. Philadelphia, 1966.

———. "That Parents Should Neither Compel nor Hinder the Marriage of Their Children and That Children Should not Become Engaged Without Their Parents' Consent (1524)." Trans. Walther I. Brandt. In *Luther's Works,* Vol. 45, *The Christian in Society,* ed. Walther I. Brandt, Philadelphia, 1962.

———. "Von Ehesachen (1530)." In *Dr. Martin Luther's sämmtliche Werke.* Vol. 23, *Dr. Martin Luther's katechetische deutsche Schriften.* Erlangen, 1938.

Mayr, Georg Karl, ed. *Sammlung der Churpfalz-Baierischen allgemeinen und besondern Landes-Verordnungen von Sr. churfürstl. Durchlaucht Maximilian Joseph IV in Justiz-, Finanz-, Landschafts-, Mauth-, Polizey-, Religions-, Militärs-, und vermischten Sachen.* 8 vols. Munich, 1784–1802.

———, ed. *Sammlung der neuest und merkwürdigsten churbaierischen Generalien und Landesverordnungen.* Munich, 1771.

Mendelssohn, Moses. "Giebt es natürliche Anlagen zum Laster?" *Berlinische Monatsschrift* 7.3 (1786): 193–204.

Michaelis, Johann David. *Mosaisches Recht.* Biehl, 1777.

Mittermaier, Carl Joseph Anton. "Beyträge zur Lehre von Verbrechen des Kindermords und der Verheimlichung der Schwangerschaft." *Neues Archiv des Criminalrechts* (Halle) 7.1 (1824): 1–45; 7.2 (1825): 304–27 and 7.3 (1825): 493–522.

———. "Der neue Entwurf des Strafgesetzbuchs für das Königreich Bayern." *Neues Archiv des Criminalrechts* (Halle) 6.2 (1823): 173–227; 6.3 (1823): 351–77.

———. "Ueber den gegenwärtigen Zustand der Strafgesetzgebung, die Gebrechen derselben und die Gesichtspunkte ihrer Verbesserung." *Archiv des Criminalrechts* (Halle), n.s., 4 (1847): 586–611.

———. "Über den neuesten Zustand der Criminalrechtswissenschaft in Deutschland." *Neues*

Archiv des Criminalrechts (Halle) 4.1 (1820): 76–107; 4.2 (1820): 157–93; 4.3 (1820): 400–428.

——. "Ueber die Einführung des Baierischen Strafgesetzbuches in Weimar mit Betrachtungen über den Werth dieses Gesetzbuches." *Neues Archiv des Criminalrechts* (Halle) 2.1 (1818): 54–64.

Montesquieu. *The Spirit of the Laws* (1748). Trans. Anne M. Cohler, Basia Carolyn Miller, and Harold Samuel Stone. Cambridge, 1989.

Mylius, Christian Otto, ed. *Corpus constitutionem Marchicarum, oder königl. Preußis. und Churfürstl. Brandenburgische. . . . Ordnungen, Edicta, Mandata, Rescripta, etc. Von Zeiten Friedrichs I . . . biss ietzo unter der Regierung Friedrich Wilhelms . . . ad annum 1736.* 6 vols. in 8. Berlin, 1737–51.

Novum Corpus Constitutionum Prussico-Brandenburgensium praecipue Marchicarum, oder Neue Sammlung Königl. Preuß. und Churfürstl. Brandenburgischer, sonderlich in der Chur- und Marck-Brandenburg, Wie auch andern Provintzien, publicirten und ergangenen Ordnungen, Edicten, Mandaten, Rescriptien etc., etc. Vom Anfang des Jahrs 1751 und folgenden Zeiten. 11 vols. Berlin, 1753–1806.

Oest, J. F. "Nöthige Belehrung und Warnung für junge Mädchen, zur allerfrühesten Bewahrung ihrer Unschuld, von einer erfahrnen Jugendfreundin." In Campe, *Allgemeine Revision*, 6:435–506.

——. "Nöthige Belehrung und Warnung für Jünglinge und solche Knaben, die schon zu einigem Nachdenken gewöhnt sind." In Campe, *Allgemeine Revision*, 6:293–434.

——. "Versuch einer Beantwortung der pädagogischen Frage: wie man Kinder und junge Leute vor dem Leib und Seele verwüstenden Laster der Unzucht überhaupt, und der Selbstschwächung insonderheit verwahren, oder, wofern die schon davon angesteckt waren, wie man sie davon heilen könne?" In Campe, *Allgemeine Revision*, 6:1–286.

——. "Versuch einer Belehrung für die männliche und weibliche Jugend über die Laster der Unkeuschheit überhaupt und über die Selbstschwächung insonderheit, nebst einem kurzen Vortrage der Erzeugungslehre." In Campe, *Allgemeine Revision*, 6:287–506.

Die Peinliche Gerichtsordnung Kaiser Karls V. von 1532. Ed. Gustav Radbruch. Stuttgart, 1975.

Peschek, Christian August. *Versuch über die Ausartung des Begattungstriebes unter den Menschen. Ein Beytrag zur Sittenlehre und Erziehungskunde.* Breslau, 1790.

Pestalozzi, Heinrich. *Über Gesetzgebung und Kindermord. Wahrheiten und Träume, Nachforschungen und Bilder.* In *Heinrich Pestalozzi; Werke . . . Gedenkausgabe zu seinem zweihundertsten Geburtstage*, ed. Paul Baumgartner. Vol. 4. Erlenbach, 1944–49.

Pufendorf, Samuel. *On the Duty of Man and Citizen* (1673). Ed. James Tully, trans. Michael Silverthorne. Cambridge, 1991.

Ramdohr, Friedrich Wilhelm Basilius von. *Venus Urania. Ueber die Natur der Liebe, über ihre Veredlung und Verschönerung.* 3 parts. Leipzig, 1798.

Rehberg, August Wilhelm. *Ueber den Code Napoleon und dessen Einführung in Deutschland.* Hannover, 1814.

Reinhold, Karl Leonhard. "Die Drey Stände. Ein Dialog." *Teutscher Merkur*, March 1792, 217–42.

Reiss, Hans, ed. *Kant's Political Writings.* Cambridge, 1970.

Rohr, Julius Bernhard. *Vollständiges Haußhaltungs-Recht, in welchem die nöthigsten und nützlichsten Rechts-Lehren, Welche so wohl bey den Land-Gütern überhaupt, derselben*

Kauffung, Verkauffung und Verpachtung, als insonderheit bey dem Acker-Bau, Gärtnerey, Viehzucht, Jagten, Wäldern, Fischereyn, Mühlen, Weinbergen, Bierbrauen, Bergwercken, Handel und Wandel und andern Oeconomischen Materien vorkommen, Der gesunden Vernunfft denen Römisch und Teutschen Gesetzen nach ordentlich und ausführlich abgehandelt werden, allen denenjenigen, so Land Güter besitzen oder dieselben zu administriren haben, höchst-nützlich und ohnentbehrlich. Leipzig, 1716.

Rößig, Karl Gottlob. *Versuch einer pragmatischen Geschichte der Oekonomie- Policey- und Cameralwissenschaften seit dem sechzehnten Jahrhunderte bis zu unsern Zeiten. Deutschland,* Part 1. Leipzig, 1781.

Rötger, Gotthilf Sebastian. *Über Kinderunzucht und Selbstbefleckung, ein Buch bloß für Aeltern, Erzieher, und Jugendfreunde, von einem Schulmanne.* Züllichau, 1787.

Rotteck, Karl, and Carl Theodor Welcker, eds. *Staats-Lexikon, oder Encyclopädie der Staatswissenschaft,* 15 vols. Altona, 1834–43.

Rousseau, Jean-Jacques. *Aemile, oder von der Erziehung.* Trans. Johann Joachim Schwabe. Berlin, 1762.

——. *Emile, or On Education* (1762). Trans. Allan Bloom. New York, 1979.

Rückert. "Über die Kunst zu gefallen. Zur Bildung des schönen Geschlechts." *Neuer Teutscher Merkur,* (September 1796), 46–60.

Salzmann, Christian Gotthilf. *Ist es Recht über die heimlichen Sünden der Jugend öffentlich zu schreiben?* Schnepfenthal, 1785.

——. *Paedagogisches Bedenken über eine Schrift des Herrn Hofraths Faust, wie der Geschlechtstrieb der Menschen in Ordnung zu bringen, und wie die Menschen besser und glücklicher zu machen.* Schnepfenthal, 1792.

——. "Preisauschreiben." In *Braunschweigisches Journal* 2 (1788): 255–56.

——. *Ueber die heimlichen Sünden der Jugend.* "Vierte unveränderte Auflage." Leipzig, 1819.

Sammlung der Gesetze, Verordnungen und Ausschreibungen für das Königreich Hannover vom Jahre 1824. Hannover, 1824.

Sarganeck, Georg. *Ueberzeugende und bewegliche Warnung vor allen Sünden der Unreinigkeit und Heimlichen Unzucht: darinnen aus Medicinischen u. Theologischen Gründen vernünftig vorgestellet wird.* 2d ed. Züllichau, 1746.

"Sch" [W. F. Graf von Schmettau]. "Nicht jeder unbeweibte verdient den Namen *Hagestolz* noch den Spott seiner Mitbürger." *Schleswigisches Journal* 1 (1793): 279–313.

Schmettau, Woldemar Friedrich, Graf von. "Ueber den Kindermord." In *Kleine Schriften.* Altona, 1795.

Schmidt, Friedrich Traugott. "Preisschrift über das Sittenverderben der Bedienten." In *Verhandlungen und Schriften,* 2:69–99.

Schwabe, Ernst. *Anweisung zu den Pflichten und Geschäften eines Stadt- oder Land-Physikus.* 2 parts. Erfurth, 1786–87.

Schwager, J. M. "Über den Ravensberger Bauer." *Westfälisches Magazin* 2, no. 5 (1786):49–74.

Seckendorff, Veit Ludwig von. *Teutscher Fürsten-Stat/ Oder: Gründliche und kurtze Beschreibung/welcher Gestalt Fürstenthümer/Graff- und Herrschafften im H. Römischen Reich Teutscher Nation, welche Landes, Fürstliche unnd hohe obrigkeitliche Regalia haben/ von Rechts- unnd löblicher Gewonheit wegen beschaffen zu seyn/Regieret/ mit Ordnungen und Satzungen/Geheimen und Iustitz Cantzeleyen/Consistoriis und andern hohen und niedern Gerichts-Instantien, Aemptern und Diensten/verfasset und versehen/ auch wie deroselben Cammer- und Hoffsachen bestellt zu werden pflegen.* Hanau, 1657.

Seehase, Wilhelm Heinrich Friedrich. *Soll man junge Leute über die eigentliche Art der Erzeugung des Menschen belehren?* Stendal, 1784.

Selle, C. G. "Von der Moralität der menschlichen Handlungen." *Berlinische Monatsschrift* 2.6 (1783): 428–35.

Sieveking, Georg Heinrich. "Fragmente über Luxus, Bürgertugend, und Bürgerwohl." In *Verhandlungen und Schriften,* 4: 163–182.

Soden, Julius von. *Geist der peinlichen Gesetzgebung Teutschlands.* 2 vols. Frankfurt, 1792.

Sonnenfels, Joseph von. *Politische Abhandlungen.* Vienna, 1777.

———. "Über das Verhältnis der Stände." In *Politische Abhandlungen,* 88–152.

———. "Über das Wort Bevölkerung." In *Politische Abhandlungen,* 231–270.

Stille, T. "Ueber den Mißrauch des Freundschafts-Kusses und der Umarmungen." *Neuer Teutscher Merkur* (November 1790): 289–301.

Stosch, S.J.E. *Versuch in richtiger Bestimmung einiger gleichbedeutender Wörter der deutschen Sprache.* 2d part. Berlin, 1780.

Das Strafgesetzbuch für das Königreich Württemberg vom 1. März 1839. Ed. Otto Schwab. Stuttgart, 1849.

Stuve, Johann. *Über die körperliche Erziehung.* Berlin, 1779.

Süssmilch, Johann Peter. *Die göttliche Ordnung in der Veränderung des menschlichen Geschlechts, aus der Geburt, dem Tode und der Fortpflanzung desselben erwiesen.* Berlin, 1742.

———. *Die Göttliche Ordnung in den Veränderungen des menschlichen Geschlechts, besonders im Tode. Durch einige neue Beweißthümer bestätiget, und gegen des Königl. Groß-Brittanischen Berg-Raths Herrn von Justi Erinnerungen und Muthmaaßungen in zweyen Send-Schreiben an selbigen gerettet.* Berlin, 1756.

Thibaut, Anton Friedrich Justus. *Beyträge zur Critik der Feuerbachischen Theorie über die Grundbegriffe des peinlichen Rechts.* Hamburg, 1802.

Thomasius, Christian. *Ernsthaffte/aber doch Muntere und Vernünfftige Gedanken u. Errinnerungen über allerhand außerlesene Juristische Händel.* Part 1. Halle, 1720.

———. *Kurtzer Entwurff der Politischen Klugheit, sich selbst und andern in allen Menschlichen Gesellschafften wohlzurathen/ und zu einer gescheiden Conduite zu gelangen; Allen Menschen/die sich klug seyn düncken/oder die noch klug werden wollen/zu höchst-nöthiger Bedürffnis und ungemeinem Nutzen.* Franckfurt, 1710.

———. *Von der Artzeney wider die unvernünftige Liebe, und der zuvorher nöthigen Erkäntniß Sein Selbst. Oder: Ausübung der Sitten-Lehre, Nebst einem Beschluß, worinnen der Autor den vielfältigen Nutzen seiner Sitten-Lehre zeiget und von seinem Begrif der Christlichen Sitten-Lehre ein aufrichtiges Bekäntniß thut* (1696). 8th ed. Halle, 1726.

———. *Von der Kunst Vernünftig und Tugendhaft zu lieben, Als dem eintzigen Mittel zu einem glückseligen, galanten und vergnügten Leben zu gelangen; Oder Einleitung der Sitten-Lehre, Nebst einer Vorrede, In welcher unter andern der Verfertiger der curiösen Monatlichen Unterredung freundlich erinnert und gebeten wird, von Sachen, die er nicht verstehet, nicht zu ertheilen, und den Autoren dermalens in Ruhe zu lassen* (1692). 8th ed. Halle, 1726.

———, ed. *D. Melchiors von Osse Testament gegen Hertzog Augusto Churfürsten zu Sachsen/Sr. Churfürstl. Gnaden Räthen und Landschafften 1556. Anitzo zum ersten mahl völlig gedruckt/Auch hin und wieder durch nützliche Anmerckungen erläutert.* Halle, 1717.

Tissot, Samuel Auguste André David. *Onanism: Or, a Treatise Upon the Disorders Produced by Masturbation: Or, the Dangerous Effects of Secret and Excessive Venery.* Trans. A. Hume. New York, 1985.

——. *L'Onanisme, ou Dissertation physique sur les maladie produites par la masturbation.* Lausanne, 1760.

——. *Tentamen de morbis ex manustrupratione.* Lausanne, 1758.

——. *Versuch von denen Krankheiten, welche aus der Selbstbestekung entstehen; aus dem Lateinischen übersetzt.* Frankfurt, 1760.

Venette, Nicolai. *Abhandlung von Erzeugung der Menschen.* Leipzig, 1711.

——. *Tableau de l'Amour: Die Geheimnisse keuscher Liebes-Wercke, In gesegnetem Kinder-Zeugen Zu Fortpflanzung des Menschlichen Geschlechts und Erhaltung der Familien.* Cologne, 1724.

Verhandlungen und Schriften der Hamburgischen Gesellschaft zur Beförderung der Künste und nützlichen Gewerbe, 7 vols. Hamburg, 1792–1807.

Villaume, Peter. *Allgemeine Theorie, wie gute Triebe und Fertigkeiten durch die Erziehung erwekt, gestärkt und gelenkt werden müssen.* In Campe, *Allgemeine Revision,* vol. 4.

——. "Über die Unzuchtssünden in der Jugend. Eine gekrönte Preisschrift." In Campe, *Allgemeine Revision,* 7:3–308.

Vogel, Samuel Gottlieb. *Unterricht für Eltern, Erzieher und Kinderaufseher: wie das unglaublich gemeine Laster der zerstörenden Selbstbefleckung am sichersten zu entdecken, zu verhüten und zu heilen.* Stendal, 1786.

——. "Weiblicher Selbstmord als eine Folge eines geheimen Lasters. (Aus dem Briefe des Arztes der Unglücklichen)." *Berlinische Monatsschrift* 10.5 (1787): 172–76.

Vollständige Sammlung der Großherzoglich Badischen Regierungsblätter von deren Entstehung 1803 bis Ende 1825. 4 vols. Karlsruhe, 1826–43.

Waßda, Nicolaus. *Lauter Wunsch für diejenigen Personen weiblichen Geschlechts, welche zu Falle kommen.* Frankfurt, 1781.

Weise, Johann Wilhelm Friedrich. "De signis mastuprationis certioribus." Med. diss., Erfurt, 1792.

Welcker, Carl Theodor. "Geschlechtsverhältnisse." In Rotteck and Welcker, *Staats-Lexikon,* 6:629–65.

Wesentlicher Inhalt des beträchtlichsten Theils der neueren Hochfürstlich-Markgräflich-Badischen Gesezgebung, oder alphabetischer Auszug aus den in den Carlsruher und Rastatter Wochenblättern befindlichen, auch mehrern andern dazu gehörigen, noch nicht gedruckten Hochfürstlich-Markgräflich-Badischen Verordnungen. Karlsruhe, 1782.

Wieland, Christoph M. "An Psyche." *Teutscher Merkur* 7 (1774): 14–33.

——. "Erklärung des Herausgebers über die im 6ten Monatsstück des T. Merk. 1791 auf der letzten Seite befindliche Note." *Neuer Teutscher Merkur,* October 1791, 113–49.

——. "Schreiben an einen Korrespondenten in Paris." *Neuer Teutscher Merkur,* October 1792, 192–223.

——. "Unterredung zwischen W** und dem Pfarrer zu ***." *Teutscher Merkur* 1 (1775): 70–96.

Wiesiger, Carl Friedrich. "Preisschrift." In *Verhandlungen und Schriften,* 2:163–75.

Winterfeld, M. A. "Über die heimlichen Sünden der Jugend. In Campe, *Allgemeine Revision,* 6:507–609.

Wolff, Christian. *Vernünfftige Gedancken von dem Gesellschafftlichen Leben der Menschen und insonderheit dem gemeinen Wesen. Zur Beförderung der Glückseeligkeit des menschlichen Geschlechtes, den Liebhabern der Wahrheit mitgetheilet* (1721). 4th ed. Frankfurt, 1736.

Zedler, Johann Heinrich. *Grosses vollständiges Universal-Lexikon aller Wissenschaften und*

❧ Bibliography ❧

Künste welche bishero durch menschlichen Verstand und Witz erfunden worden. Leipzig, 1732–50.

Zimmermann, Johann Georg. "Anmerkungen über eine Schrift zur Rettung unschuldiger Kinder. . . . " *Baldingers Neues Magazin für Aerzte* 1 (1779): 60–63.

———. *Warnung an Eltern, Erzieher und Kinderfreunde wegen der Selbstbefleckung.* Leipzig, 1779.

———. "Warnung an Eltern, Erzieher und Kinderfreunde wegen der Selbstbefleckung, zumal bei ganz jungen Mädchen." *Deutsches Museum* 1 (1778): 452–60.

Zincke, Georg Heinrich. *Anfangsgründe der Cameralwissenschaft, worinne dessen Grundriß weiter ausgeführet und verbessert wird.* 2 vols. Leipzig, 1755.

Zwingli, Ulrich. "Ordinance and Notice. How Matters Concerning Marriage Shall Be Conducted in the City of Zurich." In *Selected Works*, trans. Samuel Macauley Jackson. Philadelphia, 1901. Reprint. Philadelphia, 1972.

Secondary Sources

Andreas, Willy. "Die Einführung des Code Napoléon in Baden." *Zeitschrift der Savigny-Stiftung für Rechtsgeschichte*, Germanische Abteilung 31 (1910): 182–234.

———. *Geschichte der badischen Verwaltungsorganisation und Verfassung in den Jahren 1802–1818.* Vol. 1, *Der Aufbau des Staates im Zusammenhang der allgemeinen Politik.* Leipzig, 1913.

Applewhite, Harriet B., and Darline Gay Levy. "Reaktionen auf den politischen Aktivismus der Frauen des Volkes im revolutionären Paris von 1789 bis 1793." In *Frauen im Frankreich des 18. Jahrhunderts: Amazonen, Mütter, Revolutionärinnen*, ed. Jutta Held. Frankfurt, 1989.

Bader, Karl Siegfried. *Dorfgenossenschaft und Dorfgemeinde.* Cologne, 1962.

———. "Verbrechen, Strafe und Strafvollzug in der Landgrafschaft Heiligenberg." *Monatsschrift für Kriminologie und Strafrechtsreform* 50 (March 1967): 195–209.

Barker-Benfield, G. J. *The Horrors of the Half-Known Life.* New York, 1976.

———. "The Spermatic Economy: A Nineteenth-Century View of Sexuality. *Feminist Studies* 1.1 (1972): 45–75.

Batscha, Zwi. *Gesellschaft und Staat in der politischen Philosophie Fichtes.* Frankfurt, 1970.

———. *Studien zur politischen Theorie des deutschen Frühliberalismus.* Frankfurt, 1981.

Bauer, Leonhard, and Herbert Matis. *Geburt der Neuzeit. Vom Feudalsystem zur Marktgesellschaft.* Munich, 1988.

Baur, Veronika. *Kleiderordnungen in Bayern vom 14. bis zum 19. Jahrhundert.* Miscellanea Bavarica Monacensia, no. 62. Munich, 1975.

Baxmann, Inge. "Von der Egalité im Salon zur Citoyenne—Einige Aspekte der Genese des bürgerlichen Frauenbildes." In *Frauen in der Geschichte*, ed. Annette Kuhn and Jörn Rüsen. Vol. 3. Düsseldorf, 1983.

Becher, Ursula A. J. *Politische Gesellschaft. Studien zur Genese bürgerlicher Öffentlichkeit in Deutschland.* Veröffentlichungen des Max-Planck-Instituts für Geschichte, vol. 59. Göttingen, 1978.

Beck, Rainer. "Illegitimität und voreheliche Sexualität auf dem Land. Unterfinning, 1671–1770." In *Kultur der einfachen Leute. Bayerisches Volksleben vom 16. zum 19. Jahrhundert*, ed. Richard van Dülmen. Munich, 1983.

❧ Bibliography ❧

Becker, H.-J. "Mandat." In *Handwörterbuch zur deutschen Rechtsgeschichte*, ed. Adalbert Erler and Ekkehard Kaufmann. 4 vols. to date. Berlin, 1971–90.

Becker, Peter. *Leben und Lieben in einem kalten Land. Sexualität im Spannungsfeld von Ökonomie und Demographie. Das Beispiel St. Lambrecht 1600–1850.* Studien zur Historischen Sozialwissenschaft, vol. 15. Frankfurt, 1990.

Behringer, Wolfgang. "Mörder, Diebe, Ehebrecher. Verbrechen und Strafen in Kurbayern vom 16. bis 18. Jahrhundert." In *Verbrechen, Strafen und soziale Kontrolle. Studien zur historischen Kulturforschung*, ed. Richard van Dülmen. Frankfurt, 1990.

Berdahl, Robert. *The Politics of the Prussian Nobility: The Development of a Conservative Ideology, 1770–1848.* Princeton, 1988.

Berding, Helmut. *Napoleonische Herrschafts- und Gesellschaftspolitik im Königreich Westfalen, 1807–1813.* Kritische Studien zur Geschichtswissenschaft, vol. 7. Göttingen, 1973.

Berding, Helmut, and Hans-Peter Ullmann. "Veränderungen in Deutschland an der Wende vom 18. zum 19. Jahrhundert." In Berding and Ullmann, *Deutschland zwischen Revolution und Restauration*, 11–42.

——, eds. *Deutschland zwischen Revolution und Restauration.* Königstein, 1981.

Berding, Helmut, Etienne François, and Hans-Peter Ullmann, eds. *Deutschland und Frankreich im Zeitalter der Französischen Revolution.* Frankfurt, 1989.

Berkner, Lutz K., and Franklin F. Mendels. "Inheritance Systems, Family Structure, and Demographic Patterns in Western Europe, 1700–1900." In *Historical Studies of Changing Fertility*, ed. Charles Tilly. Princeton, N.J., 1978.

Berner, Albert Friedrich. *Die Strafgesetzgebung in Deutschland vom Jahre 1751 bis zur Gegenwart.* Leipzig, 1867.

Bettger, Roland. *Das Handwerk in Augsburg beim Übergang der Stadt an das Königreich Bayern. Städtisches Gewerbe unter dem Einfluß politischer Veränderungen.* Abhandlungen zur Geschichte der Stadt Augsburg, vol. 25. Augsburg, 1979.

Biéler, André. *L'Homme et la Femme dans la Morale Calviniste. La doctrine réformée zur l'amour, le mariage, le célibat, le divorce, l'adultère et la prostitution, considérée dans sons cadre historique.* Geneva, 1962.

Birtsch, Günter. "Die Berliner Mittwochsgesellschaft (1783–1798)." In *Über den Prozeß der Aufklärung in Deutschland im 18. Jahrhundert. Personen, Institutionen und Medien*, ed. Hans Bödecker and Ulrich Herrmann. Göttingen, 1987.

Blackbourn, David, and Geoff Eley. *The Peculiarities of German History. Bourgeois Society and Politics in Nineteenth-Century Germany.* Oxford, 1984.

Blasius, Dirk. *Der verwaltete Wahnsinn. Eine Sozialgeschichte des Irrenhauses.* Frankfurt, 1980.

Blickle, Peter. "Untertanen in der Frühneuzeit. Zur Rekonstruktion der politischen Kultur und der sozialen Wirklichkeit Deutschlands im 17. Jahrhundert." In *Vierteljahrschrift für Sozial- und Wirtschaftsgeschichte* 70 (1983): 483–522.

Bock, Gisela and Barbara Duden. "Arbeit aus Liebe—Liebe als Arbeit: Zur Entstehung der Hausarbeit im Kapitalismus." In *Frauen und Wissenschaft. Beiträge zur Berliner Sommeruniversität für Frauen, Juli 1976.* Berlin, 1977.

Bödeker, Hans Erich, and Ulrich Herrmann, eds. *Über den Prozeß der Aufklärung in Deutschland im 18. Jahrhundert. Personen, Institutionen und Medien.* Veröffentlichungen des Max Planck Instituts für Geschichte, vol. 85. Göttingen, 1987.

Bödeker, Hans Erich, and Ulrich Herrmann, eds. *Aufklärung als Politisierung—Politisierung der Aufklärung.* Hamburg, 1987.

Bosl, Karl. "Eine Geschichte der deutschen Landgemeinde." In *Zeitschrift für Agrargeschichte und Agrarsoziologie* 9.2 (1961): 129–42.

Boswell, John. *Christianity, Social Tolerance, and Homosexuality: Gay People in Western Europe from the Beginning of the Christian Era to the Fourteenth Century.* Chicago, 1980.

Boucé, Paul-Gabriel. "Some Sexual Beliefs and Myths in Eighteenth-Century Britain." In *Sexuality in Eighteenth-Century Britain,* ed. Boucé. Manchester, 1982.

Bourdieu, Pierre. "From Rules to Strategems." In *In Other Words: Essays Towards a Reflexive Sociology.* Stanford, Calif., 1990.

——. "Les stratégies matrimoniales dans le système de reproduction." *Annales, Économies, Sociales, Culturelles* 27.4–5 (1972): 1105–27.

Bovenschen, Silvia, ed. *Die imaginierte Weiblichkeit. Exemplarische Untersuchungen zu kulturgeschichtlichen und literarischen Präsentationsformen des Weiblichen.* Frankfurt, 1979.

——. *Die Listen der Mode.* Frankfurt, 1986.

Braun, Rudolf. *Industrialisation and Everyday Life* (1960). Trans. Sarah Hanbury Tenison. Cambridge, 1990.

Brecht, Martin. "Die Ulmer Kirchenordnung von 1531, Die Basler Reformationsordnung von 1629 und die Münsteraner Zuchtordnung von 1533." In *Niederlande und Nordwestdeutschland. Studien zur Regional- und Stadtgeschichte Nordwestkontinentaleuropas im Mittelalter und in der Neuzeit,* ed. Wilfried Ehbrecht and Heinz Schilling. Cologne, 1983.

Breit, Stefan. *"Leichtfertigkeit" und ländliche Gesellschaft. Voreheliche Sexualität in der frühen Neuzeit.* Ancien Régime, Aufklärung und Revolution, vol. 23. Munich, 1991.

Brown, Peter. *The Body and Society: Men, Women, and Sexual Renunciation in Early Christianity.* New York, 1988.

Brundage, James A. *Law, Sex, and Christian Society in Medieval Europe.* Chicago, 1987.

Brunner, Otto, Werner Conze, and Reinhart Koselleck, eds. *Geschichtliche Grundbegriffe. Historisches Lexikon zur politisch-sozialen Sprache in Deutschland.* 6 vols. to date. Stuttgart, 1972- .

Buchholz, Stephan. "Erunt tres aut quattuor in carne una: Aspekte der neuzeitlichen Polygamiediskussion." In *Zur Geschichte des Familien- und Erbrechts: politische Implikationen und Perspektiven. Ius Commune* 32, ed. Heinz Mohnhaupt. Tübingen, 1987.

Burghartz, Susanna. "Rechte Jungfrauen oder unverschämte Töchter? Zur weiblichen Ehre im 16. Jahrhundert." In Hausen and Wunder, *Frauengeschichte-Geschlechtergeschichte,* 173–83.

Calhoun, C. J. "Community: Toward a Variable Conceptualization for Comparative Research." *Social History* 5.1 (1980): 105–29.

Caplan, Pat. "Introduction." In *The Cultural Construction of Sexuality,* ed. Caplan. London, 1987.

Carlebach, Rudolf. *Badische Rechtsgeschichte.* 2 vols. Heidelberg, 1906–09.

Cominos, Peter T. "Late Victorian Sexual Respectability and the Social System." *International Review of Social History* 8 (1963): 18–48.

Crompton, Louis. "The Myth of Lesbian Impunity: Capital Laws from 1270–1791." In *Historical Perspectives on Homosexuality,* ed. Salvatore J. Licata and Robert P. Petersen. New York, 1980–81.

Dagger, Richard. "Rights." In *Political Innovation and Conceptual Change,* ed. Terence Ball, James Farr, and Russell L. Hanson. Cambridge, 1989.

❧ Bibliography ❧

Dann, Otto. "Die Lesegesellschaften des 18. Jahrhunderts und der gesellschaftliche Aufbruch des deutschen Bürgertums." In Herrmann, *Bildung des Bürgers*, 100–118.

——, ed. *Lesegesellschaften und bürgerliche Emanzipation: Ein europäischer Vergleich*. Munich, 1981.

Dawson, Ruth P. "The Feminist Manifesto of Theodor Gottlieb von Hippel (1741–96)." In *Gestaltet und Gestaltend. Frauen in der deutschen Literatur*, ed. Marianne Burkhard. Amsterdamer Beiträge zur neueren Germanistik, vol. 10. Amsterdam, 1980.

Demel, Walter. *Der bayerische Staatsabsolutismus 1806/08–1817. Staats- und gesellschaftspolitische Motivationen und Hintergründe der Reformära in der ersten Phase des Königreichs Bayern*. Munich, 1983.

Depauw, Jacques. "Illicit Sexual Activity and Society in Eighteenth-Century Nantes." In *Family and Society*, ed. Robert Forster and Orest Ranum. Baltimore, 1976.

Derks, Paul. *Die Schande der heiligen Päderastie; Homosexualität und Öffentlichkeit in der deutschen Literatur, 1750–1850*. Homosexualität und Literatur, vol. 3. Berlin, 1990.

Deutsches Biographisches Archiv. Ed. Bernard Fabian. Munich, 1982.

Dilthey, Wilhelm. *Zur Preussischen Geschichte*. Vol. 5 of *Gesammelte Schriften*. Stuttgart, 1985.

Dittrich, Erhard. *Die deutschen und österreichischen Kameralisten*. Erträge der Forschung, vol. 23. Darmstadt, 1974.

Dölemeyer, Barbara. "Kodifikationsbewegung" and "Kodifikationen und Projekte." In *Handbuch der Quellen und Literatur der neueren europäischen Privatrechtsgeschichte*, ed Helmut Coing. Vol. 3, part 2. Munich, 1982.

Dorwart, Reinhold August. *The Prussian Welfare State before 1740*. Cambridge, 1971.

Douglas, Mary. *Purity and Danger. An Analysis of the Concepts of Pollution and Taboo*. London, 1989.

Duden, Barbara. *Geschichte unter der Haut. Ein Eisenacher Arzt und seine Patientinnen um 1730*. Stuttgart, 1987.

——. "Das schöne Eigentum. Zur Herausbildung des bürgerlichen Frauenbildes an der Wende vom 18. zum 19. Jahrhundert." *Kursbuch* 47 (1977): 125–40.

Dülmen, Richard van. *Frauen vor Gericht. Kindsmord in der Frühen Neuzeit*. Frankfurt, 1991.

——. *Der Geheimbund der Illuminaten. Darstellung, Analyse, Dokumentation*. Stuttgart, 1975.

——. *Die Gesellschaft der Aufklärer. Zur bürgerlichen Emanzipation und aufklärerischen Kultur in Deutschland*. Frankfurt, 1986.

——. *Theater des Schreckens. Gerichtspraxis und Strafrituale in der frühen Neuzeit*. Munich, 1988.

Eisenbart, Liselotte C. *Kleiderordnungen der deutschen Städte zwischen 1350 und 1700. Ein Beitrag zur Kulturgeschichte des deutschen Bürgertums*. Göttinger Bausteine zur Geschichtswissenschaft, vol. 32. Göttingen, 1962.

Eisenhardt, Ulrich. *Deutsche Rechtsgeschichte*. Munich, 1984.

Elias, Norbert. *The Civilizing Process* (1939). 2 vols. Trans. Edmund Jephcott. New York, 1978–82.

Engelhardt, H. Tristram, Jr. "The Disease of Masturbation: Values and the Concept of Disease." *Bulletin of the History of Medicine* 48 (1974): 234–48.

Engelhardt, Ulrich. *"Bildungsbürgertum." Begriffs- und Dogmengeschichte eines Etiketts*. Schriftenreihe des Arbeitskreises für moderne Sozialgeschichte, vol. 43. Stuttgart, 1986.

❧ Bibliography ❧

Engels, Friedrich. *The Origins of the Family, Private Property, and the State* (1884). Trans. Ernest Untermann. Chicago, 1902.

Engelsing, Rolf. *Analphabetentum und Lektüre. Zur Sozialgeschichte des Lesens in Deutschland zwischen feudaler und industrieller Gesellschaft.* Stuttgart, 1973.

——. "Zur Stellung der Dienstboten in der bürgerlichen Familie im 18. und 19. Jahrhundert" In *Seminar: Familie und Gesellschaftsstruktur. Materialien zu den sozioökonomischen Bedingungen von Familienformen,* ed. Heidi Rosenbaum. Frankfurt, 1978.

Epstein, Klaus. *The Origins of German Conservatism.* Princeton, 1966.

Eriksson, Brigitte. "A Lesbian Execution in Germany, 1721: The Trial Records." In *Historical Perspectives on Homosexuality,* ed. Salvatore J. Licata and Robert P. Petersen. New York, 1980–81.

Ettenhuber, Helga. "Charivari in Bayern. Das Miesbacher Haberfeldtreiben von 1893." In *Kultur der einfachen Leute,* ed. Richard van Dülmen. Munich, 1983.

Fairchilds, Cissie. "Female Sexual Attitudes and the Rise of Illegitimacy: A Case Study." In *Marriage and Fertility. Studies in Interdisciplinary History,* ed. Robert I. Rotberg and Theodore K. Rabb. Princeton, N.J., 1980.

Fehrenbach, Elisabeth. *Traditionale Gesellschaft und revolutionäres Recht. Die Einführung des Code Napoléon in den Rheinbundstaaten.* Kritische Studien zur Geschichtswissenschaft, vol. 13. Göttingen, 1974.

——. *Vom Ancien Régime zum Wiener Kongreß.* Oldenbourg Grundriß der Geschichte, vol. 12. Munich, 1981.

Felber, Alfons. "Unzucht und Kindsmord in der Rechtsprechung der freien Reichsstadt Nördlingen vom 15. bis 19. Jahrhundert." J.S.D. diss., Universitat Bonn, 1961.

Fischer, Wolfram. *Armut in der Geschichte. Erscheinungsformen und Lösungsversuche der "Sozialen Frage" in Europa seit dem Mittelalter.* Göttingen, 1982.

——. *Handwerksrecht und Handwerkswirtschaft um 1800.* Berlin, 1955.

Fischer-Homberger, Esther. *Krankheit Frau und andere Arbeiten zur Medizingeschichte der Frau.* Bern, 1979.

Flandrin, Jean-Louis. "Comment and Controversy. A Case of Naiveté in the Use of Statistics." In *Marriage and Fertility. Studies in Interdisciplinary History,* ed. Robert I. Rotberg and Theodore K. Rabb. Princeton, N.J., 1980.

——. *Families in Former Times: Kinship, Household, and Sexuality.* Trans. Richard Southern. Cambridge, 1979.

——. "Répression et changement dans la vie sexuelle des jeunes." In *Le sexe et l'Occident. Évolution des attitudes et des comportements.* Paris, 1981.

——. *Un temps pour embrasser. Aux origines de la morale sexuelle occidentale (VIe-XIe siècle).* Paris, 1983.

Flinn, Michael W. *The European Demographic System, 1500–1820.* Baltimore, 1981.

Flossmann, Ursula. "Geschlechtsspezifische Diskriminierung und Gleichbehandlungsgebot als Strukturelemente frühneuzeitlicher Rechtsordnungen." In *Festschrift für Louis Carlen zum 60. Geburtstag,* ed. Louis C. Morsak and Markus Escher. Zurich, 1989.

Forster, Marc. *The Counter-Reformation in the Villages: Religion and Reform in The Bishopric of Speyer.* Ithaca, N.Y., 1992.

Foucault, Michel. *The Care of the Self* (1984). Trans. Robert Hurley. New York, 1988.

——. *Discipline and Punish: The Birth of the Prison* (1975). Trans. Alan Sheridan. New York, 1977.

——. *History of Sexuality*. Vol. 1, *An Introduction*. Trans. Robert Hurley. New York, 1978.

——. *The Use of Pleasure* (1984). Trans. Robert Hurley. New York 1986.

François, Etienne. "Alphabetisierung und Lesefähigkeit in Frankreich und Deutschland." In Berding, François, and Ullmann, *Deutschland und Frankreich*, 407–25.

——. "Regionale Unterschiede der Lese- und Schreibfähigkeit in Deutschland im 18. und 19. Jahrhundert." *Jahrbuch für Regionalgeschichte und Landeskunde* 17 (1990): 154–72.

Frenzel, Herbert A., and Elisabeth Frenzel. *Daten deutscher Dichtung. Chronologischer Abriß der deutschen Literaturgeschichte*. 5th ed. Vol. 1. Munich, 1969.

Frevert, Ute. *Frauen-Geschichte. Zwischen bürgerlicher Verbesserung und neuer Weiblichkeit*. Frankfurt, 1986.

Frühsorge, Gotthardt. "Die Begründung der 'väterlichen Gesellschaft' in der europäischen oeconomia christiana. Zur Rolle des Vaters in der 'Hausväterliteratur' des 16. bis 18. Jahrhunderts in Deutschland." In *Das Vaterbild im Abendland I: Rom, Frühes Christentum, Mittelalter, Neuzeit, Gegenwart*, ed. Hubertus Tellenbach. Stuttgart, 1978.

——. "Die Einheit aller Geschäfte. Tradition und Veränderung des 'Hausmutter'-Bildes in der deutschen Ökonomieliteratur des 18. Jahrhunderts." *Wolfenbütteler Studien zur Aufklärung* 3 (1976): 137–57.

Gall, Lothar. "Liberalismus und 'bürgerliche Gesellschaft.' Zu Charakter und Entwicklung der liberalen Bewegung in Deutschland." *Historische Zeitschrift* 220 (1975): 324–56.

——. *Der Liberalismus als regierende Partei. Das Grossherzogtum Baden zwischen Restauration und Reichsgründung*. Veröffentlichungen des Instituts für europäische Geschichte Mainz, vol. 47. Wiesbaden, 1968.

Garbe, Christine. "Sophie oder die heimliche Macht der Frauen. Zur Konzeption des Weiblichen bei Jean-Jacques Rousseau." In *Frauen in der Geschichte*, ed. Ilse Brehmer et al. Vol. 4, *"Wissen heißt leben . . ." Beiträge zur Bildungsgeschichte von Frauen im 18. und 19. Jahrhundert*. Düsseldorf, 1983.

Gatrell, V.A.C., Bruce Lenman, and Geoffrey Parker, eds. *Crime and the Law: The Social History of Crime in Western Europe since 1500*. Salem, N.H., 1980.

Gay, Peter. *The Enlightenment: An Interpretation*. Vol. 1, *The Rise of Modern Paganism*. New York, 1966. Vol. 2, *The Science of Freedom*. New York, 1969.

Gehrke, Heinrich. "Deutsches Reich." In *Handbuch der Quellen und Literatur der neueren europäischen Privatrechtsgeschichte*, ed. Helmut Coing. Munich, 1976.

Gerhard, Ute. *Gleichheit ohne Angleichung. Frauen im Recht*. Munich, 1990.

——. "Menschenrechte-Frauenrechte 1789." In *Sklavin oder Bürgerin? Französische Revolution und Neue Weiblichkeit 1760–1830*, ed. Viktoria Schmidt-Linsenhoff. Frankfurt, 1989.

——. *Verhältnisse und Verhinderungen. Frauenarbeit, Familie und Rechte der Frauen im 19. Jahrhundert*. Frankfurt, 1981.

Gerhard, Ute, et al., eds. *Differenz und Gleichheit. Menschen Rechte haben (k)ein Geschlecht*. Frankfurt, 1990.

Gerth, Hans. *Bürgerliche Intelligenz um 1800. Zur Soziologie des deutschen Frühliberalismus*. Göttingen, 1976.

Gesamtverzeichnis des deutschsprachigen Schrifttums, 1700–1910. Munich, 1985.

Glaser, Horst Albert. "Drama des Sturm und Drang." In *Deutsche Literatur. Eine Sozialgeschichte*, ed. Glaser. Vol. 4. Hamburg, 1980.

Gleixner, Ulrike. "Dörfliche und obrigkeitliche Ordnungen. Die Konstruktion von Geschlecht in 'Unzuchtsverfahren' im 18. Jahrhundert in Preußen (Altmark 1700–1750)." Ph.D. diss., Freie Universität Berlin, 1992.

Goldberg, Anne. "A Social Analysis of Insanity in Nineteenth-Century Germany: Sexuality, Delinquency, and Anti-Semitism in the Records of the Eberbach Asylum." Ph.D. diss., University of California, Los Angeles, 1992.

Goodich, Michael. "Sodomy in Ecclesiastical Law and Theory." *Journal of Homosexuality* 1 (Summer 1976): 427–34.

———. *The Unmentionable Vice: Homosexuality in the Later Medieval Period.* Oxford, 1979.

Goody, Jack. "A Comparative Approach to Incest and Adultery." *British Journal of Sociology* 7 (1956): 286–305.

———. *The Logic of Writing and the Organization of Society.* Cambridge, 1986.

Gothein, Eberhard. "Beiträge zur Verwaltungsgeschichte der Markgrafschaft Baden unter Karl Friedrich." *Zeitschrift für die Geschichte des Oberrheins,* n.s., 26 (1911): 377–414.

Grebing, Helga. *Der "deutsche Sonderweg" in Europa, 1806–1945. Eine Kritik.* Stuttgart, 1986.

Greenfield, Kent R. *Sumptuary Law in Nürnberg: A Study in Paternal Government.* Johns Hopkins University Studies in Historical and Political Science, series 36, no. 2. Baltimore, 1918.

Grimm, Dieter. "Die Grundrechte im Entstehungszusammenhang der bürgerlichen Gesellschaft." In *Die Zukunft der Verfassung.* Frankfurt, 1991.

———. "Die verfassungsrechtlichen Grundlagen der Privatrechtsgesetzgebung." In *Handbuch der Quellen und Literatur der neueren europäischen Privatrechtsgeschichte,* ed Hermann Coing. Vol. 3, part 1. Munich, 1982.

Grimm, Jacob, and Wilhelm Grimm. *Deutsches Wörterbuch.* Leipzig, 1877.

Habermas, Jürgen. "Further Reflections on the Public Sphere." In *Habermas and the Public Sphere,* ed. Craig Calhoun. Cambridge, Mass., 1992.

———. *The Structural Transformation of the Public Sphere: An Inquiry into a Category of Bourgeois Society.* Trans. Thomas Burger. Cambridge, Mass., 1991.

Haferkorn, Hans Jürgen. "Zur Entstehung der bürgerlich-literarischen Intelligenz und des Schriftstellers im Deutschland zwischen 1750 und 1800." In *Deutsches Bürgertum und literarische Intelligenz 1750–1800,* ed. Bernd Lutz. Literaturwissenschaft und Sozialwissenschaften, vol. 3. Stuttgart, 1974.

Hahn, Hans-Werther. "Von der 'Kultur der Bürger' zur 'bürgerlicher Kultur.' Veränderungen in der Lebenswelt des Wetzlarer Bürgertums zwischen 1700–1900." In *Armut, Liebe, Ehre. Studien zur historischen Kulturforschung,* ed. Richard van Dülmen. Frankfurt, 1988.

Hall, Lesley A. "Forbidden by God, Despised by Men: Masturbation, Medical Warnings, Moral Panic, and Manhood in Great Britain, 1850–1950." In *Forbidden History. The State, Society, and the Regulation of Sexuality in Modern Europe,* ed. John C. Fout. Chicago, 1992.

Hampson, Norman. *The Enlightenment. An Evaluation of Its Assumptions, Attitudes and Values.* Rev. ed. London, 1982.

Hardtwig, Wolfgang. "Strukturmerkmale und Entwicklungs-Tendenzen des Vereinswesens in Deutschland, 1789–1948." In *Vereinswesen und bürgerliche Gesellschaft in Deutschland,* ed. Otto Dann. Supplemental issue of *Historische Zeitschrift* (Munich) 9 (1984): 11–50.

❖ Bibliography ❖

Hare, E. H. "Masturbatory Insanity: The History of an Idea." *Journal of Mental Science* 108 (January 1962): 1–25.

Hausen, Karin. "Family and Role-Division: The Polarisation of Sexual Stereotypes in the Nineteenth Century—an Aspect of the Dissociation of Work and Family Life." In *The German Family*, ed. R.J. Evans and W.R. Lee. London, 1981.

Hausen, Karin, and Heide Wunder, eds. *Frauengeschichte-Geschlechtergeschichte*. Frankfurt, 1992.

Hayn, Hugo, and Alfred N. Gotendorf, eds. *Bibliotheca Germanorum Erotica et Curiosa, Verzeichnis der gesamten deutschen erotischen Literatur mit Einschluß der Übersetzungen, nebst Beifügung der Originale*, 9 vols. Munich, 1912–29.

Hegler, August. *Die praktische Tätigkeit der Juristenfakultäten des 17. und 18. Jahrhunderts*. Freiburg, 1899.

Hentig, Hans von. *Die Strafe*, 2 vols. Berlin, 1954–55. Published in English under the title *Punishment: Its Origins, Purpose and Psychology* (London, 1937).

Hentze, Hilke. *Sexualität in der Pädagogik des späten 18. Jahrhunderts*. Europäische Hochschulschriften, vol. 63. Frankfurt, 1979.

Hergemöller, Bernd-Ulrich. "Homosexuellenverfolgung im Mittelalter. Erscheinungsformen und Kausalfaktoren des gesellschaftlichen Kampfes gegen die 'Sodomiter.'" In *Randgruppen der spätmittelalterlichen Gesellschaft*, ed. Hergemöller. Warendorf, 1990.

Herrmann, Ulrich. "Die Kodifizierung bürgerlichen Bewußtseins in der deutschen Spätaufklärung—Carl Friedrich Bahrdts 'Handbuch der Moral für den Bürgerstand' aus dem Jahre 1789." In Herrmann, *'Bildung des Bürgers*, 153–64.

——, ed. *"Die Bildung des Bürgers"; Die Formierung der bürgerlichen Gesellschaft und die Gebildeten im 18. Jahrhundert*. Weinheim, 1989.

Hinrichs, Ernst. *Einführung in die Geschichte der Frühen Neuzeit*. Munich, 1980.

Hippel, Robert von. *Deutsches Strafrecht*. 2 vols. Berlin, 1925.

Honegger, Claudia. *Die Ordnung der Geschlechter. Die Wissenschaften vom Menschen und das Weib*. Frankfurt, 1991.

Hoof, Dieter. *Pestalozzi und die Sexualität seines Zeitalters. Quellen, Texte und Untersuchungen zur Historischen Sexualwissenschaft*. Sexualpädagogische Beiträge, Vol. 3. St. Augustin, Germany, 1987.

Hörger, Hermann. *Kirche, Dorfreligion und bäuerliche Gesellschaft*. 2 parts. Studien zur altbayerischen Kirchengeschichte, vols. 5, 7. Munich, 1978, 1983.

Hsia, R. Po-Chia. *Social Discipline in the Reformation: Central Europe, 1550–1750*. London, 1989.

Huggel, Samuel. *Die Einschlagsbewegung in der Basler Landschaft. Gründe und Folgen der wichtigsten agrarischen Neuerung im Ancien Régime*. Quellen und Forschungen zur Geschichte und Landskunde des Kantons Basellands, vol. 17/1–2. Liestal, 1979.

Hull, Isabel V. "'Sexualität' und bürgerliche Gesellschaft." In *Bürgerinnen und Bürger. Geschlechterverhältnisse im 19. Jahrhundert*, ed. Ute Frevert. Kritische Studien zur Geschichtswissenschaft, vol. 77. Göttingen, 1988.

Ilien, Albert, and Utz Jeggle. *Leben auf dem Dorfe. Zur Sozialgeschichte des Dorfes und Sozialpsychologie seiner Bewohner*. Opladen, 1978.

Im Hof, Ulrich. *Das gesellige Jahrhundert. Gesellschaft und Gesellschaften im Zeitalter der Aufklärung*. Munich, 1982.

Index deutschsprachiger Zeitschriften, 1750–1815. Ed. Klaus Schmidt. Hildesheim, 1990.

Ingram, Martin. *Church Courts, Sex and Marriage in England, 1570–1640*. Cambridge, 1987.

Jacobs, Karl-Felix. "Die Entstehung der Onanie-Literatur im 17. und 18. Jahrhundert." Med. diss., Universität Müchen, 1963.

Jacobs, Wilhelm G. *Trieb als sittliches Phänomen. Eine Untersuchung zur Grundlegung der Philosophie nach Kant und Fichte.* Bonn, 1967.

Jacquart, Danielle, and Claude Thomasset. *Sexuality and Medicine in the Middle Ages.* Trans. Matthew Adamson. Princeton, N.J., 1988.

Jauch, Ursula Pia. *Immanuel Kant zur Geschlechterdifferenz. Aufklärerische Vorurteilskritik und bürgerliche Geschlechtsvormundschaft.* Vienna, 1988.

Jordanova, Ludmilla. *Sexual Visions: Images of Gender in Science and Medicine between the Eighteenth and Twentieth Centuries.* Madison, Wis., 1989.

Kaiser, Gerhard. *Pietismus und Patriotismus im literarischen Deutschland: Ein Beitrag zum Problem der Säkularisation.* 2d ed. Frankfurt, 1973.

Kaltenstadler, Wilhelm. *Das Haberfeldtreiben. Brauch/Kult/Geheimbund, Volksjustiz im 19. Jahrhundert.* Munich, 1971.

Kaufmann, Doris. "Aufklärung, bürgerliche Selbsterfahrung und der Anfang der Psychiatrie in Deutschland." Forthcoming.

Keller, Ludwig. "Die Berliner Mittwochs-Gesellschaft. Ein Beitrag zur Geschichte der Geistesentwicklung Preußens am Ausgang des 18. Jahrhunderts." *Monatshefte der Comenius-Gesellschaft* 5 (1896): 67–94.

Kiesel, Helmuth, and Paul Münch. *Gesellschaft und Literatur im 18. Jahrhundert. Voraussetzungen und Entstehung des literarischen Markts in Deutschland.* Munich, 1977.

Kluge, Dietrich. "Die 'Kirchenbuße' als staatliches Zuchtmittel im 15.-18. Jahrhundert." *Jahrbuch für westfälische Kirchengeschichte* 70 (1977): 51–63.

Knudsen, Jonathan. *Justus Möser and the German Enlightenment.* Cambridge, 1986.

——. "On Enlightenment for the Common Man." In *"What Was Enlightenment?" Eighteenth-Century Answers and Twentieth-Century Questions,* ed. James Schmidt. Calif., 1994.

Koch, Rainer. *Grundlagen bürgerlicher Herrschaft. Verfassungs- und sozialgeschichtliche Studien zur bürgerlichen Gesellschaft in Frankfurt am Main (1612–1866).* Frankfurter Historische Abhandlungen, vol. 27. Wiesbaden, 1983.

Kocka, Jürgen. "Bürgertum und bürgerliche Gesellschaft im 19. Jahrhundert. Europäische Entwicklungen und deutsche Eigenarten." In *Bürgertum im 19. Jahrhundert. Deutschland im europäischen Vergleich,* ed. Kocka. Vol. 1. Munich, 1988.

——. "German History before Hitler: The Debate about the German 'Sonderweg.'" *Journal of Contemporary History* 23 (1988): 3–16.

Köhler, Walther. *Zürcher Ehegericht und Genfer Konsistorium.* Vol. 1, *Das Zürcher Ehegericht und seine Auswirkung in der deutschen Schweiz zur Zeit Zwinglis.* Quellen und Abhandlungen zur Schweizerischen Reformationsgeschichte, vol. 7. Leipzig, 1932.

——. *Zürcher Ehegericht und Genfer Konsistorium.* Vol. 2, *Das Ehe- und Sittengericht in den süddeutschen Reichsstädten, dem Herzogtum Württemberg und in Genf.* Quellen und Abhandlungen zur Schweizerischen Reformationsgeschichte, vol. 10. Leipzig, 1942.

Kohnen, Joseph. *Theodor Gottlieb von Hippel. Eine zentrale Persönlichkeit der Königsberger Geistesgeschichte. Biographie und Bibliographie.* Lüneburg, 1987.

Kopitzsch, Franklin. *Grundzüge einer Sozialgeschichte der Aufklärung in Hamburg und Altona.* Beiträge zur Geschichte Hamburgs, vol. 21. Hamburg, 1982.

——. "Sozialgeschichte der Aufklärung in Deutschland." In *Deutschland und Frankreich im*

Zeitalter der Französischen Revolution, ed. Helmut Berding, Étienne François, and Hans-Peter Ullmann. Frankfurt, 1989.

———. "Die Sozialgeschichte der deutschen Aufklärung als Forschungsaufgabe." In Kopitzsch, *Aufklärung, Absolutismus und Bürgertum in Deutschland.* 11–172.

———, ed. *Aufklärung, Absolutismus und Bürgertum in Deutschland.* Munich, 1976.

Koselleck, Reinhard. *Kritik und Krise. Eine Studie zur Pathogenese der bürgerlichen Welt.* Frankfurt, 1973.

———. *Preußen zwischen Reform und Revolution.* Stuttgart, 1967.

Kramer, Karl-Sigismund. *Die Nachbarschaft als bäuerliche Gemeinschaft. Ein Beitrag zur rechtlichen Volkskunde mit besonderer Berücksichtigung Bayerns.* Munich, 1954.

Kriedtke, Peter, Hans Medick, and Jürgen Schlumbohm. *Industrialization before Industrialization. Rural Industry in the Genesis of Capitalism.* Trans. Beate Schempp. Cambridge, 1981.

Krieger, Albert. *Topographisches Wörterbuch des Großherzogtums Baden.* Karlsruhe, 1898.

Krieger, Leonard. *The German Idea of Freedom: History of a Political Tradition. From the Reformation to 1871.* Chicago, 1957.

Kroeger, Gertrud. *The Concept of Social Medicine as Presented by Physicians and Other Writers in Germany, 1779–1932.* Chicago, 1937.

Kroeschell, Karl. *Deutsche Rechtsgeschichte,* 3 vols. Opladen, 1986–89.

Kuhlmann, Wolfgang, ed. *Moralität und Sittlichkeit. Das Problem Hegels und die Diskursethik.* Frankfurt, 1986.

Kunisch, Johannes. *Absolutismus. Europäische Geschichte vom westfälischen Frieden bis zur Krise des Ancien Régime.* Göttingen, 1986.

Landes, Joan B. *Women and the Public Sphere in the Age of the French Revolution.* Ithaca, N.Y., 1988.

Lang, Peter Thaddäus. "Reform im Wandel. Die katholischen Visitationsinterrogatorien des 16. und 17. Jahrhunderts." In *Kirche und Visitation. Beiträge zur Erforschung des frühneuzeitlichen Visitationswesens in Europa,* ed. Walter Zeeden and Peter Thaddäus Lang. Stuttgart, 1984.

Langbein, John H. *Prosecuting Crime in the Renaissance: England, Germany, France.* Cambridge, Mass., 1974.

Laqueur, Thomas. *Making Sex: Body and Gender from the Greeks to Freud.* Cambridge, Mass., 1990.

———. "The Social Evil, the Solitary Vice and Pouring Tea." In *Fragments for a History of the Human Body,* vol. 3, ed. Michel Feher. New York, 1987.

Laslett, Peter. *Family Life and Illicit Love in Earlier Generations: Essays in Historical Sociology.* Cambridge, 1977.

La Vopa, Anthony J. "The Revelatory Moment: Fichte and the French Revolution." *Central European History* 22 (June 1989): 130–50.

Leiser, Wolfgang. "Fürstenruhm und staatliche Integration: Geschichtsschreibung und Gesetzgebung unter Karl Friedrich von Baden." *Zeitschrift für die Geschichte des Oberrheins* 133 (1985): 211–20.

Lenel, Paul. *Badens Rechtsverwaltung und Rechtsverfassung unter Markgraf Karl Friedrich, 1738–1803.* Karlsruhe, 1913.

Liebel, Helen P. *Enlightened Bureaucracy versus Enlightened Despotism in Baden, 1750–1792.* Transactions of the American Philosophical Society, vol. 55. Philadelphia, 1965.

Lipp, Carola. "Dörfliche Formen generativer und sozialer Reproduktion." In *Dörfliches Überleben. Zur Geschichte materieller und sozialer Reproduktion ländlicher Gesellschaft im 19. und frühen 20. Jahrhundert*, Wolfgang Kaschuba and Carola Lipp. Untersuchungen des Ludwig Uhland-Instituts der Universität Tübingen, vol. 56. Tübingen, 1982.

———. "Die Innenseite der Arbeiterkultur. Sexualität im Arbeitermilieu des 19. und frühen 20. Jahrhunderts." In *Arbeit, Frömmigkeit und Eigensinn. Studien zur historischen Kulturforschung*, ed. Richard Van Dülmen. Frankfurt, 1990.

———. "Katzenmusiken, Krawalle und 'Weiberrevolution.'" In *Schimpfende Weiber und patriotische Jungfrauen. Frauen im Vormärz und in der Revolution 1848/49*, ed. Lipp. Moos, 1986.

Lipping, Margita. "Bürgerliche Konzepte zur weiblichen Sexualität in der zweiten Hälfte des 18. Jahrhunderts. Rekonstruktionsversuche am Material medizinischer und pädagogischer Texte." In *Frauenkörper. Medizin. Sexualität. Auf dem Wege zu einer neuen Sexualmoral*, ed. Johanna Geyer-Kordesch and Annette Kuhn. Düsseldorf, 1986.

Loos, Fritz, and Hans-Ludwig Schreiber. "Recht, Gerechtigkeit." In Brunner, Conze, and Koselleck, *Geschichtliche Grundbegriffe*, 5:231–311.

Luhmann, Niklas. "Soziologie der Moral." In *Theorietechnik und Moral*, ed. Niklas Luhmann and Stephan H. Pfürtner. Frankfurt, 1978.

Lukes, Steven. "Making Sense of Moral Conflict." In *Liberalism and the Moral Life*, ed. Nancy L. Rosenblum. Cambridge, Mass., 1989.

Lundgreen, Peter. *Sozialgeschichte der deutschen Schule im Überblick, 1770–1918*. Göttingen, 1980.

Maaler, Josua. *Die Teütsch spraach. Dictionarium Germanicolatinum novum* (1561). Reprint, Hildesheim, 1971.

MacDonald, Robert H. "The Frightful Consequences of Onanism: Notes on the History of a Delusion." *Journal of the History of Ideas* 28 (1967): 423–31.

Maier, Hans. *Die ältere deutsche Staats- und Verwaltungslehre*. 2d ed. Munich, 1986.

Mannheim, Karl. *Konservatismus. Ein Beitrag zur Soziologie des Wissens*. Ed. David Kettler, Volker Meja, and Nico Stehr. Frankfurt, 1984.

Marcus, Steven. *The Other Victorians*. New York, 1964.

Martens, Wolfgang. *Die Botschaft der Tugend. Die Aufklärung im Spiegel der deutschen Moralischen Wochenschriften* (1971). Stuttgart, 1982.

———. "Bürgerlichkeit in der frühen Auklärung." In *Aufklärung, Absolutismus und Bürgertum in Deutschland*, ed. Franklin Kopitzsch. Munich, 1976.

Matz, Klaus-Jürgen. *Pauperismus und Bevölkerung. Die gesetzlichen Ehebeschränkungen in den süddeutschen Staaten während des 19. Jahrhunderts*. Industrielle Welt, vol. 31. Stuttgart, 1980.

May, Georg. *Die geistliche Gerichtsbarkeit des Erzbischofs von Mainz im Thüringen des späten Mittelalters. Das Generalgericht zu Erfurt*. Leipzig, 1956.

Maynes, Mary Jo. *Schooling for the People. Comparative Local Studies of Schooling History in France and Germany, 1750–1850*. New York, 1985.

McLaren, Angus. *A History of Contraception from Antiquity to the Present Day*. Cambridge, 1990.

Medick, Hans. "Haushalts-und Familienstruktur als Momente des Produktions- und Reproduktionsprozesses." In *Familie und Gesellschaftsstruktur. Materialien zu den sozioökonomischen Bedingungen von Familienformen*, ed. Heidi Rosenbaum. Frankfurt, 1978.

———. *Naturzustand und Naturgeschichte der bürgerlichen Gesellschaft. Die Ursprünge der bürgerlichen Sozialtheorie als Geschichtsphilosophie und Sozialwissenschaft bei Samuel Pufendorf, John Locke und Adam Smith.* Kritische Studien zur Geschichtswissenschaft, vol. 5. Göttingen, 1973.

———. "Spinnstuben auf dem Dorf. Jugendliche Sexualkultur und Feierabendbrauch in der ländlichen Gesellschaft der frühen Neuzeit" In *Sozialgeschichte der Freizeit. Untersuchungen zum Wandel der Alltagskultur in Deutschland,* ed. Gerhard Huck. Wuppertal, 1980.

Meer, Theo van der. "The Persecution of Sodomites in Eighteenth-Century Amsterdam: Changing Perceptions of Sodomy." *Journal of Homosexuality* 16 (1988): 263–307.

Meisner, Heinrich Otto. *Archivalienkunde vom 16. Jahrhundert bis 1918.* Göttingen, 1969.

Mitterauer, Michael. "Gesindedienst und Jugendphase im europäischen Vergleich." *Geschichte und Gesellschaft* 11.2 (1985): 177–204.

———. *Ledige Mütter. Zur Geschichte unehelicher Geburten in Europa.* Munich, 1983.

Möckl, Karl. *Der moderne bayerische Staat. Eine Verfassungsgeschichte vom Aufgeklärten Absolutismus bis zum Ende der Reformepoche.* Dokumente zur Geschichte von Staat und Gesellschaft in Bayern, part 3, vol. 1. Munich, 1979.

Möller, Helmut. *Die kleinbürgerliche Familie im 18. Jahrhundert.* Berlin, 1969.

Möller, Horst. *Aufklärung in Preußen: Der Verleger, Publizist und Geschichtsschreiber Friedrich Nicolai.* Berlin, 1974.

———. *Vernunft und Kritik. Deutsche Aufklärung im 17. und 18. Jahrhundert.* Frankfurt, 1986.

Mooser, Josef. *Ländliche Klassengesellschaft, 1770–1848. Bauern und Unterschichten, Landwirtschaft und Gewerbe im östlichen Westfalen.* Kritische Studien zur Geschichtswissenschaft, vol. 64. Göttingen, 1984.

———. "Soziale Mobilität und familiale Plazierung bei Bauern und Unterschichten. Aspekte der Sozialstruktur der ländlichen Gesellschaft im 19. Jahrhundert am Beispiel des Kirchspiels Quernheim im östlichen Westfalen." In *Familien zwischen Tradition und Moderne. Studien zur Geschichte der Familie in Deutschland und Frankreich vom 16. bis zum 20. Jahrhundert,* ed. Neithard Bulst, Joseph Goy, and Jochen Hoock. Kritische Studien zur Geschichtswissenschaft, vol. 48. Göttingen, 1981.

Müller-Staats, Dagmar. *Klagen über Dienstboten. Eine Untersuchung über Dienstboten und ihre Herrschaften.* Frankfurt, 1987.

Münch, Paul. "Kirchenzucht und Nachbarschaft. Zur sozialen Problematik des calvinistischen Seniorats um 1600." In *Kirche und Visitation. Beiträge zur Erforschung des frühneuzeitlichen Visitationswesens in Europa,* ed. Ernst Walter Zeeden and Peter Thaddäus Lang. Spätmittelalter und Frühe Neuzeit, vol. 14. Stuttgart, 1984.

———. "Volkskultur und Calvinismus. Zu Theorie und Praxis der 'reformatio vitae' während der 'Zweiten Reformation.'" In *Die reformierte Konfessionalisierung in Deutschland— Das Problem der 'Zweiten Reformation'. Wissenschaftliches Symposion des Vereins für Reformationsgeschichte 1985,* ed. Heinz Schilling. Schriften des Vereins für Reformationsgeschichte, vol. 195. Gütersloh, 1986.

———. *Zucht und Ordnung. Reformierte Kirchenverfassungen im 16. und 17. Jahrhundert (Nassau-Dillenburg, Kurpfalz, Hessen-Kassel).* Stuttgart, 1978.

———, ed. *Ordnung, Fleiß und Sparsamkeit. Texte und Dokumente zur Entstehung der "bürgerlichen Tugenden."* Munich, 1984.

❦ Bibliography ❦

Munck, Thomas. *Seventeenth Century Europe: State, Conflict and Social Order in Europe, 1598–1700.* London, 1990.

Muster, Michael. *Das Ende der Kirchenbuße. Dargestellt an der Verordnung über die Aufhebung der Kirchenbuße in den Braunschweig-Wolfenbüttelschen Landen vom 6. März 1775.* Hannover, 1983.

Neuhouser, Frederick. *Fichte's Theory of Subjectivity.* Cambridge, 1990.

Niethammer, Lutz. "Einführung: Bürgerliche Gesellschaft als Projekt." In *Bürgerliche Gesellschaft in Deutschland,* ed. Niethammer. Frankfurt, 1990.

Nipperdey, Thomas. "Verein als soziale Struktur in Deutschland im späten 18. und frühen 19. Jahrhundert." In *Gesellschaft, Kultur, Theorie. Gesammelte Aufsätze.* Göttingen, 1976.

Norton, Mary Beth. "Gender and Defamation in Seventeenth-Century Maryland." *William and Mary Quarterly,* 3d ser., 44 (January 1987): 3–39.

Oestreich, Gerhard. "Strukturprobleme des europäischen Absolutismus." In *Geist und Gestalt des frühmodernen Staates. Ausgewählte Aufsätze.* Berlin, 1969.

Okin, Susan M. *Women in Western Political Thought.* Princeton, 1979.

Opitz, Claudia. "'Die vergessenen Töchter der Revolution'—Frauen und Frauenrechte im revolutionären Frankreich von 1789–1795." In *Grenzgängerinnen. Revolutionären Frauen im 18. und 19. Jahrhundert. Weibliche Wirklichkeit und männliche Phantasien,* ed. Helga Grubitzsch, Hannelore Cyrus, and Elke Haarbusch. Düsseldorf, 1985.

Outram, Dorinda. *The Body and the French Revolution: Sex, Class, and Political Culture.* New Haven, Conn., 1989.

Pallaver, Günther. *Das Ende der schamlosen Zeit. Die Verdrängung der Sexualität in der frühen Neuzeit am Beispiel Tirols.* Vienna, 1987.

Pateman, Carole. *The Sexual Contract.* Stanford, Calif., 1988.

Peikert, Ingrid. "Zur Geschichte der Kindheit im 18. und 19. Jahrhundert. Einige Entwicklungstendenzen." In *Die Familie in der Geschichte,* ed. Heinz Reif. Göttingen, 1982.

Peitzsch, Wolfram. *Kriminalpolitik in Bayern unter der Geltung des Codex Juris Criminalis Bavarici von 1751.* Münchener Universitätsschriften, Reihe der Juristischen Fakultät, vol. 8. Munich, 1968.

Petschauer, Peter. "Eighteenth-Century German Opinions about Education for Women." *Central European History* 19 (1986): 262–92.

Phayer, Michael Fintan. "Lower-Class Morality: The Case of Bavaria." *Journal of Social History* 8.1 (1974): 79–95.

———. *Sexual Liberation and Religion in Nineteenth Century Europe.* London, 1977.

Phillips, Roderick. *Untying the Knot. A Short History of Divorce.* Cambridge, 1991.

Pikulik, Lothar. *Leistungsethik contra Gefühlskult.* Göttingen, 1984.

Pinloche, Albert. *Geschichte des Philanthopinismus.* 2d ed. Leipzig, 1914.

Plodeck, Karin. "Zur sozialgeschichtlichen Bedeutung der absolutistischen Polizei- und Landesordnungen." *Zeitschrift für bayerische Landesgeschichte* 39.1 (1976): 79–125.

Porter, Roy. "'The Secrets of Generation Display'd': *Aristotle's Master-Piece* in Eighteenth-Century England." In *'Tis Nature's Fault. Unauthorized Sexuality during the Enlightenment,* ed. Robert P. Maccubbin. Cambridge, 1987.

———. "Spreading Carnal Knowledge or Selling Dirt Cheap? Nicholas Venette's *Tableau de l'Amour Conjugal* in Eighteenth-Century England." *Journal of European Studies* 14 (1984): 233–55.

Prüsener, Marlies. *Lesegesellschaften im 18. Jahrhundert.* Frankfurt, 1982.

Quanter, Rudolf. *Die Schand- und Ehrenstrafen in der deutschen Rechtspflege* (1901). Aalen, 1970.

Queri, Georg. *Bauernerotik und Bauernfehme in Oberbayern* (1911). Munich, 1975.

Radbruch, Gustav. *Paul Johann Anselm Feuerbach. Ein Juristenleben.* Vienna, 1934.

Radbruch, Gustav, and Heinrich Gwinner. *Geschichte des Verbrechens.* Stuttgart, 1951.

Raeff, Marc. *The Well-Ordered Police State. Social and Institutional Change through Law in the Germanies and Russia, 1600–1800.* New Haven, Conn., 1983.

Rameckers, J. M. *Der Kindermord in der Literatur der Sturm- und Drangperiode.* Rotterdam, 1927.

Raupach, Angela. "Zum Verhältnis von Politik und Ökonomie im Kameralismus—Ein Beitrag zur sozialen Theoriebildung in Deutschland in ihrer Genese als Polizei." Ph.D. diss., Universität Hamburg, 1982.

Reif, Heinz. "Väterliche Gewalt und 'kindliche Narrheit.' Familienkonflikte im katholischen Adel Westfalens vor der Französischen Revolution." In Reif, ed. *Die Familie in der Geschichte,* ed. Reif. Göttingen, 1982.

Riedel, Manfred. "Gesellschaft, bürgerliche." In Brunner, Conze, and Koselleck, *Geschichtliche Grundbegriffe,* 2:672–725.

Ritter, Gerhard A., and Jürgen Kocka, eds. *Deutsche Sozialgeschichte. Dokumente und Skizzen.* Vol. 2, *1870–1914.* 3d ed. Munich, 1982.

Rittmann, Herbert. *Auf Heller und Pfennig.* Munich, 1976.

Robisheaux, Thomas. *Rural Society and the Search for Order in Early Modern Germany.* Cambridge, 1989.

Roper, Lyndal. "Discipline and Respectability: Prostitution and the Reformation in Augsburg." *History Workshop Journal* 19 (Spring 1985): 3–28.

———. *The Holy Household: Women and Morals in Reformation Augsburg.* Oxford, 1989.

———. "Luther: Sex, Marriage and Motherhood." *History Today,* December 1983, 33–38.

———. "'Wille' und 'Ehre': Sexualität, Sprache und Macht in Augsburger Kriminalprozessen." In *Wandel der geschlechterbeziehungen zu Beginn der Neuzeit,* ed. Heide Wunder and Christina Vanja. Frankfurt, 1991.

Rosen, George. "Cameralism and the Concept of Medical Police." *Bulletin of the History of Medicine* 27 (1953): 21–42.

Rosenbaum, Heidi. *Formen der Familie. Untersuchungen zum Zusammenhang von Familienverhältnissen, Sozialstruktur und sozialem Wandel in der deutschen Gesellschaft des 19. Jahrhunderts.* Frankfurt, 1982.

Rosenberg, Hans. *Bureaucracy, Aristocracy, Autocracy: The Prussian Experience, 1660–1815.* Cambridge, Mass., 1958.

Rosenberger, Fritz Eduard. "Das Sexualstrafrecht in Bayern von 1813 bis 1871." J.S.D. diss., Universität Marburg, 1973.

Rosenthal, Eduard. *Geschichte des Gerichtswesens und der Verwaltungsorganisation Bayerns,* 2 vols. Würzburg, 1906.

Ross, Ellen, and Rayna Rapp. "Sex and Society: A Research Note from Social History and Anthropology." In *Powers of Desire: The Politics of Sexuality,* ed. Ann Snitow, Christine Stansell, and Sharon Thompson. New York, 1983.

Ruppert, Wolfgang. *Bürgerlicher Wandel. Die Geburt der modernen deutschen Gesellschaft im 18. Jahrhundert.* Frankfurt, 1983.

Sabean, David. "'Junge Immen im leeren Korb': Beziehungen zwischen Schwägern in einem schwäbischen Dorf." In *Emotionen und materielle Interessen. Sozialanthropologische und historische Beiträge zur Familienforschung,* ed. Hans Medick and David Sabean. Göttingen, 1984.

———. *Kinship in Neckarhausen.* Forthcoming.

———. *Power in the Blood: Popular Culture and Discourse in Early Modern Germany.* Cambridge, 1983.

———. *Property, Production, and Family in Neckarhausen, 1700–1870.* Cambridge Studies in Social and Cultural Anthropology, vol. 73. Cambridge, 1990.

———. "Unehelichkeit: Ein Aspekt sozialer Reproduktion kleinbäuerlicher Produzenten. Zu einer Analyse dörflicher Quellen um 1800." In *Klassen und Kultur. Sozialanthropologische Perspektiven in der Geschichtsschreibung,* ed. Robert Berdahl. Frankfurt, 1982.

Safley, Thomas Max. *Let No Man Put Asunder. The Control of Marriage in the German Southwest: A Comparative Study, 1550–1600.* Kirksville, Mo., 1984.

Scharfe, Martin. "'Soziale Kontrolle' im Dorf des vorindustriellen Zeitalters. Beitrag zur rechtlichen Volkskunde im ehemaligen Zeller Stab." *Württembergisches Jahrbuch für Volkskunde* (1961/1964): 78–83.

Schenda, Rudolf. *Volk ohne Buch. Studien zur Sozialgeschichte der populären Lesestoffe, 1770–1910.* Frankfurt, 1970.

Schieder, Elmar A. M. *Das Haberfeldtreiben: Ursprung, Wesen, Deutung.* Miscellanea Bavarica Monacensis, no. 125. Munich, 1983.

Schilling, Heinz. "'Geschichte der Sünde' oder 'Geschichte des Verbrechens'? Überlegungen zur Gesellschaftsgeschichte der frühneuzeitlichen Kirchenzucht." *Annali dell' Istituto storico italo-germanico in Trente* 12 (1986): 169–92.

———. *Konfessionskonflikt und Staatsbildung. Eine Fallstudie über das Verhältnis von religiösem und sozialem Wandel in der Frühneuzeit am Beispiel der Grafschaft Lippe.* Quellen und Forschungen zur Reformationsgeschichte, vol. 48. Gütersloh, 1981.

———. "Reformierte Kirchenzucht als Sozialdisziplinierung. Die Tätigkeit des Emder Presbyteriums in den Jahren 1557–1562." In *Niederlande und Nordwestdeutschland. Studien zur Regional- und Stadtgeschichte Nordwestkontinentaleuropas im Mittelalter und in der Neuzeit,* ed. Wilfried Ehbrecht and Heinz Schilling. Cologne, 1983.

———, ed. *Die reformierte Konfessionalisierung in Deutschland—Das Problem der 'Zweiten Reformation.' Wissenschaftliches Symposion des Vereins für Reformationsgeschichte, 1985.* Schriften des Vereins für Reformationsgeschichte, vol. 195. Gütersloh, 1986.

Schilling, Heinz, and Helmut Sydow. "Calvinistische Presbyterien in Städten der Frühneuzeit—eine kirchliche Alternativform zur bürgerlichen Repräsentation? (Mit einer quantifizierenden Untersuchung zur Holländischen Stadt Leiden)." In *Städtische Führungsgruppen und Gemeinde in der werdenden Neuzeit,* ed. Wilfried Ehbrecht. Cologne, 1980.

Schlumbohm, Jürgen. *Freiheitsbegriff und Emanzipationsprozeß. Zur Geschichte eines politischen Wortes.* Göttingen, 1973.

Schmidt, Eberhard. *Einführung in die Geschichte der deutschen Strafrechtspflege.* 3d ed. Göttingen, 1965.

Schmitz, Hermann Joseph. *Die Bussbücher und die Bussdisciplin der Kirche.* Mainz, 1883.

Schnabel-Schüle, Helga. "Kirchenleitung und Kirchenvisitation in Territorien des deutschen Südwestens." In *Repertorium der Kirchenvisitationsakten aus dem 16. und 17. Jahrhundert in Archiven der Bundesrepublik Deutschland,* ed. Ernst Walter Zeeden et al. Vol. 2, part 2. Stuttgart, 1987.

❦ Bibliography ❦

Schneiders, Werner. *Naturrecht und Liebesethik. Zur Geschichte der praktischen Philosophie im Hinblick auf Christian Thomasius.* Hildesheim, 1971.

——. *Wahre Aufklärung. Zur Selbstverständnis der deutschen Aufklärung.* Freiburg, 1974.

Schott, Robin. *Cognition and Eros; a Critique of the Kantian Paradigm.* University Park, Pa., 1993.

Schröder, Hannelore. *Die Rechtlosigkeit der Frau im Rechtsstaat, dargestellt am Allgemeinen Preußischen Landrecht, am Bürgerlichen Gesetzbuch und an J. G. Fichtes Grundlage des Naturrechts.* Frankfurt, 1979.

Schubert, Gernot. *Feuerbachs Entwurf zu einem Strafgesetzbuch für das Königreich Bayern aus dem Jahre 1824.* Schriften zur Rechtsgeschichte, 16. Berlin, 1978.

Schubert, Werner. *Französisches Recht in Deutschland zu Beginn des 19. Jahrhunderts. Zivilrecht, Gerichtsverfassungsrecht und Zivilprozeßrecht.* Forschungen zur Neueren Privatrechtsgeschichte, vol. 24. Cologne, 1977.

Schulte, Regina. "Bevor das Gerede zum Tratsch wird." In Hausen and Wunder, *Frauengeschichte-Geschlechtergeschichte,* 67–73.

——. "Kindsmörderinnen auf dem Lande." In *Emotionen und materielle Interessen. Sozialanthropologische und historische Beiträge zur Familienforschung,* ed. Hans Medick and David Sabean. Göttingen, 1984.

Schultze, Johanna. *Die Auseinandersetzung zwischen Adel und Bürgertum in den deutschen Zeitschriften der letzten drei Jahrzehnte des 18. Jahrhunderts, 1773–1806.* Berlin, 1925.

Schulze, Winfried. "Gerhard Oestreichs Begriff 'Sozialdisziplinierung in der frühen Neuzeit.'" *Zeitschrift für historische Forschung* 14.3 (1987): 265–302.

Schumann, Reinhold. "Die Auffassung des Philanthropinismus von Gesellschaft und Staat." Ph.D. diss., Universität Leipzig, 1905.

Schuster, Beate. "Frauenhandel und Frauenhäuser im 15. und 16. Jahrhundert." In *Vierteljahrschrift für Sozial- und Wirtschaftsgeschichte* 78 (1991): 172–89.

Schwartz, Friedrich-Wilhelm. "Idee und Konzeption der frühen territorial-staatlichen Gesundheitspflege in Deutschland ('Medizinische Polizei') in der ärztlichen und staatswissenschaftlichen Fachliteratur des 16.-18. Jahrhunderts." Ph.D. diss., Universität Frankfurt, 1973.

Schwarz, Joel. *The Sexual Politics of Jean-Jacques Rousseau.* Chicago, 1984.

Schwarz, Manfred. *Wechselnde Beurteilung von Straftaten in Kultur und Recht.* Vol. 1. *Die Kindestötung.* Berlin, 1935.

Scott, Joan W. "Gender: A Useful Category of Historical Analysis." In Scott, *Gender and the Politics of History.* New York, 1988.

——. "Introduction." In Scott, *Gender and the Politics of History.*

Segalen, Martine. *Historical Anthropology of the Family.* Trans. J. C. Whitehouse and Sarah Matthews. Cambridge, 1986.

——. *Love and Power in the Peasant Family: Rural France in the Nineteenth Century.* Chicago, 1983.

Segall, Josef. *Geschichte und Strafrecht der Reichspolizeiordnungen von 1530, 1548 und 1577.* Kirchhain, 1914.

Sellin, Volker. "Politik." In Brunner, Conze, and Koselleck, *Geschichtliche Grundbegriffe,* 4:789–874.

Seydel, Max von. *Bayerisches Staatsrecht.* 2d ed. 2 vols. With Josef von Grassmann and Robert Piloty. Tübingen, 1913.

Shorter, Edward. *The Making of the Modern Family*. New York, 1975.

Sieder, Reinhard. *Sozialgeschichte der Familie*. Frankfurt, 1987.

Siegert, Reinhart. *Aufklärung und Volkslektüre. Exemplarisch dargestellt an Rudolf Zacharias Becker und seinem "Noth- und Hülfsbüchlein." Mit einer Bibliographie zum Gesamtthema*. A special issue of *Archiv für Geschichte des Buchwesens*. 19 (1978): cols. 566–1347.

Simon, Christian. *Untertanenverhalten und obrigkeitliche Moralpolitik. Studien zum Verhältnis zwischen Stadt und Land im ausgehenden 18. Jahrhundert am Beispiel Basels*. Basel, 1981.

Small, Albion Woodbury. *The Cameralists, the Pioneers of German Social Polity*. Chicago, 1909.

Smith, Norah. "Sexual Mores in the Eighteenth Century: Robert Wallace's 'Of Venery.'" *Journal of the History of Ideas* 39 (1978): 419–35.

Soergel, Philip M. *Wondrous in His Saints: Counter-Reform Propaganda in Bavaria*. Berkeley, Calif., 1993.

Sombart, Werner. *Luxus und Kapitalismus*. Vol. 1 of *Studien zur Entwicklungsgeschichte des modernen Kapitalismus*. Munich, 1913.

Sommer, Louise. *Die österreichischen Kameralisten in dogmengeschichtlicher Darstellung*. Studien zur Sozial- Wirthschafts- und Verwaltungsgeschichte, vol. 12. Vienna, 1920.

Spitz, René A. "Authority and Masturbation. Some Remarks on a Bibliographical Investigation." *Yearbook of Psychoanalysis* 9 (1953): 113–45.

Staehelin, Adrian. "Sittenzucht und Sittengerichtsbarkeit in Basel." *Zeitschrift der Savigny-Stiftung für Rechtsgeschichte*, Germanische Abteilung 85 (1968): 78–103.

Stengers, Jean, and Anne van Neck. *Histoire d'une Grande Peur: La Masturbation*. Brussels, 1984.

Stolleis, Michael. *Geschichte des öffentlichen Rechts in Deutschland*. Vol. 1, *1600–1800*. Munich, 1988.

——. *Pecunia Nervus Rerum. Zur Staatsfinanzierung der frühen Neuzeit*. Frankfurt, 1983.

——. "Untertan-Bürger-Staatsbürger. Bemerkungen zur juristischen Terminologie im späten 18. Jahrhundert." In Vierhaus, *Bürger und Bürgerlichkeit*, 65–101.

Stone, Lawrence. *The Family, Sex, and Marriage in England, 1500–1800*. New York, 1977.

Straub, Albert. *Das badische Oberland im 18. Jahrhundert. Die Transformation einer bäuerlichen Gesellschaft vor der Industrialisierung*. Historische Studien vol. 429. Husum, 1977.

Strauss, Gerald. *Law, Resistance, and the State: The Opposition to Roman Law in Reformation Germany*. Princeton, ·1986.

Strobel, Engelbert. *Neuaufbau der Verwaltung und Wirtschaft der Markgrafschaft Baden-Durlach nach dem Dreissigjährigen Krieg bis zum Regierungsantritt Karl Wilhelms (1648–1709)*. Berlin, 1935.

Studien über den Philanthropinismus und die Dessauer Aufklärung. Vorträge zur Geistesgeschichte des Dessau-Wörlitzer Kulturkreises. Wissenschaftliche Beiträge der Martin-Luther-Universität Halle-Wittenberg. Halle, 1970.

Stuke, Horst. "Aufklärung." In Brunner, Conze, and Koselleck, *Geschichtliche Grundbegriffe*, 1:243–342.

Stürmer, Michael, ed. *Herbst des alten Handwerks. Meister, Gesellen und Obrigkeit im 18. Jahhundert*. Munich, 1986.

Süßenberger, Claus. *Rousseau im Urteil der deutschen Publizistik bis zum Ende der Französischen Revolution. Ein Beitrag zur Rezeptionsgeschichte*. Frankfurt, 1974.

Taylor, Peter K. "Military System and Rural Social Change in Eighteenth-Century Hesse-Cassel." *Journal of Social History* 25.3 (1992): 479–504.

Tentler, Thomas N. *Sin and Confession on the Eve of the Reformation*. Princeton, N.J., 1977.

❧ Bibliography ❧

Thalhofer, Franz X. *Die Sexualpädagogik bei den Philanthropen.* Kempten, 1907.

Theibault, John. "Community and *Herrschaft* in the Seventeenth-Century German Village." *Journal of Modern History* 64 (March 1992): 1–21.

Thompson, E. P. *Customs in Common: Studies in Traditional Popular Culture.* New York, 1991.

———. "The Moral Economy of the English Crowd in the Eighteenth Century." In *Customs in Common: Studies in Traditional Popular Culture.* New York, 1991. First published in *Past and Present* 50 (1971): 76–136.

Thudichum, Friedrich. *Ueber unzulässige Beschränkungen des Rechts der Verehelichung.* Tübingen, 1866.

Tlusty, Beverly Ann. "Gender and Alcohol Use in Early Modern Germany." Unpublished ms.

Traer, James F. *Marriage and the Family in Eighteenth-Century France.* Ithaca, N.Y., 1980.

Trepp, Anne-Charlott. "'Sanfte Männlichkeit und selbständige Weiblichkeit': Frauen und Männer im hamburgischen Bürgertum zwischen 1770 und 1840." Ph.D. diss., University of Kiel, 1993.

Ulbricht, Günter. "Der Philanthropinismus—eine fortschrittliche pädagogische Reformbewegung der deutschen Aufklärung." *Pädagogik* 20 (1955): 750–64.

Ulbricht, Otto. *Kindsmord und Aufklärung in Deutschland.* Ancien Régime, Aufklärung und Revolution, vol. 18. Munich, 1990.

Unruh, Georg-Christoph von. "Polizei, Polizeiwissenschaft und Kameralistik." In *Deutsche Verwaltungsgeschichte. Vom Spätmittelalter bis zum Ende des Reiches,* ed. Kurt G.A. Jeserich, Hans Pohl, and Georg-Christoph von Unruh. Vol. 1. Stuttgart, 1983.

Ussel, Jos van. *Sexualunterdrückung. Geschichte der Sexualfeindschaft.* 2d ed. Giessen, 1977.

Valjavec, Fritz. *Die Entstehung der politischen Strömungen in Deutschland, 1770–1815* (1951). Kronberg, 1978.

Vierhaus, Rudolf. *Deutschland im 18. Jahrhundert. Politische Verfassung, soziales Gefüge, geistige Bewegungen.* Göttingen, 1987.

———. "'Patriotismus'—Begriff und Realität einer moralisch-politischen Haltung." In Herrmann, *Bildung des Bürgers,* 119–32.

———. *Zur historischen Deutung der Aufklärung. Probleme und Perspektiven.* Bremen, 1977.

———, ed. *Bürger und Bürgerlichkeit im Zeitalter der Aufklärung.* Heidelberg, 1981.

———, ed. *Deutsche patriotische und gemeinnützige Gesellschaften.* Wolfenbütteler Forschungen, Vol. 8. Munich, 1980.

Vincent, J. M. "European Blue Laws." *Annual Report of the American Historical Association* (1897): 355–73.

Voss, Jürgen. "Der Gemeine Mann und die Volksaufklärung im späten 18. Jahrhundert." In *Vom Elend der Handarbeit: Probleme historischer Unterschichtenforschung,* ed. Hans Mommsen and Winfried Schulze. Stuttgart, 1981.

Wächtershäuser, Wilhelm. *Das Verbrechen des Kindesmordes im Zeitalter der Aufklärung. Eine rechtsgeschichtliche Untersuchung der dogmatischen, prozessualen und rechtssoziologischen Aspekte.* Quellen und Forschungen zur Strafrechtsgeschichte, vol. 3. Berlin, 1973.

Wagner, Peter. *Eros Revived. Erotica of the Enlightenment in England and America.* London, 1990.

Walker, Mack. *German Home Towns. Community, State, and General Estate, 1648–1871.* Ithaca, N.Y., 1971.

Warmbrunn, Paul. *Zwei Konfessionen in einer Stadt. Das Zusammenleben von Katholiken und Protestanten in den paritätischen Reichsstädten Augsburg, Biberach, Ravensburg und Dinkelsbühl von 1548 bis 1648.* Veröffentlichungen des Instituts für europäische

Geschichte Mainz. Abteilung für abendländische Religionsgeschichte, vol. 111. Wiesbaden, 1983.

Wasserschleben, Friedrich Wilhelm Hermann. *Die Bussordnungen der abendländischen Kirche nebst einer rechtsgeschichtlichen Einleitung.* Halle, 1851.

Wehler, Hans-Ulrich. *Deutsche Gesellschaftsgeschichte.* Vol. 1, *Vom Feudalismus des alten Reiches bis zur defensiven Modernisierung der Reformära, 1700–1815.* Munich, 1987.

Weis, Eberhard. "Die Begründung des modernen bayerischen Staates unter König Max I." In *Handbuch der bayerischen Geschichte,* ed. M. Spindler. Vol. 4, part 1. Munich 1974.

——. *Deutschland und Frankreich um 1800. Aufklärung, Revolution, Reform.* Munich, 1990.

——. *Montgelas, 1759–1799: Zwischen Revolution und Reform.* Munich, 1971.

——. "Montgelas' innenpolitisches Reformprogramm: Das Ansbacher Mémoire für den Herzog vom 30.9.1796." *Zeitschrift für bayerische Landesgeschichte* 33.1 (1970): 219–56.

Weissel, Bernhard. *Von wem die Gewalt in den Staaten herrührt. Beiträge zu den Auswirkungen der Staats- und Gesellschaftsauffassungen Rousseaus auf Deutschland im letzten Viertel des 18. Jahrhunderts.* Berlin, 1963.

Westphal, Hannelore. *Die Liebe auf dem Dorf. Vom Wandel der Sexualmoral und der Prostitution auf dem Lande.* Braunschweig, 1988.

Wettmann-Jungblut, Peter. "'Stelen inn rechter hungersnodtt.' Diebstahl, Eigentumsschutz und strafrechtliche Kontrolle im vorindustriellen Baden, 1600–1850." In *Verbrechen, Strafen und soziale Kontrolle. Studien zur historischen Kulturforschung,* ed. Richard van Dülmen. Frankfurt, 1990.

Wildvogel, Christian. *Responsa et Consilia.* Jena, 1717.

Willms, Bernhard. *Die totale Freiheit: Fichtes politische Philosophie.* Cologne, 1967.

Willoweit, Dietmar. "Struktur und Funktion intermediärer Gewalten im Ancien Régime." In *Gesellschaftliche Strukturen als Verfassungsproblem,* supplemental issue of *Der Staat* 2 (1978): 11–49.

Windelband, Wolfgang. *Die Verwaltung der Markgrafschaft Baden zur Zeit Karl Friedrichs.* Leipzig, 1917.

Wissell, Rudolf. *Des alten Handwerks Recht und Gewohnheit.* 2d ed. Ed. Ernst Schraepler. 7 vols. Berlin, 1971–.

Wittman, Reinhard. "Der lesende Landmann. Zur Rezeption aufklärerischer Bemühungen durch die bäuerliche Bevölkerung im 18. Jahrhundert." In *Der Bauer Mittel- und Osteuropas im sozio-ökonomischen Wandel des 18. und 19. Jahrhunderts,* ed. Dan Berindei. Cologne, 1973.

Wrigley, E. A. "Fertility Strategy for the Individual and the Group." In *Historical Studies of Changing Fertility,* ed. Charles Tilly. Princeton, 1978.

Wunder, Bernd. *Privilegierung und Disziplinierung. Die Entstehung des Berufsbeamtentums in Bayern und Württemberg (1780–1825).* Studien zur modernen Geschichte, vol. 21. Munich, 1978.

Wunder, Heide. *Die bäuerliche Gemeinde in Deutschland.* Göttingen, 1986.

——. *"Er ist die Sonn', sie ist der Mond." Frauen in der Frühen Neuzeit.* Munich, 1992.

Wunder, Heide, and Christina Vanja, eds. *Wandel der Geschlechterbeziehungen zu Beginn der Neuzeit.* Frankfurt, 1991.

Wurzbacher, Gerhard, and Hilde Kipp. "Das Verhältnis von Familie und öffentlichem Raum unter besonderer Berücksichtigung der Bundesrepublik Deutschland." In *Die Familie als Sozialisationsfaktor. Der Mensch als soziales und personales Wesen,* ed. Gerhard Wurzbacher. Vol. 3. Stuttgart, 1968.

Zeeden, Ernst Walter, et al., eds. *Repertorium der Kirchenvisitationsakten aus dem 16. und 17. Jahrhundert in Archiven der Bundesrepublik Deutschland.* 2 vols. to date. Stuttgart, 1982—.

Ziegler, Ernst. *Sitte und Moral in früheren Zeiten. Zur Rechtsgeschichte der Reichsstadt und Republik St. Gallen.* Sigmaringen, 1991.

Ziegler, Peter. *Zürcher Sittenmandate.* Zurich, 1978.

Zielenziger, Kurt. *Die alten deutschen Kameralisten. Ein Beitrag zur Geschichte der Nationalökonomie und zum Problem des Merkantilismus.* Beiträge zur Geschichte der Nationalökonomie, vol. 2. Jena, 1914.

Ziessow, Karl-Heinz. *Ländliche Lesekultur im 18. und 19. Jahrhundert. Das Kirchspiel Menslage und seine Lesegesellschaften.* 2 vols. Cloppenburg, 1988.

Zoepfl, Heinrich M. *Die peinliche Gerichtsordnung Kaiser Karls V., nebst der Bamberger und der Brandenburger Halsgerichtsordnung.* Heidelberg, 1842.

Zunkel, Friedrich. "Ehre, Reputation." In Brunner, Conze, and Koselleck, *Geschichtliche Grundbegriffe,* 2:1–63.

Index

❧ Index ❧

Code Napoléon (cont.)
  paragraph 340 on paternity in, 282, 336, 375,
    377–99, 401–5
  principles of, 376–77
coercion (externality)
  absolutist state's use of, 55, 56
  cameralists on, 167–70, 193–97
  and freedom of choice, 4, 193, 226, 361
  limits of, in enforcing morality, 9–10, 20, 27,
    117, 192, 193
  to prevent masturbation, 276
  See also punishments
"common good" (Gemeinwohl), 1, 4, 27, 56, 68,
  96
  cameralists' belief in, 156, 158, 159, 164–66,
    169, 182
  civil society practitioners' view of, 205, 215,
    217, 218, 220, 221, 371, 392
  as identical with government's interest, 165–
    71, 179–80
  and illegitimacy, 403–4
  police role in maintaining, 64, 125
  private sphere's displacement of, 387, 392–98
  as synonymous with male interests, 185, 190–
    92, 392
  in 19th-century ständisch society, 408–9
  See also community
community (as context for sexual behavior), 29–
  31, 36–41, 49–52, 117
  See also "common good"; harmony; honor;
    marriage: connection of, with social order;
    ständisch society
concubinage, 191, 233
  church prohibitions against, 16, 22
  by clergy, 15–16, 18, 23, 69n, 71
  decriminalization of, 339, 340, 349
  defined, 69
  as Enlightenment concern, 364, 365
  under Imperial Police Ordinances, 65
  Kant on, 307
  prosecution of, 60, 73
  punishment for, 86, 365, 367, 368
confession
  church practice of, 10, 14, 16–17, 21
  use of torture to extract, 60, 97
consensual sexual behavior (non-marital)
  cameralists' opposition to, 176
  Carolina code's concern with, 63–64
  continued criminalization of, 394–95
  courts' handling of, 58
  kinds of, 68–74
  and police power, 363–64
  punishments for, 58, 60, 79–89, 96–100
  with religious persons, 13, 69
  trend toward decriminalization of, 115–16,
    132, 321, 339, 340–42, 344, 345, 349–50,
    362, 408

  See also sexual behavior; sexual crimes; specific
    consensual sexual behaviors
conservatism, 136, 138, 140, 150–52, 299, 400
Constitutio Criminalis Carolina (Holy Roman
  Empire's criminal code), 58, 61–66, 86, 88,
  96, 113, 128, 341
constitutions
  political, 328, 334–36, 338, 358, 370
  of voluntary associations, 209
Council of Trent, 22–23, 69n
court council (Hofrat)
  of Baden, 131–33
  of Baden-Baden, 115n, 117–21
  in Bavaria, 133–37
  of the Palatinate, 116
  role of, in judicial pyramid, 60, 61, 118
  sexual regulation by, 73–74, 80, 101, 117–21,
    133–37
courts
  civil, 381–82, 385
  dependence of, on fines, 81
  in early modern period, 58–61, 65, 91–92, 97–106
  ecclesiastical, 9, 10, 14–17, 26–28
  gender differentiation in prosecutions by, 28–
    29, 56, 74, 82, 86
  higher, 385, 386
  lower, 87, 100, 126, 127, 339, 386
  marriage, 9, 25–26, 184–85
  morals, 9
  See also court council; judicial discretion; law;
    privy council; punishments; statutes; trial
    procedures
courtship, 33–34, 38–40, 49, 50, 69–71, 89
creativity (male), 249, 256, 388
crime, 135
  See also criminal codes; sexual crimes
criminal codes
  absolutist, 9, 56–57, 61–66
  compared to civil codes, 85, 371, 383–87
  educative function of, 125–26
  Feuerbach's Bavarian, 332, 339, 349–59, 371
  principles of civil society's, 407
  See also Allgemeines Landrecht; Constitutio
    Criminalis Carolina; Imperial Police Ordi-
    nances; punishments; sexual legislation;
    sexual regulation; statutes
criminals, 113, 119, 125–26, 346
customary law, 77–78, 82–88, 146n, 152, 341,
  373–74, 379, 386–87
customary practices, 3, 56, 68, 69–70, 74, 102,
  188, 189
  as basis for nationalism, 398–401
  cameralists on, 177–78, 195–97
  male domination as, 185, 186–87, 189

Dann, Otto, 207
Darjes, Joachim Georg, 164

❖ Index ❖